FROM THE LIBRARY OF

**MR LESZEK MURAWSKI**
2560 KINGSTON RD APT 1610
SCARBOROUGH ON  M1M 1L8
POTREC@ROGERS.COM

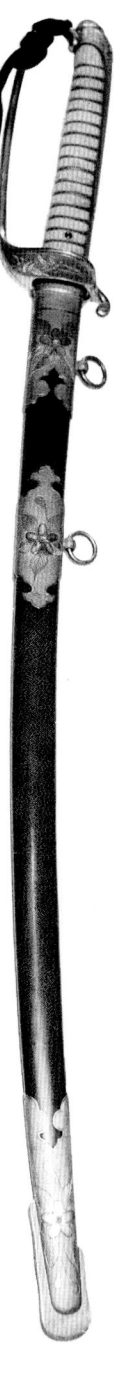

Japanese
Military and
Civil Swords
and Dirks

# Japanese Military and Civil Swords and Dirks

Richard Fuller
and Ron Gregory

Howell Press

**Dedicated to Leo Monson Jr** together with Herb Gopstein, Curt Peritz and all sword collector friends worldwide.

Copyright © 1996 Richard Fuller and Ron Gregory

First published in the UK in 1996
by Airlife Publishing Ltd

Published in the United States in 1997
by Howell Press, Inc.

ISBN 1-57427-062-1

All rights reserved. No part of this book may be reproduced or transmitted in any form or by any means, electronic or mechanical including photocopying, recording or by any information storage and retrieval system, without permission from the Publisher in writing.

Typeset by Phoenix Typesetting, Ilkley, West Yorkshire, England
Printed in Hong Kong

# Howell Press, Inc.
1147 River Road, Suite Two, Charlottesville, VA 22901.

# Contents

9   ACKNOWLEDGEMENTS

10  FOREWORD

11  INTRODUCTION

13  GLOSSARY OF TERMS AND MODERN REIGN ERAS

18  ARMY SWORDS c.1871–c.1877   Early regulation Army (fighting) sword patterns c.1871–c.1877 • Regulation c.1871 pattern Army Commissioned Officers sword • Regulation c.1873 pattern Cavalry, Artillery, Transport and Infantry Sergeant-Majors dress sword • Regulation c.1877 pattern Infantry Adjutants and NCOs sword • Regulation c.1877 pattern Cavalry, Artillery, Transport and Engineer Adjutants and NCOs sword

21  ARMY 1875 (& 1886) PATTERN OFFICERS DRESS SWORD   Regulation 1875 (& 1886) pattern Army (and Medical Corps) Commissioned Officers dress sword

24  ARMY ARTILLERY SIDEARMS   Type 1 (1886 pattern) • Type 2 • Type 3 (1885 pattern)

27  ARMY c.1886 REGULATION PATTERN NCOs SWORD

29  ARMY 1875 (& 1886) KYU-GUNTŌ   Regulation pattern Army kyu-guntō (and possible Very Senior Police Officers kyu-guntō)

35  ARMY 1875 (& 1886) PATTERN AND POSSIBLE VERY SENIOR POLICE PARADE SABRES   Regulation Army parade sabres – Possible Very Senior Civil Police parade sabres • A boys' Army parade sabre

45  ARMY CAVALRY SWORDS   Regulation 1874 pattern parade sabre for Mounted Cavalry, Transport and Artillery Officers of Field grade • 1892 regulation pattern brass-hilted (Cavalry) sabre • 1899 regulation pattern steel-hilted (Cavalry) Troopers and Army NCOs sabres • Regulation 1886 pattern Cavalry Officers sword • Regulation 1886 pattern Cavalry Officers parade sabre

54  ARMY 1934 (& 1938) SHIN-GUNTŌ   Regulation 1934 (& 1938) pattern Army Officers shin-guntō • Metal scabbards • Field scabbards • Scabbard variations • Mon • Sword knots • Purchase • Shin-guntō variations.

78  ARMY 1944 & 1945 (OFFICERS) SWORD PATTERNS   Regulation 1944 pattern Army (Officers) sword • Copper-mounted • Iron-mounted • 1945 pattern Army (Officers) Home Defence sword

83 ARMY 1935 & 1945 NCOs SWORD PATTERNS   Regulation 1935 (Type 95) pattern Army Non-Commissioned Officers shin-guntō • c.1945 pattern Army Non-Commissioned Officers sword

92 SHIN-GUNTŌ USED BY CIVIL ORGANISATIONS

94 KATANA AND WAKIZASHI FOR MILITARY USE

99 TACHI FOR MILITARY USE

100 LEATHER-COVERED SWORDS

101 ARMY DIRKS   Shōwa period dirk for military use • Officers personal dirk

103 AIR FORCE AND AIRBORNE UNIT SWORDS   Army and Naval Air Forces • Army Air Force swords • Small-sized Army shin-guntō • Naval Air Force swords • Kamikaze dirks

109 MEIJI PERIOD NAVAL SWORDS   Naval boarding cutlass • 1872 pattern Wilkinson Sword Company Naval Officers sword • Regulation 1873 pattern Commissioned Officers naval sword

113 NAVAL 1883 & 1914 KYU-GUNTŌ   Regulation 1883 pattern naval kyu-guntō • Regulation 1914 pattern Commissioned Officers naval kyu-guntō • Naval kyu-guntō variant

119 NAVAL 1883 & 1914 PARADE SABRES   Regulation 1883 and 1914 pattern Commissioned (and Petty) Officers naval parade sabres • Regulation 1883 pattern Flag Officers (Admirals) naval parade sabre • Possible Chief Petty Officers parade sabre

124 ARMY KYU-GUNTŌ FOR NAVAL USE

126 NAVAL 1937 KAI-GUNTŌ   Regulation 1937 pattern Commissioned and Warrant Officers naval kai-guntō

131 UNIDENTIFIED NAVAL AND NAVAL PRISON SWORDS   Possible Meiji period naval sword • Unidentified short pattern naval sword • 1895 Naval Prison and Shore Patrol sword (Example 1) • 1895 Naval Prison and Shore Patrol sword (Example 2)

135 SWORDS OF THE NAVAL LANDING FORCES (MARINES)   Regulation c.1873 pattern Marines and Marine Artillery Officers and NCOs sword • World War Two Naval Landing Forces swords • Shin-guntō with naval characteristics

139 NAVAL PRISON SERVICE AND NAVAL POLICE SWORDS AND DIRKS   Naval Prison Governors sword pattern • Naval Chief Prison Guards sword pattern • 1895 pattern Naval Prison Guards sword pattern • Naval Prison Governors dirk pattern • Naval Police sword pattern

141 NAVAL BANDSMEN DIRK   c.1883 pattern Naval Bandsmen dirk

143 CURRENT JAPANESE SELF-DEFENCE FORCES SWORD

144 NAVAL DIRKS   1872 Wilkinson Sword Company dirk • 1873 pattern Senior Petty Officers, Midshipmen and Junior Officers model • 1873 pattern Junior Petty Officers model • 1873 pattern Senior Petty Officers and the most Junior Commissioned Officers model • 1883 pattern Commissioned Officers model • 1883 pattern Officer Candidates naval dirk • Unidentified variation of the 1883 pattern Officer Candidates naval dirk

153　1918 Pattern Gensui (Field Marshals And Fleet Admirals) Sword

156　Imperial Household Swords And Dirks　Dirk of a Senior Official in the Imperial Household • Imperial Household Police Officers dirk • Unidentified Imperial Household sword • Parade sabre version of the Unidentified Imperial Household Officials sword

161　Diplomatic Corps Swords　Regulation Diplomatic Corps sword patterns • Diplomatic Corps sword variation with traditional blade

164　Formosan Swords And Dirks　1911 pattern Junior Officials dirk of the Government-General of Formosa • 1911 pattern Senior Officials dirk of the Government-General of Formosa • 1899 pattern Officials swords of the Government-General of Formosa

168　Korean Swords And Dirks　c.1911 pattern Junior Officials dirk of the Government-General of Korea • c.1911 pattern Senior Officials dirk of the Government-General of Korea • 1906 Officials sword of the Government-General of Korea • Possible Shinnin Officials sword of the Government-General of Korea

172　Dirks Of The Mandated Territories (South Sea Islands)　1919 pattern Junior Officials dirk of the Government-General of the Mandated Territories • 1919 pattern Senior Officials dirk of the Government-General of the Mandated Territories • 1919 Officials sword of the Government-General of the Mandated Territories

176　Swords And Dirks Of Manchukuo (Manchuria)　Junior (Civil?) Officials dirk. • Senior (Civil?) Officials dirk. • Manchukuo sword

178　Forestry Officials Dirks　First pattern Foresters model. • First pattern Senior Foresters model • Second (1903) pattern Foresters model • Second (1903) pattern Junior Foresters model • Second (1903) pattern Senior Foresters model • Possible second (1903) pattern Forestry Officials dirk of unidentified grade

182　National Railways Board Dirks　1909 pattern Junior Officials dirk • 1909 pattern Senior Officials dirk

185　Police Swords And Dirks　Police Bureau • Police badges and weapons • c.1877 Police or Patrolmans sword • c.1877 Police (Officers?) sword • Mounted Police dirk • Mounted Police hanger (Type 1) • Mounted Police hanger (Type 2) • Police dirk (Sergeants?) • Police dirk (Junior Officers?) • Police dirk (Senior Officers?) • Police sword (Senior Officers)

194　Fire Bureau Dirks　Fire Bureau • Fire Bureau badges and weapons • 1889 pattern Fire Bureau Vice-Commanders dirk • 1889 pattern Fire Bureau Commanders dirk

198　Red Cross Society Swords And Dirks　Junior Officials dirk • Senior Officials dirk • Red Cross Society swords

200 UNIDENTIFIED CIVIL SWORDS AND DIRKS  Civil Officials short sword • Ornate Civil Officials short sword • Plain full-sized Civil Officials sword • Ornate full-sized Civil Officials sword • Civil Officials, or naval, sword adapted for land warfare • Unidentified civil full dress or court sword • Unidentified dress sword of military style • Unidentified court or dress sword • Unidentified civil dirk

209 SHŌWA PERIOD PRESENTATION SWORDS  Presentation to foreign nationals • Presentation to Japanese nationals

213 MILTARY SWORD BLADES AND MARKINGS  Tamahagane gendaitō • Mill-steel gendaitō • Koa-Isshin Mantetsu-tō • Han-tanren abura yaki-ire-tō • Sunobe abura yaki-ire-tō • Mantetsu-tō • Murata-tō • Tai-sabi-kō • Machine-made • Summary of basic military blade-making methods • Army refurbishment blades • Mill-produced steels • Blade shapes • Polishing • Gendai swordsmiths • Military swordsmiths • Military inspection/acceptance and other stamps • Paper labels • Kakihan (Kao) • Seals (Kokuin) • Tang inscriptions • Ubu-ha • Terminology • Military sword fittings

233 SWORD BELTS  Army service and battle belts • Army full (and parade) dress belts • Navy service and undress belts • Navy full and parade dress belts • Civil sword belts • Suspension slings (hangers) • Suspension methods

246 SWORD SURRENDERS

252 SURRENDER DOCUMENTATION  Authorisation certificates • Details of the Japanese owner and, possibly, the swordsmith • Letters from Japanese officers in English

258 SURRENDER/TRANSPORTATION LABELS

261 COMMEMORATIVE PLAQUES

263 COLLABORATION, EMERGENCY ISSUE, REPRODUCTION AND FAKE MILITARY SWORDS  Collaboration Forces • Collaboration swords • A probable 'collaboration' sword • An enigmatic shin-guntō • Emergency issue swords • Reproduction military swords • Fake swords • Shin-guntō with silvered mounts

273 MISCELLANEOUS EDGED WEAPONS  Combination sword and pistol • Unidentified dirk • Shōwa period boys' dirk • Miniature shin-guntō • Japanese-made sword for Australian military use

278 HINTS FOR COLLECTORS

280 BIBLIOGRAPHY

283 JAPANESE SWORD SOCIETIES

285 INDEX

# Acknowledgements

The authors wish to express their gratitude to all who provided advice, photographic material and information which made the preparation of this book possible.

Special thanks is offered to: Cheyenne Noda, America, for the invaluable provision of contemporary photographs; Donald Barnes, Australia, for providing details of the many unusual items in his collection, and to Barry Thomas who photographed them; Dave Gardner, England, for his photographic assistance; Han Bing Siong, Holland, for his time and expertise in advising on, and correcting, certain sections of the manuscript, especially those relating to blade manufacture – also for permission to quote from, and refer to, his published works and forthcoming definitive article on the origin of the shin-guntō; Philip Goody, Canada, and his co-researchers for the provision, in translated form, of much material previously unknown in the West; the unknown compiler of *Imperial Japanese Daggers 1883–1945* whose work has identified such items; Clemson University, South Carolina, America; Imperial War Museum, London, England; Thomas Burke Memorial Museum, Washington, America; and the Western Australia Museum, Perth, for the reproduction of their photographs.

Others whose assistance, encouragement and kindness are much appreciated are: Trevor Duffin, Herb Gopstein, Andrew MacMillan, Neil Moir Snr, Leo Monson Jr, Curt Peritz, George Trotter, Brenton Williams, Yukio Yamaguchi.

The approval of Arms & Armour Press to reproduce drawings and photographs previously used in *Military Swords of Japan 1868–1945* is also gratefully acknowledged.

Illustrations drawn by Richard Fuller (except where otherwise credited). The credits for the photographs used refer to the individuals or institutions in whose collections the items shown are located.

# Foreword

The publication of *Military Swords of Japan 1868–1945* by the authors in 1986 (see Bibliography) created much interest among collectors worldwide generating correspondence and photographs relating to undocumented sword patterns and variations. This new material cried out to be included in a new, enlarged book also incorporating corrections and amplification of the material in the previous publication. It has, however, been necessary to reproduce a few photographs and drawings from that work since they have not been bettered. *Military Swords of Japan 1868–1945* remains a complementary reference because it contains many illustrations and photographs which have not been reused.

There is no doubt that the completion of this book is the result of international co-operation by collectors who, at their own expense, provided much photographic material for use and consideration. This is gratefully acknowledged by the authors with the hope that their efforts have not been wasted.

In 1992 one of the authors was given an invaluable booklet entitled *Imperial Japanese Daggers 1883–1945* which has been reproduced extensively in this book. It is anonymous and undated, with no indication of origin. The contents comprise excellent quality drawings together with basic captions (but no text) which indicates either access to the actual items or an unknown reference work. Enquiries have ascertained that it is American in origin and is believed to have been issued privately as a personal 'wants' catalogue. Since there is no copyright announcement it is thought permissible to reproduce a number of the original illustrations with due acknowledgement to the source. Hopefully the anonymous compiler/artist will have the forbearance to appreciate the reason for the use of this important material, and grateful thanks are hereby accorded.

A recommended book called *Swords of Imperial Japan 1868–1945* by Jim Dawson (published as this work was going to press) has permitted the definitive identification, or confirmation, for usage and dating of many swords contained herein.

Any reader who wishes to add to, or correct, information herein should direct their correspondence to the publishers who will forward it to the authors for comment.

This book is, without doubt, comprehensive, but must not be regarded as the 'definitive work' since there is so much more to learn.

Richard Fuller, Bristol, England. 1996
Ron Gregory, Milton Ernest, England. 1996

# Introduction

Why collect military Japanese swords when traditional samurai swords are older and more attractive? The answer, besides relative affordability, lies in a fascination with the history of Imperial expansion and victories, campaigns of suicidal ferocity, and retreats of terrible hardship culminating in unconditional surrender. Military swords from World War Two represent all these things plus the end of a tradition in sword warfare going back 1,000 years.

The Japanese believed the Americans were afraid of attacks by the sword because such a death would prevent them going to heaven, and they could not be reincarnated if their bodies were dismembered. The Americans, of course, realised the danger of these weapons, but for different reasons as indicated in a 1943 book called *The Jap Soldier* which was adapted from a US Army military training film:

> 'Japanese officers still favour the old-fashioned sword. You will see them leading troops with swords waving, just as in old-fashioned movie thrillers. Shoot these officers as quickly as you can, for these swords can slice a man from collar-bone to waist in a single, clean slash. Besides, Jap troops usually lose their nerve when their officers are killed, and rapidly go to pieces.'

An officer carried his sword as a symbol of authority as well as a weapon. One use is demonstrated by the following account of a competition between two Lieutenants of the 6th Infantry Division as they advanced on Nanking, China.[1] It first appeared in the *Japan Advertiser* of 7 December 1937 under the headline SUB-LIEUTENANTS IN RACE TO FELL 100 CHINESE RUNNING CLOSE CONTEST: 'Sub-Lieutenant Toshiaki Mukai and Sub-Lieutenant Takeshi Noda, both of the Katagiri unit at Kuyung, in a friendly contest to see which of them will first fell 100 Chinese in individual sword combat before the Japanese forces completely occupy Nanking, are well into the final phase of their race, running almost neck to neck. On Sunday [5 December] . . . the "score", according to the *Asahi* [a newspaper], was Sub-Lieutenant Mukai 89, and Sub-Lieutenant Noda 78.' This was later extended to 150 because referees had not been able to determine which contestant had reached 100 first. A later article showed both men with their swords and a headline reporting that Mukai had reached 106 to Noda's 105. The *Advertiser* reported Mukai's blade was slightly damaged in the competition. He explained that this was the result of cutting a Chinese in half, helmet and all. The contest was 'fun', he declared. It is not known if the above figures were final or the contest actually went on to 150.

Once Nanking fell, an orgy of rape, pillage and murder began. This included decapitation demonstrations given by sword-wielding officers.[2] 'A trial was made of old samurai swords in which it was demonstrated that none had the virtue of being able to split a man from pate to groin at a stroke.'[3]

Many cases of Allied servicemen being attacked

---

1 From *Japan's Imperial Conspiracy* by David Bergamini (Heinemann, London).
2 It would need an excellent blade to cut vertically through both skull and body with one stroke. This was not a recognised 'cut' in the old method of testing a blade on a human body, known as 'tameshigiri', (continued on page 12)

by ferocious sword-wielding Japanese officers have been documented. A typical example is recorded in the museum caption for a sword captured by the 3rd Carabiniers (Prince of Wales) Dragoon Guards.[4] 'During the regiment's service in Burma in 1945, this sword was taken by "A" Squadron after crossing the Irrawaddy in support of 2nd British Division. In the battle, a Japanese officer armed only with this sword climbed into a tank and stabbed both Captain Carnaby and his gunner before being shot by Lance Corporal Jenkins, MM, in hand to hand combat in this tank.'

An officer without his sword was disgraced and lost 'face'. Lord Mountbatten realised this, so ordered the surrender of all swords by officers and NCOs within his sphere of command. This disarmament policy was adopted in other Allied areas of operations. It was this action which brought thousands of Japanese swords to the West as souvenirs.

The Japanese currently have no interest in military swords, unless fitted with blades of artistic merit. Normal military blades, either mass produced or oil tempered, are not legally allowed into Japan and are regarded as just 'military surplus'. However, military sword mounts without blades can be returned. The Japanese continually produce books on their part in World War Two so there is obviously a great interest in that period of their history. It is therefore strange to Westerners that they do not recognise the significance of these weapons even fifty years after they were last carried in action. However, it must be realised that the Japanese post-war constitution forbids the ownership of most weapons.[5]

Dating of sword patterns has also been referenced to Japanese publications, but even these are often at variance with one another. For example, the common shin-guntō has variously been dated 1934, 1935 and 1937 by Japanese sources. Thus it has been necessary to use the most logical introduction date which is usually prefixed by 'circa' unless there is reason to believe the year given is correct. Indeed, Japanese references are not necessarily correct and are often vague in their descriptions for use.

It is considered undesirable to include valuations, not just because they become dated within twelve months, but also because of variations in value in individual countries. Instead, scarcity guidance is given based on the authors' own experience in Britain. Categorisation is as follows:

Common – frequently encountered.
Fairly common – often encountered but not in such numbers as to be regarded as 'common'.
Scarce – occasionally found (even though some patterns may have been carried in large numbers).
Rare – only a handful of examples have been noted.
Very Rare – only one or two examples have been reported (and it is assumed production, in some cases, was very limited).

A presentation inscription increases the scarcity rating of any weapon. With a common standard regulation pattern such categorisation is based upon the mountings and not the blade, which in the case of a shin-guntō, for example, can be made by individual smiths and can vary in valuation according to workmanship, age and condition. The addition of a logo or insignia (i.e. North China Joint Stock Transportation Company, airborne unit, etc.) to an otherwise totally standard regulation sword can increase the scarcity rating. Similarly, an Officers rank classification from sword mounts or colouration of sword knot may be expected to affect this rating depending upon status.

Research on Japanese military swords leads one to believe that there always seems to be at least one example which proves the exception to any (supposed) rule.

---

(continued from page 11) which required any one of eighteen different cuts graded by degree of difficulty. The Tokyo newspaper *Nichi-nichi*, of December 1937, confirms the kills in the contest between the two Lieutenants were by decapitation, which was a simple test for a blade and so was not included in the tameshigiri categories.
3 Quoted from *Japan's Imperial Conspiracy*.
4 On display at the 5th Royal Enniskilling Dragoon Guards Museum. Fourteenth-century blade with the smith's signature broken off or removed.
5 Only swords judged to be of artistic or historical merit may be privately owned, but each must be licensed annually.

# Glossary of Terms and Reign Eras

## Glossary of terms

The reader is advised to become familiar with the following basic Japanese and Western terminology which may be encountered in the text.

AIKUCHI   A dirk without a guard. See **tantō**.

AOI   The shape of the guard (**tsuba**) used with a **shin-guntō** which is said to resemble the Assarum plant.

ASHI   A scabbard or mount for suspending a sword. The suspension ring is called an 'obitori'.

BUKE-ZUKURI   A traditional style of sword with a tape-bound hilt, hand-forged blade and lacquered scabbard, e.g. **katana** and **wakizashi**.

CHAPE   The separate lower scabbard mount of a Western-style military sword scabbard.

CIVILIAN   A 'samurai' (sword or dirk), i.e. non-military.

DAI-SEPPA   The large washer next to the guard (**tsuba**); one on each side.

DRAG   A solid protusion at the end of a Western-style scabbard which prevents scabbard wear when touching the ground; also called a **shoe**.

FUCHI   The metal ferrule at the base of the grip.

HABAKI   A metal collar on the blade which acts as a wedge in the scabbard.

HAKKOU   A sun with sixteen alternating long and short rays having notched ends; see fig. 51 (ii).

HAMON   A misty white line of martensite crystals between the **yakiba** and blade surface. May be found in many shapes, each with a name.

HIASHI   A sun having sixteen rays radiating from the centre; see fig. 2 (iii), (iv).

ISHIZUKE   The scabbard chape of **shin-** and **Kai-guntō** swords.

KABUTO-GANE   The pommel of **tachi, shin-** and **kai-guntō** swords; see **kashira**.

# JAPANESE MILITARY AND CIVIL SWORDS AND DIRKS

KADOSAKURA  Cherry blossom with ten petals; see Fig. 2 (vii). A common decorative motif normally associated with Army swords.

KAI-GUNTŌ  Kai- (sea) gun (military) tō (sword). A naval sword pattern resembling the traditional **tachi**. Carried during World War Two.

KASHIRA  The pommel of a civilian **katana** and **wakizashi**. It is a cap having the hilt binding tied through each side with no provision for a sword knot.

KATANA  A traditional style of sword with a 610 to 914mm plus (24 to 36" plus) blade carried cutting edge uppermost through the waist sash; see **wakizashi**.

KIKU  The chrysanthemum blossom; see Fig. 2 (v), (vi).

KIRI  Leaves and flowers of the *Paulownia imperialis* tree; see Fig. 2 (i), (ii).

KOGAI  The skewer or head-pin carried in the side slot of a civilian sword or dagger as a companion to the **kozuka**.

KOZUKA  A small knife carried in the side slot of a civilian sword or dagger as a companion to the **kogai**.

KURIKATA  The raised wood, horn or metal knob on a civilian sword scabbard to prevent it slipping through the waist sash.

KUCHI-GANE  Scabbard throat fitting.

KYU-GUNTŌ  kyu- (proto- or first) gun (military) tō (sword). A European-style military sword, usually fitted with a traditionally shaped blade, which was common during the 1904–5 Russo–Japanese war.

LOCKETS  Separate upper and middle mounts of a Western-style military sword scabbard. Each is fitted with a suspension band or boss and a hanging ring.

MACHI  A step or notch between the blade and tang of a traditional Japanese-style blade.

MEI  The signature or inscription engraved on a blade tang.

MEKUGI  A bamboo peg that secures the hilt and blade.

MEKUGI-ANA  The hole in the blade tang for the **mekugi**. There may be more than one if a blade has been remounted.

MENUKI  An ornament secured under the hilt tape binding.

MON  A family badge.

MUMEI  An unsigned tang.

MUNE  Back edge of a traditional-style blade.

NAGA-MARU  The ovoid **tsuba** shape found on **kai-guntō** swords.

NAKAGO  The tang of a blade.

NANAKO  Background decoration of raised dots, resembling fish roe, used on civilian swords. Not to be confused with the stippled effect of tiny recessed dots commonly found on military sword fittings.

NIE  Individual discernible white martensite crystals found within the **hamon**.

NIOI  Crystals like **nie**, but much finer, forming the **hamon**.

OSHIGATA  A rubbing of the blade tang inscription done for record purposes.

POMMEL  Hilt cap of a military sword; see also **kabuto-gane** and **kashira**.

## GLOSSARY OF TERMS AND REIGN ERAS

QUILLION  The end or finial of a hilt crossguard.

RIO-HITSU  The holes in a sword guard (**tsuba**) for retention clip, **kogai, kozuka** etc.

SAKURA  Cherry blossom with five petals; see Fig. 2 (vii). A very common decorative motif used on many Japanese military swords.

SAMÉ  Rayskin used on hilts and scabbards which is characterised by rounded nodules of varying size; see **shagreen**.

SARUTE  A metal loop or cord passing through the **kabuto-gane** through which the sword knot is tied.

SAYA  The Japanese name for a scabbard.

SEPPA  Small guard washers; up to three may be found on each side of the **dai-seppa**.

SHAGREEN  A word of Turkish origin, used for sharkskin found on the hilts and scabbards, characterised by small diamond-shaped nodules; see **samé**.

SHAKUDO  A gunmetal finish applied to sword mountings, especially civilian examples, achieved through the patination of copper mixed with small amounts of gold.

SHIBABIKI  An intermediate scabbard reinforcement, binding the two halves together. It was used for decorative purposes only on **shin-** and **kai-guntō** scabbards.

SHIN-GUNTŌ  Shin- (new) gun (military) tō (sword). The most common of Army swords from World War Two based on the traditional **tachi**.

SHINOGI  Side ridge line of a traditional-shaped blade running parallel to the back and cutting edges.

SHINOGI-ZUKURI  Traditional curved Japanese sword blade having a raised ridge line (**shinogi**) and a centre of curvature midway along its length.

SHIRA-SAYA  A plain white wood keeper scabbard and hilt for storing an unmounted blade.

SHOE  Same as **drag**.

SUNAGASHI  Swept lines of **nie** found along, and within, the **hamon**-like strips of sand.

TACHI  A traditional slung sword with a 610–1,270mm (24–50") blade. The scabbard has two suspension mounts (**ashi**) to accommodate the belt hangers.

TANTŌ  A traditional dirk fitted with a guard; see **aikuchi**.

TSUBA  The guard of a civilian sword, **tantō**, and **shin-** and **kai-guntō** swords.

TSUKA  The hilt of a Japanese sword.

TSUKA-ITO  The hilt binding of a Japanese sword.

WAKIZASHI  A traditional short sword with a 300–610mm (12–24") blade, carried cutting edge uppermost through the waist sash as a companion to the **katana**.

YAKIBA  The tempered (or, more correctly, 'hardened') edge of a traditional Japanese blade which is bordered by the **hamon**.

YASURI-ME  Tang file marks.

YOKOTE  Vertical line separating the blade from the point section.

# JAPANESE MILITARY AND CIVIL SWORDS AND DIRKS

## Modern Japanese emperors and nengo

The lineage of the emperors claims unbroken descent from the first emperor, Jimmu-Tenno, who, so it is said, founded the empire in 660 BC. On acceding to the throne each new emperor gives his period of rule a reign name or 'nengo' by which his supremacy is known. After his death the emperor is also known by his 'nengo'. Thus Hirohito is now known as Emperor Shōwa. The periods since the overthrow of the 'Shogun' and restoration of the emperor as the supreme figurehead are:

| Date | Emperor | Nengo | Characters |
|---|---|---|---|
| 1868–1912 | Mutsuhito | Meiji (Enlightened rule) | 明治 |
| 1912–1926 | Yoshihito | Taishō (Great correctness or equity) | 大正 |
| 1926–1989 | Hirohito | Shōwa (Radiant peace) | 昭和 |
| 1989–Present | Akihito | Heisei (Achieving peace) | 平成 |

## Sword periods

Ancient – pre-AD 900.

KOTŌ (old swords) – 900–1596  Some references specifiy 1530 or even 1603 as the ending of this sword period but the majority use 1596 which is the commencement of the Keichō reign-era and about the time swords were confiscated from farmers and commoners. In 1600 one of the greatest blade-making centres, Osafune, was destroyed in a flood.

SHINTŌ (new swords) – 1596–1800.

SHIN-SHINTŌ (new-new swords) – 1800–1868. This period conveniently terminates at the restoration of the Emperor Mutsuhito in 1868. Not until 1876 was sword wear prohibited, after which the decline in blade manufacture occurred. Therefore 1876 could be preferred to 1868.

MODERN – 1868–1945. Modern blade dating should be by nengo, i.e. Meiji, Taishō and Shōwa.

SHINSAKUTŌ (newly made swords) – 1953–Present. Contemporary blades made after 1953 when the post-war blade manufacture prohibition was rescinded. They have an emphasis on 'art' rather than 'use'.

GLOSSARY OF TERMS AND REIGN ERAS

***Fig. 1*** Four common forms of sword knot:

    (i)    Army kyu-guntō and parade sabre. Cavalry Officers.

    (ii)    Navy kyu-guntō and parade sabre. General Officers parade sabre and kyu-guntō model.

    (iii)    Shin-guntō.
Kai-guntō.
1944 regulation Army (Officers) sword. Sometimes on Army kyu-guntō after 1934.

    (iv)    Army NCOs shin-guntō.
Cavalry Troopers and Army NCOs sabres.
Some Civil Officials swords.
(These all-leather knots are brown. There are similar British military black leather knots.)

***Fig. 2*** 'Mon' and variants used as insignia on military and civil swords; see also Fig. 51.

(i)    Kiri (Paulownia imperialis) of 5:7:5 floret type (Go-shichi no kiri). Originally used by the Imperial family but given to senior officers to denote their high rank. Found on naval kyu-guntō and parade sabres of Flag Officer (Admiral) rank, Diplomatic swords of Chokunin grade (appointment personally approved by the Emperor) plus the swords and dirks of Senior Railway Officials, the Imperial Household and Government-General of Korea.

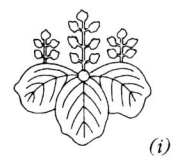
(i)

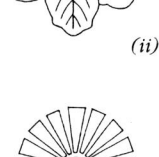
(ii)

(ii)    As (i) but the 3:5:3 floret type (Go-san no kiri) found on Diplomatic swords of Sōnin grade (standard appointment) and dirks of Junior Railway Officials.

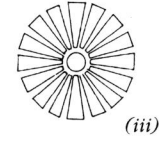
(iii)

(iii)    A sun with sixteen rays (Hiashi) previously believed to denote army General Officer rank grades. However now believed to denote the Very Senior Civil Police and Fire Bureau rank grades or, alternatively, an unidentified police unit.

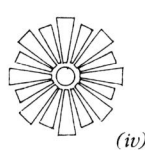
(iv)

(iv)    Variation of the sixteen-rayed sun (iii) above. Compare with the police badge in Fig. 51 (i).

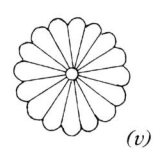
(v)

(v)    The regular form of the Imperial sixteen-petal kiku (chrysanthemum) properly called the 'Juroku kiku'. Associated with the Imperial Household and Family.

(vi)

(vi)    Sixteen-petal kiku with a further sixteen petals showing, properly called the 'Juroku yaekiku' and used by the Emperor. Found on swords believed to have been carried by members of the Imperial Household and/or officers of the Imperial Guard.

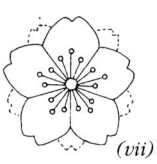
(vii)

(vii)    Sakura (cherry blossom) which is a very common decorative motif on Japanese military and Police swords. A variant with a further five petals (shown dotted), properly called the 'Kadosakura', is usually found on Army swords.

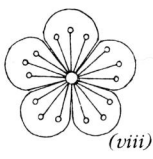
(viii)

(viii)    Ume (plum blossom) associated with Manchukuoan and Chinese Republican and Nationalist swords and dirks but not used on Japanese military swords. It is easily confused with (vii).

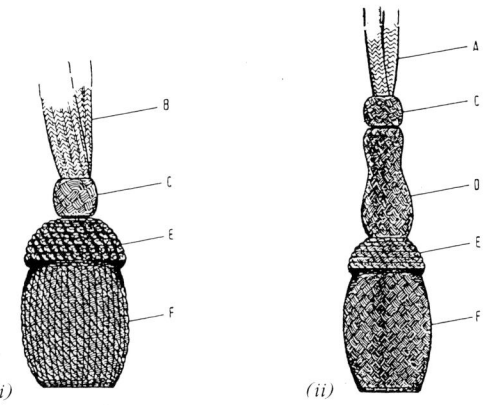

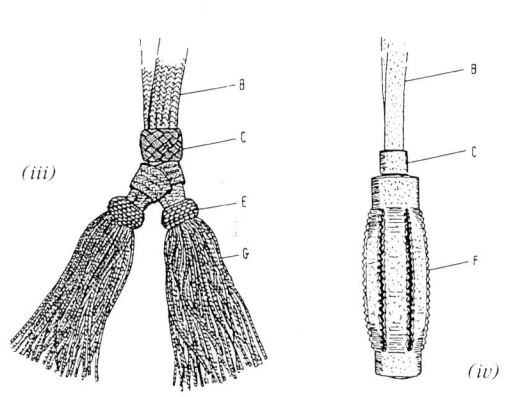

A – Cord   B – Strap   C – Slide   D – Stem
E – Crown   F – Knot   G – Tassel

# Army Swords
# c.1871–c.1877

### Early regulation Army (fighting) sword patterns c.1871–c.1877

Contemporary photographs are essential for researching the history of Japanese military swords. One dated to 1867 on page thirty-four of the *Nippon no Gunpuku* (see Bibliography) shows perhaps the earliest military-style sword located although, typically, details are indistinct. Recognisable patterns do not appear in photographs until around 1871, but actual examples are virtually non-existent, at least in the West. Those carried in the Sino–Japanese war of 1894 and by Japanese troops in the Chinese Boxer Rebellion of 1900 are also usually indistinct preventing proper identification. It is not until the Russo–Japanese war of 1904–5 that clear pictures become relatively common.

The drawings of war artists, although an invaluable guide, must be treated with great caution because of inaccuracy, mistakes and artistic licence. Consequently identification of all sword patterns up to the Army kyu-guntō have mainly been based on line drawings and dates in a Japanese book called the *Nippon no Gunso* (see Bibliography) which has proved an essential reference. However, there is reason to believe that some of the datings are inaccurate, thus the recourse to 'circa' in identification dates in this book.

The first four documented fighting swords seem to have European-style open-bar handguards with brass (probably gilded for officers) hilt mounts. Decoration appears non-existent or is possibly restricted to the sakura or kadosakura (cherry blossom variants) which appear on most Japanese military swords. The grips are black shagreen or white samē (rayskin) with intermittent brass wire binding. Hilt lengths may be longer than normal European swords to favour the Japanese style of fighting. Blade types are unknown but would be expected to be the traditional Japanese shinogi-zukuri form, either machine-made or hand-forged. The latter may be expected in officers' swords which possibly utilised older blades with habaki (blade collar) from traditional katana. Scabbards are steel, probably nickel-plated for officers or blackened for other ranks, with one or two suspension mounts fitted with hanging rings. Distinctive decorative features for various rank grades may, perhaps, be expected but have not been established.

Only one example has been reported which is similar to Fig 31(i) and could be a Warrant Officers version.[1] Plain mounts and a domed pommel as in Fig. 3 (i), (ii), (iii) with a black shagreen grip. Blackened? steel scabbard having one suspension mount. The blade, reused from an earlier sword, has a shortened tang signed by Sakata Terunobu of Higo province dated 1821. Copper habaki. Three of the first four fighting patterns seem only to vary in the handguard design:

## Regulation c.1871 Army Commissioned Officers sword

No example has been located to confirm the details shown in Fig. 3 (i).

The open-bar handguard design appears to be the same as a sword apparently carried by Police (officers) who fought on the government side in the 1877 Satsuma Rebellion (see Plates 253, 254). However, the pommel shape is different.

Presumably this pattern was carried by officers of all branches of the Army until being replaced by the kyu-guntō.

## Regulation c.1873 pattern Cavalry, Artillery, Transport and Infantry Sergeant-Majors dress sword

Nothing is known other than the details shown in Fig. 3 (ii).

## Regulation c.1877 pattern Infantry Adjutants and NCOs sword

No example has been located to confirm the details shown in Fig. 3 (iv).

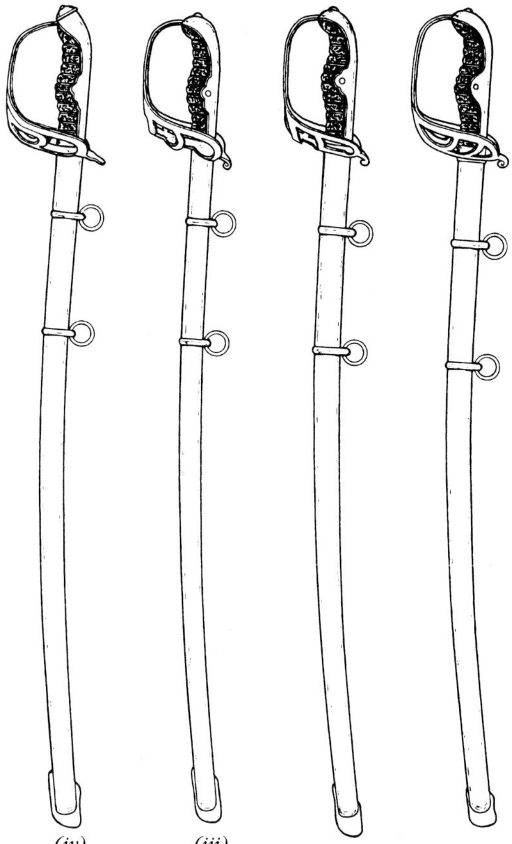

*Fig. 3 Regulation c.1871–c.1877 Army sword patterns based on illustrations in the* Nippon no Gunso *(see Bibliography):*

*(i)   c.1871 Commissioned Officers.*

*(ii)  c.1873 Cavalry, Artillery, Transport and Infantry Sergeant-Majors dress sword.*

*(iii) c.1877 Cavalry, Artillery, Transport and Engineer Adjutants and NCOs.*

*(iv) c.1877 Infantry Adjutants and NCOs.*

Presumably this, and the following item, replaced the 1873 pattern above.

---

1 Shown on page 15 of *Imperial Swords of Japan 1868–1945* by Jim Dawson.

JAPANESE MILITARY AND CIVIL SWORDS AND DIRKS

## Regulation c.1877 pattern Cavalry, Artillery, Transport and Engineer Adjutants and NCOs sword.

Again nothing is known other than the details shown in Fig. 3 (iii); see also Plate 1. Presumably this, together with the last item, replaced the 1873 pattern above.

All the above patterns appear to have been superseded by the Army kyu-guntō and Cavalry pattern swords by 1886. Photographs of such items seem to be rare but Plate 1 shows one pattern in the 1904–5 Russo–Japanese war. This implies that official dress regulations permitted their use until becoming worn out when they would be replaced by the then current pattern.

Sword knot type and colouring, in all cases, is unknown but the brown leather type in Fig. 1 (iv) was probably utilised by NCOs.

1875 may the actual introduction date for these patterns. There also appears to be a fifth pattern for mounted NCOs.

**Plate 1**  *Japanese troops entering Kinchau Castle, Korea, during the Russo–Japanese war of 1904–5. The mounted soldier (probably cavalry) on the left is of unknown rank but carries an open-bar hilted sword. It appears to be the c.1877 Cavalry, Artillery, Transport and Engineer Adjutants and NCOs pattern with a single suspension mount and leather sling. Unfortunately the sword knot is unclear. Photographs of the 1870s open-bar sword patterns are rare. (Neil Moir Snr).*

**Plate 2**  *Drawing by a Japanese war artist in the Sino–Japanese war of 1894 showing a charge by what seems to be Japanese artillerymen against Chinese soldiers. Two are carrying open-bar half-basket hilted swords which are probably either the c.1873 or c.1877 pattern NCOs sword (for Cavalry, Artillery, Transport and Infantry) with metal scabbards and acorn knots. Two are wielding Arisaka bayonets. The last man has an unidentified sidearm with ribbed grip, backstrap, inverted quillions and a brass- or steel-mounted leather scabbard. Suspension appears to be by frog. It is a different style from artillery sidearms shown in the Russo–Japanese war (see Plates 8, 9, 10). He is holding a large curved sabre with tassels which appears to be Chinese, probably picked up on the battlefield. (Richard Fuller).*

**Plate 3**  *A Japanese war artist's impression of the attack by Army Captain Matsuaki and bugler Shinekami Genjiro at the Battle of Asan in the Sino–Japanese war, October 1894. Although there may be artistic licence at work here, the Captain's sword seems to have a semi-bowl guard, ribbed grip, backstrap and, most unusually, two barrel-shaped knots. Curved blade of unokubi-zukuri form (see Fig. 59 (vi)). Metal scabbard. The pattern has not been identified. The bugler has some form of military-style dirk with a backstrap. The scabbard is probably leather with a brass or steel chape. It is carried in a leather frog. (Richard Fuller).*

# Army 1875 (& 1886) Officers Dress Sword

**Regulation 1875 (& 1886) pattern Army (and Medical Corps) Commissioned Officers dress sword**

Introduction of this Western-style sword, probably French- or American-inspired,[1] was ratified by the 1875 Imperial Government decree no. 174 (although it may possibly have been available in 1873).[2] It was modified in 1886.[4] Usage was by Army Commissioned Officers including Generals and Army Medical Officers.[3]

There were two official versions determined by the blade shapes:

(i) Epée style for full dress – narrow straight blade.
(ii) Sabre style for field use – curved blade of traditional shinogi-zukuri form.

Both have the same hilt based on the design of a European court sword. The fittings are gilded brass comprising an urn-shaped pommel, curved knucklebow and two shell-guards. The reverse guard is hinged to fold flat against the wearer's body. The knucklebow is decorated with sakura and leaves and the pommel features a raised dragonfly motif. The grip may be white or black same, shagreen or leather having brass wire set in a spiralling groove. Black horn may also be a variant but this has not been confirmed. The General Officer grades have turtle-shell grips. The obverse guard features a sun-ray motif, common to all rank variants, but the 1875 pattern has flattened ends and the modified 1886 model has notched ends. Scabbards are normally black leather, fitted with two gilded brass mounts. The mount (locket) has a decorated stud on the obverse for suspension in a frog. However, the curved blade version has a suspension band incorporating one hanging ring, the frog stud being omitted. It appears from Plate 7 that an all-metal (plated steel?) scabbard may have been an alternative for the curved blade variety. All are believed to terminate with a prominent ball finial which acts as a drag.

Rank is determined by decorative features on both the obverse guard and (leather type) scabbard fittings:

Company Officers (Lieutenant, Captain) – Sun-ray motif on handguard. Virtually plain scabbard fittings. Fig. 4 (i).

Field Officers (Major, Lt-Col, Colonel) – As last but with an ornately decorated lower scabbard mount. Decorated upper and lower grip bands.

General Officers – Scabbard and handguard decoration as for Field Officers but individual rank is determined by the presence of silver stars on the obverse guard as follows:

Major-General – Two stars (1875). One star (1886).
Lieutenant-General – Three stars (1875). Two stars (1886).

# JAPANESE MILITARY AND CIVIL SWORDS AND DIRKS

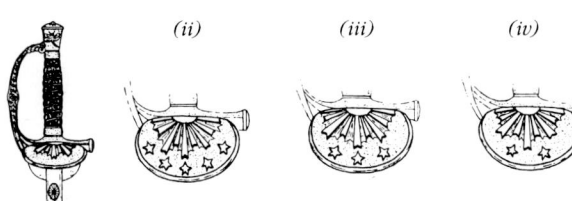

(iv)

***Fig. 4*** *Regulation 1875 pattern Army Commissioned Officers dress sword (and Army Medical Corps Officers):*

(i) *Company Officers (Lieutenant, Captain) and Field Officers (Major, Lieutenant-Colonel, Colonel) grade sword. Both had the obverse shell-guard shown. The drawing shows the Company Officers scabbard while the Field Officers scabbard chape was more ornate.*

*General Officer ranks are distinguished by the number of silver stars on the guard:*

(ii) *General – 5 no. (1875). 3 no. (1886).*

(iii) *Lieutenant-General – 3 no. (1875). 2 no. (1886).*

(iv) *Major-General – 2 no. (1875). 1 no. (1886).*

General – Five stars (1875). Three stars (1886)

Dress sword knot and colouring is unknown. However, swords worn in the field seem to have the barrel-shaped Army kyu-guntō pattern knots (Fig. 1 (i)).

Contemporary photographic records for this sword pattern are very scarce. The only pictorial evidence for the use of the curved blade version comes from photos of the 1904–5 Russo–Japanese war where it is seen carried by Army Medical Corps Officers. Full dress wear appears to have been abandoned in favour of the Army Officers kyu-guntō style parade sabre, but when this occurred is unknown. However, its appearance in the Russo–Japanese war implies retention by older Army officers and by officers of the Medical Corps. Indeed, by that time it may even have been officially sanctioned for that branch only, but this is speculative. No example has been reported with a 'cross' in the hilt ornamentation as is featured in Red Cross dirks to indicate use by that organisation (see Figs. 55, 56). No evidence to suggest wear by Army medical personnel in World War Two has been found so it may be considered obsolete before 1941 and possibly as early as 1914. Any example must be classified as rare.

This sword pattern appears to have given rise to several variants, generally unidentified. Two such items are shown in Plates 283, 284.

***Plate 4*** *Rare 1886 modified version of the 1875 pattern Army Officers dress sword of Company Officers grade. Brass fittings and black shagreen grip which has lost the wire binding in the grooves. (Han Bing Siong).*

1 Adopted by the French Army in the 1840s as Infantry Regimental and General Officers pattern and as the 1860 pattern US Army Staff and Field Officers sword.
2 Page fifty-eight of the *Nippon no Gunpuku* (see Bibliography), which was kindly translated by Han Bing Siong. It also refers to the 'strengthening and enlarging of the 1873 [dress?] system'. This could be taken to infer that the 1875 regulations acknowledged an earlier introduction date of 1873, which is that given in the *Nippon no Gunso* (see Bibliography) for this sword pattern.
3 Use by Medical Officers is confirmed in the *Nippon no Gunpuku*.
4. *Swords of Imperial Japan 1868–1945*

## ARMY 1875 (& 1886) OFFICERS DRESS SWORD

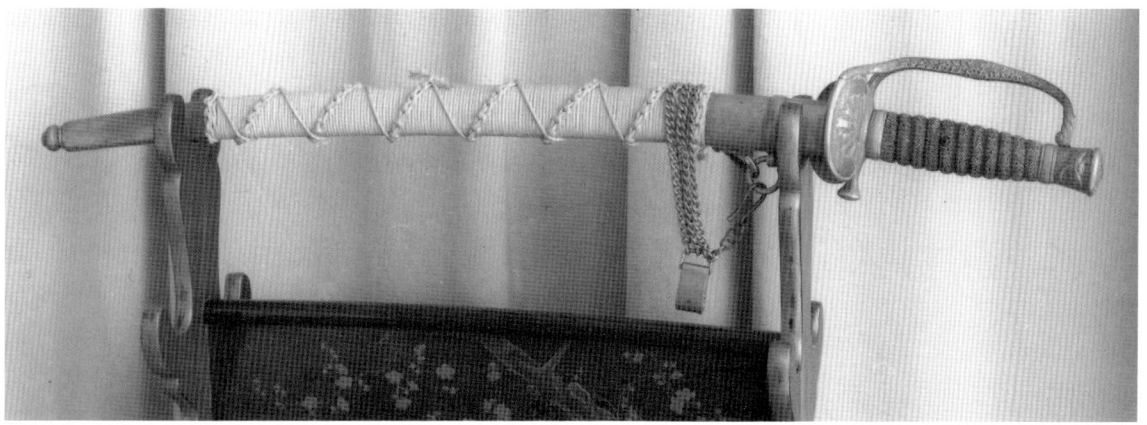

**Plate 5**  1875 (as modified in 1886) pattern Army dress sword shown in Plate 4. This example has a traditional blade reused from an older samurai sword. The brass-mounted leather-covered scabbard has been elaborately tied with white cord which, perhaps, was added as a weaving and knot exercise by an Allied seaman returning from Japan after World War Two (see Plate 110). Suspension is by a single hanging ring and chain hanger. (Han Bing Siong).

**Plate 6**  Medical Corps officer with a rare Army Officers 1875 (& 1886) pattern dress sword. It has a curved blade, probably of traditional form, in a leather scabbard having a metal locket and chape. Suspension is by means of a single leather strap. This photograph was taken in Manchuria on 1 May 1904. (Richard Fuller).

**Plate 7**  Japanese troops outside the city of Liaoyang, Manchuria in September 1904. The officer with the binoculars has a rare Army Officers 1875 (& 1886) pattern dress sword which appears to be in a steel scabbard. The knot, of indistinct type, is wrapped around the knucklebow. Suspension is by means of at least one leather strap. Presumably it has a traditional hand-forged blade if intended to be a fighting weapon. (Richard Fuller).

# Army Artillery Sidearms

In keeping with most late nineteenth-century Western armies Japan issued a sidearm or hanger (short sword) for use by artillery other-ranks. The design is based on the Roman legionary 'Gladius' which was a short stabbing sword. Concurrent use by Japanese infantry has not been confirmed. The *Nippon no Gunso* (see Bibliography) describes them as 'artillery and gunners (Hō-hei) sidearms'. They were probably intended as defensive weapons but could serve as tools for cutting wood etc. Their decline, certainly in the West, seems to have been due to the use of the rifle bayonet, although this may not have affected the artillery. Japan appears to have used at least three authorised types, of which two have been seen by the authors. For the purpose of this book they have been designated as Types 1, 2 and 3 for clarity.

## Type 1. (1886 pattern)

The brass hilt fittings comprise an obverse ribbed grip, plain reverse, prominent tang button and short crossguard which terminates with disc-shaped quillions. Manufacturing (or issue?) numbers are stamped on the crossguard reverse. Single-edged straight blade having a wide fuller on the obverse only plus the manufacturer's details and date stamped near the guard (Plate 10). The reverse of the blade is plain and may bear a single stamped Japanese character close to the guard.

Brass-mounted scabbard of black leather over a wooden liner and a steel mouthpiece. The top locket obverse has a raised frog stud which is stamped with a number which probably should match that on the crossguard. However, the example shown has different numbers because the scabbard has been interchanged at some time, although this may be a common occurrence. In this instance both the hilt and scabbard bear the same museum catalogue number.

Dimensions should be consistent since mass-produced. Hilt length 127mm (5"). Scabbard length 536mm (21⅛"). Blade length 523mm (20 9/16"). Maximum blade width 32mm (1¼"). Weight of sword 27 ounces. Weight of scabbard 9½ ounces.

The ribbed grip and pommel appear to have been copied from the Prussian M52 infantry model. The Type 1 was authorised on 25 October 1886 and officially discontinued on 11 November 1898. That which is illustrated is dated 1892 although 1893 is also known. Numbers from 12090 to 80713 are reported which indicates a great number were made, if produced sequentially. Only a few examples have been reported which confirms they are very scarce or rare. None is known with matching scabbard and crossguard numbers.

Perhaps usage was for, or preferred by, NCOs since the quality is superior to the steel-mounted Type 2 described below.

One example in a private collection has the obverse of the leather scabbard personalised by the carving of a Japanese dragon which stands out in relief and has eyes made from steel pinheads.[1] It is most unusual for a standard issue piece to be privately decorated, but whether it was done during, or after, the military service of the original owner is unknown.

## Type 2

Although based on the Type 1 this resembles a bayonet in appearance but has no provision for fixing to a rifle. The steel-mounted hilt has plain wooden grips secured by two rivets, a short crossguard with downturned quillions and a large ball pommel lacking the prominent tang button. The 534mm (21") blade has a single fuller on each side. It is also stamped and dated in the same manner as the Type 1 but the fittings are not numbered. One example examined was dated 1886.

---

[1] Donald Barnes collection.

**Plate 8** *Obverse of the Type 1 1886 pattern artillery sidearm showing the ribbed grip and fullered blade.* (Richard Fuller).

Black leather scabbard having a steel chape and top locket which has a protruding frog loop. The method of wear, which is the same as a Japanese bayonet, is by means of a frog and leather securing strap.

Probably also introduced in 1886 and abolished in 1898. Use by enlisted men is indicated by the utilitarian appearance. This model is also rare.

## Type 3 (1885 pattern)

This is known from a drawing in the *Nippon no Gunso* (see Bibliography) where described as a 'walking-out (To-ho) sidearm (see Fig. 5) plus an example on page 36 of *Swords of Imperial Japan 1868–1945* Wooden grip, brass hilt (and scabbard?) fittings and a crossguard which curves upwards. Authorised on 25 February 1885 for privates, NCOs and supervisors of some units including Artillery, Engineers and Battery Guards. Abolished on 11 November 1898.

**Plate 9** *Reverse of the Type 1 1886 pattern artillery sidearm showing the plain grip and blade.* (Richard Fuller).

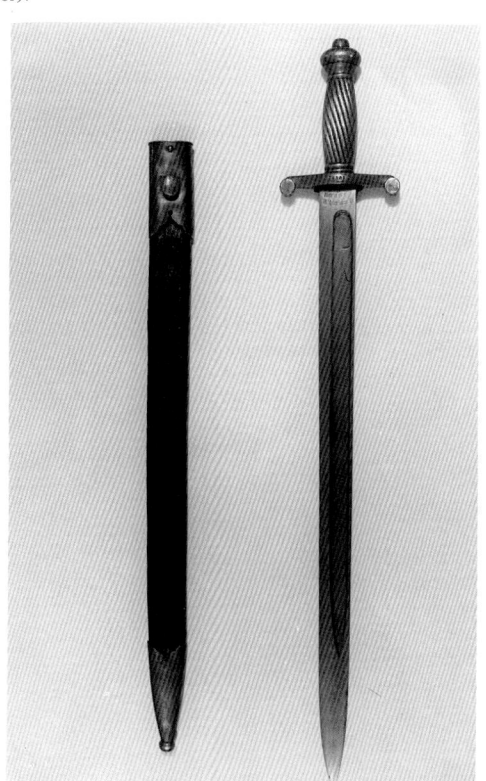

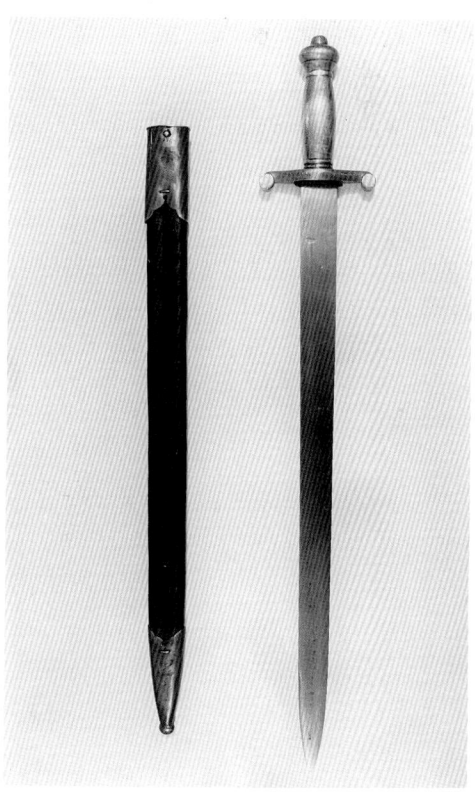

## JAPANESE MILITARY AND CIVIL SWORDS AND DIRKS

No photographic evidence for the use of any of these models after the 1904–5 Russo–Japanese war has been found.

*Plate 10* Obverse blade and crossguard markings on the Type 1 artillery sidearm (see Plates 8 and 9). The Japanese characters read, right to left, TOKYO HŌHEI KŌSHŌ (Tokyo Arsenal) and MEIJI NI-JŪ GO NEN SEI (manufactured in 1892). The lower single character is unidentified. The crossguard number is 12281 (but the scabbard frog stud is stamped 80713). (Richard Fuller).

*Fig. 5* Japanese sidearms carried around the time of the 1904–5 Russo–Japanese war. These drawings are redrawn from the Nippon no Gunsō (see Bibliography):

Type 1 (1886 pat.) – 'Artillery and gunners (Hō-hei) sidearm'. It generally matches the actual example shown in Plates 8 and 9 although the grip ribbing, blade groove and scabbard chape are different.
Type 3 (1885 pat.) – 'Walking-out (To-ho) sidearm'. This drawing is in error since the crossguard curves slightly upwards.

*Plate 11* Japanese artilleryman in the 1904–5 Russo–Japanese war with a sidearm carried in a leather frog. Unfortunately it cannot be ascertained whether it is the Type 1 or 2 model. (Richard Fuller).

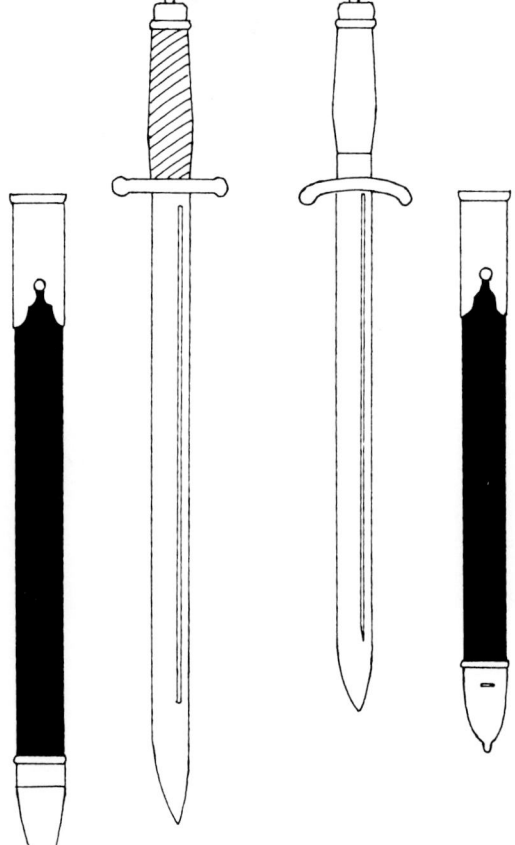

*Plate 12* Japanese soldiers caring for a wounded Russian prisoner in the 1904–5 Russo–Japanese war. The one on the right has an artillery sidearm which appears to be the brass-hilted Type 1 with a pronounced tang button as shown in Plates 8, 9, 10. The soldier on the left has an indistinct sword with a solid half-basket guard which may be the 1899 pattern Infantry NCOs sabre. (Richard Fuller).

# Army c.1886 Regulation Pattern NCOs Sword

There appears to have been an Army NCOs sword for field use which was contemporary, for a time, with the Officers kyu-guntō. Known only from an illustration in the *Nippon no Gunso* it was apparently introduced for Army NCOs by the dress amendments of 1886, presumably replacing the c.1877 pattern, and has been redrawn for Fig. 6. Use is believed to be for Infantry and Artillery with a maximum life of thirteen years until superseded by either the 1892 or 1899 pattern sabres for Infantry NCOs and Cavalry troopers.

The hilt is generally plain and lacks side-ears but no details are known of the metal used, grip material or blade configuration. However, the scabbard must have been metal, probably nickel-plated. No doubt manufacture was by one of the arsenals such as that at Tokyo.

Plate 13 shows a tantalising out-of-focus view of a sword which may be this pattern since the hilt lacks side-ears. The sword knot is the leather type (Fig. 1 (iv)) generally associated with NCOs swords of all periods. Unfortunately the guard and backstrap configuration is unclear. Curved metal scabbard with one suspension mount and a leather strap hanger.

That in Plate 14 could either be this sword pattern or the 1899 sabre but, again, details are obscured.

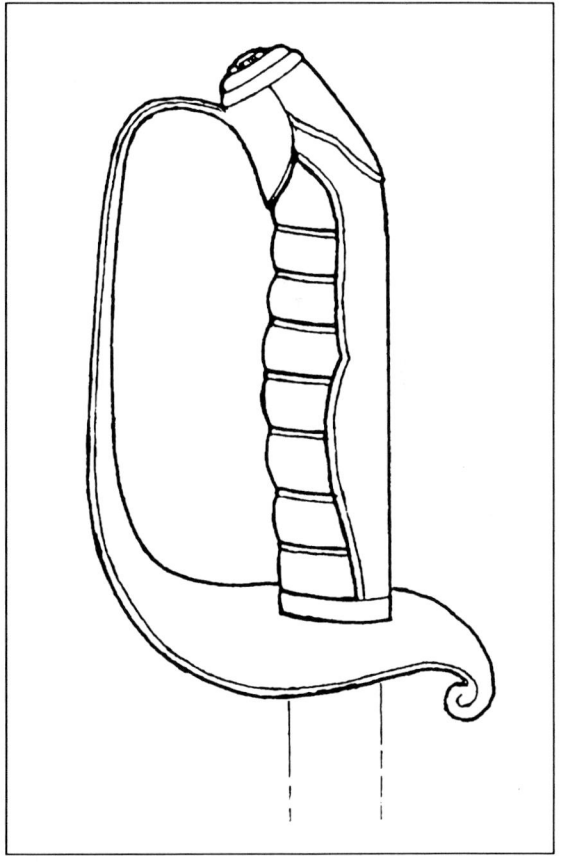

***Fig. 6***  *c.1886 regulation pattern Army Non-Commissioned Officers sword.*

# JAPANESE MILITARY AND CIVIL SWORDS AND DIRKS

***Plate 13*** *Artillerymen disembarking at Chenampo, Korea in 1905. The soldier with the sword appears to be an NCO because of the leather sword knot. The sword pattern is unidentified since the hilt lacks side ears (which would be present if it were a kyu-guntō or 1899 pattern NCOs sabre). The scabbard is steel with one suspension mount and a leather strap wrapped around in the regain position. This seems to confirm that there was a sword pattern prescribed for NCOs (both artillery and infantry) which superseded the c.1877 pattern.* (Richard Fuller).

***Plate 14*** *A Japanese soldier guarding a Russian prisoner in the Russo–Japanese war of 1904–5. His rank is unknown but probably that of a Private or NCO. He would be expected to carry the 1899 pattern Army NCOs sabre but the light colouration of the scabbard is inconsistent with the normal dark finish. Perhaps it is the same as that shown in Plate 13.* (Richard Fuller).

# Army 1875 (& 1886) Kyu-Guntō

### Regulation pattern Army kyu-guntō (and possible Very Senior Police Officers kyu-guntō)

The name kyu- (proto or first) gun (military) tō (sword) i.e. 'first military sword' is really a misnomer since it is not the 'first'. However, this name is in common usage in the West so will be retained for this book. There was probably no actual pattern name, just a year or type number. Perhaps it may be regarded as the 'first universal Army sword' since it apparently superseded the c.1871 Army Officers sword and all the c.1877 patterns (only Cavalry officers being given their own distinctive model).

The Army kyu-guntō was introduced on 24 November 1875 for all Commissioned Officer grades. On 6 July 1886 the Warrant Officers model was authorised and the Company Officers model modified.[1] It became the most common sword pattern seen in the 1904–5 Russo–Japanese war, lasting until the 1934 pattern shin-guntō was introduced. However, many were carried in action up to the end of World War Two by officers who preferred to retain them. Although carried as fighting weapons they may not have been popular as such (see naval kyu-guntō). The full dress version was represented by the much lighter Army parade sabre.

The hilt, with the exception of the handguard, is identical to the c.1877 Police (officers?) sword which would be a derivation of this pattern if introduced later (see Plate 254). The narrow obverse handguards of the three Commissioned Officers models have two pierced panels decorated with foliage and the kadosakura form of cherry blossom. All are identical to the equivalent Army parade sabre guard in Plate 34. The Police Officer variants (plates 20–23) also use the same guard design with kadosakura. The Warrant Officers version has a plain solid guard. Company, Field and General Officers models have backstrap side-ears decorated with raised kadosakura; however, the sakura is used on the side-ears of Police swords. Hilt fittings are usually unmarked but a few have the lyre-like stamp of the Suya Company of Tokyo (Fig. 61 (xxiii)) on the guard underside.

Grips are normally white samé having intermittent brass wire binding. Variations encountered are lacquered and polished white samé, black samé, black shagreen and, in rare cases, turtle-shell, although the latter is confined to swords of General Officer grade. Hilt lengths are variable to suit the owner's requirements and/or blade tangs.

Military rank grading is determined by the backstrap decorative variations tabulated below and illustrated in Plates 16 to 19.:

Warrant Officers 1886 pat. – Plain backstrap, upper panel and side-ears. Plain solid handguard. Very rare.(None have been reported).
Company Officers (2nd & 1st Lieutenants, Captain). 1875 pat. – Stippled backstrap with plain upper panel. Kadosakura on side ears. Pierced handguard. Very rare.

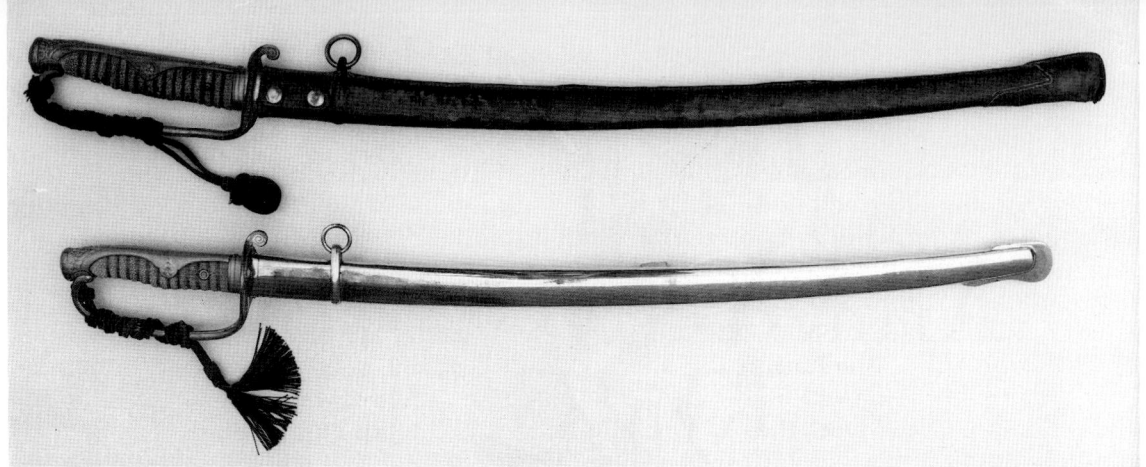

***Plate 15*** *Two 1886 pat. Army Company Officers grade kyu-gunto with white samé grips. That on the top has a steel scabbard fitted with a brown leather combat cover, unsigned Shintō period blade and correct black barrel sword knot. The bottom example has the normal plated steel scabbard, unsigned wakizashi blade (possibly Kotō period, i.e. pre-1596) and a shin-guntō pattern sword knot. (Richard Fuller).*

Company Officers. 1886 pat. – Stippled backstrap with kadosakura and leaves in upper panel. Pierced handguard. (Plate 16). Common.

Field Officers (Maj, Lt-Col, Colonel). 1886 pat. – Entire backstrap, or almost all of it, decorated with kadosakura and leaves. The upper panel is stippled. Pierced handguard. (Plate 18). Scarce.

General officer (Maj.-Gen, Lt-Gen, General). 1886 pat. – Decoration and handguard as for Field Officers. Turtle-shell grip. Very rare.

***Plates 16, 17*** *Army 1886 pat. Company Officers grade (Lieutenant, Captain) kyu-guntō identified by the small upper panel of a kadosakura (cherry blossom) and leaves. A fairly common item. This particular example, however, has the scarce black shagreen grip instead of the normal white samé. A silver wisteria mon (family badge) of the Fujiwara clan has been fixed to the lower backstrap. The shin-guntō pattern sword knot indicates this sword was carried in World War Two. (Ron Gregory).*

*Swords of Imperial Japan* (see Bibliography) adamantly states that kyu-guntō and parade sabres with the Hiashi (sun) hilt badge (Fig. 2 (iii), (iv)) are not Army General Officer grade swords. See Plates 20–23.

The blade is removable being secured to the hilt by the traditional bamboo peg, called a 'mekugi', which passes through a hole in the blade tang.[2] However, those with short hilts, or perhaps mass-produced blades, may, in rare cases, have a tapered tang threaded at the top which engages with a pommel nut in the same manner as is used on parade sabres. A brass or copper blade collar (habaki) is always used. The blade type was down to the owner's choice and may often be of some age, being reused from older samurai swords.

***Plates 18, 19*** *Scarce 1875 pat. Army Field Officers grade (Major, Lt-Col, Colonel) kyu-guntō identified by the fully decorated backstrap of kadosakura. The upper panel is plain. The grip is normally white samé but the example shown is black. (Ron Gregory).*

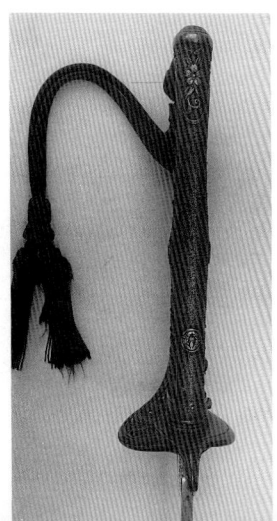 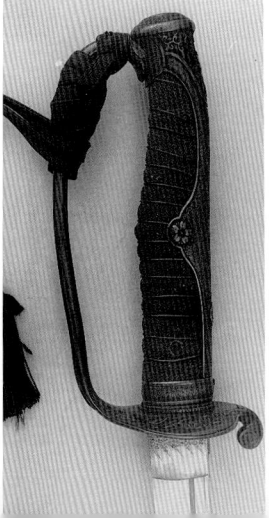 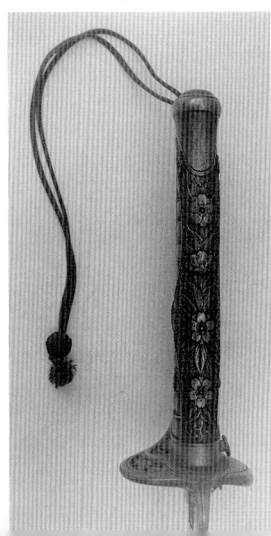 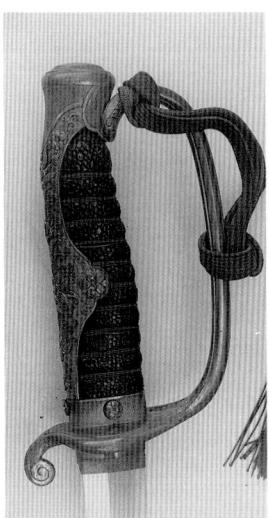

## ARMY 1875 (& 1886) KYU-GUNTŌ

Contemporary oil-tempered or hand-forged gendaitō can also be found but are in the traditional shinogi-zukuri form. A kyu-guntō with a Shōwa period blade has been found with a 3mm deep downward turned seppa (blade washer) which fits over the steel scabbard mouth to act as a seal when sheathed, as in Plate 94.

A plated steel scabbard with a wooden liner is the norm for this sword type. There may be one or two suspension bands each fitted with a hanging ring.[3] The lower band, when present, is removable and can be slid over the drag (Plate 24). Protection of the scabbard in the field was afforded by wrapping with a strip of cloth or bandage which was easily removable, or by means of a brown leather combat cover secured by a flap incorporating one or two press studs. There is no photographic evidence to support the use of wooden field scabbards in the Russo–Japanese war of 1904–5. Such scabbards, when found on kyu-guntō, appear to date from World War Two. Suspension was by means of leather straps or chain hangers (see later under 'Sword Belts').

Retention in the scabbard is by means of a spring clip which engages with a slot in the scabbard mouth. It is operated by a push button which also protrudes through the hilt collar (fuchi) reverse. Secondary retention may also be found with leather-covered scabbards. This is in the form of a leather strap riveted or sewn to the reverse of the combat cover, which is passed between the hilt and handguard to return to a press stud on the scabbard cover obverse.

Grip protection, when required, was by means of a white cloth or bandage wrapped around the grip. This was easily replaceable. Another system was the use of a leather sleeve, presumably laced up, which covered the grip but left the knucklebow and guard exposed.

Quality varies according to owners' financial means and choice. The most common option was the addition of the owner's personal mon (family badge) which is normally in the form of a small silver disc fixed to the backstrap. Alternatively one may be engraved directly on the backstrap or pommel top. The owner's family name characters could also be added in silver. (see Plate 179).

Sword knots, in the main, have been assessed from contemporary black and white photographs. Thus the colouration of the General Officers versions are uncertain but thought to be gold: Brown? leather knot and straps (Fig. 1 (iv)).–
    Uncertain. Possibly for field use.[4] See Plate 27.
Squat black barrel knot, gold slide and mid-green

---

**Plates 20, 21** *The use of sakura decoration and a Hiashi (Fig. 2 (iv)) hilt badge on this kyu-guntō was previously believed to indicate use by Army General Officer ranks. However it is now thought to represent either an unidentified Police unit or, perhaps, a very senior Civil Police rank e.g. Superintendent. A rare sword. See also Plates 22, 23, 44–47. (Ron Gregory).*

**Plates 22, 23** *Very rare kyu-guntō variant with a sun (Hiashi) badge (Fig. 2 (iii)) on the upper backstrap panel and fully decorated with sakura for the remainder of the length. This may indicate use by the most senior Civil Police rank (Superintendent-General?). The owner's silver mon is present near the fuchi (hilt collar). The pierced handguard of this sword (and in Plates 20, 21) is the same as the army kyu-guntō using kadosakura. Note the decorative details of the backstrap are not the same as the Army Field/General Officer models. (Ron Gregory).*

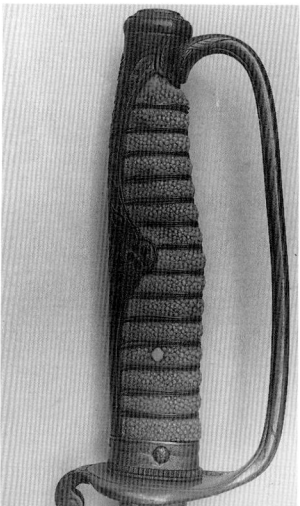

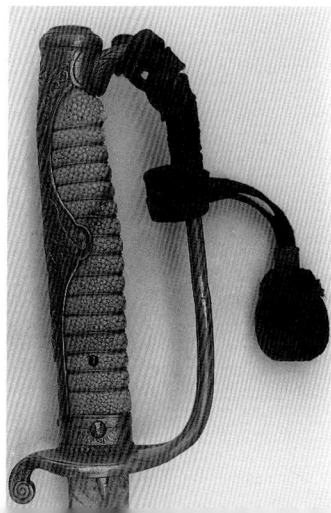

## JAPANESE MILITARY AND CIVIL SWORDS AND DIRKS

linen straps (similar to Fig.1.(i))[5] - Unknown. Possibly Warrant Officer.

Black barrel knot with gold underside, gold slide and black linen straps (Plate 15).- Company Officer and, probably, Field Officer in field uniform. (Possibly also in full dress.)

Gold? barrel knot, stem, slide and dark coloured (black?) straps (Plate 26) – General Officer in field uniform.

Gold? knot, stem, slide and cords? (Plate 83).[6] – General Officer in full dress.

Shin-guntō pattern tassels and straps (Plates 28, 29) – Coloured according to the rank of the wearer but not seen until after the introduction of the shin-guntō. (See under that section for colour coding.)

Variations of this sword pattern do exist (see Plate 179). Indeed a wakizashi length version of the Army kyu-guntō has been seen. The overall length of the sword and scabbard was only around 610mm (24"). The steel scabbard had two suspension mounts but the lower one was not removable. The blade was a traditional hand-forged wakizashi and the grip black samé. One can only assume this was intended as a parade sabre but the blade pattern is normally only found on full-sized kyu-guntō.

Dimensions vary enormously and the following are representative of the range. Overall length of sword and scabbard 893–1,045mm (35 3/16"–41 1/2"). Total weight 48–64 ounces. Blade length (from guard) 536-647mm (21 1/8"–25 1/2"). Maximum blade width 26–28mm (1"–1 11/16"). Hilt length (from guard) 168–200mm (6 5/8"–7 7/8") with an observed maximum of 273mm (10 3/4"). Scabbard length 720–795mm (28 3/8"–30 1/2"). Sword weight 28–44 ounces.

A son could carry his father's blade but whether or not it could be left in superseded mounts remains uncertain. After the introduction of the shin-guntō in 1934 it would seem unlikely that, for example, a Company grade officer would be permitted to carry his father's Field or General grade kyu-guntō (even with the correctly coloured lower grade rank tassel); but Plate 30 may disprove this assumption. However, an officer could continue to carry his own kyu-guntō regardless of rank pattern provided he used the correct grade shin-guntō knot coloration for his rank. Thus a Company Officers grade kyu-guntō can be found with a Field Officers grade shin-guntō knot, but vice versa is unlikely.

---

1 These datings and confirmation of the General officer pattern identification is given in *Swords of Imperial Japan 1868–1945* by Jim Dawson (see Bibliography).
2 Some (early examples?) may have used male/female hilt retaining screws, surmounted by kadosakura which passed through the backstrap side-ears. A Field Officers model with a Kotō period blade in the author's collection lacks both kadosakura but a hole through each side-ear has been plugged with wood and one tang hole alignment is matching. This indicates such a system was originally employed. The normal mekugi is present further down and would thus seem to be a later modification. See rear dust jacket (centre).
3 *Swords of Imperial Japan 1868–1945* states that two fixed suspension mounts were initially prescribed. Later the lower one became removable and even later (by 1904?) only one was used. However in 1932 the lower mount, if used, was ordered to be removable.
4 Plate 14, page twenty-one of *Military Swords of Japan 1868–1945* shows Army Captain Orada with a scarce black grip kyu-guntō which, for some unknown reason, appears to have a knot of this type. Whether a black grip has any significance has not been ascertained.
5 Thanks to David Morrison who allowed the authors to examine the only reported example of this knot. The barrel is shorter than the normal type and has a black base. It appears to be contemporary with the Company Officers kyu-guntō on which it was found.
6 The very light coloration could indicate silver but no authentic example has been located for verification.

---

**Plate 24** *The lower ashi (suspension band) of Army kyu-guntō and parade sabres. The slot indicates it is removable and can be slid over the scabbard drag. The oval shape of this fitting is typical of both fixed and removable ashi. The need for this second ashi appears to be determined by the use of the sword and associated sword belt. The upper fixed ashi is used with the service belt with one sling, the lower one being added for the dress belt with two slings. Kyu-guntō with the second ashi still present are scarce. (Ron Gregory).*

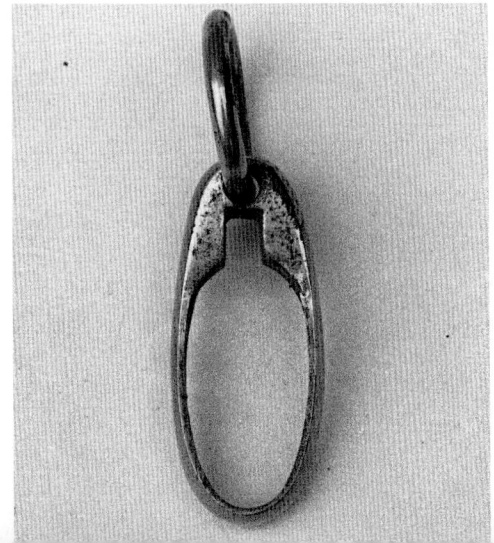

***Plate 25*** *An Army officer with a Company Officers grade kyu-guntō having the scarce black samé grip. This was taken during the Russo–Japanese war of 1904–5.* (Richard Fuller).

***Plate 26*** *General Teshima (commander of the siege artillery at Port Arthur during the 1904–5 Russo–Japanese war), in field dress. He is holding a kyu-guntō with a light coloured (gold?) General Officers barrel-shaped knot, stem, slide and darker coloured cords.* (Richard Fuller).

***Plate 27*** *General Nishi and his staff in 1904. The officer on the far right has an Army kyu-guntō of Company Officers grade (Lieutenant or Captain) and wears a red and white sash indicating he is 'Officer of the Day'. The officer in the centre with a message pouch and aiguillettes over his right shoulder also appears to have a kyu-guntō-style sword but with a leather knot, as does the sword of the person second from the right with the drinking cup hanging from his shoulder belt. Note how the swords are dragging on the ground.* (Richard Fuller).

***Plate 30*** *A seemingly unusual sword pattern which is actually an Army Field Officers grade kyu-guntō that has been modified by the removal of the knucklebow (probably because of breakage). A brass collar has been added just under the pommel to take the sword knot. The guard end of the knucklebow has been ground smooth and forms an upwards pointing quillion. A Company Officers grade shin-guntō sword knot is also attached. This sword was obtained in this condition at Johore Bahru, Malaya on 1 February 1946. It was surrendered by Second Lieutenant Kawachi together with a letter saying it had 'killed a great many men' and its value was '2,000 to 2,500 Yen'. Lieutenant Kawachi told the recipient it was made by a woman swordsmith, perhaps 'Kunishige' (1781–1800) of Bitchu province who is said to have worked under her husband's name after his death to support herself and her child. (Courtesy of Bon Dale).*

***Plate 28*** *Army officer in M90 (1930) uniform carrying a kyu-guntō with a shin-guntō pattern knot. (Richard Fuller).*

***Plate 29*** *A Japanese Army Second Lieutenant literally 'in the field' in China, 1938. He is holding an Army kyu-guntō with a shin-guntō sword knot wrapped around the knucklebow. (J. Smith).*

# Army 1875 (& 1886) Pattern and possible Very Senior Police Parade Sabres

### Regulation Army parade sabres

The Army parade sabre is a smaller, lighter version of the regulation infantry Commissioned Officers kyu-guntō for use with full and informal dress uniform. The introduction date is believed to be 1875 but only one reference has given a year.[1] At some unknown date it must have superseded the 1875 (& 1886) pattern Army Officers dress sword, but outlasted the kyuguntō as a regulation pattern since known to be in common usage during the late nineteen thirties and forties. Production must have continued well into World War Two because the Company Officers version is so very common and examples were brought back by Allied troops from Japanese-occupied areas in 1945–6 where they were also carried.

The rank grade variations are distinguishable by the degree of hilt backstrap decoration as was used on the Army kyu-guntō:

Warrant Officer 1886 pat. – Plain backstrap, upper panel and side ears. Plain solid handguard. (Plate 32). Rare.

Company Officers (2nd & 1st Lieutenants, Captain) – 1875 (very rare) and 1886 (common) models as described for the equivalent kyu-guntō models. (Plate 32).

Field Officer (Major, Lt-Col, Colonel). 1886 pat. – Entire backstrap is decorated with kadosakura and leaves. The upper panel is stippled. Pierced handguard. (Plate 33). Very scarce.

General Officer (Maj-Gen, Lt-Gen, General) 1886 pat. – Decorations and handguard as for Field Officers. Turtle-shell grip. (Plate 33). Very rare.

The use of kadosakura on guards, backstraps and side-ears of Company, Field and General Officers parade sabres is consistent with those used on the equivalent full-sized kyu-guntō models. However the Civil Police versions (Plates 44–46) have sakura but the Army Warrant Officers type is plain. Common to all rank grades is the leaf decoration around the sword knot hole at the top of the knucklebow.

Wear does not seem restricted to officers since contemporary photographs show NCOs (of at least the ranks of Sergeant and Sergeant-Major) with them (Plate 291). Probably they have the Warrant Officers version which is identified by a drawing on page nine of *Japanese Military Uniforms 1930–1945*.[2] The hilt is described as

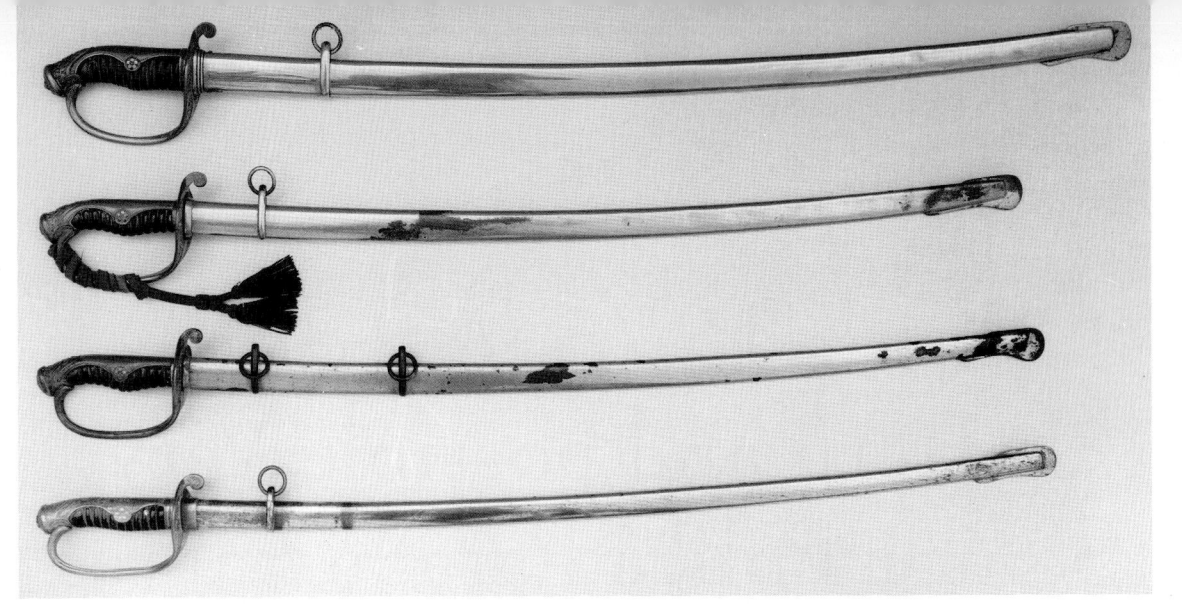

**Plate 31**  Comparison of Army parade sabre sizes. Top to bottom.
(i) Company Officers grade (Lieutenant or Captain) of unusually large dimensions (see Plate 32). Overall length 1,015mm (39¹⁵/₁₆").
(ii) Company Officers grade of average size. Overall length 895mm (35¼").
(iii) Scarce two-hanger Company Officers grade. The lower suspension mount is demountable being identical to the Army kyu-guntō type (see Plate 24). Overall length 910mm (35⅞").
(iv) Rare Police sword for Senior Officers. (see Plates 270, 271). Note the shallow inclination of the upper backstrap. A band of wear below the suspension mount indicates another was originally present. Overall length 918mm (36⅛"). (Richard Fuller).

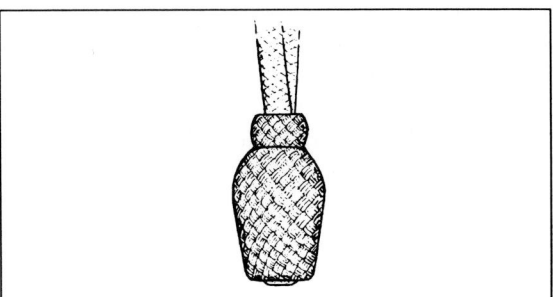

**Fig. 7**  Gold sword knot pattern shown in Japanese Military Uniforms 1930–1945 as being used for Army Company and Field Officers parade sabres.

'silver', but this is incorrect since plain brass without stippling seems usual. The decorative features on the backstrap are an edge line and two parallel lines which define the upper panel.

The D-guard hilt is difficult to remove from the blade because there is a threaded tang secured by a pommel cap which is often in the form of a (fourteen) petal chrysanthemum and a separate nut. The hilt collar (fuchi) is not a separate item, being cast integrally with the handguard. Grips are black horn, hardwood, celluloid, and in rare cases, black shagreen or turtle-shell although the last is restricted to General Officer rank grades. Intermittent brass wire binding. Brown leather washer (buffer) against the guard.

Blades are normally grooved, slender, flexible, blunt and chromium-plated. A most unusual flat-sided blade is in the author's collection. An extra cost acid-etched tempered edge (yakiba) may also be present. This is usually of a regular undulating form although variations are sometimes found (see Figs. 59, 60). Blade length, width and curvature varies, probably due to the buyer's size, choice and, possibly, different manufacturers.

A chromium-plated steel or nickel scabbard with one or two suspension bands is used. The lower band, when present, has a slot for removal over the drag exactly the same as with the kyu-guntō.[3] This allows usage with a one- or two-sling belt. Blade retention is just a push fit into the scabbard. Only the Civil Police models have been found with a push button and spring clip system, seppa (hilt washer) and habaki (blade collar).

Army parade sabres may also have the owner's family mon (badge) in the form of an engraved silver disc affixed to the lower backstrap. One rare exception in the author's collection has a brass mon in the form of a Karabana flower used by the

## ARMY 1875 (& 1886) PATTERN PARADE SABRES

**Plate 32** *(Left) Rare undecorated Army Warrant Officers parade sabre with a short blade measuring only 588mm (23¹⁵⁄₁₆"); (right) The unusually large and wide Company Officers model shown in Plate 31 (i). The hilt collar (fuchi) is a separate fitting and the blade has a scarce 'flame' pattern acid-etched yakiba (Fig. 60 (vi)). (Richard Fuller).*

guished by the use of 'police badges' on the backstrap.

The dimensions of parade sabres vary considerably although hilt lengths remain fairly consistent. Overall length of sword and scabbard 778–1,052mm (30⅝"–41⅜"). Hilt length (from inside of guard) 120–127mm (4¾"–5"). Blade length 590–875mm (23¼"–33⁷⁄₁₆"). Maximum blade width 19–24mm (¾"–¹⁵⁄₁₆"). Weight of sword 16–25 ounces. Weight of sword and scabbard 27–40 ounces.

An unusually large example of a Company Officers model is shown in Plates 31, 32. The hilt is of normal length but otherwise it is much broader and heavier than the range of figures

**Plate 33** *Very rare 1875 pattern Army General Officers grade parade sabre with fully decorated backstrap identical to the full-sized kyu-gunto version. Note the distinguishing Hawksbill turtle-shell grip. Possibly imitation turtle-shell was also used on occasions. (Patrick Lundy).*

Matsudaira family (among others) located on the pommel top.

Assembly numbers or marks are found on blade tangs but fittings are normally unstamped. Only one inspection mark has been reported which is the lyre-like logo of the Suya Company (Fig. 61 (xxiii)) located on the guard underside. There may have been other private manufacturers but it is probable that the Koishikawa/Kokura or No. 1 Tokyo Arsenals were also involved.

The sword knot pattern appears to be as described for the Army kyu-gunto until the 1930s (possibly with the introduction of the shin-gunto). However, after this a smaller gold barrel-shaped knot with cords (Fig. 7) is thought to have been used by Company and Field Officer ranks.[4] Strangely, although a common form of sword, they do not seem to be found with contemporary sword knots to verify the types used. Warrant Officers (and NCOs) may have used the brown leather knot (Fig. 2 (iv)). The use of shin-gunto knots with Army parade sabres is probably incorrect since such usage has not been verified by contemporary photographs.[5]

These swords are still, erroneously, called 'police swords' even though they can be distin-

# JAPANESE MILITARY AND CIVIL SWORDS AND DIRKS

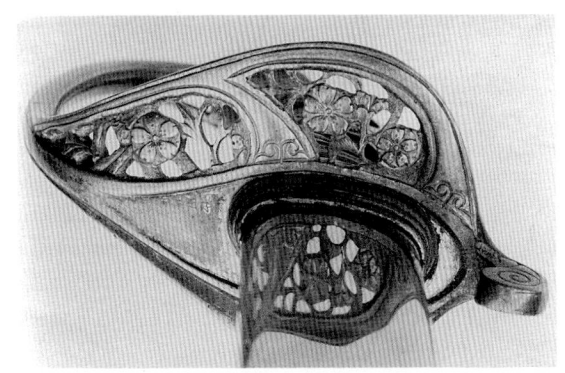

**Plate 34**  *Pierced handguard of Army Company, Field and General Officer grade parade sabres, the equivalent full-sized Army kyu-guntō and the supposed Police kyu-guntō in Plates 20–23. The right-hand panel has two kadosakura blossoms while the left has only one. (see also Fig. 2 (vii)). However the Police parade sabres, shown in Plates 44, 45, 47 have different arrangements of sakura. Compare with Plate 46. (Richard Fuller).*

**Plate 35**  *Component parts of a regulation pattern Army parade sabre. Note the tapered and threaded tang, which is a system also used on some Civil Officials swords, and the fuchi (hilt collar) which is integral with the guard. (Brenton Williams).*

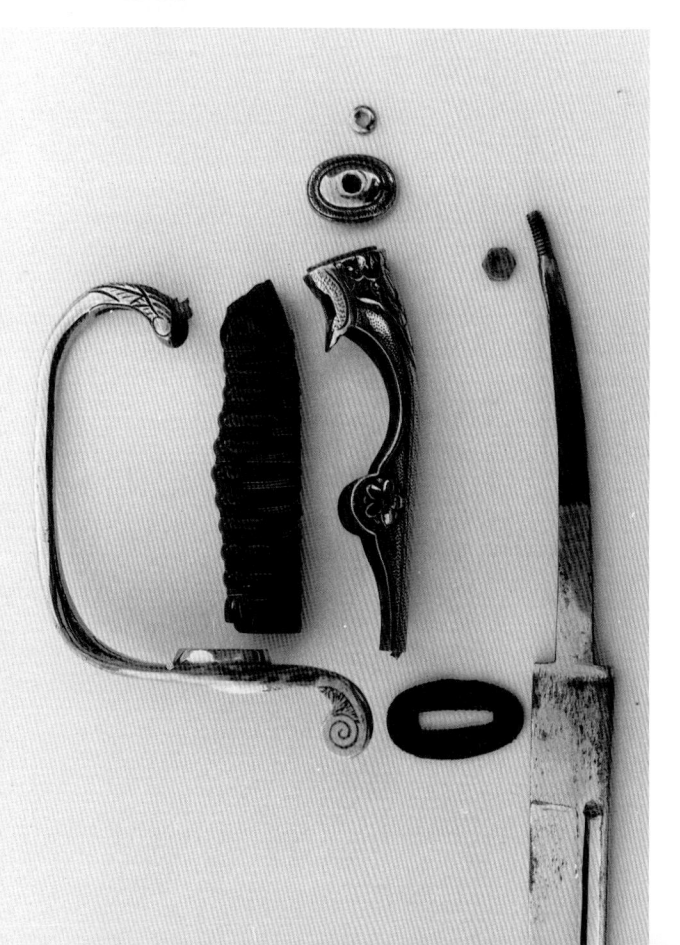

above. Overall length of sword and scabbard 1,015mm (39 15/16"). Hilt length (from inside of guard) 130mm (5 1/8"). Blade length 830mm (32 11/16"). Maximum blade width 28mm (1 1/8") Weight of sword 29½ ounces. Weight of sword and scabbard 48 ounces. This sword is near the length and weight of a full-sized kyu-guntō. One can only speculate that the owner was a very large man if this was regarded as lightweight for parade purposes. The shortest recorded is only 648mm (25½") overall including the scabbard and a hilt length of 108mm (4 1/4").

Presentation Army parade sabres are known, examples of which are listed below.[6] Such items are rare.

(i) Company Officers model. Both sides of the blade, near the hilt, are engraved in Japanese and read: 'Presented by the Shōda [or Seida] Airplane Factory Youth School [to the] Army Officers School'. A most unusual silver mon in the form of the medical insignia of a snake entwined around a winged staff is located on the lower backstrap. It is assumed that this was added before presentation which may indicate that it was given to the Army Medical School, unless it is the logo of the factory.

(ii) Company Officers model. The backstrap is engraved with a row of Japanese characters which read: 'Presentation to Mr Yoshida'. Strangely this sword has a blackened scabbard which appears to be a contemporary finish.

(iii) Field Officers model. The handguard has an engraved inscription confirming presentation by the Yoshiro Secondary School in Kumamoto Prefecture (see Plates 36, 37).

(iv) Company Officers model. The blade has a raised inscription confirming presentation to, or by, a Military Academy (see Plates 38, 39).

It seems that schools and companies bought such swords with money raised and presented them to military organisations or individuals as part of the war effort.

Although parade sabres are common they are

## ARMY 1875 (& 1886) PATTERN PARADE SABRES

### Possible Very Senior Civil Police Officers parade sabres

The hilt configuration, grip and scabbard type is the same as the standard Company and Field Officers grade models.

A raised sixteen-petal sun (Hiashi), which is believed to denote usage by Very Senior Police and Fire Bureau Officers is located in a panel on the upper backstrap (Plate 44).[7] The Hiashi is in the form of alternating long and slightly shorter rays with flattened tops (Fig. 2 (iv)). Backstrap decoration of leaves and one sakura in relief for half the length may indicate use by Superintendent grades. A fully decorated backstrap with three sakura could represent the Superintendent-General. However, these rank sub-divisions and identification are speculative.

The pierced panels of the handguard are also

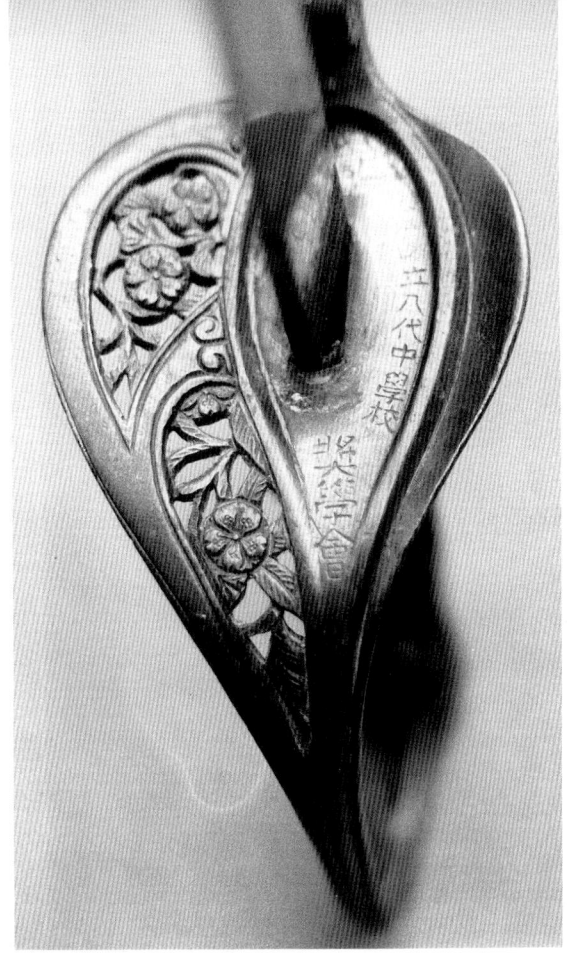

**Plate 36** *Guard underside of an Army parade sabre showing the engraved presentation inscription which reads KINEN (commemoration), SHOGAKU (scholarship), KAI (club, association), KUMAMOTO (a prefecture in Kyushu), KEN (prefecture), RITSU (public, government), YASHIRO (place name), CHUGAKKO (secondary school), ZOTEI (presentation), RIKUGUN (Army), SHIKANGAKKO (Military Academy), YUSHI (volunteer). Perhaps: A presentation to the Army Volunteer Military Academy in commemoration of the Scholastic Association of the Yoshiro Government (or Public) Secondary School in Kumamoto prefecture. This inscription obviously makes a mundane sword into a rare item. (Donald Barnes).*

**Plate 37** *Field Officers presentation parade sabre shown in Plate 36. The grip has been professionally replaced by the cast-iron handle of a child's training bayonet, perhaps due to breakage or the non-availability of a proper replacement. However, the current owner believes this was deliberately done before presentation as an individualistic act by the donors. (Donald Barnes).*

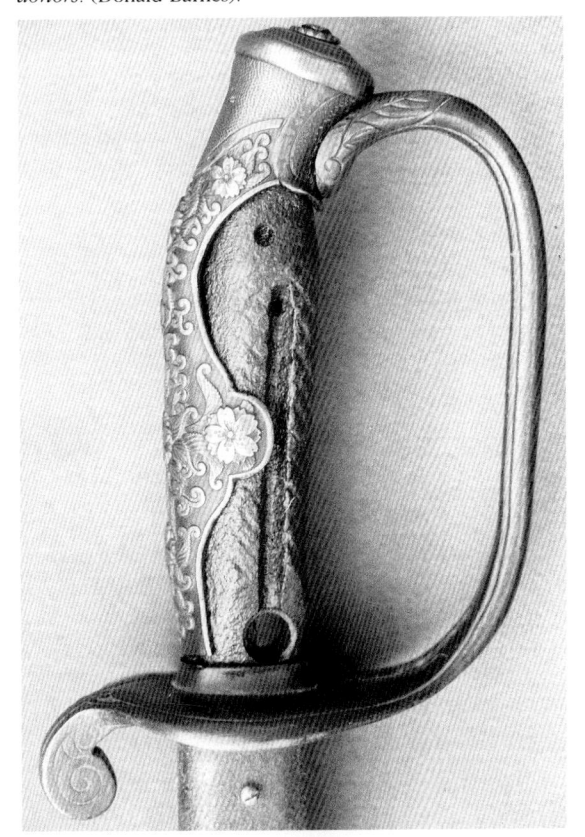

never seen in the formal surrender photographs of 1945–6. Presumably this is because they are dress and not service swords and, thus, were handed over or collected later. None have been reported with original surrender/transportation labels attached.

**Plates 38, 39** *Obverse and reverse blade shoulders of a Company Officers parade sabre showing a raised presentation inscription. Plate 38 reads ZŌTEI (presentation); Plate 39 reads RIKUGUN SHIKAN GAKKŌ (Military Academy), YŪSHI (volunteer) or USHI (a name). Thus it reads: Presentation to, or by, the Ushi Military Academy. Raised inscriptions of this type on Japanese swords are very rare. (Donald Barnes).*

distinctive, differing from those of Army officer grades by having sakura (and not kadosakura) in the reverse order (compare Plates 34 and 46).[8] Backstrap side-ears have raised sakura while those of all Army grades have kadosakura (Fig. 2 (vii)). Scabbards usually have one suspension mount but occasionally two are present. A number of variants have been found. Examples (i), (ii), (iii) below have half-decorated backstraps possibly indicative of use by officers of Superintendent grade (or equivalent).

(i) Push fit into the scabbard. The handguard and fuchi (hilt collar) are cast integrally. Leather seppa (blade washer) against the guard.

(ii) Separate fuchi incorporating a push button and spring clip for retention with the scabbard. Brass habaki and seppa against the underside of the guard.

(iii) As for (ii) but with a rough black shagreen grip and a two-hanger scabbard.

Variant (i) seems to be the basic model while (ii) is probably deluxe and (iii) appears to have extra cost features.

(iv) A most unusual variant has a fully decorated backstrap below the 'Hiashi' (as found on the full-sized kyu-guntō equivalent in Plate 22) plus a slim, sharp, hand-made blade of the rare kogarasu-zukuri shape (Fig. 59 (v)).[9] The normal length hilt has a grip of smooth lacquered black shagreen with gilded cast brass fittings of excellent quality. Sakura push button and spring clip retention system. The guard underside has the Suya Company 'lyre' stamp shown in Fig. 61 (xxii).

The blade is signed by Naohira Motosada and dated July 1890. It has a tapered tang which is

## ARMY 1875 (& 1886) PATTERN PARADE SABRES

threaded at the top and secured by both a nut and a female pommel screw surmounted by a sakura. There is also a traditional hilt securing peg (mekugi). Brass habaki (blade collar) and seppa. See Plates 44, 45 (right). Plated steel scabbard with a wood liner and two fixed suspension bands. The top of both bands are crimped to resemble bosses as used on some Police weapons (see Plate 259) rather than the normal oval type shown in Plate 24.

Overall length of sword and scabbard 745mm (29 3/16"). Hilt length (from inside guard) 123mm (4 15/16"). Blade length (from habaki) 570mm (22 7/16"). Maximum blade width 21mm (13/16"). Weight of sword 20 ounces. Weight of sword and scabbard 32 ounces.

This blade appears to have been specifically made for use in these mounts, which confirms an introduction date of at least 1890. Use by a very senior officer, perhaps the Superintendent-General?, is indicated. The combination of a signed kogarasu-zukuri blade and fully decorated backstrap parade sabre is extremely rare. Interestingly, the 1918 pattern 'Gensui' sword for Field Marshals also incorporates a kogarasu-zukuri blade, but that title was not created until May 1898.

Police parade sabres can be found with a habaki (blade collar) and spring clip retention system but these have not been reported on the Army versions.

The type of sword knot used with these swords is unknown but some form of gold bullion can,

***Plate 40*** *Army Lieutenants in M90 (1930) uniform with parade sabres. The varying lengths are apparent and notable is the very short sword in the centre. The two on the right (seated) have scarce two-hanger scabbards. Some officers have regimental numbers on their collars while others have none since they are not attached to any unit. Possibly taken at Army staff college in the early 1930s. (Cheyenne Noda).*

**Plate 41**  A portrait of the Emperor Meiji (reigned 1868–1912) holding a two-hanger Army parade sabre with a barrel knot. Suspension is by means of two straps. (Richard Fuller).

**Plate 42**  Lt-Gen Baron Kodama in full dress with a two-hanger parade sabre, c.1904–5. The knot and cords are probably all gold. This would seem to be the full dress sword knot. (Richard Fuller).

**Plate 43**  Emperor Hirohito in M90 (1930) uniform with a single-hanger parade sabre. This is almost certainly a General Officers model with the General Officers kyu-guntō gold? knot and black straps for service dress.

**Plates 44, 45** Possible Very Senior Civil Police Officers parade sabres, identified by the raised Hiashi (sun) on the top section of the backstrap. The left-hand sword is partially decorated, perhaps indicating use by an officer of Superintendent grade. That on the right is fully decorated, which may denote use by the Superintendent-General or similar high rank. These were previously thought to be Army General Officer grade swords. (Richard Fuller).

**Plate 46** Pierced handguard of a possible Very Senior Civil Police Officers grade parade sabre and Police sword for Inspectors (and above?). Distinguishable from the full-sized Police kyu-guntō equivalents, Army Officers kyu-guntō and Army parade sabres by the use of sakura with one in the right-hand panel and two in the left. Compare with Plate 34. Note that the Police parade sabres utilise a brass seppa (hilt washer) when a habaki (blade collar) is used. (Richard Fuller).

**Plate 47** Comparison of probable Police parade sabres. Left: Police Inspector (and above?) with a Hakkou (Fig. 51 (i)) upper hilt badge. Right: Possible Very Senior Police Officer (Superintendent grade?) or unidentified Police unit with a Hiashi (Fig. 2 (iv)). They can easily be confused with each other and Army parade sabres. (Donald Barnes).

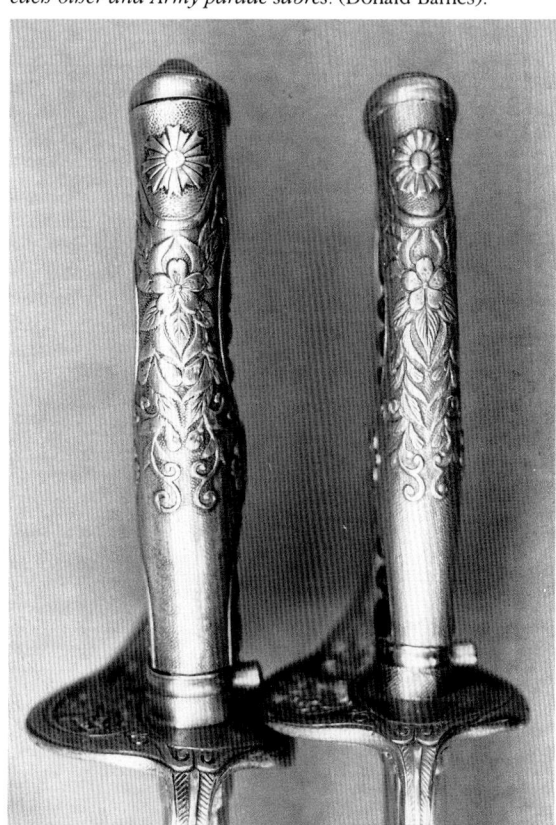

# JAPANESE MILITARY AND CIVIL SWORDS AND DIRKS

perhaps, be expected. Examples of the partly decorated version appear to be rare but the fully decorated type is very rare.

The placement of these possible Very Senior Police and/or Fire Bureau Officers kyu-guntō and parade sabres within the section on Army swords was done to compare, and differentiate between, their similarities. However reference must be made to the section on 'Police Swords and Dirks' later in this book.

## A Boys' Army parade sabre

Children, when dressed in military uniform for pageants or a school cadet force, were sometimes given swords. One such rare example is shown in Plates 48, 49. It is a half-sized Army parade sabre complete with a cord sword knot.

The grip is black-painted metal with intermittent brass wire binding. The backstrap is almost fully decorated with sakura and leaves. Hilt fittings are basically gilded copper with a brass pommel. Slim plated blade having an acid-etched yakiba. Plated metal scabbard with two suspension mounts. Overall length of sword and scabbard 540mm (21 1/4"). Hilt length 87mm (3 7/16"). Blade length 385mm (15 1/8"). Maximum blade width 13mm (1/2"). Scabbard length 453mm (17 13/16"). There is not thought to be a ranking system as was used with the full-sized versions.

---

[1] This dating is given in the *Nippon no Gunso*. See also footnote eight to this chapter. The earliest located dated photograph of a parade sabre is also 1874 (page fifty-six of the *Nippon no Gunpuku*). This means use was indeed concurrent with the 1875 pattern Army Commissioned Officers full dress sword although the parade sabre was (according to the *Nippon no Gunso*) introduced for informal wear only.

[2] Strangely this reference describes all but the General Officers model as 'silver' whereas brass, sometimes gilded, is actually found. Philip Goody has reported a nickel-plated (i.e. silvered) Company Officers hilt but this is the only such case known to the authors.

[3] The drawing in the *Nippon no Gunso* and 1874-dated photograph in the *Nippon no Gunpuku* confirm the parade sabre was introduced with two suspension mounts; but photographs of the 1904–5 Russo–Japanese war show the use of one was common practice. However, the removable lower mount may have remained available as an option up to World War Two since the shin-guntō was introduced with two.

[4] Shown as the standard pattern in *Japanese Military Uniforms 1930–1945* but no example has been found or reported although it should be common if generally worn. However, one is shown in Plate 1261, page 299, of *Imperial Japanese Army and Navy Uniforms and Equipments*.

[5] There is still an element of confusion over knot patterns for Army parade sabres. Thus details and opinions given are open to correction if necessary.

[6] Items (i) and (ii) are in the Philip Goody collection, (iii) and (iv) are in the Donald Barnes collection.

[7] Richard Fuller collection.

[8] Page 129 of the *Nippon no Gunso* illustrates the fully decorated General Officers grade model (without a 'Hiashi') together with the other officer rank variants under the heading 'Meiji 7th year enactment officers informal dress', i.e. 1874 regulation informal dress, although parade sabres are known (later) to be worn with full dress.

[9] *Japanese Military Uniforms 1930–1945* (see Bibliography), page nine, illustrates this knot for use with a Generals parade sabre. It also depicts a similar knot on page thirty-eight with vertical red zigzag stitches for use with the naval kyu-guntō, but shows the knot, stem and cords in silver.

---

**Plate 48** *A boys' parade sabre which is approximately half the size of a full-sized officers version. (Donald Barnes).*

**Plate 49** *Hilt of the boys' parade sabre in Plate 48. The backstrap decoration incorporates sakura but differs from the full-sized versions. (Donald Barnes).*

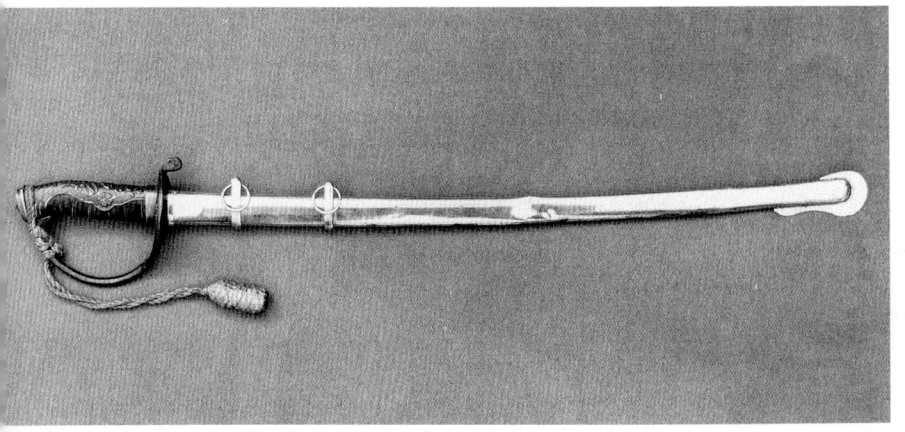

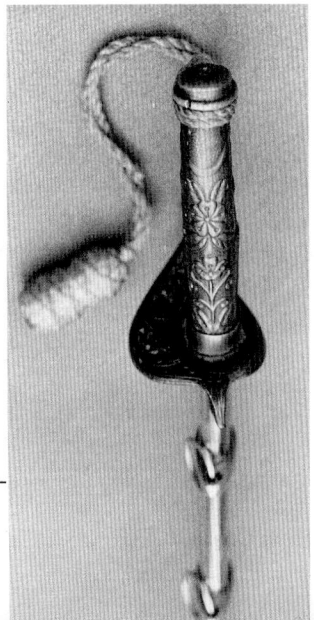

# Army Cavalry Swords

## Regulation 1874 pattern sabre for mounted Cavalry, Transport and Artillery Officers

The identification and appearance of this sword pattern is only known from page 129 of the *Nippon no Gunso*. Just the Field Officers grade (Major, Lt-Col, Colonel) is shown but there was a plainer version for Company grade officers. The main heading reads '1874 enactment officers informal dress', i.e. '1874 officers informal dress regulations', which is taken to mean walking out and general use.[1] The Infantry parade sabres are also illustrated.

The hilt has a swept three-bar handguard with a knucklebow and domed pommel. The backstrap appears to be fully decorated with what seems to be leaves and cherry blossoms although the actual form of embellishment is uncertain. White samé grip with intermittent brass wire binding. A plated blade is to be expected but details are unknown. The scabbard is probably nickel-plated steel with one or two suspension bands. The backstrap and pommel shape were retained by the later 1886 pattern Cavalry Officers parade sabre which is believed to have replaced this model.

Page fifty-six of the *Nippon no Gunso* has a photograph dated 1874 showing a Japanese Major-General (who is probably only a Major) with a sword having the same guard design, but the backstrap is obscured. The metal scabbard is straight and has two suspension mounts. The Japanese caption reads: 'The sword carried by the Major-General is a French Commissioned Officers type but had not been prescribed as a military sword [pattern] by that time'. This implies a similar sword was introduced later and this seems to conflict with the dating given in the *Nippon no Gunso*.

There are basically two types of cavalry sabre for other ranks and NCOs. One is brass-hilted which is believed to be the first pattern, and the other is steel-hilted which is the second, and final, pattern; both are mass-produced. Officers had a different and more ornate pattern.

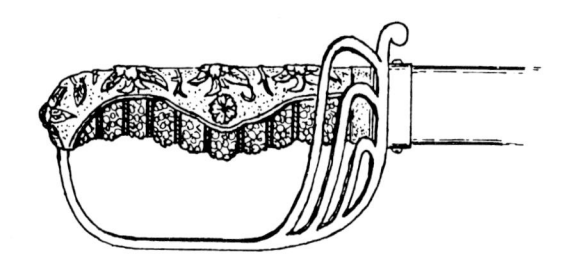

*Fig. 8   Probable appearance of the 1874 pattern parade and full-sized sabre for Cavalry, Transport and Artillery Officers of Field grade (i.e. Major, Colonel). The form of decoration is speculative.*

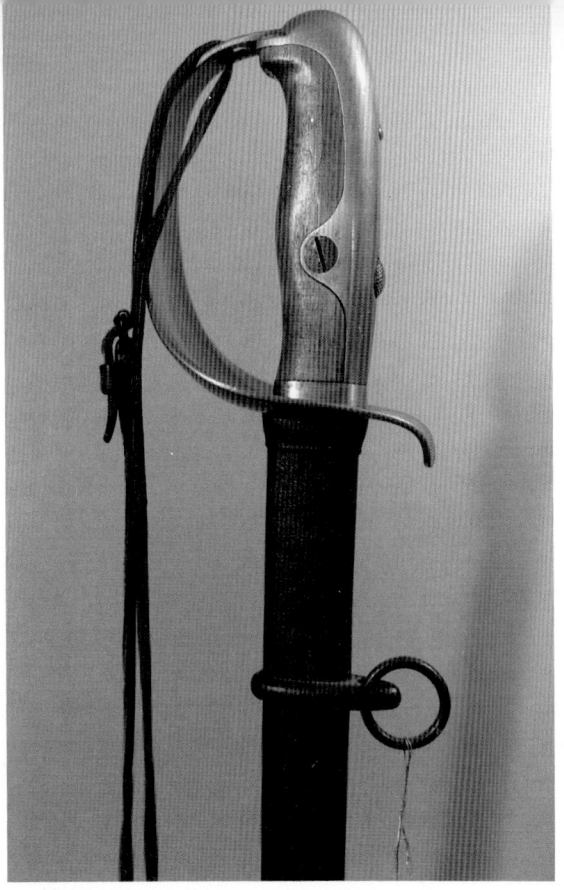

**Plate 50** *The rare 1892 regulation pattern brass-hilted (Cavalry) sabre. The leather knot on this example is adjustable.* (Patrick Lundy).

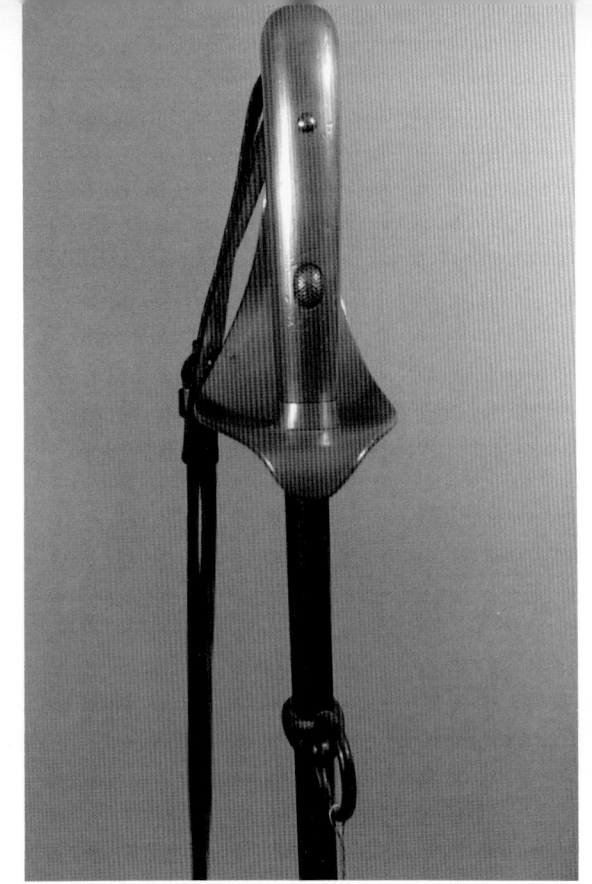

**Plate 51** *Hilt backstrap of the 1892 regulation pattern brass-hilted (Cavalry) sabre. The knurled push button and top rivet can be seen.* (Patrick Lundy).

## 1892 regulation pattern brass-hilted (Cavalry) sabre

The *Nippon no Gunso* has a drawing of the hilt of this sword with the caption 'cavalry arm military sword', but for some reason also mentions the 'revised dress regulations for 1886'. The introduction date was 19 March 1892 for use by 'mounted infantry, prison guards, military police and cavalry students.'[2] The correct designation is the 'Type 25 Army Sword'.

The backstrap, fuchi (hilt collar) and handguard are brass. The backstrap is secured by a steel screw passing through the side-ears plus a small rivet on the backstrap. A knurled push button protrudes from the backstrap which operates a spring clip for retention with the scabbard. Plain contoured wooden grip. A leather finger loop may also be present, riveted through the handguard. Mass-produced, curved blade with a full length fuller. The ricasso is stamped with what appears to be sequential production numbers which match those stamped on the scabbard drag. The 'four cannonball' stamp (Fig. 62 (i)) is normally found on the handguard. Steel scabbard with one suspension mount and a throat equipped to receive the hilt spring clip. Only a blued finish has been reported. Brown, or possibly black, leather knot and straps (Fig. 1 (iv)). Dimensions are unrecorded so it is unknown if there were two length variations.

The owner of the example in Plates 51, 52 has seen five similar swords of which the highest serial number was 16055. This seems to indicate that only a limited number were produced. Manufacture ceased with the introduction of the 1899 version, thus giving a production run of only seven years. Examples of this sword pattern are fairly rare.

## 1899 regulation pattern steel-hilted Cavalry Troopers and Army NCOs sabres

A revised version of the 1892 (Cavalry) sabre, retaining the same blade and scabbard, was introduced on 23 August 1899.[3] Japanese publications identify it as the '32 year type' which means 1899 is the year of introduction.[4]

There are two models which are identical except in overall length and weight. The hilt fittings are blued steel. Both the wooden grip and backstrap have a matching engraved chequer pattern which improved the hand-grip over the previous pattern. Retention is by means of a side-mounted spring clip. The hilt and pommel are fixed to the blade tang by nuts which have two holes and a screw with a slot, the former requiring a special tool for removal. This seems to be unique among Japanese swords. The D-shaped guard is also unusual in that the profile is slightly curved so that the outer edges turn downwards. The underside is normally marked with five small inspection marks including the centrally placed 'four cannonball' logo (Fig. 62 (i)) of the Tokyo Arsenal. There may be a small hole through the guard for a leather finger loop which is often missing. Not all have this hole. Blued steel scabbard although a drab green finish has been reported. The brass-lined throat has a protruding lug on one side which engages with the hilt spring clip. The design of the steel throat can vary in that it may, or may not, have a downturned side mount through which passes a securing screw. Raised suspension band with one steel hanging ring.

As with the previous pattern there are matching production numbers, which seem to be sequential, stamped on the blade ricasso (shoulder) and scabbard drag respectively. The lowest number reported to the authors is 1032 and the highest is 130142; both were on the Type B sword described below. These figures indicate that a large number were made.

This sword pattern can be divided into two versions with different uses:

Type A – Long size: issued to Cavalry Troopers. Overall length including scabbard 1,002mm (39½"). Weight 1.432 kg (50½ ounces).

Type B – Short size: 'For some of the NCOs of the branches other than the Cavalry.'[5] This would be infantry NCOs and particularly Superior Privates and NCOs of the Kempei (Military Police). Overall length including scabbard 920mm (36¼"). Weight 1.359 kg (48 ounces). There does, however, seem to be minor variations to these figures.

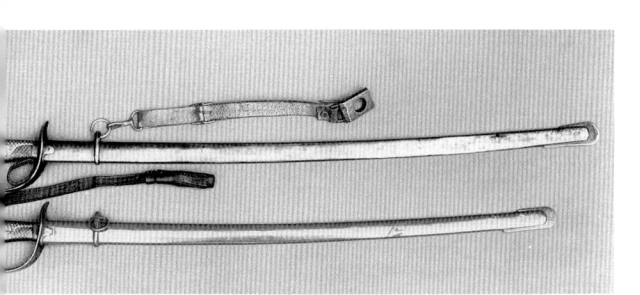

**Plate 52**  *Comparison of 1899 pattern Cavalry Troopers and Army NCOs sabres: (top) Type A, long size for Cavalry Troopers – note the leather hanger and belt slide; (bottom) Type B, short size for Infantry and Kempei NCOs. (Donald Barnes).*

**Plate 53**  *Hilt of the 1899 regulation pattern steel-hilted Cavalry Troopers and Army NCOs sabre. The chequered grip and backstrap is apparent. Incorrect sword knot pattern. (C. Halvorson).*

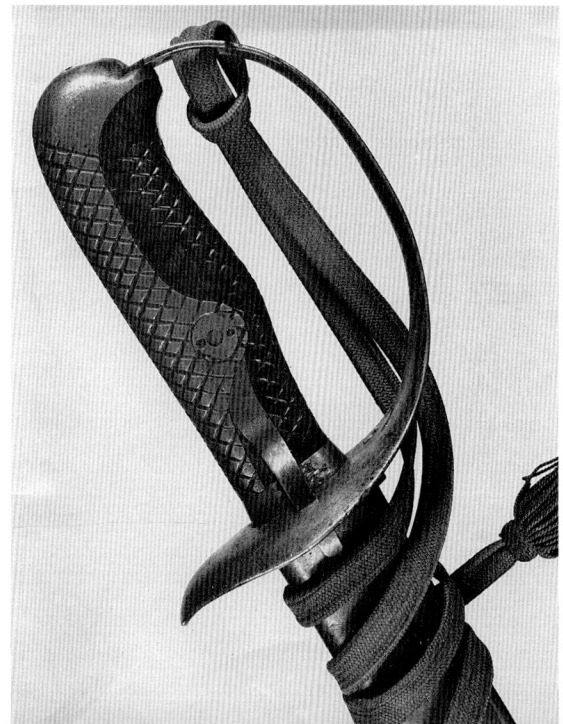

**Plate 54**  *1899 pattern steel-hilted Cavalry sabre in use. It has a leather sword knot and adjustable leather suspension strap attached to the saddle. This photograph was taken in China in 1938. (J. Smith).*

**Plate 55**  *Sergeant-Major Masaharu Morisaki of the Nagase Company in the 39th Infantry Regiment at the Battle of Ko-san, China, on 30 April 1938. This photograph proves that senior NCOs carried the 1899 pattern Army NCOs sabre which, in this case, has a protective strip of cloth or bandage bound around the scabbard.*

Both types employ a dark brown leather knot and straps (Fig. 1 (iv)). Shin-guntō knots, when found, are almost certainly post-war additions.

It is unlikely that the hilts were protected in the field since no samē or tape binding is used: however, some protection was, on occasions, given to the scabbards. Plate 55 shows a scabbard wrapped with strips of cloth or bandage. A khaki canvas non-removable shrink-fitted combat cover, now missing its leather bottom, is on a Type B sword in the author's collection. Such protection is rare and, presumably, only applicable to those swords carried on foot, i.e. the Type B version.

Examples of this sabre are now common since large numbers of surrendered swords were brought out of China in the mid-nineteen-eighties and were sold worldwide. However, measurements of such items in British collections indicate the Type B (short size) is that most frequently encountered. This is, perhaps, to be expected since the number of cavalry units that used the Type A (long size) is relatively small in comparison with infantry units.

The Japanese employed mounted cavalry up to the end of World War Two, most being stationed in north China and Manchuria. The US Technical Manual of the Japanese Forces, 1944, shows this steel-mounted model which it describes as a 'combination of a European-type hilt with a Japanese cutting blade'. The same manual states that the Military Police (Kempei) 'are equipped with a cavalry sabre[6] and pistol' since on normal duty they 'wear the usual uniform of the mounted services'. This refers to the Type B short size. However, Kempei NCOs have been photographed surrendering the 1935 pattern aluminium-hilted shin-guntō which, seemingly, superseded the Type B sword for that particular organisation. The Type B was also carried by infantry NCOs until being superseded by the aluminium-hilted shin-guntō. There is photographic evidence that usage of the Type B, in some cases, continued after 1935 (see Plate 71). The Type A seems to have continued in use until 1945.

Some sabres have been reported bearing a stamped character which indicates manufacture during the Meiji period, though they are normally undateable and none have been seen confirming Shōwa period manufacture.

An English language catalogue for the Japanese export of arms, entitled the *Taihei Kumai Catalogue A – Rifles, Machine Guns and Others*, illustrates both the long and short pattern sabres. Undated, it is believed to have been compiled around 1935. This infers both versions were exported to (and adopted by) foreign countries, but whether they were marked with the 'four cannonball' arsenal stamp is unknown. The German swordmaker Carl Eickhorn of Solingen has a full length drawing of a virtually identical sword (probably the short pattern) in the 1930 export catalogue *Military and Dress Swords for Siam*.[7] Item No. 1250 is described as a 'Mannschafssabel' (Trooper Sword). The only discernible difference between this and its Japanese-made counterpart is the scabbard throat which does not have the downturned obverse lug as shown in Plate 52. Unfortunately the reverse view is not shown to ascertain if the normal spring clip retention system was used. Probably they were not marked with the Eickhorn 'squirrel' logo although Siamese military/acceptance marks may be expected. It would be of interest to learn what other countries also used this pattern and whether or not the Japanese reissued captured stocks to their own troops after the occupation of Siam from December 1941.

A similar sword pattern having a green painted guard, green chequered plastic grip, plated blade and green-plated steel scabbard with two suspension mounts is frequently found.[8] Such items are Chinese, probably post-war Nationalist, and are often incorrectly described as Japanese. These were also brought out of China in the nineteen eighties and sold throughout the world.

## Regulation 1886 pattern Cavalry Officers sword

Cavalry Officers carried a different pattern of sword from the Troopers which according to *Swords of Imperial Japan 1868–1945* (see Bibliography) is designated the Type 19 since prescribed in 1886. This replaced the 1874 sabre for mounted Cavalry, Transport and Artillery Officers described earlier.

The gilded brass knucklebow and backstrap configuration is similar to the Army kyu-guntō but has a domed panel reflecting the design of the troopers sword. However, the slotted handguard (Plate 61) is quite distinctive.[9] White samé or lacquered shagreen grip with intermittent brass wire binding. The backstrap and pommel are decorated with kadosakura and leaves in relief while the side-ears have raised kadosakura. Normal hilt retention is by means of a removable wooden peg (mekugi), but some, possibly early, examples instead have the side-ear kadosakura mounted on a male/female securing screw. Press stud and spring clip scabbard retention system as used on kyu-guntō. Traditional shinogi-zukuri

*Plate 56  1886 pattern Cavalry Officers sword with gilded brass hilt fittings, white samé grip and a plated steel scabbard which has one suspension mount. Push button and spring clip retention. Hand-forged blade of shinogi-zukuri form which in this case is straight even though the scabbard is curved. (Ron Gregory).*

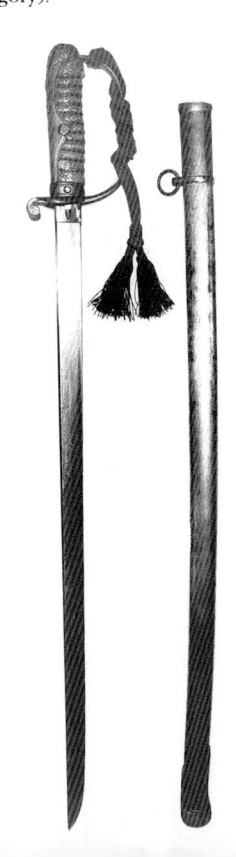

form blade which can be of some age, often being reused from an older samurai sword. Plated steel scabbard. Two suspension mounts would be expected with Cavalry swords but usually only one is found. It is uncertain if a lower one was prescribed, although that in Plate 62 has two. Possibly the lower one was removable, as with the kyu-guntō, and could have been removed for use in World War Two if the owner was transferred to a post in the Infantry. The length of the hilt and scabbard varies according to the owner's requirements and blade length.

There was a backstrap rank distinction similar to the system used on the Army kyu-guntō. Company grade Officers (Lieutenants, Captains) had backstraps partially decorated with kadosakura and leaves on the upper section and over the pommel. Backstraps of Field Officers (Major, Lt-Col, Colonel) were fully decorated. It is unknown if General Officers carried a turtle-shell grip version specifically for their use. Possibly Generals of the Cavalry had to wear the Infantry General Officers model.

A most unusual example of a fully decorated backstrap is shown in Plate 59. The stylised form of decoration seems to indicate that it was specially made.

***Plate 57*** *1886 pattern Cavalry Officers sword hilts of Company Officers grade. The backstrap is partly decorated with kadosakura and leaves. That on the right also has an ornate silver butterfly mon of the Ikeda family. The shin-guntō pattern knot indicates service in the 1930s or World War Two. (Ron Gregory).*

*Japanese Military Uniforms 1930–1945* indicates a gold acorn sword knot with horizontal red zigzag stitches and gold cords. However, this has not been confirmed.

This sword pattern was replaced by the shin-guntō in 1934 but wear was probably still permitted until becoming worn out. Cavalry officers appointed to infantry units could continue to carry them if they so wished. Indeed Lieutenant-General Baba Masao, Commander of the 37th Army in Borneo, surrendered a Cavalry Officers sword with fully decorated backstrap at Labuan, Borneo on 10 September 1945.[10] Examples of these swords are rare. A parade sabre version of this sword pattern is also known (see the following section).

***Plate 58*** *Another example of the 1886 pattern Cavalry Company Officers sword. This has a longer hilt than that shown in Plates 56, 57. Note also the decorated hilt collar (fuchi) and press button which is in the form of a sakura (cherry blossom). Steel scabbard with a protective brown leather combat cover and only one suspension mount. A blue and brown Company Officers grade shin-guntō knot is attached to the knucklebow. (Donald Barnes).*

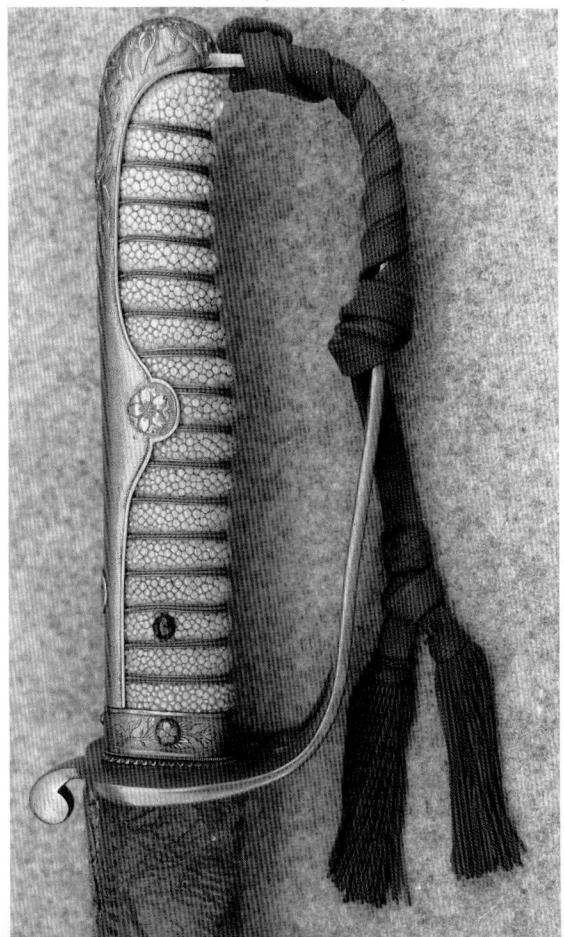

ARMY CAVALRY SWORDS

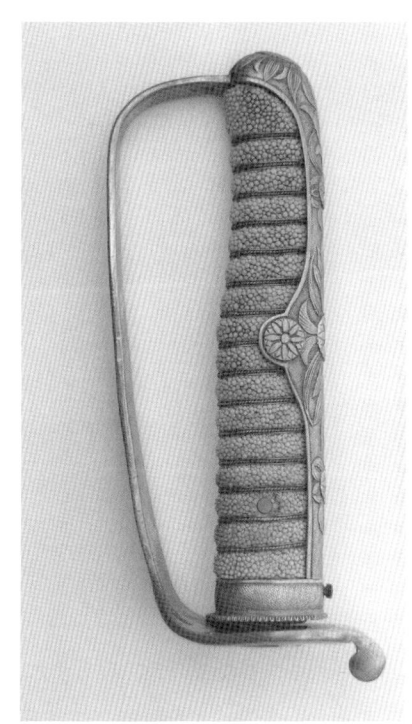

**Plates 59, 60** Most unusual variant of the rare 1886 pattern Cavalry Officers sword with brass fittings possibly for use by an officer of Field grade. The backstrap appears to be hand engraved, being decorated for virtually the entire length. The flower motif used is not the normal sakura (cherry blossom) and is not a recognisable type. Typical slotted handguard. Mass-produced blade with an unidentified stamp on the tang. Plated steel scabbard with two suspension mounts, the lower one being removable by sliding over the drag. Total length of sword and scabbard is 915mm (36"). Hilt length 205mm (8 1/16"). (Jørgen Jørgensen).

**Plate 61** Typical open-work design of the 1886 pattern Cavalry (and some Mounted Police) Officers sword guard. (Jørgen Jørgensen).

**Plate 62** 1886 Cavalry Officers sword shown in Plates 59, 60. (Jørgen Jørgensen).

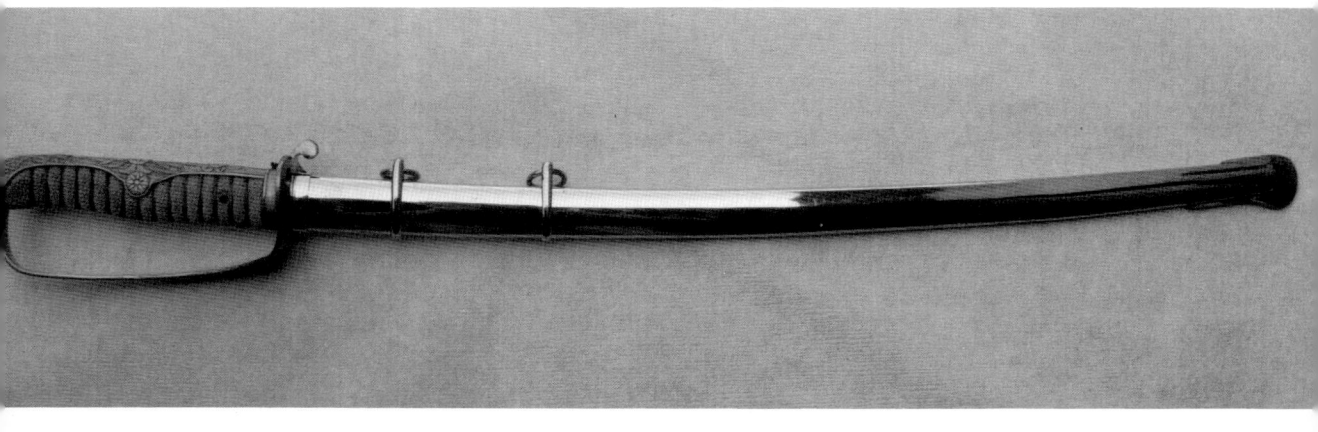

**Plate 63** *The commander of a Cavalry regiment and his Adjutant (or a regimental officer) at Hiroshima, Japan in 1904. They both have kyu-guntō style swords with single-hanger steel scabbards which are probably the 1886 pat. Cavalry Officers sword pattern but details of the guard are indistinct. The officer on the right has a light-coloured barrel-shaped sword knot. (Richard Fuller).*

## Regulation c.1892 pattern Cavalry Officers parade sabre

There is a parade sabre version of the Cavalry Officers sword which, as would be expected, is a lightweight copy of the full-sized model. The following details are based on the two examples which have been located, although photographs of others are known.

The grip can be black horn or black leather with brass wire binding in the grooves and brass hilt fittings. The obverse guard is slotted (as shown in Plate 61) and the upper section of the backstrap is decorated with kadosakura and leaves in relief, exactly as on the full-sized model. Leather washer (buffer) against the hilt. A silver mon can be found on the lower backstrap. The partially decorated backstrap indicates use by officers of Company grade. There is also a fully decorated backstrap version for use by officers of Field grade, although no example has been brought to the attention of the authors.

The flexible chromium-plated blade normally seems to have a wide groove extending from the shoulder for over two thirds of the length. That illustrated also has a short narrow groove close to the back edge which extends from the guard

**Plate 64** *Regulation 1886 pattern Cavalry Officers parade sabre. (Donald Barnes).*

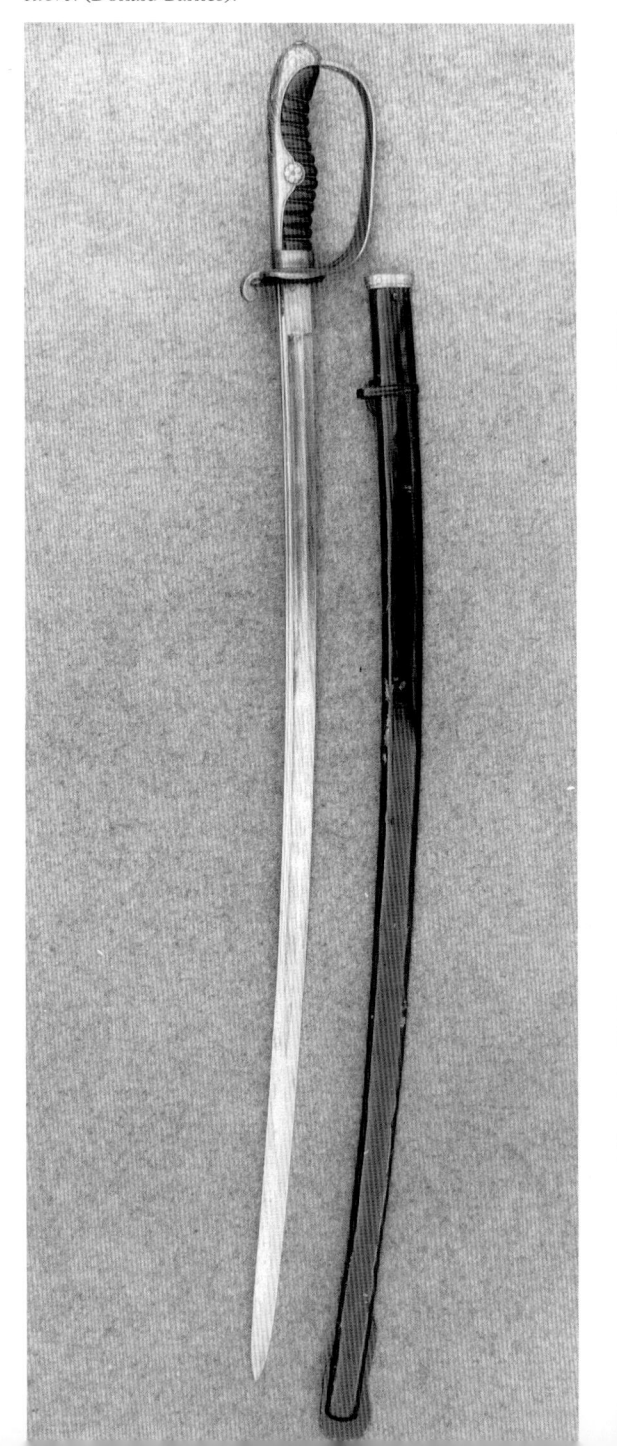

## ARMY CAVALRY SWORDS

to 40mm from the end of the large groove. Probably there are other variations as found with infantry parade sabres. Infantry-style chromium- or nickel-plated steel scabbard with a single suspension band and one hanging ring. A double hanger scabbard has not been reported. The sword in Plate 64 has a black painted finish which seems incorrect. The correct sword knot pattern is unknown.

Dimensions vary but the following are probably representative of the range. Overall length of sword and scabbard 975-1030mm (38 3/8"–40 9/16"). Hilt length 134–160mm (5 5/16"–6 5/16"). Blade length 776–827mm (30 9/16"–32 9/16"). Maximum blade width 25mm (1"). Scabbard length 817–872mm (32 3/16"–34 5/16").

The Cavalry Officers parade sabre appears to be almost as rare as the full-sized model.

1 Identified and dated to 1875 in *Swords of Imperial Japan 1868–1945* for use by all officers who served on horseback.
2 Confirmed in *Swords of Imperial Japan 1868–1945*.
3 Confirmed in *Swords of Imperial Japan 1868–1945*.
4 Prior to 1926 the Japanese Army used a designation system based on the number of elapsed years since the re-establishment of Imperial rule in 1868 (which is regarded as year one). Therefore, the thirty-second year is $1868 + 32 - 1 = 1899$.
5 The sizes and quotation are taken from *Taihei Kumai Catalogue A– Rifles, Machine Guns and Others* reproduced, edited and introduced by Fred L. Honeycutt Jr. No other swords are shown or mentioned.
6 This must refer to NCOs and possibly other ranks, since officers would carry the regulation kyu- or shin-guntô.
7 This information courtesy of Fred Stephens.
8 Illustrated in Plates 23, 24; page twenty-four of *Military Swords of Japan 1868–1945* by the authors (see Bibliography)
9 *Swords of Imperial Japan 1868–1945* illustrates two Civil Mounted Police swords with this guard pattern. Perhaps the unusual variant in Plates 59–62 of this book has a, so far, unidentified mounted use other than Army Cavalry.
10 Now in the Australian War Memorial Museum, cat no. AWM 31262. It has a General Officers grade shin-guntô sword knot and a blade by Kanenobu of Mino province, c.1650.

**Plate 65** Hilt configuration of the 1886 pattern Cavalry Officers parade sabre. (Donald Barnes).

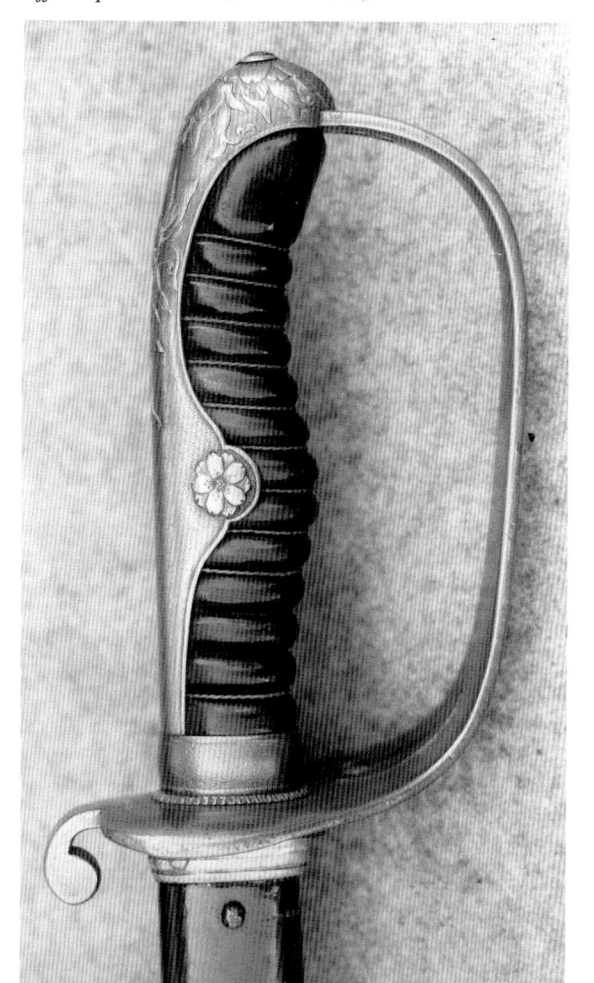

**Plate 66** Backstrap decoration of a 1886 pattern Cavalry Officers parade sabre which is believed to denote usage by an officer of Company grade. (Donald Barnes).

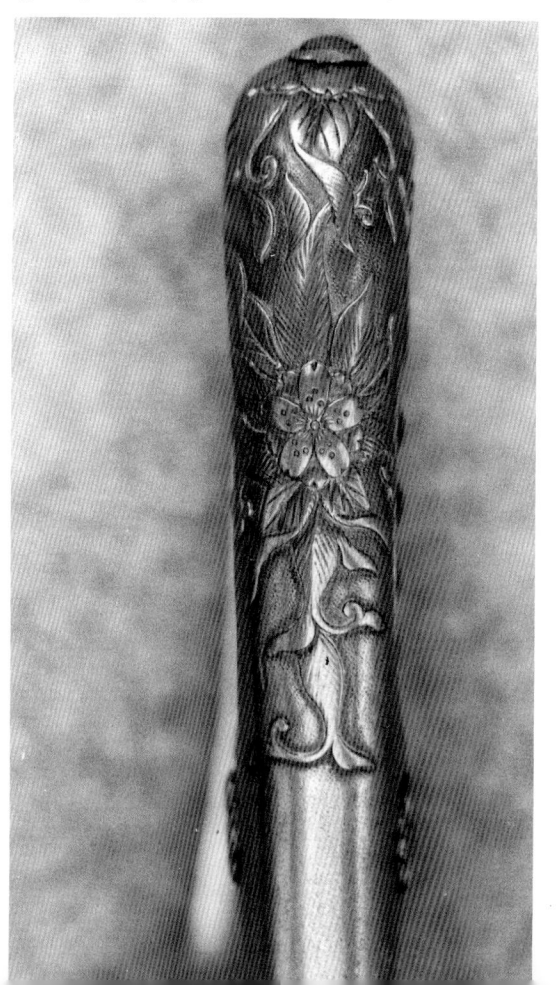

# Army 1934 (& 1938) Shin-Guntō

### Regulation 1934 (& 1938) pattern Army Officers shin-guntō

This is the most familiar of all Japanese military swords which is commonly, and erroneously, referred to by laymen as a 'samurai sword'.

The name shin- (new) gun (military) tō (sword), i.e. 'new military sword', is believed to have been popularised in the West and is now the accepted terminology among collectors. However, the *Nippon no Gunso* describes it as the 'Rikugun-no-guntō' (i.e. Army military sword) which could actually be applied to any Army sword. Thus, for clarity and differentiation purposes, the title 'shin-guntō is used throughout this book. The proper designation would seem to be the 'Type 94 (1934) pattern Army Officers sword'.

In the nineteen-thirties the Japanese thought that both Army and naval military swords should reflect the traditionalist and nationalistic ideology which had become prevalent. Thus the European-influenced kyu-guntō patterns were superseded by swords which reflected Japanese samurai traditions.[1] Like its predecessor, the shin-guntō was also a fighting weapon. According to the *Nippon no Gunpuku* the shin-guntō was authorised on 14 February 1934, based on a 'tachi' (traditional slung sword) from the Kamakura period (1185–1332).[2] Use was prescribed for Army Commissioned Officers (including those of the Cavalry) and Warrant Officers. As previously stated it replaced the Army kyu-guntō although that model was not banned from wear by those who already carried one. It was also intended to replace the use of uchigatana (traditional katana) although they continued to be worn according to personal preference. Examination of contemporary photographs confirms wear (at least on occasions) by ranks below Warrant Officer. Superior Privates, Sergeants and Sergeant-Majors have been identified with Officers shin-guntō up to about 1941 (see Plates 70, 71). It is doubtful if this was a common practice since a mass-produced aluminium-hilted shin-guntō variant was introduced for NCOs in 1935. Prior to this only the 1899 pattern Infantry NCOs sabre is thought to have been available. Perhaps wealthier NCOs had the option of purchasing an Officers shin-guntō until 1935 (and after?) in lieu of their own prescribed issue model. One can only speculate that some other ranks (i.e. Superior Private, Leading Private) could carry swords under certain circumstances of command, at least into the late nineteen-thirties. However, this seems to have been a rare occurrence and is seldom seen in photographs of the nineteen-forties. A notable example is that of a Private First Class holding a

***Plate 67*** Complete view of a typical Army Officers shin-guntō. Unsigned Shōwa period blade. Field scabbard. This sword was presented to the CO of 42nd Squadron, RAF, in Burma, 1944. The blade of this example has been greased, which is not a recommended practice. (42 Squadron Royal Air Force Museum).

***Plate 68*** Typical Army Officers shin-guntō hilt showing the kabuto-gane (pommel) with a cord sarute (knot loop), tape-bound hilt having the Army-style gilded menuki (ornaments) of three kadosakura (cherry blossoms) and the fuchi (hilt collar) decorated with sakura and leaves. The tsuba (guard) is the normal brass 'aoi' shape associated with this sword pattern. The leather combat cover, plain scabbard throat and suspension band are typical of a wooden field scabbard. (42 Squadron Royal Air Force Museum).

***Plate 69*** Second Lieutenant Namekawa Machida with his shin-guntō, sword knot and scabbard fitted with a leather combat cover. This photograph is dated 18 September 1938. (Cheyenne Noda).

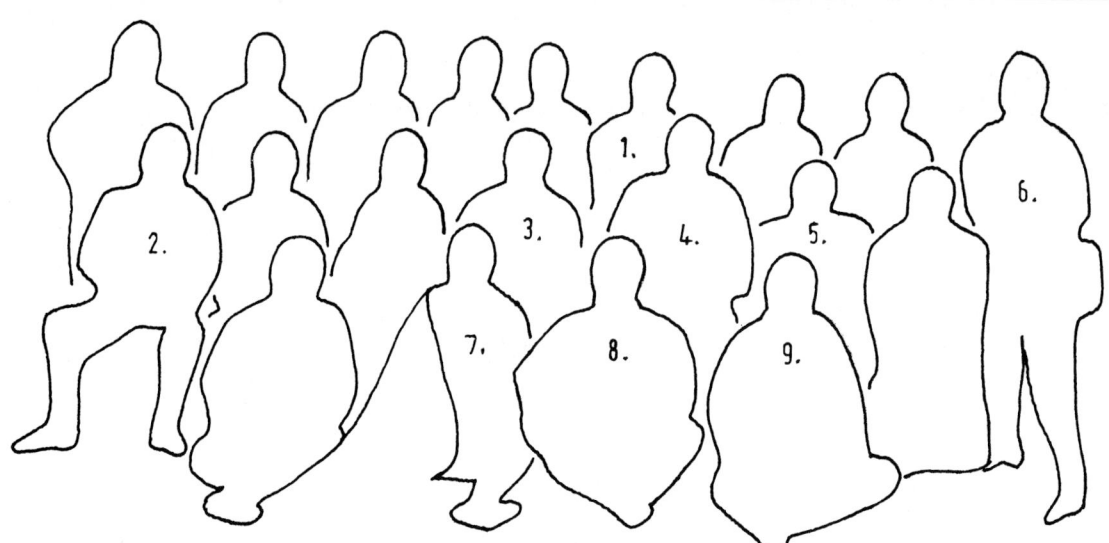

***Plate 70*** Warrant Officer Namekawa Machida and group in M90 (1930) Army field uniforms, apparently taken in China. Nearly all seem to be Superior Privates even though some have swords. This does not seem to be a group with borrowed swords since they all have suspension straps coming from sword belts.

| Rank | Sword |
|---|---|
| 1. Uncertain | Shin-guntō and knot. Protective white cloth hilt covering. |
| 2. Superior Private | Civilian wakizashi. No knot. Leather-covered scabbard. Leather suspension strap. |
| 3. Superior Private | Type indeterminate. Leather-covered scabbard. Leather suspension strap. |
| 4. Warrant Officer Namekawa Machida | Shin-guntō and knot. Protective white cloth hilt covering. Leather suspension strap. |
| 5. Superior Private | Shin-guntō and knot. Protective white cloth hilt covering. |
| 6. Superior Private | Shin-guntō. Leather combat cover to scabbard. Leather suspension strap. |
| 7. Superior Private | Shin-guntō apparently with blackened steel or civilian tsuba. Leather-covered scabbard. |
| 8. Superior Private | Unidentified. Scabbard ishizuke (chape) does not seem to be shin-guntō. |
| 9. Superior Private (Cheyenne Noda) | Civilian katana. Leather combat cover to scabbard. |

ARMY 1934 (& 1938) SHIN-GUNTŌ

***Plate 71*** *First Lieutenant Namekawa Machida and group probably taken in China and dated September 1941. They all seem to be NCOs except for the 1st Class Private holding the dog in the rear row. They are wearing M98 (1938) field uniforms.*

| Rank | Sword |
|---|---|
| 1. Sergeant-Major | 1899 pattern Army NCOs sabre. Leather knot. |
| 2. Sergeant-Major | Uncertain. Details obscure. Tassel or knot. Leather-covered scabbard. |
| 3. Sergeant-Major | Shin-guntō and knot. Protective white cloth hilt covering. Leather combat cover to scabbard. Leather suspension strap. |
| 4. Sergeant | Shin-guntō. Protective white cloth hilt covering. Leather-covered scabbard. |
| 5. 1st Lt Namekawa Machida | Shin-guntō. Protective white cloth hilt covering. Leather-covered scabbard. Leather suspension strap. |
| 6. Warrant Officer | Shin-guntō and knot. Metal scabbard with leather combat cover. |
| 7. Sergeant? | Shin-guntō and knot. Dress belt with matching suspension strap. |
| 8. Sergeant? | Uncertain. Knot. Protective white cloth hilt covering. Leather suspension strap. |

*(Cheyenne Noda)*

leather-covered sword in September 1945 which is shown in Plate 67 of *Military Swords of Japan 1868–1945* (see Bibliography).

The 1934 pattern Officers shin-guntō was prescribed with two suspension mounts (ashi) and a dress belt equipped with two slings. Examples of two-ashi shin-guntō (see later in this section) indicate that the lower one was removable while the top ashi was fixed. No example with a metal scabbard (without a combat cover) has been reported as having two matching *fixed* suspension mounts. The *Nippon no Gunpuku* says Cavalry officers, who had the same dress belt, used a chain hanger instead of the black leather and felt-backed slings, but this is debatable. It seems that the Infantry (and Artillery) required two ashi for parade purposes but possibly only one when in the field. The Cavalry, presumably, only required one for both parade and field use. In ( mid?) 1938 the regulations seem to have been amended to sanction the use of only one (fixed) ashi,[3] the lower one being abandoned.. This regularised the situation. All other fittings, however, remained the same.

It is necessary to describe the Army shin-guntō and fittings in detail because of the number of variations which occur.

The hilt has brass fittings consisting of a pommel (kabuto-gane) and hilt collar (fuchi) which are decorated ensuite with sakura (cherry blossoms) and leaves cast in relief. Background decoration is a stippled effect of very small recessed dots. There is a tarnish-resistant brown finish with the edges highlighted in gilt. The pommel sakura and leaves are often inlaid copper. Sometimes plain undecorated fittings with the usual brown finish or just a stippled background are found which seems to be indicative of later items, probably late in 1943 or 1944. A decorated brass loop (sarute) for the sword knot is pressed into a brass sleeve which passes through the pommel (kabuto-gane). This is bordered by a serrated eyelet on each side which is normally integral with the kabuto-gane. In rare cases the kabuto-gane may actually be a scabbard chape (ishizuke) which does not have the integral section (Plates 73, 74) but nevertheless has been used as a pommel. Decoration of the sarute is usually sakura, leaves and buds but variations such as clasped monkey hands and, in rare cases, flying insignia (Fig. 22) are found. They may also be plain brass, copper, steel, cord or chamois leather.

The hilt is bound with a brown tape in the

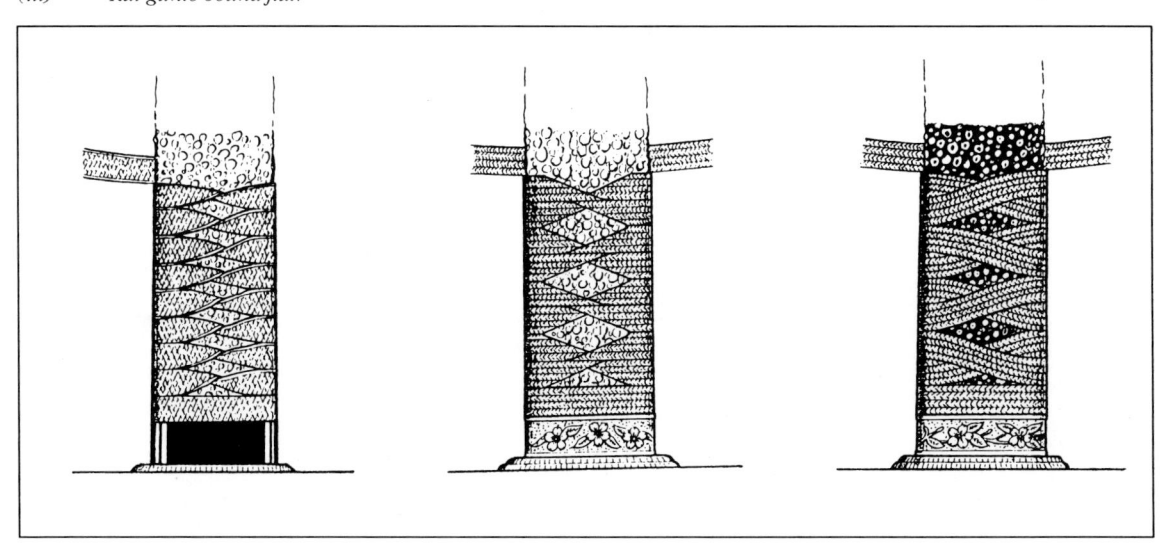

***Fig. 9*** *Comparison of common hilt binding styles found on:*
*(i)      1877 'rebellion' katana and wakizashi.*
*(ii)     Shin-guntō and kai-guntō bound with a twist.*
*(iii)    Kai-guntō bound flat.*

ARMY 1934 (& 1938) SHIN-GUNTŌ

manner used on traditional katana. This terminates with a knot, either against the kabuto-gane or tied through it (see Plates 72, 73). Sometimes other colours are found including green, blue, black and even contrasting light and dark brown. These variations do not indicate rank grades. The wooden base is usually covered with white samé (ray skin). Celluloid (fake) samé can be found on wartime swords which may be a cost or availability consideration. Other coverings such as brown shagreen (fish or shark skin), black leather and, in one genuine case, brown emery paper are normally associated with later items when samé became unavailable. A rare occurrence seen only once was the use of embossed and gilded copper sheeting emulating samé. Simulated black leather with a canvas hilt binding seems to be a post-war covering. In rare cases the wooden hilt base may have the binder's name written in ink or pencil, but normally only assembly marks are found.

On each side of the hilt, under the binding, are stamped gilded brass or copper ornaments called 'menuki'. With Army swords these are in the form

*Plate 73* Shin-guntō kabuto-gane which are both, in fact, ishizuke (scabbard chapes) utilised for this purpose. A separate sarute (sword knot loop) sleeve has been added. Scabbard fittings were presumably used because proper kabuto-gane stocks had run out during assembly. Such a feature is often overlooked by the collector and is not a very common occurrence. (Ron Gregory).

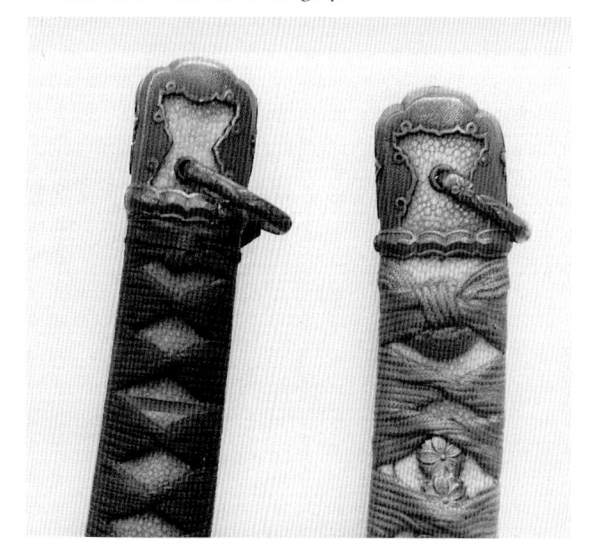

*Plate 72* Standard shin-guntō kabuto-gane with the hilt binding tied through a slot in the lower bar (left and centre) and over it (right) which prevents removal. The most commonly encountered system is for the hilt binding to be tied underneath the kabuto-gane which does allow removal or replacement. Note the central sword knot which is that of a General Officer characterised by yellow or gold zigzag stitches. (Ron Gregory).

*Plate 74* Left is a shin-guntō kabuto-gane (pommel) which is actually an ishizuke (scabbard chape). The hilt binding is tied over and through, thus securing it. This confirms it is a contemporary fitting and not a replacement. Right is a civilian-type kabuto-gane with the hilt binding taken through the sarute (sword knot loop) sleeve. The sarute is cord. The fuchi (hilt collar) is also decorated ensuite. Probably these mounts are Shōwa period, but they could be older. (Ron Gregory).

of three kadosakura which are distinct from the naval kai-guntō pattern. It is not unknown to have totally standard shin-guntō with old, or Shōwa period, civilian-style menuki, perhaps in the form of dragons or flowers etc. The hilt is secured to the blade by a removable bamboo peg (mekugi) which passes through a hole in the blade tang allowing dismantling.

The regulation cast brass guard (tsuba), which may be gilded, is known as 'aoi' or 'hollyhock' shape. On plan it is basically ovoid with four flattened sides which rise to peaks in the middle (Plate 75). Decoration consists of four raised sakura on each side and a stippled background decoration. There may be holes on each side (ryohitsu). Normal tsuba are solid but pierced ones are found, the latter rumoured to be initially restricted to senior officers. The normal thickness is 7.5mm but thicker ones are not uncommon (Plate 76). Sometimes the recessed inner surface of a solid tsuba may have a matt red finish which is, presumably, a manufacturer's option rather than an indication of any particular usage. On either side of the tsuba are washers (seppa) of varying size totalling from two to four on each side (Plate 75). In descending order of size they are a copper daiseppa which matches the shape of the raised centre of the tsuba; a brass, copper or (sometimes) silvered metal ko-seppa of oval form; and brass or aluminium seppa which are also oval. All of these will have a slot if a spring clip retention system is used. Older tsuba from traditional katana can also be found in place of the regulation military tsuba, but they do not have the normal military daiseppa.

Normally retention is with a spring clip which lies under the hilt and engages with a slot in the scabbard throat. A plain or decorated push button projects through the fuchi. If a push-fit retention is employed then the fuchi hole for the button is

**Plate 75** *Military sword tsuba and seppa. Top to bottom: 1935 pattern Army NCOs shin-guntō – brass tsuba; regulation pattern shin-guntō – brass pierced tsuba; regulation pattern shin-guntō – (left) brass solid tsuba for spring clip retention and (right) for leather strap retention; regulation pattern kai-guntō (naval sword) – copper with a blackened (Shakudo) finish. Note the brass dai-seppa with alternating copper rays. (Ron Gregory).*

# ARMY 1934 (& 1938) SHIN-GUNTŌ

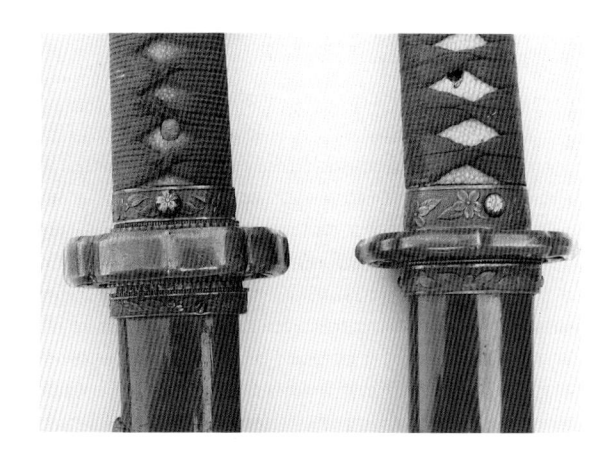

**Plate 76** *Comparisons of shin-guntō tsuba (guard) thicknesses. That on the left has an exceptionally thick rim at 13mm, while that on the right is average at 7.5mm. Such a thick tsuba is rare and was presumably specially made. It has been observed that the thicker tsuba are normally the pierced type. These swords also illustrate the centre and off-centre locations of the spring clip buttons and the two decorated types which may be found. The one on the left is better quality than the normal type button on the right. (Ron Gregory).*

absent. There are genuine examples where the seppa and tsuba have openings for a spring clip but none was used. In some cases this may mean post-war interference or the addition of new fittings.

Manufacturer's identification is generally lacking but matching numbers and characters are usually stamped on the tsuba, various seppa and fuchi bases. These are purely for assembly purposes. However, manufacturer inspection

**Plate 77** *Regulation brass shin-guntō tsuba (guard) with four stamps in seal form (Tensho script). They read vertically and from right to left: TŌ – KYŌ i.e. Tokyo, which is presumably the place of manufacture; WAKA (young) – RAI (torrent), which appears to be a nationalistic phrase probably extolling the torrent of young blood going to war. This appears to be a fairly scarce item since only a few have been located, each of them bearing identical stamps but different assembly numbers. (Alan Daniel).*

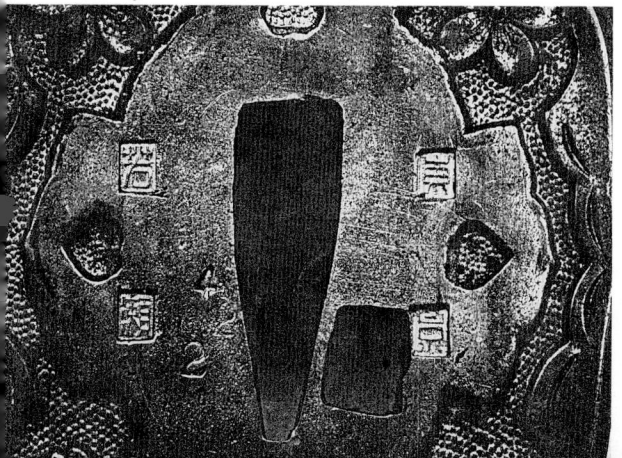

marks have been noted on tsuba and, in rare cases, on either side of the kabuto-gane as shown in Plate 78. The latter are those of the Nagoya Arsenal or No. 1 Tokyo Arsenal which are also known to have made blades. It is not known how many, or which, factories produced sword fittings other than those bearing identifiable arsenal stamps.

Solid silver fittings have been reported which must have been made to special order and are rare. Silvered fittings are also known but may have been done since the war. Acceptance of these is a matter for personal judgement.

Blades are traditional shinogi-zukuri form as used with the kyu-guntō. The tang may be signed with the smith's name, date or details relating to the place or type of manufacture. Army inspection stamps are commonly found (see Figs. 61, 62). Blade length is normally within 100mm (4") to

**Plate 78** *A shin-guntō kabuto-gane (pommel) with two stamps on the upper face and one (not shown) on the reverse. That on the left is the manufacturer's logo of the Tokyo No. 1 Arsenal (Fig. 62 (ii)) while that on the right is ⊕ which is unidentified and seems restricted to fittings of this type. The reverse stamp is the Tō inspection mark of the same arsenal (Fig. 62 (xii)). The NA inspection mark of the Nagoya Arsenal has also been noted. Sword tangs of shin-guntō which have been found with such stamped fittings seem to be dated around 1943. Such markings are uncommon. (Richard Fuller).*

125mm (5") of the scabbard length. However, old wakizashi blades 405mm (16")–610mm (24") long may be found with much longer scabbards. Types of blades will be dealt with later, but can be categorised as:

(i) Machine-made from one piece of steel. Normally associated with late war and emergency issue swords.
(ii) Combination of hand and machine forging but oil-tempered (abura yaki-ire), the bulk being made during the Shōwa period by individual smiths and often subject to Army inspection. Common.
(iii) Traditional hand-forged and water-tempered (gendaitō). Made by better class individual smiths. Scarce.
(iv) Ancestral blades from traditional tachi, katana or wakizashi, being remounted in military fittings (guntō) either at the request of individuals or by dealers. Possibly less than ten per cent of this sword pattern have these blades.

A blade collar (habaki) of brass or copper is always used. Habaki made of two pieces which slot together (Nijiu habaki) have not been reported on wartime Shōwa period blades.

Two types of scabbard are generally encountered being metal with a wooden liner or entirely of wood with a non-removable leather cover which is stitched on while wet to shrink and dry tight. The latter is termed a 'field scabbard'.

## Metal scabbards

Painted steel or alloy coloured brown, green and sometimes pale orange. Black is rarely found and is said to have been used only from 1943.[4] This colour may have been favoured by officers of the Naval Landing Forces who also carried Army-style swords. The painted finish may be matt, which is the norm, or gloss; the latter is often found with better class blades (see also scabbard variations later in this section).

Regulation fittings consist of a throat (kuchigane), suspension mount (ashi), lower strengthening band (shibabiki) and chape (ishizuke). The throat and chape are decorated ensuite with the hilt fittings. The ashi consists of two bands surmounted by a kadosakura and boss through which passes a steel or brass hanging ring (Fig. 10 (i)). The boss is brazed in and cannot be unscrewed. On occasions second lower matching demountable ashi may be found but are scarce. In most cases removal is possible without the need to take off the lower two scabbard mounts. The boss unscrews allowing the bands, which are hinged at the bottom, to fall open. There appears to be at least four variations, presumably by different makers, which are shown in Fig. 11. They are believed to be associated with the 1934 model but could have been optional for the 1938 amended model. However, naval officers in land warfare uniform have also been seen with two-ashi shin-guntō. See Plate 84 and 'Swords of the Naval Landing Forces (Marines)' later in this book.

***Fig. 10*** *Ashi (suspension mounts) for: (i) Shin-guntō metal scabbard; (ii) Kai-guntō (naval sword); (iii) 1944 regulation pattern Army sword.*

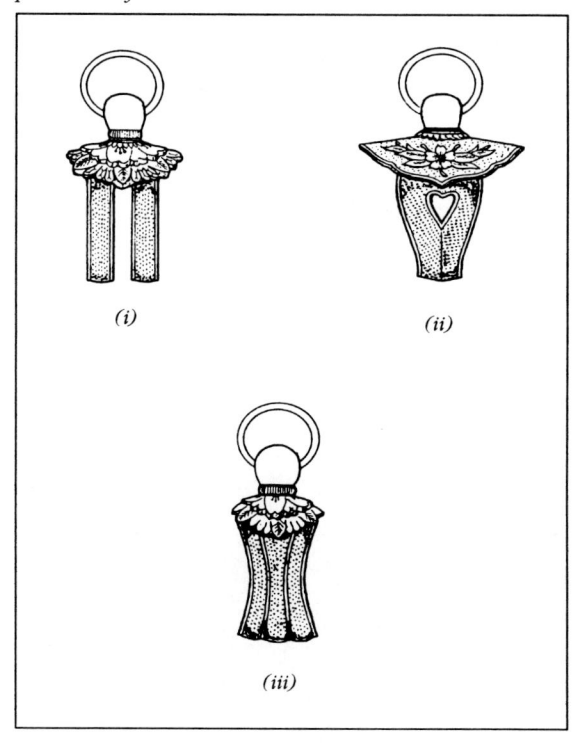

**Plate 79**  Typical shin-guntō scabbard variations. Top to bottom:
(i)  Standard painted type metal scabbard.
(ii)  Standard metal scabbard with a brown leather combat cover which has been put on while wet, stitched along the edge, and then dried to shrink tight. This is unusual and does more harm than good since the metal rusts.
(iii)  Old black lacquered katana scabbard used with a shin-guntō and covered with a removable brown leather combat cover held in place by a flap with three press studs. A field scabbard type ashi has been added which, for some unknown reason, has been fitted with two steel hanging rings in the same mount. The paper label gives the Japanese owner as Umeki Kunitaro and the silvered plaque reads: 'Presented to Captain E. F. L. Figgis by HQBMA Malaya 1945'.
(iv)  Wooden field scabbard with a brown leather cover laced up at the throat. The steel suspension mount is unusual in that the boss has a faceted finish and is pinned to the ashi allowing movement in the vertical plane. (Richard Fuller).

**Plate 81**  Large stamp on the ersatz scabbard covering of the shin-guntō in Plate 80. Unfortunately it is partly obliterated but the centre column refers to the 'patent application' or 'patent applied for'. The right-hand column appears to be the address of the unknown manufacturer in Kurume city, which is the capital of Chikugo province. (Herb Gopstein).

**Plate 80**  A late shin-guntō, from around 1944, which can be determined by the quality of fittings and materials used. The hilt covering is brown shagreen (fish skin). The kabuto-gane lacks the copper sakura decoration and the fuchi is plain. Unsigned oil-tempered blade of good quality. The field scabbard is not covered with leather but is a flexible compressed paper similar to a thick manilla card. It does not appear to be a very hard-wearing form of protection and the degree of water impermeability is unknown. This may be regarded as an ersatz measure due to the growing shortage of leather in Japan by that time. The large 'patent stamp' is clearly visible (see Plate 81). No other example of this covering has been reported. (Herb Gopstein).

A rare additional retention release system has been noted on a metal scabbard (Plates 86, 87, 88). It is a specially made elongated lever screwed to a base plate which, in turn, is screwed to one side of the scabbard. The upper end is fixed to a press stud which passes through the scabbard throat (kuchi-gane). When pressed the normal spring clip is released allowing the sword to be withdrawn. The fuchi (hilt collar) push button also acts independently if required. Presumably fitted after purchase to facilitate easier release.

A removable protective brown leather, or even green canvas, combat cover may be fitted (Fig. 13

**Plate 82** Scarce two-ashi (suspension mount) shin-guntō scabbards. The lower mount is demountable (see Fig. 11). (Ron Gregory).

**Plate 83** General Araki Sadao in full dress with a scarce two-hanger shin-guntō. Unusually, it has the gold? General Officers kyu-guntō pattern full dress sword knot which probably indicates a 1934 dating commensurate with the shin-guntō introduction. Possibly the shin-guntō coloured rank tassels were introduced a little later. (Philip Goody).

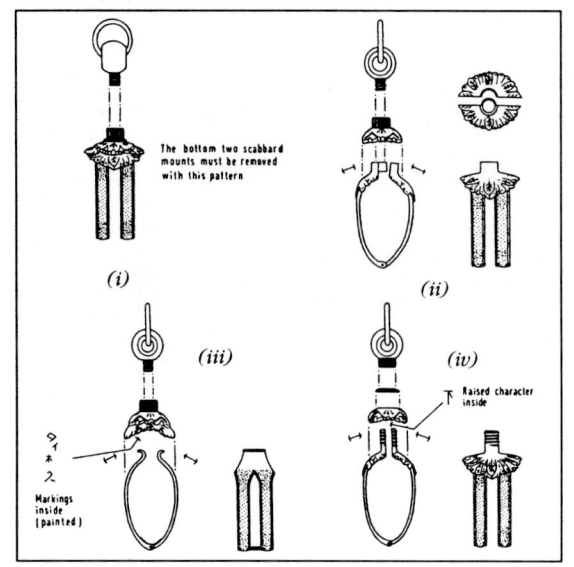

**Fig. 11** Four variations of the second lower ashi (suspension mount) which may be found with metal shin-guntō scabbards: (i) is the standard mount but the boss has not been brazed in; (ii), (iii), (iv) are hinged at the bottom allowing them to open once the top section has been unscrewed.

& Plate 90).[5] However, a non-removable brown leather cover 'shrink' fitted is an alternative, but this is fairly unusual (Plate 79 (ii)). Partial protection is sometimes found in the form of either a leather foot, like the bottom of a combat cover, shrink-fitted over the chape (ishizuke) or a plain leather sleeve located immediately below the ashi to prevent wear when held.

The wooden inner lining of a metal scabbard is in two sections stuck together with a rice-based glue called 'sokui'. Sometimes they may have details of the scabbard maker or retailer written in ink, such as 'respectfully made at the Hattori Sword Shop, Kanda', which is in Tokyo.

**Plate 84** *Japanese naval officers wearing land warfare uniform at Shanghai, China in 1937. The officer in the foreground with the binoculars has the epaulettes of a Captain. Those on the right do not seem to have the normal naval officer shoulder boards but have anchors on their caps. The man in the centre is the same officer as seen in Plates 165, 298. He carries a scarce two-hanger Army shin-guntō having the normal tape-bound white samē hilt but with a General Officers knot. Presumably he is a senior officer in the Naval Landing Forces (Marines) which would explain the Army sword. If correct, it also confirms that officers of the NLF could use the shin-guntō sword knot rank coloration system although naval rank designation was used. The officer on his left has a naval kyu-guntō with standard pattern knot, while the officer on his right has either a kai-guntō or a civilian katana. (Bill Tagg).*

## Field scabbards

These are plain wooden scabbards covered in non-removable brown leather (or sometimes pigskin) which is stitched along the back edge with a double thickness at the base (Fig. 13). Black leather is occasionally found but is believed to be indicative of use by the Naval Landing Forces.

Ashi vary, but differ from the metal scabbard type by being simpler in design (Fig. 14). They are made from brass, steel or even leather fitted with a brass or steel hanging ring. Occasionally the steel boss may be pinned through the ashi band to allow it to swivel as shown on the example in Plate 79 (iv). Only rarely are 'metal-scabbard' ashi found on field scabbards. An *ersatz* scabbard covering indicative of later use (i.e. around 1944) is shown in Plates 80, 81.

A metal throat (kuchi-gane) is normally present but often there may only be a simple brass band which can be screwed to the wooden scabbard.

The spring clip retention system is not usually employed with a field scabbard. Consequently various alternative securing systems were used:

(a) The most common is a short leather strap stitched to a leather loop which fits over the fuchi (hilt collar). This strap has one or two female press buttons which engage with male studs on the scabbard reverse. It normally passes through a hole in the tsuba (guard) but also has been found to pass around the outside. This system can also be found with metal scabbards, if fitted with combat covers when no spring clip retention was used, and also as a secondary form of retention.

# JAPANESE MILITARY AND CIVIL SWORDS AND DIRKS

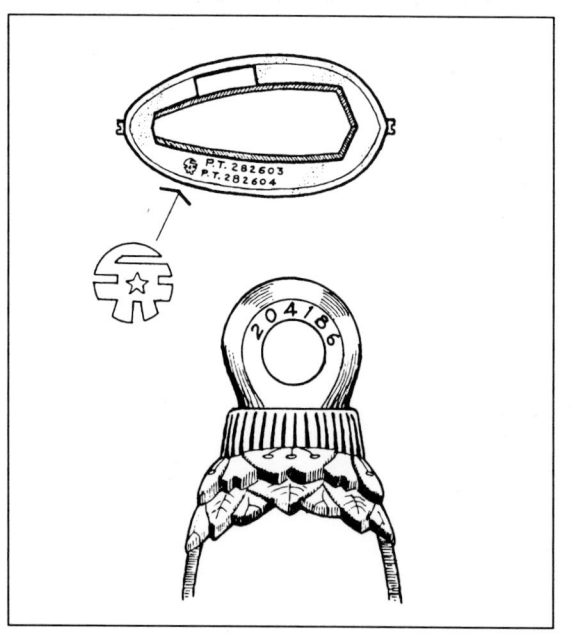

**Fig. 12** Rare markings found on shin-guntō scabbard fittings. They appear to be patent numbers which would make them early.
(i)   Top view of a kuchi-gane (scabbard throat). The stamp is unidentified.
(ii)   End view of an ashi (suspension mount). The face of the boss is flattened, which is not normal.

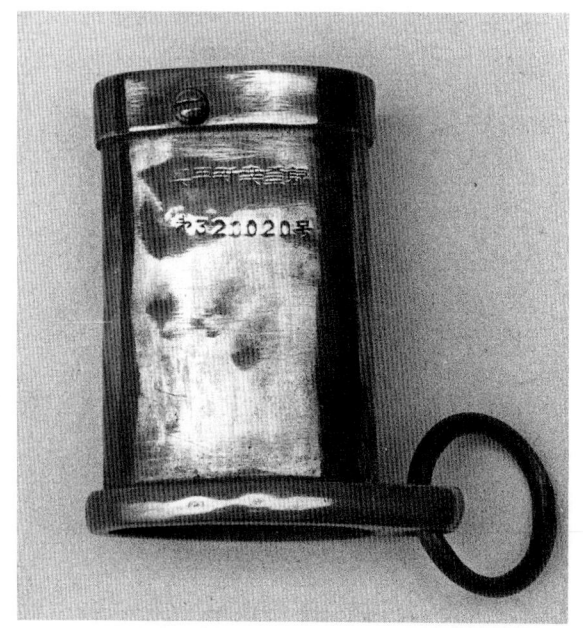

**Plate 85** Elongated brass locket for an Army field scabbard. It is stamped with Japanese characters and a patent number, 020023. The top line (unfortunately indistinct) seems to refer to the 'first new trade appliance' or 'the first of its kind'. A scarce fitting of unknown dating. It is rare to find such an engraving on a scabbard fitting. (Ron Gregory).

**Plates 86, 87, 88** A rare additional release system fixed to a metal shin-guntō scabbard. When pressed it releases the hilt spring clip allowing the blade to be withdrawn. The fuchi spring button acts independently. (Steve Wadlam).

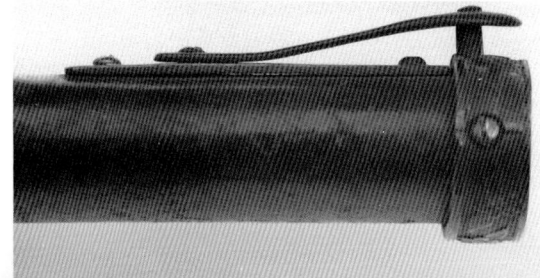

The press studs can, in fact, be American 'Antler' brand which were pre-war stocks.

(b) A long strap sewn to the leather scabbard cover which has two male studs on the base. It loops over the tsuba (or through it) and around the fuchi, returning to be fastened by two female press buttons at the end. This is scarce.

(c) A variation of (b) utilising a buckle at the base. The strap passes through a hole in the tsuba, and then returns to be secured by the buckle.

(d) Another variation has a leather strap secured to a projecting stud which is riveted to the ashi band. The free end of the strap is fixed to a metal section having a small hole at the end. It is pushed through a slot in the tsuba, returning back to be secured by the stud. This is rare.

(e) Another unusual and rare retention system has an elongated spring clip riveted to the ashi band. It protrudes from under the leather scabbard cover to engage with a slot in the tsuba (Plate 89).

An unusual field scabbard variation in the author's collection is made from a shira-saya (wooden keeper scabbard for an unmounted blade) which is covered in non-removable brown leather. It has a brass kuchi-gane (throat) with a slot for a spring clip and is fitted with two non-removable ashi (under the cover) of field scabbard design.

As with combat covers the lower end of a field scabbard cover is thickened to lessen wear. It may be further protected by the addition of a metal, usually brass, chape or drag, but this is infrequent (Plate 93).

On rare occasions a field scabbard may be found with an additional hanging ring near the bottom. This is to allow the sword to be slung across the back with the hilt projecting above the right shoulder which leaves both hands free in battlefield conditions (Plate 91). A lower ring was not always necessary since the carrying sling could have loops for sliding over the scabbard.

**Plate 89** *Shin-guntō with a special elongated spring clip protruding from a field scabbard to engage with a slot in the tsuba (guard). It is riveted to the suspension mount band. An unusual item.* (Ron Gregory).

**Plate 90** *Scarce foul weather scabbard cover of green canvas with a leather chape. This type is often tied around the middle for extra security.* (Ron Gregory).

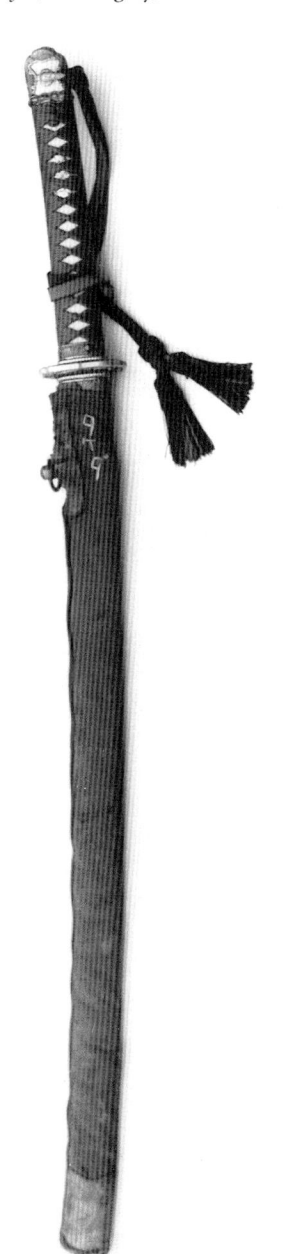

# JAPANESE MILITARY AND CIVIL SWORDS AND DIRKS

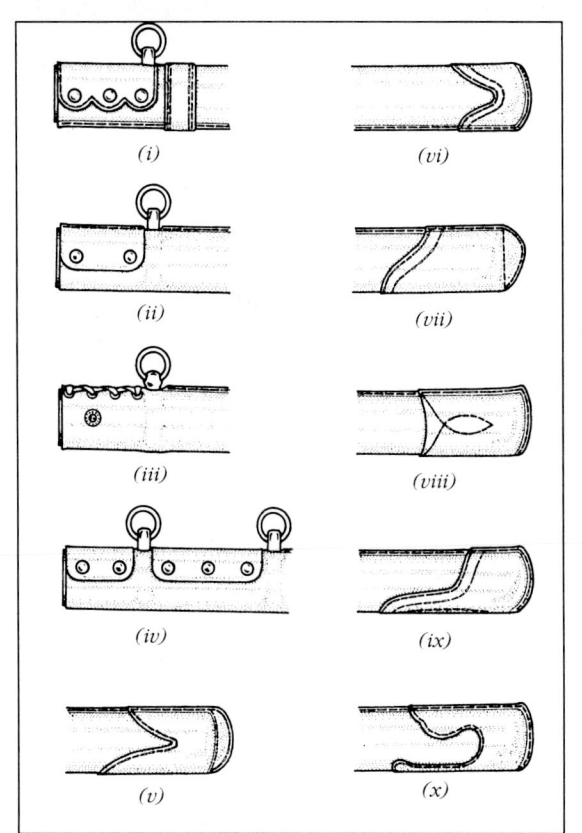

**Fig. 13** *Typical leather combat cover throats and thickened chapes: (i), (ii), (iii) are found on shin-guntō and Army kyu-guntō; (iv) is found with kai-guntō; (v) to (x) may be found with all the above varieties of swords.*

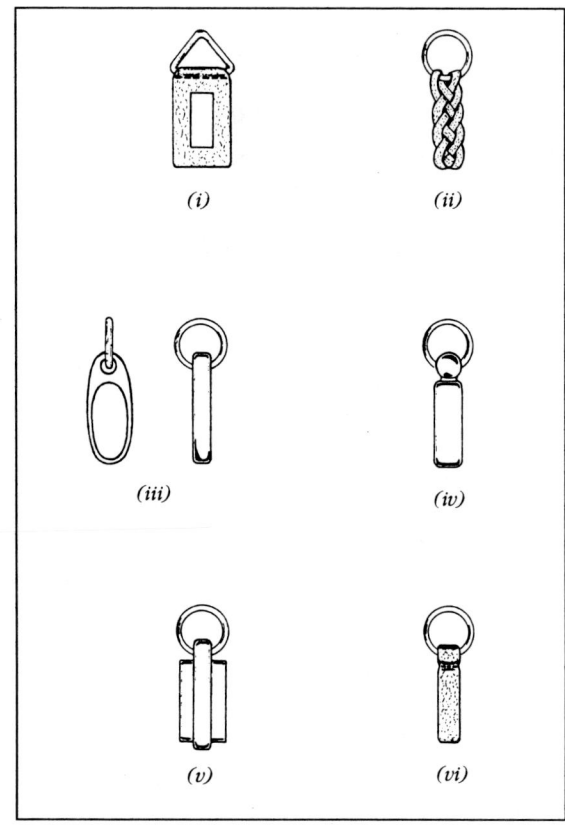

**Fig. 14** *Typical ashi (suspension mounts) used on wooden field scabbards: (i), (ii), (vi) are leather; (iii), (iv), (v) are brass or steel.*

## Scabbard variations

Scabbard finishes (a) to (e) described below may be found having the normal fittings for metal scabbards. They must have been optional items offered by retailers or, possibly, made to the purchaser's own request.

(a) Matt-finished brown lacquer over canvas on a wooden base. Gives the appearance of a metal scabbard until held. Fairly scarce.

(b) Brown lacquered shagreen (fish or shark skin) polished smooth to reveal a myriad of little white diamonds. Scarce.

(c) Thin brown leather. Rare.

(d) Samē (ray skin) lacquered dark brown to reveal white dots of varying size. Rare with Army mounts. Possibly indicative of use by the Naval Landing Forces.

(e) Black lacquer which has only been found with shin-guntō having some naval characteristics (see later under 'Swords of the Naval Landing Forces') (Plates 192, 193).

(f) Original old katana scabbard converted for military use. The rear kurikata (projecting mount used to prevent it slipping through the waist sash) could be removed, although this was not always done. A field scabbard ashi was added under a leather combat cover which is often removable

**Plate 91** *Japanese Army troops in Shanghai, China, 1937. Note that the officers or NCOs have their swords slung across their back leaving both hands free. (Bill Tagg).*

(Plate 79(iii)). This conversion was often done when an older blade was rehilted for military use, although complete katana may be found.

(g) White or black lacquered cane strips bound round metal or wooden scabbards. Presumably done when no protective leather covering was available (Plate 92).

Other optional purchase fittings for scabbards include:

(a) Ishizuke (chape) with a special thickened shoe for use with metal or lacquered scabbards (Fig. 15). The shoe is stamped on either side with Japanese characters and numbers within gilded panels. The obverse reads JITSUYŌ SHIN AN TOKKYO (the patent practical new idea) and the reverse has the patent or series number 213917. These markings are identical to those found on the equivalent kai-guntō version. Scarce.

(b) Scabbard seal formed by seppa (hilt washers) with the outer rim projecting downwards (Plate 94). The projection may be either 3mm (partly covering the scabbard throat which is recessed to receive it) or 6mm (entirely covering the throat). They form a seal when the sword is sheathed. Both are scarce.

(c) Scabbard throat having an integral hinged cover which closes, sealing the scabbard, when the blade is drawn. When the sword is sheathed the cover projects upwards through a special slot in the tsuba and acts as a retention system (Plates 95 to 98). Known as the 'IIDA SHIKI TEI GAI' (Iida model lock cover) it was invented by Mr Iida Kunitaro who ran a sword retail business (presumably before or during World War Two). He died in September 1979. Some also bear the patent number 132106. It prevents dirt and water from entering a scabbard. The standard shin-guntō tsuba is modified to accept the cover. The purpose of a brass loop, which may be fixed to the top of the tsuba, has not been established. Only a few are believed to have been made so examples are rare.

# JAPANESE MILITARY AND CIVIL SWORDS AND DIRKS

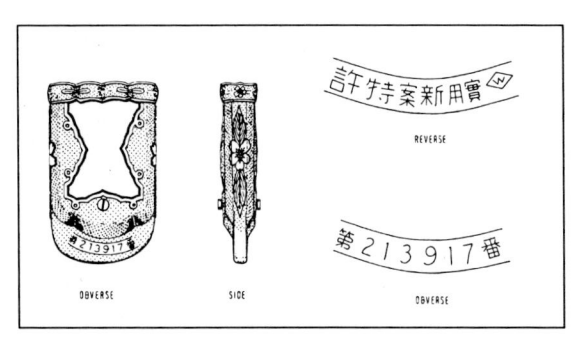

**Fig. 15** *Special shin-guntō ishizuke (chape) with a thickened shoe. The reverse markings read: JITSUYŌ (utility, practical use), SHIN (new), AN (idea), TOKKYO (patent), i.e. the patent practical new idea. The 'W' stamp is probably the manufacturer's trademark. The obverse markings read: DAI (number, order, series) 213917, BAN (number), i.e. series number 213917 which is probably the patent number. All examples found, including the naval kai-guntō version (Plate 188), have identical markings.*

Protection of the hilt from inclement weather and wear was done by one of three methods if the owner so wished:

(a) White linen or bandage wrapped around the hilt leaving the kabuto-gane (pommel) exposed (Plates 71, 99). This was only to protect the hilt binding in the field and was easily replaced by the owner when required. Contemporary photographs indicate this was a very common practice which was also used for the kyu-guntō. No genuine examples appear to have survived since it was removed or rotted away.

(b) A brown leather sleeve which covers the hilt above the tsuba but leaves the kabuto-gane exposed (Plate 102). It is cross-laced through metal eyelets along the top seam. An optional extra and scarce.

(c) A tapering leather bag which widens at the mouth to fit over the entire hilt and tsuba. It is secured by either a draw string or by a leather strap fitted with a press stud. This is known as a

**Plate 92** *Two shin-guntō scabbards covered with cane. Left is a field scabbard with plain brass fittings entirely bound with strips of black lacquered cane. Right is a standard metal scabbard wrapped with white lacquered cane. Presumably this is in lieu of a leather combat cover. (Richard Fuller and Ron Gregory).*

'foul weather cover' (Plates 100, 101). Also an optional extra and scarce. A finely woven canvas-like material has also been reported.

## Mon

As with the kyu-guntō it was permissible for the owner to display his family mon (badge) on the hilt fittings. This consisted of a silver disc about 9.5–13mm ($3/8"–1/2"$) diameter pinned or soldered to either the kabuto-gane upper edge, fuchi (hilt collar) or on one menuki (hilt ornament). Only rarely are mon found on both menuki. A brass mon on the underside of the kabuto-gane is known but this is an unusual material and location. Another rare position is on the fuchi push button. Sometimes mon[6] may be found defaced or

**Plate 93** *Shin-guntō with a leather-covered field scabbard surrendered in Burma. A brass shoe with an iron drag has been fitted to prevent wear. This unusual feature is not a regulation fitting. (Dr Terry Ingold).*

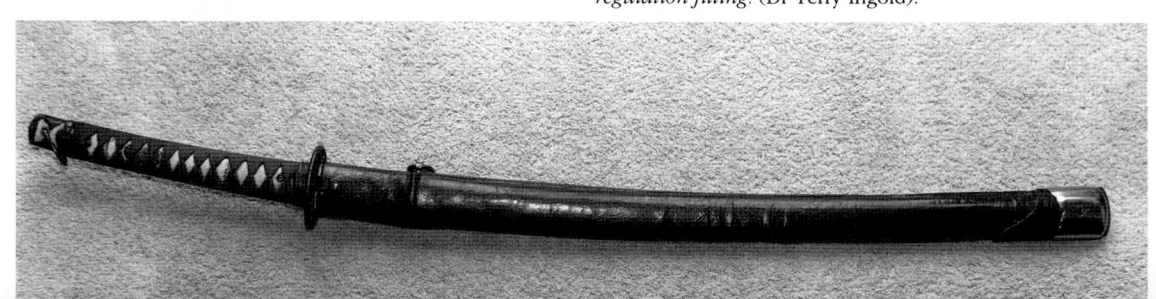

ARMY 1934 (& 1938) SHIN-GUNTŌ

**Plate 95**  *Scabbard throat sealed by the hinged spring cover. The Japanese characters read SEMBAI TOKKYO (Monopoly patent) and IIDA SHIKI TEI GAI (Iida model lock cover).*

**Plate 96**  *Underside of shin-guntō tsuba modified by the addition of an elongated slot for the passage of the cover. Note that the dai-seppa and seppa have also been modified.*

**Plate 94**  *Shin-guntō with scarce scabbard seals formed by a seppa with the outer rim projecting downwards to partially cover the scabbard throat (left) or fully cover it (right). (Ron Gregory).*

removed which was done by the owner to avoid disgrace at the time of surrender. Reference to specialist books should be made to identify the hundreds of mon and their variants used by the families of Japan.

Dimensions of these swords are, of course, variable, but the average range with Shōwa period blades are as follows. Overall length of sword and scabbard 838–1015mm (33"–40"). Total weight 38–59 ounces. Blade length 483–692mm (19"–27¼"). Hilt length 225–260mm (8⅞"–10¼"). Maximum blade width 24–38mm (¹⁵⁄₁₆"–1½"). Scabbard length 965mm–1190mm (24½"–30¼"). Sword weight 30–39 ounces.

Before describing the sword knots it is necessary to discuss the 'Rikugun Gunzoku' (literally 'Army–Civilian in military employ'). The Gunzoku were a separate organisation of civilians with their own rank structure, badges and green uniforms

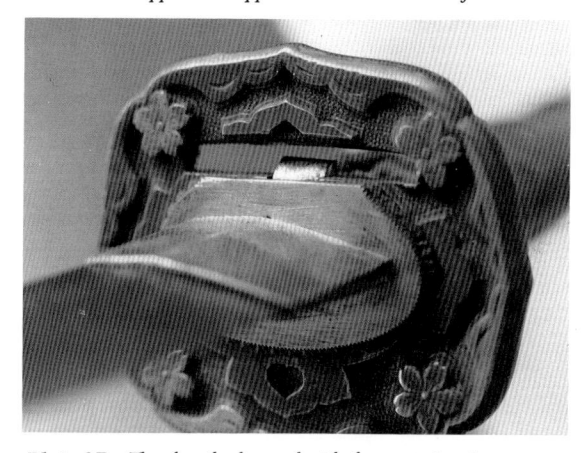

**Plate 97**  *The sheathed sword with the cover passing through the tsuba and acting as a retention clip. The use of the raised loop, visible to the left, is unknown.*

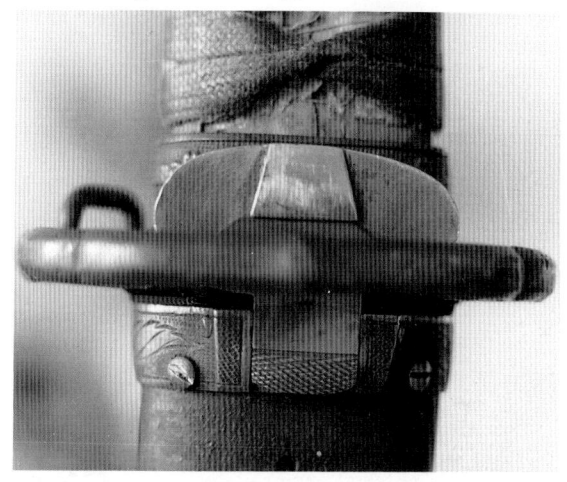

**Plates 95, 96, 97**  *Rare Iida patent scabbard seal for a shin-guntō which also acts as a retention clip. (Han Bing Siong).*

**Plate 98** Rare Iida patent scabbard seal for a shin-guntō which also acts as a retention clip as shown in Plates 95, 96, 97. The cover of this example is stamped SEMBAI TOKKYO (Monopoly patent) and DAI (number) 132106, GŌ (number, item), i.e. item number 132106, which must be the patent number. It is probably later than that stamped 'Iida model lock cover' since the patent number has been obtained. A rare fitting. (Ron Gregory).

**Plate 99** First Lieutenant Namekawa Machida in M98 (1938) Army uniform. His shin-guntō with sword knot has a protective white linen strip wrapped around the hilt. This photograph must have been taken after 1939 since he is seen as still a Second Lieutenant in May of that year. (Cheyenne Noda).

who worked for, and assisted, the Army as administrators, translators etc. They also carried regular Army pattern swords.[7] Their ranks were graded but were equivalent to those of the regular Army. The most senior rank was that of 'Shinninkan' (i.e. personally approved by the Emperor) followed by 'Chokunin' (Imperial appointment) grades 1 and 2. Both classes were collectively known as 'Shiseichōkan' (Chief Civil Administrators) and were equivalent to the Army General Officer ranks. Next came 'Sōnin' (appointment approved

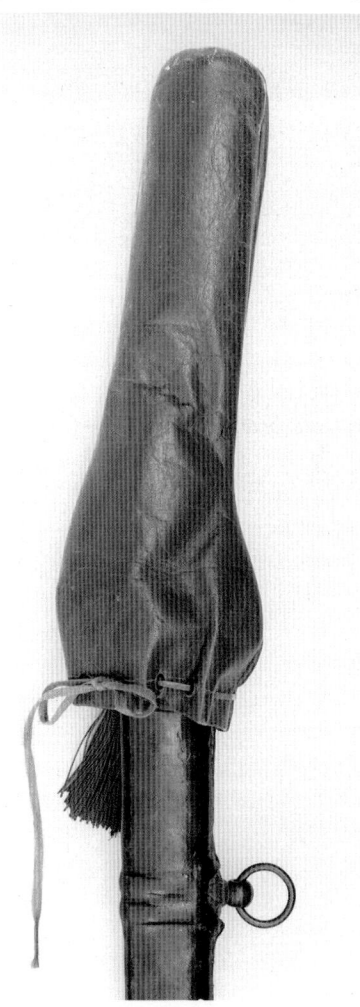

**Plate 100** Leather bag type foul weather hilt cover over a shin-guntō hilt. It is closed by a drawstring although an alternative with a leather strap and press stud is also found. (Richard Fuller).

## ARMY 1934 (& 1938) SHIN-GUNTŌ

**Plate 101** Major with a shin-guntō which has a leather foul weather hilt cover of the bag type. (Cheyenne Noda).

**Plate 102** The First Lieutenant (front right) is holding a shin-guntō with sword knot, leather foul weather hilt sleeve and suspension chain. The officer at the back left is Second Lieutenant Namekawa Machida. Both officers are dressed in the M90 (1930) Army winter uniform. This photograph was taken in Tientsin, China. (Cheyenne Noda).

**Plate 103** An Army Second Lieutenant in M98 (1938) field uniform with a drawn shin-guntō and leather-covered scabbard. Note that the sword knot is looped around his wrist. (Cheyenne Noda).

by the Emperor) grades 3 to 8 which were the equivalent to Army Field and Company grade ranks. Then came 'Hannin' (Junior Official) grades 1 to 4, equivalent to Army NCOs. 'Sōnin' and Hannin' were collectively termed 'Shiseikan' (Civil Administrators). Lastly were the rank and file called 'Koin' (Employee). It is assumed that those of Hannin grade also carried the Officers shin-guntō and not the NCOs aluminium-hilted version. Thus not all shin-guntō, including those with General Officers knots, are necessarily military.

# JAPANESE MILITARY AND CIVIL SWORDS AND DIRKS

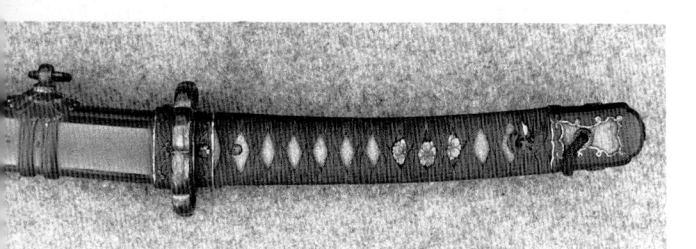

**Plate 104** *Standard shin-guntō with unusual elongated hilt and scabbard fittings. The kabuto-gane (pommel) is 52mm (norm 45mm) and the ishizuke (chape) is extremely long at 60mm (41mm norm). It is possible these fittings were specially made since the leaf decoration of the scabbard fittings is finely chiselled rather than raised, as found on normal fitments. Note also the thick tsuba (guard). The blade is signed HOKI NO KAMI SANEMORI (Sanemori, Lord of Hoki) and dated 1799. There is no question of it being a reproduction or 'parts' sword (see Plates 318, 319). (Ian Brooks).*

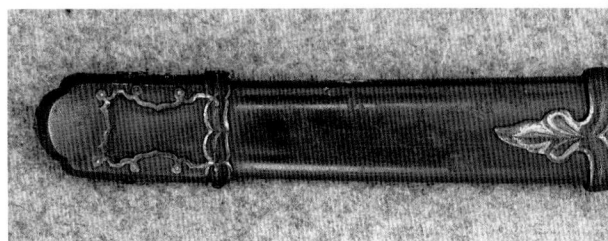

**Plate 105** *Unusually long ishizuke (chape) of the shin-guntō shown in Plate 104. (Ian Brooks).*

## Sword knots

A new-style sword knot was introduced for shin-guntō which, seemingly, was also to be used with the superseded kyu-guntō when carried contemporaneously. It consisted of linen straps with a slide and double tassels (Fig. 1 (iii)) coloured according to the rank grade of the wearer.

| Knot | Army | Gunzoku |
|---|---|---|
| Brown and red straps with yellow or gold wire zigzag stitches. Brown slide with the same stitches. Yellow tassels. | **General Officers**<br>General<br>Lieutenant-General<br>Major-General | **Shiseichōkan**<br>Shinninkan<br>Chokunin 1st grade<br>Chokunin 2nd grade |
| Brown and red straps, slide and tassels. | **Field Officers**<br>Colonel<br>Lieutenant-Colonel<br>Major | **Shiseikan**<br>Sōnin 3rd grade<br>Sōnin 4th grade<br>Sōnin 5th grade |
| Brown and blue straps, slide and tassels. (* Possibly used the same brown knot as Hannin 2nd – 4th grade) | **Company Officers**<br>Captain<br>1st Lieutenant<br>2nd Lieutenant<br>Warrant Officer | **Shiseikan**<br>Sōnin 6th grade<br>Sōnin 7th grade<br>Sōnin 8th grade<br>*Hannin 1st grade |
| Brown straps, slide and tassels. (Note: Army NCOs only used this knot when carrying traditional-style swords e.g. katana, wakizashi and Officers shin-guntō).[8] | **NCOs**<br>Sergeant-Major<br>Sergeant<br>Corporal | **Shiseikan**<br>Hannin 2nd grade<br>Hannin 3rd grade<br>Hannin 4th grade |

Probably also used by officers of the Naval Landing Forces since the same as used on the naval kai-guntō.

**Plate 106** *This shin-guntō, shown in Plates 107, 134, has an ishizuke (chape) incorporating the 'winged wheel' logo of the North China Joint Stock Transportation Company (see Plate 134) and an unusual double sarute (sword knot loop). (Dr Terry Ingold).*

Other unusual colourings are known but will be discussed later in 'Collaboration, Reproduction and Fake Swords' since they do not appear to be of Japanese manfacture.

## Purchase

An officer normally purchased his sword from a dealer or through the Army Association (or Club) known as the 'Kaikōsha'. Such a sword would be selected according to financial means and the officer's physical stature. Unfortunately no price list from any such source has been located.

In 1944 a Second Lieutenant was paid an average of 70.83 Yen[9] per month which would limit him to a fairly mundane standard sword. The basic pay for a Lieutenant-Colonel at this time commenced at 220 Yen per month. High-class hand-forged gendaitō made at the Yasukuni Shrine, Tokyo were sold direct for around 120 Yen in 1940 and 170 Yen in 1944. These Yasukuni blades, when bought at the Kaikōsha, usually sold for fifty per cent more, i.e. 180 Yen in 1940 and

**Plate 107** Side and top views of the unusual double sarute (sword knot loop) used on the shin-guntō in Plate 106. It appears to be a contemporary fitting, but why this system was used is unknown. (Dr Terry Ingold).

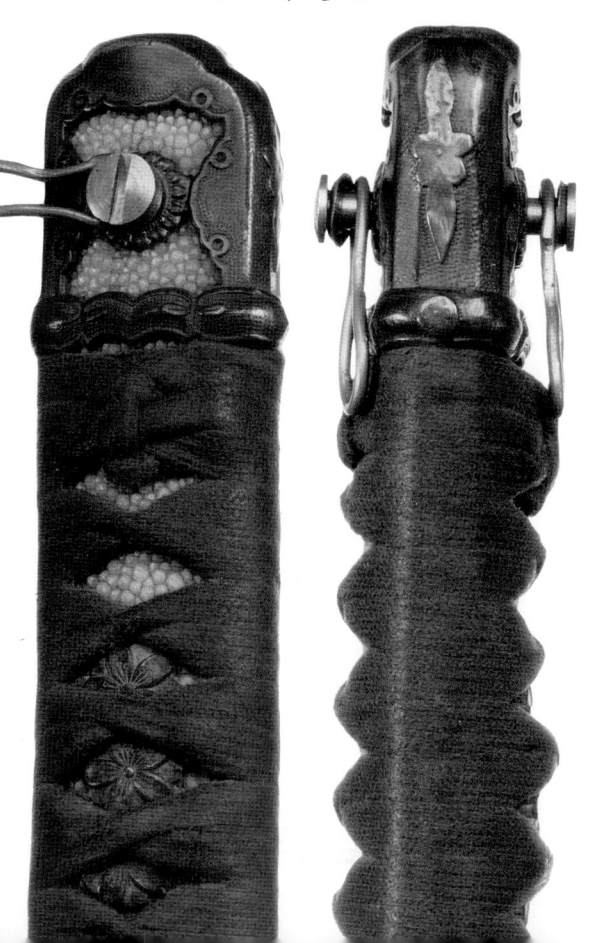

**Plate 108** Second Lieutenant Shoichi Niwa of the Nagase Company in China, May 1938. He broke his sword blade, which is in shin-guntō mounts, in hard fighting in the Battle of Ko-san. This picture clearly proves swords were actually used in battle. The replacement of such breakages could explain the rare presence of 1945 dated blades in shin-guntō mounts when they may be expected to be in 1944 Army mounts.

255 Yen in 1944.[10] Thus a Yasukuni Shrine-made blade was a great expense for even a fairly senior officer.

A naval Lieutenant confirmed that his sword, with an oil-tempered blade, cost 80 Yen in 1941 which would be on a par with the Army equivalent.

A number of shin-guntō variations have been found and are described with the various photographs used to illustrate them elsewhere in this book. There may yet be many others but care must be exercised in establishing official variations from 'collaboration', post-war 'souvenir' and 'fake' swords. Indeed this is often extremely difficult to determine and the authors' comments on such matters are open to correction if need be.

The shin-guntō is a common sword but scarcity

JAPANESE MILITARY AND CIVIL SWORDS AND DIRKS

*Plate 109* American serviceman (marine?) holding a shin-guntō picked up after a battle in the South Pacific. It still has the sword knot and a leather-covered scabbard. Often such items were booby-trapped. (Art Clarke).

## ARMY 1934 (& 1938) SHIN-GUNTŌ

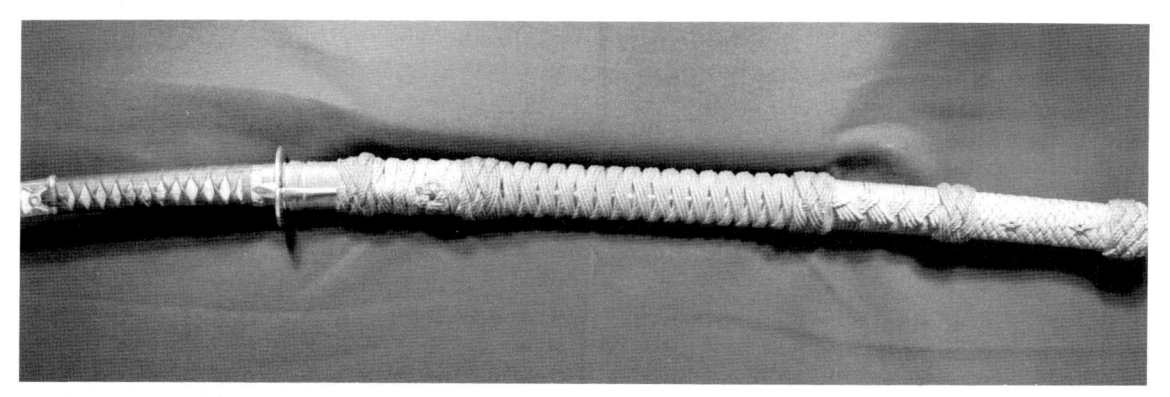

can be increased by unusual fittings or the presence of a General Officers knot. Details of surrender or capture (if genuine) are an added feature which may increase interest and enhance value for the collector. Therefore all such details should be checked for validity as far as is possible.

A sword with a well-worn scabbard and hilt suffering from grease and the sweat of the owner's hand, or wear of the suspension mount from constant carrying, indicates that it is genuine and saw military action. It may have gone through great Japanese victories such as Singapore and also through terrible hardships such as the retreat through Burma or jungle fighting in New Guinea. Such a weapon should not be dismissed because of condition when, historically speaking, it should be worth more than a near mint example whose owner may only have sat behind a desk during hostilities.

*Plate 110* A shin-guntō obtained in Japan in October 1945 by US seaman Art Clarke. He subsequently covered the scabbard with a fine example of cord weaving and knot work (known in the Navy as 'whiteline' and 'Belfast'). He also obtained several other swords which he similarly bound (but apparently not that in Plate 5) and later gave away. This work should be regarded as part of the sword's history and should not be removed in favour of the standard metal scabbard and fittings underneath. (Art Clarke).

*Plate 111* A hilt from a shin-guntō obtained from China in the nineteen-eighties. Wooden grip, steel collar, brass pommel and steel knot loop. It is believed to be a Chinese fitting either to make the hilt more substantial for Chinese military use or to convert it into an agricultural cutting implement. Several examples are known. (Richard Fuller).

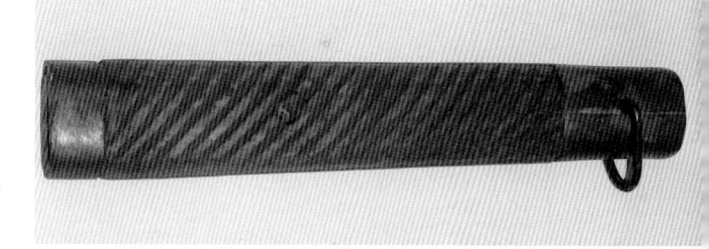

---

1 In 1978 the Dutch expert Han Bing Siong put forward the suggestion that the shin-guntō was introduced in 1933 which was different from the then existing literature. See his articles 'The Japanese and their swords', To-ken Society of Great Britain Programme 101:1978, 6–13; To-ken Bijutsu No. 264:1979, pp 54,55; No. 265, pp 59, 60; and No. 266, pp 50, 51. Shortly afterwards he found an official Japanese document (to be published in a forthcoming article) confirming that it was, in fact, 1934.
2 Translated by Han Bing Siong. Day and month specified in *Swords of Imperial Japan 1868–1945*
3 Confirmed in the *Nippon no Gunpuku*, page 101. A number of two-ashi shin-guntō have been examined which had undated Shōwa period blades. However, one totally genuine example has a blade dated 1941 which seems to indicate the manufacture of two-ashi swords continued after 1938. Conversely Hang Bing Siong, in his forthcoming article on the search for the shin-guntō's origin, will reproduce photographs dated 1934 which show officers already wearing single-ashi shin-guntō.
4 According to the *Nippon no Gunso*, but this has not been verified elsewhere.
5 The owner's name may be occasionally found written in ink on the underside of the flap. In one rare case a folded official form of rice paper was found which gave the result of an official naval inquiry into the loss of the owner's cap thus indicating use by Naval Landing Forces.
6 'Mon' is both singular and plural.
7 Han Bing Siong has ascertained from the Military History Department of the Japanese National Defence College that Gunzoku carried military swords with the same knot colouration as the regular Army. Gunzoku ranks, uniform and badges are shown in *Imperial Japanese Army and Navy Uniforms & Equipments* by Nakata (see Bibliography), page 162. Japanese text.
8 According to the researches of Han Bing Siong. Those with the aluminium-hilted shin-guntō used leather knots, although two captured officers shin-guntō have been reported with such a knot.
9 In 1941 one Yen equalled twenty-three American cents or five British pennies (i.e. 2.1 new pence).
10 *Yasukuni Shrine and the Tanren-kai* by Fujishiro Okisato (translated by Leon Kapp). To-ken Society of Great Britain Programme No. 134: 1987.

# Army 1944 & 1945 (Officers) Sword Patterns

### Regulation 1944 pattern Army (Officers) sword

The *Nippon no Gunso* (see Bibliography) has a line drawing of this pattern in a section on Army swords. It is captioned 'SHŌWA JŪ KU NEN KEI SOSEI-RANZŌ GUNTŌ', i.e. 1944 mass-produced military sword. However, *Hand Cannons of Imperial Japan* (see Bibliography) contains two photographs dated 1940 and 1942[1] which show a Colonel Namio Tatsumi[2] apparently holding an example of this sword type. A clearer, but undated, photo of the same Colonel is shown in *Japanese Military Rifles* (see Bibliography).[3] This seems to show this sword pattern but the hilt fittings appear bright and polished (perhaps brass or copper) and not dark as would be expected with the normal blackened iron mounts. *Japanese Army Uniforms 1930–1945* (see Bibliography) has a coloured drawing of an iron-mounted version under the heading 'NCOs swords' The model date given is 1935, but this appears to be incorrect, being confused with the NCOs shin-guntō which is wrongly captioned above. *Swords of Imperial Japan 1868–1945* specifies 31 May 1938 but does not state its source.

The *Naval Official Bulletin* of May 1943[5] notified the naval arsenal to manufacture swords and parts from the 'limited amount of copper'. This implies that brass (which was an essential war material) was no longer available for sword mounts and that even copper was in limited supply. This situation, no doubt, would also have applied to the Army. If the photographic dating is correct then the introduction of a brass- or copper-mounted version seems to be 1940 or before, but the iron-mounted version probably superseded it in 1944. The above reference to usage implies the iron-mounted version was introduced for NCOs. However the observed use of plain brown shin-guntō knots and some good quality signed blades infers private purchase, possibly as a prescribed alternative to the Officers shin-guntō previously available to wealthier NCO ranks. Brass shortage may also have dictated use by new Warrant and Commissioned Officers when the mounts for their version of the shin-guntō could no longer be produced.

### *Copper-mounted*
Only one copper-mounted version has been reported which, unfortunately, does not prove that it was a separate model. The possibility exists that it is a prototype or manufacturer's variation. However, no brass-mounted version has been reported.

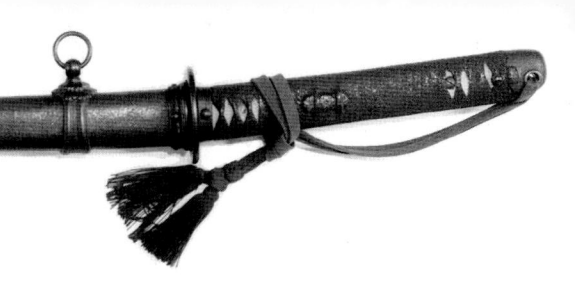

*Plate 112* Regulation 1944 pattern Army (Officers) sword. (Ron Gregory).

The general appearance is the same as the common iron-mounted version described below. All hilt fittings are made of solid copper except the tsuba (guard) which is brass, plated with copper and finished with a red lacquer. Retention with the tang is by a single wooden peg and not two screws as with the iron-mounted version. A Shin-shintō (1800–1868) period blade signed by Kanetada is utilised.

The scabbard is wood finished with a rough textured brown lacquer. The 1944 pattern ishizuke (chape) and kuchi-gane (throat) are copper. However the ashi (suspension mount) is that of a shin-guntō scabbard but is also made of copper. A dark brown leather combat cover is also fitted.

A surrender/transportation label confirms ownership by a Morimoto Zensaburō of a unit in the 38th Division.[6]

*Iron-mounted*
Hilt and scabbard mounts are blackened iron which have a stippled effect decoration of very small recessed dots.[7] The kabuto-gane (pommel) has a large offset hole for the sword knot, the straps of which are stitched together underneath (Fig. 20 (i)) after one is passed through. Examples with a sarute (knot loop) are very scarce. One has been found with an oval brass sarute and some may be cord (see Plate 115). The grip is bound in the distinctive 'battle style' (Katemaki) which exposes the blackened steel shin-guntō pattern menuki (hilt ornaments) of three kadosakura. The binding may be green or brown often heavily lacquered orange-red or dark brown. Artificial celluloid same is normally used over the wooden base. The hilt is secured by two widely spaced dome-headed screws with the heads on opposite sides. The fuchi is decorated with sakura and leaves, and has a push button which operates the spring clip retention system. Another button can be found in the kuchi-gane (scabbard throat) which also releases the spring clip. An oval blackened steel tsuba (guard) is used. However an ornate open-work type (Fig. 16)[8] was, apparently, originally intended perhaps for the copper-mounted version. Probably it was to be copper (or brass) but no example has been reported to confirm adoption.

Blades are shinogi-zukuri form which vary in quality and may even have the star stamp (Fig. 61 (x)). If signed and dated they seem to range from 1942 up to June 1945.[9] The widely spaced tang peg holes often help to identify blades which had these mounts. No example of a remounted old blade has been reported in the iron-mounted version. Sometimes a scabbard seal formed by a projecting seppa, as shown in Plate 94, may also be found. Whether 1942 blades indicate an earlier introduction than 1944 or they were taken from storage is unknown.

Scabbards may be either steel, with a wooden liner, painted light khaki, olive green or pale orange; or they may be rough textured lacquered canvas over a wooden base coloured either brown or black. There are three fittings which are a kuchi-gane (throat) decorated ensuite with the

*Fig. 16* The *Nippon no Gunso* shows a drawing of the 1944 pattern Army (Officers) sword with this flamboyant tsuba (guard) design. Since no example or photograph has been found to confirm the details, it is assumed this must be based on the original design but was never introduced, the more mundane plain blackened steel tsuba being preferred.

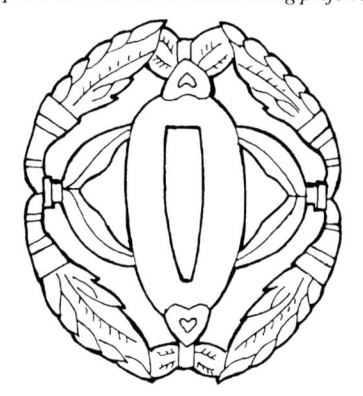

JAPANESE MILITARY AND CIVIL SWORDS AND DIRKS

**Plate 113** *1944 pattern Army sword (regulation pattern) with lacquered hilt binding. Note the two press buttons for release. The rough finished lacquered scabbard is also apparent.* (Ron Gregory).

**Plate 114** *Regulation pattern 1944 Army (Officers) sword with unlacquered green tape hilt binding. This example only has one spring clip button. Painted metal scabbard.* (Richard Fuller).

fuchi, ashi (suspension mount) which has a single wide band reducing in width at the centre (Fig. 10 (iii)) and an ishizuke (chape) which has a sakura with a steel rivet set in the centre. The use of a shibabiki (strengthening band) was abandoned. Leather combat covers were also used.

Dimensions appear to be fairly consistent except in weight because of scabbard types. Overall length of sword and scabbard, 1,000mm (39 3/8"). Hilt length 254mm (10"). Blade length 665mm (26 3/16"). Scabbard length 730mm (28 1/4"). Weight of sword and scabbard 55–60 ounces.

The sword knot seems to be a plain brown shin-guntō type. The previous ranking system may have been abandoned. Possibly those swords with

ARMY 1944 & 1945 (OFFICERS) SWORD PATTERNS

***Plate 115*** *Maj-Gen Gracey presents an Army (Officers) shin-guntō to Captain H. W. Parry, 1st Battalion (Russel's) Kumaon Regiment at Saigon, Indo-China, on 10 January 1946. The sword in the foreground is a 1944 pattern Army Officers with sarute (knot loop) which is unusual since they are normally absent with this pattern. The third from the left is a civilian katana mounted for the war.* Imperial War Museum.

heavily lacquered hilt bindings and lacquered wooden scabbards were favoured by the Naval Landing Forces but, again, this is speculation.

Contemporary photographs showing this pattern in use are virtually non-existent although the current availability of the iron-mounted version indicates that it must have been fairly common (at least by 1945). Only one photograph of a General Officer with such a sword has been reported

### 1945 pattern Army (Officers) Home Defence sword

The general appearance of this sword seems to indicate a more utilitarian version of the 1944 pattern Army Officers sword. Perhaps it may be termed the Army Officers Home Defence pattern since it was reputed to have been made for the expected American invasion of Japan in 1945. No reference to the use of this sword in occupied areas has been located.

Plain blackened steel hilt and scabbard mounts. Matching ishizuke (chape) and kabuto-gane (pommel) with pointed ends and slightly raised

Standard shinogi-zukuri blade form with two widely spaced holes although only the lower one is used for the mekugi peg. The author's example is oil-quenched, heavy with 'full dress' file marks and Japanese numbers stamped on the back edge of the tang. The other known example has a 'Mantetsu' (made from Manchurian iron) blade which does not, necessarily, imply Manchurian assembly. Wood-lined steel scabbard having a dark chocolate-brown finish and three mounts consisting of a kuchi-gane (throat), ashi and ishizuke. The latter has a centrally placed steel rivet head on each side. The type and colouration of sword knot is unknown. Although utilitarian the workmanship and fit are good.

Dimensions appear fairly consistent with those shown in Plate 116. Overall length of sword and scabbard 1,016mm (40"). Hilt length 263mm (10 3/8"). Blade length 679mm (26 3/4"). Scabbard length 749mm (29 1/2"). Weight of sword and scabbard 63 ounces.

The general appearance is of a prescribed pattern either contemporary with, or superseding, the 1944 pattern Army (Officers) sword. Production was probably limited with a likely use by new officers of the last Army draft in May 1945. The war planners had hoped to supply enough swords by September of that year for defensive purposes. This pattern also appears contemporary with the late-war Army NCOs sword in Plate 130. Only two examples are known to the authors which indicates a very rare classification.

**Plate 116** *Reputed 1945 pattern Army (Officers) Home Defence sword. This example was rescued in Japan from a pile of swords destined for destruction.* (Richard Fuller).

flattened sides. The ashi (suspension mount), however, is brass being painted or lacquered black. The hilt is bound with a dyed wine-red braid in 'battle style' (katemaki) over a similar coloured canvas (fire hose?). Thin blackened (tin?) menuki (hilt ornaments) of typical shin-guntō style. Single wooden hilt retention mekugi (peg). Oval blackened steel tsuba (guard) which is stamped with Arabic numbers and a black steel seppa (washer) on each side. Normal push button and spring clip retention system. Steel sarute (knot loop).

1 Page 100 & 188.
2 Chief Officer of the 1st Laboratory of the 1st Section of 1st Army Technical Research Institute in 1942. For the last six months of the war he was the Superintendent of the Torimatsu factory of the Nagoya Arsenal.
3 Page 135.
4 However usage, or if supplementary to, or superseding the Officers shin-guntō is not stated.
5 *The Changes of the Landing Forces Uniforms* by Etsuko Yagyu. Information and translation provided by Philip Goody.
6 This division was isolated in the New Britain area by 1944.
7 Copper-plated iron fittings have also been reported but appear to be very scarce.
8 Illustrated by a line drawing in the *Nippon no Gunso*. Use is incongruous for a 1944 utilitarian sword but may, perhaps, be expected on one of an earlier date, unless it was only for prototype use.
9 This is the latest date observed by the authors.

# Army 1935 & 1945 NCOs Sword Patterns

## Regulation 1935 (Type 95) pattern Army Non-Commissioned Officers shin-guntō

The correct designation of this sword pattern is the 'Type 95 pattern Army NCOs sword' since authorised on 16 September 1935[1]; although better known to collectors as the NCOs shin-guntō because it resembles the Commissioned Officers model.

The hilt is a cast aluminium replica of the regulation 1934 pattern Army Officers shin-guntō replicating the kabuto-gane (pommel), samē, hilt binding and menuki (hilt ornaments) (see Plate 125 for assembly details). All aluminium parts are painted in imitation of the colouration of the shin-guntō hilt. It is secured to the blade tang by a single brass dome-headed screw plus a male-female screw system through the kabuto-gane which also accepts a triangular sarute (knot loop). The plain, separate fuchi (hilt collar) is usually copper, sometimes iron or steel and, in rare cases, brass, although aluminium has been reported. The earliest examples (perhaps the first six thousand) have unpainted copper die-cast hilts (Plate 117) which have been annealed to produce a protective coating of oxide. In this case they are secured to the tang by the pommel screw system only. Production of these (fittings only?) seems restricted to the Suya Company of Tokyo, sub-contracting for the Tokyo Kokura (or Koishikawa) Arsenals prior to 1936.

Two types of tsuba (guard) are found on aluminium-hilted swords:

(i) Brass 'aoi' (hollyhock) shape as found on the shin-guntō but plain except for a stippled background decoration of small recessed dots. There is a decorative opening on each side with smaller upper and lower holes. The upper allows the spring clip to pass through while the lower is for the sword knot.

(ii) Plain oval blackened steel with only one opening which is for the spring clip.

It was assumed that the different tsuba types were manufacturers' individual variations or the steel pattern was later. However, as can be seen from Fig. 17, both brass and steel tsuba have been found on Kokura- and Nagoya-made blades which seems to dispel both theories. No evidence has been located to indicate that either tsuba type represents a rank distinction.

Scabbards are steel painted olive-green or khaki

JAPANESE MILITARY AND CIVIL SWORDS AND DIRKS

**Fig. 17**  *Typical fuchi (hilt collar) and blade markings observed on Army NCOs shin-guntō.[6] Tabulation in numerical order intimates that a factory block numbering allocation is likely.[7] (See also Fig. 62).*

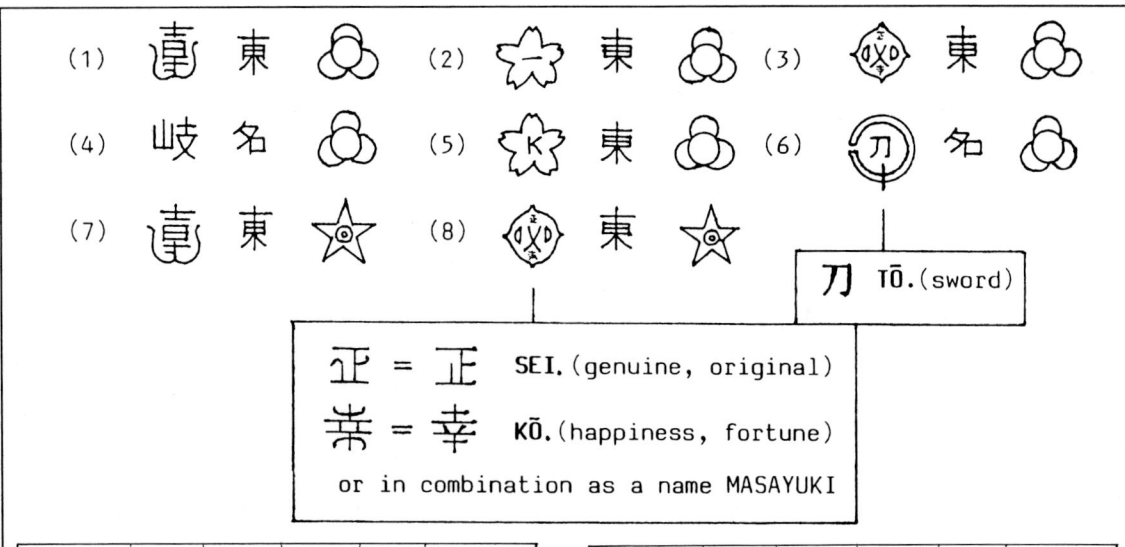

(1) 壽 東 ◯◯◯    (2) ✿一 東 ◯◯◯    (3) ◇ 東 ◯◯◯

(4) 岐 名 ◯◯◯    (5) ✿K 東 ◯◯◯    (6) 刀 名 ◯◯◯

(7) 壽 東 ★    (8) ◇ 東 ★

刀 TŌ. (sword)

正 = 正  SEI. (genuine, original)
幸 = 幸  KŌ. (happiness, fortune)
or in combination as a name MASAYUKI

| Blade numbering | Fuchi stamps | Hilt type | Fuchi type | Tsuba type | Manufacturing Arsenal |
|---|---|---|---|---|---|
| 340, 383, 1610, 4413, 4899, 5432 東, 5869 | (1) | Copper | Copper | Brass | Kokura |
| 名 10615 | (4) | Aluminium | Copper | Brass | Nagoya |
| 14175 東 / 14354 東 | (1) | " | " | " | Kokura |
| 17751 東 | (2) | " | " | " | Kokura |
| 22604 東 / 23523 東 | (1) | " | " | " | Kokura |
| 24930 東 | (3)[8] | " | " | " | Kokura |
| 26204 東 | None | " | Iron | Steel | Kokura |
| 名 26947 / 名 37118 | (4)[9] | " | Copper | Brass | Nagoya |
| 38254 東 / 39023 東 | (5) | " | " | " | Kokura |
| 40991 東 | (1) | " | " | " | Kokura |
| 名 47079 | None | " | Iron | Steel | Kokura |
| 50540 東 / 50642 東 | (1) | " | Copper | Brass | Kokura |
| 53195 東 | None | " | Iron | Steel | Kokura |
| 57964 東 | (3) | " | Aluminium? | Brass | Kokura |
| 59144 東 | None | " | Iron | Steel | Kokura |
| 名 61427 | None | " | " | " | Nagoya |
| 名 61963 | (4) | " | Copper | Brass | Nagoya |
| 名 62904 | None | " | Iron | " | Nagoya |
| 名 67147 | (4) | " | Copper | " | Nagoya |

| Blade numbering | Fuchi stamps | Hilt type | Fuchi type | Tsuba type | Manufacturing Arsenal |
|---|---|---|---|---|---|
| 68920 東 | (2) | " | " | " | Kokura |
| 75579 東 | (3) | " | " | " | Kokura |
| 名 77512 | (4) | " | " | " | Nagoya |
| 名 78622 | None | " | Iron | Steel | Nagoya |
| 名 82009 | (6)[10] | " | Copper | Brass | Nagoya |
| 名 81642 | None | " | Iron | Steel | Nagoya |
| 名 84937 | (6) | " | Copper | Brass | Nagoya |
| 94258 東 | (3) | " | " | " | Kokura |
| 95227 東 | None | " | Iron | Steel | Kokura |
| 名 104339 | (6) | " | Copper | Brass | Nagoya |
| 113341 東 | None | " | Iron | Steel | Kokura |
| 名 116049 / 名 130338 | None | " | " | " | Nagoya |
| 132666 東 | (7)[11] | " | Copper | Brass | Kokura |
| 137269 東 | (3) | " | " | " | Kokura |
| 139680 東 | (8) | " | " | " | Kokura |
| 141384 東 | (2) | " | " | Steel | Kokura |
| 144436 東 | (8) | " | " | Brass | Kokura |
| 145817 東 | (8) | " | " | " | Kokura |
| 147156 東 | (7) | " | " | " | Kokura |

— 84 —

## ARMY 1935 & 1945 NCOs SWORD PATTERNS

and fitted with a wood liner. Copper-hilted swords have been reported with painted brass scabbards. Steel or brass throat (kuchi-gane) with a projecting lug which engages with the hilt spring clip. The top of the throat is stamped with the same numbers as found on the blade although the accompanying inspection mark is not always present. The frequent mismatching of blade and scabbard numbers occurred in post-war years because they were separated at sword dumps or in the hands of dealers. Single suspension band with a steel hanging ring.

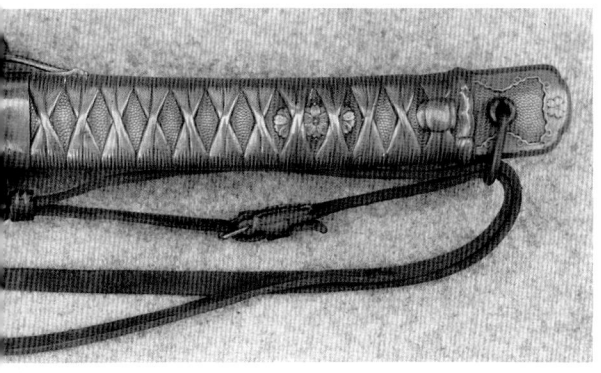

**Plate 117** NCOs shin-guntō with a brass tsuba (guard) and the correct version of the leather sword knot. Note that it passes through the lower tsuba slot and then through the metal sarute (knot loop), being secured by a buckle. This sword is unusual in that the hilt is unpainted and manufactured of copper. Other examples are known and appear to pre-date the normal aluminium-hilted type since the blade numbering is usually low (see Plates 119, 120). Dimensions are within a few millimetres of the aluminium-hilted model. (Donald Barnes).

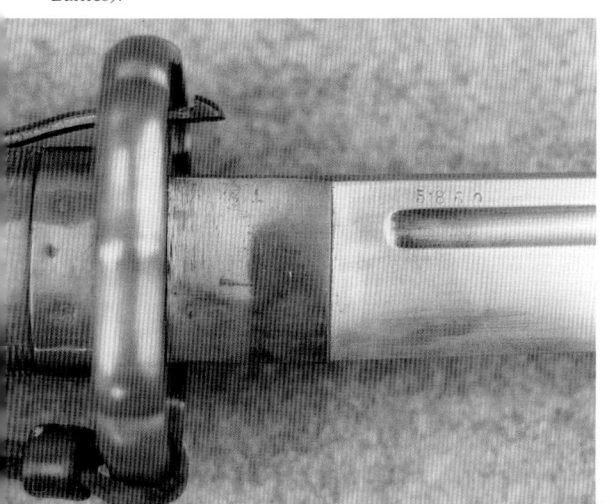

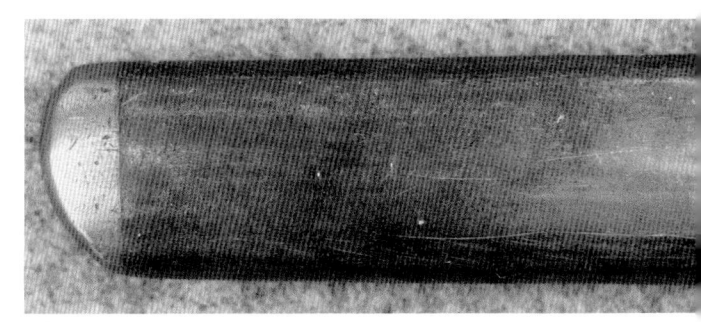

**Plate 118** Scabbard end of the copper-hilted NCOs shin-guntō in Plate 117. A brass cap has been fitted to the end of the scabbard instead of the shoe (drag). This seems to be a feature of this type of sword. (Donald Barnes).

**Plates 119, 120** Numbering on the blade of the copper-hilted NCOs shin-guntō in Plates 117, 118. This is most unusual in that it has two different numbers. The first, located in the usual place above the blade groove, is 5869 but lacks a following arsenal mark (see Plate 123 for a comparison). The second number, 2023, is larger in size and located on the other side of the blade close to the habaki. However, this does have the Japanese katakana character for 'zero' in front. The fuchi (hilt collar) is stamped with the normal 'four cannonball' logo of the Koishikawa/Kokura Arsenal. It seems probable that the number 5869 is that of the manufacturer while 2023 is an Army issue number. (Donald Barnes).

# JAPANESE MILITARY AND CIVIL SWORDS AND DIRKS

Aluminium-hilted models have long steel scabbard shoes (Fig. 18) but those with copper hilts do not; instead they terminate with either a brass cap (Plate 118) or reduce to form a thickened drag with a rounded end. The shape of the scabbard shoe and positioning of the throat-securing screw (as shown in Fig. 18) also differentiates Kokura and Nagoya Arsenal produced swords.[2]

A brown, shrink-fitted, leather combat cover has been found which is possibly representative of a Warrant Officer since it was accompanied by a surrender/transportation tag for a man of that rank.

Retention with the scabbard is by a steel spring clip set on the top edge of the hilt, projecting through the tsuba and engaging with a slot in the protruding scabbard throat. However, Plate 126 shows a very scarce variation where the spring clip is situated on the side of the hilt and the scabbard throat fitting is relocated accordingly. (This system was also used on the late-war replacement pattern shown in Plate 131.) Only late-number Nagoya-made blades have been found with the side clip system. Examination of Fig. 17 infers Nagoya introduced this feature not long before they ceased production, but Kokura carried on with the normal edge clip.

Machine-made blade with a narrow full length groove on either side. Brass habaki (blade collar) which on copper-hilted swords is notched at the top so the sides extend just beyond the machi (blade notches).

Arabic (Western-style) serial numbers are stamped on one side above the blade groove and near the habaki. These are accompanied by a factory inspection stamp which is either the 東

**Plate 121** *1935 pattern Army NCOs shin-guntō made by the Kokura Arsenal (top) and Nagoya Arsenal (bottom). (Donald Barnes).*

**Fig. 18** *Basic manufacturing differences between 1935 pattern Army NCOs shin-guntō swords made at the Kokura and Nagoya Arsenals.*
*Top: Kokura – TO inspection stamp. Blade numbering is read parallel to the groove. Scabbard screw on reverse. Lower edge of scabbard shoe (drag) is slightly curved.*
*Bottom: Nagoya – NA inspection stamp. Blade numbering is read parallel to the back edge. Scabbard screw on front. Lower edge of scabbard shoe has a pronounced curvature.*

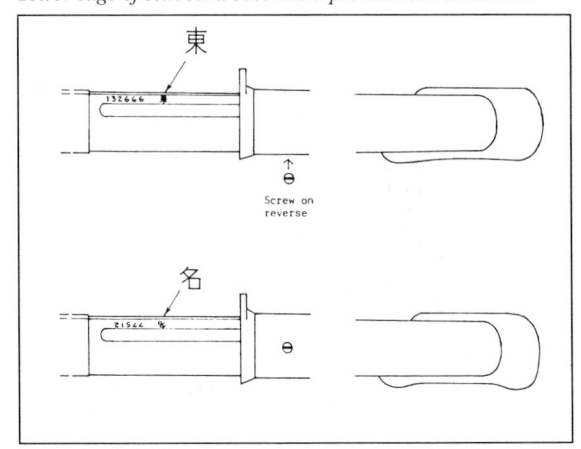

(TŌ) character used by the Kokura Army Arsenal or the 名 (NA) character of the Nagoya Army Arsenal (see Fig.18). It is this and the centre matching fuchi stamp which can be said to identify the manufacturing or supervising arsenal. However, blades with copper hilts are generally numbered only and lack such a stamp. It would appear from swords in collections that this numbering is a sequential system thus being individual to each sword and would probably allow dating if the manufacturing production figures could be located (see Fig. 17). The lowest number noted on a copper-hilted sword is 340 and the highest 5869. The lowest number reported on the aluminium-hilted version with the normal edge spring clip is 6276 and the highest 149726. The lowest reported side spring clip example is numbered 131820 and the highest 134089, which

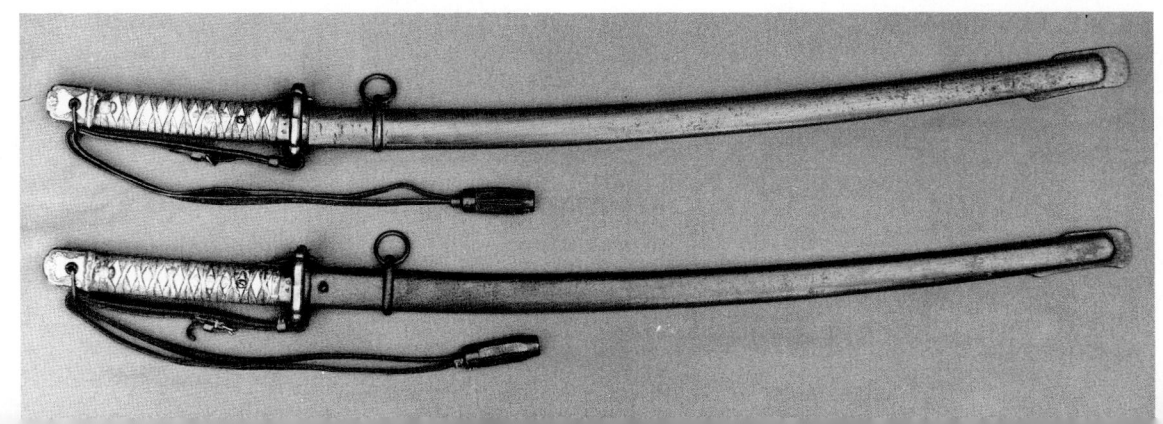

## ARMY 1935 & 1945 NCOs SWORD PATTERNS

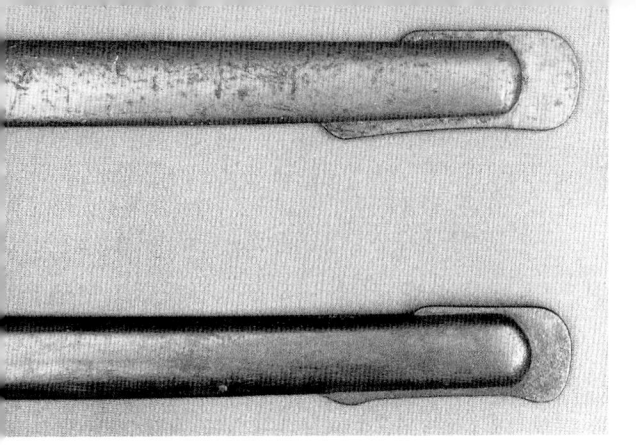

*Plate 122* Scabbard shoe of the NCOs shin-guntō shown in Plate 121. That on the top indicates manufacture by the Kokura Arsenal while that on the bottom is made by the Nagoya Arsenal. (Donald Barnes).

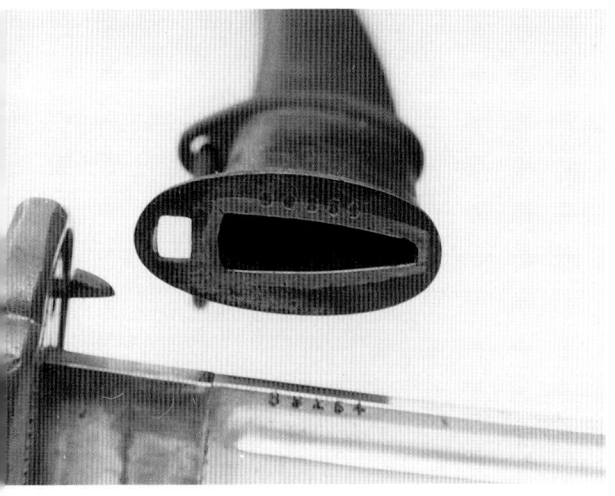

*Plate 123* Matching numbers on the blade and scabbard throat of a 1935 pattern Army NCOs shin-guntō. The TŌ inspection stamp of the Kokura Arsenal is just visible to the right of the blade numbering. (Richard Fuller).

seems to be about the end of the Nagoya production figures. (The replacement c.1945 pattern described later has numbers in the two to three hundred thousand range.)

There are anomalies in every supposed rule. An aluminium-hilted model numbered 1067 東 has been reported which is within the copper hilt range. Either copper and aluminium hilts were produced simultaneously, which seems unlikely, or the original hilt has been replaced, perhaps because of damage in action. Another aluminium-hilted sword has the number 1059181 for some unknown reason, which is well outside any known numbering range. Possibly both Kokura (Tokyo) and Nagoya Arsenals were allocated number blocks for production purposes. From the serial numbers in Fig. 17 it may be deduced that around 150,000 of these swords were made over a ten-year period, which is an amazing number for a modern army. It is believed that Kokura (near Tokyo) and Nagoya Arsenals manufactured blades (and scabbards?) but the production of hilt fittings was contracted out to private companies. Possibly the 1st Tokyo Arsenal later made fittings for Kokura-produced blades since their mark has been seen on NCOs fuchi. The arsenals are assumed to have supervised the final assembly of the swords.

Copper or coppered aluminium fuchi (hilt collars) have three stamps. Eight combinations have been noted (Fig. 17) although there may be more. Steel fuchi are usually unmarked (see also Fig. 62). The right-hand stamp is normally the 'four cannonball' logo ⊛ of Kokura. However, both the centre stamp and blade stamp may be that of Nagoya 名 together with the Nagoya scabbard characteristics. The reason for this is unknown. Late examples can be found with the 1st Tokyo Arsenal logo ☆, but the scabbards have Kokura characteristics.[3] The centre mark is the inspection mark of either Kokura 東 or Nagoya 名, but it matches that found on the blade. This must indicate the supervising arsenal since scabbard manufacture characteristics also seem to match. The six different left-hand stamps observed seem to represent sub-contractors who probably made the hilt fittings. Only the 'lyre-like' stamp of the Suya Company of Tokyo (Fig 17) has been identified. Unstamped iron fuchi appear on both Kokura- and Nagoya-made swords but the significance of this, if any, is unknown.

The ubiquitous brown leather barrel knot (Fig.1 (iv)) seen on many sword patterns is retained for this sword. Some have been found with a whistle inside the knot to allow the owner to blow commands. There are basically two types: straps having a buckle and claw for use with a brass tsuba (Plate 121); and unbroken straps for use with swords having a steel tsuba. The latter are secured by the sarute (knot loop) and then just looped around the hilt.

— 87 —

JAPANESE MILITARY AND CIVIL SWORDS AND DIRKS

Dimensions are constant to within about 3mm (¹⁄₈") in overall length and half an ounce in weight. Overall length of sword and scabbard 965mm (38"). Total weight 60 ounces. Hilt length 219mm (8⁵⁄₈"). Blade length 673mm (26½"). Maximum blade width 27.8mm (1³⁄₃₂"). Scabbard length 737mm (29"). Sword weight 38 oz.

Although mass-produced this sword pattern was both a fighting weapon and a symbol of rank. There seems little doubt the purpose of introduction was to replace the 1899 pattern Infantry NCOs (Type B) sabre. General usage is for Infantry and Kempei (Military Police) NCOs as their equivalent of the Officers regulation 1934 pattern shin-guntō. However, photographs dating from 1936 to 1941 show some Superior and Leading Privates as well as NCOs and Warrant Officers carrying this sword pattern. Privates of the Imperial Guard also, appar-

*Plate 124* Typical manufacturer's inspection stamp on the fuchi (hilt collar) of a 1935 pattern Army NCOs shin-guntō. That on the right is the 'four cannonball' logo of the Kokura Arsenal, Tokyo. The small centre stamp is the inspection mark of the same arsenal but the purpose of the tsuba-like mark on the left is unknown. The fuchi of this example is apparently aluminium. Note the excellent detailing of the die-cast hilt. (Curt Peritz).

*Plate 125* Dissembled hilt of the 1935 pattern aluminium-hilted NCOs pattern shin-guntō showing the component parts and wood liner. They comprise a steel sarute (knot loop) with an eyelet on each side, a copper fuchi (hilt collar) incorporating a steel spring clip and an 'aoi'-shaped brass tsuba (guard) with a seppa (washer) on each side. An oval tsuba of blackened steel is also commonly found. The hilt is die-cast aluminium made in two halves, welded together and finished so that the side seams are only visible internally. Detailing is excellent with a painted finish resembling the Officers version. The braid is brown, the samé is matt-aluminium and the menuki (hilt ornaments) are yellow. This is secured to the blade tang by a single dome-headed screw (not shown). (Ron Gregory).

*Plate 126* 1935 pattern Army NCOs shin-guntō with a scarce side-mounted spring clip retention system which appears to have been introduced by the Nagoya Arsenal towards the end of their production run. The steel fuchi (hilt collar) has three indistinct stamps. Matching blade and scabbard numbers 134089 名 . (Sergio Pelone).

ently, carried it when wearing the blue full dress greatcoat.[4] Warrant Officers may have had the option of carrying this, or the Officers shin-guntō, depending upon their means since this is an 'issue' sword whereas the shin-guntō was privately purchased.

The *Nippon no Gunso* (see Bibliography) describes this pattern as a 'Sergeant-Majors sword (Military Police NCO: Long service Sergeant: Cavalry)'. No reference to use by the cavalry has been found elsewhere and it seems unsuitable for mounted use. However there is a possibility that cavalry NCOs carried this as representative of their rank when on foot.

Production appears to have ceased by (or during) 1945 because of the shortages of aluminium, with the late-war steel-mounted version being introduced as an alternative. There is a rumour that, initially, examples were manufactured in England or Germany for the Japanese government, but absolutely no evidence to support this has been located, and it would seem highly unlikely given the Japanese expertise in sword production.

In rare cases a 200mm (7⅞") removable brown leather sleeve incorporating a lower triangular hanging ring may be found.[5] This is for conversion from a one-hanger to a two-hanger sword but it is now believed to be a Chinese addition, either on weapons captured during the war to render them suitable for their own use, or possibly for use after the Japanese surrender. Again, in rare cases,

**Plate 127** Superior Private (left) and Sergeant (right) with 1935 pattern NCOs shin-guntō with leather knots. That on the left can be seen to have the knot straps fitted with a buckle for use with the brass tsuba. This photo is dated 29 August 1940. The scabbard shoe (drag) patterns and lack of visible scabbard screws indicate that both swords were made at the Kokura Arsenal. (Richard Fuller).

**Plate 128** Superior Privates (front row) in M90 (1930) uniform with 1935 pattern NCOs shin-guntō which can be determined by the scabbard type. The two on the left have protective white cloth wrapped around the hilts. The man on the left (second row) is a Sergeant with a katana while the others in the same row are Commissioned Officers with shin-guntō. This photo is dated 21 July 1936 or 1937. (Richard Fuller).

# JAPANESE MILITARY AND CIVIL SWORDS AND DIRKS

this fitting may be found on Officers shin-guntō metal scabbards. All such swords had been obtained in China during the nineteen-eighties.

The aluminium-hilted version is common but the copper-hilted version is scarce. It is recommended that the collector checks for matching blade and scabbard serial numbers if a complete item is required. Reproductions of the aluminium-hilted pattern are now common. See 'Reproduction swords' later in this book.

## c.1945 pattern Army Non-Commissioned Officers sword

The shortage of aluminium is believed to have necessitated a replacement for the Army 1935 pattern NCOs shin-guntō in late 1944 or, more likely, 1945. The resulting pattern is even more utilitarian than its predecessor.

Plain blackened steel hilt mounts consisting of a kabuto-gane (pommel) having a large hole for a sword knot, a fuchi (hilt collar) and circular tsuba (guard). Checkered natural or black-finished wooden grips fixed to the blade tang by two widely spaced screws which have their heads on opposite sides. A central blackened steel lug is recessed into the wood on each side. Side-mounted spring clip.

One-piece factory-made blades of traditional shinogi-zukuri shape are the norm. These are stamped near the brass habaki (blade collar) with one or two Japanese characters plus Arabic numbers in the two to three hundred thousand range. These numbers seem to be sequential.

There are two scabbard types each having one suspension band with a hanging ring and a protruding throat lug for the hilt retention clip. Colouring is either black, brown or olive green. The steel type is similar to the 1935 pattern NCOs shin-guntō with a Nagoya Arsenal pattern shoe (drag) (see Plate 122, bottom). The lacquered wood type has an elongated blackened steel locket incorporating a suspension mount, similar to that in Plate 85, but lacking a separate throat. Riveted blackened steel chape with a thickened

**Plate 129** *Army Corporal with an aluminium-hilted 1935 pattern NCOs shin-guntō which has a steel tsuba (guard) and leather sword knot. It is carried in the regain position. The leather suspension strap passes around the scabbard in the normal manner but seems to be supported by a jacket flap and not the belt. (J. Jackson).*

shoe similar in principle to the shin-guntō special ishizuke shoe shown in Fig. 15.

The normal NCOs leather sword knot with unbroken strap appears to have been used

Dimensions seem to be fairly consistent. Overall length of sword and scabbard 1,006mm (39⁵⁄₈"). Hilt length 260mm (10¼"). Blade length 673mm (26½"). Scabbard length 737mm (29"). Weight of sword with steel scabbard 60 ounces.

Markings vary and may indicate the manufacturer. Swords with steel scabbards have been found with the NA stamp (Fig. 62 (xiii)) of the Nagoya Arsenal on the fuchi and blade tang. An example with a lacquered scabbard, and blade numbered 301011, has the NI and HE stamps shown in fig. 61 (xxxiii) and (xxxv) respectively.

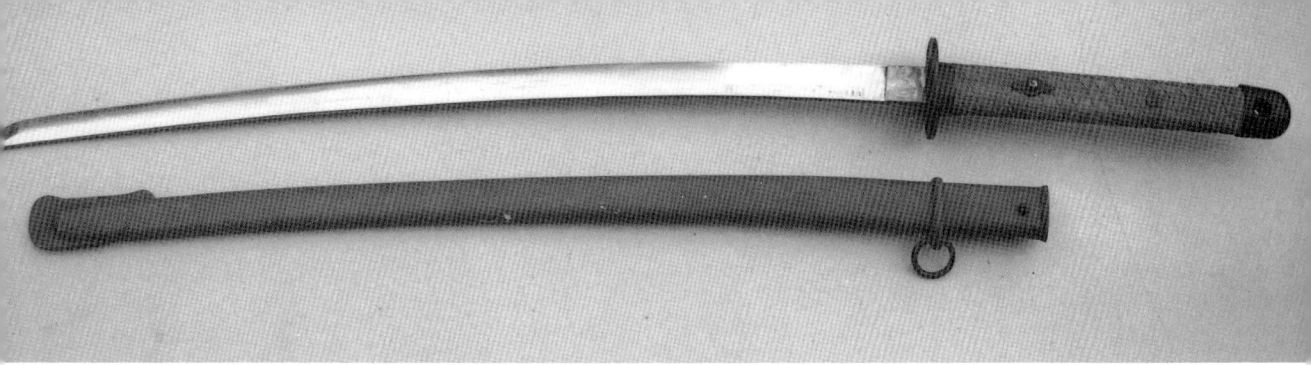

**Plate 130**  c.1945 pattern Army NCOs sword and scabbard. (Ron Gregory).

The latter is used by the Heigo factory of the Jinsen Arsenal in Korea, but it has not been determined if this represents that maker when found on swords. This stamp is also repeated on the scabbard chape. The NI stamp 'when found in the proximity of an arsenal symbol or manufacturer's markings indicates that the weapon has been adapted for military use by a special wartime inspection standard as a "second class arm".'[12] That shown in Plate 130 is numbered 211611 which is repeated on the scabbard mouth. There is also a small indistinct mark reminiscent of the Seki stamp (Fig. 61 (ix)). The scabbard shoe can be seen to be the Nagoya Arsenal type.

Even in 1945 swords were still required for men drafted into the Army to defend Japan against the expected American invasion. The quality and style of this pattern along with the blade and scabbard numbering indicates almost certain use by NCOs. They were probably restricted to the home islands but may, possibly, have been issued to some troops in Korea and/or Formosa. Until recent years these swords were not seen in Britain but are now becoming somewhat more common. Many seem to have come from America where they are more abundant, probably because they were obtained during the American occupation of Japan.

**Plate 131**  Hilt of the c.1945 Army NCOs sword. (Ron Gregory).

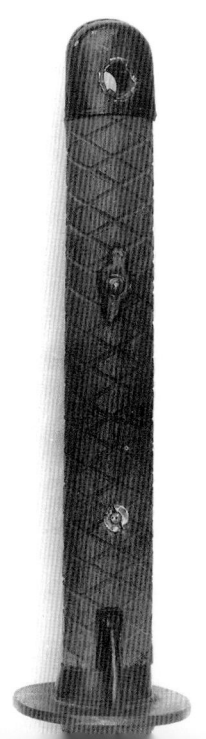

---

1 Introduction date stated in *Swords of Imperial Japan 1868–1945* (see Bibliography).
2 These differences were observed by Donald Barnes who has examined over one hundred of these swords but found no exception to the rule. He also noted the distinguishing features of the copper-hilted model.
3 The principal mark is frequently the 'four cannonball' mark of Kokura used from 1933–1945. However, their own inspection mark '小' is not found, whereas that shared by both Kokura and Tokyo Arsenals, 東, is common. Thus it could be that Kokura was the principal producer overseeing swords produced at Tokyo and Nagoya.
4 *Japanese Military Uniforms 1930–1945*.
5 Shown in Plate 52 of *Military Swords of Japan 1868–1945* by the authors.
6 The authors wish to thank Donald Barnes, who recorded the bulk of this tabulated information.
7 This limited random sample may indicate a factory block number allocation system, e.g. Kokura 20,000–26,500, Nagoya 26,501–37,500, Kokura 37,501–60,000 etc. However, these numerical bands are purely speculative.
8 The details of the tsuba-like left-hand fuchi mark are unclear but it seems to contain two Japanese characters. The upper is 正 which can be read as SHO (correct), SEI (original) or a MASA (a name). The lower one is indistinct but is believed to be 義 which can be read as GI (righteousness, integrity) or YOSHI (a name). When read in combination they can be read as SEIGI (right, correct meaning) or MASAYOSHI (a name). The authors believe the former interpretation is the favourite, but it has been suggested that the latter meaning is applicable (perhaps the name of the principal inspector?).
9 Although the principal right-hand fuchi stamp is that of Kokura, the sword characteristics indicate manufacture at the Nagoya Arsenal in Owari province. The left fuchi character is GI (abbreviation) for Gifu in Mino province. The reason for stamps representing three different locations is unknown.
10 The left-hand fuchi stamp represents a sword in circular form with the character 刀 (TŌ) meaning 'sword'.
11 The right-hand fuchi stamp is the logo of the No. 1 Tokyo Arsenal which was associated with Kokura.
12 Quoted from *Military Rifles of Japan*, page 15, second edition, by Fred Honeycutt Jr and F. Patt Anthony (see Bibliography) although, apparently, debateable.

# Shin-Guntō Used By Civil Organisations

Officials of some large private or government-controlled companies or organisations appear to have worn uniforms with their own insignia and, possibly in some cases, swords. This may be a limited practice since no photographic evidence of sword wear has been located. Shin-guntō, which seem to come into this catagory, are described below.

Plates 132, 133, 134 show swords carried by Japanese officials of the North China Joint Stock Transportation Company (Ka hoku kotsu kabushiki kaisha). This was a joint Chinese–Japanese company set up in 1938 which employed 80,000 Chinese and 30,000 Japanese to run the railways of north China. The company logo was a 'winged wheel' (Fig. 19 (iii)) which has mistakenly been thought to indicate Air Force usage. On rare occasions this logo has been found on a kabuto-gane (pommel), ishizuke (chape) and stamped on a blade tang. The degree of seniority required to wear such swords is unknown.

Another major company which certainly manufactured swords for the Army and, presumably, themselves is the South Manchurian Railway Company (Mantetsu Kaisha). Although their logo (Fig. 19 (ii)) has not been reported on sword mounts it has been found on a few shin-guntō blade tangs. Plate 136 shows a typical example. So far it has only been found on blades dated 'spring, summer and winter 1938' which was prior to full Army control in the early nineteen-forties. See also the section on military sword blades and markings later in this book.

Perhaps it may be expected that officials of the Japanese-controlled Central China Railway (Ka chū tetsu-do) also carried swords marked with the logo of that organisation (Fig. 19 (i)) although none has been reported to the authors.

The extent of this practice is unknown and there may be other organisations which followed suit. Swords bearing company logos must be considered rare.

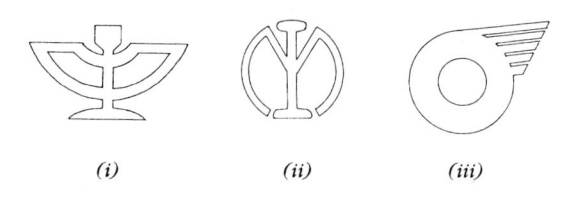

*(i)*          *(ii)*          *(iii)*

**Fig. 19** *Civil badges on military swords.*
*(i)*     *Central China Railway (Ka chū tetsu-do). This has not, so far, been reported on a sword but can, perhaps, be expected in view of (ii) and (iii) being seen.*
*(ii)*     *South Manchurian Railway Company (Mantetsu Kaisha). Only found stamped on shin-guntō blade tangs dated 1938. Rare.*
*(iii)*     *'Winged wheel' logo of the North China Joint Stock Transportation Company (Ka hoku kotsu kabushiki kaisha) which operated the railways in north China. Found on shin-guntō fittings and blade tangs. Very rare.*

**Plate 132** Kabuto-gane (pommel) of a shin-guntō featuring the 'winged wheel' logo of the North China Joint Stock Transportation Company on the back edge (left) and around both sides of the sarute (knot loop) opening (right). The blade of this particular example also has the logo stamped on the blade tang (Plate 133). Only two similar swords have been reported, but they differ in that the logo is situated only on each side of the ishizuke (chape) (see Plates 106, 134). (Rubens Rotelli).

**Plate 134** Specially made ishizuke (chape) of a shin-guntō which has the 'winged wheel' logo of the North China Joint Stock Transportation Company (Ka hoku kotsu kabushiki kaisha) on both sides which makes it very rare. There are no other markings to relate it to this company. This sword also has a most unusual sarute (sword knot loop). See also Plates 106, 107. (Dr Terry Ingold).

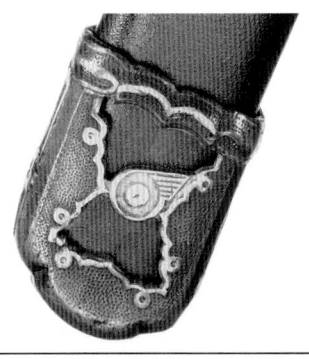

**Plate 135** An employee (probably junior) of the North China Joint Stock Transportation Company. The 'winged wheel' logo of this organisation can be seen on his cap. (Trevor Duffin).

**Plate 133** The tang of the shin-guntō in Plate 132. It is signed SEKI ISHIHARA KANENAO SAKU, i.e. made by Ishihara Kanenao of Seki who was a Shōwa period smith. It bears the inverted logo of the North China Joint Stock Transportation Company under the signature. Above the signature is a common 'sho' stamp (not shown) indicating Army inspection and acceptance prior to c.1942. (R. Rotelli).

**Plate 136** Tang of a blade in standard shin-guntō mounts. Unsigned, but dated, it has an unusual stamp which is the logo of the South Manchurian Railway Company. The assumption is that these blades were made in Manchuria by the SMRC, but they could have been made in Japan for their use. The zodiacal dating system is used and reads: SHŌWA (reign era name), TSUCHINOE-TORA (15th year of the cycle), FUYU (winter) – winter of the 15th year of the zodiacal cycle in the Shōwa era, i.e. 1938.

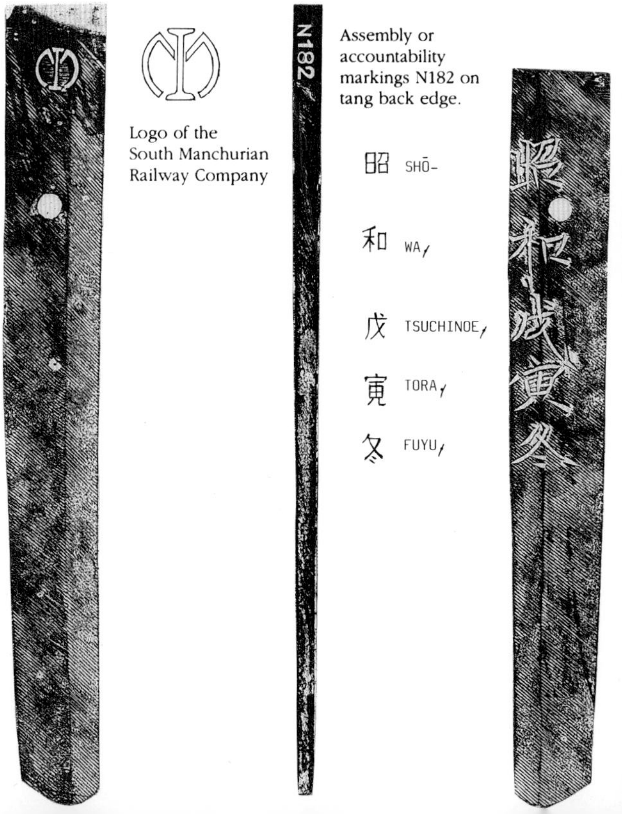

Logo of the South Manchurian Railway Company

Assembly or accountability markings N182 on tang back edge.

昭 SHŌ-
和 WA,
戊 TSUCHINOE,
寅 TORA,
冬 FUYU,

# Katana and Wakizashi for Military Use

Military swords are fairly often found with older blades reused from earlier samurai swords (i.e. katana and wakizashi). Less common are entire katana and wakizashi adapted for Army or naval use.

Modifications can involve all three items listed below, although (i) is the most frequent:

(i) One or two suspension mounts (ashi) slid over the scabbard which is then covered with a leather combat cover. Fig. 14 shows a number of such ashi types.
(ii) Removal of the kurikata which is the knob projecting from a scabbard to prevent it from slipping through the waist sash.
(iii) Addition of a metal sarute (sword knot loop) to the hilt near the kuchi-gane (pommel of a civilian sword). Fig. 20 (ii).

A fully mounted old katana is known with its original shira-saya covered with a sheet of copper, finely creased to resemble leather and patinated. There is a snake skin band around the throat with a custom-made brass hanger and ishizuke (chape). Presumably done for service in World War Two.

Such swords may be any age or quality.

The early Japanese Army and Navy, up to around 1871, initially carried such swords through a waist belt or in a leather frog.[1] This practice was discontinued when military pattern swords were prescribed. Plate 139 shows a katana being carried in the 1904–5 Russo–Japanese war, but from photographic evidence this seems to be a rare occurrence. It does not seem to have become a recognised practice again until the 1930s, presumably when the armed forces were drastically increased and reservists called up. Army dress regulations relating to the wearing of such swords appear lax which allowed officers to carry such weapons if they preferred, although the Navy dress code forbade it (see under 'Naval Kai-guntō'). Many, no doubt, were family heirlooms while others were purchased from dealers.

As the war with China progressed and Western nations began to press for a withdrawal, a resurgence of Japanese nationalism and traditional attitudes occurred. This included an interest in the old samurai sword patterns. Consequently katana were produced with modern fittings and blades. These were bought by officers, or by their families as a present, and adapted for military use as described above. They could be mounted with either original traditional sword fittings or modern

---

[1] These frogs are extremely rare since they do not seem to have survived. Only one possible example is known and is shown in Plate 2 and Fig. 45 of *Military Swords of Japan 1868–1945* (see Bibliography). Richard Fuller collection.

## KATANA AND WAKIZASHI FOR MILITARY USE

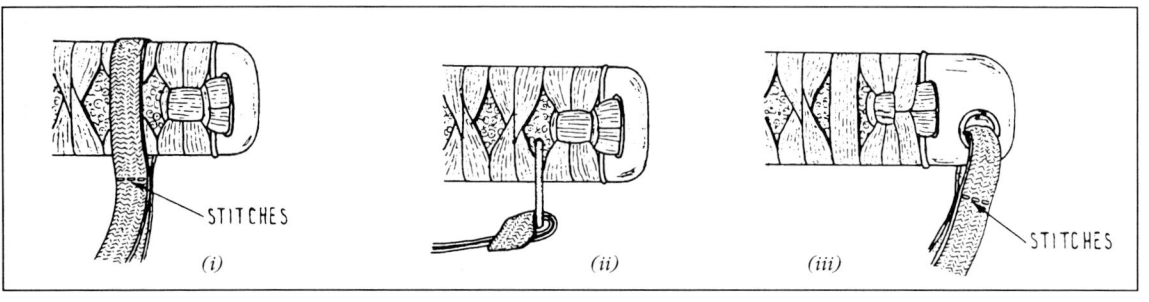

**Fig. 20** *Method of securing sword knots to those swords which are not fitted with a sarute (knot loop): (i) traditional katana or wakizashi; (ii) as (i) but by adding a sarute; (iii) 1944 regulation pattern Army sword.*

**Fig. 21** *Leather cap stitched over the kashira (pommel) of a civilian katana. It protects the decorative kashira and incorporates a leather loop for the sword knot.*

mass-produced tsuba (guard), fuchi (hilt collar) and kuchi-gane (pommel), often decorated ensuite. The most common Shōwa period decorative features are:

(i) Brass mounts with raised sakura (cherry blossoms). Plate 141 (left).
(ii) Brass mounts with raised bamboo leaves having a browned or silver finish. Plate 141 (centre).
(iii) Blackened steel mounts with raised seashells and starfish, although the tsuba (guard) may have a different decoration such as waves. Plate 141 (right).
(iv) Brass fuchi and kuchi-gane with engraved tendrils.

Hilts are bound in the traditional manner with either black or blue-green braid. The menuki (hilt ornaments) may also be of Shōwa period manufacture. Scabbards are black or coloured lacquer over a wooden base and are complete with

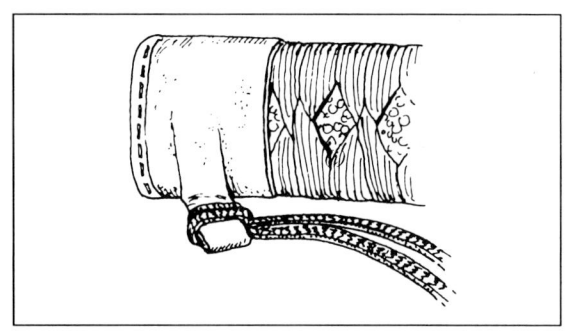

**Plate 137** *Traditional samurai weapons mounted for military use in World War Two. Top: A wakizashi (short sword) having a removable protective brown leather combat cover for the scabbard which also incorporates a suspension ring. A leather retention loop fits over the fuchi (hilt collar) with a short strap which passes through a hole in the tsuba (guard) to engage with a press stud on the combat cover. The hilt is protected by a removable brown leather foul weather cover which, in this case, is tightened by a drawstring. Bottom: A tantō (dirk with a guard) which has been fitted with a non-removable brown leather combat cover and press stud retention. Dirks mounted for military wear are rare. Both items still retain the kurikata (knob to prevent slippage through the waist sash). These may often be removed for ease of fitting the covers. (Ron Gregory).*

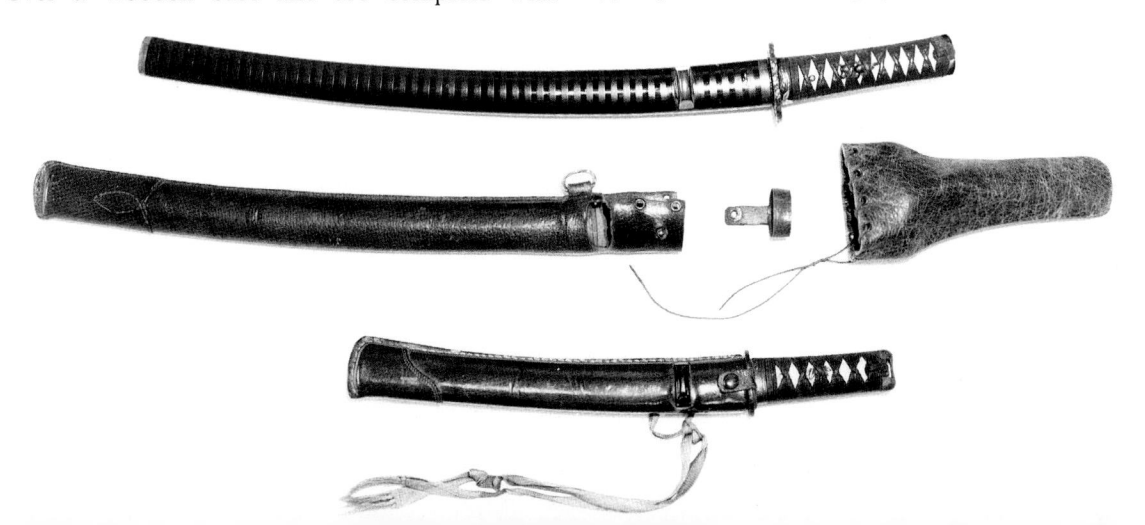

JAPANESE MILITARY AND CIVIL SWORDS AND DIRKS

*Plate 138* A civilian wakizashi (short sword) with its black lacquered scabbard covered with a brown leather combat cover having two suspension mounts. The use of a brown cover suggests Army usage but the presence of two hangers indicates probable use by the Naval Landing Forces. The blade is unsigned but dated to c.1600. (Western Australia Museum W74-19).

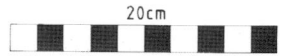

*Plate 139* General Okasaki (left) during the Russo–Japanese war of 1904–5 has a two-hanger kyu-guntō with a gold? sword knot and black straps. However, the officer in the right foreground has a traditional katana, with tape-bound hilt and leather-covered scabbard, which seems to be a most unusual occurrence during this period. (Richard Fuller).

*Plate 140* The officer on the right has a civilian katana with a tightly fitted leather hilt cover. The outline of the hilt binding underneath can clearly be seen. The scabbard is also covered in leather. This was taken in China in the nineteen-thirties.

— 96 —

*Plate 141  Shōwa period tsuba and fuchi from katana made in the 1930s and 1940s. (Ron Gregory).*

kurikata (projecting sash mount). Often the lacquer covering is thin and cracks easily. Sometimes a blue or gold (Fig.61 (xxxiv)) paper quality control label of the Seki Cutlery Manufacturers (or Industrial) Society is found stuck on a scabbard. Adaptation for war is by the addition of a field scabbard type ashi and leather combat cover.

Blades are normally signed and of quite good quality although they usually seem to be oil-tempered. Plate 142 shows a good example of such a sword which has a blade horimono (carving) which is rare on shōwa period blades. The presence of the military 'shō' stamp on the tang seems to indicate that such swords could also be bought through the 'Army Officers Club' (Kaikosha).

Shōwa period katana obtained from World War Two are often mistaken for true samurai swords.

*Plate 142a, b  Shōwa period katana having a blade engraved with a horimono of a dragon chasing the sacred jewel. The tang is signed MITSUNOBU SAKU, i.e. made by Mitsunobu, with a 'Shō' stamp (Army acceptance prior to c.1942). The mass-produced kashira (pommel) and fuchi (hilt collar) are brass decorated with bamboo leaves. Normally a brass tsuba decorated ensuite is found, but on this example an older tsuba has been used. It is most unusual to find a Shōwa period blade with a horimono. (Geoff Foletta).*

JAPANESE MILITARY AND CIVIL SWORDS AND DIRKS

**Plate 143** *An Army Lieutenant inspects his sword after a battle with Chinese forces in Manchuria on 2 March 1932. It appears to be a civilian katana.*

# Tachi for Military Use

A tachi is a traditional slung sword, having two suspension mounts (ashi), and was the inspiration for the design of military shin- and kai-guntō. Ashi design is distinctive and normally features a slot for the belt loop instead of a separate hanging ring. Unlike katana and wakizashi their scabbards do not seem to have been adapted for military use in World War Two. No contemporary photographs of officers carrying such swords have been located and none is apparent in sword surrender ceremonies.

Two Shōwa period tachi with possible military connections are known although neither has been personally examined by the authors:

(i) Standard shin-guntō with a red painted metal scabbard fitted with two ashi of tachi style.[1] Shōwa period blade by Asano Kanezane. All hilt and scabbard fittings have been silvered.
(ii) Typical traditional civil style Itomaki-no-tachi which is distinguished by the upper third of the reddish-brown scabbard being bound with brown tape exposing a brownish-gold brocade cloth beneath in exactly the same manner as the hilt.[2] Distinctive ashi of tachi style. Gilded iron or steel hilt and scabbard fittings engraved with leaf decoration and tachi-style tsuba (guard). All removable hilt fittings, including the tsuba and silver habaki (blade collar) are stamped with the assembly number 134. Civilian menuki (hilt ornaments) of dogs fighting. The 'Koa Isshin Mantetsu' inscribed blade (see later under 'Military Sword Blades and Markings') is dated 1941 and also stamped 134 on the tang back edge.

The shin-guntō fittings on example (i) would seem to indicate military use but, more likely, it was intended for presentation or exhibition. The 'Itomaki-no-tachi' shows no signs of service wear. However, the matching assembly numbering indicates the hilt fittings and blade are contemporary.

It would not be difficult to convert a shin-guntō to a tachi, as in example (i) above, for post-war financial gain, but (ii) is much harder. All such swords must be closely examined before purchase, checking for wear under the fittings, new paintwork and possibly modern silvering or gilding. See also 'Shōwa Period Presentation Swords' later in this book.

---

1 Jørgen Jørgensen collection.
2 Thomas A. Bassier collection.

# Leather-Covered Swords

Some swords are found entirely covered with non-removable brown leather. See plates 145, 150. This is an easy, cheap way of adapting a plain wooden hilt and scabbard for use. Generally they are of poor quality but there are exceptions such as Plate 150. If a shira-saya (plain wooden keeper hilt and scabbard for an unmounted blade) is used then the blade quality can be good, although this is not always the case. This can be recognised by having slightly flattened sides whereas normal wooden scabbards are rounded.

The leather covering is fitted and stitched when wet, shrinking tight when dry. A kabuto-gane (pommel) may be fitted and left exposed. Sword retention is by means of a leather strap from the hilt which engages with a raised stud on the scabbard covering. Ashi (suspension mounts) are fitted to the scabbard before it is covered and are of the type shown in Fig. 14. Variations may be encountered without a tsuba or kabuto-gane. Better quality items were made in Japan while poor quality examples appear to have been made in the field, perhaps as 'emergency or collaboration swords'.

# Army Dirks

The Army had no prescribed pattern of dirk, but an old tantō (dirk with a guard) may be encountered which has been adapted for military use by the addition of a leather cover to the scabbard (Plate 137). Another type found has a dirk blade in shira-saya (wooden keeper mounts) covered entirely in leather (Plates 144 to 146). The latter may have a hand-forged Shōwa period blade. Both types are fitted with a wide leather belt loop which obviously implies use. No example of a fully mounted tantō with a Shōwa period blade has been reported. Other dirk types encountered may be confused with the kamikaze dirk, but they may not be mounted for wear. See Plate 147 for an example.

An officer could, and did, take several edged weapons on active service. No photograph of an Army officer carrying a dirk has been seen but such an item could easily be carried for protection when off duty. It is also equally possible that a dirk was preferred by Army Air Force officers when flying, in lieu of an unwieldy sword. A good quality traditionally mounted tantō with a leather-covered scabbard is known with a plaque which reads: 'Family knife of honour. Presented to Lieut. Colonel L.M. Coffey, British Int. Corps, by Maj. General Gonpachi Yoshida, Chief of Staff 15th Army. Sept. 25th Banpong, Siam 1945'.[1] Examples of dirks adapted for Army use are rare.

## Shōwa period dirk for military use

A rare and unusual dirk probably made for an Army or Air Force officer in World War Two is shown in Plates 144 to 146.

Shira-saya[2] covered in brown leather for military use. The scabbard reverse has a large leather belt loop stitched on. The hilt obverse is fitted with a strap riveted to the hilt for retention purposes. It is fitted with a press cap which engages with a raised stud on the scabbard. The hand-forged Shōwa period tantō blade was secured to the hilt by a peg which was covered by the leather cover thus preventing removal. Forcible removal by a previous owner has snapped the peg, also resulting in the loss of a habaki (blade collar). Overall length of hilt and scabbard 291mm (11 7/16"). Blade length 183mm (7 3/16"). Tang length 90mm (3 1/2").

One side of the tang is engraved with Japanese calligraphy, but the intended meaning to the English language speaker is unclear. It can be read in two ways: TENKA (under heaven), MUTEKI (matchless), RAIFU (thunder wind) or KAMINARI-KAZE (lightning storm), i.e. a thunderstorm unequalled under heaven;[3] or TENKA (the whole country), MU (negation), TEKI (enemy, foe), RAI (thunder), FU (wind) or KAZE (storm), i.e. (like a) thunderstorm the whole country is against the enemy. Perhaps both interpretations are open to question.

This dirk appears to be for personal use since there were no regulation patterns for officers of the Army or Army Air Force. If the first interpretation is correct then it could mean it was carried by an Air Force officer.

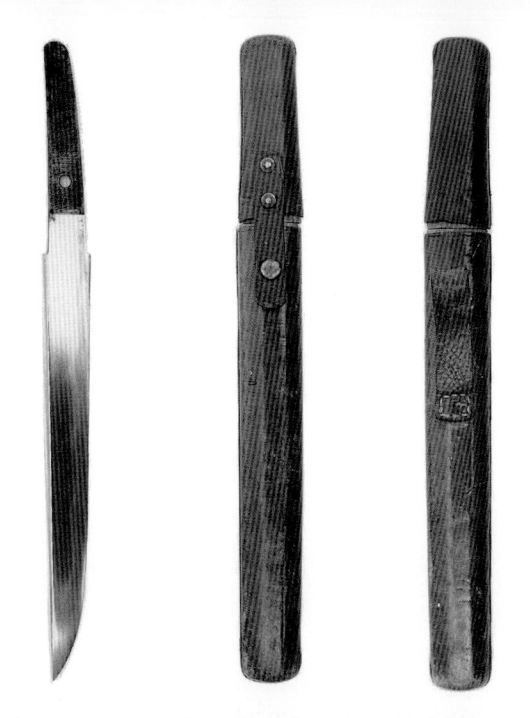

**Plates 144, 145, 146** *A Shōwa period dirk blade in leather-covered shira-saya (for military use).* (Richard Fuller).

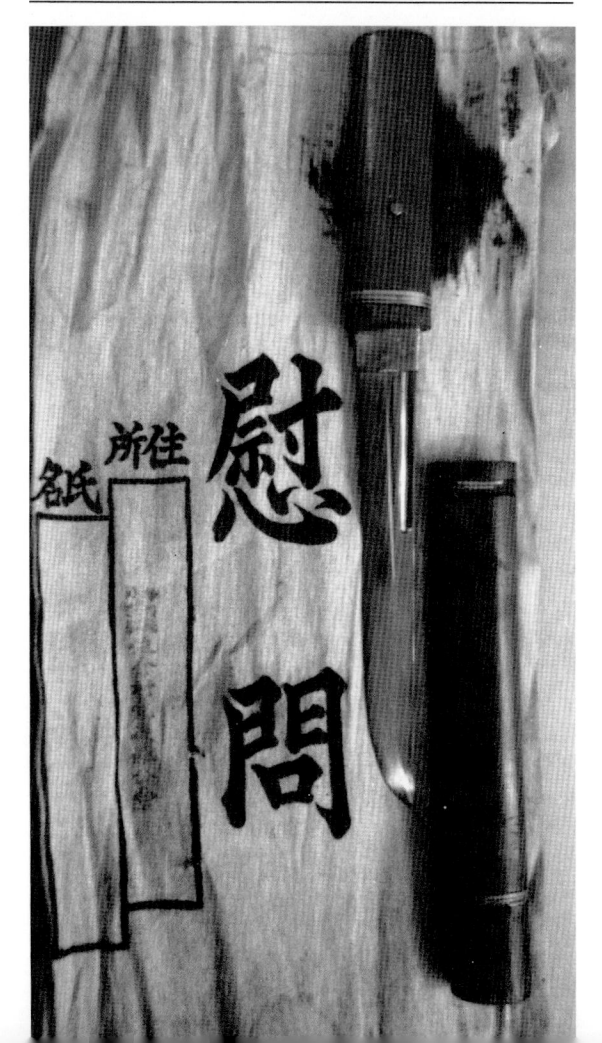

Hand-forged Shōwa period dirk blades appear to be rare but always seem to be in shira-saya. No example has been reported in Shōwa period tantō or aikuchi mounts (except for the kamikaze form) and no other examples in shira-saya have been seen mounted for military use.

## Officers personal dirk

An aikuchi (dirk without a guard) found at a Japanese naval base in China by an American soldier is shown in Plate 147. It resembles the kamikaze dirk style but is not thought to be for that usage.

The hilt and scabbard are wood with brass wire binding. Silver habaki (blade collar). Unsigned hand-forged blade with two grooves. The upper groove runs out of the back edge at the machi (shoulder) which indicates a shortened blade. The dirk was found wrapped in the cloth on which it lies. The large characters read IMON, i.e. condolences. The left-hand column is headed SHOZAI, i.e. location, and apparently contains shipping instructions (to?) China. The far left column is headed SHIMEI, i.e. surname, but no name is present. This cloth implies the owner was killed and that the dirk is part of his effects.

This does not appear to be for military use since there is no form of cover or suspension. Officers often took with them their personal edged weapons in addition to their normal military swords and dirks. It is rare for such dirks to be found with documentation.

---

1 This may have been a private presentation rather than a surrender since this officer did not formally surrender his sword until the 11 January, 1946 at Bangkok.
2 Plain wooden 'keeper' hilt and scabbard identified by the flattened sides and distinct from a field scabbard which is more rounded.
3 This could be a reference to the kamikaze storm unleashed on the Allied fleets of Okinawa. Conventional non-suicide escort aircraft also participated.

---

**Plate 147** *An Officers personal dirk with its cloth wrapping.* (Alton Glazier).

# Air Force and Airborne Unit Swords

## Army and Naval Air Forces

Both the Army and Navy had their own air forces which were independent of each other. Ranks and uniforms were the same as their parent service but with some variations in flying or trade insignia. The Army Air Force was very small before the outbreak of hostilities with China, but by 1940 had grown to 30,000 men. The Navy air arm was initially confined to carrier units but was expanded when land bases became necessary during Japan's expansion in the Pacific war.

## Army Air Force swords

There was no separate prescribed sword pattern for the Army Air Force, the Army shin-guntō being carried. This could be personalised if required by the addition of a 'flying' or 'airborne' (paratroop) motif. These are rare, but examples noted are:

(i) Specially made sarute (sword knot loop) featuring the flying insignia of a stylised peregrine falcon with outstretched wings cast in relief (Fig. 22 (iii)).
(ii) A 'winged parachute and sakura' engraved on

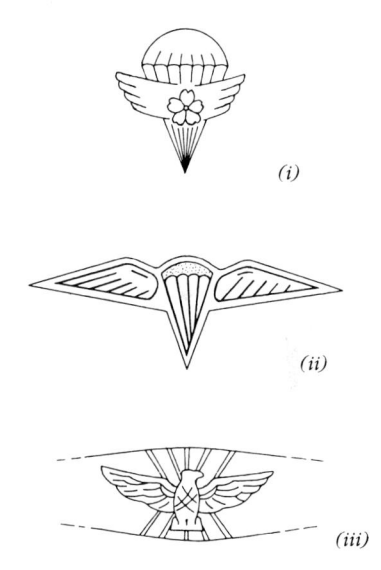

***Fig. 22*** *Airborne and flying insignia (unofficially?) added to full-sized shin-guntō:*
*(i)         The official badge of the small, but élite, Army airborne (paratroop) units. Engraved on the kabuto-gane (pommel).*
*(ii)        Variation of the Army airborne badge found engraved on the leather cover of a scabbard (see Plate 151).*
*(iii)       Army flying insignia found on specially made sarute (sword knot loop).*

the kabuto-gane (pommel) (Fig. 22 (i)).
(iii) Leather scabbard cover embossed with a 'winged parachute' (Plate 151).

**Plates 148, 149** *Rare small-sized Army shin-guntō believed to have been carried by Air Force officers. The example shown is of excellent quality with silver metal hilt and scabbard mounts. A hand-forged Shintō period blade and black lacquered scabbard.* (L. A. Elsener Jr).

The élite airborne units were small and their use restricted. Accounts of their actions confirm that officers, at least, carried swords presumably strapped across the back during descent. A contemporary wartime photograph indicates that some fighter planes had a removable external panel in the fuselage in which a sword could be clipped for the duration of the flight.[1] Some photographs show pilots with swords climbing into planes. However, an Army Air Force kamikaze pilot said, 'we were forbidden to take swords into the cockpits of our planes as they might affect the gyroscope'.[2] He also confirmed that he left his sword in the barracks along with his personal effects when he went on the final, but aborted, mission. However, *Japanese Military Uniforms 1930–1945* (see Bibliography) illustrates a Second Lieutenant in a summer flying suit which has two special short parallel slits through which a full-sized shin-guntō is carried.

### Small-sized Army shin-guntō

A short shin-guntō approximately two thirds, or less, normal size may have been carried by some Army Air Force officers when on flying duty. The brass fittings and tsuba (guard) are typical of shin-guntō with metal scabbards and are proportional to the reduced scale of the sword.

Overall length of sword and scabbard is around 610–660mm (24"–26") which would enable such items to be carried in cramped aircraft cockpits. However, no contemporary photographs have been located showing such swords in use.

Three variations have been reported:

(i) Green painted metal scabbard and a factory-made shinogi-zukuri blade having an acid-etched yakiba (tempered edge) as found on parade sabres. Solid tsuba. No sarute (sword knot loop). This is believed to be the standard version.
(ii) Brown painted metal scabbard also with an acid-etched blade. Pierced tsuba. This example has a sarute and a standard blue/brown Company Officers grade knot. However the straps are shorter than normal and commensurate for use with such a short sword. Better overall quality than item (i) above.[3]
(iii) Silver shin-guntō style fittings with a black lacquered scabbard (Plates 148, 149). Hand-forged Shintō period blade. No sarute. This seems to have been specially made for a person of senior rank, perhaps as a presentation peice.

Variants (i) and (iii) have a squat appearance because the hilt is short. Variant (ii) has a longer hilt and is better proportioned. One example of variant (i) is shown in Plate 1266, page 300, of *Imperial Japanese Army and Navy Uniforms and Equipments* (see Bibliography) where it is captioned 'a short sword for use in the air'. This is the only documented reference located by the authors. Another such sword is shown on page 50 of *Swords of Imperial Japan 1868–1945*.

Presumably numbers and popularity were limited with many being destroyed in crashed planes. This would explain their apparent rarity.

It must be noted that short shin-guntō with remounted wakizashi blades are not necessarily for Air Force use and they normally have full-sized fittings.

**Plate 150**  *A good quality unsigned Shintō period wakizashi blade in wooden mounts adapted for military use by the addition of a brown leather covering and ashi (suspension mount). A standard shin-guntō brass sarute (knot loop) has also been fitted. The tsuba (guard) is also of some age but is from, or for, a fighting sword since the design includes three characters which read BUUN (the fortunes of war) and NAGA (RAKU) (a long time or forever). Such a short sword is unusual and would seem unsuitable for normal active service. It may, however, have been carried by an officer of the Army Air Force although there are no markings to confirm this supposition.* (Dean Dennis).

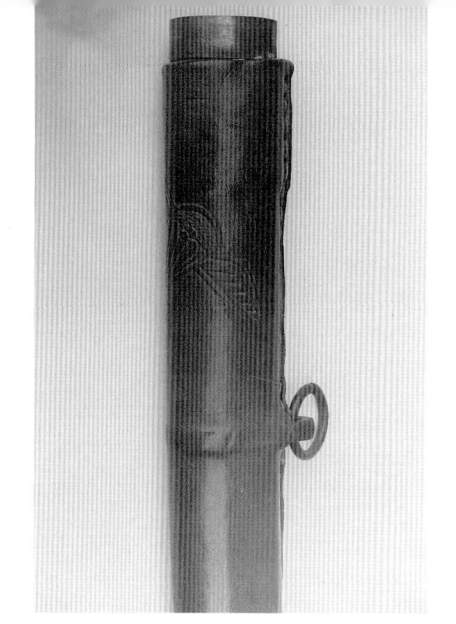

**Plate 151**  *Shin-guntō field scabbard with an engraved parachute and wings which indicates use by an airborne officer. This is a contemporary engraving and is a very rare occurrence. The hilt sarute (knot loop) of this sword is also decorated with the Army flying insignia shown in Fig. 22 (iii).* (Ron Gregory).

## Naval Air Force swords

There was no separate prescribed sword pattern for the naval air arm and no naval swords have been reported with any form of flying motifs.

An unusual example of a hybrid sword which may have been for Navy Air Force use is known from a collector's photographs but has not been personally examined or verified by the authors. It seems to be a small-sized shin-guntō measuring 635mm (25") overall in the scabbard. All fittings are Army shin-guntō except for the ishizuke (chape) and kabuto-gane (pommel) which are the naval kai-guntō pattern. The metal scabbard is painted a very dark brown. A hand-forged Shintō blade of good quality is used but it has a tapered and threaded tang indicating possible original use in Civil Officials sword mounts at some time. However, retention with the hilt is by the normal bamboo securing peg (mekugi).

It is assumed that only Commissioned Officers, Warrant Officers and, possibly, Chief Petty Officers could take swords on active flying duty.

# JAPANESE MILITARY AND CIVIL SWORDS AND DIRKS

The collector must be aware that it is possible to cut down a full-sized shin-guntō to make a small version but the fittings would be full-sized. Therefore all examples of small Air Force swords must be carefully examined and compared with regular-sized swords before purchase.

## Kamikaze dirks

The Army and Navy had separate air forces which operated independently until late in the war. Initially the use of suicide tactics by piloted aircraft was favoured by the Navy Air Force. Such suicide attacks were known as kamikaze (divine wind) or more properly 'Shimpu'.[4] The Navy formed the first official 'Tokko-Tai' (Special Attack Force)

***Plate 152*** *Rare kamikaze pilots dirks. That on the right is complete with a wrist cord and brown leather combat cover having a neck suspension cord. The example on the left has its protective linen bag in which it was probably presented. (Ron Gregory).*

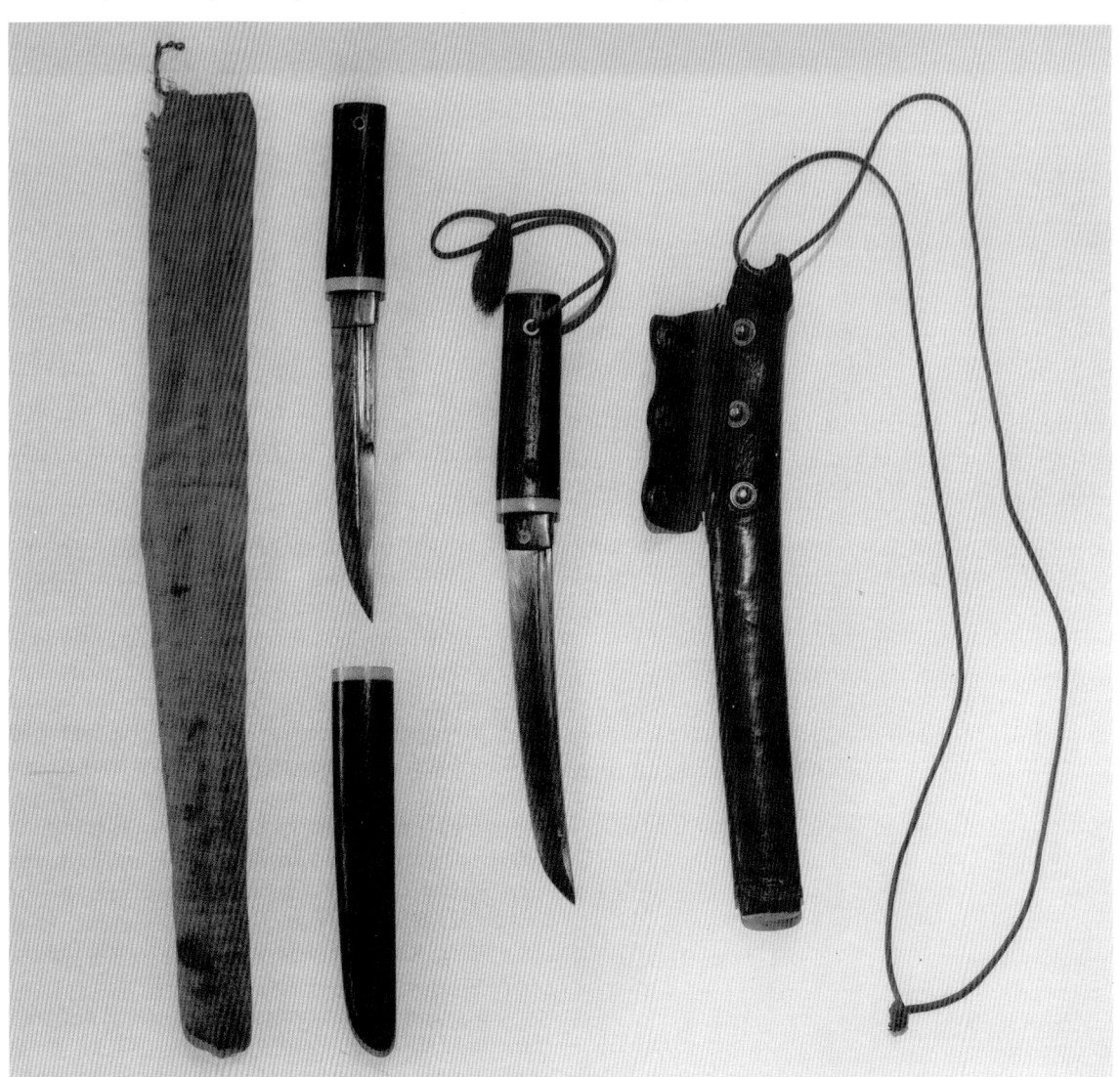

from volunteers, the full name being 'Shimpu Tokubetsu Kogetai' (Divine Wind Special Attack Force). The Army followed suit with its own 'Sword Brandishing Special Attack Force'. The first organised attack against Allied warships was on 25 October 1944, and the last on 6 January 1945. Later suicide tactics became compulsory for all pilots so ordered and many mass attacks were made. There were other manned suicide weapons such as the 'ohka' (piloted rocket bomb), 'kaiten' (suicide torpedo) and 'shinyo' (explosive motor-boats).

It is known that some kamikaze and kaiten pilots were presented with a form of edged weapon generally assumed to be a dirk. Post-war accounts of such awards seem to indicate that they were restricted to Navy personnel during the initial Kamikaze and Kaiten campaigns. No account of an Army presentation ceremony has been located by the authors. The following accounts appear to be typical.[5] Vice-Admiral Miwa Shigeyoshi, on 7 November 1944, presented kaiten pilots with a hachimaki (white headscarf) and a 'wakizashi, the short sword traditionally carried by samurai and used in the act of seppuku' (ritual suicide). At 0800 the following morning they marched off 'with swords at their right sides, wakizashi in their left hands'. At 0900 the submarines sailed on the first kaiten mission (of the war) with the kaiten pilots standing in the open hatches of their torpedoes 'brandishing their swords'. On 3 December 1944 Admiral Toyoda Soemu presented each pilot of the first ohka unit with a white hachimaki and 'a short sword engraved with the recipient's name'. This occurred towards the end of their training period.

No Shōwa period wakizashi in naval or civilian mounts has been reported which could indicate presentation to kaiten pilots. It is also believed that ohka pilots, as well as kamikaze pilots, received dirks although none has been reported with the recipient's name thereon. A contemporary photograph shows kaiten pilots with newly presented dirks in shira-saya (plain wooden keeper mounts) and holding full-sized kai-guntō. Thus the aforementioned reference to wakizashi seems

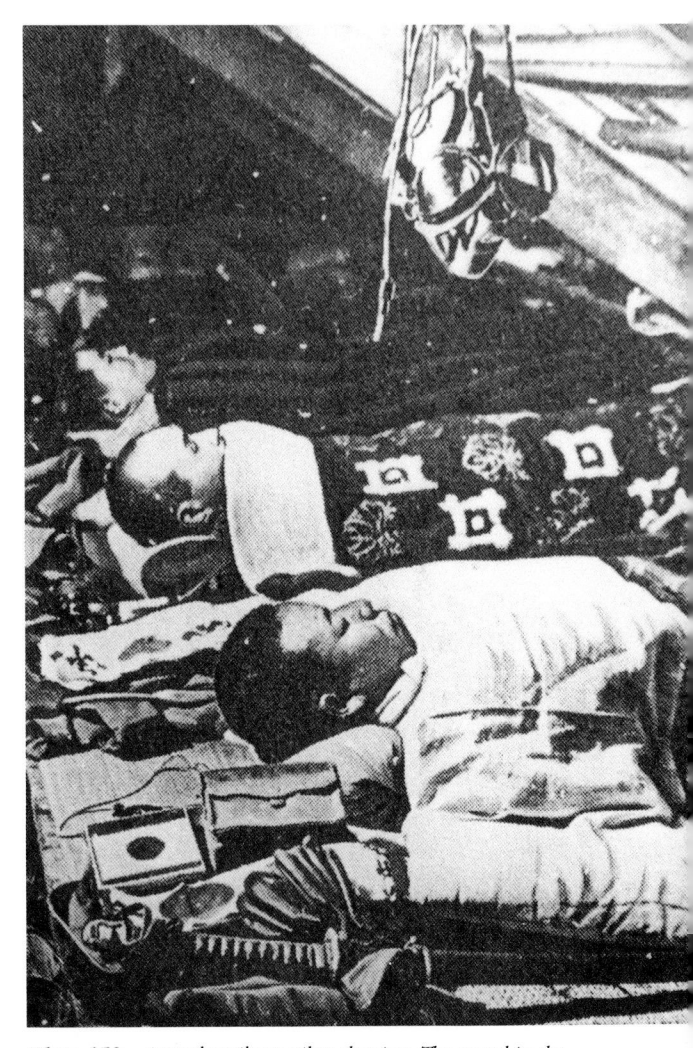

*Plate 153* Army kamikaze pilots sleeping. The sword in the foreground is a full-sized shin-guntō with the sword knot wrapped around the hilt near the kabuto-gane (pommel). Note the hachimaki (head band) between the first two men. (J. Arlott).

incorrect. These dirks were carried by the recipients on their suicide missions, which explains why none have been located.

Bona fide kamikaze dirks are a rare find. The two original examples shown in Plate 152 are verified by the presence of the original accessories. That on the left has the original linen bag in which it would have been presented while that on the right is complete with its brown leather combat cover which covers it entirely. The long cord is for hanging round the neck and the short cord through the hilt is for securing to the wrist. Reputedly such dirks were for cutting the jugular before the plane crashed into its target. However they were probably more symbolic than practical since a pilot would require all his skill to operate his machine up to the moment of impact.

All seemingly genuine examples reported are based on the traditional aikuchi (dagger without a guard used for suicide, particularly by women). None has been observed to be identical. Normally both the removable hilt and scabbard are rosewood with ivory or bone collars. Scabbards can also be black lacquered wood. Blades are handforged or machine-made but fitted with a habaki (blade collar). Some are engraved with patriotic inscriptions such as 'go forth and your deeds will be recited in history'.

Dimensions vary. Overall length of dirk and scabbard 235–254mm (9¼"–10⅜"). Hilt length 83–92mm (3¼"–3⅝"). Blade length 137–159mm (5⅜"–6¼"). Scabbard length 156–175mm (6⅛"–6⅞").

It may be assumed that, if presented en masse, there was a supplier, or suppliers, who could provide considerably more than one dirk at a time. However, no reference to official sanction or a prescribed pattern has been seen or reported. Perhaps the senior officers concerned in the presentation ceremonies funded the items themselves as a mark of respect for 'those about to die'.

A few kamikaze dirks were recovered from crashed planes or the bodies of pilots, while others seem to have been obtained in Japan after the Allied occupation. There is an unfortunate tendency among collectors and dealers to assume that any dirk remotely resembling a kamikaze aikuchi must have been intended for that purpose. Japanese officers often owned more than one edged weapon and this may include dirks for personal use (see Plates 144 to 147). There are also many tourist dirks sold as letter openers which match the general description but do not, normally, have a habaki. However, some could fool an inexperienced collector.

A post-war 'adjustment' of a genuine dirk to become kamikaze is also possible. For example, a dirk blade in white wood shira-saya (keeper mounts) is known with a sarute (knot loop) from a shin-guntō and a leather NCOs sword knot.[6] All relevant factors must be considered before kamikaze use can be attributed.

---

1 Information courtesy of Han Bing Siong. Presumably swords could be carried inside the body of a bomber without problem.
2 *I Was a Kamikaze* by R. Nagatsuka (see Bibliography). Presumably this does not apply to the kamikaze dirk although nowhere does he state that Army pilots were presented with such items.
3 Information courtesy of Stephen Yap.
4 Kamikaze appears to be a term applied by Allied personnel; shimpu refers to suicide and is more correct.
5 Both are taken from *Suicide Squads* by Richard O'Neill (Salamander Books, London, 1981).
6 Illustrated in Plate 6, page 47, of *Aeronautica* by A.J. Marriott-Smith (Arms & Armour Press, London, 1989).

# Meiji Period Naval Swords

The Imperial Japanese Navy was regarded as secondary to the Army and was not even separate until 1872 when the Navy Ministry was established. The Navy General Staff was not created until 1893 although the Army General Staff was founded in 1878. For a considerable period manpower was obtained from voluntary sources whereas the Army was manned by conscription.

The earliest prescribed naval sword mentioned in the Japanese references consulted is the 1873 pattern for officers, although undocumented examples have been found which could be earlier but, so far, have not been dated. They have thus been loosely termed 'Meiji period naval swords', i.e. in the period 1868–1912. The naval kyu-guntō patterns, although Meiji, have been described under their own heading.

Proper identification and dating of the types with the integral cross guard sword knot rings and loose, or protruding, pommel rings have not been fully established. The design concept seems to be based on eighteenth-century European and American hunting swords or, more likely, some early nineteenth-century British naval dirks which utilised chains instead of knucklebows. Some Chinese soldiers are known to have used a similar pattern during, at least, the first quarter of the twentieth century but they could be of Japanese manufacture (Plate 272). See the sections on 'Unidentified Naval Swords' and 'Unidentified Civil Swords and Dirks' later in this book. Therefore use, with the exception of the Naval Police and Naval Prison Service, is unknown as are the sword knot patterns which may be regarded as essential with this hilt type.

### Naval Boarding cutlass

No example of a Japanese naval boarding cutlass has been located to confirm that such a thing existed. However, Plates 154, 155, dated 1904, from contemporary English language publications, apparently show such a weapon in use. Both drawings are by the British war artists R.C. Woodville[1] and depict the same event. A Japanese seaman, who was the first to leap on board a Russian destroyer, slashed a Russian officer (probably the captain of the *Steregushti*) who had just appeared on deck and then threw him over the side. The artist, who would not have been present during this action, has possibly used artistic licence by basing the cutlass on a Russian type. The Japanese seaman is shown holding a cutlass with a curved blade which has a wide single fuller (groove). The large bowl-guard has a ring quillion which is associated with attachment to a rifle. This infers duel usage as a sword bayonet.

There is a cutlass which has a blackened steel half-basket guard with three large open panels. The black grips are smooth (Bakelite?) secured by three brass rivets. Curved single-edged fullered blade with a falchion-shape tip. The leather scabbard has iron throat and chape fittings. Leather strap and button attachment for a frog. The scabbard leather may be branded with a Japanese

# JAPANESE MILITARY AND CIVIL SWORDS AND DIRKS

**Plate 154, 155**  *War artist's impressions of Japanese seamen using a naval boarding cutlass during the 1904–5 Russo–Japanese war. (Richard Fuller).*

character or mark on one side near the throat. Erroneously mistaken for a Japanese pattern it is in fact a Netherlands Colonial Infantry sword captured, in some numbers, by the Japanese and reused by their own, or collaborating, forces.[2]

The existence of Japanese cutlass patterns must therefore be regarded as speculative until either the naval dress regulations can be located or a bona fide example with Japanese manufacture markings is found.

## 1872 pattern Wilkinson Sword Company Naval Officers sword

The English company of Wilkinson Sword Ltd illustrates a Japanese Admirals sword, belt and buckle in their pattern book dated 2 January 1872.[3] By 25 January they had 'proved, embossed and mounted' one Admirals and two Commanders swords[4] for an S. Harada, presumably as patterns for the approval of the Japanese Navy. However, the design seems to have been rejected in favour of the c.1873 pattern naval sword since none has been reported.

The design is closely based on the 1846 pattern Royal Navy sword with the only major difference, seemingly, being the obverse hand guard cartouche insignia. This is a foul anchor, set over two crossed flowers (cherry blossoms?), with a rope entwined around the cross stay. This also features on the design for the Admirals gilded brass belt clasp which has a surround of a laurel wreath (Fig. 69). The sword has a half-basket guard, backstrap with lion's head pommel and white shagreen grip. Black leather scabbard with three engraved mounts and a straight blade

# MEIJI PERIOD NAVAL SWORDS

presumably suitably etched with maritime designs. It appears that the belt badge was not adopted for use on any sword but was in current usage on belt buckles (see Plates 292, 293) at least for NCOs and/or ratings, but how long this lasted is unknown.

## Regulation 1873 pattern Commissioned Officers naval sword

Western, and particularly British, influence became very strong in the organisation and uniforms of the Japanese Navy by the early 1870s. This is reflected in the design of the first known prescribed naval sword pattern of 1873 which is clearly based on the American (and French) swords of the period. The *Nippon no Gunso* (see Bibliography) describes it as a 'naval sword for full dress wear by Commissioned Officers' with an introduction date (i.e. 'change in regulations') of December 1873. However, according to *Swords of Imperial Japan 1868–1945*, the actual authorisation date was 14 November 1873.

The hilt, guard shape, and brass-mounted leather scabbard are typically Western but the distinctive blade type and sakura (cherry blossom) decoration are typically Japanese. This sword pattern is one of only a very few Japanese naval swords which have been found to feature a foul anchor design incorporating two interlocking rings (Fig. 23 (v)). Why this was not used on other Japanese naval swords, which normally incorporated only one ring in the anchor motif, is unknown.

Gilded brass hilt fittings comprise a half-basket guard pierced with sakura and foliage, a knuckle-bow, fuchi and pommel. The latter is decorated with a band of laurel leaves and is surmounted by a sakura and foul anchor (Plate 158). The fuchi is engraved with waves. White samé grip with brass wire binding in the grooves but no backstrap. The known examples and a Japanese drawing indicate the short hilt is the norm. Unusual style blade of unokubi-zukuri form distinguished by a wide, short groove reducing to a long narrow one which gives a false top edge. It is unknown if this is the

**Fig. 23** *Foul anchor motifs observed on the following naval swords and dirks:*
(i)  Unidentified short pattern naval sword.
(ii)  1895 pat. Naval Prison (and Shore Patrol) sword (Example 1).
(iii)  1895 pat Naval Prison (and Shore Patrol) sword (Example 2).
(iv)  Variation of the 1883 pattern Naval Officer Candidates dirk. Perhaps a Petty Officer Candidates version of (v).
(v)  1873 pattern Commissioned Officers naval sword, 1883 pattern Naval Officer Candidates dirk and a possible Chief Petty Officers parade sabre.
(vi)  Army kyu-guntō for naval use.

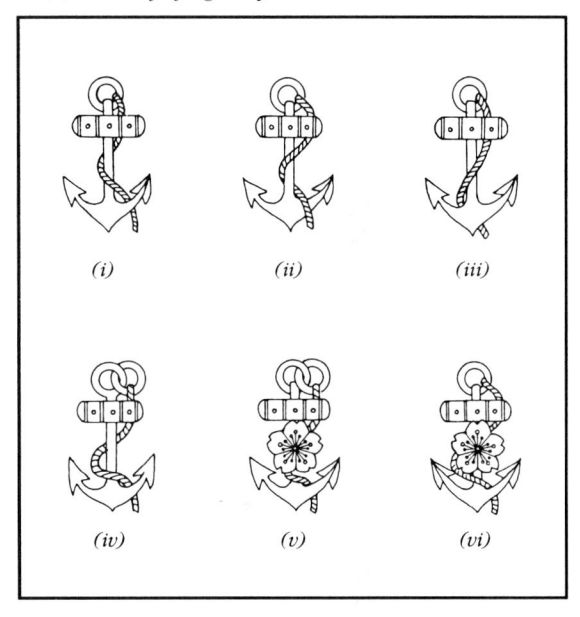

standard blade style for this sword pattern although noted on all known examples. No habaki (blade collar) was utilised. Black leather scabbard having three gilded brass mounts decorated ensuite with four raised sakura and engraved leaves. The type of sword knot is unknown. No parade sabre version is known.

Dimensions may have varied but those of the sword illustrated are as follows: Overall length of sword and scabbard 933mm (36¾"). Hilt length 133mm (5¼"). Blade length 672mm (26⁷/₁₆"). Maximum blade width 25mm (1"). Scabbard length 787mm (31").

Presumably decoration of fittings was the same for all Commissioned Officer ranks. Petty Officer ranks appear to have been given a plain version

## JAPANESE MILITARY AND CIVIL SWORDS AND DIRKS

with a metal scabbard having roped suspension bands (same as Fig 24 (i)?). A particularly ornate and short version with an old wakizashi blade is also known (from an auction catalogue). The scabbard decoration is standard for this pattern but both lockets have been fitted with suspension bands in the form of interwoven rope. The hilt is similar to the 1883 pattern naval kyu-guntō with a backstrap but the knucklebow is roped as is the obverse quillion and outer edges of the handguard. It would seem to be a specially made combination of both patterns either for presentation purposes or, possibly, as a very early transitional version of the replacement 1883 model.[5]

Examples of this sword pattern must be regarded as very rare.

---

1 Richard Caton Woodville (1856–1927) was a prolific military illustrator for newspapers and periodicals. He mainly worked at his studio from written reports and is known for his realism, often using original military equipment as a model to ensure accuracy. Whether he did this for the, then current, Russo–Japanese war is doubtful.
2 Identified in *Swords for Sea Service* vol. 1 page 192, and vol.2 Plate 122. Wrongly described as a variant of the American 1917 Model Naval Cutlass in the *American Sword 1775–1945* by H. L. Peterson.
3 Shown in *A Pictorial History of Swords and Bayonets* by J. R. Wilkinson-Latham (Ian Allan Ltd, 1973).
4 Wilkinson Sword issue nos. 18221,2,3 respectively.
5 It is possible that this sword is a manufacturer's mistake based on the newly issued dress regulations and not the official illustrated specification.

---

**Plate 157** *Hilt and top scabbard locket of the rare 1873 pattern Naval Officers sword. The hilt style is typical of many French (and American) swords of the same period. (Ron Gregory).*

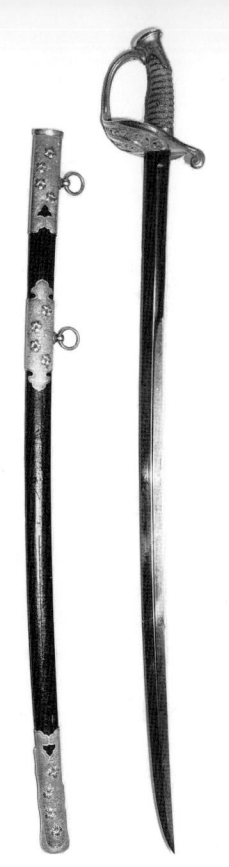

**Plate 156** *Rare 1873 pattern Commissioned Officers naval sword. The unokubi-zukuri blade style on this example is signed by Naotake who worked around 1865–68. (Ron Gregory).*

**Plate 158** *Guard design and pommel decoration of the 1873 pattern Naval Officers sword. The foul anchor, limited to the pommel cap only, incorporates a sakura with two interlocking rings above the cross stay, which is unusual since normally only one ring was used on Japanese naval items. (Ron Gregory).*

# Naval 1883 & 1914 Kyu-Guntō

## Regulation 1883 pattern naval kyu-guntō

Three, or possibly four, variations of a new sword pattern, drawn in the *Nippon-no-Gunso*, were authorised on 20 October 1883[1] to replace the 1873 pattern naval sword. They all have white samé grips, gilded brass hilt fittings and scabbards with three gilded mounts. Type and decoration depended upon the rank grade of the wearer as is detailed below.

The name kyu-guntō (i.e. 'first military sword') is not correct but has come into common usage in the West and will, therefore, be retained in this publication for ease of description. There appears to be no proper name other than a naval sword with the probable introduction date designation.

### Type 1 – Flag Officers grade[2]
Solid half-basket guard having the obverse decorated with raised sakura (cherry blossoms) and leaves. The upper backstrap and all three scabbard mounts are decorated with raised 5:7:5 floret kiri (*Paulownia imperialis*) flowers used as a sign of rank by Flag Officers (Fig. 24 (iii)). Gold sword knot (possibly plain) with bullions (ringlets) and cords.

### Type 2 – Junior and Senior Commissioned Officers grades[3]
The same as Type 1 but decorated with sakura and leaves only (Fig. 24 (ii)). Silver or gold? barrel-shaped knot (possibly with red zigzag stitches), elongated stem, slide and plain cords (Fig. 1 (ii)).

### Type 3 – Superior Petty Officers (and Warrant Officers?)
This may, in fact, be the 1873 pattern which also lacks a backstrap. The obverse guard is decorated with sakura and leaves but the scabbard mounts are plain except for roped suspension bands (Fig. 24 (i)). Gold acorn knot (possibly plain), elongated stem and cords. *Japanese Military Uniforms 1930–1945* (see Bibliography) has a drawing of a similar sword with a black grip and plain suspension bands. The English caption reads 'Navy Sergeant-Major's sword (old model)'. *Swords of Imperial Japan* indicates this is the second pattern introduced on 26 February 1914 but abolished on 3 October 1919 in favour of the universal 1914 pattern naval kyu-guntō. However roped suspension bands may still have been used

### Type 4 – Petty Officers
It is uncertain whether this is a separate version since it appears to be identical to the Superior Petty Officers sword (Type 3), but possibly the obverse guard is undecorated. Gold fringed knot, elongated stems and cords.

# JAPANESE MILITARY AND CIVIL SWORDS AND DIRKS

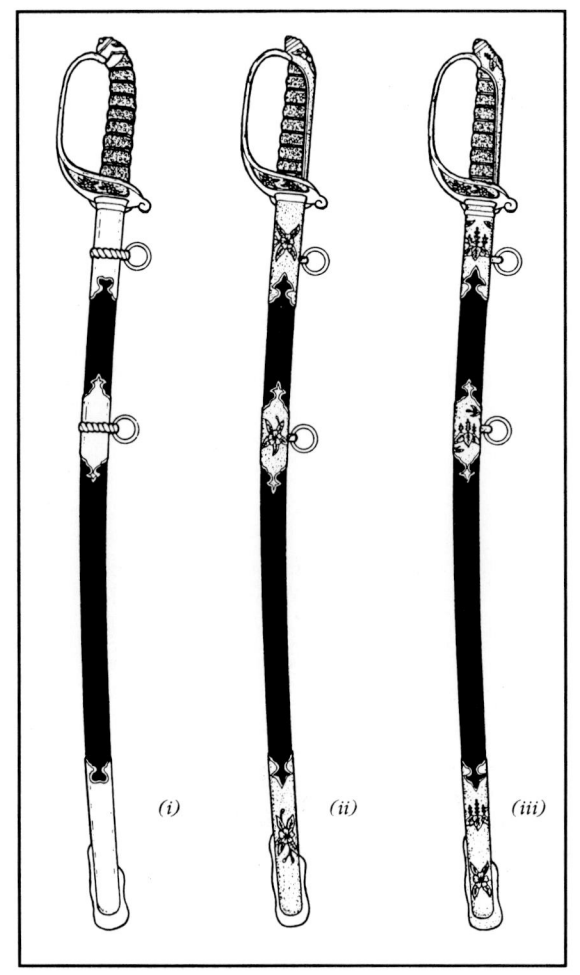

**Fig. 24** Regulation 1883 pattern naval kyu-guntō sword patterns:
(i)   Superior (and Junior) Petty Officers. (1873 model?)
(ii)  Senior and Junior Commissioned Officers.
(iii) Flag Officers (Admirals).
There were equivalent parade sabre versions of all three sword types. About 1914 that shown in (ii) became the standard model for all Commissioned Officers; the other two became obsolete.

No examples of Types 1, 3 and 4 have been reported to the authors, although parade sabre versions of Types 1, 2 and 3 are known.

The Commissioned and Flag Officers versions would be expected to have hand-forged blades of shinogi-zukuri form (possibly reused from older samurai swords) secured to the hilt by the traditional bamboo peg. The wooden scabbards could be covered with black leather or shagreen. A samé scabbard with this sword pattern has not been noted although used with the replacement kai-guntō. Probably the Petty Officers versions had machine-made blades and black leather scabbards. Blades may not be removable, but this is speculation. Retention in the scabbard, on all models, would be a small folding reverse guard flap which engages with a raised stud projecting from the rear of the top scabbard locket.

The Type 2 model became universal for all Commissioned Officer ranks from 26 February 1914 and for Superior Petty Officers from 3 October 1919. Unless blade dating allows, it is not possible to distinguish a 1883 version from the post-1914 version and examples are very scarce. All other variations must be regared as very rare.

**Plate 159**  Vice-Admiral Kamimura, during the 1904–5 Russo–Japanese war. He has a naval kyu-guntō which appears to be the 1883 Flag Officers pattern with the kiri (Paulownia imperialis) on the fittings. (Ron Gregory).

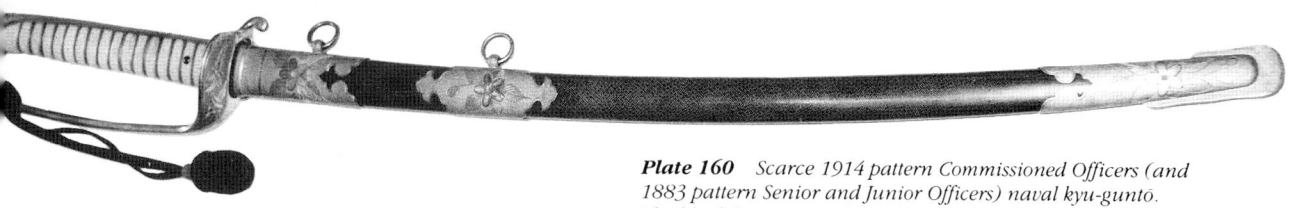

**Plate 160** Scarce 1914 pattern Commissioned Officers (and 1883 pattern Senior and Junior Officers) naval kyu-guntō. The black knot is, possibly, incorrect since it is the Army kyu-guntō pattern. (Ron Gregory).

## Regulation 1914 pattern Commissioned Officers naval kyu-guntō

Three of the 1883 versions of the naval kyu-guntō became obsolete in 1914 and 1919[4] in favour of a single pattern, the Type 2, 1883 pattern Junior and Senior Commissioned Officers model (Fig. 24 (ii)). Flag Officers had to adopt this pattern thus losing their rank distinction unless it was indicated by the sword knot (see below). Petty Officers (with the probable exception of Senior Petty Officers) appear to have lost the right to carry a sword in 1919. There is no indication that the wear of the previous patterns was banned (except, perhaps, for Petty Officers) or required replacement until worn out.

Blade type, scabbard and decoration remained the same as the 1883 model. However, a new sword knot, of the type shown in Plate 166, appears to have been introduced. This has a red base and vertical bright red zigzag stitches to the knot, stem and slide. There is uncertainty about a ranking system, although it is possible since the folllowing colorations have been found. All have the red stitches (i) gold knot, stem, slide and cords

**Plate 161** Hilt reverse of the 1914 (& 1883) Commissioned Officers naval kyu-guntō. The rear hinged flap is folded downwards over the locket stud. (Ron Gregory).

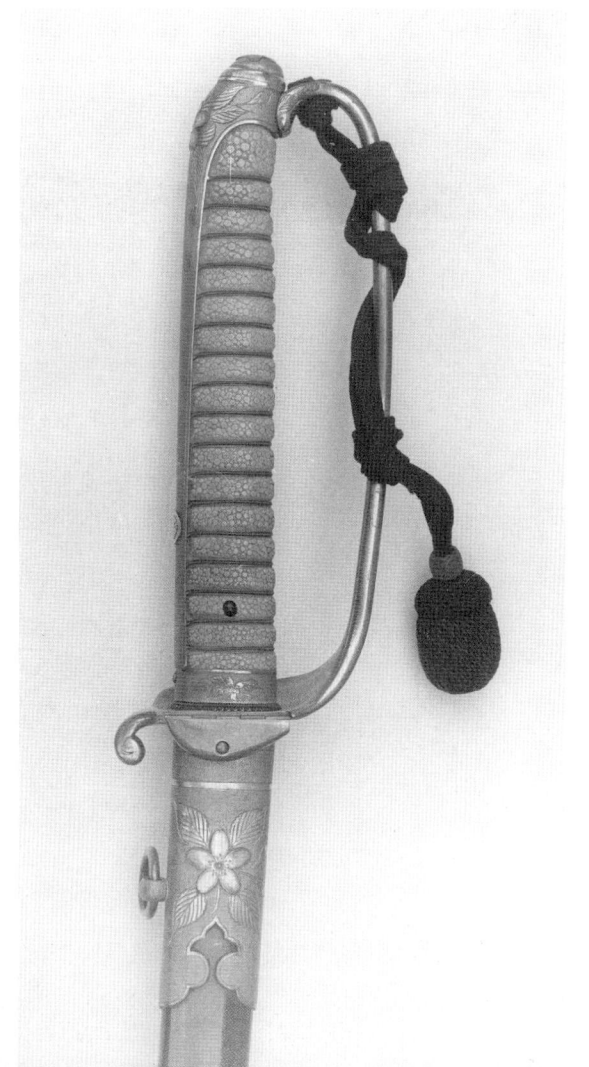

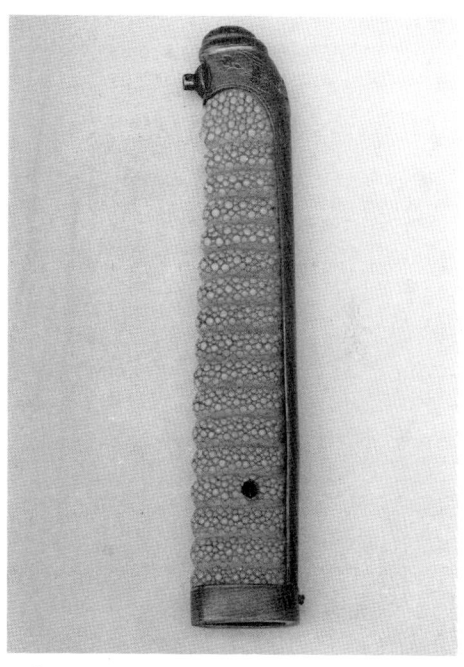

**Plate 162** White same grip and brass backstrap of a standard 1883 & 1914 pattern naval kyu-guntō. Normally the pommel has a slot for engagement with the knucklebow but in this case there is a protruding lug which has a small hole through it, possibly for a pinned fitting. However, it could be that this particular hilt never had a knucklebow and was just fitted with a small sarute (sword knot ring) which is also missing. If correct, this would be an unknown variation. (Ron Gregory).

# JAPANESE MILITARY AND CIVIL SWORDS AND DIRKS

(although normally believed to be associated with Army General Officers parade sabres); (ii) silver knot, stem, slide and gold cords; (iii) off-white knot, stem, slide and gold cords; (iv) off-white knot, stem, slide and cords.[5] The gold and silver is bullion wire over a silk base while the white seems to be a fabric. Sometimes the Army kyu-guntō knot with black cords is found with this sword pattern, but no contemporary photographic evidence has, so far, been located to confirm that it was not a later, incorrect, addition.

The naval kyu-guntō was unpopular as a fighting weapon since regarded as being unbalanced when raised above the head and on the down-stroke. The knucklebow prevented a proper two-handed grip. Consequently it was replaced by the kai-guntō in 1937, basically to satisfy the combat requirements of the Naval Landing Forces.[6]

This sword pattern is identical to its 1883 predecessor. All hilt and scabbard mounts are gilded brass. The obverse guard is solid being decorated externally with raised sakura (cherry blossoms) and leaves. Scabbard retention is by means of a small downward-folding rear guard which engages with a raised stud on the upper scabbard locket. The backstrap is plain except for an upper panel of a sakura with four radiating leaves and a raised sakura on the pommel. White same grip with intermittent brass wire binding.

Blades of varying quality may be found which can be of some age. The example photographed

**Plate 163** *Unusual naval kyu-guntō pommel decoration of a sakura and leaves. Normally only a raised sakura is featured.* (Donald Barnes).

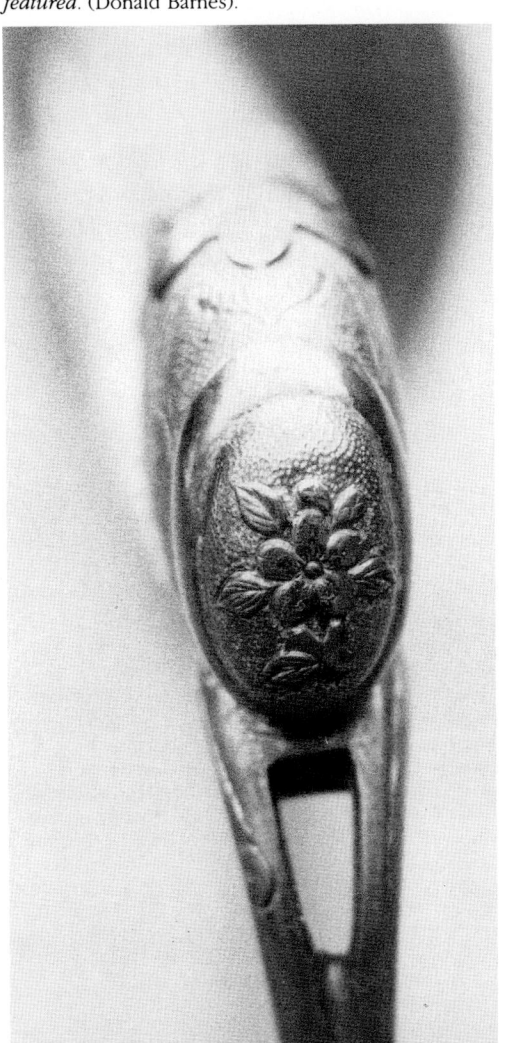

**Plate 164** *Vice-Admiral Hasegawa Hitoshi (left), naval commander at Shanghai, who supported the Army landings by General Matsui Iwane (right), C-in-C Shanghai Expeditionary Force in 1937. This photograph was taken at Army field headquarters in 1938. Hasegawa holds a naval kyu-guntō.* (Han Bing Siong).

has a traditional blade of shinogi-zukuri form signed by Sukesada and dated 1579. Late examples may be found with Shōwa period blades. A removable bamboo or wooden peg (mekugi) is used to secure the hilt and tang. Black leather or lacquered shagreen-covered wooden scabbard which has three mounts decorated ensuite with sakura and radiating leaves in relief.

Dimensions vary according to the wishes of the purchaser. Sword and scabbard length of example shown 991mm (39⅝"). Hilt length 241mm (9½"). Blade length 689mm (27⅛"). Sword and scabbard weight 56 ounces.

As previously stated, examples of these swords are very scarce.

## Naval kyu-guntō variant

A most unusual and rare short naval kyu-guntō variation is shown in Plates 166 to 168. It is presumed to have been specially made rather than being representative of a separate model.

The obverse guard is pierced and decorated with two large sakura and leaves. It also has two small holes for a sword knot which is a feature not found on Japanese military swords but is very common on British Royal Navy dress swords. The knucklebow is also decorated with sakura and leaves which is not normal practice. A wakizashi-length blade is signed by Arimitsu of Osafune in Bishū province and is dated 1596. Black leather scabbard having three mounts decorated ensuite with engraved sakura blooms, leaves and stems.

It also has a surrender/transportation tag which

**Plate 165** *Shanghai, 1937. Senior Army and naval officers on board a warship. Front row (seated) from left to right: 1st, 2nd, 4th are naval officers with naval kyu-guntō; 3rd, 7th, 9th are Army officers with shin-guntō; 5th is General Matsui Iwane, C-in-C Shanghai Expeditionary Force, whose sword is indistinct; 6th is Vice-Admiral Hasegawa Hitoshi, commander of naval forces at Shanghai, with a naval kyu-guntō; 8th is the officer shown in Plates 84, 298. He is in dark naval uniform but with the land warfare shoulder belt and has a scarce two-hanger Army shin-guntō having a General Officers knot. His cap badge is an anchor and not the normal Navy Officers badge of an anchor, sakura and wreath. It seems likely he is the commander of the Imperial Marines who took part in the Shanghai campaign. 10th is a naval officer with a naval parade sabre. (Bill Tagg).*

translates as YAMADA TSUKASA TAISA, i.e. (naval) Captain Yamada Tsukasa. Above in English is written 'Rear Admiral Yamada'.[7] This sword was the property of Australian Major-General E. J. Milford, GOC 7th Australian Division.

Overall length of sword and scabbard 800mm (31½"). Hilt length 150mm (5 15/16"). Blade length 589mm (23¼"). Maximum blade width 27mm (1 1/16"). Scabbard length 589mm (23 3/16").

---

1 This dating is given in *Swords of Imperial Japan 1868–1945* (see Bibliography).
2 *Flag Officers*: Rear Admiral, Vice-Admiral, Admiral, Fleet Admiral. There was no rank of Commodore in the Japanese Navy.
3 *Junior Officers*: Warrant Officer, Cadet, Midshipman, Ensign, Sub-Lieutenant, Lieutenant. *Senior Officers*: Lieutenant-Commander, Commander, Captain.
4 These dates are given in *Swords of Imperial Japan 1868–1945*.
5 The all-white knot is rumoured to represent Flag Officers (Admirals) grade but this has not been confirmed. White could be an alternative of silver, but this is uncertain.
6 *The Changes of the Landing Forces Uniforms 1937–1940* by Etsuko Yagyu which was provided in translated form by Philip Goody and his co-researchers.
7 This does not seem to be the same as Rear-Admiral Kamada Michiaki whose kai-guntō was presented by General Milford to the Australian War Memorial Museum (cat. no. AWM 20323).

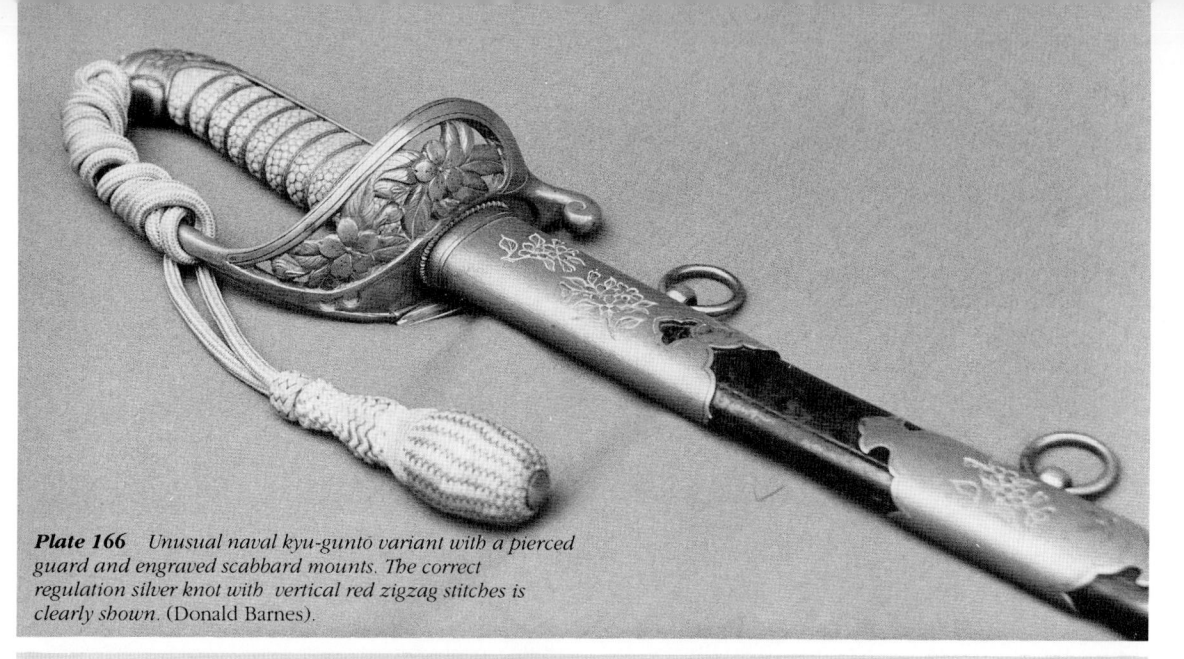

**Plate 166** *Unusual naval kyu-guntō variant with a pierced guard and engraved scabbard mounts. The correct regulation silver knot with vertical red zigzag stitches is clearly shown. (Donald Barnes).*

**Plate 167** *Pierced guard of the naval kyu-guntō in Plate 166. The two holes in the guard for the sword knot cords is a feature normally not encountered on Japanese naval swords. (Donald Barnes).*

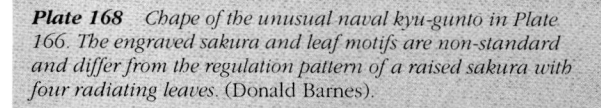

**Plate 168** *Chape of the unusual naval kyu-guntō in Plate 166. The engraved sakura and leaf motifs are non-standard and differ from the regulation pattern of a raised sakura with four radiating leaves. (Donald Barnes).*

# Naval 1883 & 1914 Parade Sabres

### Regulation 1883 and 1914 pattern Commissioned (and Petty) Officers naval parade sabres

Naval parade sabres are smaller lightweight versions of the 1883 and 1914 full-sized naval kyu-guntō patterns which were carried by all ranks of Commissioned Officers (and Petty Officers up to 1919) for dress and walking-out occasions, although the exact circumstances of wear have not been established. They were not intended as fighting weapons, which is obvious when one sees their slender, flexible, blunt, chromium-plated blades.

Privately purchased, certainly in the case of Commissioned Officers, they could be subject to extra cost embellishments such as an acid-etched tempered edge (Fig. 60) or quality variations. However, the design was fairly consistent following the design of the current naval kyu-guntō. There are no manufacturer's inscriptions. The only markings likely are assembly numbers or stamps on the tang and hilt fittings such as that of the Toyokawa Naval Arsenal mark (Fig. 62 (xvii)), Suya Company (Fig 61(xxiii)) and unidentified Fig. 61 (xiii).

The first patterns appear to have complemented the 1883 naval kyu-guntō sword patterns with the equivalent rank distinctions for Superior (and Junior) Petty Officers, Warrant, Senior and Junior Commissioned Officers, and Flag Officers (Admirals). The plain 1883 Petty Officers model with black grip appears to have roped scabbard bands and a backstrap (Plate 170) although the full-sized version does not. The 1914 model is similar but has 'arrow' shaped scabbard projections/recesses. In 1914 the Junior and Senior Commissioned Officers model also became standard for Flag Officers. However the 1883/1914 pattern Petty Officers model did not become obsolete until 1919. They were carried up the end of World War Two although no parade version of the traditional-styled kai-guntō (introduced in 1937) was produced. However, production must have continued until 1944 at least, since such a common item, indicating that a great many were made. Becoming a naval officer was expensive because a full-sized sword, parade sabre and naval dirk were all prescribed items of dress.

Four types of sword knot were available, depending upon rank grade, with the 1883 pattern naval kyu-guntō (see that entry for details). These were available for the equivalent parade sabre versions but were smaller. After 1914 only one pattern of knot became available in keeping with the single multi-rank Officers sword. Again this was smaller in size but consisted of plain silver bullion cords with a slide, stem and barrel-shaped

**Plate 169** *Undated Japanese naval group with ranks assessed from their cuff bands. Standing left to right: Chief Petty Officer with 1883 pat. Petty Officers parade sabre; unidentified rank; Sub-Lieutenant with naval kyu-guntō. Seated left to right: Sub-Lieutenant with Naval Officers parade sabre; First Lieutenant with naval parade sabre. (Cheyenne Noda).*

knot displaying vertical red zigzag stitches. The knot has a red base. Whether or not there are colour variations, as found with the 1914 naval kyu-guntō is unknown.

Hilt and scabbard fittings are gilded brass. The grip is white samé having an intermittent brass wire binding. Retention is by means of a small folding flap on the hilt reverse which engages with a raised stud on the top scabbard locket. All fittings are decorated with sakura and leaves in relief identical to the 1914 pattern naval kyu-guntō.[1] Flexible chromium-plated blade of two types (Fig. 59 (ii), (iv)) which may have the extra-cost acid-etched yakiba (tempered edge), usually in the regular undulating form (Fig. 60 (i)). A wooden scabbard is covered with either black leather or black or brown lacquered shagreen. The shagreen scabbard seems to indicate a deluxe model since a brass habaki (blade collar) is normally also fitted.

Dimensions of examples checked seem remarkably consistent when compared with the variations in sizing of Army parade sabres. Lengths would be expected to vary in accordance with the owner's height, but there is apparently little difference from the following average measurements. Overall length of sword and scabbard 813mm (32$^{11}$/$_{16}$"). Hilt length (to inside of guard) 122mm (4$^{13}$/$_{16}$"). Blade length 635–660mm (25"–26"). Maximum blade width 19mm (¾"). Weight of

---

1 The leaves on the foremost guard sakura may be either four or six in number. This may be no more than a design variation and has not been reported on the full-sized naval kyu-guntō. Four seems to be the norm.

---

**Plate 170** *Close-up of Plate 169. The parade sabre on the left is the 1883 pattern Petty Officers model. Hilt details are unclear but probably reflect the guard sakura decoration of the full-sized version. However, this sword does appear to have the addition of a backstrap. The scabbard mounts clearly differ from the Officers pattern on the right in that they have raised, roped suspension bands and heart-shaped (boar's eye) recesses. The barrel-shaped knot is similar to the Officers version but appears darker with black cords and a light-coloured (gold?) slide. (Cheyenne Noda).*

# NAVAL 1883 & 1914 PARADE SABRES

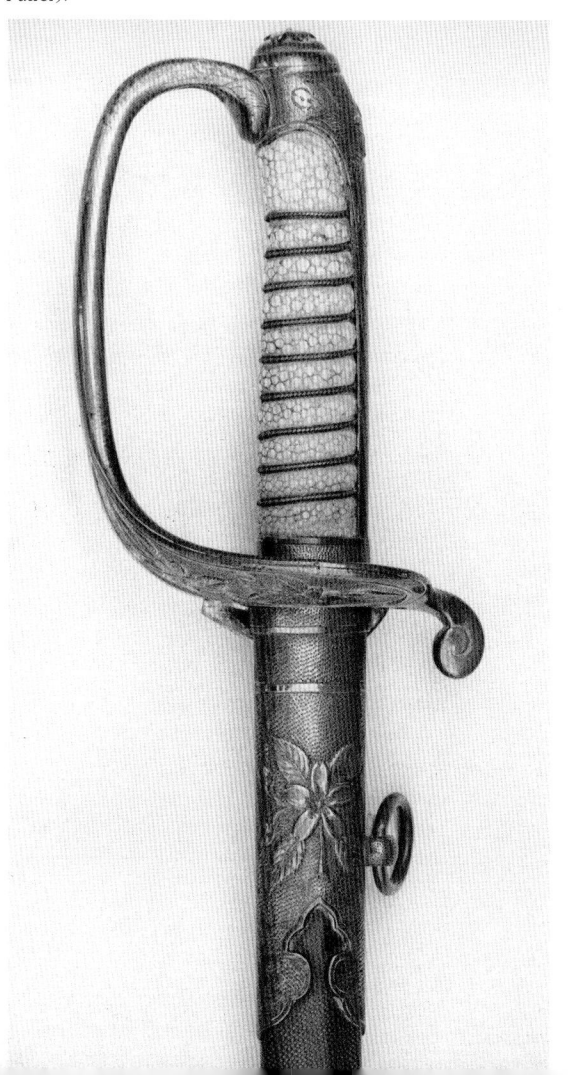

**Plate 171**  Typical 1914 regulation pattern Commissioned Officers naval parade sabre. (Richard Fuller).

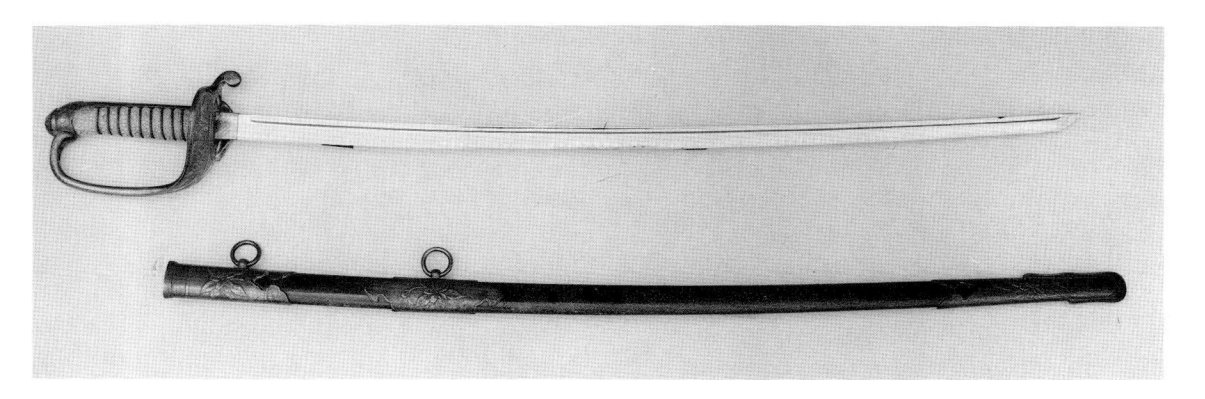

**Plate 172**  Hilt and top locket of the regulation 1914 pattern Commissioned Officers naval parade sabre. The typical naval decoration of a sakura (cherry blossom) with four radiating leaves is shown. The scabbard of this example is shagreen which is evident from the myriad of little diamonds. (Richard Fuller).

**Plate 173**  Guard underside of the regulation pattern Commissioned Officers naval parade sabre showing the typical decoration of sakura (cherry blossoms) and leaves set in one large panel. This is exactly as found on the full-sized Naval Officers kyu-guntō pattern. (Richard Fuller).

sword and scabbard 25 ounces.

Examples of both the standard and deluxe Commissioned Officers versions are fairly common.

## Regulation 1883 pattern Flag Officers (Admirals) naval parade sabre

Flag Officers were permitted to carry parade sabres which reflected their rank grade from 1883 to 1914 when this distinction is known to have been discontinued. However, it is possible that although the equivalent naval kyu-guntō was

# JAPANESE MILITARY AND CIVIL SWORDS AND DIRKS

**Plates 174, 175**  *Backstrap and side view of the rare 1883 pattern Flag Officers (Admirals) naval parade sabre showing the 5:7:5 floret kiri associated with that rank grade. (Brenton Williams).*

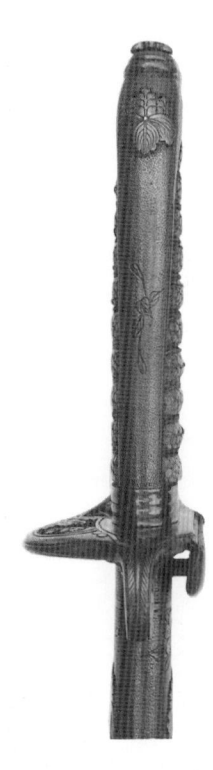

**Plate 176**  *Pierced handguard of the 1883 pattern Flag Officers naval parade sabre shown in Plates 174, 175. The decoration incorporates a 5:7:5 floret kiri and is totally different from the standard Commissioned Officers version. (Brenton Williams).*

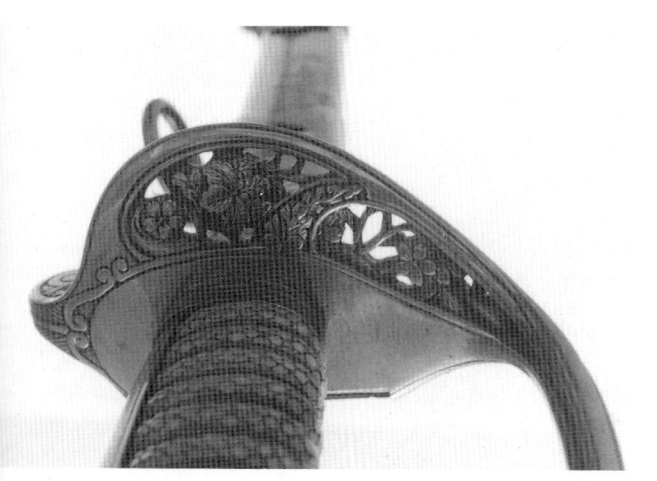

discontinued, the practice of wearing the parade sabre version survived somewhat longer.

A smaller version of the 1883 Flag Officers naval kyu-guntō, it even utilised the same backstrap and scabbard decorative features. Rank distinction is by means of the 5:7:5 floret kiri (Fig. 2 (i)) which are located on the backstrap, handguard, front and reverse of all three scabbard mounts. The obverse handguard of the example illustrated is pierced which is not a feature thought to be found on the equivalent full-sized kyu-guntō. Plate 176 shows the inside of the guard. The larger panel incorporates a 5:7:5 kiri and a kadosakura while the smaller panel only has a single kadosakura. Another example has a solid guard with the 5:7:5 kiri.

Gilded brass mounts, white samé grip and black leather-covered scabbard. Lacquered shagreen is also known. Normal rear-hinged flap and stud retention system. Chromium-plated blade which, on this example, is the double groove type shown in Fig. 59 (iv), but it does not have a habaki (blade collar). The brown kai-guntō knot must be a later addition.

Dimensions probably vary slightly. Hilt length of example shown 127mm (5"). Blade length 610mm (24"). Scabbard length 648mm (25½").

Such swords must be classified as rare.

## Possible Chief Petty Officers parade sabre

A most unusual naval parade sabre variant is shown in Plates 177, 178. The handguard is pierced and decorated with sakura and leaves similar to an Army parade sabre. It also features a sakura surmounting a foul anchor which is repeated on the upper backstrap (Plate 178). The backstrap motif also has a surround of leaves and the anchor has two interlocking rings (Fig. 23 (v)). This differs from the Army kyu-guntō for naval use shown in Plate 180 which has no surround and only one anchor ring. White samē grip with intermittent brass wire binding. Naval parade sabre guards are normally solid and lack any anchor motifs. Black leather scabbard with gilded brass mounts but decorated only with stippling.

An unidentified Japanese reference illustrates a similar parade sabre, although the backstrap motif lacks the leaf surround and both the anchor ring (or rings) and handguard detail are indistinct. The short caption just refers to a 'naval Chief Petty Officers sabre'. Identification is thus unconfirmed.

**Plate 177** *Underside of a possible Warrant and/or Chief Petty Officers parade sabre handguard showing the pierced sakura and leaf decoration with a foul anchor surmounted by a sukura.* (Rubens Rotelli).

It may be the parade version of the 1883 (Warrant? and) Superior (Chief) Petty Officers sword. However both these ranks had white grips while Petty Officer ranks had black grips. A similar sword, classified as unidentified, is shown on pages 78, 79 of *Swords of Imperial Japan 1868–1945* although the scabbard is decorated. Contemporary photographs of this pattern in wear have not been located. A very rare sword type.

On 3 October 1919 Petty Officers lost the use of a separate pattern and Chief Petty Officers carried the Commissioned Officers model..

**Plate 178** *Backstrap of the possible Warrant and/or Chief Petty Officers parade sabre shown in Plate 177. A raised foul anchor with two interlocking rings at the top is surmounted with a sakura (cherry blossom).* (Rubens Rotelli).

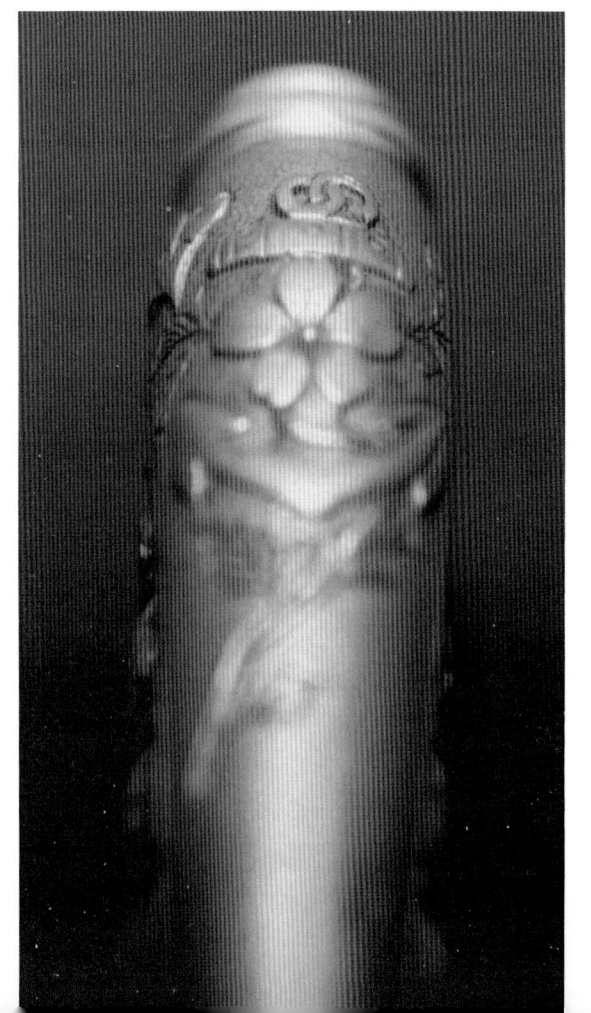

# Army Kyu-guntō for Naval Use

This variant of the army kyu-guntō may have predated, or was contemporary with, the 1883 naval pattern kyu-guntō. Such speculation is based on two examples of the 1875 Army pattern kyu-guntō featuring a raised foul anchor surmounted by a sakura (cherry blossom) on the upper backstrap. The anchor only has one ring at the top (Fig. 23 (vi)).[1]

The example shown in Plates 179, 180 has a white samē grip and a blue/brown shin-guntō sword knot. The obverse guard is pierced in the normal Army fashion. Army-style plated steel scabbard with two suspension mounts and a leather combat cover. Another reported example has the same anchor motif but a shagreen-covered wooden scabbard of the type used with the 1873 pattern Naval Officers sword shown in Plates 156, 157. Whether or not this is the correct scabbard type for this sword variant is unknown. Page thirty-eight of *Japanese Military Uniforms 1930–1945* (see Bibliography) has a drawing of a similar sword with a two-hanger steel scabbard but a black grip and a brown kai-guntō sword knot. The brief caption, in Japanese, translates as 'naval sword at [or from] the beginning [or inception]'. The meaning is unclear but seems to infer an early introduction date. Possibly the steel scabbard version was still used during World War Two by members of the Naval Landing Forces through personal preference, despite being a superseded pattern.

The pre-1942 Petty Officers grade cap badge is similar to the anchor and sakura used on this sword.[2] This may be coincidental, but use of the steel scabbard version by Senior Petty Officers cannot be ruled out without definitive information.

---

1 Note that the anchor arms continue through to the tip of both flukes and not just the right-hand fluke as occurs in the double ring anchor type in Fig. 23 (v).
2 Illustrated on page 43 of *Japanese Military Uniforms 1930–1945*. However, it differs from that used on this sword in that the rope does not continue below the sakura.

***Plate 179 (opposite)*** *Foul anchor and sakura on the backstrap of the Army kyu-guntō for naval use.* (Donald Barnes).

***Plate 180*** *The sword on the left is the very rare Army kyu-guntō for naval use which is differentiated by the foul anchor and sakura on the upper backstrap. It is compared with an Army Company Officers grade kyu-guntō on the right. This has the owner's name, Ota, applied in silver at the base of the backstrap, which is an unusual occurrence.* (Donald Barnes).

# Naval 1937 Kai-guntō

## Regulation 1937 pattern Commissioned and Warrant Officers naval kai-guntō

In 1935 Rear Admiral Koizumi Chikaharu, a sword expert, was requested by the Naval Artillery School to design a sword to replace the unpopular naval kyu-guntō which was judged unsuitable for use in combat. Article 24 of the Naval Dress Code (1937?) forbade the wearing of a 'long sword with military uniform at the time of war, training etc.' This referred to the popular use of civilian katana when worn with naval uniform. Thus they became prohibited since they broke naval dress regulations.

The Marco Polo Bridge (or China) Incident of July 1937 was a forewarning of war and precipitated urgent action to adopt a more suitable pattern. Therefore Imperial Ordinance no. 614 of October 1937 ordered the change to Admiral Koizumi's draft design which was based on the traditional tachi (slung sword). In the West it is now known as the kai-guntō, i.e. 'sea military sword'. This could be used to describe any naval sword but it has generally become accepted for this particular pattern. The actual designation is probably the 'Type 97 (1937) pattern Naval Officers sword'.

The Navy submitted a paper to the Japanese cabinet detailing the reason for change.[1] The 'existing long sword is not appropriate for practical use. It is necessary to adopt a convenient sword as quickly as possible which will be issued to the Landing Forces.' It was also stated that the Japanese sword was considered to be an incarnation of the samurai and the Yamato spirits, but the naval kyu-guntō did not reflect this.[2] Use was for Naval Officers, Special Service Officers and Warrant Officers but Ensigns, Midshipmen and Senior Petty Officers are also seen carrying this pattern; however, Junior Petty Officers were not entitled to wear it.

The design and specification describing all aspects and fittings of the sword was passed to the manufacturers on 7 December 1937 by means of Military Duty Order no. 161. The blade must be curved with a length determined by the user's height or his acquired school of swordsmanship.[3] The desirable length was to be more than 57cm (22½"). The shortest hilt length was to be 17cm (6¹¹⁄₁₆") and the scabbard should be more than 60cm (23⅝"). Therefore general usage did not commence until early 1938.

The gilded brass or copper hilt and scabbard fittings are quite distinctive, and are easy to distinguish from the Army shin-guntō (Fig. 10 and Plates 184 to 186). The decoration of sakura and leaves is normally in relief since the fittings are cast. However, engraved fittings are occasionally found, some of which could be hand-done. The

NAVAL 1937 KAI-GUNTŌ

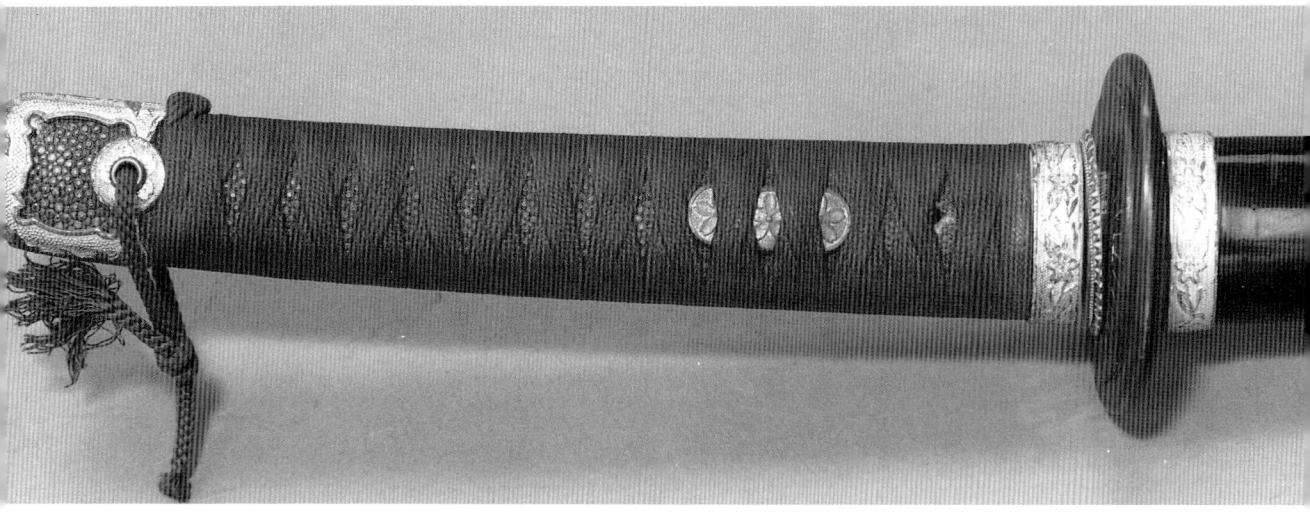

*Plate 181* Hilt of a standard kai-guntō with gilded brass fittings decorated ensuite with cherry blossoms (sakura) and leaves. The sakura and leaves on the kabuto-gane (pommel) are inlaid in copper. The menuki (hilt ornaments) are the typical naval type of three sakura with circular borders. Brown flat bound tape. Same base lacquered to give a black finish. The sarute (sword knot loop) is, in this instance, made from cord. (Clemson University, South Carolina).

*Plate 182* Upper section of a kai-guntō scabbard made of wood with a black lacquer finish. The kuchi-gane (throat) is decorated ensuite with the fuchi (hilt collar). Typical and distinctive kai-guntō style ashi (suspension mounts), each with a heart-shaped (boar's eye) opening and upper section decorated with sakura and leaves. (Clemson University, South Carolina).

*Plate 183* Lower section of a kai-guntō scabbard showing the shibabiki (strengthening band) which is distinguishable from the Army shin-guntō type by being a sakura and leaf design. The ishizuke (chape) is identical to the kabuto-gane (pommel). (Clemson University, South Carolina).

hilt is bound with a brown tape usually flat (Fig. 9), or with a twist (Fig. 9), over black samē (rayskin). Menuki (hilt ornaments) are three overlapping sakura, each bordered by a circle. The plain tsuba (guard) is ovoid in shape (known as 'naga-maru') being made of copper or brass with a dark blue-black shakudo finish. On either side is an ovoid copper dai-seppa in the form of sun rays with an alternating plain and stippled finish. Some have the rays alternating in copper and brass (Plate 75). Two or three brass seppa (washers) are then found on each side.

Blades are the traditional shinogi-zukuri form manufactured by any of the methods described later in the section on 'Military Sword Blades and Markings'. A brass or copper habaki (blade collar) is always present. Often a naval blade is distinguished by an 'anchor in a circle' stamp (Fig. 62 (xvi)) of the Toyokawa Naval Arsenal. In 1943 the Yokohama Naval Arsenal began to forge blades for distribution through the various naval clubs. These blades are officially described as 'Kikusui' and 'Kamakura'. The former is forged by the traditional method (probably at the Minatogawa Shrine forge) and sold at 250 Yen each, while the latter are the utilitarian stainless steel type at only 100 Yen each. 'Short swords' (presumably dirk blades) were also made of stainless steel for 15 Yen each.

Scabbards are wooden with a black finish of either lacquer over a leather base, polished samē or shagreen. The type probably depended on cost. Metal scabbards are not used.[4] A removable black combat cover can be found but is scarce (Plate 195). Suspension is by means of two ashi, of distinctive appearance having heart-shaped (boar's eye) openings on the sides, for use with a double sling belt. Scabbards with only one ashi are found with no indication that a second ashi was ever fitted. Usually these are the wooden field type covered with a non-removable black (and sometimes brown) leather cover. These were favoured by officers of the Naval Landing Forces who could wear Army uniforms and one-sling Army belts if they wished (see under 'Swords of the Naval Landing Forces'). Retention with the scabbard is either by means of a press button in the fuchi (hilt collar) and spring clip or just a push fit. Secondary retention with naval swords is rare. Plate 186 shows a most unusual system.

There was no rank distinction with this sword pattern since only a plain brown shin-guntō-type sword knot (Fig 1 (iii)) is worn.

A kai-guntō with a pure white samē scabbard and gold mounts has been reported but no other details are known. This is most unusual and must have been specially made, perhaps for presentation purposes.

By May 1943 the government had implemented a drive to obtain metal from civilians and temples to offset the shortage of essential war materials. This affected sword production and the naval arsenals were instructed to manufacture sword parts from the limited amounts of available copper (since brass had become an essential material for shell cases etc.). The lack of manpower, as well as materials, prompted further reductions in standards. A naval order dated 27 March 1945 stopped the use of gilding, samē and 'hairline engraving and carving'. Only one ashi (suspension mount) was to be fitted and the use of leather was to be avoided if possible. Indeed the order specified that scabbards were to be covered with imitation materials (and even bark) which was to be painted black. It is doubtful if there was much demand for naval swords by this time since the surface fleet had virtually ceased to exist and the only call for such items would be for defence.

Poorly made kai-guntō (Plate 326) are sometimes found, often being described as the late 'naval NCOs pattern'.[5] They do not comply with the 1945 regulations for late-war swords and, in the authors' opinion, are of non-Japanese manufacture, since very crudely constructed and using an excessive amount of brass for late war issue swords.

Kai-guntō are seen with service dress and land warfare uniform. They were probably not carried on board ship because of their size, the dirk being preferred. However, they were certainly taken into normal and midget submarines because several have been recovered from such vessels.

NAVAL 1937 KAI-GUNTŌ

*Plate 185* Kai-guntō ishizuke (chape) pattern with thickened drag. It is stamped in a panel with the patent or series number 213917. The obverse is also stamped JITSUYŌ SHIN AN TOKKYO, i.e. the patent practical new idea. These markings are identical to the shin-guntō version (Fig. 15). (Curt Peritz).

*Plate 184* Unusual brass kai-guntō fittings on the same sword. Both ashi (suspension mounts) have 12mm wide (5–7mm norm) boar's eye recesses. Note the shagreen scabbard covering characterised by a myriad of small white diamonds. The elongated kabuto-gane (pommel) is actually an ishizuke (chape) with a separate central sarute mount. The ishizuke (not shown) is identical. Compare with Plates 181, 182. They may be specially made or, possibly, limited production items. (Robert Dragos).

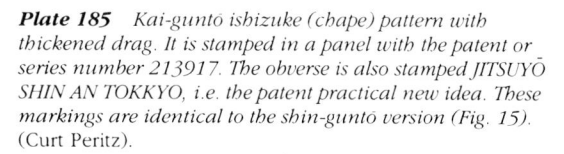

Indeed the first sword taken during World War Two belonged to Lieutenant Kazuo Sakamaki IJN who commanded the midget submarine M19. He was captured, along with his sword, off Waimanalo, Oahu, Hawaii during the Japanese attack on Pearl Harbor on 8 December 1941, thus becoming the first prisoner taken by the United States. It is a totally standard example with an unsigned blade and is now in the US Naval Academy Museum, Annapolis (cat. no. 42. 45).[6]

JAPANESE MILITARY AND CIVIL SWORDS AND DIRKS

***Plate 186*** *Unusual secondary retention system on a kai-guntō utilising a rope and hook. This would seem to have been added by the officer himself since it has not been seen on any other sword.* (Ron Gregory).

Dimensions, as would be expected, are variable. Overall length of sword and scabbard 977–987mm (38½"–38⅞"). Total weight 52–56 ounces. Blade length 660–694mm (26"–27⁵⁄₁₆"). Average blade width 33mm (1¼"). Hilt length 248–259mm (9¾"–10³⁄₁₆"). Scabbard length 708–728mm (27⅞"–27¹¹⁄₁₆"). Sword weight 39–45 ounces.

A short example with an old wakizashi blade and full-sized fittings has a hilt length of only 216mm (8½") and a scabbard length of only 584mm (23"). Such short kai-guntō are unusual. See also 'Air Force and Airborne Unit Swords' earlier in this book.

1 The information relating to the kai-guntō introduction, dress regulations and Yokosuka Arsenal have been taken from *The Changes of the Landing Forces Uniforms 1937–1940* by Etsuko Yagyu, which was kindly provided in translated form by Philip Goody and his co-researchers. Refer also to 'Kai-guntō. Its introduction and rationale' by Philip Goody, Japanese Sword Society of the United States Newsletter, vol. 26, no. 6, 1995. *Swords of Imperial Japan 1868–1945* gives an introduction date of 1934 which must be regarded as incorrect.
2 'Yamato-no-kuni' was the ancient name for Japan.
3 The school of fencing has previously not been considered by the authors as a reason for choosing the length of a 'military blade'.
4 Only one exception has been reported which was, apparently, owned by Lt-Gen Akinaga Tsutomu (Chikara), GOC 6th Division, Solomons. It is a kai-guntō with a brown painted alloy scabbard which has naval fittings. A General Officers shin-guntō knot is also present. There is no record that he was ever a naval officer so the reason for this occurrence is unknown. The Shintō period blade by Sukehiro appears to be a fake signature. Although a letter from Lt-Gen Sir William Bridgeford confirms ownership (he received it at Torokina, on Bougainville Island, in September 1945) it could, perhaps, have belonged to a senior divisional staff officer if he obtained more than one sword at that ceremony. It now resides in a private collection in Australia. The report of Akinaga's death in *Shokan* (see Bibliography) is incorrect.
5 Such an item is in the British National Maritime Museum (cat. no. 358) and is said to have come from a Petty Officer on a Japanese warship at Singapore in 1945. Probably it is a local, or Indian-made, fake produced at the end of the war for sale as a 'genuine' Japanese souvenir.
6 Illustrated in Plate 72, page 55, of *Military Swords of Japan 1868–1945* by the authors (see Bibliography).

# Unidentified Naval and Naval Prison Swords

Some of the items in this section have not been positively associated with any naval branch or unit although they possess naval characteristics or markings.

## Possible Meiji period naval sword

This sword has the general appearance and feel of a fighting weapon, perhaps some form of cutlass (Plate 187). This opinion is reinforced by the presence of an issue number and the naval feature of rear folding guard, although the latter has been found on later civil governmental parade sabres. Dating and condition suggest Meiji period (1868–1912) but a later date is possible.

Brass hilt fittings with a small obverse folding guard pierced to receive a scabbard stud. Downturned front quillion and up-turned rear quillion incorporating a large ring, set in a vertical plane for the sword knot. Black samé grip which originally had wire in the spiral groove. Raised sakura (cherry blossom) on the pommel over a female screw which engages with the threaded tip of the tang. There would have been a brass ring for the sword knot set in the raised pommel loop. Plain circular brass menuki (hilt ornaments) surmounting male and female screws which pass through a hole in the blade tang. The pommel obverse is stamped '80', which seems to be an issue number, while the reverse is stamped with three indistinct and unidentified marks.

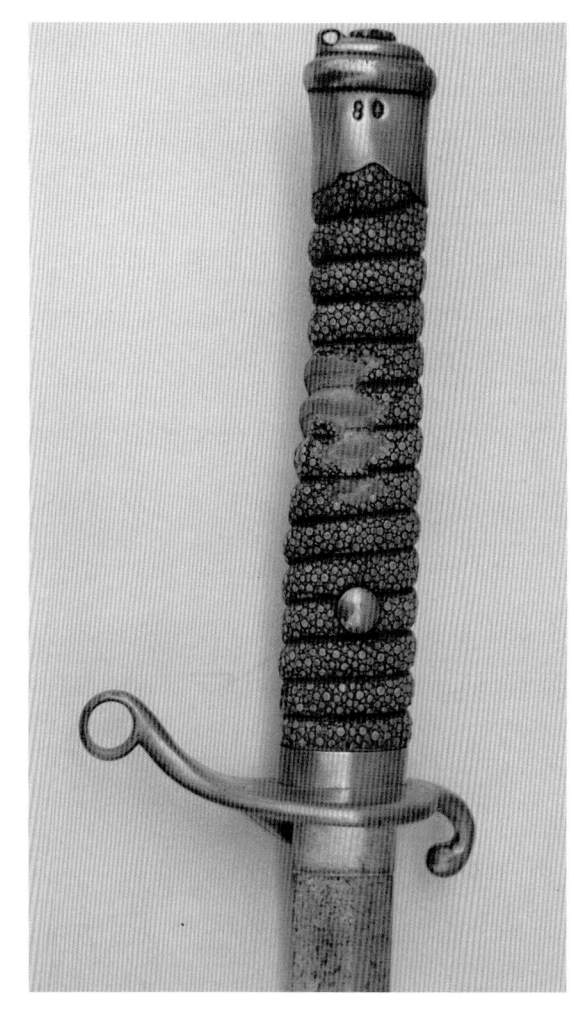

**Plate 187** *Unidentified Meiji period sword which is thought to be naval.* (Richard Fuller).

The unsigned blade is straight, which is a most unusual occurrence, but is of traditional Japanese style with a raised ridge line (shinogi). Copper habaki (blade collar). The scabbard, unfortunately missing, would probably have been of black leather with brass mounts incorporating a raised stud on the reverse of the top locket to engage with the hilt flap. Hilt length 191mm (7½"). Overall length of blade to guard 597mm (23½"). Maximum blade width 25mm (1"). Weight 29 ounces.

A very rare item because no other identical example has been located. Indeed, the straight blade could make it extremely rare if not a normal feature of this sword pattern.

## Unidentified short pattern naval sword

The sword in Plates 188, 189 has plain brass hilt fittings, originally gilded, with a backstrap, side-ears decorated with a raised discs on each side and a pommel incorporating a protruding ring for the sword knot. Inverse crossguard which is elongated at the rear and terminates with a large sword knot loop set in a vertical plane. Heavily lacquered black samé grip with brass wire binding in the grooves. Separate fuchi (hilt collar) incorporating a push button with a spring clip which engages with a slot in the scabbard mouthpiece. The hilt is secured to the blade by a pommel nut, the tang being threaded for this purpose.

Traditional-style blade of shinogi-zukuri form, probably factory-made since no temper line is evident, and a brass habaki (blade collar). Nickel-plated metal scabbard having a wooden liner, two suspension mounts and an engraved foul anchor (Fig. 23 (i)) on the obverse in the area of the drag (Plate 158). Hilt length 114mm (4½"). Blade length (to habaki) 483mm (19"). Scabbard length 549mm (21⅝").

The foul anchor design is similar to that used on the larger examples featured later in this section. Possibly this could indicate usage by naval cadets (see note two at the end of this chapter) or Naval Police. Dating is difficult and the sword may be later than it seems, perhaps into the nineteen-thirties. See Plate 278, which shows a similar sword that has been adapted for land warfare.

**Plate 188** *Unidentified short pattern naval sword.* (Brenton Williams).

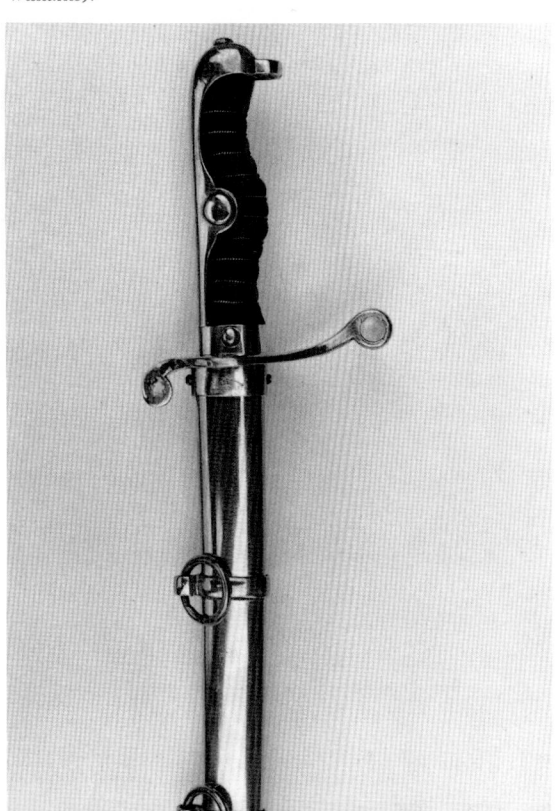

**Plate 189** *Engraved foul anchor on the scabbard of the unidentified short pattern naval sword.* (Brenton Williams).

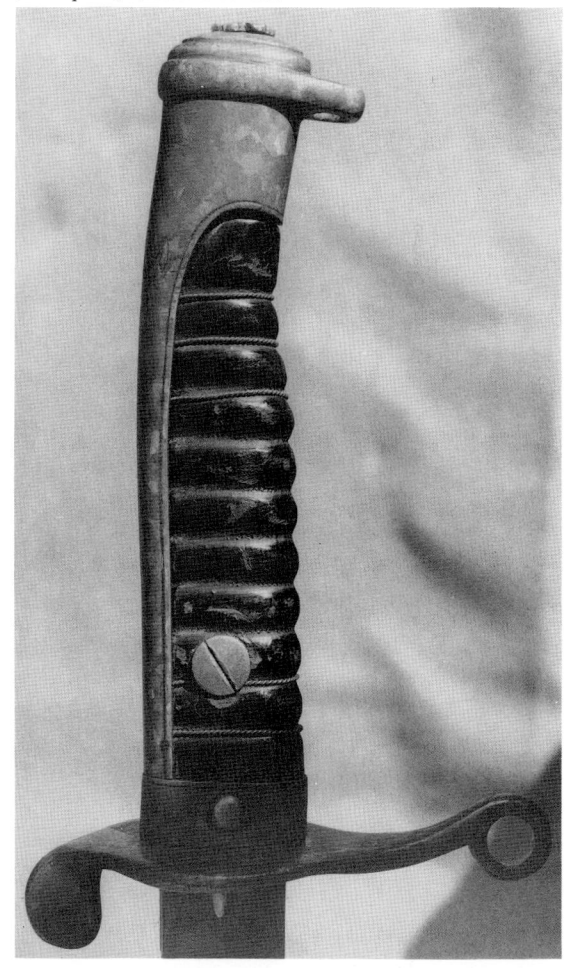

UNIDENTIFIED NAVAL AND NAVAL PRISON SWORDS

## 1895 pat. Naval Prison and Shore Patrol sword (Example 1)

Plain brass hilt fittings having a browned finish. A foul anchor (Fig. 23 (ii)) is engraved on the upper part of the straight backstrap which also has a decorative edge line. The pommel, surmounted by a raised sakura (cherry blossom), has a raised protruding band incorporating a circular hole for the sword knot. Dark brown/black leather-covered grip with intermittent brass wire binding. The small guard has inverted quillions with a large ring at the rear, set in a vertical plane, for the sword knot. The hilt is fixed to the blade by a brass male/female screw system terminating with a plain disc on one side and a slotted screw head on the other. Push button and spring clip scabbard retention system. Brown leather washer (buffer) against the guard. See Plates 190–192.

Contemporary blade of traditional shinogi-zukuri form, probably arsenal-made, with a brass habaki (blade collar). Wood-lined nickel-plated steel scabbard having two suspension bands, each with a steel hanging ring. The obverse is engraved near the drag (shoe) with a foul anchor which matches that on the backstrap (Fig. 23 (ii)). The throat band, secured by two screws, has a scalloped edge.

Dimensions of the few known examples are fairly consistent. Overall length of sword and scabbard 835mm (32⁷⁄₈"). Hilt length (from inside the guard) 152mm (6"). Blade length (including habaki) 635mm (25"). Maximum blade width 23mm (¹⁵⁄₁₆"). Weight of sword 24 ounces. Weight of sword and scabbard 39 ounces.

The correct knot is thought to be the brown leather Army NCOs type (Fig. 1 (iv)). One example in a private collection[1] is complete with a brown leather sword knot and a black leather sword belt. Both the handguard and belt buckle reverse are stamped '17' which confirms they are, in fact, associated items. The circular brass buckle has the same engraved foul anchor motif as the sword (Fig. 23 (i)) but lacks the usual roped border found on other naval belt buckles. This example is also unusual in that the unsigned blade is Kotō period.

Another sword has been found with the number '59' stamped on the obverse scabbard drag.

Naval cadets, at least during the 1930–45 period, used an unbordered cap badge with a similar foul anchor design[2] but they have not been observed with a sword specifically for their own use. *Swords of Imperial Japan 1868–1945* identifies this sword pattern as that used by Naval Prison Guards from 1895 and Naval Shore patrols from 1899. See Fig. 26 (i) of 'Naval Prison Service and Naval Police Swords and Dirks' later in this book.

The buckle motif for Petty Officers (Fig. 70 (iv)) and naval bandsmen (Fig. 71 (iii)) is similar but both have a roped border. The former carried their version of the 1883 naval kyu-guntō while the latter are not known to have worn a sword of any type. Swords of this type appear to be very scarce.

**Plate 190**  *1895 pat. Naval Prison and Shore Patrol sword (Example 1).* (Richard Fuller).

**Plate 191** *Engraved foul anchor on the backstrap of the 1895 pat. Naval Prison and Shore Patrol sword. (Example 1) in Plate 190.* (Richard Fuller).

**Plate 192** *Engraved foul anchor on the scabbard of the Naval Prison sword in Plate 190.* (Richard Fuller).

## 1895 pat. Naval Prison and Shore Patrol sword (Example 2)

This item is virtually identical to Example 1, including a foul anchor design engraved on the backstrap and scabbard (Fig. 23 (iii)). Usage is assumed to be the same. It has the number '93'

stamped inside the handguard, which is probably for issue purposes.

Brass hilt fittings with a black leather grip having intermittent brass wire binding. Light, machine-made blade of shinogi-zukuri form but with a flattened back edge. Tapered blade tang threaded at the top where it is secured by the pommel cap. Thin brass habaki (blade collar). Blade length 650mm (25 9/16"). Blade width at habaki 26mm (1").

Manufacturing quality is poor..

1 Donald Barnes collection.
2 Illustrated on page 57 of *Japanese Military Uniforms 1930–1945* (see Bibliography) under the heading 'Navy Officer School'. It shows the lower right-hand anchor arm continuing through to the tip of the fluke while the left-hand fluke is plain. This may be a distinguishing feature for cadets since the Meiji period 'double ring' anchor (Fig. 23 (v)), which is also found on Officer Candidates dirks, is the same. The right-hand fluke of Fig. 23 (iv)) is indistinct but also seems to match (v). However, examination of other Japanese naval badges (including Fig. 23 (vi)) and buttons indicates this feature is unusual since they have both flukes plain or the arms continue through both. Compare also the entwined ropes of Fig. 23 (i) to (iii). They are probably just variations on a theme, although (i) is virtually identical to the c.1930–45 Naval Cadets cap badge.

**Plates 193, 194** *The hilt and backstrap of the 1895 pat. Naval Prison and Shore Patrol sword (Example 2). The engraved foul anchor is also repeated near the scabbard drag as shown on Example 1.* (Anton Krahenbuhl).

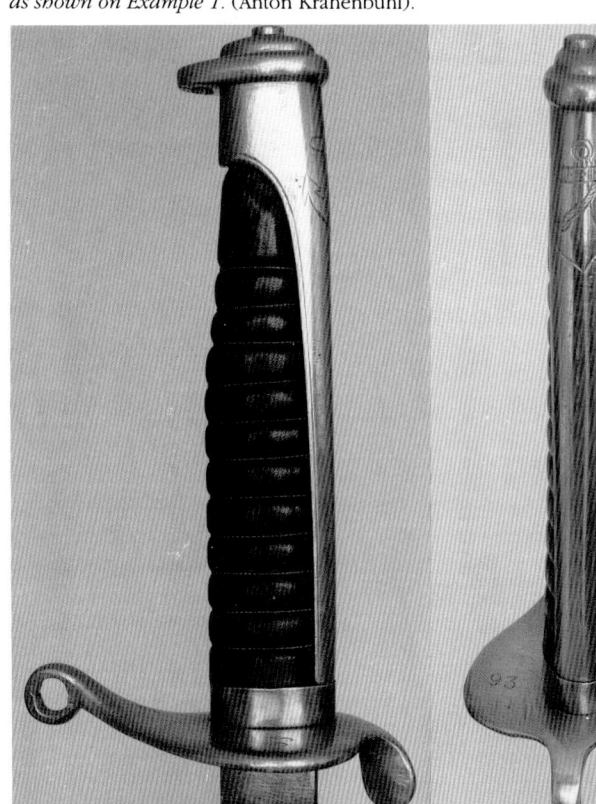

# Swords of the Naval Landing Forces (Marines)

Marines (Rikusentai) seem to have no prescribed sword pattern of their own apart from the c.1873 pattern shown in Fig. 25. After this was made obsolete around 1883, or so it is thought, they seem to have carried a mixture of swords as is indicated by their mixed function.

## Regulation c.1873 pattern Marines and Marine Artillery Officers and NCOs sword

The *Nippon no Gunso* (see Bibliography) illustrates a sword purely for officers and NCOs of the Marines and Gunners (Marine Artillery) although no photographs or actual examples have been seen to verify the details in Fig. 25.

It has a (brass?) half-basket guard, pommel, knucklebow and white samē grip without a backstrap. The obverse of the guard is engraved with what appears to be a central sakura (cherry blossom) and radiating leaves. The scabbard is metal with two roped suspension bands, each having a single hanging ring. Blade type is unknown.

Presumably this pattern was superseded by the 1883 naval kyu-guntō patterns, or army kyu-guntō for Naval use (Plate 179). Although traditional katana mounted for military use were more popular.

## World War Two Naval Landing Forces swords

The Joint Army and Navy uniform chart (JAN No.1) of September 1943 which was issued by the United States Military Intelligence says:

> 'Strictly speaking the Japanese have no Marine "Corps"; anyone in the Navy may be detached from regular shipboard duties for landing and policing operations. However, the need for large numbers of men for such duty means that a "Corps" performing Marine functions exists, though from an administrative viewpoint they remain regular Navy personnel. Except for the use of Navy insignia, Marine uniforms for Officers and Men is the same as that now used by the Army; but enormous individual variations may be expected. [Naval insignia is used] but some units may even use Army rank insignia. The least variable identifying features are a gold anchor on the cap or helmet.'

After the Pacific conquests they were reorganised for defensive and garrison duties, actually becoming anti-landing forces. The chart illustrates two officers (Ensign and Lieutenant) in tropical

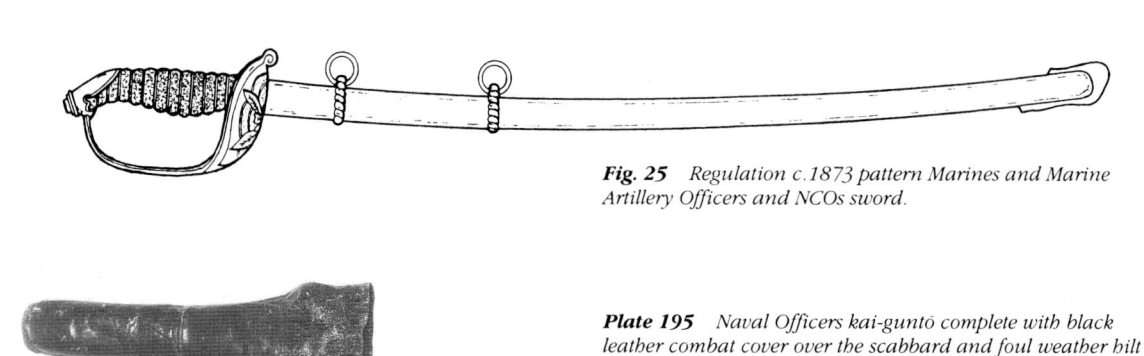

# JAPANESE MILITARY AND CIVIL SWORDS AND DIRKS

**Fig. 25** *Regulation c.1873 pattern Marines and Marine Artillery Officers and NCOs sword.*

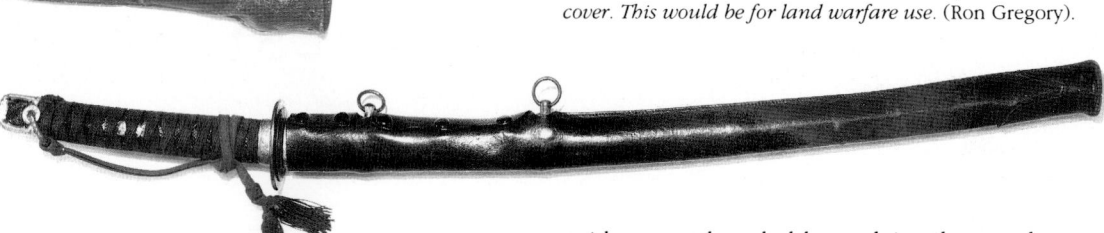

**Plate 195** *Naval Officers kai-guntō complete with black leather combat cover over the scabbard and foul weather hilt cover. This would be for land warfare use. (Ron Gregory).*

Army uniform with a narrow Army-style leather sword belt; however, the number of slings is not shown. No doubt the naval land warfare sword belt was also worn. Thus Army shin-guntō carried by naval officers and single-ashi (suspension mount) kai-guntō may be explained in this context (although late-war kai-guntō reverted to one ashi). The 1944 pattern Army (Officers) sword may perhaps also have been carried by NLF Officers, but it was not specifically intended for their use and no photographs of such usage have been located. Indeed, a special Army kyu-guntō, as shown in Plate 179, may also have been used in some cases. The brown sword knot worn with kai- and shin-guntō swords would be expected.

Naval Landing Forces personnel had more occasions to carry, and use, their swords in action than the regular sea-serving naval officers. It is said they did not favour the naval kyu-guntō for fighting and therefore preferred traditional mounted swords until the introduction of the kai-guntō in 1937. This seems to be confirmed by photographic evidence and probably explains the naval use of Army shin-guntō which became available in 1934, some three years before the kai-guntō. See Plates 84, 165, 198, 298.

One of the favourite methods of carrying a sword in battle was by means of a sling across the back, thus leaving both hands free. This may explain a kai-guntō in a private collection which has the entire scabbard close-bound with narrow strips of black leather.[1] The metal mounts have been placed over this and then painted to match the leather. The two suspension mounts (ashi) are widely spaced. The ring bosses have been mounted sideways and the hanging rings welded tight so that they remain in a vertical plane but are also sideways. The tsuba (guard) and dai-seppa (large guard washers) are steel and not the usual copper. The sideways position of the suspension rings is a most unusual occurrence and seems only to be explained if carried across the shoulders. However, no other example has been reported and no contemporary photographs have been seen of slung swords with the rings in this position, although this sword is, without doubt, totally genuine.

**Plate 196** *Kai-guntō in an Army-style brown leather-covered field scabbard with one ashi (suspension mount). The hilt has a white samē covering instead of the black normally associated with naval swords of this type. All hilt mounts are standard pattern kai-guntō. This was probably used by a naval officer in the Naval Landing Forces (Marines). (George Trotter).*

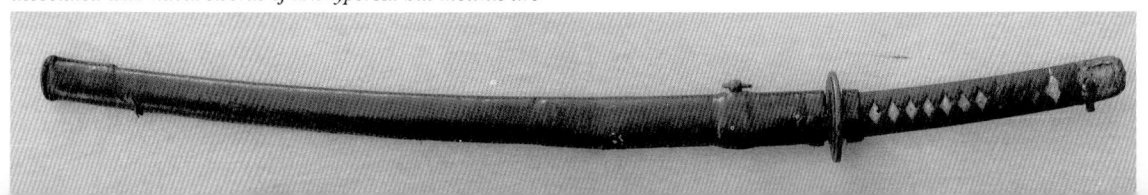

**Plate 197** Naval Landing Forces and Army troops in China, 1939. The saluting NLF officer in the foreground carries a civilian katana with a leather-covered scabbard and a single suspension mount. The officer immediately behind him holds a normal kai-guntō with two suspension mounts. The man to his left appears to be Army with a sword, of indeterminate type, having the leather bag type foul weather hilt cover. (Philip Goody).

1 Philip Goody Collection.

**Plate 198** Surrender of naval elements in Saigon to Sub-Lt Martin, the youngest Royal Navy officer present on 24 November, 1945. Four Petty Officers surrendered their swords but officers were allowed to keep theirs. The two swords on the table are standard kai-guntō, but that being handed over by a Chief Petty Officer has an Army tsuba (guard) and seems to be a scarce two-hanger Army shin-guntō with a leather-covered scabbard. He is wearing land warfare uniform which probably explains why such a sword is carried. Imperial War Museum.

## Shin-guntō with naval characteristics

This sword type is basically a 1934 pat. Army shin-guntō but has certain naval characteristics.

The kabuto-gane (pommel), menuki (hilt ornaments), kuchi-gane (scabbard throat), single ashi (suspension mount), shibabiki (strengthening band) and ishizuke (chape) are all standard shin-guntō pattern. However, the scabbard is wooden with a glossy black lacquered finish over a canvas base, the hilt is covered with a black canvas under a brown tape binding, and the oval tsuba (guard) is blackened steel. These three features are normally associated with the naval kai-guntō. Metal hilt and scabbard fittings are usually bright or gilded brass. The blades in these mounts always seem to be factory-made in traditional shinogi-zukuri form with the 'anchor-in-circle' stamp of the Toyokawa Naval Arsenal (Fig. 62 (xvi)) on the tang.

A number of these swords have appeared in recent years but only one was noted to have the standard kai-guntō tsuba and dai-seppa with the sun ray pattern. Another is known which has the ashi boss in the shape of a cylinder, but the reason for this is unknown. The tsuba and seppa can have matching assembly numbers.

The correct coloration of the sword knot is unknown although plain brown would be expected.

The 'mixed' appearance seems to indicate usage by officers and/or Warrant Officers of the Naval Landing Forces since conforming with the available information on the 'mixed dress' of that arm. However, the use of canvas hilt covering instead of samé suggests mid- or late-war production perhaps as a joint Army/Navy sword since the NLF had ceased to function as an offensive unit. Alternatively the Toyokawa Naval Arsenal may have been reduced to making swords solely for the Army when the demand for kai-guntō decreased along with severe naval battle losses. In any event no contemporary photographs have been seen showing this pattern in wear or being surrendered.

Examples currently sold in Britain seem to have emanated from America and none has been reported from British veteran sources. They could have been obtained from storage in Japan by occuping troops, but the authors suspect they are post-war assemblies, perhaps using surviving surplus blades and modern hilt/scabbard fittings. Low relief decoration, poorly finished seams, bright finish and lack of overall wear lends credence to this opinion.

*Plates 199, 200* Shin-guntō with naval characteristics. (Alan Clayton).

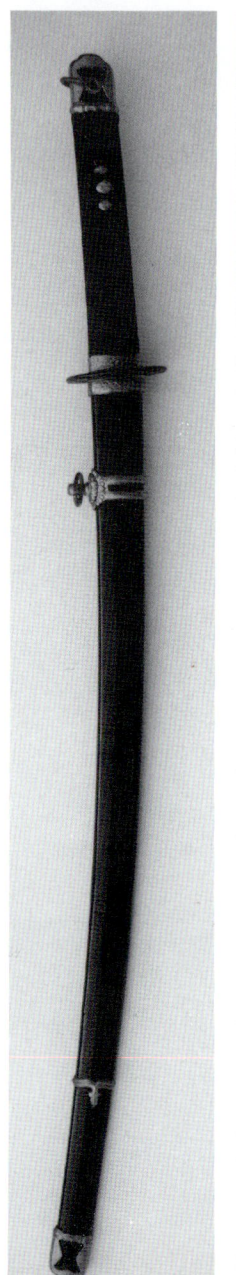

# Naval Prison Service and Naval Police Swords and Dirks

The Naval Prison Service, which was under the control of the naval Judge Advocate, wore light blue uniforms and distinctive sword patterns. The Navy Police, also controlled by the Judge Advocate, wore a similar uniform but different insignia from the prison service. Little has been learned about either.

*Japanese Military Uniforms 1930–1945* (see Bibliography) contains drawings of swords and dirks used by these service arms but detailing is, unfortunately, poor. However, they have been redrawn for Fig. 26. Two of the illustrated sword patterns have upturned rear quillions with integral rings for the sword knot but, unusually, they appear to be in the horizontal plane. Backstraps and scabbards seem to be undecorated.

The introduction dates are unknown except for the Naval Prison Guards and Shore Patrol sword which was introduced in 1895 (see pages 133, 134). The date of discontinuance is unknown.

Sword belts were black leather with the clasp designs shown in Fig. 71.

## Naval Prison Governors sword pattern
Fig. 26 (iii)
Gilded brass hilt fittings consisting of a separate pommel, white samé grip with a spiral brass wire binding and a decorated obverse guard (possibly pierced). There is no backstrap. Black (leather?) scabbard with gilded brass fittings consisting of a chape, two lockets and a separate throat. Each locket has a raised suspension band with a brass hanging ring. The fittings appear to be undecorated and have either semi-circular or heart-shaped (boar's eye) recesses. Gold bullion sword knot with tassels.

This sword pattern appears very similar, if not identical, to the 1883 pattern Petty Officers sword shown in Fig. 24 (i). However, the scabbard designs are different.

## Naval Chief Prison Guards sword pattern
Fig. 26 (ii)
Brass hilt and scabbard fittings. The hilt has a backstrap, black grip with intermittent wire binding and a cross guard with inversed quillions. The pommel has a projecting band incorporating a hole for a sword knot while the rear quillion has a large ring also for the sword knot. Black (leather?) scabbard with three mounts, the upper two having raised suspension bands and hanging rings. The fittings appear to be undecorated and have either semi-circular or heart-shaped (boar's eye) recesses. Gold barrel-shaped sword knot and cords.

# JAPANESE MILITARY AND CIVIL SWORDS AND DIRKS

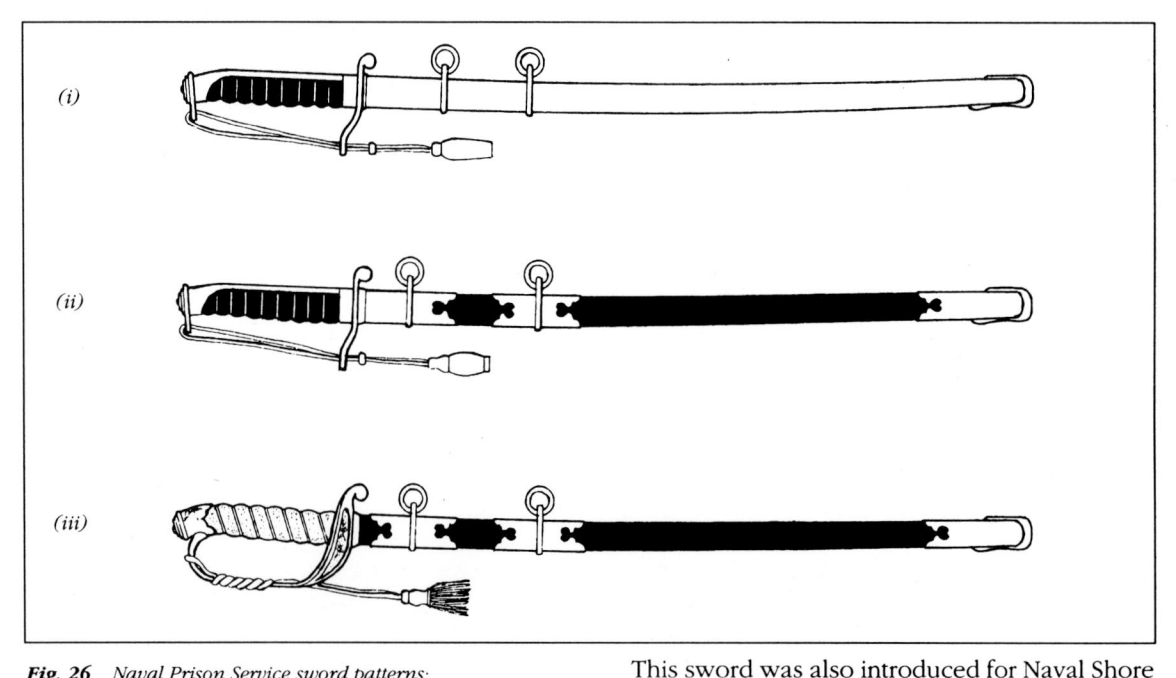

***Fig. 26*** *Naval Prison Service sword patterns:*
*(i)*       *Prison Guard and Shore Patrol (Naval Police).*
*(ii)*      *Chief Prison Guard.*
*(iii)*     *Prison Governor.*

***Fig. 27*** *Probable appearance of the Naval Prison Governors dirk based on that shown in* Japanese Military Uniforms 1930 –1945 *with sakura menuki (see Bibliography).*

## 1895 pat. Naval Prison Guards sword
Fig. 26 (i)
The brass mounted hilt is the same as used with the Chief Guards pattern. Nickel- or chromium-plated steel scabbard having two raised suspension bands and hanging rings. Gold elongated acorn sword knot and cords, although the Army leather NCOs type (Fig. 1 (iv)) may also have been used.

This sword was also introduced for Naval Shore Patrols from 1899. Examples are shown in Plates 190 – 194. although the quillions are set in the vertical plane.

### Naval Prison Governors dirk pattern
Fig. 27
This is believed to be similar to the standard 1883 pattern Commissioned Officers naval dirk but may be distinguished by a stippled decoration only and scabbard mount recesses which are heart-shaped (boar's eye) instead of the usual arrowhead form.[1] The pommel is in the form of a cap and is not pierced. Sakura menuki

The details given for this dirk pattern must be regarded as speculative.

### Naval Police sword pattern

This appears to be identical to the Naval Prison Guards pattern described above.

---

1 Forestry and Fire Officials dirks are the only other known patterns to have 'boar's eye' recesses.

# Naval Bandsmen Dirk

Naval bandsmen carried a separate dirk from 1883, or possibly 1896,[1] which remained in use until around 1940 and, possibly, through World War Two. Presumably naval band officers and senior NCOs also carried a sword when necessary. Since no specific type for band use has been located it may be assumed that the standard regulation naval pattern applicable to their rank was worn.

## 1883 pattern Naval Bandsmen dirk

This is a curved version of the naval 1883 pattern Senior Petty Officers and most Junior Officers model (Fig. 28). Only one example has been reported but the following details are believed to be generally applicable to all.

Hilt and scabbard fittings are plain gilded brass. Black samē, or perhaps shagreen, grip with intermittent brass wire binding. Short crossguard with inversed quillions and a plain backstrap. The blades, in the main, are probably machine-made but this is the only regulation naval dirk pattern to have a curved blade. Black leather-covered, or possibly lacquered, wooden scabbard. The upper mount has opposing hanging rings and the chape has a pronounced shoe (drag). Both fittings have arrow-shaped recesses.

A photograph of a naval band taken in 1938 clearly shows this dirk pattern carried in the regain position (Plate 201). It seems likely that such items were issued so some form of numbering may, perhaps, be expected. The known example has a silver mon on the backstrap which is indicative of private purchase by an officer or, possibly, an NCO.

Examples of this dirk pattern must be considered as being very rare.

**Plate 201** *The 1883 pattern Naval Bandsmen dirk being carried in Manchukuo (Manchuria), February/March 1938.* (Philip Goody).

---

1 Identified, but undated, in *Japanese Military Uniforms 1930–1945*. Dated as 1883 in *Imperial Japanese Daggers 1883–1945*. However, the *Nippon no Gunpuku* dates it as 1896 with the caption (naval) 'Military bandsman: Military music student sabre'. The introduction date is thus unconfirmed.

# JAPANESE MILITARY AND CIVIL SWORDS AND DIRKS

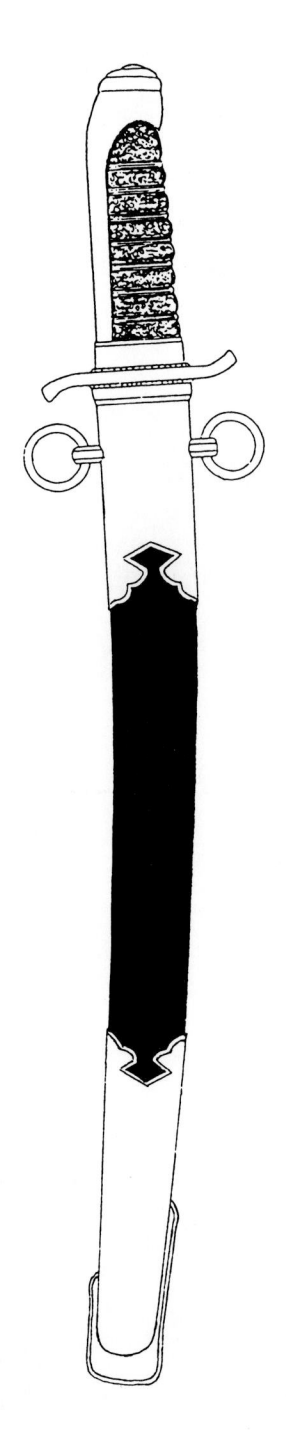

**Fig. 28**  *1883 pattern Naval Bandsmen dirk.* (Imperial Japanese Daggers).

# Current Japanese Self-Defence Forces Sword

Occasionally some officers of the modern Japanese Self-Defence Forces (JSDF) wear swords. The design is very similar to the naval parade sabre with a World War Two black leather scabbard and gilded brass mounts. Only one example has been examined by the authors. This was made by the English firm of Wilkinson Sword Ltd although it is likely there are other manufacturers. Differences noted between this and the former naval parade sabre are a straight blade and the scabbard decoration which is engraved and not in relief as on pre-1945 examples. The sakura and leaf motif has been retained.[1]

This model is now universal, being the only sword pattern carried by the land, air and maritime arms of the JSDF.

Sub-section 4 of Section 24 of the JSDF dress regulations[2] confirms Self-Defence officials/officers can wear ceremonial swords as follows:

(i) Military Attaché: when in full dress in a foreign country.
(ii) A commander of a training squadron and Officers and Warrant Officers so ordered by the commander: when in full dress in foreign countries or on long-distance cruises.
(iii) A leader of a guard-of-honour: when performing a guard-of-honour ceremony in full ceremonial uniform or performing the same duty on a long-distance cruise with a training squadron.
(iv) When so ordered by the Chief-of-Staff: when it is required for international courtesy.

Perhaps it is worth nothing that no World War Two veteran can, or will, appear in public with a military mounted sword from that period. They are regarded as 'war swords' and are forbidden under the current Japanese pacifist constitution.

---

1 Illustrated in Plate 88 (far left) of *Swords in Colour including other Edged Weapons* by Robert Wilkinson-Latham (see Bibliography), although the text wrongly describes it as 'Japanese Navy late nineteenth century'.
2 Courtesy of the Japanese Self-Defence Force. Translated by Yukio Yamaguchi. The approximate current strength of serving personnel is: Ground – 148,700 (thirteen divisions); Maritime – 43,000 (160 vessels); Air – 44,300 (460 aircraft).

# Naval Dirks

### 1872 Wilkinson Sword Company dirk

The Wilkinson Sword Company of England are believed to have made a dirk for approval by the Japanese Navy in 1872 (at the same time as their swords). However, no illustration has been located and it is certain that adoption was never sanctioned.

On 15 December 1873 two types of naval dirks were introduced for different rank grades.[1] No examples of either have been located to confirm the details given.

### 1873 pattern Senior Petty Officers, Midshipmen and Junior Officers model

A drawing based on the known information is shown in Fig. 29.

All hilt and scabbard fittings are gilded brass. The hilt has a backstrap, flattened pommel and short straight crossguard. White samé grip with intermittent brass wire binding. Straight blade of uncertain form but probably the same as the later 1883 revision. A habaki (blade collar) was probably not used. Black leather (covered?) scabbard with hanging rings on each side of the top locket and a chape without a drag (shoe). The very early examples may have had fixed rings. All metal fittings are plain except for the pommel top and, possibly, a decorative edge line to the scabbard mounts.

Use by Midshipmen seems also to have been from 1873 and probably continued after it was discontinued for the other rank classes mentioned above.[2] It may have lasted until the 1883 Commissioned Officers model was prescribed for all Commissioned Officer ranks in 1914.

### 1873 pattern Junior Petty Officers model

Similar in appearance to the Senior Petty Officers model but with steel mounts. It is uncertain if the scabbard is leather with steel mounts or is entirely constructed of steel. The former seems likely.

1873 pattern dirks were phased out and replaced by new and revised patterns. They were introduced on 20 October 1943.[3] It is unknown if Junior Petty Officers either continued with their 1873 pattern for a time or lost the right to carry a dirk.

### 1883 pattern Senior Petty Officers and the most Junior Commissioned Officers model

This was a minor revision of the 1873 pattern for

# NAVAL DIRKS

This pattern was worn along with the 1883 Commissioned Officers model until being superseded by it. However, the date when this occurred is unknown but may have been around 1914 when the sword patterns are known to have been revised.

Examples of these dirks are rare.

***Plate 202*** *1883 pattern Senior Petty Officers and the most Junior Commissioned Officers naval dirk.* (Herb Gopstein).

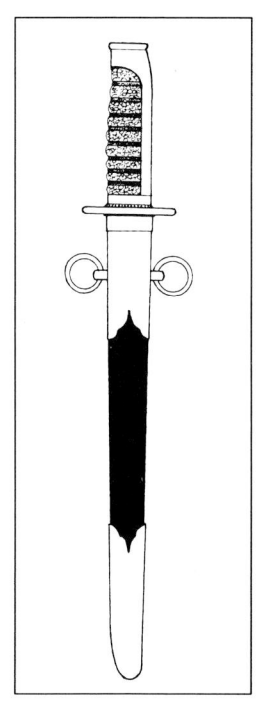

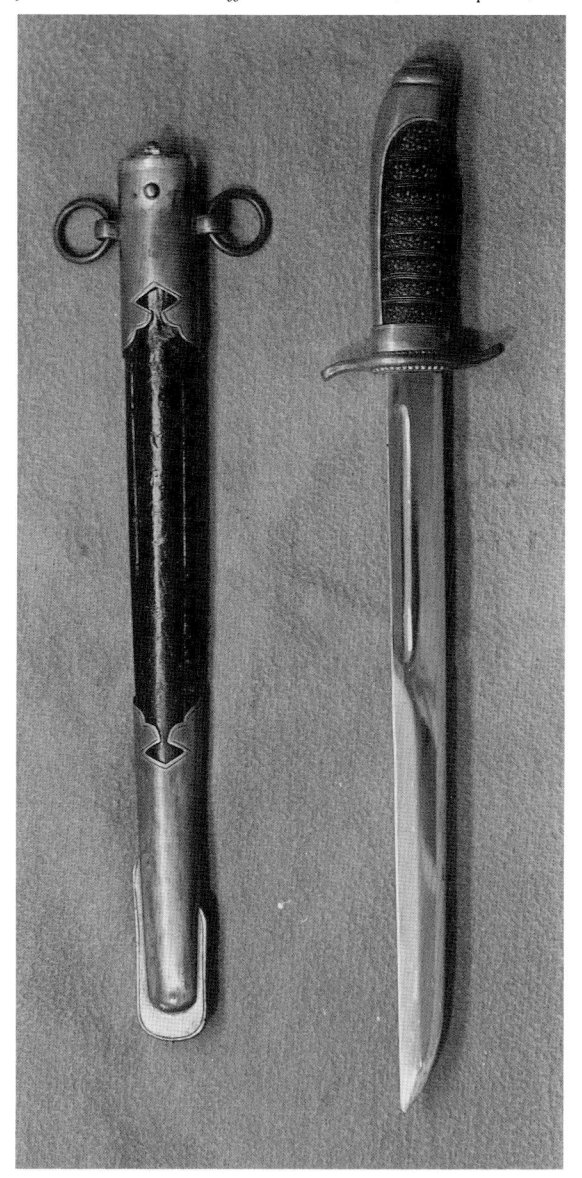

***Fig. 29*** *Probable appearance of the 1873 pattern Senior Petty Officers and Junior Commissioned Officers naval dirk. Midshipmen may have had a crossguard with inversed ends.*

the same ranks. The only modifications were to introduce a domed pommel and crossguard with inversed ends.

The example in Plate 202 has a brown samē grip with a brown lacquered leather scabbard. A push button with protruding spring clip is located on the scabbard locket reverse for retention with a slot in the crossguard. Single-edged, plated blade with a narrow groove extending from the ricasso for approximately half the blade length and then changing to a false top edge.

Dimensions could presumably vary but probably not by much. Overall length of dirk and scabbard shown 419mm (16½"). Hilt length 257mm (10⅛"). Blade length 257mm (10⅛"). Blade width 20mm (⁸/₁₀"). Scabbard length 311mm (12¼"). Total weight 14 ounces.

Another example has been found with a black horn grip and scabbard of black leather over a wooden liner.

Naval bandsmen used a curved version as has previously been described.

JAPANESE MILITARY AND CIVIL SWORDS AND DIRKS

## 1883 pattern Commissioned Officers model

This is a new pattern based on the traditional tantō (dirk with a guard) which became the most common of all naval dirks. Initially introduced for Commissioned Officers above the most junior grade on 20 October 1883.[4] Later, possibly 1914, it superseded the 1883 Senior Petty Officers/Junior Commissioned Officers dirk to become the universal pattern for all Commissioned Officers, Senior Petty Officers and Midshipmen.[5] Wear continued until the end of World War Two with a number of variations being found. Flag Officers (Admirals) also appear to have carried the standard model with no indication of rank, although a better quality may, perhaps, be expected.

The grip is tapering with a spiral groove and brass wire binding. A pommel cap is usually surmounted by a raised sakura (cherry blossom). The grip covering is normally white samé (ray skin). Sometimes black samé is found although the significance of this, if any, has not been discovered. Gilded brass crossguard with inversed ends. Mass-produced plated and grooved blade fixed to the hilt by a male-female screw system surmounted by sakura which form menuki (hilt ornaments). Brass habaki (blade collar). The

**Plate 203** *Typical standard 1883 pattern Commissioned Officers naval dirk. This example has a leather scabbard. A common item. (Mike Hadlum).*

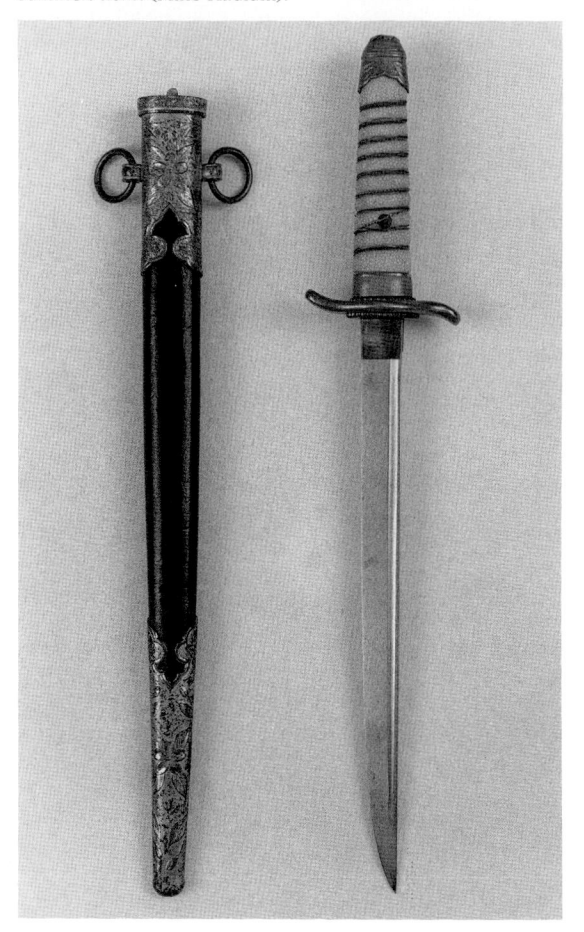

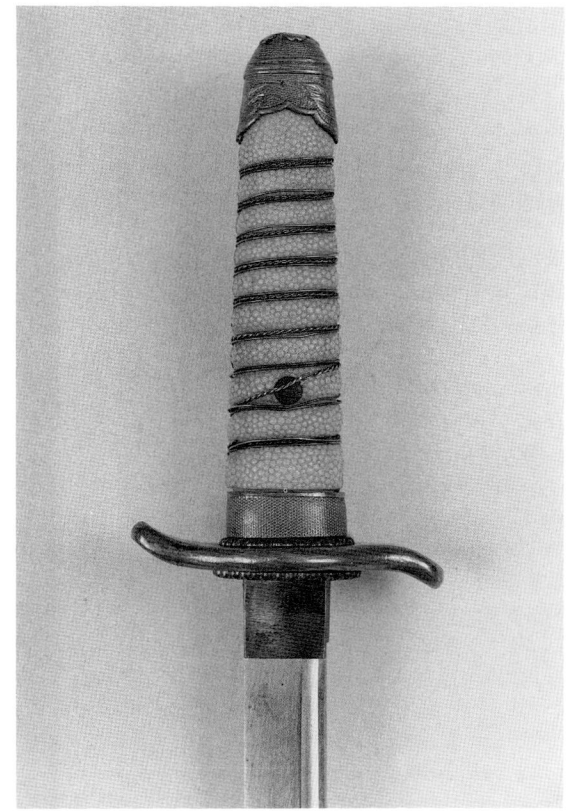

**Plate 204** *Hilt detail of the standard 1883 model Commissioned Officers naval dirk. Normally the blade is fixed to the tang with a male-female screw system which passes through to the other side and terminates with a brass sakura (cherry blossom). However a plain wooden peg is used on this example. The fuchi (blade collar) of this example has only a stippled decoration. (Mike Hadlum).*

# NAVAL DIRKS

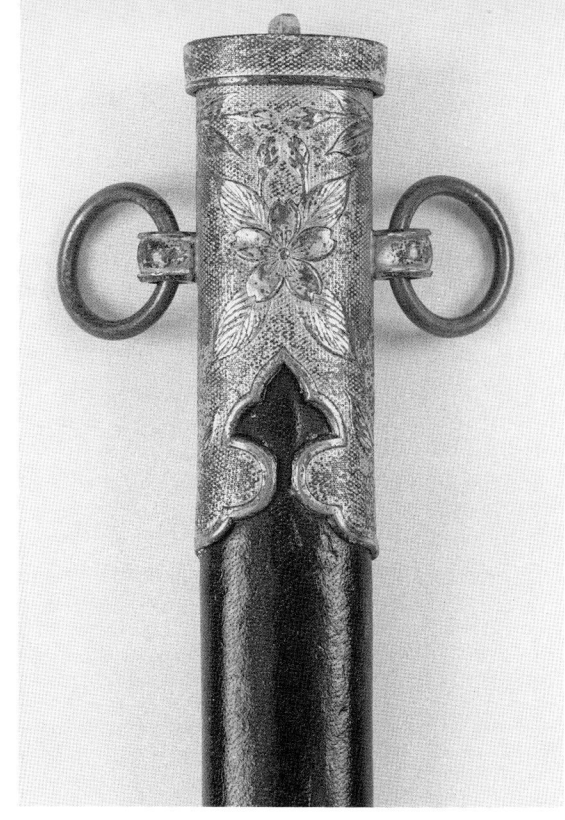

**Plate 205**  *Top scabbard locket of a standard 1883 model Commissioned Officers naval dirk showing the typical naval decoration of a sakura (cherry blossom) with four radiating leaves and two buds which is also found on naval swords. Retention is by means of a spring clip set in the scabbard which projects into the hilt crossguard, the release button being on the reverse of the scabbard locket.* (Mike Hadlum).

**Plate 206**  *Pommel cap of a standard 1883 model Commissioned Officers naval dirk showing the typical sakura (cherry blossom) in relief* (Mike Hadlum).

tapering wooden scabbard may be covered with black or brown leather or lacquered shagreen. Two gilded brass mounts decorated ensuite with sakura and leaves in relief, and a stippled background. The upper mount (locket) has opposing hanging rings. Reverse push button and spring clip which projects upwards to engage with a slot in the crossguard. This system became standard on nearly all Japanese military and civil dirks.

Quality and style of decoration varies. The basic model is shown in Plates 203 to 206 but the normal deluxe version has a decorated fuchi (hilt collar) and a more elaborately decorated pommel as shown in Fig. 30. More elaborate versions, as shown in Figs. 32, 33, 34, could be purchased according to the financial means of the individual officers.

There are thought to be a number of manufacturers including private companies, but only the Toyokawa Naval Arsenal (Fig. 62 (xvii)) has been identified. The underside of some crossguards have stamps which are believed to be trademarks (see Fig. 61 (xiii), (xiv), (xv), (xxiv)). However, most are unmarked.

Examples with old tantō, or hand-forged blades are found only rarely (Fig. 34). These are usually wider than standard since the fittings had to be specially made. Silver family mon forming the menuki have been seen on one example.

Naval dirks with contemporary hand-forged blades were awarded as prizes, perhaps on behalf of the Emperor, by the Naval Academy and by individuals (see under 'Shōwa period presentation swords and dirks' later in this book). The name, or details, of the donor was normally engraved on the habaki (blade collar). Unfortunately the recipient is rarely mentioned.

By the end of the war, materials such as brass and samé became scarce. Therefore late-war dirk quality became much poorer omitting the habaki

# JAPANESE MILITARY AND CIVIL SWORDS AND DIRKS

and utilising moulded celluloid grips imitating samē which could even include the grip wire and menuki. Celluloid crossguards and pommels, gilded or copper-plated, were also employed. Blade construction was simplified by omitting the groove and tapering the tang which was threaded at the top to engage with a pommel cap surmounted by a sakura (Fig. 31). A very late version with a celluloid grip over a wooden liner has a moulded plastic scabbard and hilt fittings painted to resemble gilding. The fuchi and pommel are separate celluloid items glued to the grip. The only metal items are the seppa, scabbard throat and hanging rings. A plain unplated blade is secured by a wooden peg which passes through both sides of the integral grip sakura menuki. No habaki or spring clip retention system is used. Wooden scabbard covered in thin black leather.[6]

**Plate 207** *1883 pattern Commissioned Officers naval dirk with a lacquered shagreen scabbard and black samē grip. This is probably a special purchase variation rather than having any special significance. The hangers appear to be post-war additions and are probably not Japanese. (Ron Gregory).*

No doubt there are other celluloid and metal combinations.

Some government and civil organisations used similar style dirks with the same sakura and leaf decoration as the Navy. This has often resulted in confusion which, hopefully, this book will clarify to some extent.

Even mass-produced dirks were highly regarded by their owners as is evidenced by the following reminiscences of naval Medical Officer Lieutenant Ozeki of the Naval Landing Forces:[7]

> The war ended for me as an Australian PoW on a tiny island south of New Guinea. I was stripped of

**Plate 208** *Early, and scarce, variation of the 1883 pattern Commissioned Officers naval dirk with white samē grip and shagreen scabbard. Scabbard fittings are decorated with a number of sakura (cherry blossoms) which are reminiscent of the 1873 model Commissioned Officers naval sword (see Plate 160). The open panels of the pommel and scabbard fittings are a very distinctive shape. The general impression is that this is an early version of this dirk pattern (perhaps 1883–1914 when the naval sword pattern was superseded). Other virtually identical versions are known with menuki (hilt ornament) in the form of plain discs (instead of sakura) and triple lozenge-shaped chrysanthemums. (Ron Gregory).*

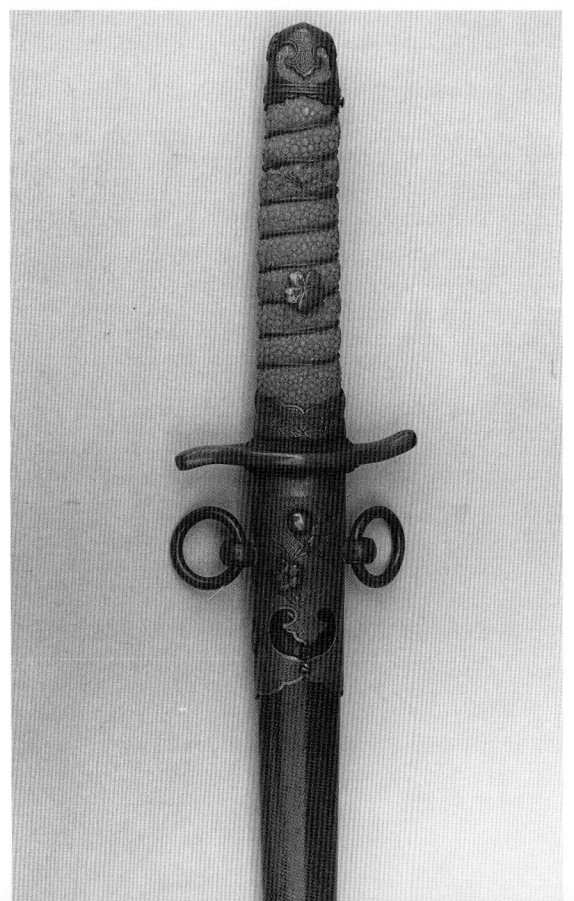

all my equipment by souvenir-hunting Aussies. The only thing I wish they wouldn't have taken was my naval dagger. That is a naval officer's soul and honour . . . I still think about that dagger daily. The naval dirk is a symbol of not only his authority but social status and even virility. No woman could resist a man in white with a dagger at his side. We had a saying that a naval dagger was a charm that kept away the three evils: Disease, Evil spirits and Ugly women.'

**Plate 209** *Japanese war artist's drawing of naval guns in action on a Japanese warship in 1904. The officer on the far right is in summer service dress. Both are clearly shown with the regulation 1883 Commissioned Officers naval dirk which indicates they were carried in action. (Richard Fuller).*

**Plate 210** *This photograph confirms that 1883 pattern Naval Officers dirks were carried on board Japanese warships. It shows dirks, hangers, belts and caps hung from hooks in an officers' ward room during World War Two. (Richard Fuller).*

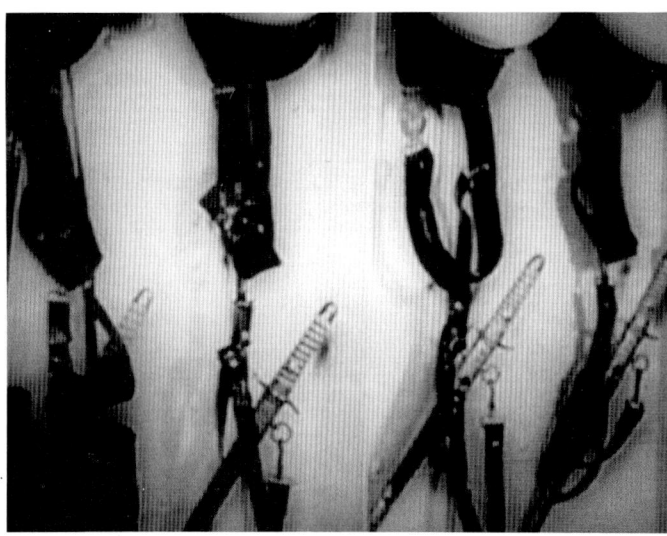

## 1883 pattern Officer Candidates naval dirk

Little is known regarding the ornate dirk pattern shown in Fig. 35 which was presumably worn on full dress occasions by Officer Cadets (Candidates) at Etajima Naval College[8] or other approved naval educational establishments.

The introduction date is given as 1883[9] but when it was phased out, or if modified, is unknown. Possibly a short-lived pattern. The design is totally unlike other Japanese dirks since it has a most unusual, and distinctive, large canted pommel. Similarly the blade shape, known as unokubi-zukuri, is not found elsewhere. The only known exception is that shown in the next section which may be a Petty Officer Candidates version.

No example has been located so it is assumed the fittings are gilded brass with a white samé grip and black lacquered wooden scabbard. All fittings including the hilt backstrap are decorated with sakura and leaves (see Fig. 35). However, the pommel top and one side of the locket have the same foul anchor design with interlocking rings (Fig. 23 (iv)) as found on the 1873 Commissioned Officers naval sword pattern.

This must be regarded as a very rare dirk.

# JAPANESE MILITARY AND CIVIL SWORDS AND DIRKS

## Unidentified variation of the 1883 pattern Officer Candidates naval dirk

A less ornate dirk, obviously based on the 1883 pattern Officer Candidates naval dirk, is shown in Plates 211 to 213. Whether it is a later version or different model used by Petty Officer candidates (which seems more likely) is unknown. The overall impression is of a fighting weapon rather than a dress dirk. 'It seems that when Midshipmen received the same pattern dirk [as Commissioned Officers] they had a longer weapon.'[10] Whether that statement was actually intended to mean this particular pattern is unknown, but no other regulation Naval Officers dirk has been located with such an unusually long blade.

Brass hilt fittings consisting of a large canted pommel and a backstrap engraved with a roped border and foul anchor having two interlocking rings (Fig. 23 (iv)). Black lacquered wooden grip with brass wire in the grooves. Short crossguard with inverse ends and a wide fuchi (hilt collar) which have been cast integrally. Brass male and female dome-headed screws pass through the fuchi to secure the hilt to the tang. The crossguard underside is stamped '108' in Western-style numbers which is probably for issue purposes. Small unidentified Japanese assembly marks have been scratched on. No spring clip retention system is utilised.

Unsharpened machine-made unokubi-zukuri blade which is unplated and of substantial construction being a maximum of 7mm thick. No habaki (blade collar) is used. There is a leather washer against the crossguard. The tang tapers, becoming curved and very narrow at the end (as in Fig. 35) to engage with a hole in the pommel crown; however it is not threaded. Japanese

**Fig. 30**  *1883 pattern Commissioned Officers naval dirk. Additional decoration to the fuchi (hilt collar) indicates this is a deluxe model which may be expected to have a lacquered or samé-covered scabbard. (Imperial Japanese Daggers).*

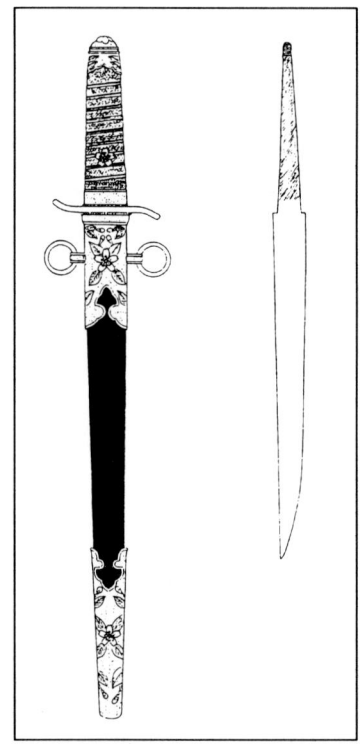

**Fig. 31**  *Late World War Two version of the 1883 pattern Commissioned Officers naval dirk. This has a moulded celluloid grip and plain blade with a tapered threaded tang. (Imperial Japanese Daggers)*

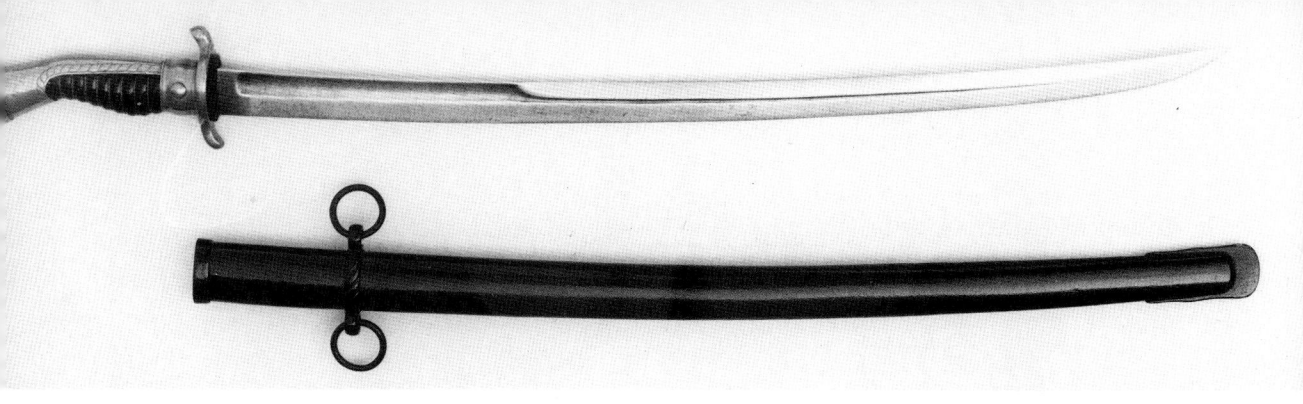

assembly numbers and marks are scratched on, above and below the tang screw hole. Black (possibly repainted) alloy scabbard. It has a separate throat, roped steel suspension band, opposing hanging rings and a shoe. There is no provision for a knot. It may be more correct to refer to this as a hanger or short sword rather than a dirk because of the blade length.

Overall length of dirk and scabbard 669mm (26⁵/₁₆"). Hilt length 120mm (4¾"). Blade length 520mm (20⁷/₁₆"). Scabbard length 555mm (21⅞"). Total weight of dirk and scabbard 26 ounces.

**Plate 211** *Variation of the 1883 pattern Officer Candidates naval dirk with a blade of unokubi-zukuri shape. Usage is uncertain but is is a very rare item. (Richard Fuller).*

This is the only example of this dirk pattern located and thus must be considered very rare.

1 Dating and usage is confirmed in *Swords for Sea Service* by May and Annis (see Bibliography). However, use by Midshipmen is not mentioned.
2 The introduction date is also confirmed in the *Nippon no Gunso* (see Bibliography) where it is identified as being for Midshipmen only. However, the crossguard is drawn with inversed ends. The *Nippon no Gunpuku* also shows the same drawing and states use was by Midshipmen; however, that gives the introduction date as 1887.

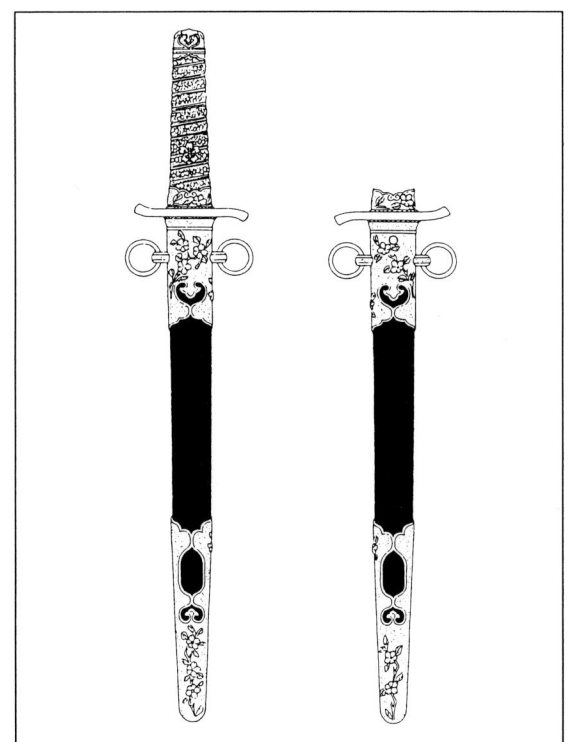

**Fig. 32** *Obverse and reverse of another early variant of the 1883 pattern Commissioned Officers naval dirk. (Imperial Japanese Daggers).*

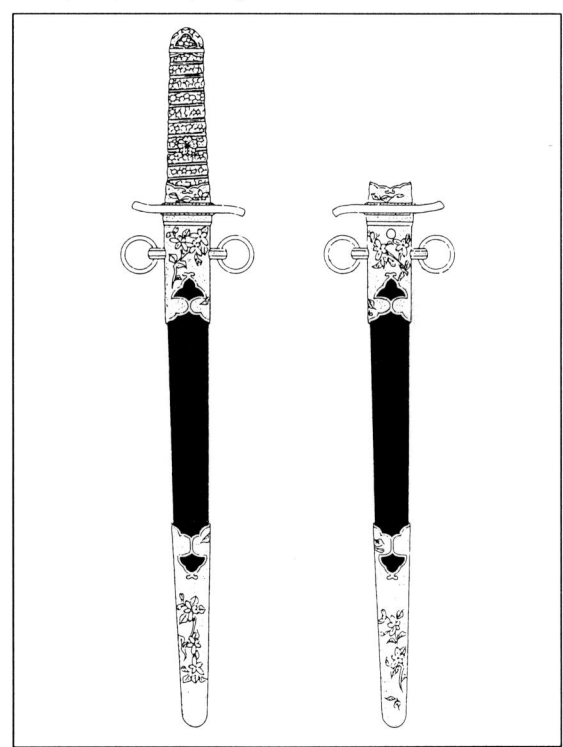

**Fig. 33** *Obverse and reverse of an early 1883 pattern Commissioned Officers naval dirk variation similar to that shown in Plate 208. (Imperial Japanese Daggers).*

# JAPANESE MILITARY AND CIVIL SWORDS AND DIRKS

***Plates 212, 213*** *Hilt details of the variant 1883 pattern Officer Candidates naval dirk showing the distinctive and unusual canted pommel and engraved backstrap foul anchor which incorporates two interlocking rings. (both Richard Fuller).*

---

3 Confirmed in *Swords for Sea Service* by May and Annis.
4 According to *Swords for Sea Service* by May and Annis.
5 The *Nippon no Gunsō* (see Bibliography) first illustrates this dirk model together with the four 'naval kyu-guntō sword variations which it dates as c.1896 but these are now known to be 1883.
6 Sergio Pelone collection.
7 Issue no. 149 of the *Banzai* bulletin. 1994. Translated by Dan King.
8 The educational Museum of the Japanese Maritime Self-Defence Force at Etajima could not identify this, or the following dirk pattern, because it 'needed very special knowledge'. Therefore one can only conclude that there are no examples in the JMSDF museum.
9 Shown as a crude drawing under this date on page 140 of the *Nippon no Gunpuku* (see Bibliography) and captioned as such in *Imperial Japanese Daggers 1883–1945*.
10 Quoted from *Swords for Sea Service* by May and Annis.

---

***Fig. 34*** *Obverse and reverse of an early variant of the 1883 pattern Commissioned Officers naval dirk. The wide hilt and scabbard are indicative of the use of an old tantō blade. (Imperial Japanese Daggers).*

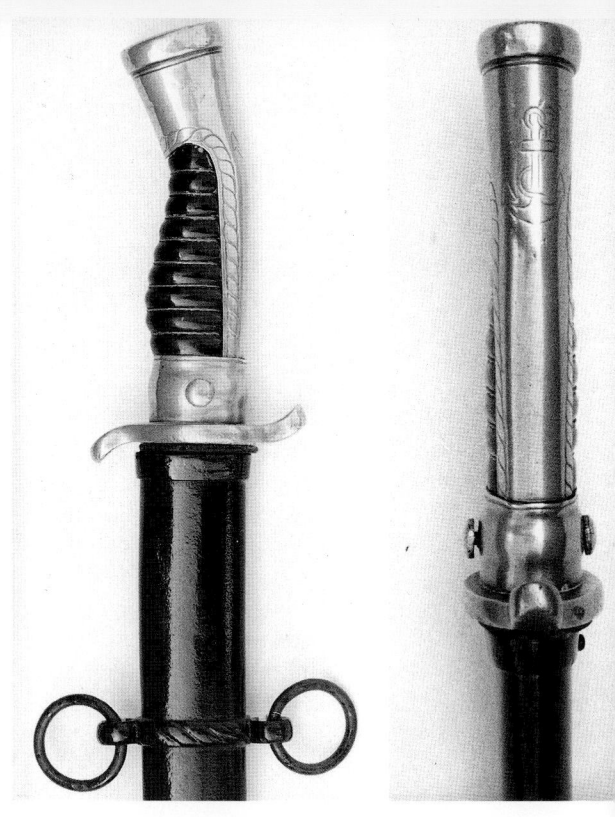

***Fig. 35*** *Obverse and reverse of the very rare 1883 pattern Officer Candidates naval dirk. (Imperial Japanese Daggers)*

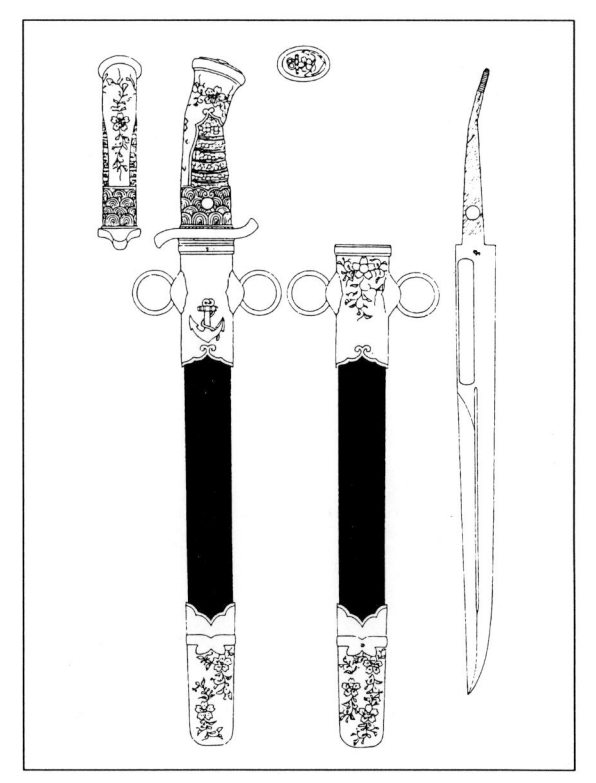

# 1918 Pattern Gensui (Field Marshals and Fleet Admirals) Sword

The honorary title of Gensui (Field Marshal or Fleet Admiral) was created in May 1898.[1] It was rarely awarded, and then only to distinguished full Admirals or Generals who were appointed to the Gensuifu (Board of Field Marshals and Fleet Admirals). This august body acted in an advisory capacity on military matters to the Emperor. However, there was no specific uniform or rank distinction and the recipient's current command remained unchanged.

Those appointed received a Gensui-kishō (Gensui badge) and a Gensui-tō (Gensui sword), at least from 1918.[2] The latter was personally presented by the Emperor and it is likely the former was presented at the same time. The Gensui-kishō (Gensui badge) was worn on the right breast of the normal full dress uniform. It is a gold, silver and enamelled oval badge featuring crossed red and white rising-sun flags, the staffs of which are tied with a blue ribbon. Surmounting the upper portion are purple *Paulownia* (kiri) flowers above three kiri leaves. The whole item is topped by a single raised gold chrysanthemum (kiku).[3] The reverse is inscribed 'MEIJI SAN JŪ ICHI (NO) GATSU SEITEI', i.e. enacted (or established) in May 1898.[4]

The regulation Gensu-tō was authorised by an Imperial decree of the Emperor Taishō dated August 1918.[5] The design is traditional, based on the kenukigata-tachi carried by Fujiwara Hidesato who defeated the rebel, and self-proclaimed, emperor Taira Masakado in AD 940. This actual sword still exists at Ise where it is designated as 'Important Cultural Property'. Fig. 36 is drawn from a photograph of the Gensui-tō of the World War Two Field Marshal Hata Shunroku.[6]

The metal saya (scabbard) and hilt (tsuka) are made of dark bluish-black rōgin[7] with matching ornately decorated gold (or gilded brass?) fittings and edge straps. Both sides of the saya and tsuka have raised, but widely spaced, juroku-kiku (Fig. 2 (v)) in gold. On each side of the hilt (tsuka) is a narrow decorative band which widens at the ends. This is called a kenukigata (hair tweezer shape) from which this style of sword gets it name. Unfortunately details of the ornate tsuba (guard) have not been located. The traditional-style sword knot (tsuyu-no-o) consists of gold cords, which pass through the pommel (kabuto-gane), and terminate with metal ends of gold. The saya (scabbard) has a kuchi-gane (throat), shibabiki (strengthening band), ishizuke (chape) and two

**Plate 214** 'Gensui Hakushaku Tōgō Heihachirō', i.e. Fleet Admiral Count Tōgō Heihachirō, who was Japan's greatest Admiral and C-in-C Combined Fleet at the time of his victory over the Russian Second Pacific Squadron (formerly the Baltic Fleet) at the Battle of Tsushima in May 1905. This photograph was probably taken not long before his death on 30 May, 1934. His 'Marshals' badge is located immediately above the lower decoration on his right. The sword is the 'Gensui' pattern, but because it is edge on details are unclear. (Brenton Williams).

**Plate 215** Unidentified Fleet Admiral holding his Gensui sword at the funeral of Admiral Yamamoto Isoroku in 1943. Although specific details are unclear it is obviously of tachi form with two ashi (suspension mounts). (Philip Goody).

The only other reported example has a blade of the same shape which indicates that it may be prescribed for this pattern. The grooves stop short of the gold habaki (blade collar) where a gold juroku-kiku is inlaid in relief. At least one Shōwa period smith, Kotani Yasunori, made these blades during the period 1935–45 when he was an instructor at the Yasukuni Shrine School for swordsmiths.[8] Unfortunately it has not been ascertained if the tang was engraved with a presentation inscription or recipient's name, although the smith's name (and date?) may be present. Presumably all the fittings were handcrafted but the actual decorative design used and artisans involved have not been identified. A special full-dress belt and buckle (Fig. 66) was also worn with this sword (refer to the chapter on 'Sword Belts' later in this book).

Well-known recipients are Fleet Admiral Tōgō Heihachiro (Plate 214), victor over the Russian Fleet at Tsuchima in 1905, who was probably one of the first. Field Marshal Terauchi Hisaichi became a Gensui in June 1943 and it is known that the blade for his Gensui-tō was made by Yasunori. On 30 November 1945, Terauchi, as C-in-C Southern Army, surrendered two swords to Lord

ashi (suspension mounts). The latter have hanging rings (for use with a sword belt) which are features not found on old tachi.

Each blade is believed to be specially handforged by a leading contemporary smith. That owned by Field Marshal Hata is the rare kogarasu-zukuri (little crow shape) as shown in Fig. 59 (v).

*Fig. 36  1918 pattern Gensui-tō (Field Marshals and Fleet Admirals sword) based on the tenth-century kenukigata-tachi.*

Mountbatten. One of these is a kenukigata-tachi closely resembling a Gensui-tō but is 'silver' mounted with a blade dated 1292.[9] This is believed to be a family sword. Probably he did not surrender his Gensui-tō because of its association with the Emperor, and its current whereabouts is unknown.[10]

Admiral Yamamoto Isoroku, C-in-C Combined Fleet, was shot down and killed on 18 April 1943. His funeral procession was accompanied by a naval officer carrying Yamamoto's Gensui-tō (Plate 216), but since promotion to Fleet Admiral was posthumous he probably never actually saw it. A widely published painting of Yamamoto in full dress shows this sword (edge on) but, again, it must have been painted after his death.

The Gensui-tō of Field Marshal Hata Shunroku is apparently on display in a Japanese museum with the blade exposed.[11] The museum caption confirms the title of Gensui, up to his appointment in 1944, was only awarded to seventeen people. Therefore it is probable that no more than a dozen or so Gensui-tō were made since not authorised until 1918, although the title was created in 1896. They must be regarded as the rarest of all prescribed Japanese military swords with an extremely high probability that none exists outside Japan.

*Plate 216  The orders and decorations of Admiral Yamamoto Isoroku being carried on cushions at his state funeral in 1943. The naval officer in front carries Yamamoto's Gensui sword which was posthumously presented. (Philip Goody).*

1 *Orders & Medals of Japan and Associated States* by James W. Peterson (see Bibliography).
2 However, as Han Bing Siong will put forward in a forthcoming article, Gassan Sadakazu is reported as having made the Emperor Meiji's Gensui-tō in 1906 assisted by Gassan Sadakatsu. Also in that year Gensui-tō were made for Marshal Oyama and Admiral of the Fleet Tōgō. Thus the introduction date of 1918 would seem open to correction unless presentation military pattern swords were used for this purpose.
3 *Orders & Medals of Japan and Associated States* by James W. Peterson.
4 Details of this inscription were provided by Han Bing Siong.
5 The *Nippon no Gunpuku* (see Bibliography) which was kindly brought to the authors' attention by Philip Goody and translated by Han Bing Siong.
6 Provided by Keith Boothroyd.
7 The scabbard material was identified by Han Bing Siong. Rōgin (literally 'misty silver') is an alloy of silver, copper, lead and tin.
8 'Yasunori' by Han Bing Siong, To-ken Society of Great Britain Programme no. 91: 1976.
9 Now in Lord Mountbatten's home of Broadlands, England. Illustrated on page 153 of *Mountbatten, Eighty Years in Pictures* (Macmillan, London, 1979).
10 Han Bing Siong, ibid.
11 Hata became a Field Marshal in June 1944 (not 1943 as reported in *Shokan*). From April 1945 he was C-in-C 2nd General Army, HQ Hiroshima, responsible for the defence of Kyushu, Shikoku and western Honshu. Tried and sentenced to prison as a Class A war criminal. Died 1962. Biographical details of Hata and other Gensui mentioned in this section can be found in *Shokan* by Richard Fuller (see Bibliography).

# Imperial Household Swords and Dirks

Identification of such items is extremely difficult because of a lack of definitive documentary evidence. It has therefore been necessary to formulate an opinion based on the presence of certain decorative features. Further complications arise because of the plethora of persons, officers and organisations associated with the well-being and protection of the Palace institutions. Basically they comprise:

(i) Imperial Family Councillors: adult male members of the Imperial family.
(ii) Privy Councillors (Jushin): twenty-six elder statesmen appointed by the Emperor.
(iii) Lord Privy Seal: to give day-to-day political advice to the Emperor and control such things as the Imperial archives, tombs, shrines, peerage, etc.
(iv) Grand Chamberlain: to advise the Emperor on matters of state, diplomacy, health etc. He controls the Board of Chamberlains (stewards, butlers etc.), various court bureaux such as ceremonials, physicians, stables, recreations and the Household of the Crown Prince, Empress and Dowager Empress.
(v) Imperial Household Minister: supervises and manages the Imperial Treasury, Maintenance and Works Bureau etc.
(vi) Security: Imperial police and fire services for the Imperial palaces. Possibly this was controlled by either (v) or (viii).
(vii) Chief Imperial Aide-de-Camp: to advise the Emperor on military matters and be responsible for other aides-de-camp.
(viii) Imperial Guards: part of the Army but directly responsible to the Emperor.

It is to be expected that many people connected with the above functionaries could wear swords and dirks when in the presence of the Emperor or on full dress occasions.

The motif or mon associated with the Imperial family is the kiku, i.e. sixteen-petal chrysanthemum. The most common form is properly called the **Juroku kiku** (Fig. 2 (v)). A similar mon, which may be confused with it, is the **Hiashi**, i.e. sixteen-rayed sun (Fig. 2 (iii), (iv)) which may represent very high ranking officers in the civil police force. The Emperor, Empress, Crown Prince and, it seems, the Imperial Household used a kiku version having a further sixteen petal tips showing which is called the **Juroku yaekiku** (Fig. 2 (vi)). This was also used on the Imperial Guard cap badge, certainly during the Meiji period, but was later changed to a 'star within a wreath'. On 30 September 1869 the Juroku kiku was forbidden to the royal princes to avoid confusion with the Juroku yaekiku.[1] Instead they were ordered to use one of fifteen, fourteen (or less) petals or the 'reversed chrysanthemum' called the Ura kiku.

Another mon is the **kiri** (*Paulownia imperialis*)

## IMPERIAL HOUSEHOLD SWORDS AND DIRKS

which may be found in two forms:
(i) 5:7:5 (five florets on each side and seven in the centre above three leaves, Fig. 2 (i)). This is associated with Government Officials, Diplomats and naval Flag Officers (Admirals).
(ii) 3:5:3 (three florets on each side with five in the centre over the same leaves as above, Fig. 2 (ii)). This is associated with lower ranking Diplomats.

Thus military-style sword and dirk patterns with either the Hiashi or a kiri of either type may represent a senior person or Government Official. The presence of a Juroku kiku or Juroku yaekiku indicates almost certain use by a member of the Imperial Household (and possibly the royal family), as does a kiri if used in combination with any form of kiku.[2]

It may be expected that Imperial Aides-de-Camp and Privy Councillors used the swords of the services from which they originated, but other Household members may have had special edged weapons. All encountered, or shown in this section, must be regarded as very rare.

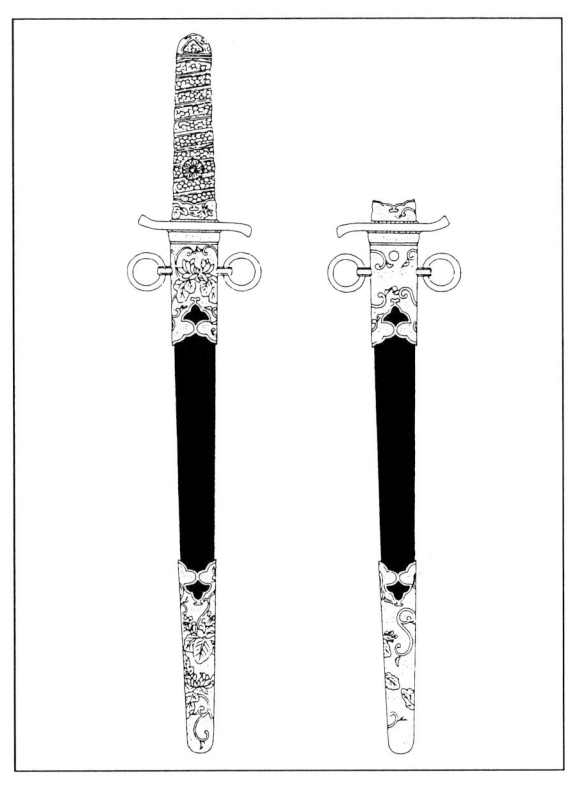

*Fig. 37* Obverse and reverse of a dirk of a Senior Official in the Imperial Household. (Imperial Japanese Daggers).

### Dirk of a Senior Official in the Imperial Household

This ornate dirk, shown in Fig. 37, is based on the 1883 Commissioned Officers naval dirk.[3] The grip is probably white samé but the scabbard type and colouration is unknown. The menuki (hilt ornaments) are in the form of a kiku (but which one is uncertain). The top scabbard mount is decorated with an open (peony?) blossom while the lower one has a 5:7:5 floret kiri. Press button and

**Plate 217** *The Emperor Mutsuhito (Meiji) who ruled from 1868 to 1912, in full dress Army uniform and a court sword of European style. It has a large pommel, knucklebow and down-turned shell-guard. Details are obscure since this may be a painting because photographic portraits of the Emperor were not allowed at that time. The hilt, guard and knucklebow appear to be entirely inlaid or embossed, possibly with the Imperial Paulownia (kiri) flower on the guard. It was probably made just for his usage and is not a specific pattern.* (Richard Fuller).

spring clip retention system.

Note the similarity to the 1909 pattern National Railways Senior Officials dirk.

## Imperial Household Police Officers dirk

A very distinctive item but none has been located to enable a full description to be given.[4] However, from Fig. 38 it may be ascertained that the hilt features the Juroku kiku (Fig. 2 (v)) on the pommel and menuki. The backstrap is decorated with kiri leaves and tendrils plus 5:7:5 floret kiri (Fig. 2 (i)) on the side-ears. The scabbard appears to be metal, possibly chromium-plated, with a chape which is probably gilded brass. The latter is also decorated with a raised Juroku kiku. Suspension must have been by means of a frog since there is no hanging ring.

## Unidentified Imperial Household Officials sword

This very rare and ornate sword pattern resembles the Army Officers kyu-guntō but is believed to have been carried by (very?) senior officials connected to the Imperial Guard or Imperial Household (Police?) because of the decorative features. Only two examples have been reported which are identical except for the method of blade manufacture. The Tokyo National Institute for Cultural Properties confirms these were not used by members of the Imperial family but, unfortunately, does not state (or know?) who actually wore them.

Gilded cast brass mounts, probably hand-finished. The backstrap is richly sculptured with leaves and the Juroku yaekiku. The obverse hand-guard is also decorated with a pierced design of Juroku yaekiku (Fig. 2 (vi)). The fuchi (hilt collar) is engraved with leaves and has a protruding kiri leaf-shaped push button for the spring clip retention system. A white samé grip has gilt wire binding in the grooves.

The blade shape is unusual being kogarasu-zukuri form which is double-edged near the point and single-edged for the rest of its length. There

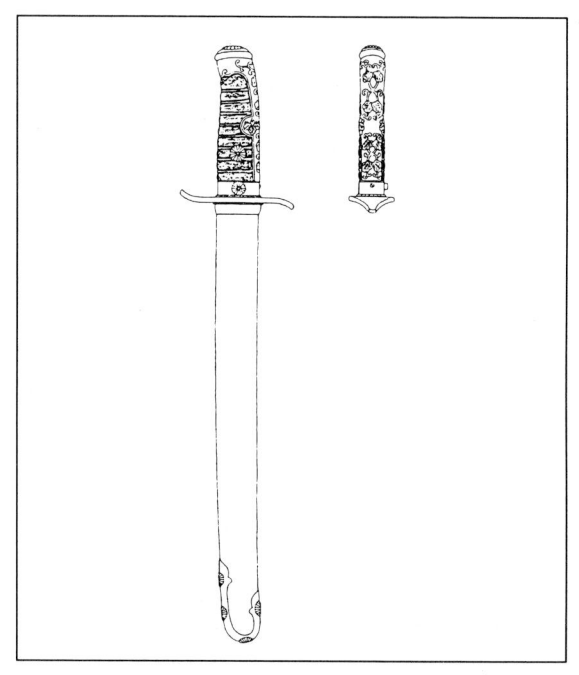

*Fig. 38* Imperial Household Police Officers dirk (Imperial Japanese Daggers).

**Plate 218** Very rare and ornate sword believed to have been carried by a senior official of the Imperial Household. (Brenton Williams).

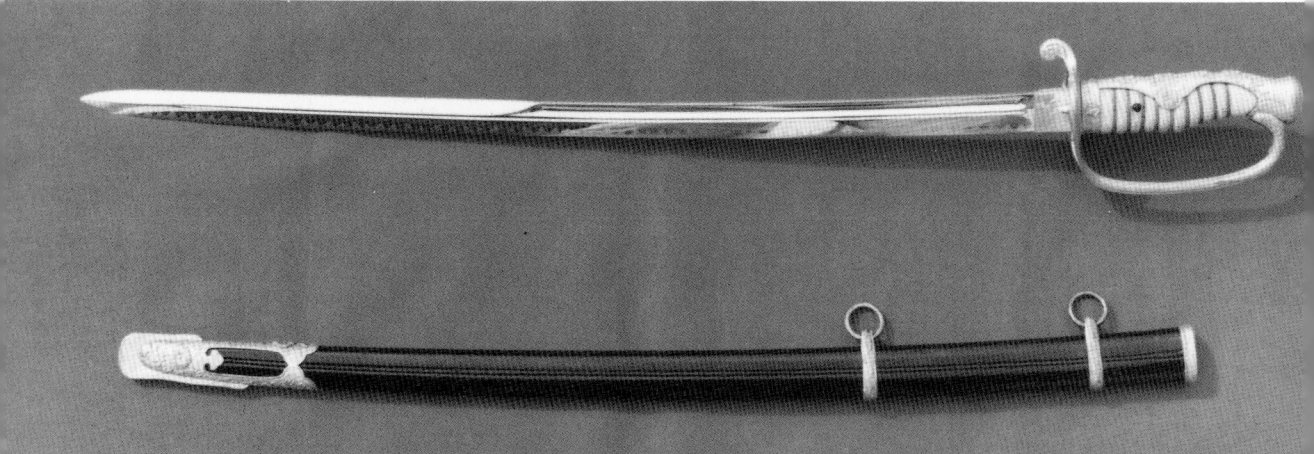

is a narrow centrally placed groove running the full length of the blade and a wider groove extending from the hilt for just over half the blade length (Fig. 59 (v)). The example shown is chromium-plated with a false acid-etched yakiba (tempered edge). The only other known example has a hand-forged blade of the same shape. Gilded copper habaki (blade collar). Black leather scabbard with gilded brass throat and two raised suspension bands all decorated ensuite with the fuchi. The gilded brass chape has a drag and is also decorated with embossed Juroku yaekiku and leaves. It has an open panel exposing the scabbard leather. Hilt length of example shown 124mm (4⅞"). Blade length 556mm (21⅞"). Blade width at habaki 19mm (¾"). Scabbard length 610mm (24"). A parade sabre version is shown in Plates 223 to 225.

The Juroku yaekiku was also used by the Imperial Guard which was founded in 1871. The general military appearance lends credence to the idea that it was carried by high-ranking officers of that élite unit but no reference to a separate Guard sword pattern has, so far, been discovered by the authors. However, the fact that there are full-sized and parade sabre versions does seem to indicate military connections.

The sword illustrated was 'liberated' from Japan by an Australian serviceman who served in the occupation forces.

**Plate 221** *Underside of the handguard of the Unidentified Imperial Household Officials sword. The obverse is pierced with a design of Juroku yaekiku chrysanthemum and leaves set in two panels in the same fashion as the normal Army kyu-guntō and parade sabre. The guard is also engraved with the Japanese characters for Watanabe, which is the owner's surname.* (Brenton Williams).

**Plate 219** *Hilt of the Unidentified Imperial Household Officials sword. Note the retention push button in the fuchi (blade collar) which is in the form of a kiri leaf.* (Brenton Williams).

**Plate 220** *Backstrap of the Unidentified Imperial Household Officials sword showing the excellent quality of the deeply sculptured backstrap which features the Imperial Juroku yaekiku and leaves.* (Brenton Williams).

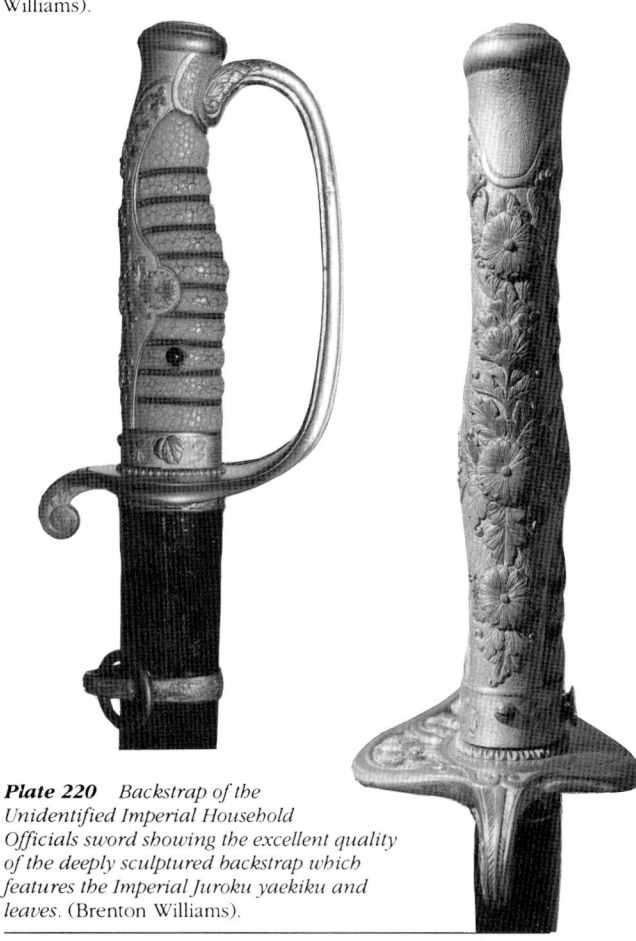

**Plate 222** *Scabbard ishizuke (chape) of the Unidentified Imperial Household Officials sword showing the Juroku yaekiku chrysanthemum decoration and leaf design.* (Brenton Williams).

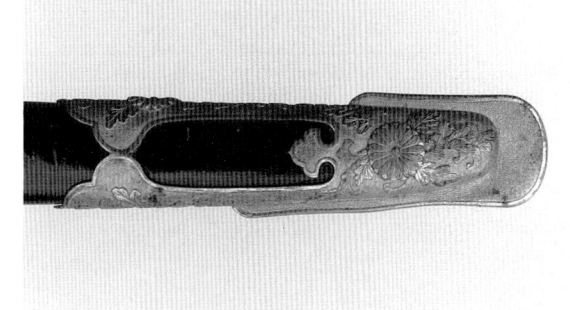

**Plate 223**  *Parade sabre version of the Unidentified Imperial Household sword. (Donald Barnes).*

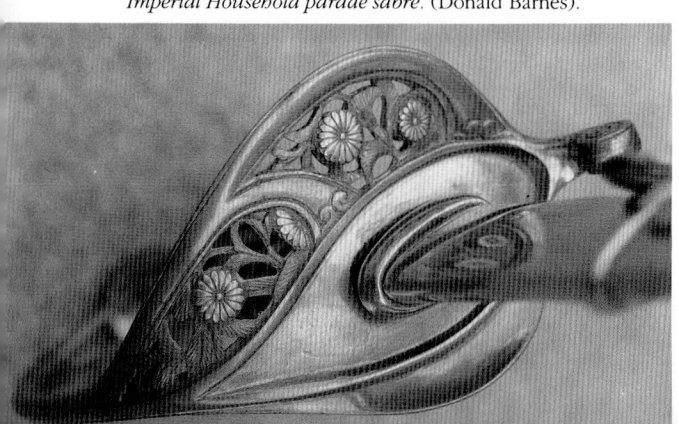

**Plate 224**  *Backstrap of the parade sabre version of the Unidentified Imperial Household sword. (Donald Barnes).*

## Parade sabre version of the Unidentified Imperial Household sword

This is a smaller and lighter version of the full-sized sword shown previously but is obviously intended as a parade sabre.

The gilded brass hilt has a wire-bound turtle-shell grip with an ornate backstrap featuring four chrysanthemum blossoms which, in this case, seem to be of the Juroku kiku type.[5] The obverse handguard has two pierced panels featuring kiku but differs from the full-sized model in that the larger front panel has two full blossoms. Compare with Plate 221 where the front panel only has one kiku. Whether this represents a rank differential is unknown. A light chromium-plated blade has a wide groove extending from the shoulder for about two thirds of the length. Chromium-plated steel scabbard with one suspension mount and a single hanging ring. Detailing of the hilt decoration is not as good as the full-sized version.

Overall length of sword and scabbard 900mm (35 7/16"). Hilt length 134mm (5 5/16"). Maximum blade width 23mm (15/16"). Scabbard length 752mm (29 5/8").

This is also a very rare sword pattern.

**Plate 225**  *Handguard underside of the Unidentified Imperial Household parade sabre. (Donald Barnes).*

1  Page 26 of *Japanese Heraldry* by R. Lange.
2  Hiroi Yuuichi, director of the Department of Archives at the Tokyo National Institute of Cultural Properties, has confirmed that swords made for the Emperor and aristocracy should be hand-made or hand-engraved. That in plates 218 to 222 is cast so was not made for members of the Imperial family.
3  Identified in *Imperial Japanese Daggers 1883–1945* but no further explanation is given.
4  Identifed in *Imperial Japanese Daggers 1883–1945* but no further explanation is given.
5  The turtle-shell grip is used on Army General Officer kyu-guntō and parade sabres, reinforcing the opinion that high ranking officials or officers used this pattern.

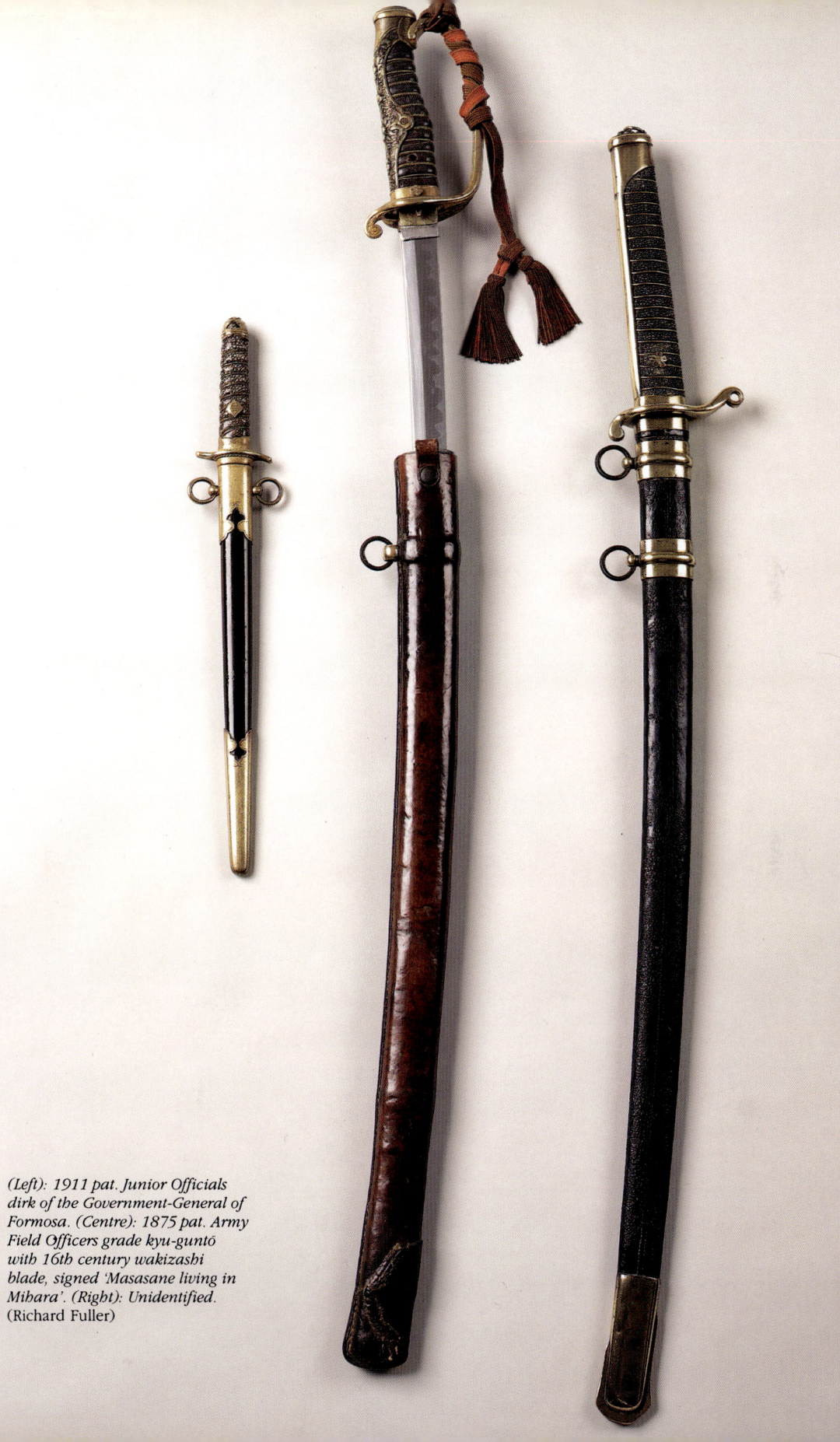

*(Left): 1911 pat. Junior Officials dirk of the Government-General of Formosa. (Centre): 1875 pat. Army Field Officers grade kyu-guntō with 16th century wakizashi blade, signed 'Masasane living in Mihara'. (Right): Unidentified. (Richard Fuller)*

**Plate i** 1937 pattern Naval Officers kai-guntō with a samē (rayskin) scabbard. (Richard Fuller)

**Plate iii** An Officers personal dirk with its cloth wrapping. (A Glazier).

**Plate iv** c.1945 pattern Army NCOs sword and scabbard. (R Gregory).

**Plate v**   Unusual brass kai-guntō fittings. Both ashi (suspension mounts) have 12mm wide (5–7mm norm) boar's eye recesses. Note the shagreen scabbard covering characterised by a myriad of small white diamonds. The elongated kabuto-gane (pommel) is actually an ishizuke (chape) with a separate central sarute mount. The ishizuke (not shown) is identical. Compare with Plates 181, 182. They may be specially made or, possibly, limited production items. (Robert Dragos).

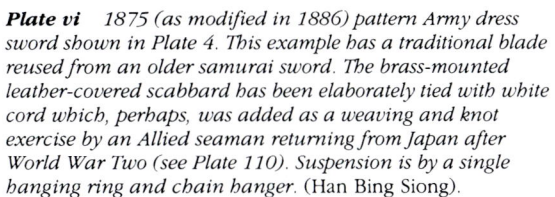

**Plate vi**   1875 (as modified in 1886) pattern Army dress sword shown in Plate 4. This example has a traditional blade reused from an older samurai sword. The brass-mounted leather-covered scabbard has been elaborately tied with white cord which, perhaps, was added as a weaving and knot exercise by an Allied seaman returning from Japan after World War Two (see Plate 110). Suspension is by a single hanging ring and chain hanger. (Han Bing Siong).

**Plate vii**   Rare 1886 modified version of the 1875 pattern Army Officers dress sword of Company Officers grade. Brass fittings and black shagreen grip which has lost the wire binding in the grooves. (Han Bing Siong).

**Plate viii**  Pierced handguard of the 1883 pattern Flag Officers naval parade sabre shown in Plates 174, 175. The decoration incorporates a 5:7:5 kiri and is totally different from the standard Commissioned Officers. (Brenton Williams).

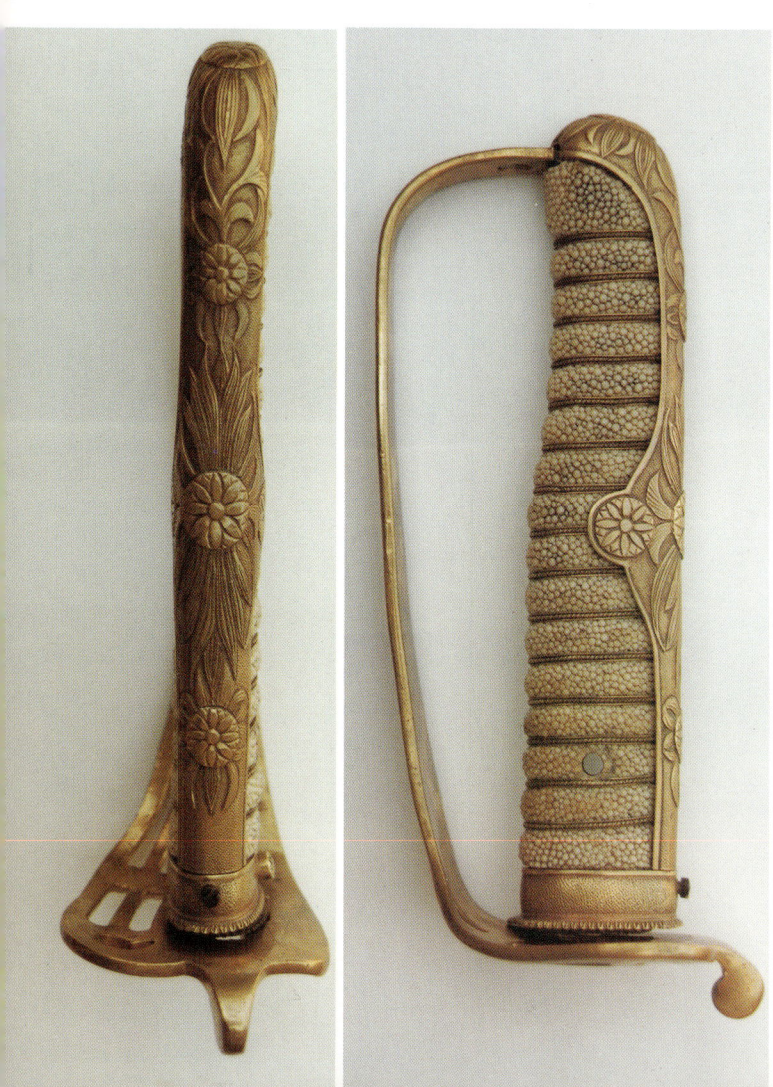

**Plate ix**  Very rare 1875 pattern Army General Officers grade parade sabre with fully decorated backstrap identic to the full-sized kyu-guntō version. Note the distinguishing turtle-shell grip. Possibly imitation turtle-shell was used on occasions. (Patrick Lundy).

**Plates x**  Most unusual variant of the rare 1886 pattern Cavalry Officers sword with brass fittings possibly for use b an officer of Field grade. The backstrap appears to be han engraved, being decorated for virtually the entire length. flower motif used is not the normal sakura (cherry blossom and is not a recognisable type. Typical slotted handguard. Mass-produced blade with an unidentified stamp on the t Plated steel scabbard with two suspension mounts, the lou one being removable by sliding over the drag. Total length sword and scabbard is 915mm (36"). Hilt length 205mm (8 1/16"). (Jørgen Jørgensen).

*Plate 199*  Shin-guntō with naval characteristics. (Alan Clayton).

*Plate 188*  Unidentified short pattern naval sword. (Brenton Williams).

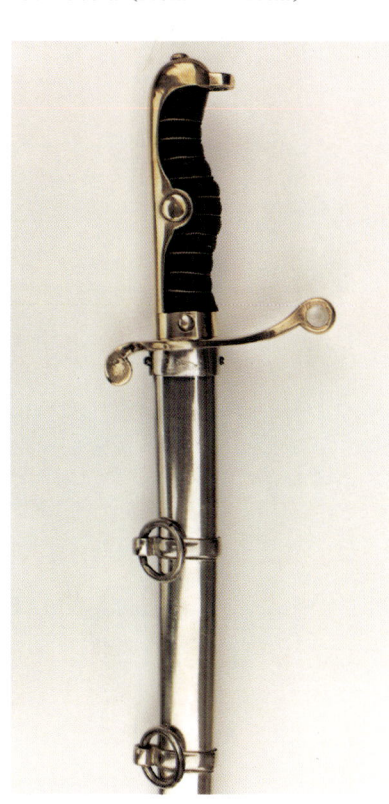

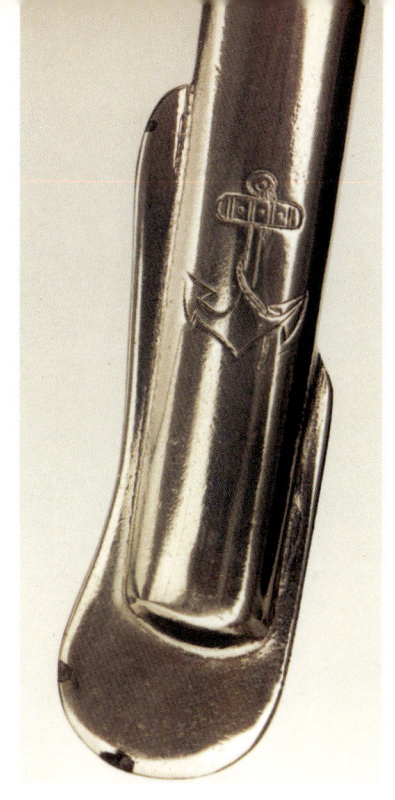

*Plate xiii*  Engraved foul anchor on the scabbard of the unidentified short pattern naval sword. (Brenton Williams).

*Plates xiv*  Backstrap and side view of the rare 1883 pattern Flag Officers (Admirals) naval parade sabre showing the 5:7:5 floret kiri associated with that rank grade. (Brenton Williams).

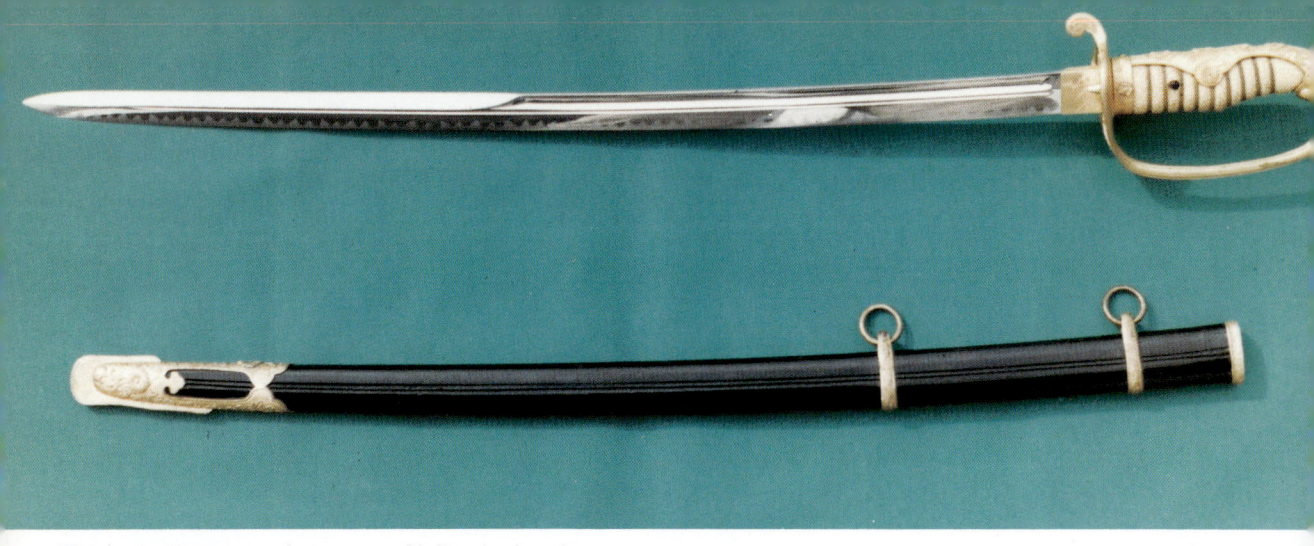

**Plate xvi**  *Very rare and ornate sword believed to have been carried by a senior official of the Imperial Household. (Brenton Williams).*

**Plate xvii**  *Hilt of the unidentified Imperial Household Officials sword. Note the retention push button in the fuchi (blade collar) which is in the form of a kiri leaf. (Brenton Williams).*

**Plate xix**  *Underside of the handguard of the unidentified Imperial Household Officials sword. The obverse is pierced with a design of Juroku yaekiku chrysanthemum and leaves set in two panels in the sa fashion as the normal Army kyu-guntō and parade sabre. The guard is also engraved with the Japanese characters for Watanabe, which is the owner's surnan (Brenton Williams).*

**Plate xviii**  *Backstrap of the unidentified Imperial Household Officials sword showing the excellent quality of the deeply sculptured backstrap which features the Imperial Juroku yaekiku and leaves. (Brenton Williams).*

**Plate xx**  Hilt obverse and scabbard of an unidentified civil full dress or court sword. (Alan Clayton).

**Plate xxi**  Reverse of the unidentified civil full dress or court sword. (Alan Clayton).

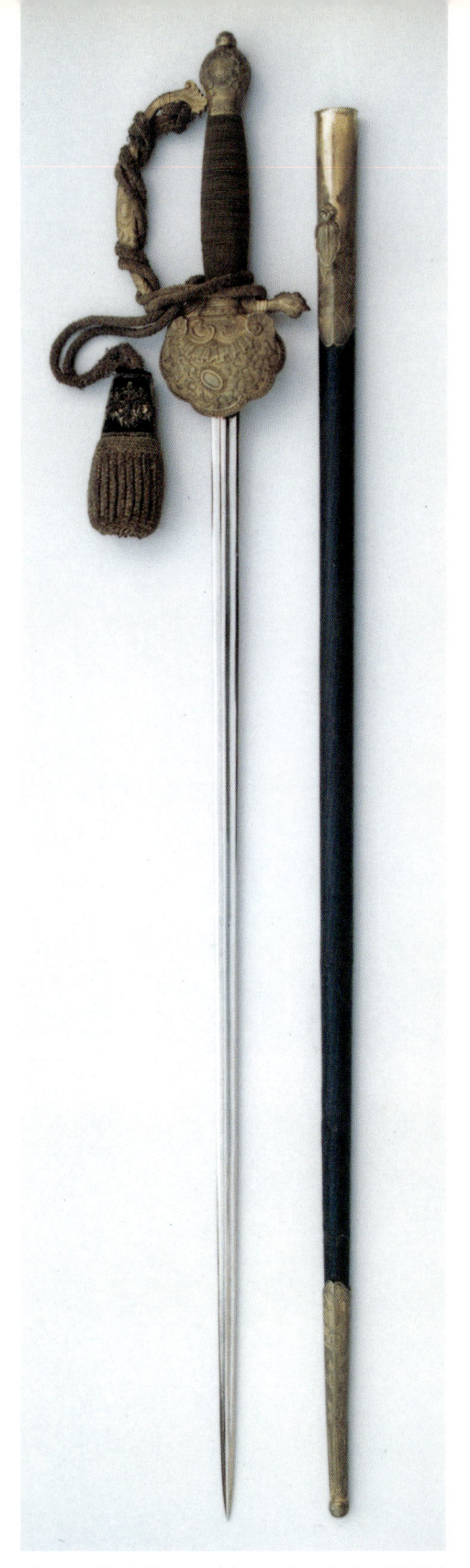

**Plate xxii**  Full view of the unidentified civil full dress or court sword. (Alan Clayton).

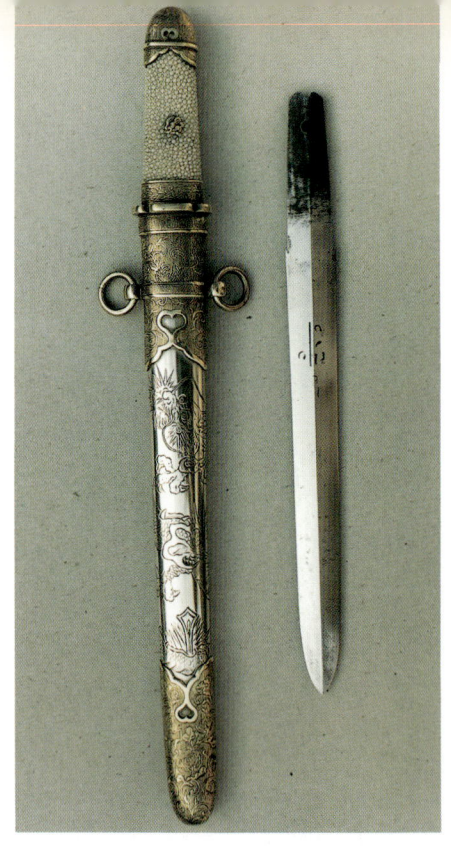

**Plate xxiii** Ornate unidentified dirk, possibly made for presentation purposes. (Brenton Williams).

**Plate xxiv** Obverse of the ornate dirk in Plate 330 showing the assembled blade with the double copper habaki (blade collar) (Brenton Williams).

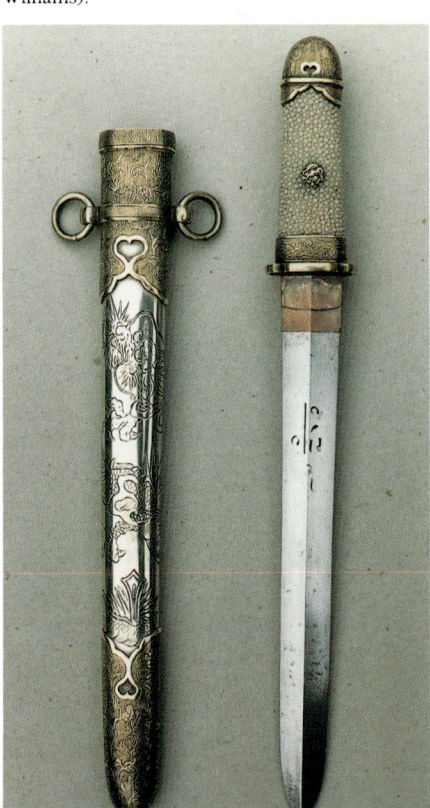

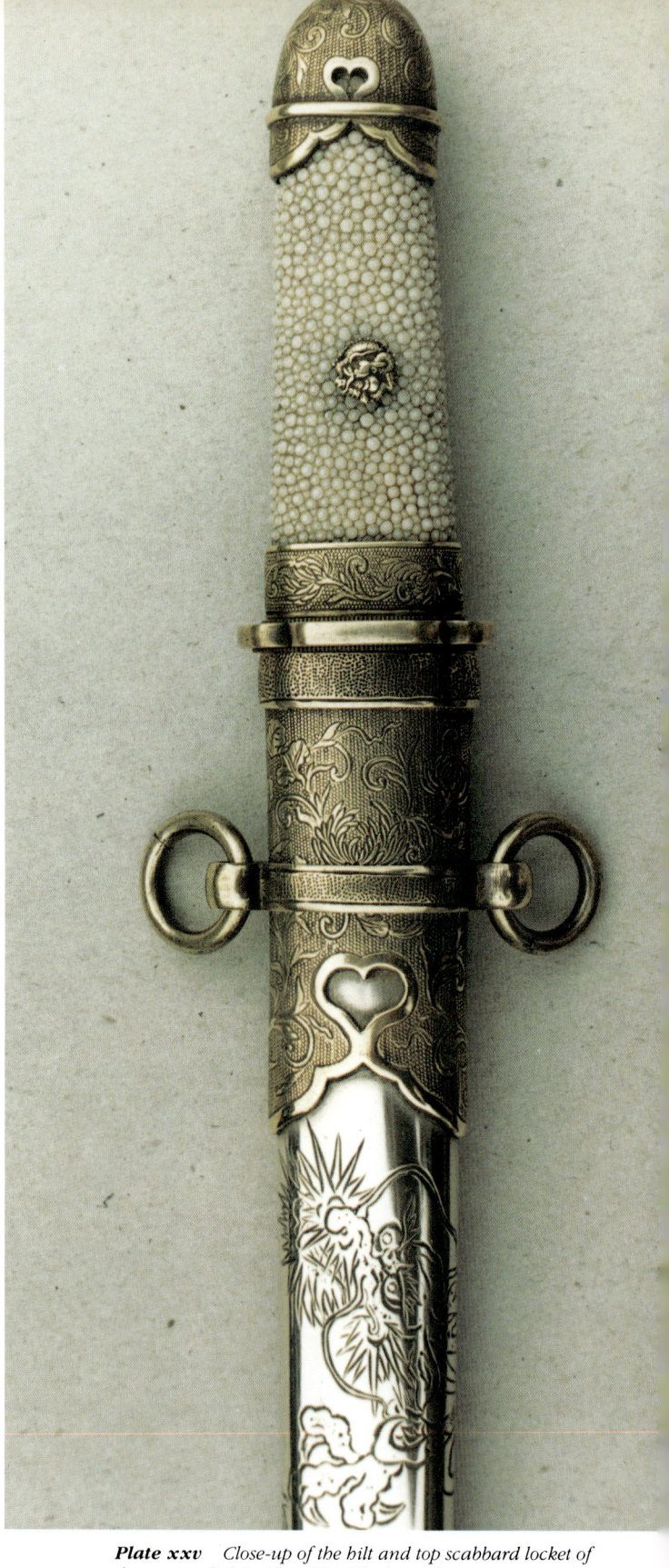

**Plate xxv** Close-up of the hilt and top scabbard locket of the ornate dirk in Plate 330. The brass fittings appear to be hand-engraved. The gold curled dragon menuki is in the centre of the grip. (Brenton Williams).

# Diplomatic Corps Swords

## Regulation Diplomatic Corps sword patterns

Members of the Diplomatic Corps (Kakkoku-koshi) carried dress swords suspended either by a black velvet frog from a white silk shoulder belt (Plate 227) or a silver and brown striped frog from a black-faced leather waist belt.

There were two grades of this sword distinguishable by the form of kiri (*Paulownia imperialis*) used in the decoration.[1] The junior rank of Sōnin (standard appointment) utilised a 3:5:3 kiri (Fig. 2 (ii)); the senior rank of Chokunin (appointment personally approved by the Emperor) used a 5:7:5 kiri (Fig. 2 (i)).

All hilt and scabbard fittings are gilded brass. The grip of the Sōnin version is tightly wrapped with fine silver wire plus a thicker gold banding. Both wrap and banding wire are gold on the Chokunin model. The grip of both types are fitted with gilded side straps. A raised kiri of the appropriate rank form is present on each side of the spherical pommel. The decorated knucklebow terminates with a Ho-ho bird (or phoenix) head quillion. Differences in the central knucklebow motif have been noted. Normally a kiri is used but a kiku (chrysanthemum), indicating Imperial family or court use, is known.[2] Large down-curved obverse shell-guard pierced with a kiri bearing the requisite number of florets according to rank and a small up-turned reverse guard. Narrow, straight, oval section plated blade either plain or etched with a foliate design and a 5:7:5 kiri near the hilt (Fig. 39). The normal pattern of this etching seems similar for both Sōnin and chokunin versions. However, diamond and hexagonal section blades have been found on Sōnin swords which also had different foliage etching without a kiri. Blade decoration in the Western style has only been reported on one other sword type and that is shown in Plate 283.

Black leather-covered wooden scabbard with two mounts. The locket obverse is partially decorated and has a frog stud in the form of a leaf. The chape obverse is fully engraved and terminates with a ball finial. A variation in the scabbard engraving between the two grades has been noted but it is uncertain whether a rank differential is intended or only a manufacturer's variation. The gold bullion knot and straps shown in Plate 226 are assumed to have been used by both rank grades.

It is unlikely that dimensions varied by much. Overall length of sword and scabbard shown 794mm (31¼"). Hilt length 149mm (5⅞"). Blade length 559mm (22"). Maximum blade width 13mm (½"). Scabbard length 648mm (25½"). Weight of sword and scabbard 22 ounces.

Such swords are seen carried with the full Diplomatic Corps dress uniform which has kiri richly embroidered in gold bullion on the jacket (Plate 230).

Examples of either rank grade are rare.

---

1. The two grades were unfortunately transposed in the first edition of *Military Swords of Japan 1868–1945* by the authors but were corrected in all later editions.
2. Illustrated on pages 102, 103 of *Swords of Imperial Japan 1868–1945*.

# JAPANESE MILITARY AND CIVIL SWORDS AND DIRKS

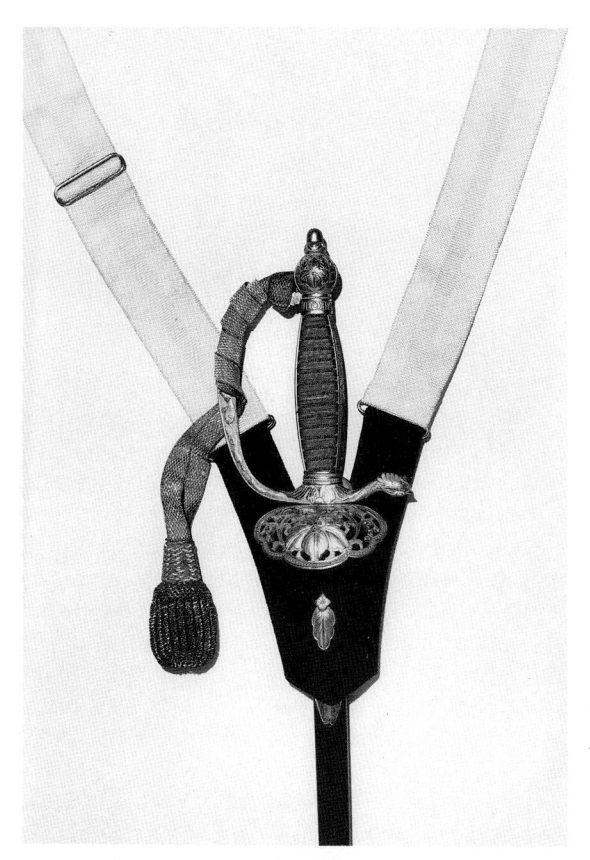

**Plate 226** Rare Diplomatic Corps sword of Chokunin (appointment personally approved by the Emperor) grade. (Ron Gregory).

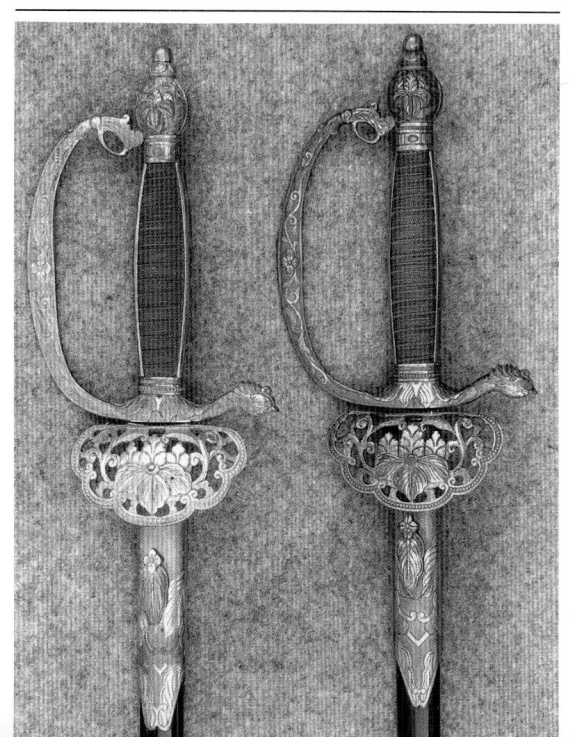

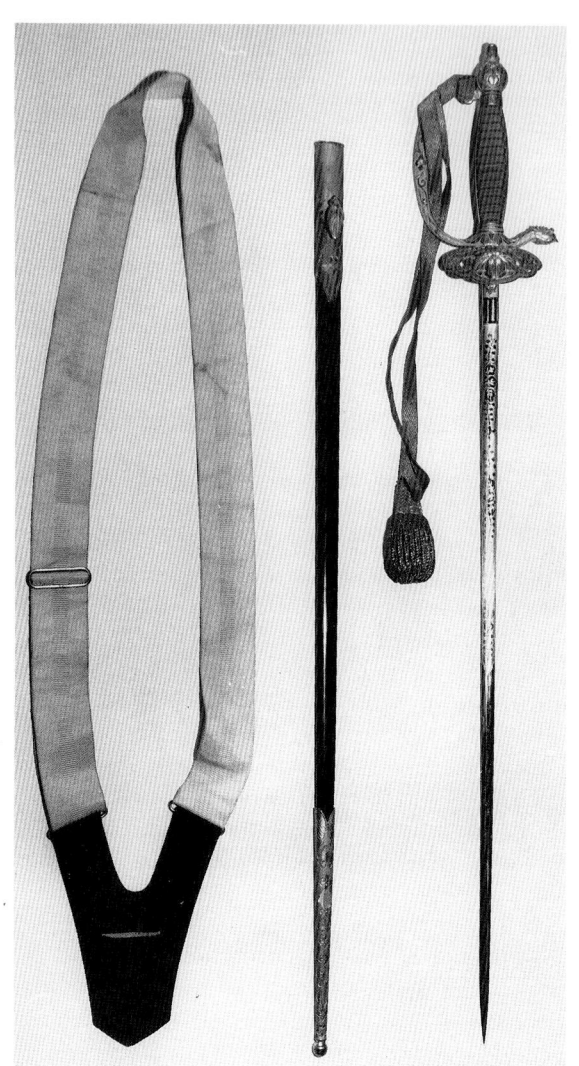

**Plate 227** Rare Diplomatic Corps sword of Chokunin grade and accoutrements consisting of the suspension belt and frog, scabbard, knot and etched blade. (Ron Gregory).

**Plate 228** Both grades of the Diplomatic Corps sword. That on the left is the junior grade Sōnin (standard appointment) and features a kiri flower of the 3:5:3 floret type. The grip wire binding is silver. The example on the right is the senior grade Chokunin (appointment personally approved by the Emperor) and has the kiri of the 5:7:5 floret type. The grip wire binding is gold. Scabbard fittings are identical. (Donald Barnes).

## Diplomatic Corps sword variation with traditional blade

A very rare variation of the Diplomatic Corps (Kakkoku-koshi) dress sword is shown in Plate 229.

Gilded brass hilt mounts decorated in relief with foliage and featuring a large *Paulownia* flower (kiri) of the 5:7:5 floret form on the obverse shell-guard. The reverse guard is plain and hinged to fold down against the body. White samé grip with gilded wire in the grooves.

Unsigned Shintō period blade of good quality attributed to the smith Korekazu. It has been remounted for the former Japanese owner in these mounts and was presumably a family blade or heirloom. Black lacquered scabbard with gilded brass fittings consisting of a kuchi-gane (throat), two separate ashi (suspension mounts), each fitted with a brass hanging ring, a shibabiki (strengthening band) and an ishizuke (chape) having a drag. All fittings are richly decorated ensuite and feature an embossed kiri of the 5:7:5 floret type. It has full length gilded brass scabbard side straps which is a feature only seen on the Gensui (Field Marshals and Admirals) sword pattern.

A superb quality item, it must have been carried by a person of very high rank. This may be confirmed by the use of the 5:7:5 floret kiri which was used by a person of Chokunin grade. He may also have had military connections or rank because of the style of this sword and the use of a traditional blade.

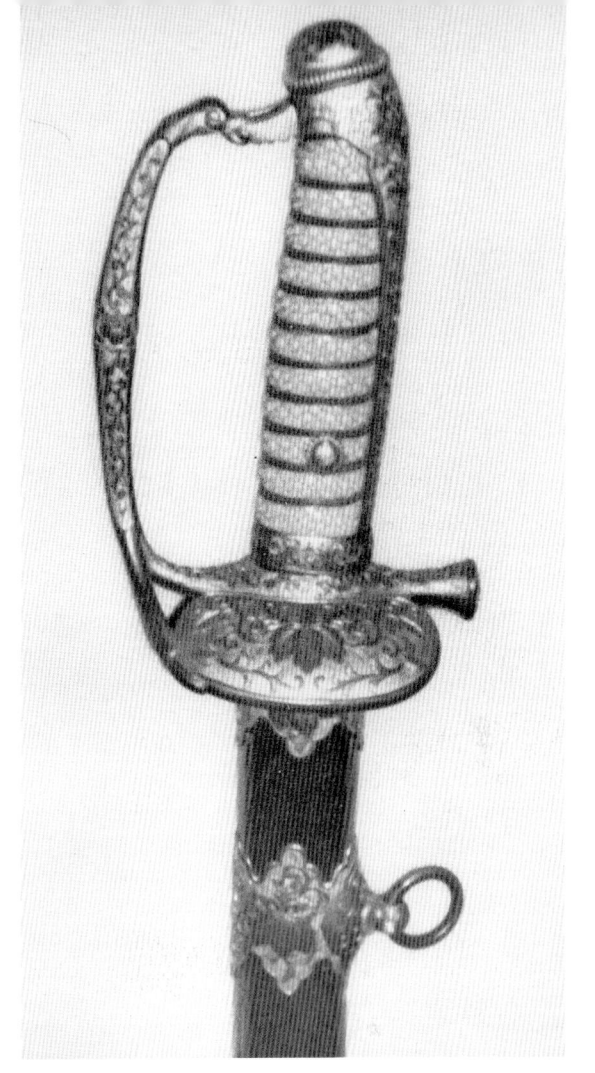

**Plate 229** *Very rare variation of the Diplomatic Corps (kakkoku-koshi) dress sword with a traditional hand-forged blade. (Keith Hostler).*

**Plate 230** *Hirota Koki, Prime Minister of Japan from 9 March 1936 until 23 January 1937, in full Diplomatic dress uniform. The hilt of his Diplomatic sword can be seen. The richly embroidered jacket features kiri of the 5:7:5 type.*

**Fig. 39** *Normal blade-etching design found on both rank versions of the Diplomatic Corps sword*

# Formosan Swords and Dirks

Formosa (Taiwan) was ceded to Japan by China in 1895, and was ruled by the Japanese with the establishment of a Government-General and the accompanying bureaucratic system. Uniforms of officials of this organisation are shown bearing a 'double triangle' badge (Fig. 51 (vi)) which appears to have been adopted by the Japanese as a motif for Formosa.[1] This badge is present on a sword and dirks which closely resemble the Japanese naval parade sabre and 1883 pattern Commissioned Officers naval dirk respectively. However, these dress weapons were carried by Government-General officials and are not naval weapons. There are three rank classes: Hannin (Junior), Sōnin (Emperor approved) and Chokunin (Imperial appointment). Two patterns of dirk were authorised in 1911[2] but the sword patterns were introduced in 1899.

## 1911 pattern Junior Officials dirk of the Government-General of Formosa

All hilt fittings are gilded brass entirely decorated with stippling. The pommel cap has a pierced panel on each side and is decorated with a sakura (cherry blossom) and leaves. The grip is polished lacquered black same with gilt wire binding and menuki (hilt ornaments) fixed to male and female hilt-securing screws. These menuki are in the form of the Formosan 'double triangle' badge. The underside of the crossguard on the example shown is stamped with Japanese characters which can also be found on the Formosan parade sabre in Plate 235. They read KYŌTŌ ECHIZEN-YA SEI, i.e. made in the Echizen shop in Tokyo. In this case 'kyōtō' means the 'eastern capital' of Tokyo because different characters are used for the city of Kyoto.

Standard naval dirk machine-made grooved blade fitted with a brass habaki (blade collar). The scabbard has a wooden base and is finished with a dark brown/black lacquer. It is unknown if other scabbard coverings, such as leather or shagreen, were permitted. Both mounts are decorated only with stippling. Normal scabbard push button and spring clip retention.

Overall length of dirk and scabbard shown 410mm (16 1/8"). Hilt length 107mm (4¼"). Blade length (to crossguard) 251mm (10¼"). Scabbard length 302mm (11 15/16"). Weight of dirk and scabbard 10 ounces.

Wear would be by officials of Hannin grade (equivalent to Army officers of Company grade).

Since no other example has been reported, it would seem to be very rare.

## 1911 pattern Senior Officials dirk of the Government-General of Formosa

This has the same scabbard as the Junior Officials model. However, the hilt differs in that the pommel cap has no pierced panels and the grip is possibly white same. See Fig. 40 (ii).

***Plate 231*** *1911 pattern Junior Officials dirk of the Government-General of Formosa. (Richard Fuller).*

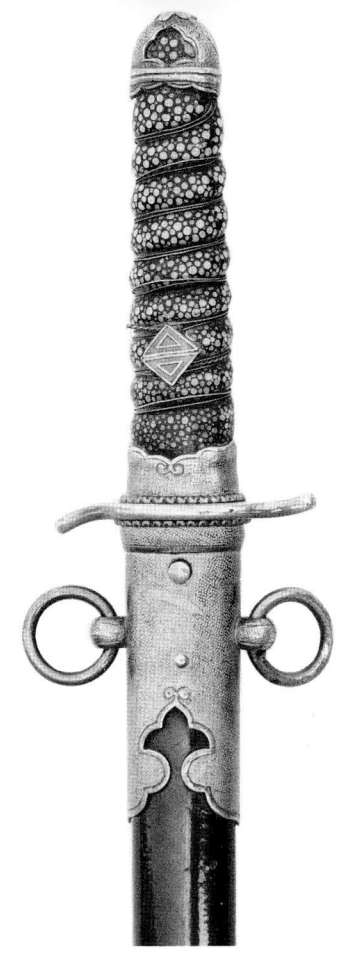

***Plate 232*** *Hilt of the 1911 pattern Junior Officials dirk of the Government-General of Formosa. (Richard Fuller).*

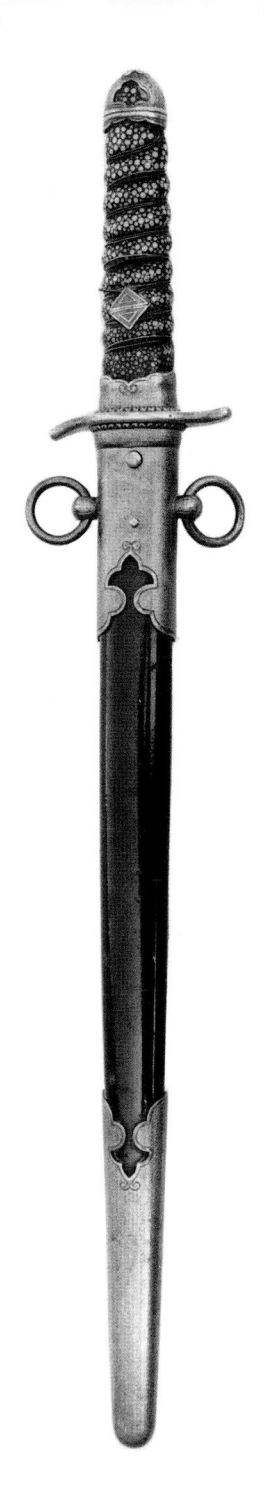

***Plate 233*** *Close-up of the Formosan 'double triangle' badge located on both sides of the grip of the Junior and Senior Officials dirks of the Government-General of Formosa (and also on the hilt side-ears of the equivalent swords). (Richard Fuller).*

JAPANESE MILITARY AND CIVIL SWORDS AND DIRKS

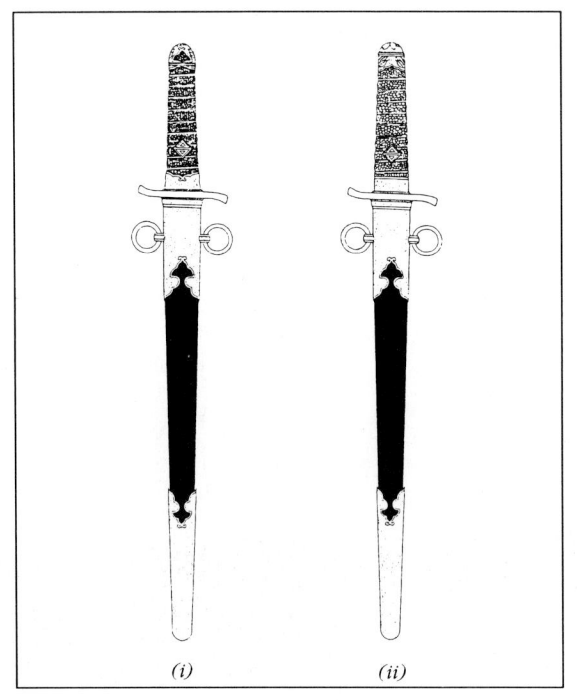

***Fig. 40*** *1911 pattern dirks of the Government-General of Formosa (Taiwan): (i) Junior Official; (ii) Senior Official.* (Imperial Japanese Daggers).

No example has been located so, perhaps, it may be classified as very rare. Use was by Sōnin officials (equivalent of Army officers of Field grade) but it is uncertain if those of Chokunin grade also carried a dirk (which would be more ornate).

## 1899 pattern Officials swords of the Government-General of Formosa

*Swords of Imperial Japan 1868–1945* gives an introduction date of 17 February 1899 for the two known sword patterns. The Hannin (Junior) Officials model has plain stippled mounts and a black grip. The Sōnin (Senior) Officials model has sakura and leaf decorated handguard and upper backstrap with a white grip.

Hilt fittings are gilded brass with background stippling. The only sakura (cherry blossom) on the

***Plate 234*** *1899 pattern sword of a Hannin (junior) official in the Government-General of Formosa.* (P. Faarvang).

# FORMOSAN SWORDS AND DIRKS

entire Hannin sword surmounts a female pommel screw which allows the hilt to be disassembled. The backstrap has side-ears with raised Formosan 'double triangle' badges on each side. Small folding rear guard which engages with a raised stud on the reverse of the top scabbard locket. The underside of the guard near the knucklebow may be stamped with the same Japanese characters as the dirk which reads KYŌTŌ ECHIZEN-YA SEI, i.e. made in the Echizen shop in Tokyo. Not all examples of this sword are found with this inscription which appears to be strictly limited to Formosan swords and dirks.

Mass-produced chromium-plated blade which can have the optional acid-etched yakiba and is fitted with a brass habaki (blade collar). However, a signed hand-forged blade of similar dimensions dated 1899 and made from a rifle or musket barrel by the Meiji period smith Motosada has been found in these mounts. Scabbard of black leather or polished black or brown shagreen over a wooden liner with three gilded brass mounts. The Hannin model has raised suspension bands, each incorporating a hanging ring and fittings with 'heart-shaped' (boars eye) recesses.[3] The Sōnin scabbard appears identical to the 1914 pat. naval officers parade sabre.

Dimensions are probably variable. Hilt length of example shown 125mm (5"). Blade length 675mm (26 9/16"). Maximum blade width 20mm (¾").

Beige-coloured sword knot and cords similar to that in Fig. 7.

Only a few examples of this sword pattern have been reported so they may be considered as rare.[4]

---

1 Shown in *Imperial Japanese Army and Navy Uniforms and Equipments* by Nakata (see Bibliography). However, no edged weapons are illustrated.
2 According to *Imperial Japanese Daggers 1883–1945*.
3 The recesses (cut-outs) and projections of the scabbard fittings for standard naval kyu-guntō, parade sabres and dirks have been likened to an arrow for descriptive purposes only and the word is not intended to be an accurate reflection of the shape since there appears to be no proper term. Perhaps it is somewhat reminiscent of a stylised 'yari' (traditional pole arm) but the side blades normally curve downwards or are straight out.
4 The Royal Navy Museum, Portsmouth, England has a Hannin officials sword on display, captioned 'a typical Japanese naval sword'.

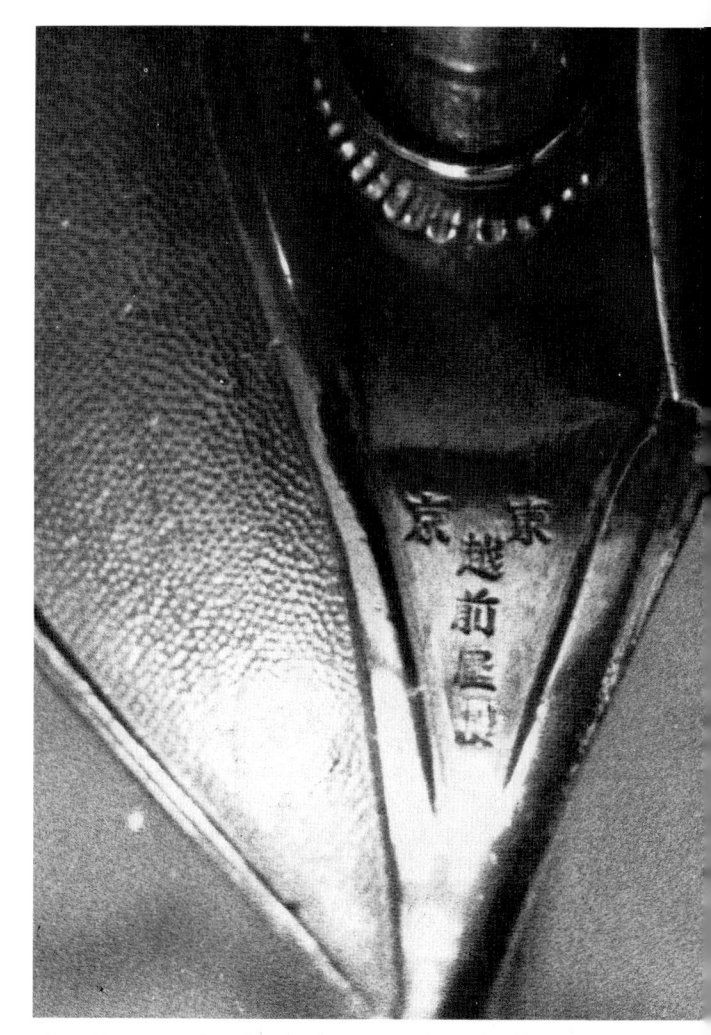

**Plate 235** *Guard underside of a Hannin (Junior) Officials pattern sword of the Government-General of Formosa. The manufacturer's inscription is shown which reads KYŌTŌ ECHIZEN-YA SEI, i.e. made at the Echizen shop in Tokyo. (P. Faarvang).*

# Korean Swords and Dirks

Korea (Chōsen) was always coveted by the Japanese and became the object of several military expeditions. It was the scene of the Sino–Japanese war of 1894–5. The 1895 treaty of Shimonoseki forced the Chinese to concede Formosa and the Pescadores Islands to Japan. However, Korea remained nominally independent under its own king but was controlled by the Japanese. By 1905–6 Japan had declared Korea to be a 'protectorate' which prompted the king to protest unsuccessfully to the 1907 International Peace Conference at The Hague. The assassination of the Japanese Resident Governor-General by a Korean nationalist in 1909 incurred full annexation and the appointment of a Military Governor-General in July 1910, accompanied by full authoritarian rule. All public officials, including elementary school teachers, were forced to wear uniforms and swords.[1]

Officials of the Government-General wore their own uniforms and dress weapons which are distinguished by the use of the 5:7:5 floret kiri (Fig. 2 (i)), although this motif was also used on dirks of the Japanese National Railways Board. Rank classes were Hannin (Junior), Sōnin (Emperor approved), Chokunin (Imperial appointment) and Shinnin (personally approved by the Emperor). The latter is equivalent to a full Army General.

The Korean national emblem is a red and blue 'double comma' known as the 'taeguk' (or 'yin-yang'). This symbol has been reported on the spring clip push button of a parade sabre style sword which has the backstrap in the form of a dragon's body and the head as the pommel (Plate 236). It has been described as a Korean Army Officers sword from the period of the Japanese occupation.[2] However, this pattern is known to be that used by Imperial Chinese Army officers.[3] The use of the 'yin-yang' could suggest use by Korean Army officers while Korea was under Chinese control up to 1895 and possibly as late as 1905.[4] More likely it was added as an auspicious symbol for a Chinese officer. Several other examples are known, although they all lack the 'yin and yang', but all seem to be of Japanese manufacture. This makes them post-1892 since that is the year Japan commenced the manufacture of swords to the order of foreign countries.

### c.1911 pattern Junior Officials dirk of the Government-General of Korea

Such an item is presumed to exist because there is a Senior Officials model, but no information or description has been located. Possibly the grip is black samē.

Use would be by officials of Hannin grade.

### c.1911 pattern Senior Officials dirk of the Government-General of Korea

Based on the 1883 pattern Commissioned Officers

# KOREAN SWORDS AND DIRKS

appointment) authorised on 2 February 1906 and confirmed again after annexation on 31 May 1911. Only examples of parade-style swords are known.

The Hannin version has a raised 5:7:5 floret kiri on each backstrap side-ear and a raised sakura on the pommel but is otherwise plain except for background stippling. The Sōnin and Chokunin versions have additional 5:7:5 on the upper back-

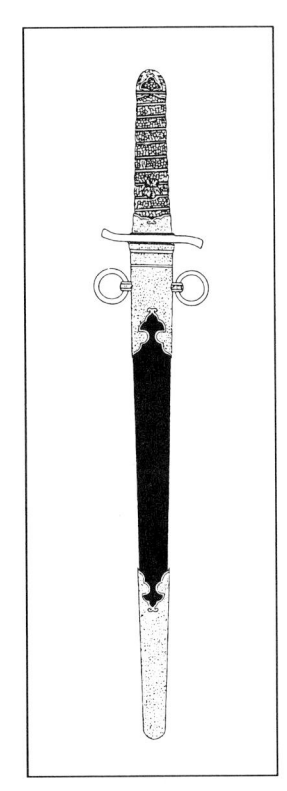

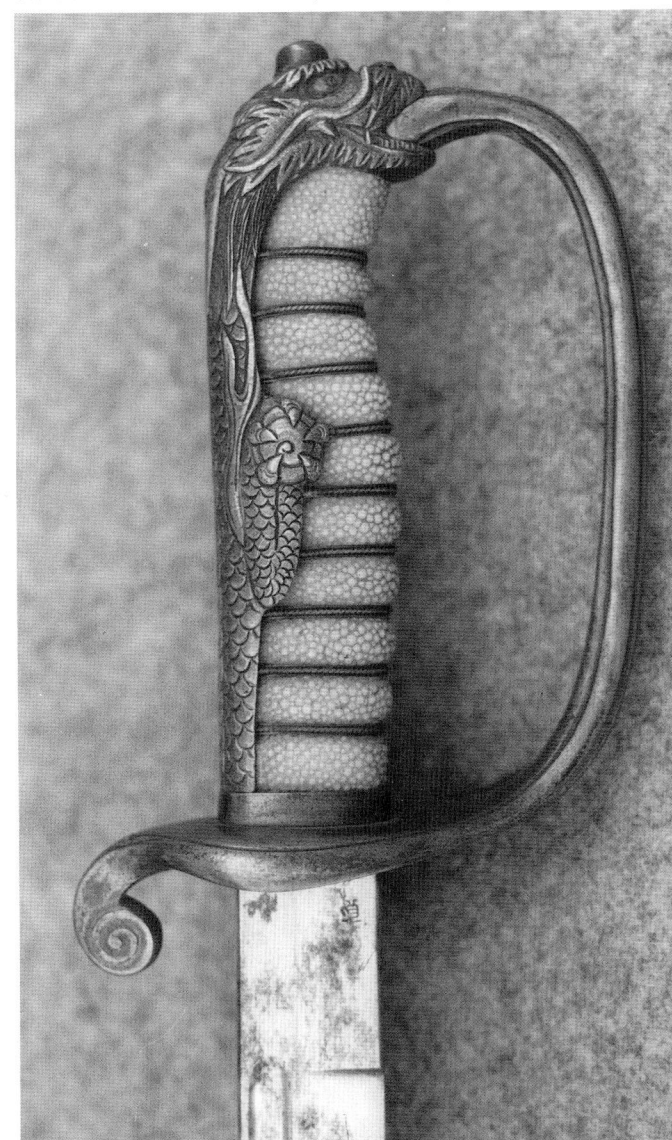

*Fig. 41* c.1911 pattern Senior Officials dirk of the Government-General of Korea. (Imperial Japanese Daggers).

naval dirk and only known from the drawing in Fig. 41.[5]

Gilded brass fittings decorated only with stippling except for the pommel cap which has a raised sakura (cherry blossom). Samē-covered grip, probably white, with brass wire binding and menuki (hilt ornaments) of the 5:7:5 floret kiri.

The gilded brass scabbard mounts are stippled. Presumably the usual spring clip retention system is used. The scabbard is assumed to be black or brown lacquered wood or possibly leather.

Use was probably by officials of Sōnin grade.

## 1906 pattern Officials swords of the Government-General of Korea

*Swords of Imperial Japan 1868–1945* states there were swords for Hannin (Junior), Sōnin (Emperor approved) and Chokunin (Imperial

*Plate 236* Dragon-hilted Imperial Chinese Army Officers sword worn up to the overthrow of the Manchu Emperors (Ching dynasty) in 1911–12. Possibly this pattern may also have been carried by Korean officers prior to c.1905 (see text). The quality and construction details, including a white samē grip and acid-etched yakiba (tempered blade edge), clearly indicates Japanese manufacture. The only marking on this example is an unidentified Chinese or Japanese character on the blade shoulder. (Donald Barnes).

**Plate 237**  *1911 pattern Hannin (Junior) Officials sword of the Government-General of Korea. The sword knot is a post-war addition. (Richard Fuller).*

**Plate 238**  *The kiri (Paulownia imperialis) flower on the hilt side-ears of all Korean Government-General sword patterns. It has five florets on each side and seven in the middle. (Richard Fuller).*

strap and each scabbard mount plus leaves and tendrils. The solid handguard of the Hannin version is plain but the Sōnin model features a raised leaf and multi-bud motif which is more ornate on the Chokunin sword. All models have white grips.

Normal grooved single-edged parade sabre blade with a false acid-etched yakiba (tempered edge). The blade of the illustrated example has never been plated. The tang tapers to terminate with a threaded portion which engages with the pommel screw. Black leather or lacquered shagreen scabbard having three gilded brass mounts with the usual arrow-shaped recesses/projections. The upper and middle lockets both have a brass hanging ring. Strangely the example shown has a plated steel Army parade sabre type scabbard having one suspension mount which is a perfect fit for both retention and length. Neither the blade nor scabbard interchange with numerous other Army and Navy parade sabres the authors have tried. Thus, it appears that for some unknown reason this particular steel scabbard may be correct for this sword. Possibly it indicates either police or military use. Gold (or silver?) bullion sword knots.

Dimensions are probably variable. Overall length of sword and scabbard shown 875mm (34 7/16"). Hilt length 130mm (5 1/8"). Blade length 650mm (25 9/16"). Maximum blade width 20mm (3/4").

The very few examples known indicate all grades may, perhaps, be considered as very rare.

## Possible Shinnin Officials sword of the Government-General of Korea

Identification of this ornate full-sized sword is tentative and has been assessed from the decorative details on the only reported example.[6] Therefore the conclusion is open to question since no corroborating photographic or documentary evidence has been located.

The general appearance is similar to a Naval Officers kyu-guntō but the hilt, which lacks a backstrap, resembles that in Fig. 24 (i). Gilded brass pommel, knucklebow, guard and fuchi (hilt collar) with a white samé grip and brass wire in the grooves. The back of the pommel has a raised 5:7:5 kiri (Fig. 2 (i)). The solid handguard is decorated with a groups of three engraved kiri leaves from which radiate a total of three stems of wisteria(?) flowers.[7] A small hinged flap on the

# KOREAN SWORDS AND DIRKS

reverse engages with a protruding stud on the scabbard.

Wood-lined chromium-plated steel scabbard with three gilded brass mounts. The upper two each have a single loose suspension ring. Decoration of the top mount consists of engraved tendrils and leaves plus a raised 5:7:5 kiri on each side. The centre and bottom mounts are decorated ensuite with a single tendril and leaves similar to the bottom mount of the Fire Bureau dirks in Fig. 54. The scabbard mount recesses resemble the normal arrow style on naval kyu-guntō but differ in that the points are flattened. The slightly curved blade is a wider and heavier version of that used on parade sabres (Fig. 59 (i)). It is unplated and has a narrow full length groove with a narrow straight yakiba (tempered edge). The tang tip is threaded to engage with a female pommel screw. Gilded brass habaki (blade collar). Gold bullion sword knot and cords. Blade length (from guard) 692mm (27¼"). Hilt length (from inside guard) 141mm (5 9/16").

The decorative features and blade configuration indicate civil, rather than military use. The 5:7:5 kiri could represent senior rank but, in this case, is believed to signify use in Korea by the most senior Japanese official rank of Shinnin (personally approved by the Emperor).[8]

A very rare item.

---

1 *Soldiers of the Sun* by Meirion and Susie Harries (see Bibliography). Unfortunately it is unknown what sword patterns were prescribed for such usage.
2 In an American militaria sales catalogue.
3 Three rank versions are illustrated in *Die Chinesiche Armee* published by Moritz Ruhl, Leipzig, Germany, 1910. The introduction date is not given. Research is currently on-going for a book on twentieth-century Chinese military swords where it is hoped to discuss and illustrate this sword type further.
4 The Korean Army was disbanded by the Japanese during the period 1906–9 and not reformed.
5 Identified by *Imperial Japanese Daggers 1883–1945*.
6 The authors wish to express their gratitude to Arthur Brand who brought this sword to their attention.
7 Possibly the leaves and flowers represent a Tōgiri (Chinese *Paulownia*) which is very similar and would reinforce the Korean theory.
8 The equivalent Army ranks to Chokunin and Shinnin are Maj/Lt-General and a full General respectively.

---

**Plate 239** *Guard underside of the 1911 pattern Hannin Officials sword of the Government-General of Korea. There are no manufacturer's inspection marks. (Richard Fuller).*

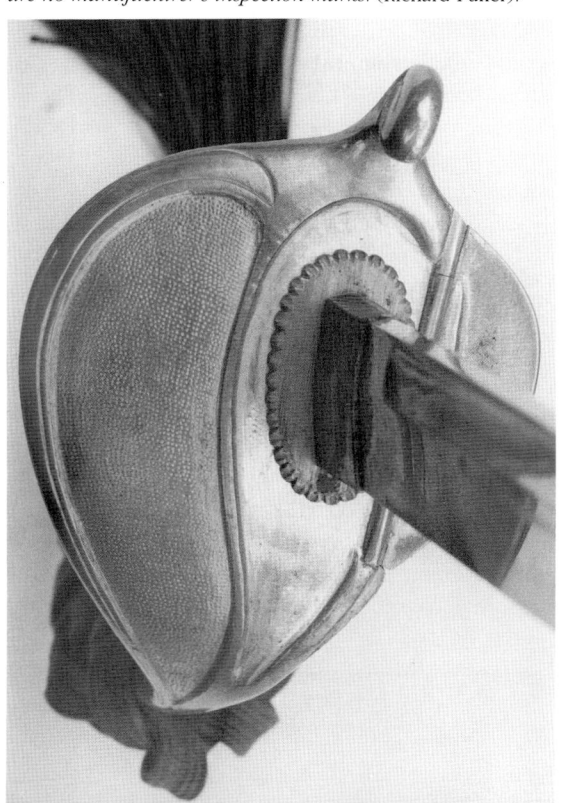

**Plate 240** *Photograph of Korean Prince Min-Yun-Huan, Commander-in-Chief of the Korean armed forces, which was taken about 1904. He wears a Japanese Army style dress uniform with cap and a Japanese style Army parade sabre with two hangers. Unfortunately the hilt decoration cannot be determined to ascertain if there are any distinguishing features. (Richard Fuller).*

# Dirks of the Mandated Territories (South Sea Islands)

In 1918 the captured German territories in the Pacific were mandated to Japan for their part in World War One. These consisted of the Mariana, Caroline and Marshall Islands. They were subsequently lost by Japan during World War Two. A Government-Generals Department was established to run the vast area involved. The wearing of swords and dirks was authorised in 1919, to accord with the administrations dress regulations.

### 1919 pattern Junior Officials dirk of the Government-General of the Mandated Territories

As with other governmental dirks this is based on the 1883 pattern Commissioned Officers naval pattern, but is only known from the drawing in Fig. 42.[1]

Gilded brass fittings decorated only with stippling except for the pommel cap which has a raised sakura (cherry blossom). The grip is samē but colouration is uncertain. The menuki (hilt ornaments) are in the form of a kadosakura within a multi-leaf wreath similar to that in Fig.51(vii) which presumably represents this government organisation (Fig. 51 (viii)).

### 1919 pattern Senior Officials dirk of the Government-General of the Mandated Territories

Senior Officials would be expected to wear a dirk but no example or description has been located. A more ornate version of the Junior Officials model is likely, retaining the same menuki badge, but having a different coloured grip.

### 1919 pattern Officials swords of the Government-General of the Mandated Territories

*Swords of Imperial Japan 1868–1945* illustrates two parade sabre-style swords for this use which were authorised on 22 August 1919.

The Hannin (Junior) Officials version has gilded brass hilt and scabbard mounts decorated only with stippling and a raised kadosakura within a multi-leaf wreath (similar to Fig.51(viii)) on each

## DIRKS OF THE MANDATED TERRITORIES (SOUTH SEA ISLANDS)

backstrap side-ear. A raised sakura surmounts the pommel. Black grip. Leather or lacquered shagreen scabbard with raised suspension bands and distinctive U-shaped recesses to all mounts. Plated blade with an optional acid-etched yakiba.

The Sōnin (Senior) Officials model has identical side-ear decoration plus a sakura with radiating leaves on the upper backstrap, handguard and each scabbard mount. White grip. 1914 naval parade sabre-style scabbard with arrow-shaped recesses/projections.

Both versions have a small folding rear hilt guard and projecting scabbard stud as used on naval scabbards.

No references to Chokunin (there being no Shinnin) rank swords are known.

All examples of swords and dirks for this Government-General organisation must be regarded as very rare.

*Swords of Imperial Japan 1868–1945* confirms the authorisation of swords for the Kwantung Leased Territories (Kanto Government). These were introduced for Japanese civil officials on 29 August 1906. The emblem used was similar to Fig.51(viii).

The same reference states that swords were authorised for Japanese officials of Tsingtao on 16 October 1917 until Japan's voluntary withdrawal on 10 December 1922. However the motif used is unknown. It may be similar to that in Fig.51(viii) or, perhaps, be two sakura, from which emanate buds, over a wreath consisting of three large leaves on each side. An unidentified parade sabre with the latter motif on the hilt side-ears is shown on page 139 of that reference. The grip is black, all fittings are stippled and the scabbard mounts have boars eye (heart-shaped) recesses. Obviously a Hannin (junior grade) officials sword pattern. A dirk with the same emblem is also known.

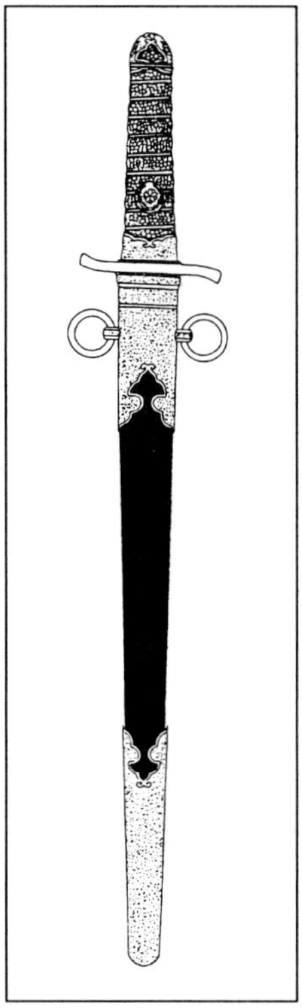

***Fig. 42*** *1919 pattern Junior Officials dirk of the Government-General of the Mandated Territories (South Sea Islands) with a sakura within a multi-leaf wreath sakura. (Imperial Japanese Daggers).*

---
1 Identified by *Imperial Japanese Daggers 1883–1945*.

# Swords and Dirks of Manchukuo (Manchuria)

The Japanese became heavily involved in Manchuria during the Russo–Japanese war of 1904–5. However, the 1905 treaty of Portsmouth forced a withdrawal from Manchuria proper to the Liaotung peninsula, which became known as the 'Kwantung Leased Territories'. The Kwantung (Kanto) government was established in 1905 and the 'Kwantung Army' in 1906. The South Manchuria Railway zone from Port Arthur to Changchun also remained under Japanese control and acted independently as a Japanese colony.

The Japanese extended their influence until invading and occupying southern Manchuria and then the northern area in 1932. The country was renamed 'Manchukuo' on 18 March of that year under the protection of the Japanese Kwantung Army. A figurehead in the form of the deposed Chinese Emperor Pu-Yi was appointed by the Japanese. He was crowned Emperor Kang-te on 1 March 1934.

The formation of Manchukuo was accompanied by the introduction of uniforms, medals and accoutrements. Uniform dress regulations, in the form of line drawings, confirm Japanese style swords and dirks were prescribed[1]. The patterns adopted were (a) Kyu-guntō. (Emperor Kang-te has been photographed with this type). (b) Parade sabre. (c) Sabre type incorporating a sword knot ring in the rear quillion as shown in Plate 243. (d) Field Marshals style 'Kenukigata-tachi'. (e) Two forms of dirks with hilt backstraps.

Unfortunately the lack of page numbering and poor reproduction of the author's copies do not allow translation of the captions to confirm identification or rank grades. Hilt backstraps designs, possibly for the Guard Police, have been reproduced in Fig. 44. Other backstrap designs are illustrated in the regulations but use has not been established.

Crossed Manchukuoan flags often appear on hilt backstraps (Fig.44). The main ground is yellow with an upper corner canton divided into four horizontal stripes which are, from top to bottom, red, blue, white and black. These five colours represent the races of Manchuria i.e. Koreans, Manchus, Japanese, Mongols and Chinese respectively.

The most common motif found on these edged weapons is the 'Plum blossom' (Fig. 2(viii)) which may also be present on Chinese Republican and Nationalist dress swords and dirks. Fig. 44 shows two other Manchukuoan motifs being the Manchurian Sorghum (Kaoliang) and stylised Orchid blossom.

Examples of Manchukuoan swords and dirks seem to be very rare. Those located by the authors appear, not surprisingly, to be Japanese made. Whether some were manufactured locally is unknown.

Commissioned Manchukuoan officers, NCOs,

# SWORDS AND DIRKS OF MANCHUKUO (MANCHURIA)

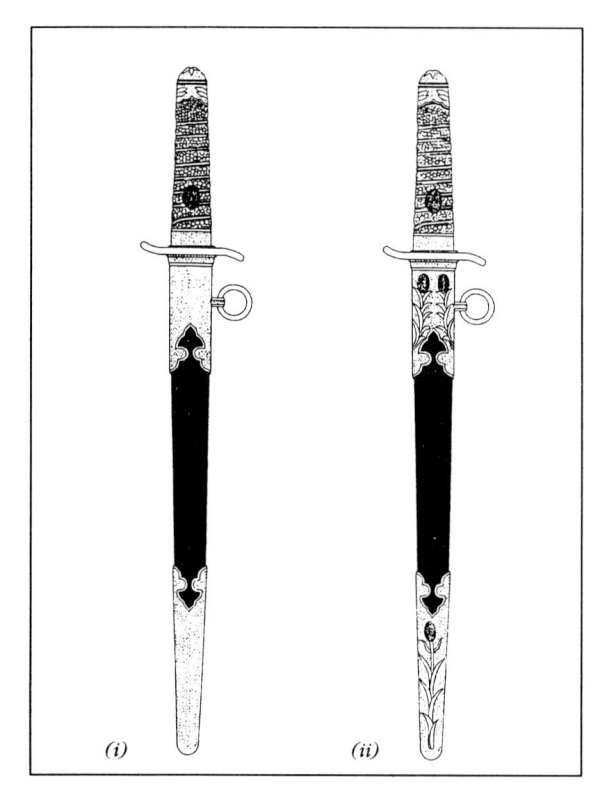

*Fig. 43  c.1932 pattern dirks of (Civil?) Manchukuo Officials: (i) Junior Officials; (ii) Senior Officials. with Sorghum-head menuki (Imperial Japanese Daggers).*

police, civil and palace officials seem to have carried swords and dirks in accordance with the previously mentioned dress regulations. However the dirks shown in Fig. 43 and Plate 241 (since not included) were probably worn by Japanese officials of the Manchurian Governor-Generals Department and not by Manchukuoan personnel.[2]

Both the following dirks are based on the Japanese 1883 pat. Naval Commissioned Officers model but incorporate only one suspension mount.

## Junior (Civil?) Officials dirk

Gilded brass fittings decorated with stippling only. White samé grip with brass wire binding and menuki (hilt ornaments) set over a male and

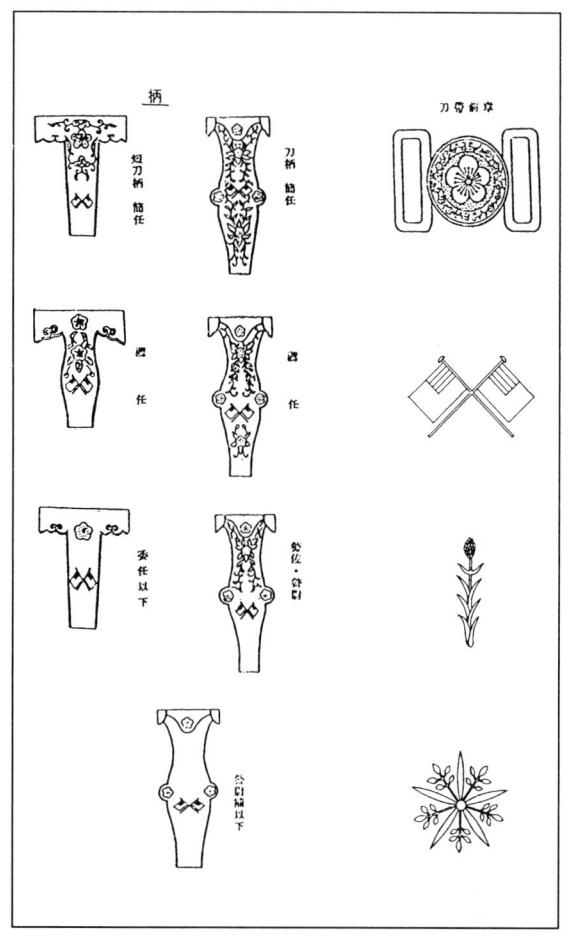

*Fig. 44  Extract from the Manchukuo (Manchurian) uniform dress regulations illustrating backstrap designs of dirks (left) and swords (right) which are believed to represent the four seniority grades of the Guard Police. Right is the (dress?) sword belt buckle with a plum blossom motif. Added below are the crossed Manchukuoan flags, Manchurian Sorghum and stylised orchid blossom, all associated with Manchukuo swords, medals and insignia.*

female hilt-securing system. The design of the menuki represents a head of the Manchurian Sorghum. The pommel cap is surmounted by a raised five-pointed star. The scabbard of the example shown is covered with black shagreen and the top locket incorporates a push button spring clip retention system. Note that only one suspension ring is used. Standard plated grooved dirk blade. Since only one example has been located it, perhaps, can be considered as very rare.

— 175 —

JAPANESE MILITARY AND CIVIL SWORDS AND DIRKS

***Plate 241*** *c.1932 pattern Junior (Civil?) Officials dirk of Manchukuo (Manchuria). (Ron Gregory).*

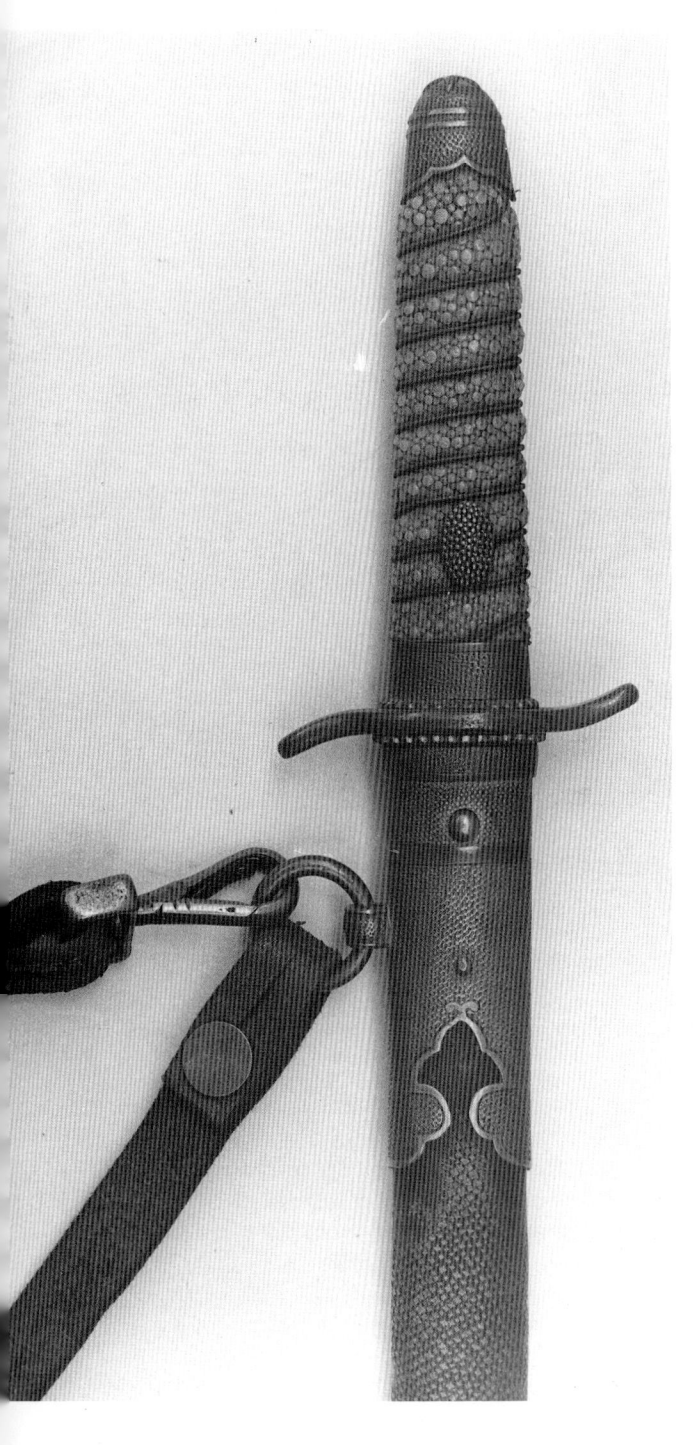

***Plate 242*** *Hilt detail of a Junior (Civil?) Officials dirk of Manchukuo (Manchuria) clearly showing the Manchurian Sorghum head menuki (hilt ornament). (Ron Gregory).*

## Senior (Civil?) Officials dirk

The hilt appears to be identical to the Junior Officials model. However, the scabbard fittings are much more ornate featuring Manchurian Sorghum heads, stalks and leaves.

No example has been located so, again, it appears to be very rare.

## Manchukuo sword

At first glance this item appears to be a Japanese-made Civil Officials sword. However, closer examination of decorative detail indicates use in Manchukuo. The hilt backstrap design is shown in the Manchukuoan dress regulations (Fig. 44) and is believed to represent the lowest Guard Police rank entitled to carry such weapons. Probably post 1934.

Gilded brass hilt fitting having a stippled background decoration. The upper backstrap features a 'plum blossom' motif which is also repeated on each side-ear (Fig. 2 (viii)). Two crossed Manchukuoan flags are situated in the middle of the backstrap. Small solid guard which terminates at the rear with a ring set in the vertical plane. Note that the rear section of the guard is not inverted upwards to the extent found on many of the Japanese civil swords shown elsewhere in this book. The pommel cap also has an extended fitting with a hole for the sword knot. Wooden grip with a black lacquered finish and brass wire in the grooves. Push button and spring clip scabbard retention system. Factory-made blade without any markings. Plated steel scabbard with a wooden liner. The sword knot shown is the black Japanese army kyu-guntō type which seems incorrect. A brown or black leather Japanese style NCOs knot is indicated in the dress regulations. The classification must be very rare.

---

1 Obtained by Ugo Pericoli for the film *The Last Emperor* with copies kindly provided by Philip Jowett. Dateable pages are from 1932 to 1938.
2 Identified as 'Manchurian Officers dirks' in *Imperial Japanese Dirks 1883–1945*.

**Plates 243, 244**  *Hilt and backstrap of a Manchukuo sword for possible Guard Police use. See Fig. 44. (Patrick Lundy).*

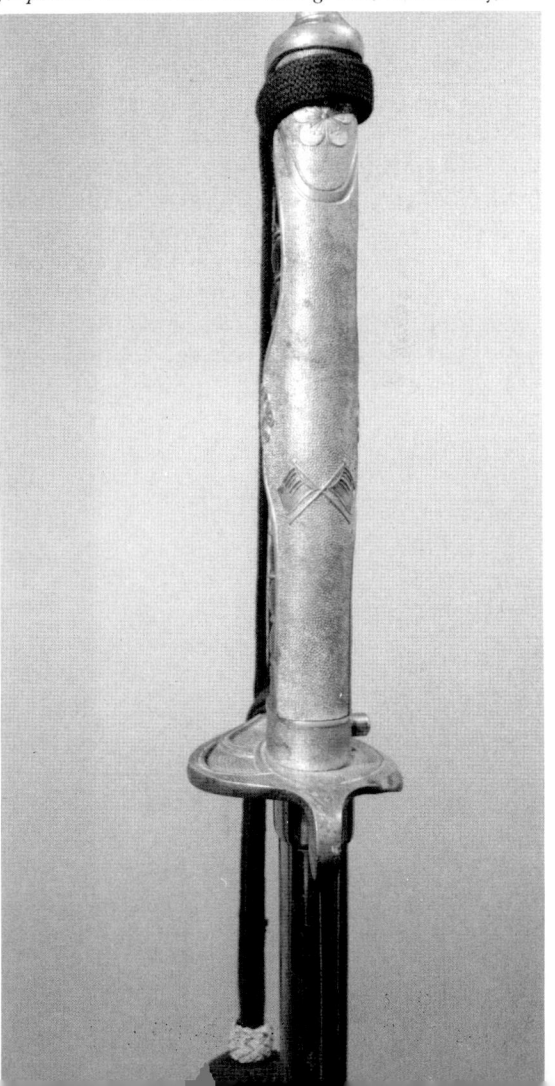

# Forestry Officials Dirks

Forestry Officials, who were controlled by the Ministry of Agriculture and Forestry, were apparently authorised to carry dirks, but the use of swords has not been confirmed. The circumstances of dirk wear is unknown but usage may have continued until 1945.

There appears to be two patterns of dirks subdivided into rank models.[1] The first is nineteenth-century, probably being introduced in the late eighteen-eighties. The second was introduced in 1903. Previously they have erroneously been identified as 'transitional naval dirks' because of the sakura and leaf decoration. However, unlike naval dirks all hilts have backstraps, and scabbard mounts feature heart-shaped (boar's eye) recesses. Examples of the first pattern must be regarded as very rare, but several examples of the second pattern are known so, perhaps, they must be classified as rare. It is also probable that all patterns had plated blades as standard, although hand-forged traditional blades appear to have been optional.

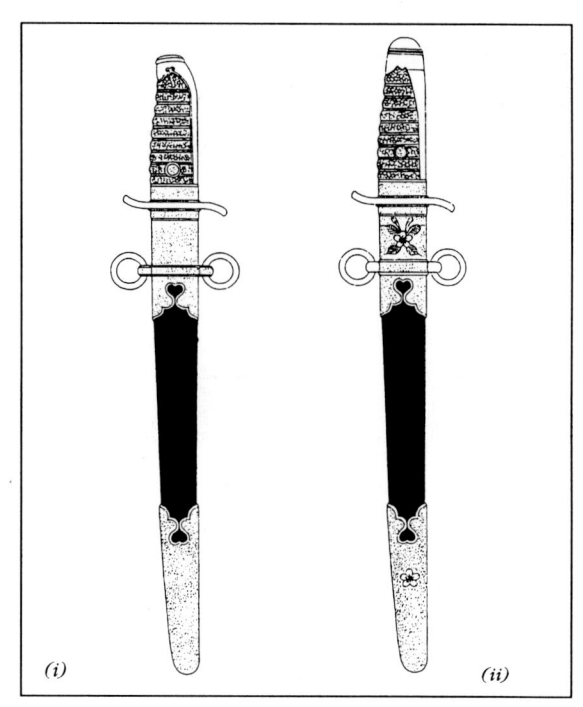

**Fig. 45** *First pattern (Meiji period) Forestry Officials dirks: (i) Foresters (silver-plated); (ii) Senior Foresters (gilded).* (Imperial Japanese Daggers).

### First pattern Foresters model

The basic model shown in Fig. 45(i) has a (black?) samē grip, plain backstrap and flattened pommel. The scabbard is probably wood with a black leather covering or has a black lacquered finish. The backstrap and pommel are plain but the fuchi (hilt collar) and scabbard have a stippled decoration. All hilt and scabbard fittings have a plated silver finish.

### First pattern Senior Foresters model

This is basically the same as the Foresters model but is distinguished by a sakura with four radiating leaves on the top scabbard mount and a pronounced dome pommel. Fig. 45(ii). The grip is probably white samē. The bottom scabbard mount only has a sakura. All hilt and scabbard fittings are gilded.

# FORESTRY OFFICIALS DIRKS

## Second (1903) pattern Foresters model

This is a slimmer version of the equivalent grade first pattern model. All fittings are plain and have a plated silver finish. Fig. 46(i).

An unusual example with a black samē grip and curved hand-forged blade of shinogi-zukuri form is shown in Plates 245, 246. The pommel is surmounted by a raised sakura. The blade is fitted with a habaki (blade collar). Black leather scabbard. Overall length of dirk and scabbard 487mm (19 3/16"). Hilt length 117mm (4 5/8"). Blade length 327mm (12 7/8"). Maximum blade width 21mm (13/16").

**Fig. 46** *Second (1903) pattern Forestry Officials dirks: (i) Foresters (silver-plated); (ii) Junior Forestry Officials (silver-plated). (Imperial Japanese Daggers).*

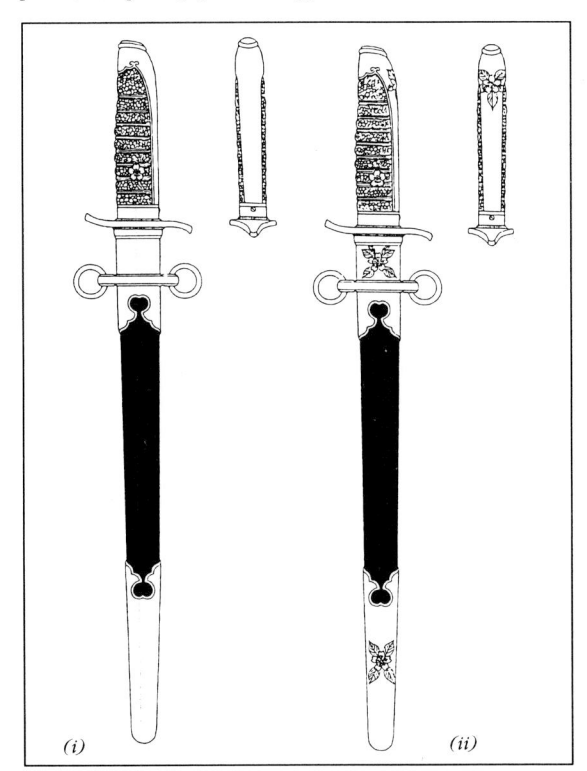

## Second (1903) pattern Junior Foresters model

Similar to the Foresters model but with the addition of a sakura and leaf decoration on the backstrap and both scabbard fittings. All fittings are believed to have a plain background with a plated silver finish. Fig. 46(ii).

**Plate 245** *Hilt of a second (1903) pattern Foresters dirk. (Donald Barnes).*

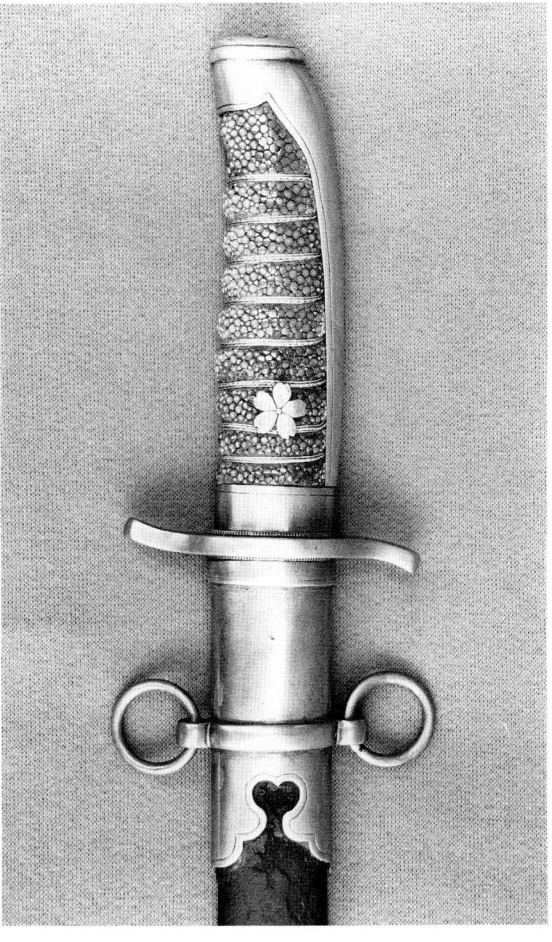

**Plate 246** *Rare and unusual curved blade variation of the second (1903) pattern Foresters model dirk with plated silver fittings. (Donald Barnes).*

JAPANESE MILITARY AND CIVIL SWORDS AND DIRKS

## Second (1903) pattern Senior Foresters model

Identical to the Junior Foresters model except that the scabbard has a stippled decoration and all metal fittings are gilded. Fig. 47.

The example photographed has a white samé grip with a sakura menuki (hilt ornaments) surmounting male and female hilt-securing screws. The fuchi (hilt collar) and crossguards are made of gilded steel. There is an unidentified stamp (Fig. 61 (xv)) on the guard underside. Machine-made, straight grooved blade with a brass habaki (blade collar). Black lacquered wooden scabbard with gilded fittings. Push button and spring clip retention system.

Overall length of dirk and scabbard 413mm (16¼"). Hilt length 106mm (4 3/16"). Blade length to guard 256mm (10 1/8"). Maximum blade width 18mm (11/16"). Weight of dirk and scabbard 10½ ounces

**Fig. 47** *Second (1903) pattern Senior Forestry Officials (gilded) dirk.* (Imperial Japanese Daggers).

**Fig. 48** *Possible second (1903) pattern Forestry Officials dirk of unidentified grade.* (Brenton Williams).

## Possible second (1903) pattern Forestry Officials dirk of unidentified grade

Forestry Officials dirks are one of only three known types with heart-shaped (boar's eye) scabbard mount recesses.[2] The example illustrated would thus seem to belong to this organisation although it lacks the sakura and leaf decoration. However, all scabbard and hilt mounts are entirely decorated with a stippled effect of tiny recessed dots. This implies its grade lies between the Junior (ii) and Senior (iii) Foresters models since gilded, but there may be some other unidentified, but associated, branch of this service.

Gilded brass fittings. White samé grip. Standard grooved and plated blade with an acid-etched temper line. Black leather scabbard. Overall length of dirk and scabbard 406mm (16").

1 Identified in *Imperial Japanese Daggers 1883–1945*.
2 The others are the Fire Bureau Vice-Commander and the Naval Prison Governors dirks, although the latter does not have a backstrap.

# FORESTRY OFFICIALS DIRKS

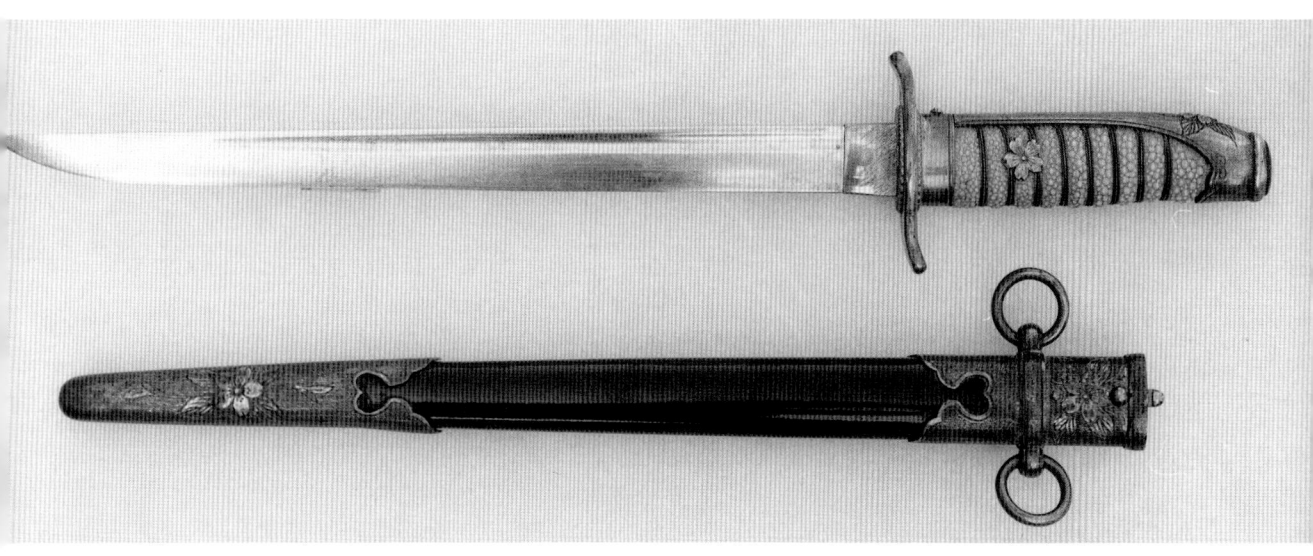

***Plate 247*** *1903 pattern Senior Forestry Officials dirk with gilded fittings and black lacquered scabbard. (Richard Fuller).*

***Plates 248, 249*** *Hilt and top scabbard locket of the 1903 pattern Senior Forestry Officials dirk. (Richard Fuller).*

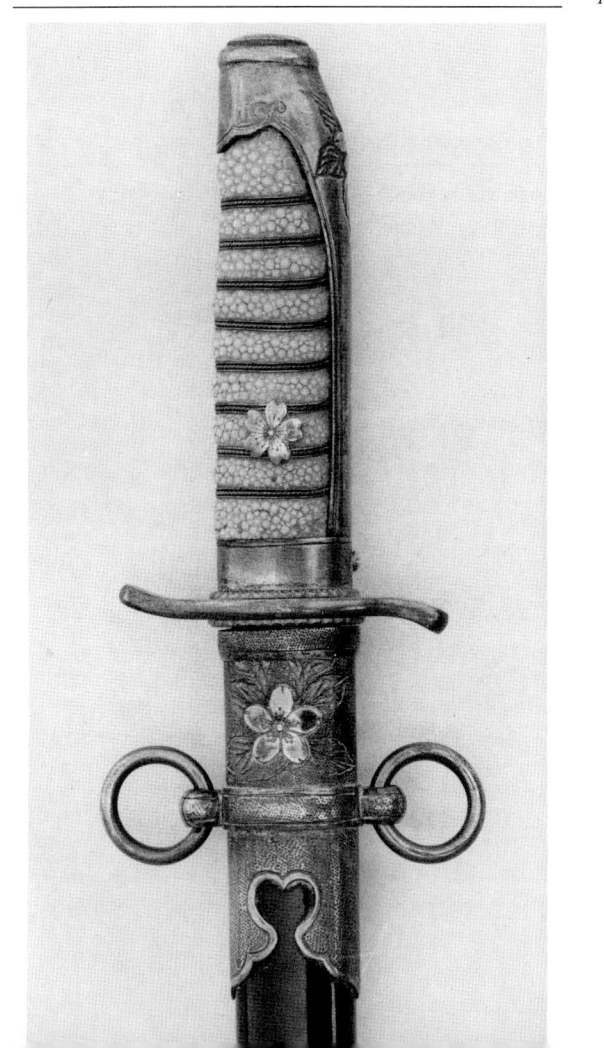

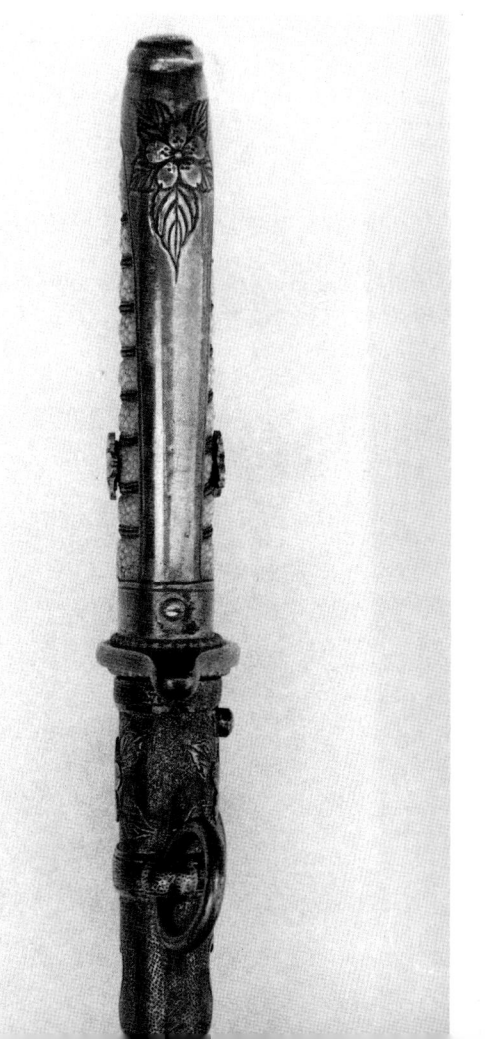

# National Railways Board Dirks

The Japanese National Railways Board authorised its officials to carry dirks. Wear was probably restricted to ceremonial occasions, but this has not been confirmed. Two models of dirks were introduced in 1909 for both Junior and Senior Officials.[1] *Swords of Imperial Japan 1868–1945* illustrates a National Railways sword identified by an engine drive-wheel motif on the backstrap side-ears

## 1909 pattern Junior Officials dirk

Several examples of this dirk are known which are virtually identical except for the scabbard covering.[2]

Gilded brass mounts, black samé grip and black leather or black lacquered shagreen scabbard. The menuki (hilt ornaments) are located on the normal male and female hilt-securing screws. They are in the form of a 5:7:5 floret kiri (Fig. 2 (i)). Both scabbard mounts are engraved with the 5:7:5 floret kiri although the top locket of that shown in Fig. 49 has the 3:5:3 version. It is unlikely that there were two models for this rank grade so the drawing is thought to be in error in this respect. Standard dirk push button and spring clip retention system. Plated steel blade usually with an acid-etched yakiba and a brass habaki (blade collar).

A rare item which has often erroneously been described as a naval Flag Officers (Admirals) dirk.

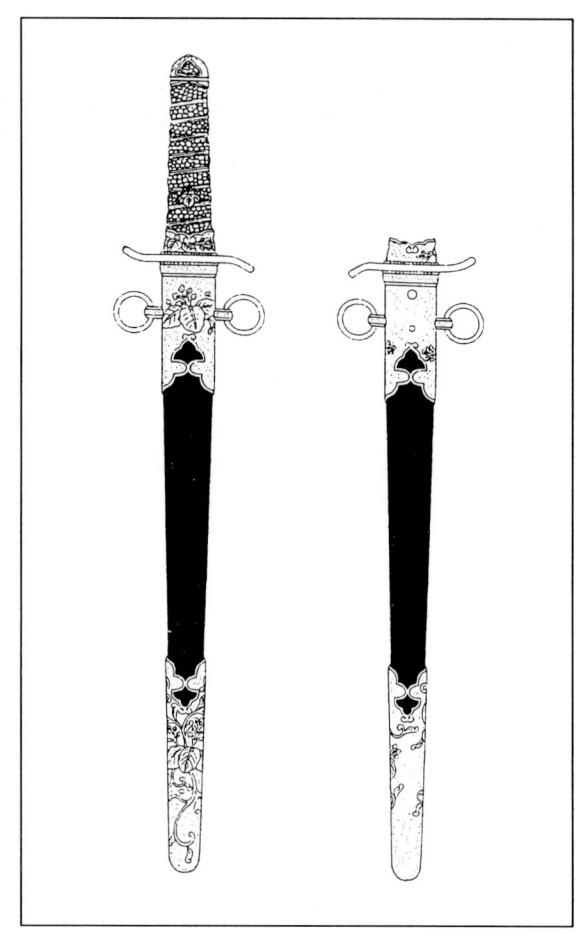

*Fig. 49* Obverse and reverse of the 1909 pattern National Railways Board Junior Officials dirk. (Imperial Japanese Daggers).

# NATIONAL RAILWAYS BOARD DIRKS

## 1909 pattern Senior Officials dirk

No example has been located but it appears from Fig. 50 to be a more ornate version of the Junior Officials model. The hilt fittings are the same but the grip may be white samē. However, the scabbard mounts have the addition of engraved open (peony?) blossoms. Press button spring clip retention system.

This must be classified as very rare. Note the similarity to the Imperial Household Senior Officials dirk in Fig. 37.

---

1 Identified as such in *Imperial Japanese Daggers 1883–1945*.
2 A Japanese company in Tokyo currently produces an exact reproduction of this dirk with a shagreen scabbard. Only its mint condition distinguishes it from an original.

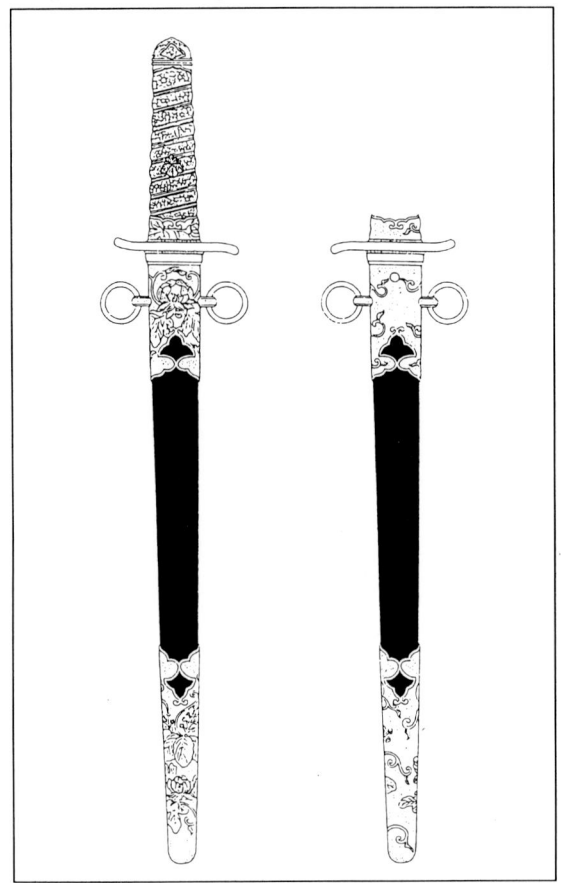

**Fig. 50** *Obverse and reverse of the 1909 pattern National Railways Board Senior Officials dirk.* (Imperial Japanese Daggers).

**Plate 250** *Rare 1909 pattern National Railways Board Junior Officials dirk. The menuki (hilt ornaments) is in the form of a five 5:7:5 floret kiri. This is also engraved on the upper and lower scabbard mounts. Gilded brass hilt and scabbard fittings. Black lacquered leather scabbard. Plated steel single-edged blade with an acid-etched yakiba (tempered edge).* (Ron Gregory).

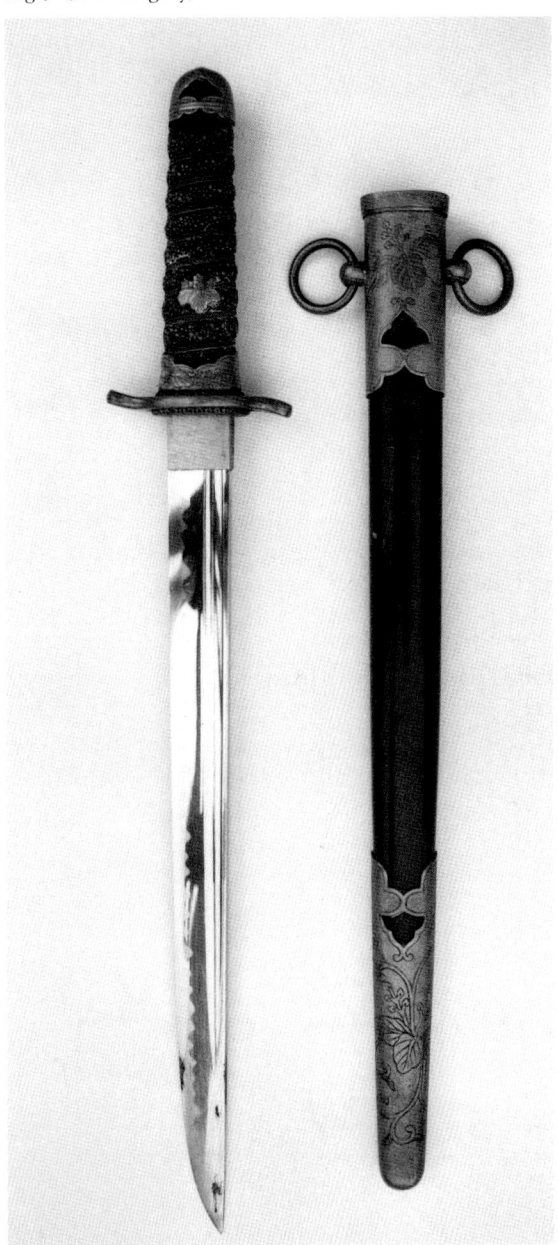

# JAPANESE MILITARY AND CIVIL SWORDS AND DIRKS

**Plate 251**  Top scabbard locket and fuchi (hilt collar) of the 1909 pattern National Railways Board Junior Officials dirk. This example has a black lacquered shagreen scabbard. (Donald Barnes).

**Plate 252**  Bottom scabbard mount of the 1909 pattern National Railways Board Junior Officials dirk. (Donald Barnes).

# Police Swords and Dirks

## Police Bureau

Prior to the Edo period (1600–1868) policing was performed by samurai and groups of local citizens.[1] Under the shogunate, from 1600, town magistrates with samurai status were appointed to act concurrently as judge, prosecutor and chief of police. Also appointed were police sergeants (Yoriki) and policemen (Doshiro) who were sword-carrying samurai, the former being mounted. They were assisted by detectives (Maekashi) who were often outcasts or former criminals and were armed only with a 'jitte', which was a metal truncheon or sword breaker.

In 1872, after the commencement of the Meiji period (1868–1912) a former samurai, Kawaji Toshiyoshi, was sent to Europe to study Western policing systems. He returned in 1873 and recommended reorganisation based on the Prussian and French police systems which was accepted and implemented with the establishment of the Home Ministry (Naimushō) in 1873. This set up and controlled the Police Bureau (Keihokyoku) although general duties were managed at prefectural level under a local governor. In 1874 the Tokyo Metropolitan Police Department (Keishichō) was founded. A Ministry of Justice (Shihōshō) was also formed to separate judicial matters from police control. However, police responsibilities far exceeded those relating to criminal matters since they also controlled fire brigades (1881–1948) and regulated public health, construction, factories, issuing permits and licences etc.

During the Satsuma Rebellion of 1877 the government lost a large proportion of their main forces and reserves. Therefore, to make up numbers, ex-samurai were recruited into the national police force and then used in battle apparently organised into brigades. The Tokyo police, in particular, were heavily engaged and fought with swords. Whether they used traditional katana or issue swords such as those shown in Fig. 52 is uncertain. By 1883 the police consisted of 23,000 'educated' men controlled by the Police Bureau. Around this time they were reorganised with the formation of a training school and were dispersed from garrisons to local stations and villages.

1928 saw the establishment of the Special Higher Police (Tokubetsu kōtō keisatsu, which was abbreviated to Tokko) in all prefectures.[2] They were also known as the 'Thought Police'. Their job was to investigate and censor political activities thought prejudicial to the State. They were independent and ruthless, reporting directly to Tokyo and not to prefectural headquarters. Uniforms were dark (blue?) with distinguishing striped armbands. Swords, and possibly dirks, were carried by officers at least.

The outbreak of fighting in China in 1937 led to an increase in police responsibilities which included labour mobilisation, control of transport, regulating political meetings, publications and the

# JAPANESE MILITARY AND CIVIL SWORDS AND DIRKS

cinema etc. The Military Police (Kempei) were under the command of the armed forces but were not restricted to military matters. They also assisted the civil police, especially in cases involving illegal political activities. The political influence of the military grew after 1931, thus enabling the Kempei to become more powerful. They even assumed normal police functions which led to disagreement with civil police officers. This state of affairs lasted until the end of World War Two in 1945, after which the police were totally reorganised in accordance with American recommendations.

## Police badges and weapons

Uncertainty still surrounds the use of badges shared, or used separately, by the Police and Fire Bureaux.

Those shown in Fig. 51 (i) to (iv) are known to be Police but *Imperial Japanese Daggers 1883–1945* also illustrates (iii) on Fire Bureau dirks, thus indicating concurrent use by the latter organisation. Fig. 51 (i) is reported to be used by pre-1945 Mounted Civil Police[3] while Fig. 51 (ii) is Civil Police above the rank of Assistant Inspector.[4] However, Fig. 51 (iii) is definitely known to be the current Police badge but is assumed to have been previously used by ranks up to Assistant Inspector. Figs. 2 (iii), (iv) are thought to represent the most senior Police/Fire Bureau ranks but could indicate usage by an unidentified Police organisation. See pages 31, 39–43. Thus there is still an element of

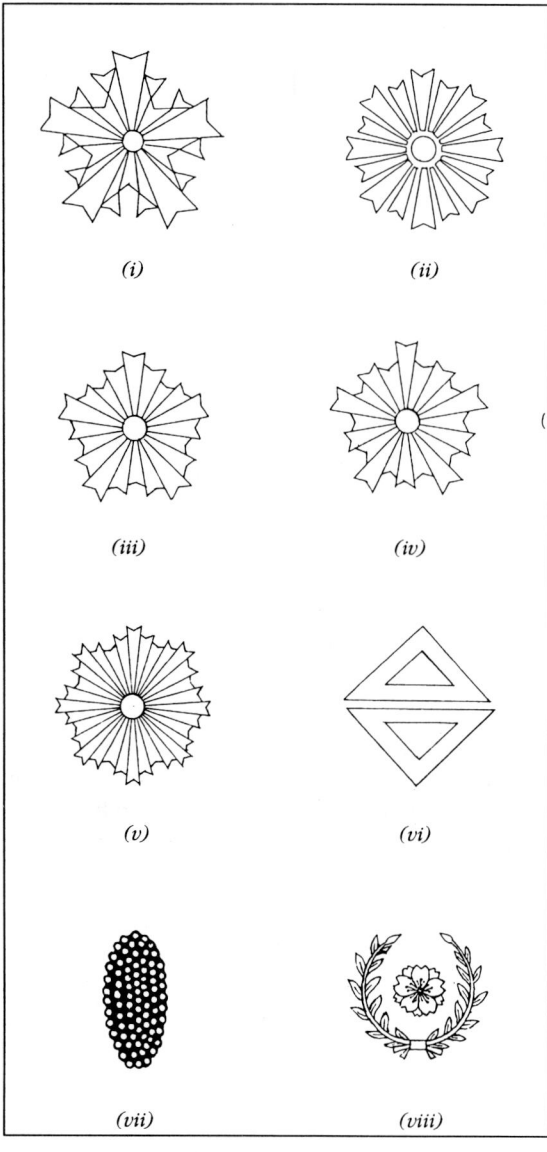

**Fig. 51** *Badges and insignia. With the exception of (iv) and (v), which could be confused with others shown, they have all been found on swords and/or dirks. See also Fig. 2 (iii), (iv).*

(i) Pre-1945 Mounted Civil Police although exclusive use by this branch has not been confirmed.
(ii) Civil Police for Inspectors (and above?). (Known as a 'Hakkou' it consists of sixteen alternating long and short 'notched' sun rays.)
(iii) Civil Police (service dress?) probably up to, and including, Assistant Inspector. Fire Bureau. Post-WW2 Police rank badge. Also found on the 1875 pattern Army Officers dress sword.(Twenty 'notched' arrows or rays of variable lengths.)
(iv) Associated with the standard cap badge of the Police, c.1911, but appears to have been superseded by (iii) at an unknown date. (Twenty 'notched' arrows or rays of variable lengths.)
(v) Army Military and Civil Police (full dress). Army full dress uniform cap badge. Cap badge of officials of the Korean and Formosan Government-Generals, c.1911. Order of the Rising Sun. (Thirty-two 'notched' arrows or rays of variable lengths.)
(vi) Government-General of Formosa, post-1910.
(vii) Manchurian Sorghum (Kaoliang) head.
(viii) Government-General Departments of the Kwantung Leased Territories and, perhaps, Tringtao. A multi-leaf wreath version was used by the Mandated Territories (South Sea Islands) Government-Generals Department.

# POLICE SWORDS AND DIRKS

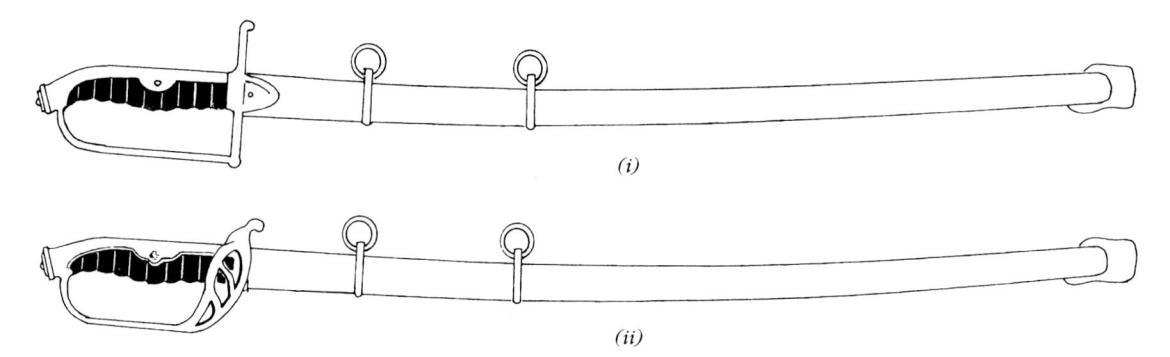

***Fig. 52*** *Satsuma Rebellion (1877) period Police swords: (i) Police or Patrolmans sword; (ii) probable Officers sword.*

uncertainty over the identification of these badges. Therefore, the edged weapons shown in this section are assumed to be Police until evidence to the contrary is produced. No evidence has been located to confirm that the Military Police (Kempei) carried edged weapons which had a distinguishing badge. Therefore, it is believed that they carried standard military swords.

Photographs of the 1920s and 1930s show uniformed police carrying swords whilst engaged in crowd control. Unfortunately, as so often happens, they are too indistinct to permit positive identification of patterns. The variation in type, size and decoration seems to indicate an evolution of patterns. Naturally the assumption is that the more ornate a weapon, the more senior was the owner.

Three types of weapon bearing the Police badges are encountered which can be categorised as follows:

Dirks – They are assumed to be for 'walking-out' (off duty?) purposes.
Hanger – These are short swords which may have been service weapons. Possibly they were superseded by full-sized swords.
Swords – These seem to be of the parade sabre type.

The two sword patterns shown in Fig. 52, and described below, are based on drawings in the *Nippon no Gunso* (see Bibliography). The heading for both refers to the '3rd Independent (flying) Brigade' at the time of the Satsuma Rebellion in 1877. The caption to Fig. 52 (i) indicates that this is a Police unit which would have fought for the government. It is probable that the swords shown are earlier and were not introduced in that year. Neither appear to have any form of Police badge.

### c.1877 Police or Patrolmans sword

Nothing is known regarding this sword pattern except for the drawing in Fig. 52 (i). The caption reads 'JUNSA HAITŌ', i.e. sword carried by Police or patrolman. The hilt configuration is unlike any other known Japanese sword pattern and is decidedly European in appearance.

### c.1877 Police (Officers?) sword

This sword (Fig. 52 (ii)) is drawn (together with the last item) in the *Nippon no Gunso* but does not have a separate caption. Because of the similarity with the Army kyu-guntō it is thought that use was by officers. Indeed the backstrap and pommel configuration is identical to the 1875 pat. Company Officers kyu-guntō which may have been the basis for this sword pattern and was contemporaneous with it. However, the curved-bar handguard appears to be the same as the c.1871 Army Commissioned Officers sword. Presumably there were more ornate versions for Senior ranks. What replaced it, and when, is unknown.

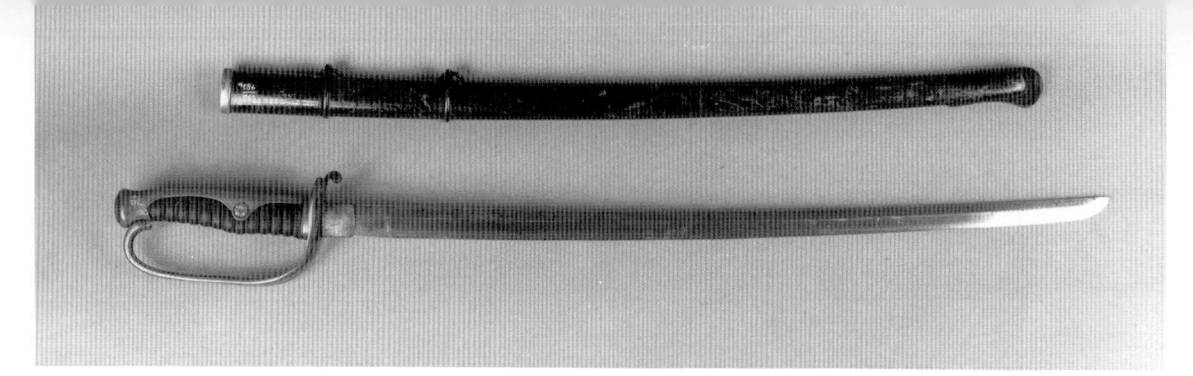

**Plate 253** *Satsuma Rebellion (1877) period Police (Officers?) sword. (Courtesy of Thomas Burke Memorial, Washington State Museum, cat. no. 8.7E195).*

An actual example is shown in Plates 253, 254. It differs from the drawing only in that the handguard is flat and is not semi-bowl or cupped, but that may be artistic licence to show the guard design. The hilt fittings are brass with an open curved-bar guard of European influence. Black shagreen hilt having intermittent brass wire binding. A spring clip, with a press stud in the form of a sakura, is set in the fuchi (hilt collar). It engages with a slot in the scabbard mouthpiece. The hilt is secured to the blade tang by a bamboo peg plus a male-female screw system through the backstrap side-ears which terminate with kadosakura on both sides.

The blade is standard shinogi-zukuri form which, in the known example, is Kotō period (pre-1596) and has been shortened. Brass habaki (blade collar). A steel scabbard with two suspension mounts appears to be the normal military type. However, the item shown has a coating of dark brown lacquer of some age but it is probably not contemporary since a chromium- or nickel-plated finish would be expected.

Dimensions no doubt varied. Overall length of hilt and scabbard shown 965mm (38"). Hilt length (from base of habaki) 187mm (7³⁄₈"). Blade length 711mm (28"). Scabbard length 775mm (30½").

Since this is the only example known to the authors it may be regarded as very rare.

The identification of Mounted Police edged weapons is based on the presence of the badge shown in Fig. 51 (i). It would be expected that they also carried some form of fighting sword or sabre, but only the dirk and hangers described in this section have been reported. Dating of these weapons is uncertain.

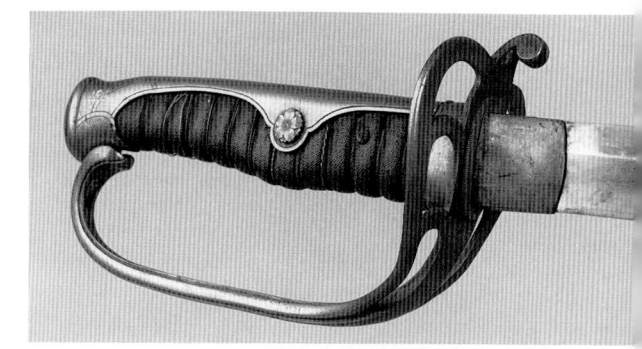

**Plate 254** *Hilt of a Satsuma Rebellion (1877) period Police (Officers?) sword. Note the backstrap and pommel configuration which is identical to the Army 1875 pat. Company Officers kyu-guntō pattern. (Courtesy of Thomas Burke Memorial, Washington State Museum, cat. no. 8.7E195).*

**Fig. 53** *Mounted Police dirk, possibly a Junior Officers model. (Brenton Williams).*

POLICE SWORDS AND DIRKS

## Mounted Police dirk

Brass mounted hilt with a tendril and leaf decoration to the upper backstrap. A raised Mounted Police badge (Fig. 51 (i)) is also featured. The remaining backstrap and fuchi (hilt collar) have a stippled decoration of tiny recessed dots. Short crossguard with inverted ends. White samé grip with intermittent brass wire binding. Nickel-plated scabbard having a raised suspension band and a single hanging ring. Machine-made single-edged blade.

The backstrap configuration and tendril decoration is similar to the dirk patterns in Plates 261 and Fig. 54, although the hilt badges are all different. The general appearance suggests use by an officer of lower or middle rank.

## Mounted Police hanger (Type 1)

Two versions of this scarce sword pattern have been seen varying only in the length and grip covering. The shorter one is that normally encountered. It is unknown if the different lengths represent rank seniority, different use or are merely a matter of personal preference.

Hilt fittings are plain brass having a brown ed finish. The backstrap edge profile is curved and has a decorative line around the edge. A raised Mounted Police badge (Fig. 51 (i)) is situated on the upper backstrap. The raised protruding pommel band incorporates a ring for the sword knot. All short versions have been found with a black leather-covered grip and intermittent brass wire binding while that of the only long version examined is covered in black samé. A small obverse guard has two panels on the underside decorated with raised dots. The quillions are

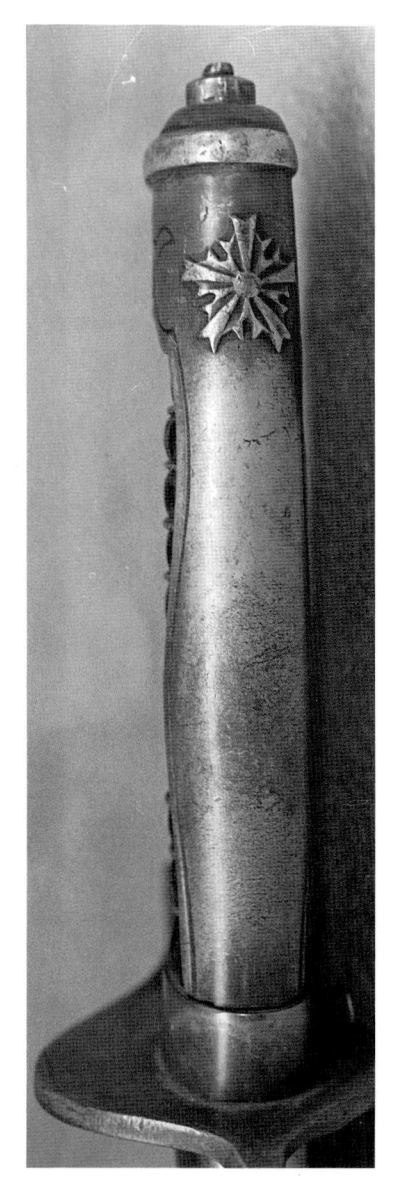

**Plate 256** *Backstrap of a Mounted Police hanger (Type 1) showing the identifying Mounted Police badge.* (Richard Fuller).

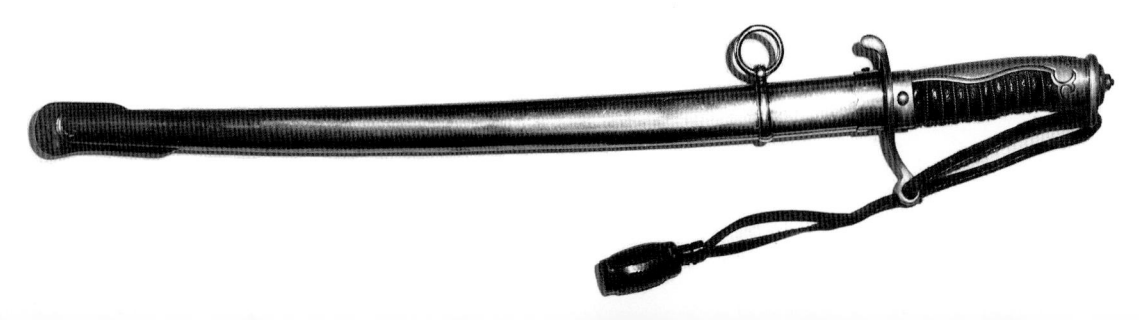

**Plate 255** *Mounted Police hanger or short sword (Type 1) complete with its original dark brown leather knot.* (Ron Gregory).

## JAPANESE MILITARY AND CIVIL SWORDS AND DIRKS

inverted but the rear is large and incorporates a ring, in the vertical plane, for the sword knot. Push button and spring clip scabbard retention system. Brown leather washer (buffer) against the guard.

The blade type is traditional shinogi-zukuri form with a tapered threaded tang which engages with a female screw acting as a pommel cap. These often appear to be contemporary hand-made with a narrow straight hamon of ko-nie. Brass habaki (blade collar). Wood-lined nickel-plated steel scabbard having a raised suspension band and one hanging ring. The throat band, secured by two screws, has a scalloped edge.

Dimensions given are for the short and long versions respectively. Overall length of sword and scabbard 620mm (24½"); 753mm (29¹³⁄₁₆"). Hilt length (from inside the guard) 127mm (5"); 150mm (5⅞"). Blade length (including habaki) 456mm (18"); 542mm (21⁵⁄₁₆"). Maximum blade width 23mm (¹⁵⁄₁₆"); 26mm (1"). Weight of sword 16½ ounces; 21½ ounces. Weight of sword and scabbard 23½ ounces; 27½ ounces.

The short dark brown knot shown in Plate 255 loops through the pommel crossguard. This is believed to be original and the correct system of tying.

Usage is believed to be by police officers of lower or middle rank since decoration is minimal.

An identical sword with the badge shown in Fig. 51(iv) is also known.

## Mounted Police hanger (Type 2)

This short sword is similar to that categorised as the Type 1 but has certain differences. These are the upper backstrap which is inclined, the presence of side-ears and decorative details, although the Mounted Police badge (Fig. 51 (i)) is still present. Brass hilt mounts and black leather grip. Press button and spring clip retention system.

Machine-made grooved blade. Brass habaki (blade collar). The scabbard is missing but is assumed to be steel with one or two hanging rings. The blade tang is stamped '63' while the guard underside is stamped '64'. These are assembly numbers but the mismatch appears to have occurred during the original assembly.

Overall length of hilt and blade 684mm (26⁵⁄₁₆"). Blade length 540mm (21¼"). Maximum blade width 21mm (¹³⁄₁₆").

Again this appears to be a 'pattern' since the presence of assembly numbers indicates more than one was made. Use is assumed to be by an officer of lower or middle rank. Whether the Type 1 and Type 2 represent manufacturers' variations or different usage is a matter for conjecture.

Police dirks are believed to have been carried by various ranks but were differentiated by the degree of decoration and at least two badges. They seem to be Fig. 51 (iii) - Sergeants and Junior Officers (up to Assistant Inspector) and Fig.51 (ii) - Senior Officers (Inspectors and above).

Patrolmen appear to have carried swords up to World War Two but none have been located to confirm details.

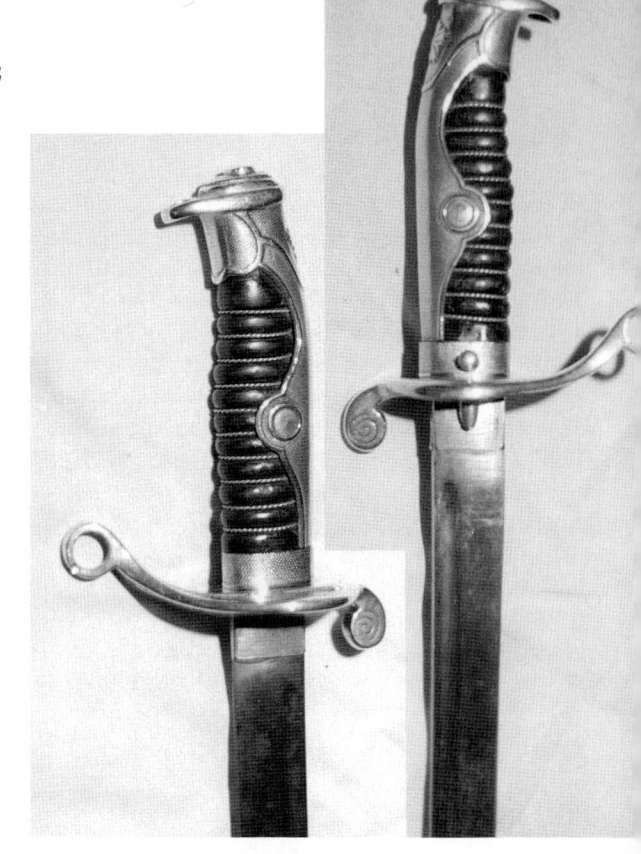

**Plates 257, 258** *Mounted Police hanger or short sword (Type 2). (Alan Heniger).*

## POLICE SWORDS AND DIRKS

## Police dirk (Sergeants?)

Plates 259, 260.

Plain brass hilt with a raised badge (Fig. 51 (iii)) on the upper backstrap. Black samē or leather grip with intermittent brass wire binding. Push button spring clip retention. Short crossguards with inverted ends. Nickel-plated steel scabbard having a raised suspension band and one hanging ring. Single-edged machine-made blade with a brass habaki and, sometimes, an acid-etched yakiba. The backstrap configuration is slightly different from dirks of other organisations but is similar to the Mounted Police sword in Plate 255. The plainness of the hilt fittings indicates use by lower ranks. It is possible that dirk wear by patrolmen was not authorised.

**Plates 259, 260** *Backstrap and hilt of a Police dirk for Sergeants?* (Courtesy of Brenton Williams).

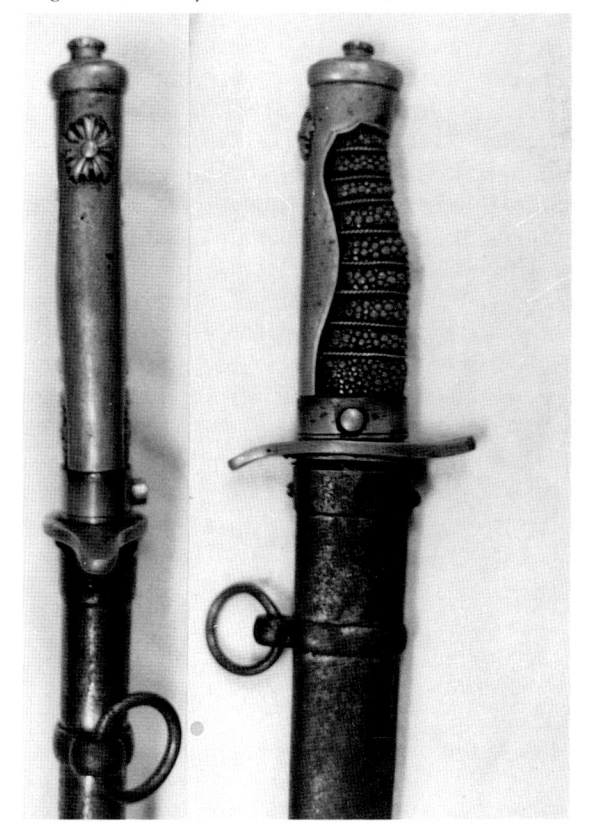

## Police dirk (Junior Officers)

This dirk is identical to the Senior Officers model shown in Plates 261, 262 but features the lower ranks badge (Fig. 51 (iii)) and lacks the leaf/tendril decoration. However the flower blooms are retained above and below the hilt badge.

## Police dirk (Senior Officers)

Only one example has been located so it is unknown if there are variations or if the pattern shown is typical. This is similar to, or based on, the 1889 pattern Fire Bureau Commanders dirk (see Plate 268).

The hilt backstrap has an upper decorated panel of leaves and tendrils plus the 'Hakkou' badge of sixteen alternating long and short 'notched' rays (Fig. 51 (ii)). White samē grip with intermittent brass wire binding and sakura menuki (hilt ornaments) which are fixed to male-female hilt-securing screws. Short crossguard with inverted ends. All hilt fittings are gilded brass. Push button spring clip retention system. The nickel-plated steel scabbard has a raised suspension band and two opposing hanging rings. Single-edged, straight mass-produced blade with a long narrow groove parallel to the back edge. Brass habaki (blade collar).

Perhaps very Senior Officers (Superintendent or equivalent) had even more ornate dirks.

**Plate 261** *Police dirk for Senior Officers with a steel scabbard. The distinguishing feature is a backstrap badge of sixteen alternating long and short 'notched' rays (Hakkou).* (Alan Clayton).

JAPANESE MILITARY AND CIVIL SWORDS AND DIRKS

*Plate 262* Backstrap decoration of the Senior Officers Police dirk shown in Plate 261. The distinguishing 'Hakkou' badge is apparent. (Alan Clayton).

## Police sword (Senior Officers)

Use of this sword pattern is believed to be for Inspectors (and above?). The appearance is that of an Army General Officers grade parade sabre and, indeed, the hilt side-ears with sakura and pierced handguard design are identical to that found on that sword model.

Hilt fittings are gilded brass. The backstrap is decorated for about three quarters of its length with sakura and leaves. Press stud and spring clip retention system. Black shagreen or lacquered wood grip with intermittent brass wire binding. Nickel-plated steel scabbard with one suspension mount although a band of rust indicates a lower one may have been present on that shown in Plate 31 (iv). There are, however, certain differences from normal parade sabres:
(i) The backstrap badge (Fig. 51 (ii)).
(ii) The shallow angle of inclination of the upper backstrap which is less than normal parade sabres.
(iii) A slim, slightly curved, unplated blade of traditional shinogi-zukuri form is utilised and fitted with a brass habaki (blade collar) and seppa (blade washer).
(iv) The plain wide scabbard throat band. (see Plate 31 (iv)).

Dimensions probably varied. Overall length of sword and scabbard in Plates 270, 271 918mm (36$^1$/$_8$"). Hilt length (from inside of guard) 124mm (4$^7$/$_8$"). Blade length (including habaki) 741mm (29$^1$/$_{16}$"). Maximum blade width 18mm ($^{11}$/$_{16}$"). Weight of sword 20 ounces. Weight of sword and scabbard 32 ounces.

Possibly a version with a fully decorated backstrap was made for the rank of Superintendent-General.

A full-sized kyu-guntō version of this sword pattern seems to exist since one example matching this decorative description has been reported in an American auction catalogue. The blade was reused from a Shintō period wakizashi and the long hilt has a grip of black samē or shagreen. The design of the upper backstrap badge appears to be the same as Fig. 51 (ii) and the plated scabbard, apparently, has two fixed suspension mounts. These, and all other Police swords and dirks, appear to be rare. Probably most were destroyed at the end of the war. However, Police items seem to be more common in the United States than Britain and Australia. Identification of all items in this chapter is, by necessity, subjective and tenuous, being open to correction as necessary.

---

1 The information relating to the histories of the Police and Fire Bureaux was kindly provided by the Japan Information and Cultural Centre, London.
2 Their actual formation is believed to be in 1911.
3 The authors are indebted to Yukio Yamaguchi who obtained the stated identities of badges (i) and (ii) from the Japanese Metropolitan Police Headquarters.
4 The information supplied said 'a badge for civil police ranking above an Assistant Inspector', so it must be assumed that this rank was not included. Current ranks are: Policeman (Patrolman), Senior Policeman, Sergeant, Assistant Inspector, Inspector, Superintendent, Senior Superintendent, Chief Superintendent, Superintendent Supervisor and Superintendent General. Presumably there was a similar structure prior to 1945.

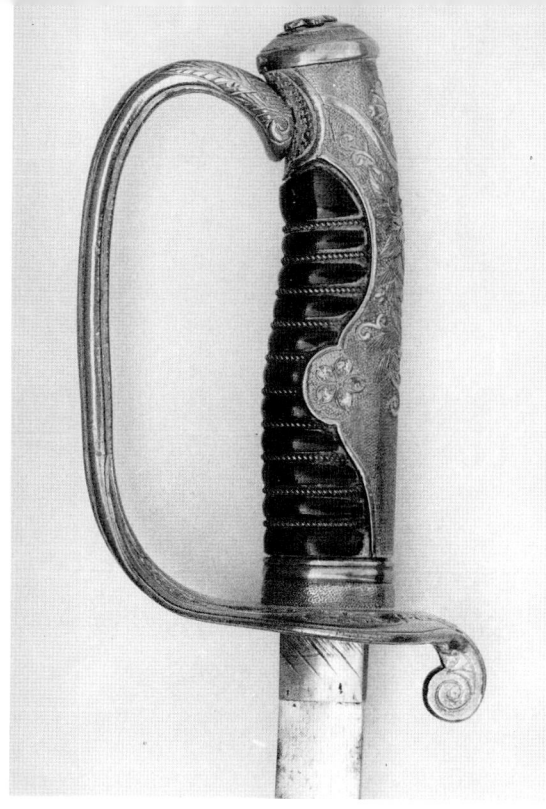

**Plates 263, 264** *Hilt and backstrap of a Senior Officers Police sword for Inspectors (and above?) which could be mistaken for that of an Army general officer. However, it has a shallow inclined backstrap, unplated blade of shinogi-zukuri form and a badge of sixteen alternating long and short 'notched' rays ('Hakkou'). (Richard Fuller).*

**Plates 265, 266** *Backstrap and hilt of a Police sword. The backstrap badge detailing is unclear but could be that used by Senior Officers since the decorative details are identical. This has a black same grip. (Patrick Lundy).*

# Fire Bureau Dirks

## Fire Bureau

Until 1718 organised firefighting units were restricted to the great castles and shrines, especially Edo (Tokyo). After this date volunteer units were formed from commoners to fight large-scale fires in the capital. Not until after the Meiji Restoration of 1868 were professional firefighting companies (Shōbōgumi) formed. In 1881 they were placed under the control of the Tokyo Metropolitan Police Office. In 1939 they became known as 'Keibōdan', but still remained under Police control until 1948.

## Fire Bureau badges and weapons

Fig. 65 (i) shows a motif identified with the Fire Bureau but the introduction date is unknown and it has not been reported on edged weapons. That shown in Fig. 51 (iii) is assumed to be associated with the Fire Bureau since *Imperial Japanese Daggers 1883–1945* (see Bibliography) shows it on the 1889 model Senior Officers dirk patterns. Only dirk patterns are known which were probably worn with full or parade dress.[1] No examples of swords bearing this badge have been located to indicate that Fire Bureau officers also carried them.

---

[1] Both patterns are identified by *Imperial Japanese Daggers 1883–1945* (see Bibliography).

## 1889 pattern Fire Bureau Vice-Commanders dirk

This dirk (Fig. 54 (i)) is similar in form to the later 1903 Forestry Officials pattern. The hilt has a partially decorated backstrap featuring the 'twenty arrow or ray' badge shown in Fig. 51 (iii). White

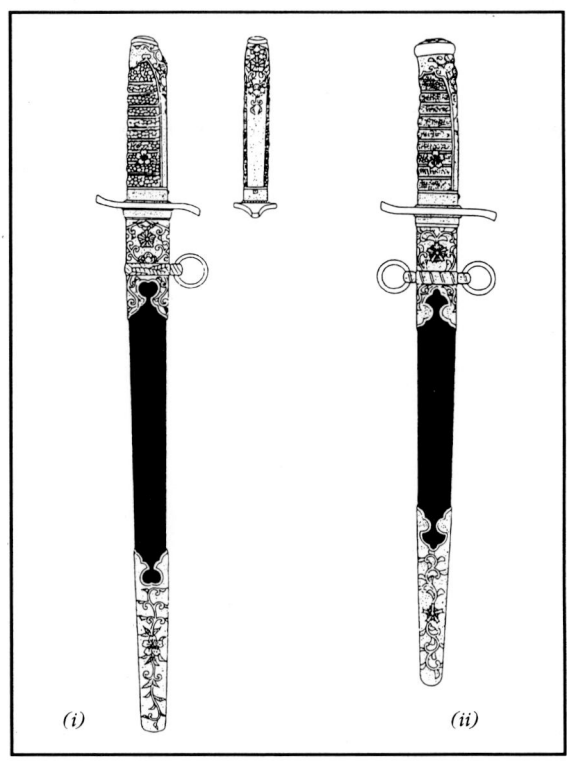

*Fig. 54*   *1889 pattern Fire Bureau dirks: (i) Vice-Commander ; (ii) Commander.* (Imperial Japanese Daggers).

same grip with intermittent brass wire binding. Sakura menuki (hilt ornaments). Gilded brass fittings and crossguard which has inverted ends. Plain pommel cap. Lacquered or leather-covered scabbard with two gilded mounts decorated with sakura and tendrils. Heart-shaped (boar's eye) recesses. Roped suspension band with one hanging ring. The top locket features the same badge as the backstrap. The blade would be expected to be single-edged, machine-made.

No example has been located to confirm the details shown so it must be considered as rare or, perhaps, very rare.

## 1889 pattern Fire Bureau Commanders dirk

A Senior Officers dirk, in most other civil organisations, is a more ornate version of the Junior Officers version. However, in this case, it is a different pattern and also appears to be slightly shorter. Fig. 54 (ii).

The hilt has a backstrap, large domed pommel, white samē grip and crossguards with inverted ends. The crossguard underside of the example photographed has a stamp (Fig. 61 (xxiv)) which is possibly that of the manufacturer or retailer. The pommel has a raised sun (Hiashi) badge of sixteen long and short rays with flattened tops (Fig. 2 (iv)) thought to represent the most senior officer rank grade. The backstrap is decorated with leaves and tendrils for approximately three quarters of the length and also features the same badge as the pommel. Sakura (cherry blossom) menuki (hilt ornaments).

Normal single-edged grooved and plated blade. Retention in the scabbard is by a push fit. The scabbard of the example in Plate 267 is black leather with two ornately decorated mounts although there are differences between it and the mounts shown in Fig. 54 (ii). The upper mounts of both have a roped suspension band with two opposing hanging rings and a raised 'twenty ray or arrow' badge of the type shown in Fig. 51 (iii). However, the scabbard mount recesses of that in Plate 267 are of a design not seen on any other

*Plate 267* Probable 1889 pattern Fire Bureau Commanders dirk and scabbard. The scabbard mount recesses differ in shape from that in Fig. 54 (ii) and the lower mount has a sakura rather than the 'twenty ray' badge. (Mike Hadlum).

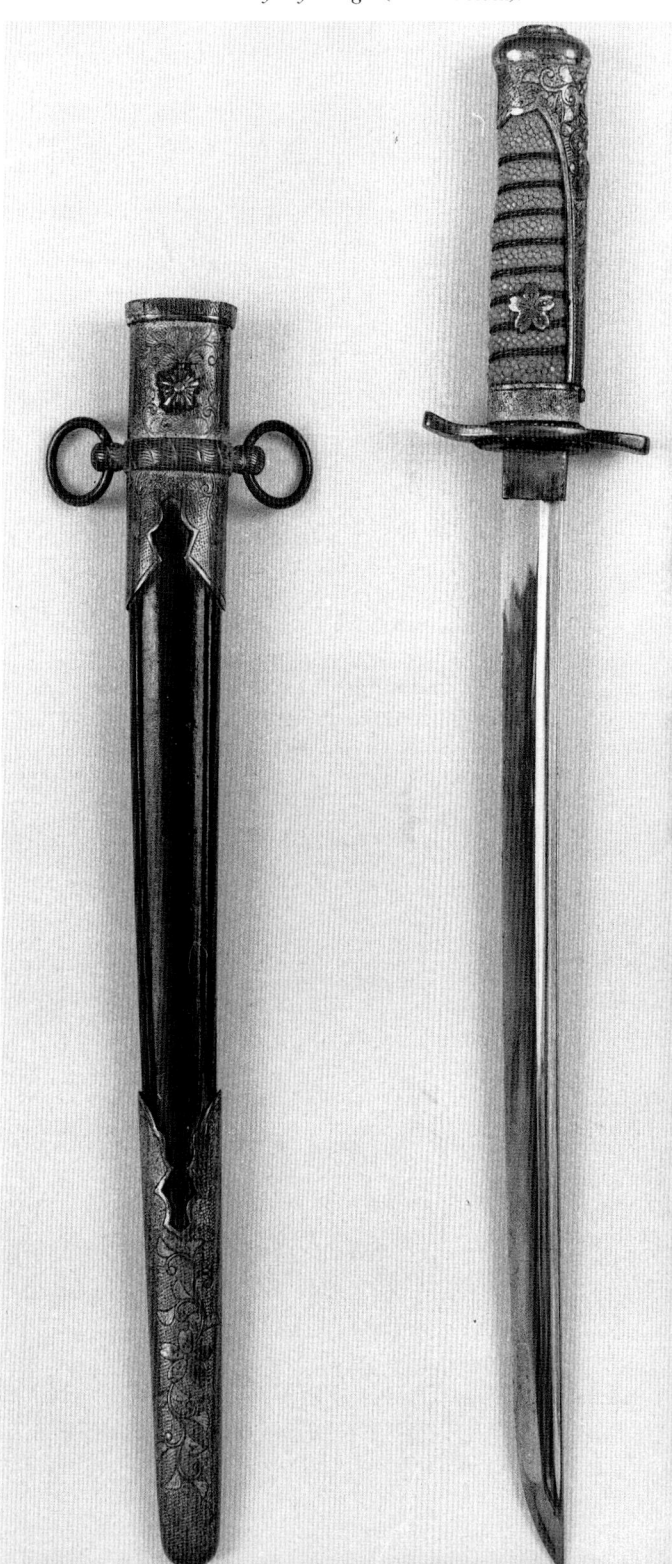

dirk pattern and differ from the 'arrow' pattern shown in Fig. 54 (ii). The lower mount of the item photographed only has a sakura instead of the 'twenty ray' badge on the drawn example. Whether these differences indicate another rank variation or even an unidentified dirk pattern is unknown, so tentative identification as a Fire Bureau Commanders dirk has been made at this time. The hilt badges on this model seemingly signifies use by a very senior officer, while the scabbard badge represents the Fire Bureau.

Again, such dirks appear to be very rare.

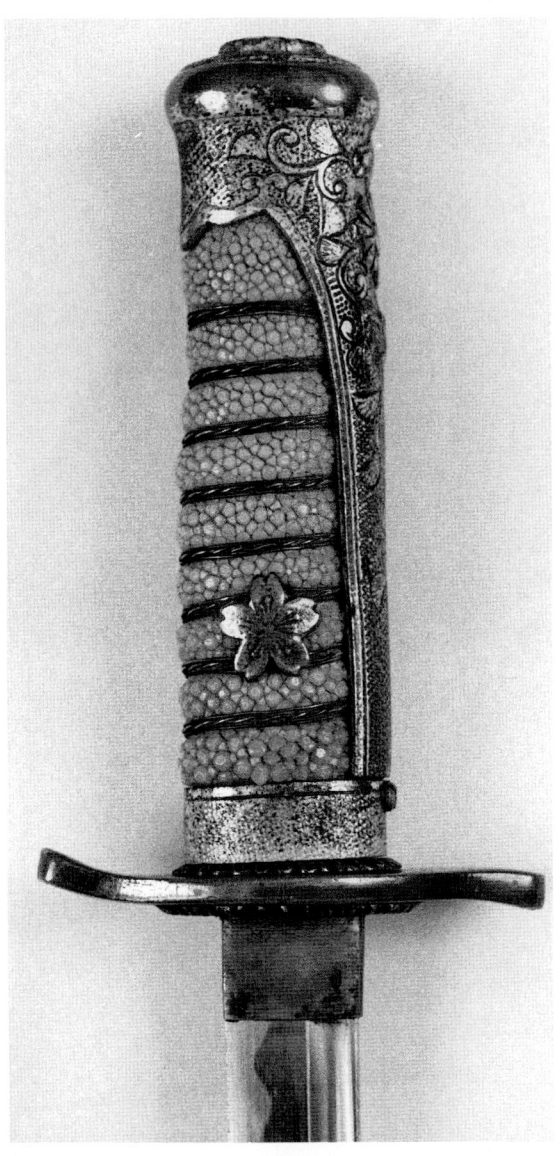

**Plate 268**  Hilt of the 1889 pattern Fire Bureau Commanders dirk. (Mike Hadlum).

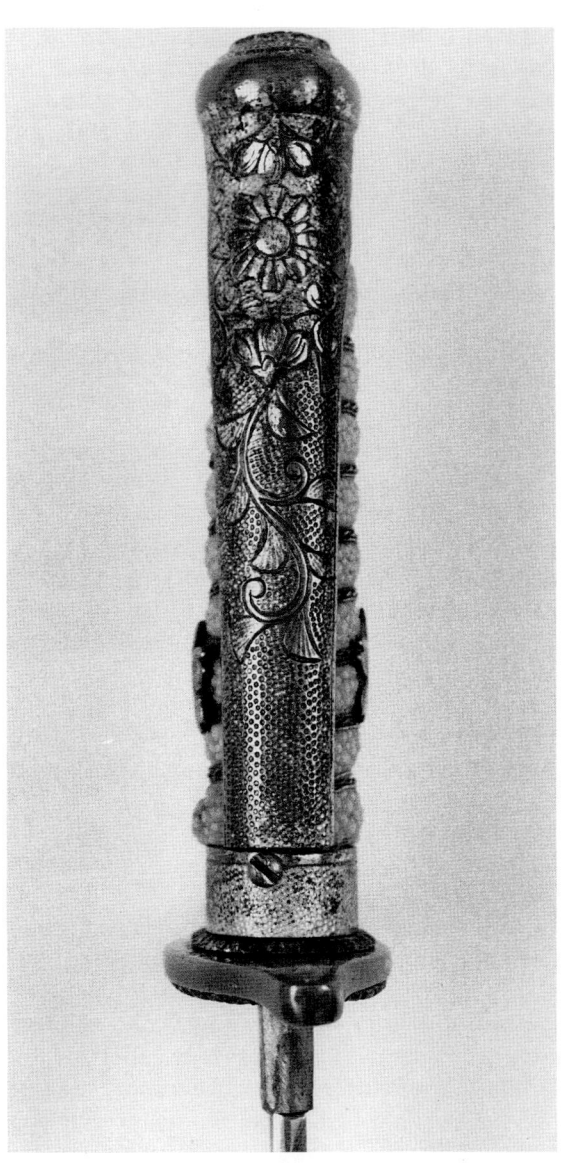

**Plate 269**  Backstrap of the 1889 pattern Fire Bureau Commanders dirk. The version of the sixteen-rayed sun (Fig. 2 (iv)), probably indicative of use by a very senior officer, is visible near the top. (Mike Hadlum).

FIRE BUREAU DIRKS

**Plate 270** Pommel of the 1889 pattern Fire Bureau Commanders dirk showing the 'sun badge' probably used by very senior officers. (Mike Hadlum).

**Plate 271** Richly decorated top scabbard mount of the 1889 pattern Fire Bureau Commanders dirk. The raised 'twenty arrow or ray' badge (Fig. 51 (iii)) is believed to be that used by the Fire Bureau. (Mike Hadlum).

— 197 —

# Red Cross Society Swords and Dirks

The 'Hakuaisha' (Philanthropic Association) was founded in 1877 to provide medical aid to the sick and wounded from both sides in the 1877 Satsuma Rebellion. In 1886 it was affiliated to the International Red Cross Society and changed its name to the Red Cross Society of Japan. Imperial recognition and sanction was given in 1902.

Certain officers of the Red Cross Society of Japan were authorised to carry dirks as is evidenced by the two known patterns. Presumably there were two grades since the known examples show the same rank variations found with other civil organisations although two separate patterns are used. The introduction date is unconfirmed but is probably 1886 or 1902, with wear probably lasting until 1945.

## Junior Officials dirk

Details are only known from one example which is assumed to be representative of this model.[1]

Gilded brass hilt fittings consisting of a pommel and backstrap with side-ears, fuchi, crossguard with inverted ends and a seppa (washer) on each side. The pommel has a raised cross on the top and the backstrap is engraved with bamboo leaves. Each side-ear has a bamboo flower in relief. White samé grip secured to the blade tang by a wooden mekugi (peg), and intermittent brass wire binding. The fuchi (hilt ferrule) is plain and has a projecting spring clip button. Plain brown

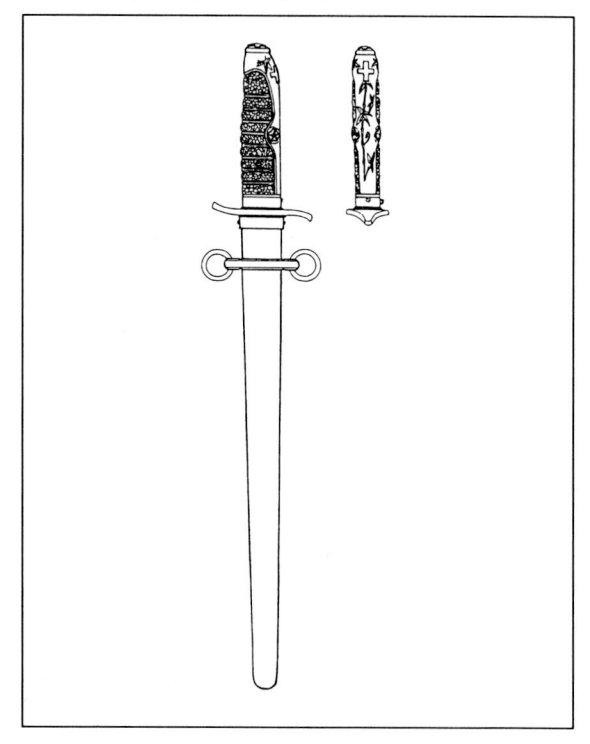

**Fig. 55** *Junior Officials dirk of the Red Cross Society of Japan based on an actual example.*

# RED CROSS SOCIETY SWORDS AND DIRKS

painted metal scabbard with a raised suspension band and opposing hanging rings. Single-edged, plain unfullered machine-made blade with a brass habaki (blade collar).

Dimensions are assumed to be fairly consistent. Overall length of dirk and scabbard shown 410mm (16"). Hilt length 106mm (4 1/8"). Blade length 272mm (10 11/16"). Weight of dirk and scabbard 15 ounces.

Examples of this dirk must, perhaps, be regarded as very rare.

## Senior Officials dirk

Only a few examples of this dirk model have been reported, so it must be considered as rare.[2] The overall configuration is based on the 1883 pattern Commissioned Officers naval dirk pattern

Gilded brass hilt fittings having a pierced pommel decorated with a phoenix bird surmounted by a raised cross. Turtle-shell grip with a spiral groove and brass wire binding. The hilt is secured to the blade tang by a male and female screw system having a bamboo flower menuki (hilt ornament) on each side. The fuchi (hilt ferrule) is decorated with bamboo leaves. Standard dirk crossguard having inversed ends and a seppa (washer) on each side.

The black leather-covered scabbard (which appears to be the norm) has two gilded brass mounts decorated ensuite with bamboo leaves. The upper mount has a single hanging ring and a press stud clip for retention with the hilt. Single-edged unfullered blade which may have an acid-etched yakiba (tempered edge). Brass habaki (blade collar).

Dimensions are assumed to be fairly consistent. Overall length of dirk and scabbard 420mm (16½"). Hilt length 115mm (4½"). Blade length 265mm (10½"). Weight of dirk and scabbard 10½ ounces.

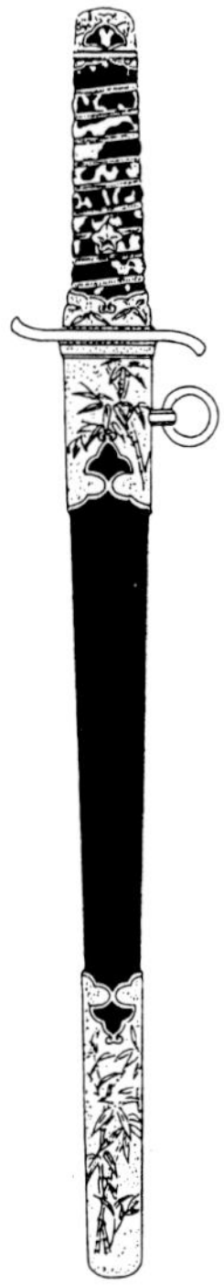

*Fig. 56* Senior Officials dirk of the Red Cross Society of Japan. (Imperial Japanese Daggers).

## Red Cross Society swords

It seems that Senior Officials, at least, wore swords when in full dress. A photograph of Vice-President Baron Hanabusa, taken around 1904, shows him with what appears to be an 1875/1886 pattern Army Commissioned Officers dress sword. Unfortunately the decorative details cannot be seen. However, it is known that this pattern was also carried in the field by Army Medical Corps officers during the 1904–5 Russo–Japanese war. Whether or not the same pattern, or another, featuring a 'cross' motif was prescribed for the Red Cross officials has not been resolved by the authors.

---

1 Martin Hirons collection.
2 Identification of this model is confirmed by *Imperial Japanese Daggers 1883–1945*.

# Unidentified Civil Swords and Dirks

There are a number of swords and dirks which have, so far, defied identification. They may be plain or ornate but do not have identifiable military and civil decoration or motifs. It has been assumed that the examples shown in this section are, in general, 'civil', i.e. for use by officials in government-controlled departments or organisations, although their specific functions have not been established. Any opinons given by the authors are speculative and thus open to correction when, or if, information is eventually forthcoming.

Dating of these items is open to question but most, from their condition, appear to be Meiji (1868–1912). However, production in some cases may have continued up to, and including, the Shōwa era, i.e. post-1926.

Plate 272 shows two Chinese soldiers, probably c.1912–1928, with a sword pattern which has inverse quillions fitted with a rear integral sword knot ring and a protruding pommel also pierced for the knot.[1] These are features normally only associated with some Japanese civil and naval swords. If such (undecorated) weapons were made in Japan and exported to China then confusion and mistaken identity will inevitably occur. However, the quality of Chinese-made swords is generally inferior to Japanese workmanship which should enable a distinction to be made. It must be noted that Japanese-manufactured swords for use by the Chinese are known, but are not within the scope of this book.

No photographs of Japanese carrying this sword type have been located, although three examples are pictured in Plates 1252–4 and 1262 of *Imperial Japanese Army and Navy Uniforms and Equipments* (see Bibliography). They are all captioned 'BUNKAN YŌ KEN', which literally translates as 'Civil Official – use – sword'. See also 'Swords and dirks of Manchukuo (Manchuria)' earlier in this book.

## Civil Officials short sword

A typical sword reputedly carried by civil officials (of unknown type) is shown in Plates 273, 274. Dating is believed to be late nineteenth century but no contemporary photographs of such swords being worn have been located.

That shown has plain brass hilt mounts and a black samé-covered grip which originally had brass wire binding in the grooves. A small solid handguard has inverse quillions, the reverse being sharply upturned to terminate with a ring set in the vertical plane. The pommel is believed to have a small loose brass ring (replaced on this example)

---

[1] First brought to the authors' attention by Anton Krahenbuhl since used on the jacket cover of *The Military Dimension of the Chinese Revolution* by Edmund S. K. Fung (University of British Columbia Press, 1980). Unfortunately it was not captioned or mentioned in the text.

***Plate 272***  *Two Chinese soldiers with a sword type which was thought to be exclusively for Japanese civil and naval use. This rare photo is from an undated postcard which is just captioned 'Chinese soldiers'. Their unit and ranks have not been established and their cap badges do not seem to be Nationalist (Kuomingtang). It is thought that they are probably Republican, which would date the picture between 1912 and 1928. The sword pattern is that which has inverse quillions incorporating a rear sword knot ring and a protruding pommel also pierced for the knot. Dark (leather?) grip and a backstrap which lacks side-ears. Elongated barrel-shaped knot (black?) and cords with a gold or silver slide. It is of course possible that these swords were supplied by, or bought from, Japan.* (Cheyenne Noda).

for the sword knot. The hilt is secured to the blade tang by plain silvered brass dome-headed male-female screws.

Unsigned blade of traditional shinogi-zukuri form. Brass habaki (blade collar). Steel scabbard, probably originally nickel-plated, with two raised suspension bands and steel hanging rings. Wooden liner. Push fit retention with the blade. The back edge of this blade tang, fuchi (hilt collar) and inside of the wooden grip have small notches in a group of five and two. This is a somewhat unusual system of assembly markings although it

***Plates 273, 274***  *Civil Officials short sword.* (Richard Fuller).

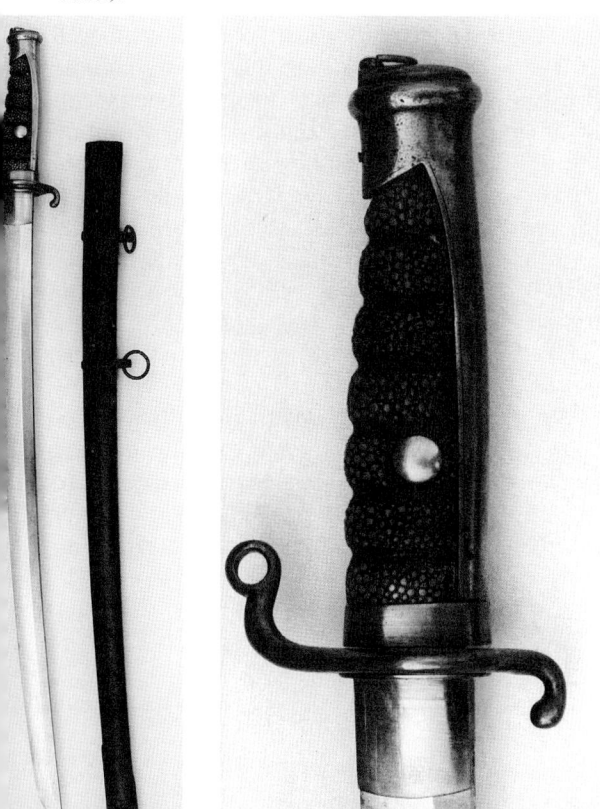

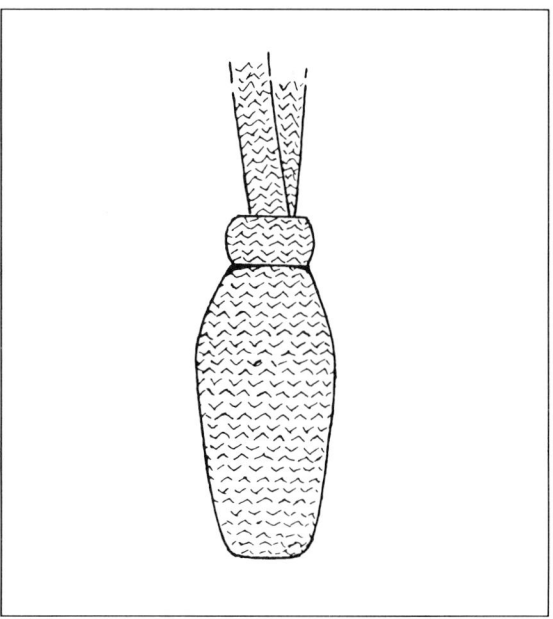

***Fig. 57***  *Tan or dark gold knot and cords seen on a Civil Officials sword of a type similar to that in Plate 273. It is unknown if this is representative of all civil swords, or just the type it was found with.*

# JAPANESE MILITARY AND CIVIL SWORDS AND DIRKS

can be found on other sword patterns. The normal method is by stamped numbers or characters.

Overall length of sword and scabbard shown 790mm (31 1/16"). Hilt length 150mm (5 7/8"). Blade length (to habaki) 564mm (22 3/16"). Tang length 163mm (6 7/16"). Scabbard length 640mm (25 1/4"). Weight of sword and scabbard 41 ounces.

Other examples noted have identical hilt configurations and hilt-securing screws, although the upper backstrap grip return is not so angular as that shown and is more rounded. However, they are thought to be representative of the same sword pattern.

Possibly a rank distinction exists since three decorative variations have been seen: (i) plain (as above); (ii) small area of engraved foliage on the backstrap near the pommel; and (iii) fully engraved backstrap of four sakura separated by tendrils and leaves. Version (ii) had a longer hilt than normal, but all blades were around the same length.

The correct sword knot pattern is unknown, but one or both cords (or straps) would appear to pass through the pommel and quillion rings.

All variations seem to be very scarce.

## Ornate Civil Officials short sword

An ornate example of a probable Meiji period short sword thought to have been carried by civil officials is shown in Plate 275.

Gilded brass hilt fittings decorated with cherry blossoms (sakura) and leaves. There is a small loose ring attached to the pommel reverse for a sword knot. Inversed guard with raised kadosakura on the top obverse. White samé grip with brass wire binding and sakura menuki (hilt ornament). Traditional unsigned Shintō period blade of shinogi-zukuri form. Good quality engraved brass habaki (blade collar). Black leather-covered scabbard with three gilt brass mounts, each decorated ensuite with sakura and leaves. The richness and quality of decoration indicates use by a person of high rank. The crossguard shape is unlike any other known sword. The general impression is that it was specially made and, thus, is not representative of an officially prescribed pattern.

## Plain full-sized Civil Officials sword

The sword in Plate 276 has the usual inverted handguard quillion configuration incorporating a sword knot ring but is distinguished by a longer hilt than is normally encountered with similar mounts.

Plain brass hilt fittings with a long backstrap (without side-ears). The pommel is surmounted by a raised sakura and incorporates a small raised mounting which has a small loose ring for the sword knot. Black samé grip having (replacement) brass wire in the grooves. A brass male-female securing screw passes through the hilt and blade which terminates either side with sakura menuki (hilt ornaments). Unsigned wakizashi length blade of shinogi-zukuri form. Copper habaki (blade collar). Scabbard of black lacquered leather over a wooden liner. Plain brass mounts consisting of a throat, two suspension bands with steel hanging rings and a chape which has a shoe (drag). Push fit retention with the blade. It is unknown if the brown leather sword knot shown is correct for this pattern.

Overall length of sword and scabbard 930mm (36 5/8"). Hilt length 219mm (8 5/8"). Blade length (to habaki) 517mm (20 3/8"). Scabbard length 710mm (27 15/16"). Weight of sword and scabbard 32 ounces.

Dating is probably Meiji or Taishō (i.e. 1868–1926). Use is unknown but the general appearance suggests military (naval?) association. The undecorated mounts may indicate low officer rank of NCO grade. An unusual and very rare item.

**Plate 275** *Ornate Civil Officials short sword.* (Roy Lindus).

**Plate 276** *Full-sized Civil Officials sword with plain mounts and a wakizashi blade. The hilt length is much longer than is usually found with swords which have this type of mount.* (Richard Fuller).

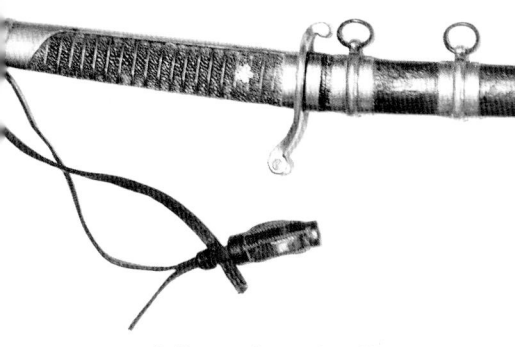

## Ornate full-sized Civil Officials sword

The obverse and reverse of a probable upper ranked Civil Officials sword are shown in Plates 277a, b.

The copper hilt fittings were originally gilded. They are engraved with sakura (cherry blossoms) and leaves. The upper backstrap panel is decorated with a sun and crescent moon set among clouds and the domed pommel has a raised sakura. Both side-ears have a raised silver sakura and the separate fuchi (hilt collar) is engraved with flowers and leaves. Small handguard with inverse quillions, the reverse being longer and terminating in a ring set in the horizontal plane. Normally swords of this type have the quillion ring set in the vertical plane, as can be seen from other examples illustrated in this book. Originally there must have been a sarute (sword knot ring) fixed to the small protruding pommel loop. Silver sakura form the surrounds to the wooden peg (mekugi) which secures the hilt and tang. Black samé grip with brass wire binding in the grooves.

An unsigned wakizashi length Kotō period (pre-1596) blade has been reused from an older sword. Wood-lined plated steel scabbard with two suspension bands each having a steel hanging ring. Push fit retention with the blade.

Overall length of sword and scabbard 927mm (36½"). Hilt length 162mm (6⅜"). Blade length 584mm (23").

This is a very rare and ornate version of this scarce sword type. Exact usage is unknown but suggests wear by a person of upper rank perhaps with military connections since most Civil Officials swords are short. Dating is also uncertain, but late nineteenth or early twentieth century (i.e. Meiji) is thought likely.

**Plates 277 a, b** *Hilt of an ornate full-sized Civil Officials sword. Note that, in this case, the reverse quillion has the sword knot ring set in the horizontal plane.* (Ron Gregory).

# JAPANESE MILITARY AND CIVIL SWORDS AND DIRKS

## Civil Officials, or naval, sword adpated for land warfare

A good example of a sword type reputed to have been carried by civil officials is shown in Plate 278. It is very similar to the unidentified naval sword pattern shown in Plate 188 but has been adapted for military use in the field by the addition of a non-removable shrink-fitted leather combat cover to the metal scabbard and a shin-guntō pattern sword knot. These imply it was also carried in World War Two. It may, in fact, be a naval pattern but examination of the scabbard would be needed to ascertain if an engraved foul anchor is present. Unfortunately the length is unknown.

Plain brass mounts with hilt side-ears featuring a raised disc on each side. The pommel incorporates a protruding ring for the sword knot and is surmounted by a sakura. Inverse crossguard which is elongated at the rear and terminates with a ring set in the vertical plane for the sword knot. Black shagreen grip with brass wire in the grooves. Unsigned Shintō period blade of shinogi-zukuri form having a sanbon-sugi hamon of nioi, i.e. the tempered edge undulates in the 'three cedars' pattern and is formed of fine martensite crystals.

Dating of the mounts is uncertain, but the adaptation for World War Two indicates reuse.

**Plates 278** *Civil Officials, or naval, sword adapted for land warfare. (Private collection).*

**Plate 279** *White samé grip and brass backstrap of a Civil Officials sword which is profusely engraved with sakura (cherry blossoms) and leaves. (Ron Gregory).*

UNIDENTIFIED CIVIL SWORDS AND DIRKS

*Plate 280* Hilt obverse and scabbard of an unidentified civil full dress or court sword. (Alan Clayton).

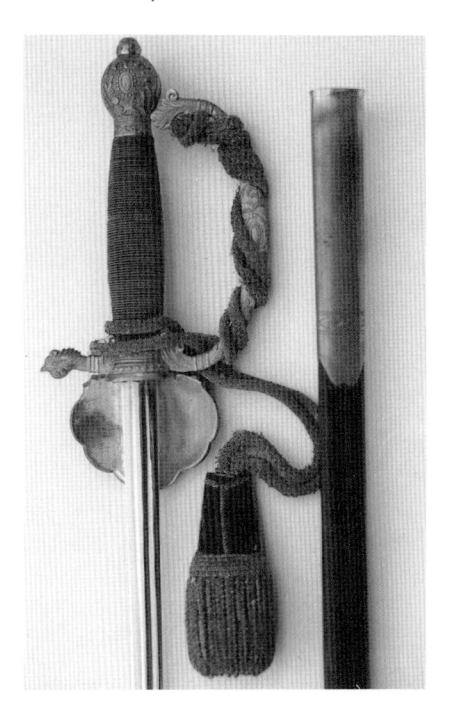

*Plate 282* Full view of the unidentified civil full dress or court sword. (Alan Clayton).

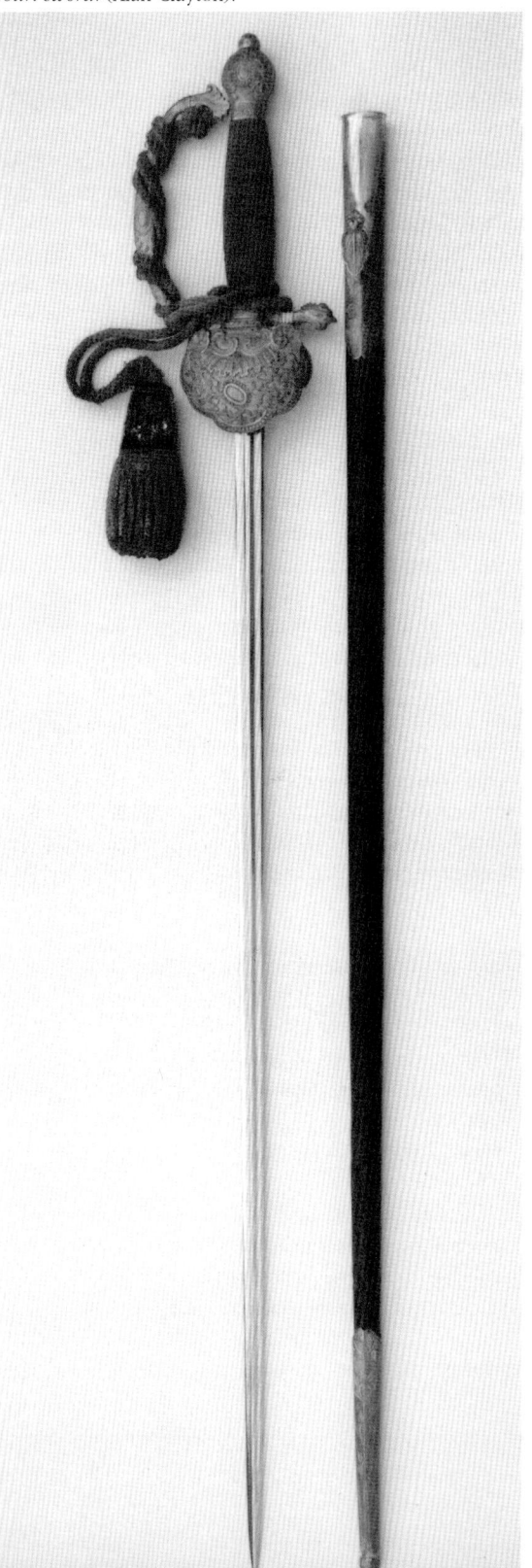

*Plate 281* Reverse of the unidentified civil full dress or court sword. (Alan Clayton).

JAPANESE MILITARY AND CIVIL SWORDS AND DIRKS

## Unidentified civil full dress or court sword

Plates 280, 281, 282. (Previous page)

This very rare dress sword appears to be Japanese but is of unknown usage.

It is similar in appearance to the diplomatic sword patterns. Hilt and scabbard fittings are gilded brass and the grip is tightly bound brass wire. The quillion is a cockerel's head which is a Japanese feature. The pommel, shell-guard and knucklebow are each richly decorated with raised tendrils and what may be a badge comprising an oval ring surrounded by raised dots. However, this has not been related to any particular office or organisation.

The gold bullion sword knot has an upper black velvet panel surmounted by what appears to be a bullion wire *Paulownia* (kiri) flower of the 3:5:3 floret type, normally associated with officials of Sōnin (standard appointment) rank. Narrow, straight, double-fullered, plain plated blade. Black leather scabbard which must be suspended by means of a frog in the same manner as the diplomatic swords.

Since not identifiable there is the possibility that this is an export piece for use by a Far East government or court such as Manchukuo or Imperial/Republican China. However, it certainly seems to be of Japanese manufacture.

## Unidentified dress sword of military style

The limited number of examples reported indicate a prescribed pattern probably for use as a court sword.

From Plate 283 it is seen to closely resemble the 1875 pattern Army Officers dress sword in Fig. 4.

Wire bound black horn grip. Heavily gilded brass hilt and scabbard mounts. The obverse shell guard has raised sun rays which, like the 1875 pat. Army dress sword, have flattened ends. The pommel side is plain (lacking a dragonfly motif) although there is an ornamental edge banding

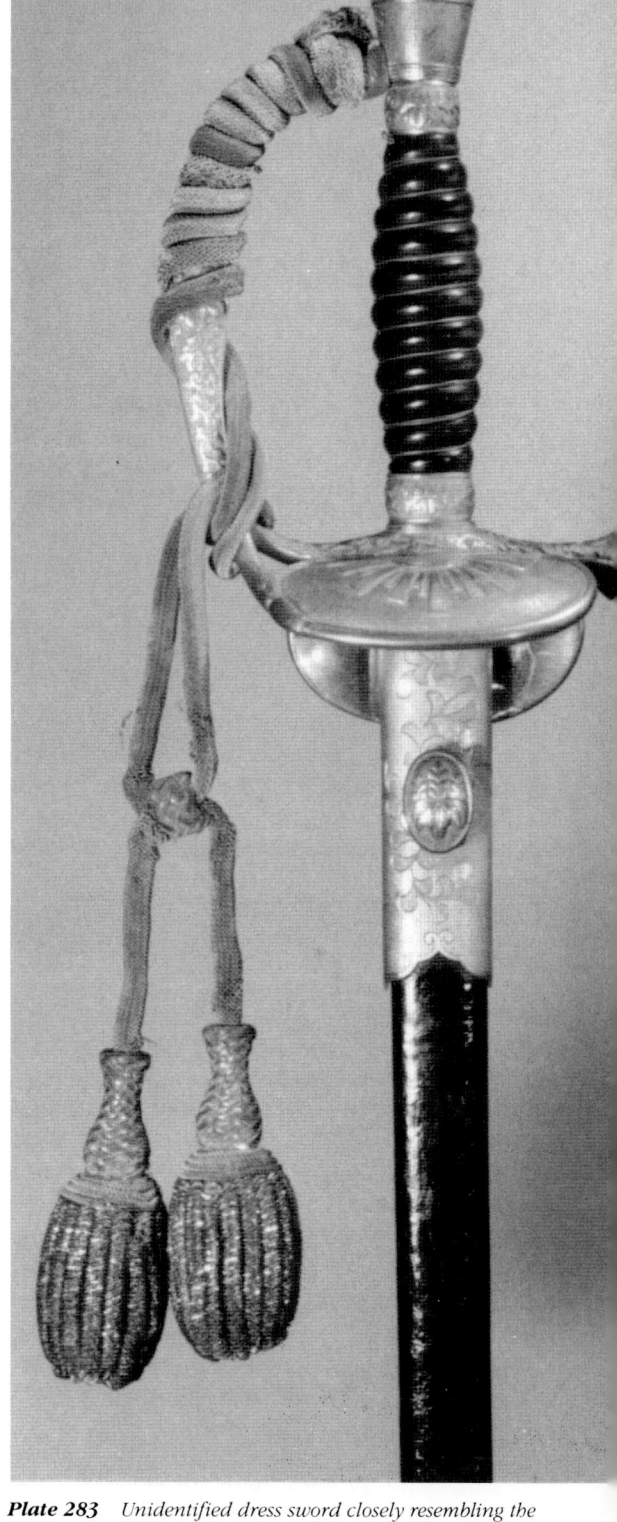

**Plate 283** *Unidentified dress sword closely resembling the 1875 Army Officers pattern. Note the unusual double knot.* (Patrick Lundy).

similar to 'Greek fret'. Small folding rear guard.

A total of ten 5:7:5 'Kiri' mon (Fig .2 (i) in relief are present on the top and lower portion of the pommel, fuchi (hilt collar), centre of the knucklebow and scabbard frog stud. The hilt and scabbard fittings are also decorated ensuite with vines, which are in relief on the former and engraved on the latter.

Black lacquered leather scabbard with a top locket and chape similar to that used on the army dress sword.

Straight, narrow, plated oval section blade decoratively etched in European fashion with a number of seven-floret 'Kiri' and stylised half-blooms. A 5:7:5: 'Kiri' is located on either side near the guard.

Several examples are known with double gold bullion sword knots and cords, as shown in Plate 283, which suggest they are the norm for this sword type. A double knot has not been reported on any other Japanese sword patterns, although one is shown in a drawing (Plate 3) from the Sino-Japanese war of 1894.

The dimensions of a typical example are as follows but probably varied according to the height of the wearer:- Overall length of sword and scabbard 835mm (32⁷⁄₈"). Hilt length 150mm (6"). Blade length 627mm (24¹¹⁄₁₆"). Scabbard length 685mm (27").

Whether there is also a version with the lower ranking 3:5:3 'Kiri' is currently unknown.

One can only speculate that use was by a person of high government or civil rank. Dating is also unknown. Examples must be considered as very rare.

## Unidentified court or dress sword

This is a very rare sword known only from the example illustrated in Plate 284. The design is based on the 1875 pattern Army Officers dress sword.

Gilded brass mounts with an urn pommel, knucklebow and large down-curved shell-guards, the reverse being hinged to fold flat against the

**Plate 284** *Unidentified court or dress sword.* (Mike Quigley).

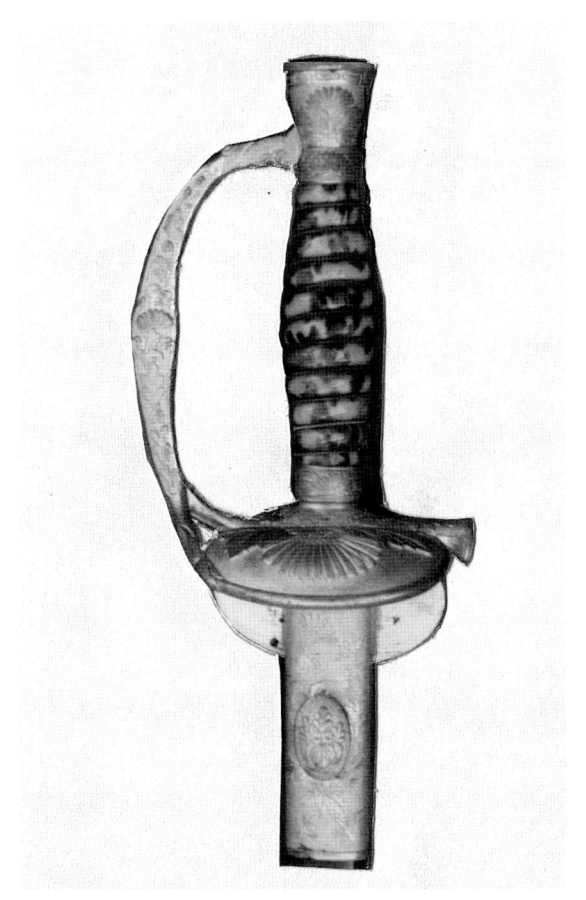

body. The knucklebow, pommel and fuchi (hilt collar) are decorated ensuite with foliage and open (chrysanthemum?) blooms. The obverse shell-guard appears to be similarly decorated with the same motif. Turtle-shell grip with gilt wire binding. A narrow straight blade is used. Black leather scabbard with gilded brass locket and chape which are decorated ensuite with the hilt fittings. Raised frog stud which features a 5:7:5 floret kiri (Fig. 2 (i)).

Use by a person of high rank, perhaps attached to the Imperial Court or Household, is a possibility. The same open flower design is also very prominent on the embroidered full dress coat of cabinet ministers who are known to have carried dress swords of unconfirmed type, although the

# JAPANESE MILITARY AND CIVIL SWORDS AND DIRKS

diplomatic sword pattern may, perhaps, be expected.

## Unidentified civil dirk

The design of this dirk, shown in Fig. 58, is closely based on the 1883 pattern Naval Officers dirk.

All hilt and scabbard fittings are gilded brass. The grip is black samé and the menuki are in the form of sakura (cherry blossoms). The pommel is pierced and also decorated with sakura. Black leather scabbard. The fittings have arrow-shaped recesses but are decorated only with a stippled effect of tiny impressed dots. Two opposing suspension rings. Plain, straight, machine-made blade with notches on the tang for assembly purposes. Overall length 483mm (19").

The black grip, stippled decoration and lack of scabbard sakura suggests use by an official of one of the Government-General departments responsible for the administration of an unidentified Japanese-controlled territory.

Only one example of this dirk has been reported.

**Fig. 58** *Unidentified civil dirk probably for use by an official in an unknown Government-General department.* (Brenton Williams).

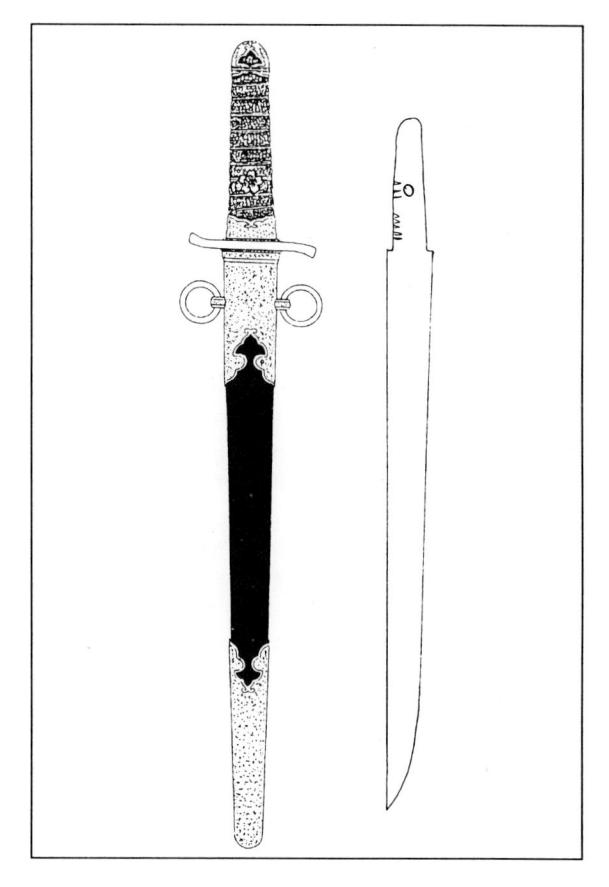

# Shōwa Period Presentation Swords and Dirks

The Japanese have a long tradition of presenting swords as rewards for services rendered or as a mark of respect. This was continued when the Western nations became established in Japan, with foreign dignitaries and heads of state becoming recipients. Even during World War Two swords were presented to foreigners. In the Shōwa era, blades were sometimes made for competition prizes (such as horse racing) or as gifts to temples and shrines. These are not included within the term 'presentation' for the purposes of this book. Similarly, surrendered swords and their handing over do not come into this category.

Basically there are two categories of presentation (both civilian and military mounted) swords which are:

(i) Specially made blade and fittings. Details of presentation are not etched on the blade surface, as is done with Western swords, but may be found engraved in Japanese on the tang together with details of the swordsmith. This provides proof of authenticity, especially if chiselled in the smith's own handwriting.

(ii) Standard sword and fittings. Documentary evidence is required to support presentation of these items.

From the limited information available it seems that foreign and Japanese military personnel were generally presented with military mounted swords while civil and diplomatic persons were given swords of traditional form. Bona fide examples of 'presentation' swords are very rare, and those inscribed to named foreign nationals are extremely rare. The following have been brought to the authors' attention since they mainly relate to military items.

## Presentation to foreign nationals

(1) Five Finnish Army officers who visited Japan and Manchuria were presented with shin-guntō. Two have been examined by a Finnish collector who has supplied the following details.[1]

Both are standard shin-guntō with Field Officers red and brown sword knots. Both are signed KOA ISSHIN (single-mindedly praying for the development of Asia) MANTETSU SAKU KORE WO (made of Mantetsu, i.e. Manchurian iron). They probably got these in Japan and not Manchuria (see the section on 'Koa Isshin Mantetsu' blades later in the following chapter). The tang edge markings respectively are リ10八 (i.e. RI 108) and リ 110 (i.e. RI 110). They are believed to be batch and serial numbers. Presumably RI 109 is one of the other three swords. Since totally standard with normal tang inscriptions they were not specially made for presentation and were probably taken from stock.

(2) Tang inscription of a shin-guntō: 'Presented [to] Colonel Mr Kaira [from] Colonel Kanegawa. December 8, 1942. Made by Akitomo'. This was presented by a Japanese Colonel Kanegawa to a military representative of Finland, Colonel Kaila ('r' being used since there is no 'l' in Japanese) while he was on an official visit to Japan.

(3) Tang inscription on a shin-guntō: 'Presented to his Excellency the Governor of Bhamo in Burma. Izawa Akira of Fukuoka City in Great Japan. Respectfully made by Moritsugu Norisada living at Fukuoka in Chikuzen'. Bhamo is on the Irrawaddy River in north Burma. It is unclear whether Izawa Akira is the recipient (who would probably be the Japanese military governor) or he actually presented it to a collaborating Burmese national, such as the mayor.

(4) Lieutenant-General Yamashita Tomoyuki has been photographed presenting a sword in shira-saya (plain wooden storage scabbard and hilt) to Feldmarschall von Brauchitsch, C-in-C German Army, in Berlin, February 1941. The shira-saya has painted Japanese characters which probably gives details of the swordsmith but they are, unfortunately, unclear. No doubt it was an old blade, but its fate is unknown.

(5) On 11 November 1940 in the Indian Ocean a British merchant ship, the *Automedan*, was attacked and boarded by Captain Bernhard Rogge of the German surface raider *Atlantis*. A search of the ship revealed intelligence documents and naval cyphers in the strong room and a bag containing the top secret British defence appraisal for the Far East ('Far Eastern Appreciation') in the chart room. It had been removed from the strong room and placed in a handy location for dumping in the sea in the case of an emergency. Unfortunately the bridge crew were killed by a salvo from the *Atlantis* before this could be done. Rogge recognised the great importance of these documents and sent them to the German naval attaché in Tokyo. He in turn showed them to the Vice-Chief of the Japanese Naval Staff after authorisation from Berlin. The contents were assessed by the C-in-C of the Combined Fleet, Vice-Admiral Yamamoto Isoroku, who revised his appreciation of Allied capabilities and amended his future offensive strategy. He now realised the British forces were far weaker than thought: there were no combined Allied defensive plans and the Philippines could not be adequately defended if the main American Pacific Fleet was annihilated.

Eighteen months later, just after the fall of Singapore, Rogge was presented with a sword on behalf of the Emperor for services rendered. By this time he was a Rear-Admiral. The circumstances of the actual presentation are unknown but it seems to have occurred in Germany, the ceremony probably conducted by the Japanese ambassador.

The sword is a shin-guntō with a Field Officers red and brown sword knot.[2] Details of the blade are unknown but the silver habaki (blade collar) is engraved with a 3:5:3 floret kiri (Fig. 2 (ii)) which has two Japanese characters in the centre. Presumably they confirm it is an Imperial presentation or gift. The mounts and tsuba are standard shin-guntō form but are made from grey metal (silver?). Brown metal scabbard.

This, apparently, is one of only three such swords awarded to Germans by the Emperor.[3] The other two were presented to Reichsmarschall Hermann Göring and General-Feldmarschall Erwin Rommel.[4]

(6) Achmed Soekarno, who became President of Indonesia, was a fervent nationalist and pro-Japanese during World War Two. He was presented with a sword, which must have been after 1943, although the date and details surrounding this are unknown.

It is an ornate weapon of excellent quality being a copy of a traditional kenukigata-no-tachi and made specially for presentation purposes.[5] The solid silver hilt and scabbard fittings are hand-engraved ensuite with cherry blossoms (as used by the Army) and tendrils in high relief on a ground of nanako (dots like fish roe). The fuchi (hilt collar) is signed 'all fittings made by Miyata Nobuaki, 1943'. The scabbard is gold-dusted nashiji lacquer also decorated with cherry blossoms and tendrils of silver lacquer.

The 699mm (27½") blade is signed 'made by Shoshichi-i Miyamoto Kanenori, aged 92'. This is a true gendaitō made by a top smith who became a 'Teishitsu gigein' (member of the Imperial Art Academy) in 1906, which is perhaps comparable to the modern 'National Living Treasure'. It was made in 1921 since he died in 1926, aged 97.

## Presentation to Japanese nationals

(1) Tang inscription of a shin-guntō: 'Presented, in remembrance, to Colonel Oda by the officers of the 30th Infantry Regiment. In Harbin on 1 August 1942. Kanenobu *(who is the swordsmith)* living in Nōshu. July 1941.' The presentation inscription has been added to a standard shin-guntō which must have been bought for the occasion. Presumably it was given to mark this officer's transfer or promotion. Harbin is in Manchuria.

(2) Tang inscription of a large blade obtained from China in the nineteen-eighties in poor condition (so the type of mounts are unknown): 'A lucky day in November 1937. Respectfully made by Akihide of the Order of Merit 4th Class. At the landing forces field headquarters of China Theatre Fleet commander His excellency Vice-Admiral Hasegawa Kiyoshi'.[6]

Vice-Admiral Hasegawa Kiyoshi commanded the fleet which landed 1,300 sailors and marines to protect Japanese interests just outside, and in, the International Settlement at Shanghai. He supported the landings of the Shanghai Expeditionary Army on 23 August 1937 which led to the Japanese occupation of Shanghai by 12 November 1937.

This unique and historically interesting blade could have been made to the Admiral's own order, but it seems to have been made for presentation to him by persons unknown in recognition of his victory at Shanghai since it was made in the same month. It is extremely rare for the smith's personal award to be stated. Possibly the Army commander, General Matsui Iwane (who became known as 'the butcher of Nanking'), also received such an award. Matsui and Hasegawa are photographed together at field headquarters in 1938 with the latter holding a long naval kyu-guntō (Plate 167). Whether or not it is this sword is unknown.

(3) Vice-Admiral Yamamoto Isoroku was awarded a substantial sum of money by the Emperor for his success at Pearl Harbor in lieu of an award which he did not want. He commissioned a swordsmith, Sakai Ikkansai Shigemasa, from his home town of Nagaoka to make ten identical hand-forged dirk (tantō) blades with the famous 'Z' signal ('the fate of the Empire depends upon this battle') engraved on the blade.[7] This was part of Admiral Nelson's signal at Trafalgar and thereafter abbreviated by the signal flag for 'Z'. It was adopted by Admiral Togo at Tsushima, and later by Admiral Yamamoto himself.

The tangs are engraved with the Admiral's signature 'Yamamoto Isoroku' on one side and the swordsmith's signature on the other. The habaki are inscribed 'Imperial gift'. They were presented to his chiefs of staff and to those officers who assisted him in his victories, although all the recipients are unknown. However, Vice-Admiral Ugaki Matome is known to be one.[8] Two such dirks are in a private collection in America.

After Yamamoto's death in April 1943, his widow commissioned another Nagaoka swordsmith, Endo Mitsutada, to make ten similar tantō. The money had come as a gift from the Emperor and the work was supervised by the Imperial household which is indicated by an inscription on the habaki of each. The metal used in the blades was from the number one gun of Admiral Togo's flagship, the *Mikasa*. Delivery was not made until almost the end of the war by which time two of the intended recipients had been killed. Two of these dirks were retained by Yamamoto's widow and are now in a private collection in America.

(4) A tang of a sword bearing the date 'summer 1938' and the logo of the South Manchurian Railway Company (Fig. 17 (ii)) has the additional inscription ZŌ HAMAMOTO KAKKA, i.e. presented to His Excellency Hamamoto. It also has a good luck slogan, which reads 'praying for eternal fortune in war'. Research indicates that it was presented to Lt-Gen Hamamoto Kisaburo who was commander of the 3rd Independent Garrison Unit in Manchuria from March to November 1938.[9]

(5) Swords presented by schools or companies to individuals or military organisations with money raised for the war effort. They are often engraved with details of the donor and sometimes that of the recipient. Some examples have been described in the section on 'Army parade sabres (see Plates 36–39). Examples of shin-guntō may have such information engraved on the tangs but are rare and must not be confused with blades made to special order. In some cases, so it is believed, the donors expected the return of their swords upon the successful conclusion of the war.

(6) Vice-Admiral Kusaka Juichi, C-in-C 11th Air Fleet, at Rabaul in New Britain, bestowed swords on deserving recipients under his command. At least four were presented, for heroic actions during the period 1942–3, to one Ensign and three Petty Officers. Commander Hori Tomoyoshi was an eyewitness when Ensign Kojima received his. He recalls: 'It was not a guntō [military sword] but it was a dagger in a plain wooden sheath, so to speak. It was a sword for self-defence. So that it cannot be carried like an officer'. A photograph of Chief Petty Officer Kudo, one recipient, shows him holding a 'sword', but details are unclear.[10] This seems to be a katana in shira-saya (plain wooden keeper mounts) with his citation wrapped around the upper section. Vice-Admiral Kusaka presumably ordered and paid for these items privately and may have awarded either a dirk or sword in shira-saya at different times.

It would be interesting to learn what other examples of presentation swords and dirks still survive undocumented in collections or museums.

---

1 The authors wish to express their appreciation to Stig Manderbacka for providing the information for items (1) and (2).
2 This is now in a private collection in Germany but it has apparently not been examined by an authority on Japanese swords, so it has basically been assessed from polaroid photographs.
3 *German Raiders of World War II* by Karl Muggenthaler (Robert Hale, 1971).
4 The whereabouts of these swords are unknown. No report of a Japanese sword among Göring's treasure caches has been found. Rommel's son Manfred confirmed that his father's sword was 'liberated' from his parents' home by the Allies at the end of World War Two.
5 See 'The Japanese and their swords', To-ken Bijutsu no. 266 p. 51, and item no. 008 in *Japanese Zwaarden in Nederlands Bezit* (Japanese swords in Dutch Collections) by Han Bing Siong.
6 This is a correction to the reading given on pages 101, 102 of *The Oshigata Book* by the authors.
7 The details in this section are taken from the article 'The "Zed" tanto' by R. B. Caldwell, published in the Newsletter of the Japanese Sword Society of the United States, vol. 21 No. 4.
8 Ugaki, carrying this dirk, committed suicide by flying on the last kamikaze mission of the war after hearing the Emperor's surrender broadcast. His body was never officially found although this may be untrue and the dirk could have survived. See *Shōkan* by R. Fuller (see Bibliography) under the naval entry for 'Ugaki Matome'.
9 The authors wish to thank Stephen Yap for furnishing the details of this rare sword.
10 These details and the photograph are contained in the article 'Military Ceremonial Swords' by Henry Sakaida, *Banzai Bulletin* no. 153, March 1995.

# Military Sword Blades and Markings

One of the joys of collecting Japanese swords of any type is the expectation of owning a blade of considerable age and a unique construction. The hand forging and folding of steel to produce a blade with soft inner steel, back and side steel of varying hardness and a razor-sharp hard-tempered edge (resulting in the ultimate cutting weapon) is every collector's ideal. Unfortunately this does not apply to the bulk of blades in military mounts.

In 1876 an Imperial edict (Haito-rei) abolished the right of the samurai to carry swords. Not only was the samurai caste forced into rapid decline but the swordsmiths' skills were unwanted and many turned to other trades such as producing cutlery or decorative metalwork for export or tourists. Some survived by making high-class blades to order, but many of the traditional blade-making skills became lost.

Apart from the traditional old blades, most worn in modern military mounts are either mass-produced and machine-made, in part or in whole, or were manufactured by methods which included some, but not all, traditional processses. Consequently the class and cutting ability of such blades is inferior to the older types.

As the armed forces increased in number so blade-making techniques were adapted by various individuals or companies to simplify production and to meet demand. Thus by the outbreak of World War Two there were many smiths of mixed ability and training who worked either at their own forges, small co-operatives, or in military arsenals (Zōheishō). Those under direct military control had to submit their blades for military inspection and acceptance. It is uncertain if those who worked individually also had to supply blades to the military on a quota basis. If so, they were probably also inspected and stamped. Blades made and sold privately would not, necessarily, bear military stamps.

The Shōwa period smith, Asano Kanezane, confirmed in a letter that he worked at Seki in Nōshu province (Mino prefecture) at his own premises.[1] In 1942 he, and others in Seki, came under the control of the Army Blade Department (Army Sword Co.) which appears to explain the introduction of the 'Seki' stamp (Fig. 61 (ix)). This organisation appears to have been formed to co-ordinate the manufacture and acceptance of blades in the centres where they were supplied direct to the Army. Many forges were associated with branches of the National Technical School which probably taught blade-making to metalwork students.

Essential for the production of a 'true' Japanese sword is the quality of steel used. 'Tamahagane' is made from Japanese sand iron at a charcoal-fired 'tatara' (traditional smelter). During the old sword (Kotō) period, swordsmiths often made

# JAPANESE MILITARY AND CIVIL SWORDS AND DIRKS

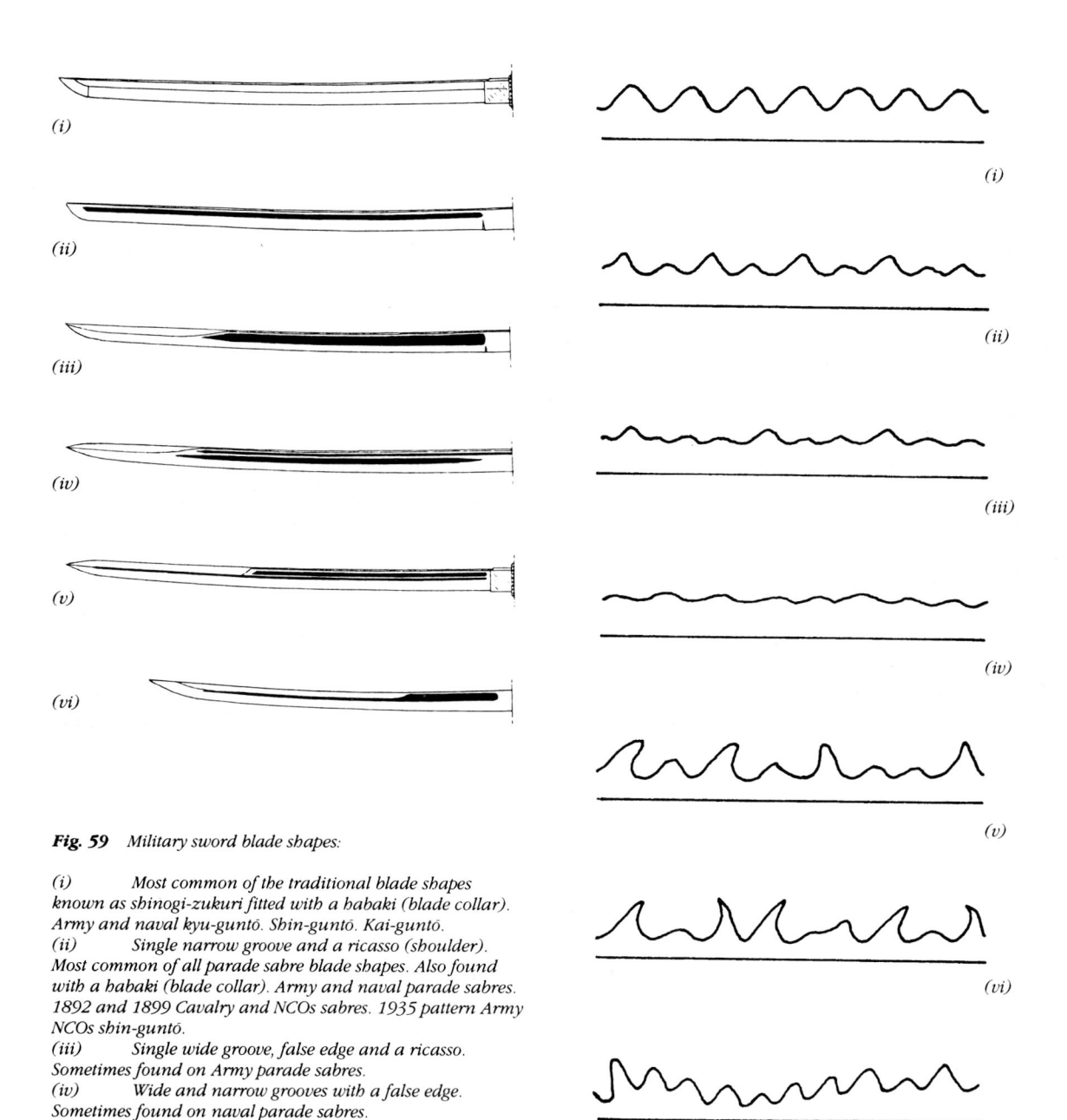

**Fig. 59** Military sword blade shapes:

(i) Most common of the traditional blade shapes known as shinogi-zukuri fitted with a habaki (blade collar). Army and naval kyu-guntō. Shin-guntō. Kai-guntō.
(ii) Single narrow groove and a ricasso (shoulder). Most common of all parade sabre blade shapes. Also found with a habaki (blade collar). Army and naval parade sabres. 1892 and 1899 Cavalry and NCOs sabres. 1935 pattern Army NCOs shin-guntō.
(iii) Single wide groove, false edge and a ricasso. Sometimes found on Army parade sabres.
(iv) Wide and narrow grooves with a false edge. Sometimes found on naval parade sabres.
(v) Short-wide and long-narrow grooves with a false edge known as kogarasu-zukuri ('little crow style'). A rare shape. Usually fitted with a habaki. Imperial Guard (or Household?) swords and 'Gensui-tō' (Field Marshals and Fleet Admirals swords).
(vi) Wide groove reducing to a narrow one known as unokubi-zukuri. A very scarce shape. c 1873 Naval Officers sword. 1883 Naval Candidates dirk.

**Fig. 60** Typical acid-etched yakiba patterns (which are variations on a theme) observed on Army, naval and civil parade sabre blades. Example (i) is the most common, while (v) and (vi) appear to be the scarcest. Possibly there are also other unrecorded variants.

214

tamahagane themselves at their own tatara. These smiths were known as 'ō-kaji'. During the later Kotō period, and certainly during the Shintō period, swordsmiths bought ready-made tamahagane from a tatara. Such smiths were called 'ko-kaji'. Thus an ō-kaji fully controlled the quality of the steel he required.

A traditional Japanese blade is made from a hard, high carbon content, steel (kawagane) folded (orikaeshi) and hammered by hand many times to eliminate impurities and produce laminations, or layers, which can show as a grain (hada). This may be wrapped around a softer, low carbon content, steel (shingane) which becomes the core. After hand forging into shape, a blade was covered with a special clay; the area for the yakiba (hardened edge usually referred to as 'tempered') was given a thinner application than the upper section and back edge. When the clay had dried, the blade was heated to the required temperature and then plunged into water. This could make, or break, a blade since the sudden shock could crack the yakiba (cutting edge) so formed. These processes produced an aesthetically pleasing but razor-sharp cutting blade which could absorb the forces of a hard blow without breaking.

An important effect was the formation of a line of martensite crystals between the yakiba and the main blade surface (jigane). This is known as the 'hamon' which consists of small crystals called 'nioi' and larger ones called 'nie', but the latter are not always present. Nioi give the appearance of a narrow white line, while nie crystals are discernible to the naked eye.[2] Another effect produced by the lamination of the steel is a grain (hada) visible on the blade surface, which in some cases is very flamboyant. Other features may be found in these hand-forged blades, such as 'chikai', 'kinsuji', 'sunagashi', 'utsuri' etc., but recourse to specialist books is recommended for explanation.

Hand-forged blades made by traditional methods and using traditional materials after 1876 (i.e. after the Haito-rei sword prohibition) are called 'gendaitō, literally 'present age sword'.

In the sixteenth century imported Asian and Western steel appeared, becoming popular for blade-making as an additive to the traditional tamahagane. By the twentieth century, smiths working under military control were issued with mill-produced steel which was often made from scrap such as railway lines. Apparently this could be folded a few times in the mill before distribution, thus producing a laminated steel which could again be folded several times by the better smiths at their forges.

The traditional blade manufacturing method was entirely by hand, eye and experience with no mechanisation or even a thermometer. Military blade-making, by necessity, utilised factory techniques in arsenals and some machine hammering in the smaller forges. This, along with tempering in oil, produced blades of varying quality. Mass production of blades, used with issue pieces such as cavalry sabres, involved little or no skill. However, officers required blades of better quality so elements of factory and hand production were combined, terminating with a quenching in (whale?) oil. There was less risk of cracking since it was a slower cooling process than water hardening, and greatly lessened the risk of failure. Some smiths started to develop their own techniques, even producing blades in 'anti-rust steel' (probably 'stainless'). Other manufacturing methods were also introduced in the late nineteenth and twentieth centuries (see later in this section), all of which generally involved oil tempering or quenching the entire naked blade in oil.

An English language magazine, probably just pre-World War Two, sold in Gifu (Mino) prefecture and called *Japan Today and Tomorrow* published the following small articles:

### [Watanabe, Noted Swordsmith]

Isokichi Watanabe[3] is an eminent swordsmith, being the leader of the To-ken Tanren-kai [an association of swordsmiths] in Seki-machi, Gifu, which is active in supplying superior swords, the demand for which has considerably increased. The association also features information and advice regarding swords.

**[Eminent Sword Maker]**
The increasing demand for swords forged by the new process[4] has enabled the Seki-no-Magoroku Tokensho, in front of Seki-machi station, Gifu, to undertake mass production thereby making swords available at very reasonable prices.

Adjacent to the above articles was an advert for 'The Seki Token K.K. Ltd, dealers in Japanese swords'. Presumably they were retailers as distinct from manufacturers.

It has been reported that thirty thousand swords a year were being made at the peak of World War Two, which reduced to eight thousand at the end.[5] The occupation forbade the manufacture of swords entirely, but General MacArthur is reported to have given permission for swords to be finished for GI souvenirs so as not to throw men out of work until they could find alternative employment.[6] Indeed, a blade signed and dated 1946 has been found but it had never been tempered. Certain old wives' tales are associated with the mystique of Japanese swords taken by Allied troops as souvenirs. A typical example is: 'Traditionally the sword belonging to a father or grandfather was melted down to form the cutting edge of the blade owned by the son or grandson.'[7]

Blades of considerable age can be found in guntō (military mounts). They are either family heirlooms remounted for war or were bought from dealers. Probably less than ten per cent of Officers shin-guntō are fitted with pre-twentieth century blades. A number of post-war Japanese–English language publications have stated that no 'old' blades (i.e. Kotō or Shintō period) were carried in World War Two, although the Japanese authors must have known that this was untrue.

The following sections are a synopsis of the primary blade-making methods thought to have prevailed during the 1930s and 1940s which vary from traditional hand-forged to mass-produced with a number of categories in between. They are listed (according to the authors' opinion) in descending order of quality. The best of all may, for ease of identification, be termed 'tamahagane gendaitō' (although the true definition may just be 'gendaitō'). The second best, and technically almost as good, has no specific name but, again for ease, the authors have classified as 'mill-steel gendaitō'. However, since 'tamahagane' is not used then the term 'gendaitō' is, in the strictest sense, incorrect; but is retained in this book because it conveys to the reader that traditional hand forging and water hardening was still the main process involved.

## Tamahagane gendaitō

Some top-class smiths appear to have been exempt from military service and were allowed to work in the traditional water tempering manner using domestically produced steel (tamahagane) made at a traditional smelter (tatara)[8] from domestic sand iron or ore.[9]

Tamahagane lacks a homogeneous carbon content which thus allows a grain (hada) formed by laminations to still be visible even after folding fifteen times (i.e. 32,768 layers). This is not possible with homogeneous carbon content mill-produced steel when the laminations will become invisible after six to nine folds.[10] 'Sunagashi'[11], which is sometimes found, also results from a lack of homogeneous carbon and cannot be produced using unmodified mill steel.[12]

This class of blade is a true gendaitō and thus a true Nihontō (Nippontō), i.e. Japanese blade. However, they are said by some experts to be inferior to most Kotō and Shintō period blades. Such blades would be privately sold or made to special order and were highly regarded. They are not believed to bear military inspection/acceptance stamps of any kind even if ordered or bought through military channels. Tamahagane gendaitō were regarded as works of art as well as weapons and, consequently, were expensive.

Blade-making in this fully traditional manner was allowed to re-commence in 1953 under licence. Smiths have to serve a full apprenticeship. Their numbers are strictly limited with production restricted by law to twenty-four finished blades per man per annum regardless of type, i.e. tantō, katana or tachi. Quality is excellent. Such blades are very expensive with, in some cases, a waiting period of up to seven years.

## Mill-steel gendaitō

There is another form of hand-forged blade made traditionally which can visually and physically produce all the features of tamahagane gendaitō but is not considered by some experts to be true Nihontō or even gendaitō. The difference lies with the metal used, which in this case was produced at a steel mill smelter and could even be imported Western scrap.

Such steel has a homogeneous carbon content which, as previously stated, cannot be laminated to any degree without loss of grain. Therefore carbon is added by the swordsmith in a process called 'orosu' to vary the carbon content.[13] The resultant steel (known as 'oroshi-gane') is folded, hammered and water-tempered in the full traditional manner becoming capable of producing all the characteristics of true Nihontō including multi-laminations, nioi, nie, sunagashi etc. Such blades appear to be visually indistinguishable from tamahagane gendaitō except, perhaps, to the eyes of Japanese blade experts.

Chris Bowen was told by a swordsmith, who made blades during the war, that an established swordsmith acting as a 'shinsa-in' (examiner) selected swords to be bought by the Army. According to this information the shinsa-in personally stamped blades which passed his examination with a 'Star' stamp (Fig. 61 (x)). Probably this applied to mill-steel gendaitō and, perhaps, some better quality 'han-tanren abura yaki-ire' blades. This stamp is generally associated with blades made in the nineteen-forties. Another rare stamp noted on reputedly good quality undated blades which may possibly be in this category is that of Tokyo/Koishikawa/Kokura Arsenal (Fig. 62 (i)), although normally thought to be associated with mass-produced items. These are believed to have been made in, and possibly restricted to, the late nineteen-twenties. However, the stamp could have been added sometime after manufacture (elsewhere?) for assembly purposes.

As in the case of tamahagane gendaitō there are several methods of construction using hardened steels. The basic is 'maru gitae' (one grade steel), the next is 'kobuse gitae' (two steels of different hardness), while even more complex methods are possible. Probably 'maru gitae' is the most common structure of mill-steel gendaitō.

Some Shintō period blades stated on their tangs that 'namban tetsu' (foreign or barbarian steel) was used in their construction. These are regarded as true Nihontō. This is probably because such steel was added to tamahagane rather than forming the entire blade.[14] Thus, in theory, if tamahagane and mill-steel were mixed the resultant blade should also be regarded as true Nihontō, although it is believed that this has not successfully been carried out even by post-war smiths. Mill-steel gendaitō should also, in the writer's opinion, be highly regarded since the smith's full skill went into the production.

## Koa-Isshin Mantetsu-tō

'Mantetsu' is a play on words since the meanings are interrelated. It can be translated as (a) South Manchurian Railway; (b) Manchurian iron; (c) Full of iron; and (d) Meet the (demand) for iron. The consensus of opinion is that (b) is the intended reading when used in blade tang inscriptions, but it does not necessarily imply manufacture of the blade in Manchuria.

Recent information indicates there were two grades of Mantetsu blades. The superior type being made in Japan while the inferior grade was made in Manchuria (Manchukuo). Both types have tangs which are dated by the zodiacal method (using a sixty-year cycle) but may be distinguished by the main inscription. Those made in Japan read KOA ISSHIN (a patriotic phrase meaning 'single-mindedly praying for the development of Asia')[15] plus MANTETSU SAKU KORE WO ('made this of Mantetsu'). Those made in Manchuria generally read MANTETSU (NO) KITAU TSUKURU KORE WO ('worked this by forging with Mantetsu') and may have the 'Nan' stamp (Fig. 62 (xx)) of the Mukden Arsenal.

'Koa-Isshin Mantetsu' blades are a complex construction made by the insertion of a soft steel core into a tube of high carbon content steel which was quenched in water to produce a hamon of nie as well as nioi.[16] Indeed a hamon of pure ko-nie (small nie) has been seen. They have a good cutting ability and their shape is rather elegant, being reminiscent of Kotō period blades. Manchurian-made Mantetsu blades are said to be rolled only and oil-tempered (see 'Mantetsu-tō' later in this chapter). They are wide, heavy and possibly have a hamon looking like nioi.

The South Manchurian Railway Company logo (Fig. 61 (xix)) has been found on tangs which have no inscription except for the zodiacal manufacturing date of 1938 (no other year has been reported). These are generally wide and heavy but have been found with a hamon of pure ko-nie. The method of manufacture is possibly the same as the 'Koa-Isshin Mantetsu' blades, but it is unknown if they were made in Japan or Manchuria although the former is suspected.

It may be surmised that the South Manchurian Railway Company commenced blade production in the late nineteen-thirties possibly using a complex construction. This method was also adopted in Japan using imported Manchurian steel. However, the Army takeover of the South Manchurian Railway in the early nineteen-forties probably dictated a speedier production method which necessitated one-piece oil-tempered blades.

The term 'abura-yaki' means 'oil hardened' which can be applied to all blades which are not water-tempered. Oil hardening (tempering) allows a more rapid blade production to meet demand with a consequent loss of quality. There were a number of processes but the best may, perhaps, be classified as 'laminated or folded abura yaki-ire' which involved some hand forging using mill-produced steel. The other, and more common, process involves hammering and drawing out a single piece of mill-steel without folding, which is known as 'sunobe'. All such items are frequently encountered bearing a swordsmith's signature, date and military stamp.

In the opinion of the Dutch expert Han Bing Siong only blades made according to the traditional folding and forging procedure, known as 'orikaeshi-tanren', can withstand the shock of water quenching. Thus a *partly folded* and *water-hardened* category between mill-steel gendaitō and han-tanren abura yaki-ire should not be possible. However, he believes 'Koa-Isshin Mantetsu' blades can withstand the shock of water quenching because they are made from two steels of different hardness.

## Han-tanren abura yaki-ire tō

Literally 'partly forged oil-hardened blade', i.e. partly laminated (forged) and hardened in oil.

The best of oil-tempered blades are those made from mill-steel which has been folded a few times by the smith to produce a laminated construction, but not to the extent of the gendaitō classes because of the loss of grain. This worked steel may, perhaps, be termed 'han-tanren tetsu' (partially folded steel).[17] Quenching of the cutting edge (yakiba) is in oil. This produces a conspicuous nioi-like[18] hamon (but not nie) and possibly a fine grain (hada) which may be hardly discernible.

Quality varies, although some by better class, trained smiths are good. The amount of hand forging involved may also vary according to the individual smith's ability. These are frequently, and erroneously, described as gendaitō.

## Sunobe abura yaki-ire tō

Literally 'drawn and hammered oil-hardened' i.e. drawn out, hammered and hardened in oil.

Sunobe (hammered and drawn but not folded) mill-steel blades with oil-tempered yakiba are the most common of 'abura yaki-ire' blades. Normally a nioi-like hamon is produced but no grain (hada) is visible. Visually they may be hardly discernible from han-tanren abura yaki-ire, although inferior, and are often called 'Shōwa-tō' (i.e. Shōwa blades). However, there is one type which visually shows the features of grain, nioi, some ko-nie (small nie) and even sunagashi which are features often associated with, and used to identify, gendaitō. Gary Purkiss (on page thirty of the Japanese Sword Society of the United States Newsletter, vol. 25 no. 4) says:

> 'Some of these blades do exhibit what appears to be a grain, but on closer examination, one will find there is no oxide boundary between the layers of metal and this characteristic must appear on a blade which is forge-welded in the atmosphere. It must be remembered that not all Western steel has no life in it. What appears to be grain is an amalgam of high and low carbon steel similar to crystalline Indian damascus steel, but this is formed in the smelter, not the smithy. When these blades are quenched they never show ji-nie, ara-nie or normal nie. Sometimes a very small ko-nie is visible at the boundary of the hamon, on occasions fine sunagashi appears, but it never goes deep into the hamon; and these blades always exhibit a very shiny surface not found even on blades of Western steel which were forged in the traditional manner.'

Thus the grain is only a surface feature formed in the foundry and is probably due to the amalgam of low and high carbon content steels. It is the opinion of Han Bing Siong that the prescence of some ko-nie and sunagashi is coincidental, and again due to the steel used. These features have caused great confusion among collectors who, naturally, mistake such blades for gendaitō.

Machine hammering into shape appears to have been used to various extents depending upon the smith's technique since most are believed to have been made at individual forges or small co-operatives rather than on arsenal assembly lines.

There are numerous simplified manufacturing processes, some of which are described in the following sections. Others reported are 'Shin-an Tokkyo Nihontō' (newly patented Japanese swords), 'Rutsubo kou seisaku shin nihontō' (new Japanese sword made of crucible steel), 'Nippon Tokusho Tōken'. (Japanese special swords), 'Tokkyo guntō' (patented Army swords), 'Jitsuyo-tō' (practical swords) etc.[19] Whether or not they are all 'abura yaki-ire' is unknown.

## Mantetsu-tō

As previously explained 'Mantetsu-tō' (Manchurian iron blades) without the additional 'Koa-Isshin' inscription were made by, or for, the Army in Manchuria (Manchukuo) at the South Manchurian (Second Mukden) Arsenal.

The swordsmith Nobuhira (Keith Austin) says that contrary to popular belief railway lines were not used. Local high-grade iron ore was smelted into pig-iron at the Anshan Ironworks south of Mukden. It was then converted into a 'special steel' which resisted the intense cold which rendered a blade brittle and liable to break. The steel was 'rolled into basic shaped rods [i.e. shinogi, mune etc.] This was then cut into the right lengths, tapered, kissaki and nakago pounded out, tempered, polished and signed.'[20] The composition of the 'special steel' is unknown. Possibly a nioi-like hamon could be produced. Therefore these blades are a simplified (one-piece) construction quenched in oil and virtually machine-made since rolled into shape. Thus they cannot be classified as 'sunobe' (drawn and hammered). The steel used may, perhaps, make them superior to 'Murata-tō', but this is debatable.

A 'Nan' stamp (Fig. 62 (xx)), which is the inspection stamp of the Mukden Arsenal, may be found above the inscription. This seems to have appeared in the nineteen-forties, seemingly after the Army takeover of the South Manchurian Railway Company. The rare 'Ren' stamp (Fig. 61 (xxviii)) has also been observed, but only on a blade dated 1944 which indicates it is late-war.

'Kinzoku kenyujo-tō' (abbreviated to 'Kinetō') is a blade specifically designed for the sub-zero temperatures of Manchuria and Siberia.[21] It may be that the Manchurian-made Mantetsu blades fall within this category.

## Murata-tō

A process invented by Tsuneyoshi Murata, a famous firearms maker, around the beginning of the twentieth century. It is basically a one-piece steel bar, oil-hardened, but has no visible hamon of nioi or nie. A yakiba (tempered edge) is clearly visible but merges into the blade surface (jigane). Such blades may be signed and dated.

It is unknown if they are sunobe, just drawn or rolled, but the absence of a hamon would seem to make them inferior to Mantetsu-tō. Manufacture was probably at the Koishikawa (Tokyo) Arsenal where Murata pattern rifles were made, although it is quite likely outside semi-skilled smiths also adopted the process.

## Tai-sabi-kō

Literally 'anti-rust steel', which is a type of stainless steel. Such blades may sometimes be found in Army mounts but are normally associated with blades made at the private Tenshozan Forge (Company) of Kamakura which made swords for the Navy. Thus they are commonly found in kai-guntō mounts and would seem to be virtually machine-made. The kanji (characters) for this metal may be included in the tang inscription. Tenshozan also had its own stamp (Fig. 62 (ix)).

The smith Fujiwara Kanenaga, formerly Kawamura Eijiro, who worked at the Tenshozan Forge was the manager of the Taika Electric Company of Manchuria. He, and Uejima Meiichi, using steel from Gyushindai in southern Manchuria, made these and are said to have brought out a hamon which was previously thought impossible with this type of blade.[22] This presupposes that there was also a real yakiba with nioi, although this feature has not been reported. However, a 'well-defined yakiba' (without nioi) has, apparently, been seen.

Another term found on blade tangs is 'Fushukō', i.e. stainless steel.

## Machine-made

Normally wholly machine-made in an arsenal from a single piece of hammered steel which is fully quenched in oil (without a clay covering) or, possibly, just allowed to cool in air. No folding is involved and there is no tempered edge. Since not drawn out by hammering, the term 'sunobe' does not apply.

Generally mounted as 'issue' swords such as cavalry sabres and NCOs shin-guntō. Thinner flexible chromium-plated versions are used for parade sabres which may also have a false, acid-etched, yakiba apparently offered as an extra cost option (see Fig. 60).

## Summary of basic military blade-making methods
(In descending order of quality)

(1) Tamahagane gendaitō – Traditionally made steel (tamahagane). Hand-forged. Water-hardened. Nioi and/or nie. Grain.

(2) Mill-steel gendaitō – Mill-produced steel processed to form 'oroshi-gane'. Hand-forged. Water-hardened. Nioi and/or nie. Grain.

(3) Koa-Isshin Mantetsu-tō – Insertion method. Water-hardened. Nioi and/or ko-nie. Grain?

(4) Han-tanren abura yaki-ire tō – Partially forged. Oil-hardened. Nioi-like hamon. Fine grain.

(5) Sunobe abura yaki-ire tō – Drawn and hammered. Oil-hardened. Nioi-like hamon. (Possibly some ko-nie). Surface grain only.

(6) Mantetsu-tō – Rolled. Oil-hardened. Nioi-like hamon. No grain.

(7) Murata-tō – Rolled? Oil-hardened. Yakiba but no hamon. No grain.

(8) Tai-sabi-kō – Stainless steel. Oil-hardened. Possible yakiba but no hamon. No grain.

(9) Machine-made – Entirely quenched in oil. May be plated. Optional acid-etched yakiba.

The precedence of (6), (7), (8) is, perhaps, open to question.
(1) to (8) may be signed and dated.
(2) [and (4)?] may have a 'star' stamp.
(4) to (8) frequently have military inspection/acceptance stamps.

## Army refurbishment blades

Sword refurbishment units accompanied the Army throughout the occupied areas. Besides repairs to binding and scabbards they also undertook blade manufacture, utilising the various methods previously described (and probably others as well) according to the abilities of the Army swordsmiths and the availability of materials.

Some swordsmiths appear to have moved to occupied areas in an independent capacity to make blades under contract to the Army. Indeed *Nakajima Monogatari* by Francis Boyd explains how one such smith, called Muneyoshi Nakajima,[23] moved to Peking around 1942 and set up a forge where he employed twelve Chinese craftsmen and a Chinese swordsmith. He was contracted to supply three hundred blades per month, which he did, plus the occasional blade made to special order. British railway lines were used if marked 'Sheffield' because the upper section was already folded (laminated). The lower section was discarded. These were stolen by the Chinese and sold to the smith on the black market. Interestingly Nakajima would temper all three hundred in one night without a clay covering by passing the yakiba area through a fire until red hot and then quenching. Quality was thus debatable, but 'railway line' swords, apparently, could resemble old Bizen swords and sell for more than the standard production items.

Individual smiths may have signed their own tangs but not necessarily stating the place of manufacture. Certainly the authors have never seen any inscribed 'made in Peking'.

Blades made by smiths who were worked independently or in refurbishment units in other areas are known. For example: 'Takakazu, Lord of Tomari in Yamato [*an honorary title*] at Saigon while following the Army. October 1942', and 'Ishihara Kanetada on Singapore Island. February 1945'.

## Mill-produced steels

Traditionally made tamahagane was used only for gendaitō. All other blades were made from steel produced in the Western manner at various steel works. Quality naturally varied, as did the raw materials which could be scrap Western steel or domestic and imported iron ores.

Occasionally Shōwa period tang inscriptions include a reference to the steel or ore used in the blade. Examples noted are; 'Mantetsu' (Manchurian iron); 'Kaimen iron' (from Manchuria); 'Anti-rust steel from Taika' (in Manchuria); 'Stainless steel from Niishin' (not identified); 'Sand iron from Tottori prefecture' (in Japan); 'Yasuki steel' (from Izumo province in Japan); 'Steel from a gun of the battleship *Mikasa*' (used regularly by only one smith, Minamoto Hideaki); 'Gunsui steel' (from Gunma prefecture, Japan). Gunsui-hagane was a limited production electro-refined steel which was developed during World War Two as one possible substitute for tamahagane. However, it does not seem to have been very successful.

## Blade shapes

Fig. 59 shows various blade shapes which are found in military sword fittings. The most common is the traditional shinogi-zukuri which was used with wakizashi, katana and tachi and remained popular for Army and Naval Officers swords because of the proven suitability as a cutting weapon. Other single-edged grooved patterns were introduced especially for mass-produced swords. Two rare forms of traditional shape are also shown in Fig. 59 (v), (vi), although use seems very limited.

## Polishing

Blades of traditional shinogi-zukuri form received a polish to bring out the construction features such as 'hada', 'nie' and 'nioi' which are so important to the appearance of a good blade. Polishing was an art carried out by trained craftsmen who worked by hand using special stones of varying degrees of hardness. During the war years only the best blades received this treatment. The bulk were probably machine-polished in part or in whole. Women were also employed for this work in military establishments as is clearly shown in Plate 285.

## Gendai swordsmiths

Over 800 swordsmiths of varying ability are said to have worked during the Shōwa period, but how many of these continuously made tamahagane gendaitō (true Nihontō) is unknown.

The Army invited private swordsmiths (Kaji) to submit examples of their work for inspection and testing. The latter included cutting (tameshigiri), sharpness, bending and impact. If the blade passed the tests, the smith was designated 'Rikugun Jūmei Tōshō' (i.e. Army sword craftsman of note) and became eligible to receive 7.5kg (16½lb) of sought after tamahagane for each blade he produced. Some 'Kaji' apparently signed and submitted quality blades produced by other smiths to qualify. Consequently not all 'Rikugun Jūmei Tōshō' could produce gendaitō and adopted other methods, although signing their tangs in a manner to suggest they were of traditional manufacture.[24] Research has revealed that 209 wartime smiths of this status were registered in Seki alone.[25]

Imura Kasho published a list of what, in his opinion, are the top twenty 'eminent Shōwa Gendai-swordsmiths'.[26] They are, in descending order: 1. Gassan Sadakatsu; 2. Horii Toshihide; 3. Takahashi Yoshimune; 4. Kasama Shigetsugu; 5. Watanabe Kanenaga; 6. Kurihara Akihide; 7. Kajiyama Yasutoshi; 8. Amada Sadayoshi; 9. Shibata Ka; 10. Kajiyama Yasutoku; 11. Miyaguchi Toshihiro (Yasuhiro); 12. Imai Sadashige; 13. Morioka Masataka?; 14. Tsukamaoto Okimasa; 15. Endo Mitsuoki; 16. Moritsugu Norisada; 17. Fujita Tadamitsu; 18. Nakao Tadatsugu; 19. Ikeda Yasumitsu; 20. Chikushu Nobumitsu. This list is at variance with other scholars who may place the smiths in different orders, but the names are generally compatible.

Included in the list are four smiths who worked at the Nippon-tō Tanrenkai. This important centre was established at the Yasukuni Shrine, Toyko in July 1935 under the patronage of the Army to produced tamahagane gendaitō by traditional methods from tamahagane made at its own tatara in Shimane prefecture. It was also intended to prevent the loss of true blade-making and rediscover some of the old techniques which were said to have been lost. Formed as a non-profit organisation and a swordsmith school, it consisted of five smithies employing approximately thirty people over an eleven-year period until closure in November 1944. Approximately 8,000 blades were produced during this period, all highly regarded and now greatly sought after by modern collectors.

Although these blades, like those by other well-known swordsmiths, were subjected to examination if made available through military channels, they were never stamped. Each smith signed with just the two characters of his name and the date. A resident smith, or student who became qualified and worked at the shrine, was honoured with the use of the character 靖 (YASU) which he incorporated into his art name. The following list gives the art names of instructors and students plus the period in which they worked as qualified swordsmiths at the shrine.[27] The production figures are of particular interest.

## MILITARY SWORD BLADES AND MARKINGS

| | | |
|---|---|---|
| Yashuhiro | 靖廣 | – Instructor, 1933–37. Approx. 500 blades. |
| Yasutoku | 靖德 | – Instructor, 1933–40. Approx. 1,250 blades. |
| Yasumitsu | 靖光 | – Instructor, 1933–40. 1,100 blades. |
| Yasunori | 靖憲 | – Swordsmith, 1935–45. 1,600 blades. |
| Yasutoshi | 靖利 | – Swordsmith, 1939–41. 350 blades. |
| Yasunobu | 靖延 | – Swordsmith, 1939–45? 1,000 blades. |
| Yasushige | 靖繁 | – Swordsmith, 1939–45? Approx. 850 blades. |
| Yasuyoshi | 靖吉 | – Swordsmith, (first signed Yasuharu 靖春) 1940–45? Approx. 700 blades. |
| Yasuoki | 靖興 | – Swordsmith, 1940–45. Approx. 750 blades. |
| Yasutake | 靖武 | – Swordsmith, 1944–45. Ten blades. |
| Yasuyō | 靖要 | – Swordsmith, 1944–45? Approx. ten blades. |

There were other students, including Moriwaki Masataka (see below), who do not appear to have become fully qualified during their time at Yasukuni.

Another important centre was founded at the Minatogawa Shrine near Kobe by the Navy in 1940.[28] The head instructor was Moriwaki Masataka who worked there for four and a half years, producing about 1,000 hand-forged blades which were issued by the Naval Academy. Blades made at this shrine are distinguished by a stamp of a 'chrysanthemum blossom floating on water', which is known as the 'Kiku-sui' (Fig. 61 (xvi)) above the signature. According to the information acquired from Chris Bowen in Japan they were tamahagane gendaitō, but the Navy did not have its own tatara. Presumably some surplus tamahagane from the Shimane tatara was issued for naval use. Other respected associations were formed, among which were the Nihontō Tanren Denshujo (Japanese Sword Forging Institute), Tokiwamatsu Tanren Kenkyu Jo, Hanazwa Tanren Jo, Okura Tanrenjo etc.

## Military swordsmiths

A smith who worked for the Army was known as a 'Rikugun Tōshō', literally 'Army sword artisan'. A number appear to have been fully trained, with students of their own. Some must have made mill-steel gendaitō. Many were probably no more than former cutlers or metalworkers of indifferent ability who may even have been conscripted. The

**Plate 285** *A rare wartime photograph of women blade polishers at work in an unknown arsenal or centre. They appear to be polishing by hand with the blade tip resting on a block. Perhaps each undertook a different stage of work.* (Philip Goody).

great proportion of wartime smiths were 'Rikugun Tōshō' and produced blades by the various oil-tempered methods previously described.

The largest manufacturing centre of such items appears to be Seki where a collection of smithies worked as independent companies to supply the Army (and to a lesser extent the Navy). This may be regarded as the Japanese equivalent of Solingen in Germany which was the sword and dagger manufacturing centre for the Third Reich. Prior to 1941 they probably worked on a contract basis supplying blades on a quota system and were allowed to sell a number, or any excess, privately or accept commissions. Some smiths entered and won various blade-making competitions, although the class of blade submitted has not been established. In late 1941 or early 1942 the Army Blade Department (Army Sword Co.) took control of these small companies and controlled production which, presumably, limited private dealings.

Even prison labour was utilised for sword production in association with the Army Blade Department. For example, the chief warden of Okayama prison (in Bizen province) was Chounsai Emura (Nagamitsu), who was also a swordsmith. He opened a forge at the prison in the nineteen-forties, apparently taking prisoners as students and using others for polishing. Another prison where a similar system worked was Takayama (in Hida province) where blades were made by the smiths Hattori Masahiro and Ishihara Masanao. Blades made here have an abnormally thick 'kissaki' (blade point) which swells out in the manner found on old armour-piercing swords. The reason for this feature on modern blades is unknown. Another unusual, and unique, feature of Takayama blades is the inclusion of the prisoner-polisher's name in the inscription. A number of different names have been found but, so far, never more than once.

The United States Strategic Bombing Survey of January 1947 for the 'The Japanese wartime standard of living and utilization of manpower' Table JJJ gives the following figures for 'prisoners in prison workshops' engaged in 'swordsmithing':

March 1941 – No figure (nil?), March 1942 – 240, March 1943 – 290, March 1944 – 303, March 1945 – 380, August 1945 – No figure. These must consist of hammermen, polishers etc. Blade production figures have not been ascertained..

## Military inspection/acceptance and other stamps

Many blades in shin- and kai-guntō mounts are found with a small stamp on the blade tang above the smith's signature although, sometimes, one may be found on an unsigned blade. A number, but probably not all, of these stamps are shown in Figs. 61, 62. The authors believe that some are military inspection and/or acceptance stamps but others may relate to specific retailers or to the (patented?) process by which the blade was made.

They seem to be a phenomenon of the Shōwa era (post-1926), probably originating in the late nineteen-thirties and lasting up to 1945 since not seen on blade tangs from the Meiji and Taishō periods. Military stamps appear to have been added at central collection centres, presumably after some form of visual inspection, to indicate 'acceptance' or 'receipt' by the military.[29] Information from Japan on the true purpose and meaning of these stamps is lacking, so they have been assessed, in general, from the 'oshigata' (tang rubbings) of over one thousand Shōwa period blades. Stamped numbers may occasionally be found on tangs but they are probably batch numbering for record purposes. Painted numbers and characters appear to be for assembly purposes.

The Army arsenals which produced swords are Kokura, Koishikawa (both in Tokyo), Tokyo No. 1, Osaka and Nagoya. The naval arsenals are Toyokawa, Yokohama and Yokosuka. Most seem to have used identifying inspection/acceptance stamps, but it has not been possible to identify them all with certainty. Sword-producing arsenals abroad were Mukden in Manchuria and apparently Jinsen in Korea. The latter is known to have

MILITARY SWORD BLADES AND MARKINGS

produced bayonets, but no blade confirming manufacture in that centre has been reported. There were also Japanese-controlled arsenals in Nanking and Tientsin, China producing bayonets, but whether or not they made swords is unknown.

A high blade breakage rate in China may have necessitated an inspection system and mark commencing with the prolific 'Shō' stamp.

The 'Shō' (abbreviation for 'Shōwa') stamp (Fig. 61 (i)) seems to be general military (probably Army) stamp of no specific blade-making centre used prior to late 1941 or early 1942. The earliest observed date is May 1940. Most seem to be 'sunobe abura yaki-ire' (drawn, hammered and oil-tempered mill-steel) and not arsenal-produced machine-made. Use is thought to be restricted to blades sold through the Army Officers Club (Kaikosha)[30], which presumably means they could be bought 'off the shelf'.

Swordsmiths came under the control of the Army Blade Department around late 1941 or early 1942. The 'Shō' stamp seems to have been abandoned in favour of stamps relating to specific blade-producing centres.[31] The most common of these is that of 'Seki' (Fig. 61 (ix)) which is normally seen on blades dating from December 1941.[32] Neither the 'Shō' or 'Seki' stamps indicate the method of blade manufacture, only that they are not tamahagane gendaitō.

Other stamps are found although most have an unknown or indeterminate significance. Not all appear to be military and at least four shown may represent private manufacturers and/or retailers, e.g. Fig. 61 (xvii), (xviii), (xxii), (xxiv). It has been suggested by Japanese sources that those incorporating Roman lettering (e.g. Fig. 61 (xiv), (xxi)) represent the owner's initials[33], but this seems most unlikely since (xiv) has been found on both Army and naval items.

The 'Tan' stamp (Fig. 61 (v)) is the Japanese character meaning 'to forge'. This is believed to indicate a hand-forged blade, possibly mill-steel gendaitō, but could also indicate a lesser quality partially forged blade. Whether or not it is a military stamp is open to question. Such blades are usually signed by smiths living at Seki in Nōshū province, and the earliest noted date is 1942. The term 'forged' is sometimes used in the inscription.

The 'Shin gane iru' stamp meaning 'genuine inserted steel' (Fig. 61 (vi)) must also refer to the manufacturing process.[34] The classification of this blade is uncertain, but is probably oil-tempered.

The 'Star' stamp (Fig. 61 (x)) is believed to have been added by an Army gendai swordsmith inspector appointed by the Army to buy good quality blades from individual swordsmiths. Some tang inscriptions refer to Seki and the Tokyo No. 1 and Osaka Arsenals. It is thought to be associated with mill-steel gendaitō (see under that heading) and possibly better quality han-tanren abura yaki-ire blades. The earliest date noted is 1937, which may be an anomaly since all other dated examples seem to be post-1942.

The Nagoya Arsenal appears to have produced sword blades.[35] A tiny 'Na' (abbreviation for Nagoya) stamp (Fig. 61 (xiii)) is sometimes found on signed blades whose inscriptions normally make no reference to a possible place of manufacture. This stamp is associated with firearms made by that arsenal. No inscribed tang (stamped or not) referring to Nagoya has been reported. All seem to be oil-tempered.

A small block of Japanese characters and numbers in columns is, sometimes found stamped near the tang end of signed blades, often in conjunction with a 'Shō' stamp. Unfortunately the right-hand column of the few checked was always indistinct, thus preventing a full translation. The centre column reads: 'Item number 211659'. This is standard to all and therefore may be a patent or registration number. The left-hand column is difficult to understand but seems to relate to the manufacturing process: HŌ (wrap, cover with) *or* KURUMU (wrap, tuck in), TETSU (steel), TANREN (forging, temper), TŌ (sword) *or* KATANA (blade), IN (seal, stamp). Perhaps the meaning is '[this] seal [confirms] this blade was forged [by] the concealed steel [process]'. Possibly this signifies that different grades of inner and outer steel were used. The occasional presence of a 'Shin gane iru' stamp (Fig. 6 (vi)) also reinforces this theory. The indistinct column could relate to a particular

## JAPANESE MILITARY AND CIVIL SWORDS AND DIRKS

***Fig. 61*** *Stamps found on military sword/dirk tangs and fittings (see also Figs. 17, 19, 62).*

(i) 'Shō' (abbreviation of 'Shōwa') stamp. Post-1926 military (normally Army) inspection and/or acceptance stamp used until around late 1941. Very common.

(ii) 'Gi' stamp. Probably an abbreviation of 'Gifu prefecture'. Possibly used on blades made, or inspected, outside Seki which was also in Gifu. Earliest date noted is May 1944. Rare.

(iii) 'Kami' (meaning 'God') stamp. Significance unknown. Found only on a shin-guntō tsuba (guard). Very rare.

(iv) 'Hisa' stamp. Significance unknown. Found on a naval dirk crossguard.

(v) 'Tan' (or 'Kitau') stamp, literally 'to forge' or 'forged'. See main text. Very scarce.

(vi) 'Shin gane iru' stamp, literally 'genuine steel put in', i.e. genuine inserted steel. This must refer to the blade-making process and was, perhaps, used by only one unidentified maker or retailer.

(vii) 'Five Measures' stamp, literally Go (5) – To (measure of capacity: One To = 3.97 (Imperial gallons). Significance unknown. Very rare.

(viii) 'Matsu' stamp found associated with tang batch or issue numbers. Significance unknown. Appears limited to blades (both signed and unsigned) found in 1944 pattern Army mounts. Rare.

(ix) 'Seki' stamp. Military (Army) inspection and/or acceptance stamp for blades made at Seki in Nōshu (Mino) province. Appears after December 1941. Very common.

(x) 'Star' stamp. Military inspection and acceptance stamp. Believed to be associated with mill-steel gendaitō and, perhaps, better quality ban-tanren abura yaki-ire blades. See main text. Generally post-1942. Scarce. (Also used as a 'materials' stamp on firearms.)

(xi) 'Dai' (or 'Tai') stamp. Significance unknown. Has only been found on blades dated 1945. Very rare.

(xii) 'Wa' stamp. Probably indicates manufacture in an occupied area, most likely by a collaborating force. Found on poor quality rolled or hammered blades.

(xiii) Probably a naval inspection and/or acceptance mark. Found on naval parade sabre and dirk guards. Possibly associated with the Toyokawa Naval Arsenal.

(xiv) Unidentified. Found on a naval dirk crossguard and Army kyu-guntō guard.

(xv) Unidentified. Found on 1903 pattern Forestry Officials dirk crossguard.

(xvi) 'Kikusui' (chrysanthemum on water). Located above the signatures of smiths who worked at the Navy-controlled Minatorgawa Shrine forge from 1940. (Also adopted as a kamikaze motif in 1944, but does not imply this usage when found on a blade.)

(xvii) Large unidentified mark found only once above a signature. Possibly a retailer's logo.

(xviii) Unidentified. Noted only on the reverse of signed, but undated, tangs (one of which had a 'Seki' stamp) by the Shōwa period smith Shimada Yoshisuke. Probably the logo of a private manufacturer/retail company.

(xix) Logo of the South Manchurian Railway Company. Only noted on tangs dated 1938. Scarce.

(xx) Logo of the North China Joint Stock Transportation Company. Found only on specially made shin-guntō fittings and once on a signed tang. Very rare.

(xxi) Small unidentified stamp noted only on blades by the smith Takehisa (one dated 1943) but was used three times on each. Possibly the Chigusa Factory of the Nagoya Arsenal.

(xxii) Seal stamp which has been found only once on the reverse of an undated Shōwa period blade. Probably a retailer's trademark. It reads NIHON (Japan), TORA (tiger), GO (which is suffix meaning 'title' or 'item'). Meaning uncertain but possibly an 'item by Tiger of Japan'.

(xxiii) Logo of the Suya Company of Tokyo. Often found in conjunction with Fig. 62 (i), (xii). It appears to be associated with Kokura, Koishikawa and Tokyo Arsenals when working as a sub-contractor making military sword fittings (and blades?).

(xxiv) Unidentified. Reported on 1889 pattern Fire Bureau Commanders and naval dirk crossguards. The latter was also in conjunction with the Toyokawa Naval Arsenal stamp shown in Fig. 62 (xvii).

(xxv) Small unidentified tang stamp on an unsigned Shōwa period blade.

(xxvi) Small, and generally, indistinct 'I' stamp. Cursive form of 伊 meaning 'that one'. Perhaps used to indicate the maker is who he says. Has been found below the Toyokawa Naval Arsenal stamp (Fig. 62) (xvi) and above an inscription reading INANAMI 伊奈波 (presumably a name) which incorporates the same character.

(xxvii) Small and unidentified stamp. Noted only on a blade by Semimaru Masahiro dated April 1944. (Does not appear to be a poorly struck Na 名 stamp, as in 'Nagoya'.)

(xxviii) Unidentified. Noted only once on a Mantetsu tang dated spring 1944. Perhaps 'Ren' 連 meaning 'company, party', which could be a reference to the South Manchurian Railway Company.

(xxix) Unidentified. Noted on the special thickened ishizuke (chape) sometimes found on shin- and kai-guntō scabbards. Possibly a manufacturer's logo.

(xxx) Unidentified. The Tō character means 'sword'. Found only on a shin-guntō kabuto-gane (pommel) in conjunction with the 1st Tokyo Arsenal logo (Fig. 62 (ii)).

(xxxi) Unidentified. Noted only once on the top of a shin-guntō kuchi-gane (throat) (see Fig. 12). Possibly a trademark.

(xxxii) Small and unidentified stamp. Reported only once on an unsigned Kotō period katana blade where it was stamped under the habaki (collar). This had been shortened and was in shira-saya. Perhaps the logo of a private company which retailed it before, or during, the war.

(xxxiii) 'Ni' stamp (meaning 'two'). Believed to indicate use as a second class military weapon when found in conjunction with a manufacturer's mark or arsenal stamp. Noted in conjunction with (xxxv) on a c.1945 pattern Army NCOs sword blade.

(xxxiv) Gold paper quality control label found on Shōwa period lacquered scabbards. It confirms inspection by the Seki Cutlery Industrial Society (see text). Probably early 1940s. Very scarce.

(xxxv) 'He' stamp. Inspection mark of the Heigo factory of the Jinsen (Inchon) Arsenal, Korea. Noted only in conjunction with (xxxiii) but may have another significance since Korean manufacture of swords is, so far, unconfirmed.

MILITARY SWORD BLADES AND MARKINGS

i ii iii iv v
vi vii viii ix x
xi xii xiii xiv xv
xvi xvii xviii xix xx
xxi xxii xxiii xxiv xxv
xxvi xxvii xxviii xxix xxx
xxxi xxxii xxxiii xxxiv xxxv

227

# JAPANESE MILITARY AND CIVIL SWORDS AND DIRKS

| Manufacturer's logo | Principal inspection mark | Manufacturer's logo | Principal inspection mark |
|---|---|---|---|
| (i) Tokyo Artillery (prior to April 1923) Koishikawa (Tokyo) Army Arsenal (April 1923–Nov 1933) Kokura Army Arsenal (After Nov 1933) (Koishikawa and Kokura used this mark simultaneously during the 1929–35 period) | (x) 七 Small Arms Manufacturing Factory of Tokyo Army Arsenal; 2nd Factory of Kokura Army Arsenal after November 1933 (SHICHI character meaning 'seven') | (v) Osaka Army Arsenal | |
| | (xi) 小 Supervisory Section of Kokura Army Arsenal after March 1935 (KO character abbreviation of Kokura) | (vi) Toyokawa Naval Arsenal | (xvi) Toyokawa Naval Arsenal |
| (ii) 1st Tokyo Arsenal (formed 1936 from the reorganised Koishikawa Arsenal) | (xii) 東 Department of Control (Chief Inspector) Kokura and Tokyo Arsenals (and factory identification for Nagoya Army Arsenal until 1936) see also (xix) below (TŌ character abbreviation of Tokyo) | (vii) Nambu Rifle Manufacturing Co. Chuo Kogyo Co. Ltd | (xvii) Toyokawa Naval Arsenal |
| (iii) 2nd Tokyo Arsenal | | | (xviii) 南 Kokubunji Factory of Chuo Kogyo Co. Ltd after Nov 1944 (NA character probably an abbreviation of Nambu) |
| (iv) Nagoya Army Arsenal 1923–45 | See also (xii) above | | (xix) 東 Factory of Chuo Kogyo Co. Ltd 1936–45; see also (xii) above (TŌ character) |
| | (xiii) 名 Department of Control (Chief Inspector) Nagoya Arsenal (NA character abbreviation of Nagoya) | (viii) Mukden Arsenal, Manchuria, 1930s–1945 | (xx) 南 Department of Control (Chief Inspector), Mukden Arsenal (NA character meaning 'south') |
| | (xiv) リ Toriimatsu Factory of Nagoya Army Arsenal (Katakana character for RI) | (ix) Tenshozan Company, Kamakura | |
| | (xv) 千 Chigusa Factory of Nagoya Army Arsenal (CHI character abbreviation of Chigusa) | | |

manufacturing company. Blade quality seems to be oil-tempered (abura yaki-ire).

Blades made by, or for, the South Manchurian Railway Company may be stamped with the company's logo (Fig. 61 (xix)), but this has only been found on blades dated 1938. Another Manchurian stamp is 'Nan' (Fig. 62 (xx)) meaning 'south', which was used by the Mukden Arsenal. This only appears on Mantetsu blades, probably made under Army supervision in the nineteen-forties.

On rare occasions combinations of stamps are found on different sides of the same tang, e.g. 'Seki' and 'Star' (noted September 1944 and January 1945); 'Seki' and 'Gi'[36] (Fig. 61 (ii)) stamps (noted May 1944 to May 1945).

Mass-produced machine-made blades for the Army were manufactured at the Tokyo and Koishikawa (Tokyo) Arsenals (c.1870–1933) and Kokura Arsenal (1929–1945). The 'four cannon-

*Fig. 62 Manufacturing and inspection symbols found stamped on military swords, bayonets and firearms. (Not all have been found on swords.)*
Note: The above stamps have been observed as follows: blade tangs – (i), (ix), (xiii), (xvi), (xx); military sword fittings – (i), (ii), (xi), (xii), (xiii), (xvii). See also Fig. 17.

ball' stamp (Fig. 62 (i)) was used by all. However, only one signed, but undated, blade by a swordsmith, Masayasu of Bishū province, has been found bearing this stamp. None of his dated wartime blades has been reported with a stamp of any kind. Indeed, some first-rate smiths controlled blade-making, and worked, at arsenals, e.g. Gassan Sadakatsu at Osaka, Yoshihara Kuniie at Tokyo and Moritake Yasuhiro at Kokura.[37] However, none of their blades has been reported with a stamp. Probably they continued to make tamahagane gendaitō while at these arsenals.

The Navy Officers Association or Club (Suikōsha) also supplied swords. The Navy also controlled blade-making as is evidenced by the 'anchor in circle' stamp (Fig. 62 (xvi)) of the Toyokawa Naval Arsenal. They are abura yaki-ire (oil-hardened) and possibly a type of stainless steel. Another Toyokawa Arsenal stamp of an 'anchor within a sakura' (Fig. 62 (xvii)) is said to be the naval equivalent of the Army 'Shō' stamp.[38] However, this appears incorrect since what should be a fairly common stamp has not been reported on blade tangs, only on naval sword and dirk fittings. No stamps relating to Yokosuka have been identified on blades.

It is not unknown for a military inspection/acceptance stamp to have been removed from a tang during post-war years to deceive a collector into thinking the blade is older than Shōwa, and thus is not of wartime manufacture. This may be detected by a small area of unnatural rust or non-contemporary file marks above an inscription.

## Paper labels

Small paper labels are sometimes found stuck on Shōwa period (i.e. post-1926) lacquered scabbards which have been fitted with leather combat covers. They are rare and only two types have been recorded.

(i) A circular blue and white label in English and Japanese. The outside reads 'The Seki Cutlery Manufacturers Society. Seki. Gifuken [i.e. Gifu prefecture]. Japan. (Passed)'. One has also been found stuck on a blade tang. The use of English and inclusion of 'Japan' seems to indicate an export item which is clearly not the case with a sword. Possibly they are pre-war but were used up on swords after the cessation of normal Japanese exports to the West.

(ii) The above society also issued a gold quality control or inspection label for lacquered scabbards. It has three lines of small embossed Japanese kanji (characters) which are normally indistinct or obliterated by wear from the combat cover (see Fig. 61 (xxxiv)). All but the two top left-hand characters have been translated and read

KENSA . . . ? (Inspection . . . ?); SEKI HAMONO KŌGYŌ KUMIAI (Seki Cutlery Industrial Society); GIFU KEN SEKI CHO (Seki town in Gifu prefecture). Perhaps a replacement for (i) in the early nineteen-forties.

## Kakihan (or Kao)

A fully qualified smith could retain the tradition of chiselling his blade tang with a personal stylised mark known as a 'kakihan'. This is unique to each individual and may, perhaps, be described as an 'artist's seal'. It cannot be read as a normal Japanese character or name and is quite distinctive in formation.

Fig. 63 shows some examples which have been found on signed Shōwa period blades. A kakihan is placed under the smith's signature. It is assumed they are restricted to tamahagane gendaitō and mill-steel gendaitō. Rarely is one found on a blade which also has a military inspection/acceptance stamp.

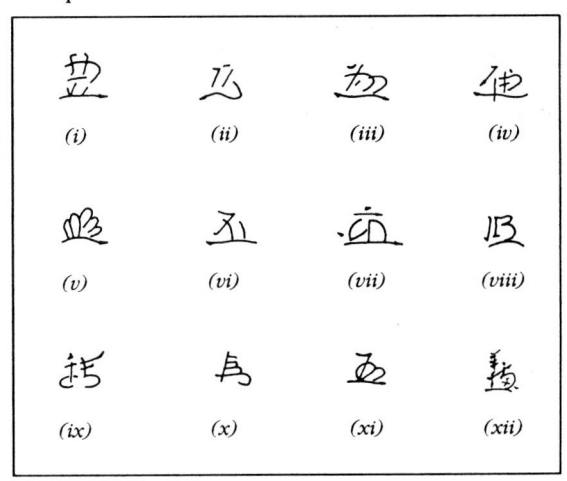

*Fig. 63* Typical engraved swordsmiths' kakihan. The examples shown have been found on Shōwa period blades. Only (i) has been noted in conjunction with an Army inspection or acceptance stamp, in this case that of Seki. (i) Okada Kaneyoshi; (ii) Tessai? Shirō Kunimitsu; (iii) Fujiwara Masatane; (iv) Ishidō Mitsunobu; (v) Morimichi; (vi) Hara Morinobu; (vii) Minamoto Moritaka; (viii) Ichihara Nagamitsu; (ix) Gassan Sadakatsu; (x) Kawanao (Minamoto) Sadashige; (xi) Tenryushi Sadakiyo; (xii) Kanemitsu.

JAPANESE MILITARY AND CIVIL SWORDS AND DIRKS

## Seals (Kokuin)

Another system, perhaps, used by smiths of slightly lesser ability than 'Jumei Tōshō' (sword craftsmen of note) or for school/forge identification is a stamped 'seal'. This is a recessed cartouche normally containing one or both characters of the smith's name and is placed under the inscription. It was added when the tang was red hot and thus is sometimes called a 'hot stamp' by collectors.

Examples are shown in Fig. 64. They are generally associated with Shōwa period blades which seem to be better quality han-tanren- or sunobe abura yaki-ire (and possibly mill-steel gendaitō). Although fairly scarce they are frequently found on blades which also have military inspection/acceptance stamps. Perhaps used by a qualified Army swordsmith (Rikugun Tōshō) who was head of, or the senior smith at, the forge. Although entitled to use one, a smith did not always do so. Possibly it signified his best work or a blade made without the aid of others, e.g. students. However some blades made at one gendai association, the Tokiwamatsu Tanren Kenkyu Jo, occasionally have an identifying stamp of this kind.

## Tang inscriptions

Smiths of all abilities could engrave details of their name, and often, their place or province of work. If signed on both sides of a tang, then one inscription is most likely the date of manufacture.

Shōwa period smiths abandoned the traditional convention of signing their name on a certain side according to the type of blade. With the blade forward and cutting edge downwards 'katana and wakizashi' were signed on the left and tachi were signed on the right. A smith could vary his 'art name' (nanori) several times during his working life, thus reference must be made to specialist Japanese and English language reference works. Unfortunately little is known, or has been published, on the personal history of the great majority of Shōwa period smiths, especially those of average ability.

It has been noticed that certain blades have identically formed inscriptions when a man would normally be expected to show some variation in character formation or spacing each time he signed. This is particularily noticeable in some Mantetsu inscribed blades. It can only be assumed that a template, or printed inscription on rice paper as an overlay, was used by an unskilled person.

Tang inscriptions may contain additional information which can increase interest and value.[39] This may include: (i) manufacturing method and type of steel; (ii) a special location, such as a shrine, where it was made; (iii) religious or patriotic phrase or slogan; (iv) details of the person who ordered the blade or for whom it was made; (v) presentation details.

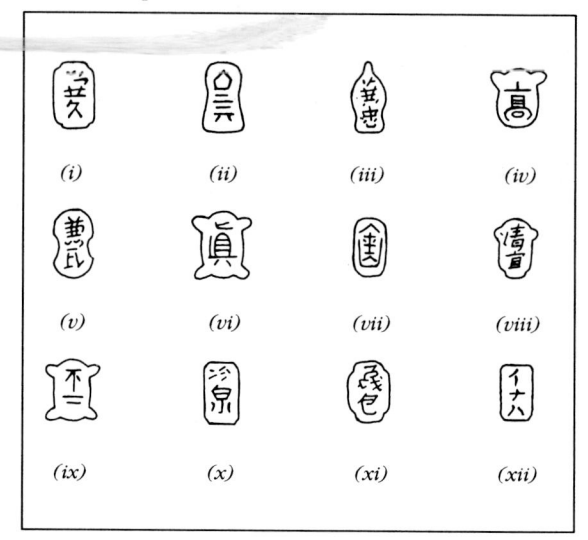

**Fig. 64** Typical swordsmiths' seal stamps ('hot stamps') which can be found on Shōwa period blades. They are often found in conjunction with Army inspection or acceptance stamps. (i) Ozawa Kanehisa; (ii) Kanenari; (iii) Ishibara Nyudō Kanetada; (iv) Matsuda Kanetaka; (v) Yoshida Kaneuji; (vi) Asano Kanezane; (vii) Kojima Katsumasa; (viii) Nagamura Kiyonobu; (ix) Nagamura Kiyonobu, but using the characters for 'Fuji'; (x) Suetsugu Shigemitsu; (xi) Fujiwara Yoshikane; (xii) Kanesaki Itsuryushi Toshimitsu, using the characters for 'Inaba' which is a province. This indicates he was descended from Hamabe Toshinori (1745–1810) who founded a school, the members of which used the character 壽 (Toshi) to begin their names.

## Ubu-ha

The cutting edge may be blunt under the habaki (blade collar) and for a short distance in front of it. This is known as 'ubu-ha' and its presence may be used as a guide to identifying a Shōwa period blade. However, it is not a feature unique to Shōwa blades since observed on some of those of the Shintō period, and has been reported on Kotō blades.

Basically this is an unsharpened section of blade deliberately left by a polisher, but the reason is speculative. Perhaps one of the following: (i) to prevent the edge of the 'habaki' from splitting;[40] (ii) because that section of blade is not used; (iii) to prevent the blade, in that area, from breaking or chipping; (iv) to allow the blade thickness to be increased to regularise with the tang thickness. Blades which have been repolished normally lose this feature, thus it is uncommon with earlier examples. Blades with only the original wartime polish would be expected to retain it, although some have been found without.

## Terminology

There is often dissension, even in Japanese books, over the proper terminology for Shōwa period blades. Terms often mentioned are:

**Shōwa-tō** (literally 'Shōwa sword'). This is often used disparagingly for any machine-made or oil-tempered class of blade made in the Shōwa era. It actually applies only to sunobe abura yaki-ire made during the period 1926–45.

**Gendaitō** (literally 'present age sword' or 'modern sword'). This could encompass any type of blade but is restricted to hand-forged blades made by traditional methods and materials after 1876 (although 1926 is sometimes preferred).

**Guntō** (literally 'military sword'). This refers to military mounts and not the type of blade.

Other terms of note relating to blades are **Abura** (oil), **Mizu** (water), **Sunobe** (drawn and hammered), **Tanren** (forged), **Tō** (sword), **Yaki-ire** (hardening).

## Military sword fittings

Many mass-produced fittings such as seppa (hilt washers), tsuba (guards) and fuchi (hilt collars) have markings in Japanese characters or Western numbers. These are normally for assembly purposes and are not necessarily manufacturers' identification stamps, although seppa are found bearing the Roman letters TEC and the mark of the Toyokawa Naval Arsenal (Fig. 62 (xvii)).

In fact manufacturers' marks are very rare on military sword fittings but the Koishikawa/Kokura 'four cannonball' stamp (Fig. 62 (i)) is common on cavalry/NCOs sabres and NCOs shin-guntō. Manufacturers' or possibly retailers' marks are sometimes seen on the underside of naval and civil dirk crossguards (see Fig. 61) but only one has been identified, the inscription on swords and dirks of the Government-General of Formosa which reads 'Made at the Echizen shop in Tokyo' (Plate 235).

No list of military sword fitting manufacturers has been located. It is therefore assumed that, in general, they were produced by private companies working under contract or at certain arsenals such as Tokyo. Some swords have been found with higher class mounts of standard form which appear to have been made to special order. However, it is important to note that most well-sculptured fittings (e.g. Field Officers kyu-guntō backstrap) are die-cast and not hand-engraved, although they were probably hand-finished.

Plate 78 shows a shin-guntō kabuto-gane (pommel) with the manufacturing and inspection marks of the No. 1 Tokyo Arsenal (Fig. 62 (ii), (xii)). Others have been found with that of Nagoya (Fig. 62 (x)) which was also used in conjunction with Fig. 62 (xii). A few naval parade sabre guards have been found with either the Suya Company logo (Fig. 61 (xxiii)), the 'anchor within a sakura' mark of the Toyokawa Naval Arsenal (Fig. 62 (xvii)) or a sakura superimposed over an anchor (Fig. 61 (xiii)). Refer also to Fig. 17.

# JAPANESE MILITARY AND CIVIL SWORDS AND DIRKS

Much of the information in this section on blades and markings is, by necessity, conjectural. Therefore any corroborating, additional or corrective material would be appreciated by the authors.

---

1 *Military Swords of Japan 1868–1945* by Richard Fuller and Ron Gregory (see Bibliography). Kanezane appears to be fully qualified but is not believed to have made wartime tamahagane gendaitō. Some of his blades from that period seem to be han-tanren abura yaki-ire, but no hamon with nie has been reported which might indicate mill-steel gendaitō. His Army blades may be sunobe abura yaki-ire.
2 The only difference between 'nioi' and 'nie' is size. They are both formed at the same temperature, but keeping the blade longer at the required temperature before quenching in water allows the martensite crystals to grow, becoming visible as nie.
3 This does not appear to be his 'art name' and he has not been identified as a swordsmith.
4 Unfortunately the process is not explained.
5 *Return of the Black Ships* by Decker (Vantage, 1978).
6 *Return of the Black Ships* by Decker.
7 Quoted from *A Doctor's War* by Aidan MacCarthy (Robson Books, 1979).
8 This could be surplus tamahagane made for the Yasukuni Shrine swordsmiths school which had its own tatara in Shimane prefecture for producing steel. Mr Han Bing Siong's researches indicate that, from 1933, this was the only tatara in Japan.
9 Japanese Sword Society of the United States newsletter articles: 'Gendaito' by Arnold Frenzel, vol. 20 nos. 4 & 6; 'The state of the art. Contemporary Japanese swordsmiths' by Craig A. Bird, vol. 18 no. 4.
10 'The significance of the Yasukuni Shrine for the contemporary sword history', Parts IV, V by Han Bing Siong, To-ken Society of Great Britain Programme nos. 114, 115 (1989).
11 'Sunagashi' is not an uncommon effect which can be found on hand-forged water-tempered blades made from steel which does not have a homogeneous carbon content. It is a number of short parallel lines of nie (giving the appearance of floating sand) along the hamon and parallel to it.
12 'The significance of the Yasukuni Shrine for the contemporary sword history', Part V by Han Bing Siong, To-ken Society of Great Britain Programme no. 145 (1989).
13 This process is discussed in 'The enigma of stamps on contemporary Japanese swords (revisiting the premises necessary)' by Han Bing Siong, To-ken Society of Great Britain Programme no. 157 (1992). He also stated that it was used by swordsmiths to add or reduce the carbon content of tamahagane as they deemed necessary.
14 'The enigma of stamps on contemporary Japanese swords (revisiting the premises necessary)' by Han Bing Siong.
15 'On the study in Europe of Japanese swords' by Han Bing Siong, Bulletin of the Japanese Sword Society of the United States, 1980–1981, pages 61–62.
16 'Koa-Isshin' blades were, according to the Japanese references checked by Han Bing Siong, made in Japan by a complex construction method.
17 Reference to the *Gendai Tōkō Meikan* by Ono Tadashi and *Teikoku Rikukaigun Guntō Montogatari* by Okochi Tsunehira, which were brought to the authors' attention by Han Bing Siong.
18 Han Bing Siong in his article 'The enigma of stamps on contemporary Japanese swords' suggests that oil tempering does not produce a true nioi since rapid cooling in water is required to produce it (and nie).
19 'The wartime Japanese sword' by Malcolm E. Cox, Japanese Sword Society of the United States Newsletter, vol. 27. no. 1 (1995).
20 'Southern Manchurian Railway' by Nobuhira, Sacramento Japanese Sword Club Newsletter, 1993. Unfortunately the composition of the 'special steel' mentioned is not stated.
21 'A further explanation of Gendaitō/Showatō' by Malcolm E. Cox, To-ken Society of Great Britain Programme no. 156 (1992).
22 Information courtesy of Gordon Bailey.
23 His art name (nanori) was, apparently, Yoshikuni.
24 'A further explanation of Gendaitō/Showatō' by Malcolm E. Cox. However, a blade inscription never states that it is made from tamahagane. In rare cases the signature style may be flamboyant and cursive, called 'sōsho' script. This is difficult to relate to the normal form of Japanese characters. Apparently it indicates the smith was a 'man of learning' (thus being fully trained) so the blade could be (but not necessarily is) a tamahagane gendaitō.
25 'Amahide: who was this gendai smith?' by Malcolm E. Cox, Japanese Sword Society of the United States Newsletter, vol. 24 no. 6 (1992).
26 *Shinshintō Taikan*, page 375, vol II (second edition). Translated and listed by Han Bing Siong in his article 'The significance of the Yasukuni Shrine for the contemporary sword history', Part II, To-ken Society of Great Britain Programme no. 142. Entry no. 13 is given as Morioka Masayoshi who actually died in 1921. Mr Han is of the opinion that this is a mistake and that it should, presumably, be Morioka Masataka who won four successive special awards after the war, and during it was a 'Rikugun Jūmei Tōshō'.
27 'Yasukuni Shrine and the Tanren-kai' by Fujishiro Okisato (translated by Leon Kapp), published in the To-ken Society of Great Britain Programme no. 134 (1987). This also gives a history of each smith, financial details and blade production costs. Reference must also be made to 'The significance of the Yasukuni Shrine for the contemporary sword history' Parts I–V by Han Bing Siong, To-ken Society of Great Britain Programme nos. 141–145 incl. (1989–90). The Yasukuni forges were actually closed for relocation but this was never completed before the war ended.
28 'Masataka Gendaitō' by Bob Colman, Japanese Sword Society of the United States Newsletter, vol. 13 no. 1. Moriwaki Masataka is not the same as Morioka Masataka.
29 Malcolm Cox's correspondence with Mr Uchiyama in Japan. The latter is adamant that such stamps indicate 'receipt' and not 'acceptance of quality'.
30 'A further explanation of Gendaitō/Showatō' by Malcolm E. Cox.
31 On rare occasions both 'Seki' and 'Shō' stamps have been found on the same tang, but the reason is unknown.
32 Two of three blades dated 1940 by Toshimasa have been found with 'Seki' stamps. Another of his blades dated 1942 also has such a stamp whereas one dated 1943 lacks it. Either the introduction date is earlier than generally believed or, as seems likely, the 1940 blades were, for some reason, not submitted for Army inspection until later.
33 Malcolm Cox's correspondence with Mr Uchiyama in Japan. The latter consulted two 'experts' who concluded that, with the popularity of the English language in pre-war Japan, it is likely that such personalisation was added by university-educated men with an appreciation of English. However, this is still conjectural and, in the authors' opinion, is most improbable.
34 Previously given in *Military Swords of Japan 1868–1945* by the authors as 'Ma kane hisa', meaning 'made from old steel'. This is now known to be incorrect. An error in the reading of the last kanji (character) has now been identified by Han Bing Siong, which changes the overall meaning to that given in the text.
35 'A further explanation of Gendaitō/Showatō' by Malcolm E. Cox.
36 Previously given as 'Chimata' in *Military Swords of Japan 1868–1945* by the authors, but Han Bing Siong has suggested that it is the first character of the kanji denoting the prefecture of Gifu, formerly Mino, where Seki is located.
37 'The enigma of stamps on contemporary Japanese swords' by Han Bing Siong.
38 'A further explanation of Gendaitō/Showatō' by Malcolm E. Cox.
39 *The Oshigata Book* by the authors (privately printed limited edition, 1985) shows many such tangs with full English translations.
40 Many habaki on Shōwa period blades are partially split, so this reason is doubtful.

# Sword Belts

Sword belts are essential accoutrements but are seldom seen. All Army service and dress belts must be regarded as rare and naval service belts are even rarer. Naval full dress belts seem to be extremely rare. Belts with slings have one of them equipped with a brass regain hook to enable the sword to be suspended by its hanging ring thus leaving the hands free. Many belts, especially those used with civil swords, remain unrecorded. Refer also to the section on 'Reproduction swords' for details of some modern reproduction naval sword belts.

The following charts are by no means complete and must be taken as a basic guide. Dimensions given are an average.

## Army service and battle belts

These are seldom photographed in wear because they are normally hidden under the jacket with only the slings exposed.

| Sword pattern | Belt | Buckle |
| --- | --- | --- |
| Katana and wakizashi | Leather frog suspended from a shoulder or waist belt | Unknown |
| 1871 Officers pattern | Black or brown leather having two slings | Circular two-piece construction; motif unknown |
| 1892 and 1899 Cavalry Troopers and, possibly, Infantry NCOs sabres. | 44mm (1¾") wide brown leather. One leather sling (which can be adjusted for length) suspended from a brass slider (Fig. 67) | Rectangular steel buckle with one claw |
| 1934 & 1938 Shin-guntō (Officers) – Artillery and Infantry (also Cavalry Officers) | Brown leather; Average 76mm (3") wide; one leather or chain sling (Plate 287a) | Rectangular steel buckle with two claws; two small buckles may also be found (Plate 287a) |
| Shin-guntō (Officers) and possibly senior NCOs – Infantry | Green or khaki canvas 76mm (3") wide with sling as last (Plate 287b) | Rectangular steel buckle with two claws |
| Shin-guntō (NCOs and Warrant Officers)[1] – Infantry | Brown leather 41mm (1⅝") wide with one leather sling (Plate 287c) | Rectangular steel buckle with one claw |

# JAPANESE MILITARY AND CIVIL SWORDS AND DIRKS

**Sword pattern**

1886 pattern Cavalry Officers[2] (andpossibly infantry NCOs)

**Belt**

Brown leather 41mm (1⅝") wide with one leather sling; there is an external tongue to cover the buckle (Plates 288, 290)

**Buckle**

Rectangular steel buckle with one claw

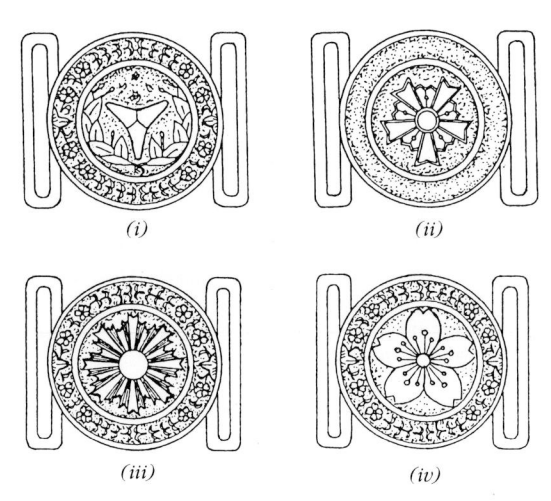

(i)  (ii)

(iii)  (iv)

***Fig. 65*** *Gilded brass belt buckles:*

(i) Fire Bureau; c.WW2 but introduction date unknown.
(ii) Civil Defence Corps, WW2.
(iii) 1934 pattern Army parade sword belt for officers of all grades, Warrant Officers and probably Sergeant-Majors. Officers of the Army Judge Advocate.
(iv) Army Preparatory School. Shōwa period (and possibly earlier).

***Fig. 66*** *1918 pattern Gensui (Field Marshals and Fleet Admirals) full dress sword belt buckle.*

***Fig. 67*** *Adjustable brown leather sling for the 1892 and 1899 pattern Cavalry sabres. The belt slider is brass (see also Plate 52)*

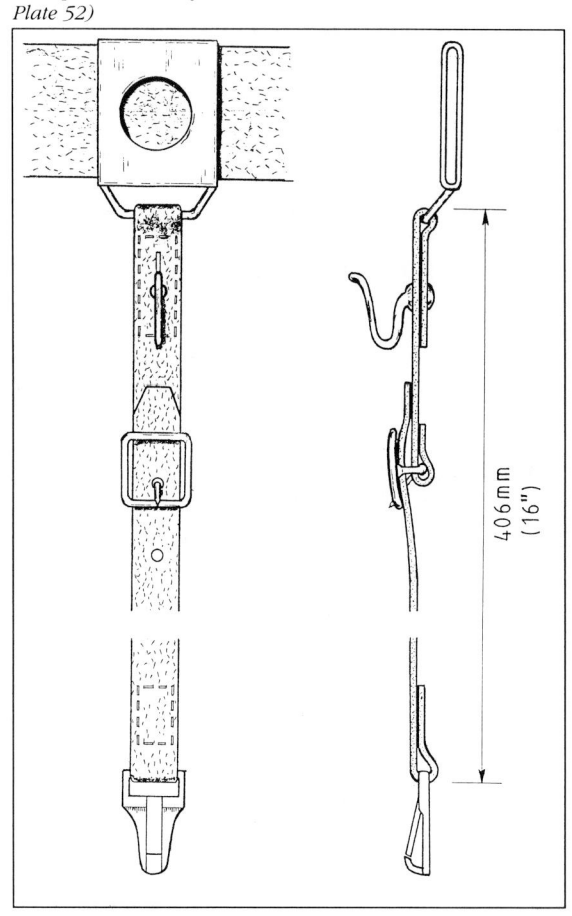

406mm (16")

***Plate 286*** *Gilded brass Army Officers parade belt buckle for use with the 1934 pattern shin-guntō. (Ron Gregory).*

## Ubu-ha

The cutting edge may be blunt under the habaki (blade collar) and for a short distance in front of it. This is known as 'ubu-ha' and its presence may be used as a guide to identifying a Shōwa period blade. However, it is not a feature unique to Shōwa blades since observed on some of those of the Shintō period, and has been reported on Kotō blades.

Basically this is an unsharpened section of blade deliberately left by a polisher, but the reason is speculative. Perhaps one of the following: (i) to prevent the edge of the 'habaki' from splitting;[40] (ii) because that section of blade is not used; (iii) to prevent the blade, in that area, from breaking or chipping; (iv) to allow the blade thickness to be increased to regularise with the tang thickness. Blades which have been repolished normally lose this feature, thus it is uncommon with earlier examples. Blades with only the original wartime polish would be expected to retain it, although some have been found without.

## Terminology

There is often dissension, even in Japanese books, over the proper terminology for Shōwa period blades. Terms often mentioned are:

**Shōwa-tō** (literally 'Shōwa sword'). This is often used disparagingly for any machine-made or oil-tempered class of blade made in the Shōwa era. It actually applies only to sunobe abura yaki-ire made during the period 1926–45.

**Gendaitō** (literally 'present age sword' or 'modern sword'). This could encompass any type of blade but is restricted to hand-forged blades made by traditional methods and materials after 1876 (although 1926 is sometimes preferred).

**Guntō** (literally 'military sword'). This refers to military mounts and not the type of blade.

Other terms of note relating to blades are **Abura** (oil), **Mizu** (water), **Sunobe** (drawn and hammered), **Tanren** (forged), **Tō** (sword), **Yaki-ire** (hardening).

## Military sword fittings

Many mass-produced fittings such as seppa (hilt washers), tsuba (guards) and fuchi (hilt collars) have markings in Japanese characters or Western numbers. These are normally for assembly purposes and are not necessarily manufacturers' identification stamps, although seppa are found bearing the Roman letters TEC and the mark of the Toyokawa Naval Arsenal (Fig. 62 (xvii)).

In fact manufacturers' marks are very rare on military sword fittings but the Koishikawa/Kokura 'four cannonball' stamp (Fig. 62 (i)) is common on cavalry/NCOs sabres and NCOs shin-guntō. Manufacturers' or possibly retailers' marks are sometimes seen on the underside of naval and civil dirk crossguards (see Fig. 61) but only one has been identified, the inscription on swords and dirks of the Government-General of Formosa which reads 'Made at the Echizen shop in Tokyo' (Plate 235).

No list of military sword fitting manufacturers has been located. It is therefore assumed that, in general, they were produced by private companies working under contract or at certain arsenals such as Tokyo. Some swords have been found with higher class mounts of standard form which appear to have been made to special order. However, it is important to note that most well-sculptured fittings (e.g. Field Officers kyu-guntō backstrap) are die-cast and not hand-engraved, although they were probably hand-finished.

Plate 78 shows a shin-guntō kabuto-gane (pommel) with the manufacturing and inspection marks of the No. 1 Tokyo Arsenal (Fig. 62 (ii), (xii)). Others have been found with that of Nagoya (Fig. 62 (x)) which was also used in conjunction with Fig. 62 (xii). A few naval parade sabre guards have been found with either the Suya Company logo (Fig. 61 (xxiii)), the 'anchor within a sakura' mark of the Toyokawa Naval Arsenal (Fig. 62 (xvii)) or a sakura superimposed over an anchor (Fig. 61 (xiii)). Refer also to Fig. 17.

# JAPANESE MILITARY AND CIVIL SWORDS AND DIRKS

Much of the information in this section on blades and markings is, by necessity, conjectural. Therefore any corroborating, additional or corrective material would be appreciated by the authors.

---

1 *Military Swords of Japan 1868–1945* by Richard Fuller and Ron Gregory (see Bibliography). Kanezane appears to be fully qualified but is not believed to have made wartime tamahagane gendaitō. Some of his blades from that period seem to be han-tanren abura yaki-ire, but no hamon with nie has been reported which might indicate mill-steel gendaitō. His Army blades may be sunobe abura yaki-ire.
2 The only difference between 'nioi' and 'nie' is size. They are both formed at the same temperature, but keeping the blade longer at the required temperature before quenching in water allows the martensite crystals to grow, becoming visible as nie.
3 This does not appear to be his 'art name' and he has not been identified as a swordsmith.
4 Unfortunately the process is not explained.
5 *Return of the Black Ships* by Decker (Vantage, 1978).
6 *Return of the Black Ships* by Decker.
7 Quoted from *A Doctor's War* by Aidan MacCarthy (Robson Books, 1979).
8 This could be surplus tamahagane made for the Yasukuni Shrine swordsmiths school which had its own tatara in Shimane prefecture for producing steel. Mr Han Bing Siong's researches indicate that, from 1933, this was the only tatara in Japan.
9 Japanese Sword Society of the United States newsletter articles: 'Gendaito' by Arnold Frenzel, vol. 20 nos. 4 & 6; 'The state of the art. Contemporary Japanese swordsmiths' by Craig A. Bird, vol. 18 no. 4.
10 'The significance of the Yasukuni Shrine for the contemporary sword history', Parts IV, V by Han Bing Siong, To-ken Society of Great Britain Programme nos. 114, 115 (1989).
11 'Sunagashi' is not an uncommon effect which can be found on hand-forged water-tempered blades made from steel which does not have a homogeneous carbon content. It is a number of short parallel lines of nie (giving the appearance of floating sand) along the hamon and parallel to it.
12 'The significance of the Yasukuni Shrine for the contemporary sword history', Part V by Han Bing Siong, To-ken Society of Great Britain Programme no. 145 (1989).
13 This process is discussed in 'The enigma of stamps on contemporary Japanese swords (revisiting the premises necessary)' by Han Bing Siong, To-ken Society of Great Britain Programme no. 157 (1992). He also stated that it was used by swordsmiths to add or reduce the carbon content of tamahagane as they deemed necessary.
14 'The enigma of stamps on contemporary Japanese swords (revisiting the premises necessary)' by Han Bing Siong.
15 'On the study in Europe of Japanese swords' by Han Bing Siong, Bulletin of the Japanese Sword Society of the United States, 1980–1981, pages 61–62.
16 'Koa-Isshin' blades were, according to the Japanese references checked by Han Bing Siong, made in Japan by a complex construction method.
17 Reference to the *Gendai Tōkō Meikan* by Ono Tadashi and *Teikoku Rikukaigun Guntō Montogatari* by Okochi Tsunehira, which were brought to the authors' attention by Han Bing Siong.
18 Han Bing Siong in his article 'The enigma of stamps on contemporary Japanese swords' suggests that oil tempering does not produce a true nioi since rapid cooling in water is required to produce it (and nie).
19 'The wartime Japanese sword' by Malcolm E. Cox, Japanese Sword Society of the United States Newsletter, vol. 27. no. 1 (1995).
20 'Southern Manchurian Railway' by Nobuhira, Sacramento Japanese Sword Club Newsletter, 1993. Unfortunately the composition of the 'special steel' mentioned is not stated.
21 'A further explanation of Gendaitō/Showatō' by Malcolm E. Cox, To-ken Society of Great Britain Programme no. 156 (1992).
22 Information courtesy of Gordon Bailey.
23 His art name (nanori) was, apparently, Yoshikuni.
24 'A further explanation of Gendaitō/Showatō' by Malcolm E. Cox. However, a blade inscription never states that it is made from tamahagane. In rare cases the signature style may be flamboyant and cursive, called 'sōsho' script. This is difficult to relate to the normal form of Japanese characters. Apparently it indicates the smith was a 'man of learning' (thus being fully trained) so the blade could be (but not necessarily is) a tamahagane gendaitō.
25 'Amahide: who was this gendai smith?' by Malcolm E. Cox, Japanese Sword Society of the United States Newsletter, vol. 24 no. 6 (1992).
26 *Shinshintō Taikan*, page 375, vol II (second edition). Translated and listed by Han Bing Siong in his article 'The significance of the Yasukuni Shrine for the contemporary sword history', Part II, To-ken Society of Great Britain Programme no. 142. Entry no. 13 is given as Morioka Masayoshi who actually died in 1921. Mr Han is of the opinion that this is a mistake and that it should, presumably, be Morioka Masataka who won four successive special awards after the war, and during it was a 'Rikugun Jūmei Tōshō'.
27 'Yasukuni Shrine and the Tanren-kai' by Fujishiro Okisato (translated by Leon Kapp), published in the To-ken Society of Great Britain Programme no. 134 (1987). This also gives a history of each smith, financial details and blade production costs. Reference must also be made to 'The significance of the Yasukuni Shrine for the contemporary sword history' Parts I–V by Han Bing Siong, To-ken Society of Great Britain Programme nos. 141–145 incl. (1989–90). The Yasukuni forges were actually closed for relocation but this was never completed before the war ended.
28 'Masataka Gendaitō' by Bob Colman, Japanese Sword Society of the United States Newsletter, vol. 13 no. 1. Moriwaki Masataka is not the same as Morioka Masataka.
29 Malcolm Cox's correspondence with Mr Uchiyama in Japan. The latter is adamant that such stamps indicate 'receipt' and not 'acceptance of quality'.
30 'A further explanation of Gendaitō/Showatō' by Malcolm E. Cox.
31 On rare occasions both 'Seki' and 'Shō' stamps have been found on the same tang, but the reason is unknown.
32 Two of three blades dated 1940 by Toshimasa have been found with 'Seki' stamps. Another of his blades dated 1942 also has such a stamp whereas one dated 1943 lacks it. Either the introduction date is earlier than generally believed or, as seems likely, the 1940 blades were, for some reason, not submitted for Army inspection until later.
33 Malcolm Cox's correspondence with Mr Uchiyama in Japan. The latter consulted two 'experts' who concluded that, with the popularity of the English language in pre-war Japan, it is likely that such personalisation was added by university-educated men with an appreciation of English. However, this is still conjectural and, in the authors' opinion, is most improbable.
34 Previously given in *Military Swords of Japan 1868–1945* by the authors as 'Ma kane hisa', meaning 'made from old steel'. This is now known to be incorrect. An error in the reading of the last kanji (character) has now been identified by Han Bing Siong, which changes the overall meaning to that given in the text.
35 'A further explanation of Gendaitō/Showatō' by Malcolm E. Cox.
36 Previously given as 'Chimata' in *Military Swords of Japan 1868–1945* by the authors, but Han Bing Siong has suggested that it is the first character of the kanji denoting the prefecture of Gifu, formerly Mino, where Seki is located.
37 'The enigma of stamps on contemporary Japanese swords' by Han Bing Siong.
38 'A further explanation of Gendaitō/Showatō' by Malcolm E. Cox.
39 *The Oshigata Book* by the authors (privately printed limited edition, 1985) shows many such tangs with full English translations.
40 Many habaki on Shōwa period blades are partially split, so this reason is doubtful.

# SWORD BELTS

## Army full (and parade) dress belts

General Officers in full dress are often seen wearing a waist sash which covers the belt, thus photographs of such officers with their belts visible have not been located.

| Sword pattern | Belt | Buckle |
|---|---|---|
| 1875 pattern Officers dress sword | Coloured belt with a frog suspended by two short straps: | |
| | **General**: Scarlet and purple | Interlocking circular gilded brass with unknown motif |
| | **Maj-Gen; Lt-Gen:** Horizontal bands of purple, white, purple, white, purple | Ditto |
| | **Field Officer:** Red | Ditto |
| | **Company Officer:** Navy blue | Ditto |
| 1875 (& 1886) pattern Kyu-guntō | Uncertain; probably the same as for shin-guntō below | |
| 1918 pattern 'Gensui' (Field Marshal) sword | Horizontal bands of gold, white, gold, white, gold; Two matching slings | Interlocking circular gilded brass with a kiku (chrysanthemum) motif; Fig. 66 |
| 1934 (& 1938) pattern Shin-guntō (Officers) | Black leather facing with coloured felt lining (as below); 29mm (1⅛") wide; two (1934 pattern), or one (1938 pattern) matching slings. (Cavalry officers are said to have used a single chain hanger with this belt). | |
| | **General & Field Officers:** Red | Interlocking circular gilded brass with a thirty-two sun ray motif; Fig. 65 (iii) |
| | **Company Officer:** Blue | Ditto |
| Shin-guntō (and probably kyu-guntō) | **Judge Advocate:** Horizontal bands of red (narrow), gold (wide), red (narrow), gold (wide), red (narrow); Matching slings | As last |

# JAPANESE MILITARY AND CIVIL SWORDS AND DIRKS

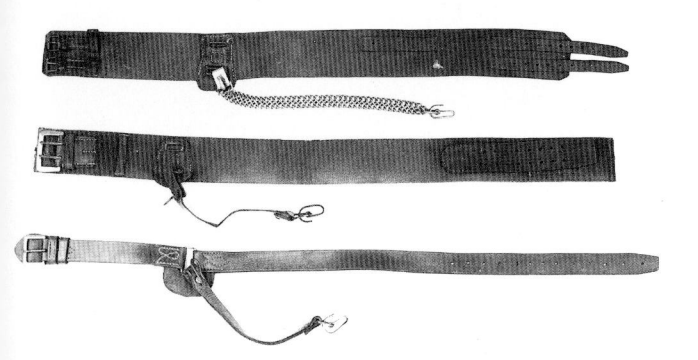

**Plate 287** *Three Army Infantry sword belts. Top to bottom:*

*(i) Officers brown leather undress pattern used on active service. This example has two separate straps and buckles instead of the normal single one. Worn under the tunic.*
*(ii) Officers (and probably senior NCOs) green canvas undress and 'battle' (service) pattern. Worn under the tunic.*
*(iii) Warrant Officers (and NCOs) brown leather service pattern. Worn outside the tunic. Note the protective flap to prevent rubbing by the reverse stud of the regain hook. See also endnote 1.*

*Such belts are now difficult to obtain since they were not surrendered with the swords or taken as trophies. Possibly many made their way from Japan after the war.* (Richard Fuller).

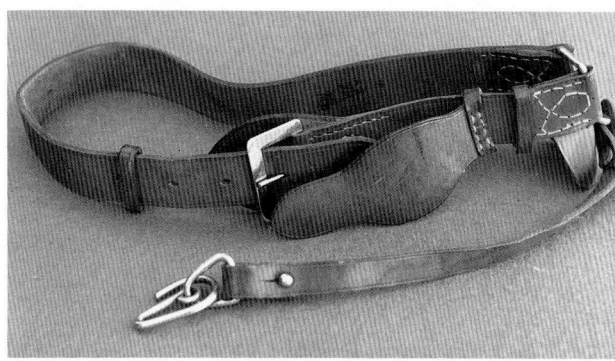

**Plate 288** *Brown leather sword belt with an external tongue which covers the buckle and tucks into the belt loop. It is reputed to be used by Cavalry Officers but may also have been used by Infantry Warrant Officers. This item has the owner's name, which appears to read Kiyomoto, marked in ink on the inside. Worn outside the tunic. See also Plate 290* (Brenton Williams).

## Navy service and undress belts

All naval service and undress belts are black patent leather 38–41mm (1½"–1⅝") wide, with two slings of different lengths, varying only in the clasp motif. These were also used for dirks. Circular gilded brass buckles are generally of the interlocking form with the centre clasp passing through a slot in the buckle.

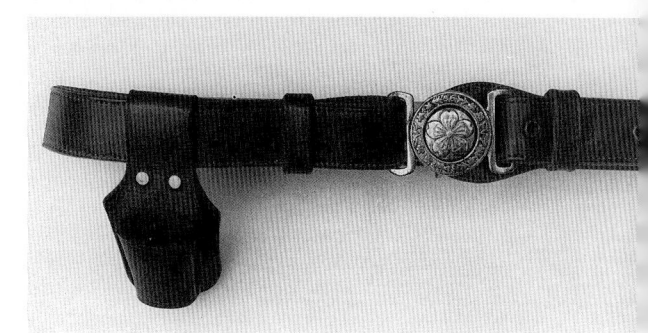

**Plate 289** *Very unusual brown leather belt with red felt lining fitted with a brown leather frog. Gilt brass buckle decorated with a sakura (cherry blossom). It is of small size which implies use by a young person. The frog has no provision for a weapon with a locket stud. This is, in fact, the dress belt of an Army Preparatory School cadet, and the frog is a flag holder.* (Ron Gregory).

| Sword pattern | Belt | Buckle |
| --- | --- | --- |
| c.1873 Marines | Unknown; probably black leather with two slings | Fig. 70 (vi) |
| 1873 pattern Naval Officers | Black leather with two slings | Possibly Fig. 69 |
| 1883 naval kyu-guntō | **Admiral of the Fleet:** Black leather with two slings | Uncertain; possibly same as Flag Officer below. The following have a silver centre motif: |
|  | **Flag Officer:** Ditto | Fig. 70 (i) |

SWORD BELTS

| Sword pattern | Belt | Buckle |
|---|---|---|
| | **Senior Officer:** Ditto | Fig. 70 (ii) |
| | **Junior Officer:** Ditto | Fig. 70 (iii) |
| | **Petty Officer:** Ditto | Fig. 70 (iv) |
| 1914 naval kyu-guntō and 1937 kai-guntō | Black leather with two slings | Fig. 70 (v) (for all ranks) |
| 1937 kai-guntō (Marines and Naval Landing Forces) – land warfare | **Officers:** Wide brown leather with one or two slings and a cross belt (Fig. 72, top) | Large rectangular steel buckle with two claws; the belt has three parallel rows of holes |
| | **Petty Officers:** Wide brown leather with one or two slings (Fig. 72, bottom) | Long rectangular steel buckle with one claw |

***Plate 290*** *Sergeant with tropical hat (topi), shin-guntō and sword knot. The scabbard is metal with a protective leather cover which has been shrink-fitted, which is unusual since most are removable. This is discernible because it is tightened over the scabbard throat and suspension band. He wears the Cavalry Officers (and Infantry NCOs) pattern brown leather sword belt (see Plate 288). The circular collar badge with a star in the centre indicates he is an officer candidate. (Cheyenne Noda).*

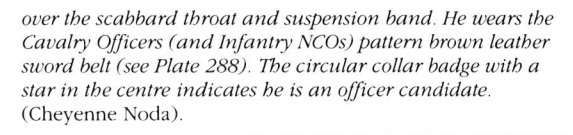

***Plate 291*** *Two Japanese in M98 (1938) Army field uniforms. The collar rank patches seem to be those of Sergeant-Majors (Captains are similar but with outer bands of yellow, but these are not visible). Both have dress sword belts and spurs (Infantry officers and sometimes senior NCOs could be mounted). The sword on the left appears to be a civilian katana since the kurikata (waist sash knob) protrudes above the suspension mount. A leather combat cover has been fitted to the scabbard and a shin-guntō knot wrapped around the hilt. The sword on the right is an Army parade sabre, but no knot can be seen. (Cheyenne Noda).*

# JAPANESE MILITARY AND CIVIL SWORDS AND DIRKS

## Navy full and parade dress belts

All are patent black leather with two slings. They vary in function according to the coloured bullion lace facing on the front and belt clasp motif.

| Sword pattern | Belt | Buckle |
|---|---|---|
| Wilkinson's 1872 pattern (not adopted) | **Flag Officer:** Gold laurel leaves (not adopted) | Fig. 69 |
| c.1873 Marines | **Senior Officers:** Three bands of scarlet? and two of gold (Fig. 68 (i)) | Fig. 70 (vi) |
| | **Junior Officers:** Two bands of scarlet? and one of gold (Fig. 68 (ii)) | Fig. 70 (vi)? |
| 1873 pattern Naval Officers | Unknown | Possibly Fig. 69 |
| 1918 'Gensui' sword[3] | **Admiral of the Fleet:** Three bands of red (possibly with gold central stripes) and two of white (Fig. 68 (iii)) | Interlocking circular gilded brass with a kiku (chrysanthemum) motif (Fig. 66) |
| 1883 naval kyu-guntō | As below: | Interlocking circular gilded brass with a silver motif: |
| | **Flag Officer:** Two bands of black and one of gold (Fig. 68 (iv)) | Fig. 70 (i) |
| | **Flag Officer (Reserve):** Two bands of black and one of gold (with a diagonal grain) (Fig. 68 (v)) | Fig. 70 (i) |
| | **Senior Officer:** Three bands of black and two of gold (Fig. 68 (vi)) | Fig. 70 (ii) |
| | **Senior Medical Officer:** Two bands of red, one of black and two of gold (Fig. 68 (vii)) | Fig. 70 (ii) |
| | **Junior Officers:** Two bands of black and one of gold (Fig. 68 (viii)) | Fig. 70 (iii) |
| | **Petty Officer:** As for the service belt | Fig. 70 (iv) |
| 1914 naval kyu-guntō and 1937 kai-guntō | The 1883 rank facings are believed to have been retained | Fig. 70 (v) for all ranks (central motif is brass) |

## SWORD BELTS

Naval arm of service colours (by 1943)[4] which may be present on full dress belts as edge bands:
Black – Line
Blue – Military band
Green – Judge Advocate
Mauve – Engineering
Red – Medical, Pharmacy, Dental
White – Paymaster

**Fig. 68**  Key: B =Black, G = Gold, R = Red (or scarlet), W = White.
Naval and Marines dress sword belt facings.
c.1873 Marines and naval gunners:
    (i)    Senior Officers
    (ii)   Junior Officers
Naval Officers worn with the 1883 pattern kyu-guntō:
    (iii)  Admiral of the Fleet
    (iv)  Flag Officers (Admirals)
    (vi)  Flag Officers in the Reserve
    (vi)  Senior Officers
    (vii) Senior Medical Officers
    (viii) Junior Officers

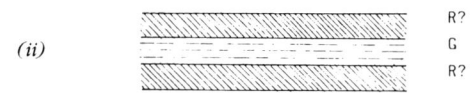

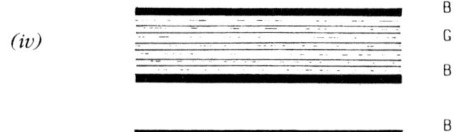

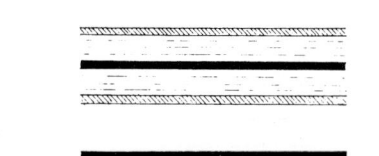

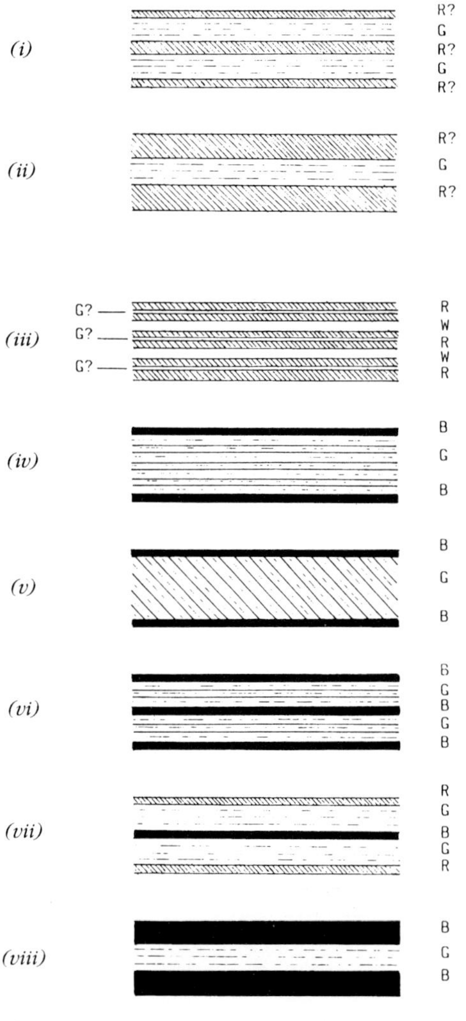

**Fig. 69**  1872 pattern naval sword belt clasp, probably for commissioned officers. This design is shown in the Wilkinson Sword pattern book for 1872 with their design for a Japanese naval sword.

**Plates 292, 293**  Rare Imperial Japanese naval belt buckle. Pressed brass. Probably that of a Non-Commissioned Officer or rating. The motif is believed to be the first used by the Japanese Navy, but the prescribed period of wear has not been determined. The Nippon no Gunso (see Bibliography) indicates a foul anchor, with a sakura (cherry blossom) above, was in use on officers caps as early as 1870 which continued in use through World War Two. (P. Faarvang).

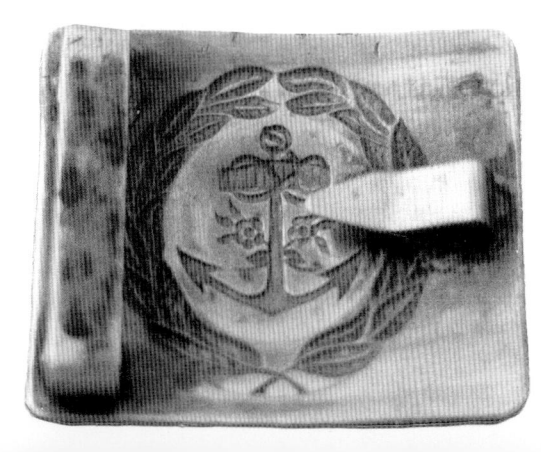

## JAPANESE MILITARY AND CIVIL SWORDS AND DIRKS

**Fig. 70** *Naval and Marines gilded brass sword belt buckles; (i) to (iv) have raised central motifs of silver:*

(i)   Flag Officers (Admirals), 1883–1914, 5:7:5 kiri.
(ii)  Senior Officers, 1883–1914, 3:5:3 kiri.
(iii) Junior Officers, 1883–1914.
(iv)  Petty Officers, 1883–1914.
(v)   All Commissioned Officer ranks, 1914–1945. This superseded all of (i) to (iv). It is made entirely of brass.
(vi)  Marines and Gunnery Officers, c.1873–1883. The outer motto reads 'Nippon kai ho hei tai' (Japanese gunnery units and marines). The example shown may be for senior officers with a different inner motif for junior officers.

---

**Plate 294** *Unidentified gilded brass naval sword belt buckle. The flower motif seems Japanese but this is probably not the case. The rear hook fitting is similar to the British Royal Navy pattern, and not the insert system normally found on Japanese naval belts. (Ron Gregory).*

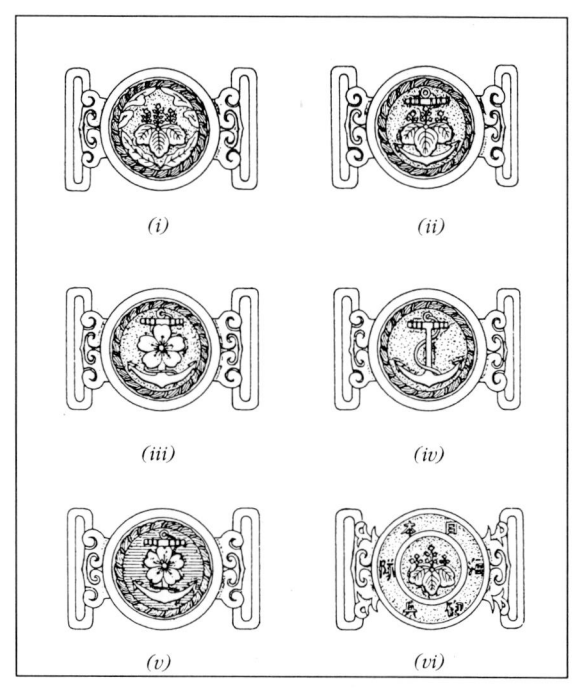

**Plate 295** *Two black patent leather naval service belts. That on the top has a brass buckle with the 1914 clasp design for all Commissioned Officer ranks (Fig. 70 (v)). The belt on the bottom has the unidentified clasp design shown in Plate 294. Note that this has the British system of a hook on the reverse which engages with a slot in the side piece, while the item above is the normal Japanese type which interlocks by passing through the buckle. (Ron Gregory).*

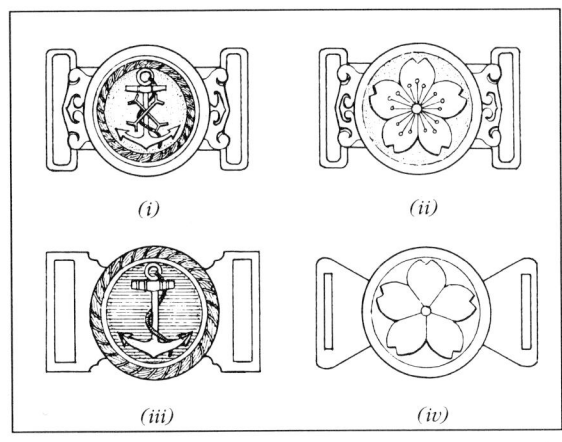

**Fig. 71**  Naval belt buckles for use with black leather sword belts:

(i)   Governor of a naval prison; gilded brass.
(ii)  Chief guard and guard of a naval prison; gilded brass.
(iii) Naval band officer; gilded brass. (There is also a silvered brass version with a brown leather belt which lacks sword suspension attachments. Usage is conjectural. Perhaps cadets?)
(iv)  Navy police. Silvered brass or white metal, with brass belt mounts.

**Fig. 72**  Naval Landing Forces brown leather sword belts for land warfare. (Top) Officers. The centre row of holes engage with a raised stud located just behind the buckle. (Bottom) Petty Officers. One or two slings may be used.

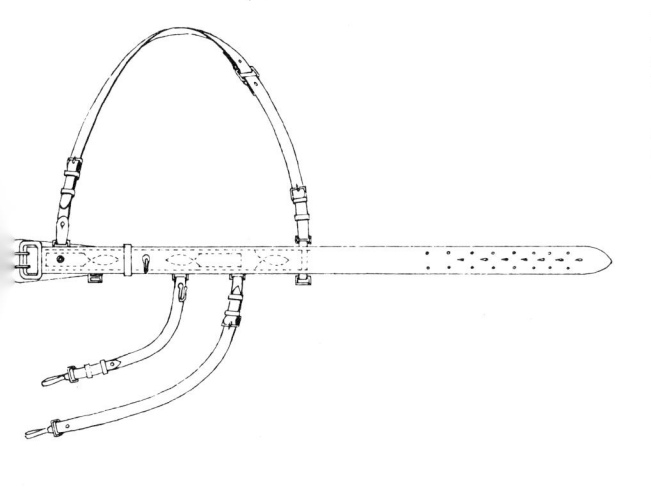

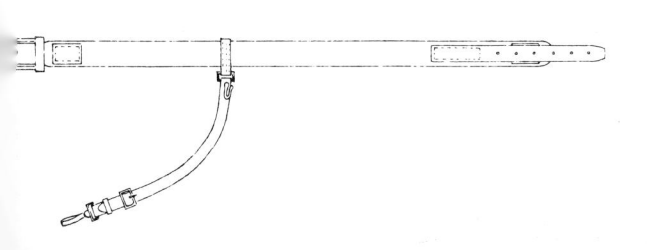

**Plate 296**  Vice-Admiral Heichachiro Togo, C-in-C Combined Fleet and Japan's most famous Admiral, photographed in 1904. The gold facing pattern of his Flag Officers sword belt is apparent, and the clasp motif should be that shown in Fig. 70 (i), but, strangely, appears to be stamped $\overset{A}{23}$ (see Plate 297). (Richard Fuller).

**Plate 297**  Enlargement of the belt buckle shown in Plate 296. There is no sign of the central motif and it appears to be stamped $\overset{A}{23}$. This photograph is taken from vol. 1 of Japan's Fight for Freedom (see Bibliography) published in 1904, but no credit is given for its origin. Whether retouched and a photographer's or source mark added is unknown, but no other suggestions have been made to explain this strange clasp. The profusely illustrated set of three volumes contains no other pictures with similar markings. (Richard Fuller).

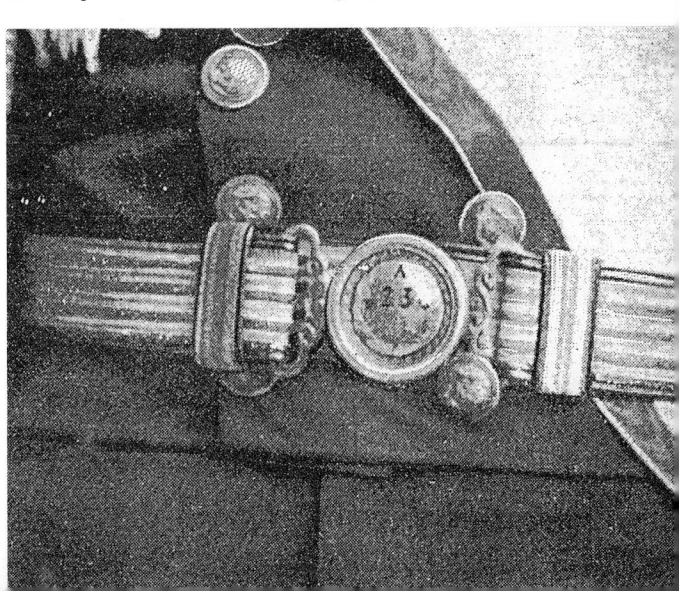

**Plate 298** *Naval officers in land warfare uniform at Shanghai in 1937. The officer in the centre is of high rank and is shown in Plates 84, 165. He has a scarce two-hanger Army shin-guntō. Probably they are Imperial Marines and the choice of sword represents their mixed function, but this is speculation. The naval land warfare leather sword belt pattern, clearly shown, is identified by the three rows of parallel holes and shoulder strap. It is interesting to note that the centre officer has a wide rectangular buckle while the others are narrower and have rounded corners. Whether this is a rank distinction is unknown.* (Bill Tagg).

## Civil sword belts

Information on belts for civil swords is generally lacking. They can be a shoulder or waist type. The latter are probably bullion-faced for full dress or plain leather with bullion-faced slings for undress.

An unidentified undress belt 'said' to be Japanese (but not confirmed) in the author's collection is brown leather 20mm ($^{13}/_{16}$") wide with chequered decoration over the outside surface. There are two slings of similarly decorated brown leather faced with gold lace and having a narrow central black strip. No regain hook was ever fitted. Rectangular steel buckle with one claw.

Since virtually every country in the world had military and civil sword belts, identification as Japanese must be done with extreme caution.

| Sword pattern | Belt | Buckle |
|---|---|---|
| Diplomatic Corps | V-shaped black velvet frog suspended from a white watered silk shoulder belt Plates 226, 227) | None |
|  | V-shaped frog with vertical alternating silver bullion and brown (cloth?) stripes; leather waist belt with black? lace | Rectangular buckle and single claw |
| Unidentified | Plain brown leather belt with two brown leather slings, each faced with bands of gold, red (narrow), silver, red (narrow), gold | Steel 'figure of eight' (or 'snake') shape |

# SWORD BELTS

## Suspension slings (hangers)

These may sometimes be found already attached to military swords. They are as follows:

*Army*
(i) Plain brown leather – service and battle dress.
(ii) Plaited brown leather – service and battle dress. Usually four strands.
(iii) Nickel- or chromium-plated brass chains – service and battle dress. (A single 20–23mm wide interlinked chain is the most common but separate double, treble and even quadruple chains are known but are rare. The multi-chain in Plate 299 is the only reported example.)
(iv) Black leather with a coloured felt backing – full (and parade) dress, and possibly for walking-out.

*Navy*
(i) Black patent leather – service dress.
(ii) Black leather with coloured bullion lace facing – full and parade dress.
(iii) Black leather with black felt backing – possibly for dress use by Chief Petty Officers.

Army and Navy leather and chain hangers are detachable, so may be found separately. Those of the naval police and naval prison guards, for example, are integral with a wide loop which slides over, or is stitched, to the belt. Thus the latter are unlikely to be encountered. Some leather slings are also adjustable for length, particularly that used with the 1892 and 1899 pattern Cavalry Troopers and, possibly, the infantry NCOs sabres.

The suspension spring clips at the ends of slings also vary in pattern. Usually they are brass or steel and quite short. Occasionally an Army version of extreme length may be found which appears to be early or Russo–Japanese war period. Naval suspension clips are normally brass spring-operated (Plate 300) while Army spring clips, when found, can be more substantial, longer and of a different pattern. Army service belt hangers usually have a coiled hook for suspension as shown in Plate 299.

The army hanger belt clip is also quite distinctive being wide, spring-operated and fitted with a regain hook on the rear. A short chain and hook

**Plate 299** *Various suspension straps and chains for Army swords. Top to bottom:*

(i)   Nickel-plated single interwoven chain 457mm (18") long.
(ii)  Very unusual multi-chain of eight strands 508mm (20") long.
(iii) Brass single interwoven chain 380mm (15") long.
(iv)  Black leather with the unusual feature of two spring clips at the top, instead of the usual wide clip, and regain hook.
(v)   Brown leather.
(vi)  Three strand brown plaited leather. (Brenton Williams).

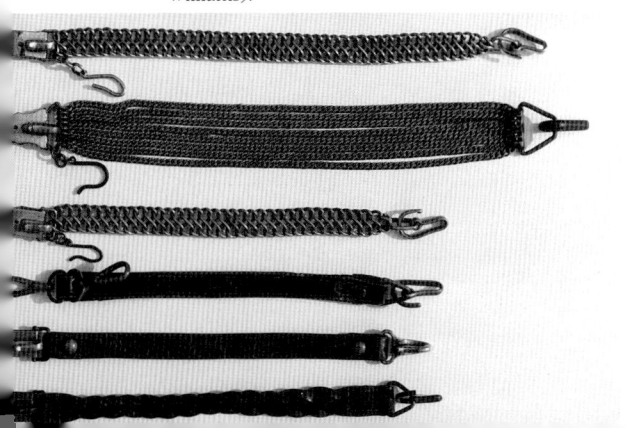

**Plate 300** *Suspension straps and a chain which are not all they seem. Top to bottom:*

(i)   Genuine black patent leather Japanese naval hanger. Black felt backing, brass spring clip and regain hook.
(ii)  Modern Japanese copy of a plaited brown leather Army hanging strap. It only has two strands and lacks a regain hook.
(iii) Wide brown leather strap with a thin lacquered spring clip. The obverse has an engraved twelve-petal chrysanthemum and the reverse has four illegible ink characters. Wide belt loop. The 'intuitive feel' is that it is not of Japanese manufacture.
(iv)  Unidentified sword chain hanger (probably for European use) which is easily mistaken for Japanese.[5] The spring clip has a non-Japanese feature of a locking nut. A short chain with a regain hook, missing from this example, sometimes has a manufacturing stamp specifying France or Germany.

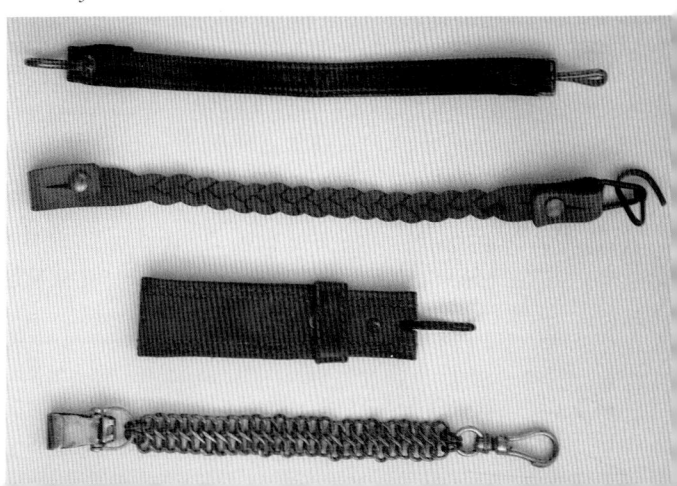

# JAPANESE MILITARY AND CIVIL SWORDS AND DIRKS

(see 'suspension methods') can also be found fixed to the belt clip of some hangers.

Various Army full (and parade) dress belt hanger fixing combinations have been noted:

(i) The strap passes through the metal belt loop and is secured by a regain hook which has a stud on the rear. Coiled hook or spring-operated suspension clip for the sword.
(ii) Wide Army-style belt spring clip with a regain hook on the rear and sometimes an additional short chain with a hook. Coiled hook or a thick oval-style brass spring-operated suspension clip for the sword.
(iii) One rare example has two brass spring clips at the top. One is for the belt fixing and the other is for regain purposes. Coiled suspension hook for the sword. Plate 299 (iv).

Civil belts may not have sword clips or hooks but, instead, have a short piece of leather which passes through the scabbard hanging ring to return to a buckle on the reverse of the sling.

## Suspension methods

Basically there are two ways in which swords were carried:

(i) Regain position, i.e. one scabbard hanging ring is looped over a hook situated at the top of the front short (or single) suspension sling. This allows the weapon to be supported without also being held.
(ii) Suspended by both (or the single) suspension slings. The weapon then swings free and needs to be held.

Dirks:

(i) Hilt towards the rear. The rear long sling is attached to the upper scabbard hanging ring which, in turn, is looped over the regain hook of the front sling. The short front sling is attached to the opposing underside ring. Both slings are on the outside of the dirk (Fig. 73, top). This is the

**Fig. 73** *Methods of carrying a naval dirk and single-hanger sword. (Top) A naval dirk in the regain position which was the normal manner of wear. (Bottom) An Army parade sabre with the full dress belt and being carried in the regain position. Extra support is given to this belt by means of a short material strip which is suspended from a stud on the full dress coat.*

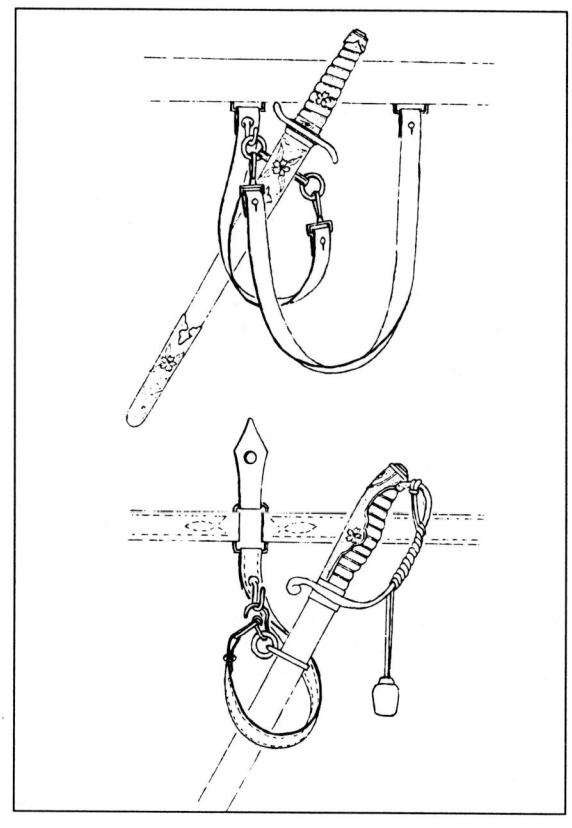

**Fig. 74** *The method of carrying a two-hanger sword (in this case a kai-guntō in the regain position.)*

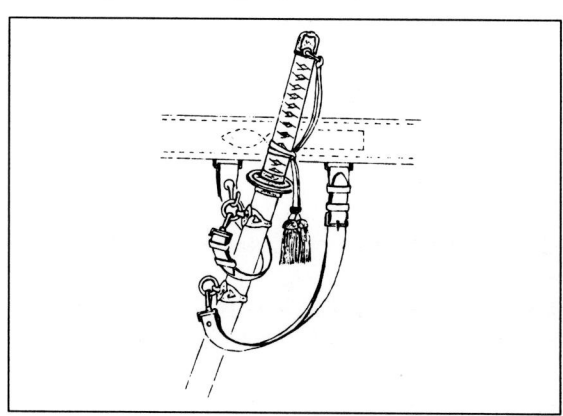

normal manner of carrying a naval dirk.
(ii) Hilt towards the rear. The short front sling is attached to the upper scabbard hanging ring which, in turn, is looped over the retain hook of the same sling. The rear long sling is attached to the opposing underside ring. Used by cadets at naval officers school.[6]
(iii) Hilt towards the rear. Suspended by the front short sling which is attached to the upper hanging ring. The rear long sling is attached to the opposing underside ring. Thus the dirk is unrestrained and hangs free. *Japanese Military Uniforms 1930–1945* indicates that naval Military Band dirks are worn in this way since the front sling is not shown with a regain hook. However those in Plate 202 may be in the regain position, although details are indistinct, which is contradictory if correct.

Swords (single suspension mount):

(i) Suspended by the sling only and allowed to hang free.
(ii) The sling is wrapped under and around the scabbard and then attached to the scabbard hanging ring by the coil-type clip. This clip is then hooked over the regain hook (Fig. 73, bottom). See also Plate 129.

Some chain and dress hangers have an additional hook at the end of a short chain which is fixed to the sling belt clip (Plate 299). This appears to be for additional security as it is hooked over the scabbard hanging ring. Alternatively it allows the sword to be held in the regain position without the use of the regain hook.

Swords (two suspension mounts):

(i) Supported by the slings only. The short front sling is attached to the upper scabbard hanging ring while the rear long sling is attached to the lower ring. The sword then hangs with the hilt pointing forward. In the case of naval police this was the only way the sword could be carried because there was no regain hook on the front sling.

(ii) The front short sling passes under and around the scabbard and then is attached to the upper hanging ring. This ring is looped over the regain hook of the same sling. The rear long sling passes across the front of the scabbard and is attached to the lower ring. This holds the sword in the regain position with the hilt towards the rear (Fig. 74).
(iii) As for (ii) but the short front sling is not passed under the scabbard. This appears applicable only to naval prison guards.

Dress Army belts are afforded extra support when worn with full dress uniform. A short strip of jacket material is suspended from a stud on the coat and looped over the metal loop between the two belt sections (Fig. 73, bottom).
Alternative methods of carrying a sword in the field are:

(i) A long adjustable leather strap with loops at each end. These fit over the hilt and scabbard respectively of shin- or kai-guntō patterns allowing the sword to be slung across the back as in Plate 91.
(ii) Some Army leather sword belts have a wide and angled leather loop stitched on near the buckle. The scabbard can be inserted through this, while still attached to the sling or hanger, thus rendering the sword rigid and freeing both hands.[7]

---

1 *Japanese Military Uniforms 1930–1945* (see Bibliography) illustrates the same belt for both Warrant Officers and NCOs but differentiates in that the former has a plaited leather sling with a small protective flap underneath, while the latter has a plain leather sling and no flap. However, that in Plate 287 (iii) of this book, which is original, has the flap and a plain sling. It may be that NCOs were issued with the version without the flap. The plaited type of sling may not be indicative of rank.
2 Identified as such in *Imperial Japanese Army and Navy Uniforms & Equipments* (see Bibliography) but not confirmed by any other reference studied.
3 A colour photograph (tinted?) of Admiral of the Fleet Heihachiro Togo shows him wearing such a belt. The clasp centre is a kiku but the remainder of the features are unclear. See *Imperial Japanese Army and Navy Uniforms & Equipments*, Plate 264, page 100.
4 These colours are shown in *Japanese Military Uniforms 1930–1945*.
5 Wrongly described as a French Air Force dirk hanger in *Collecting the Edged Weapons of the Third Reich*, vol. III, by L.T.C. Thomas M. Johnson, page 349.
6 This manner of wear is shown in *Japanese Military Uniforms 1930–1945*.
7 This method of wear is shown in Plate 103 of *Military Swords of Japan 1868–1945* (see Bibliography).

# Sword Surrenders

*Kogun* (see Bibliography) gives the following numbers of Army officers estimated to be on active duty as of 15 August 1945:

| Grade | Regulars | Reserves, Recalled & Retired | Total | Full Strength Authorised total |
|---|---|---|---|---|
| Generals (& Field Marshals) | 19 | 2 | 21 | 21 |
| Lt-Gen | 384 | 100 | 484 | 560 |
| Maj-Gen | 623 | 575 | 1,096 | 1,432 |
| Colonels | 2,247 | 4,054 | 6,301 | 7,096 |
| Commissioned officers of all ranks | – | – | 250,000 | 336,629 |

Naval figures have not been established.

It is estimated that there were approximately 5,500,000 Japanese under arms at the time of surrender (including those on the mainland of Japan). Of these 680,879[1] were in South-East Asia and 1,283,240[2] were in China. After deducting the Army commissioned officers total above there are an estimated 5,250,000 other ranks. If one assumes five per cent of these were NCOs entitled to carry swords then 262,000 were available. This gives a total of approximately 512,000 officers and NCOs available to surrender swords. The estimate of Japanese military killed in action from 1937 to 1945 is 1,140,429, with a further 240,000 missing in action and thus assumed to be dead.[3] Taking an average of nine per cent officers and NCOs gives a further 124,238 swords captured, destroyed or returned to Japan with personal effects. Thus an estimated total of 636,239 military swords were carried during the period 1937 to 1945. Possibly this is low since it does not take into account those of naval officers, ownership of more than one sword, parade sabres, dirks and replacements for loss or damage. The true figure may be in excess of 1,000,000.

It was Lord Mountbatten, Supreme Allied Commander South-East Asia, who insisted that all Japanese officers and NCOs in the area under his command be instructed to hand over their swords

SWORD SURRENDERS

upon their surrender. This was to humiliate them in retaliation for the Japanese ill-treatment of Allied prisoners of war. An officer without his sword lost face and the respect of his subordinates. Properly constituted ceremonies were conducted so that the handing over could formally take place.[4] The number of Allied and Japanese troops involved varied tremendously. The usual procedure was for the Japanese to parade under the watchful eyes of Allied armed guards. Other ranks would already be disarmed. Officers would parade carrying their swords. The senior officer (or officers in order of descending seniority) would unclip the sword, walk towards a table covered with a Union Jack flag, hand it over to the Allied senior officer designated to accept the surrender, salute and return to his position. Other junior officers (and NCOs if required) would move forward singly, or in ranks, and lay their swords down on the ground or a large mat. There were of course variations to this procedure.

The senior Allied officer in charge could then award these swords to other officers under his command at the same ceremony or later. Sometimes they were given to civilians who had suffered under the Japanese or who had helped in the war effort. The swords on the ground were collected and stored for distribution later as thought fit. This was either to officers or other ranks as official souvenirs. The surplus was destroyed.

***Plate 301   A collector's dream.*** *This remarkable photograph shows an estimated **750 visible** confiscated swords at the main storage facility in Osaka, Japan, in 1946. The actual number is probably two to three times more. They all seem to be traditional katana and wakizashi with a few sword-sticks in the front left. The American Sergeant is holding a blade in shira-saya (plain wooden storage mounts). The labels apparently had the names and addresses of the owners (see also Plate 302). They were either distributed as souvenirs or were destroyed. How many swords did the Sergeant bring back? None!* (David Scott).

Sometimes an attempt to grade blades according to age and swordsmiths was made using Japanese experts in the Army, but this was rare. The better quality items were presented to the more senior recipients. Swords in the American theatre of operations were also confiscated.

The Russians and Chinese must have collected enormous numbers of swords from surrendered Japanese troops, but the actual figures are unknown. The Central Museum of the Armed Forces of the USSR confirmed that most of those taken from the Japanese Kwantung Army in Manchuria were destroyed. However, it has been reported that some were shipped back to Russia where a few ended up in museums. Huge numbers must have been available in China. Some may have been reused by Chinese forces but the great majority was probably destroyed. A store of several hundreds of swords (most Cavalry/NCOs sabres and NCOs shin-guntō) plus bayonets, rifles and even field guns was found stored in China during the nineteen-eighties. They were brought out en masse for sale to Western collectors. Why they survived so long has not been ascertained, although it is probable they were kept as reserve equipment by the Chinese but became outdated and forgotten.

It is reported that many officers who returned home immediately after the war arrived still carrying their swords. Possibly they came from places like Korea and Formosa which only had a token Allied presence.

The bulk of these surrenders occurred in September or October 1945 but went on to at least November. Nationalist and communist activity, especially in Indo-China and Indonesia, resulted in fully armed Japanese troops being retained under the control of British officers to keep order and offer armed resistance if necessary. Officers were permitted to retain their swords for the duration of the emergency but handed them over (usually to their British commanders) before repatriation to Japan. This occurred in 1946 which explains this late date found on some documentation.

Surrender ceremonies may only have involved the handing over of just a few swords, but larger ones involved perhaps several hundred as appears to be the case at Kuala Lumpur airfield, Malaya, in September 1945. Area Army, Army, Divisional, and Brigade commanders generally surrendered singly or in very small numbers. However twenty Generals and two Admirals including the 18th Area Army Commander-in-Chief, Lt-Gen Nakamura Akita, surrendered their swords at a ceremony presided over by Maj-Gen G. C. Evans, GOC 7th Indian Division, at Bangkok, Siam on 11 January 1946.[5] This is the largest ceremony by such high-ranking officers known to the authors.

General MacArthur, Supreme Allied Commander Far East, ordered that all Japanese were to be disarmed which included the confiscation of all swords, both military and civilian, i.e. old samurai swords retained in private ownership. All Japanese were ordered to hand in their swords at collection points like police stations or face a prescribed punishment. They were then taken to a central collection store to await disposal. Consequently many old, valuable items of great artistic merit were given up. These were distributed as souvenirs or destroyed. Fortunately this loss of historical and artistic swords was stopped within a few years, but not before many were lost. However, military swords were permanently banned and even today sword ownership is strictly licensed. Indeed blades judged to be of no artistic merit, such as military oil-tempered blades, are not allowed in Japan, even on a temporary basis, for repolishing. They are seized and destroyed by the Japanese Customs.

The number of swords surrendered or confiscated can never be known. Figures are not generally available, but it is known that 7,000 swords and dirks were found among stores in a hundred and fifty mile-long tunnel system at the great military base of Rabaul in New Britain. Some 11,000 swords were reported collected in Siam (Thailand). The official American estimate of swords and sabres taken in the south-west Pacific and Japan gives 661,621 captured and surrendered. These would also include samurai swords

**Plate 302**  *Confiscated military swords at the main storage facility in Osaka, Japan in 1946. At least 270 can be seen but the actual number present must be higher. They appear to have been sorted into naval kai-guntō (top right) and Army shin-guntō. Only a very few have sword knots. The labels apparently had the names and addresses of the owners. It seems they were separated from the civilian swords in Plate 301. (David Scott).*

confiscated from civilians. Some 372,609 were dispersed as trophies, to museums and technical use. The remaining 289,012 were destroyed. The true figure for swords, of all types, taken by the Allied nations must be well in excess of 2,000,000 (but excludes those kept hidden and retained by the Japanese population).[6] Destruction was normally by furnace after cutting in half. Another way was to dump them at sea from barges or garbage scows.

Swords which were presented or taken as souvenirs may be marked either by their original owners or by the recipient to indicate their origin or circumstances of presentation. The systems normally found are: (i) documentation; (ii) labels; and (iii) metal plaques.

It must be remembered that an officer could, and often did, own more than one sword which could be surrendered or presented on different occasions.[7] Examination of surrender events confirms this was often true, especially among senior officers. Admiral Yamamoto Isoroku is reported to have owned eight or nine swords.

Although the days of the samurai were long gone, many officers had some education and experience with sword usage and etiquette. When handing a sword to another person it was customary for the donor to hold it horizontally in the flat of the palms with thumbs underneath and the cutting edge facing towards his own body with the hilt on his left. This rendered the sword effectively 'dead' and in a peaceful mode. The receiver should then turn the sword to a similar position. It is noticeable that some officers personally surrendered their swords with the cutting edge towards the recipient, which is an aggressive act. Possibly this was done in ignorance, which is doubtful in the case of senior officers, or as a calculated insult even though it would not be recognised as such by the Allied officer concerned. Lt-Gen Takehara (Plate 303) is doing it correctly, although his thumbs are on top.

On occasion the sword may be wrapped in a silk bag (Plate 305) which is a sign of respect. However, Field Marshal Terauchi Hisaichi, C-in-C of Southern Army, went even further by presenting Lord Mountbatten with two swords in a wooden box, which was a mark of special esteem. This appears unique since it has not been reported anywhere else. This ceremony was at Saigon, Indo-China, on 30 November 1945. Terauchi had two family swords specially flown in from Japan for the occasion. One was a wakizashi (short sword) with a fifteenth-century blade which was subsequently presented by Mountbatten to King George VI and is now in Windsor Castle. The other was a silver-mounted tachi (slung sword) with a blade dated 1292 which is now in Mountbatten's home of Broadlands. The whereabouts of his shin-guntō[8] and Gensui-tō (Marshals sword) are unknown.

---

1 *The Life and Times of Lord Mountbatten* by J. Terraine.
2 *History of the Sino–Japanese War 1937–45* compiled by Hsu Long-hsuen and Chang Ming-kai (Taiwan, 1971).
3 *World War II Almanac 1931–1945* by R. Goralski (Hamish Hamilton Ltd, 1981).
4 A list of over eighty-five such events is given in *Shōkan* by Richard Fuller (Arms & Armour Press, London, 1992).
5 Strangely neither the Imperial War Museum nor the Australian War Memorial Museum has a photographic record of this event. The swords were surrendered to invited senior Allied officers but a list of the participants has not been located. However the names and ranks of all the Japanese officers involved are given in *Shōkan* (see above).
6 Tony Pfeiffer in his article 'How many swords?', Japanese Sword Society of the United States Newsletter, vol. 26 no. 2, has suggested 9,900,000 to 13,200,000 Japanese swords survived after World War Two, but this seems excessive.
7 *Shōkan* (see above) records details of some of the swords of Shōwa period Generals and Admirals plus where and when they were surrendered. The location of Japanese armies, divisions and mixed brigades at the end of the war is also tabulated.
8. He may have owned more than one shin-guntō.

**Plate 303**  *Lt-Gen Takehara Saburo, GOC 49th Division, surrenders his sword to Maj-Gen W. A. Crowther, GOC 17th Indian Division, at Thaton, Burma, last week of October 1945. It is a shin-guntō with a civilian tsuba (guard), but it seems to be without a knot.* Imperial War Museum.

**Plate 304**  *French civilian Lucette Mus, liaison officer between resistance groups and, latterly a Japanese prisoner, is presented with an Army Officers shin-guntō complete with knot by Maj-Gen Gracey, Chief of the Allied Control Commission, at Saigon, Indo-China on 26 November 1945. There are five aluminium-hilted NCOs shin-guntō with leather knots in the foreground group of seven swords. These are all the swords of Kempeitai (Military Police) officers and NCOs who surrendered at a ceremony immediately prior to this presentation.* Imperial War Museum.

---

**Plate 305**  *General Itagaki Seishiro (far left), C-in-C 7th Area Army, his Chief of Staff Lt-Gen Ayabe Kitsuji (second from left) and staff officers at the Kuala Lumpur, Malaya surrender ceremony on 22 February 1946. The first three officers on the left are presenting their swords in bags which is a sign of respect and an unusual occurrence. The fourth has a kyu-guntō and the fifth a shin-guntō. All have labels attached. General Itagaki handed his sword to Lt-Gen Messervy. It has a blade signed Kanemoto (second generation of Seki, c.1450) which is now in the British Museum. Lt-Gen Ayabe handed his sword to Brigadier C. P. Jones. It is a shin-guntō with a General Officers tassel which is now in the Royal Engineers Museum. (Lt-Col West and courtesy of Peter Eyers).*

# Surrender Documentation

There are several types of documentation which may be found accompanying swords surrendered in groups or individually presented to Allied officers as a final token of surrender and mark of respect.

(i) *Authorisation certificate*: British servicemen and officers had to receive official authorisation to retain a sword taken from the battlefield or after a surrender ceremony. This does not give details of the actual sword but only the date, name and rank of the recipient plus the place where it was obtained. Typical examples are shown in Plates 306 to 310.

Unfortunately it appears that these certificates were not always accepted by the British Customs and some swords were confiscated even though possession was not illegal. Many returning servicemen were told they could be charged with attempting to import an illegal weapon. This story was often spread by souvenir-hunting seamen who would swap for cigarettes saying they were prepared to take the risk knowing that they would have no problem. Alas many servicemen preferred to throw their swords overboard and, in consequence, it is said there are more in Liverpool and Southampton harbours than in Britain. Others were cut in half in order to smuggle them inside kit bags. They would be welded together later.

(ii) *Details of the Japanese owner and, possibly, the swordsmith*: This may be in both Japanese and English. It was supplied by the Japanese officer together with a translation for the handing over or presentation. Most are dated 1946 after service under British officers. A particularly detailed example is shown in Plate 311. The English section, with the original spelling, reads:

BRIEF HISTORY

DATE OF MANUFACTURE: About 1500–1550 (Koto)
MANUFACTURE: Anonymous. (Judged by a connoisseur as 'Seki-mono'.)
LAST OWNER: Captain H. Takemura
HISTORY: In the year of Keityo (about 350 years' age), given to the ancestor of Takemura family by his Lord for his meritorious services in war, and has since been kept by the family, who had succeedingly been samurai to the Lordship of Shin-shu, Takato-Han.

This sword was surrendered to Capt Gerard Warren, Royal Engineers, Movement Control Saigon at 0900 hrs on 23 January 1946, at Port Headquarters by Capt H. Takemura, officer in charge of the Phnom Penh detachment of the ODERA Shipping Unit, French Indo-China.

(iii) *Letters from Japanese officers in English*: These give details of swords to be surrendered or presented. Again these are often dated 1946.[1] All such letters from the Japanese owners are historically invaluable since they often show the esteem

## SURRENDER DOCUMENTATION

in which even Shōwa period blades were held, and the reluctance to surrender a most valued possession and symbol of authority. The following letter relates to a sword surrendered to the 1st Battalion of the West Yorkshire Regiment at Mudon in Burma. It now resides in the museum of that regiment. The blade has since been examined by an expert who has stated that, unfortunately, it is in fact a sixteenth-century blade with a contemporary fake tang inscription:

> 'Sir, It is my express wish that my sword surrendered on 1 November 1945 be presented to Lieutenant-Colonel H.H. Crofton, commanding 1st Battalion The West Yorkshire Regiment. This sword was beaten in AD 1400 by Morimitsu Osafune of Bizen for Benticki Yamaguchi of Kyōto and has been handed down as a family heirloom since that time. It is now qualified as a national treasure.
> (Signed) SABURO OJIMA Colonel.
> Officer attached to HQ Japanese Army in Burma Area.'

The next two letters refer to a sword surrendered by a W. Taketomi, of unknown rank, to Lieutenant D.S.O. Williams, RA, at Pradjoe, Sumatra, 4 February 1946. The first is from an Army Captain and the second is from Taketomi himself. All original spelling and grammar has been retained:

**Plate 306** *Locally typed British Army certificate authorising a Private A. Smith, stationed in Siam, to retain a captured or surrendered sword and a pair of binoculars.* (Ron Gregory).

'This is a "samurai" sword of, with a blade of excellently tempered steel. The blade was made by one of Japan's best swordsmiths family that of Fujiwara Tadayoshi – at Hizen no Kuni and is about 350 or 400 years old, and is not marked with any number to show which of the generations of the Tadayoshi family made it. That may mean, according to Captain Hashida that the sword is among the first that the Tadayoshi swordsmiths produced. Its excellent temper is shown by the "midare" a wave-like marking on the blade.

Hashida Capt.

(This is the best I can do with my poor knowledge of swords)'

Simple and poor explanation regarding the Sword.

I'm very glad and satisfied to hear that my sword has been delivered to Sir, an English Officer. I am very sory and ashamed that I cannot explain in detail about Japanese swords, but I will try to relate very shortly, as far as I can in my poor knowledge as follows.

As you already know well Japanese swords (katana) are divided into different classes: in one side 'the old ones' and in the other side 'the new ones'. Roughly speaking the former are those which were made on the age tracing back to the past about five hundred years from the present, the main part of which was the age of the famous 'Tokugawa Government' being long about three hundred years, and the latter are those which were made in the age tracing back to the past more farther.

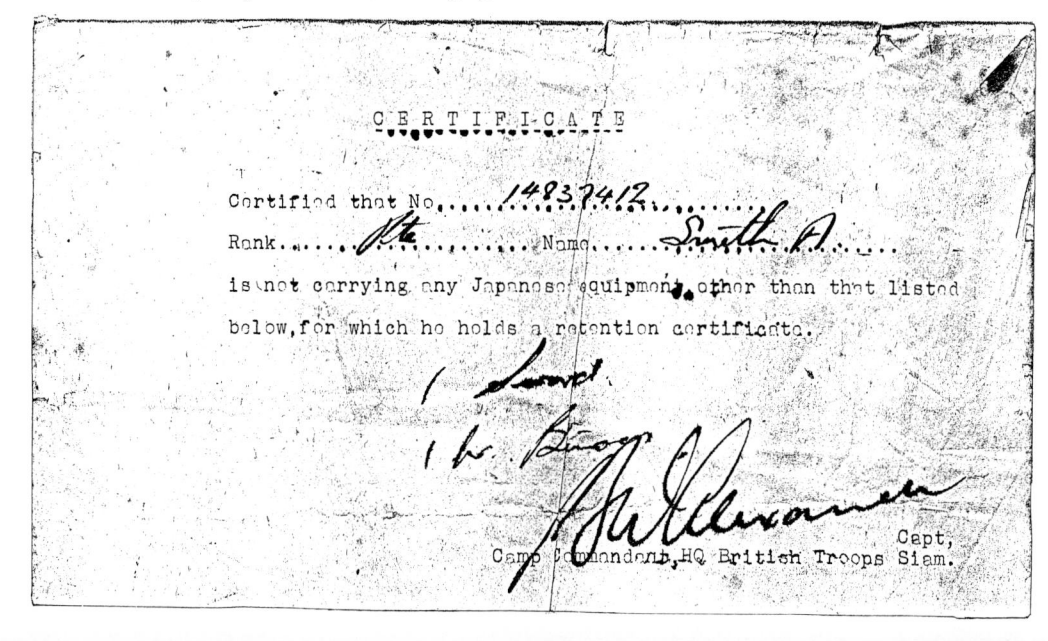

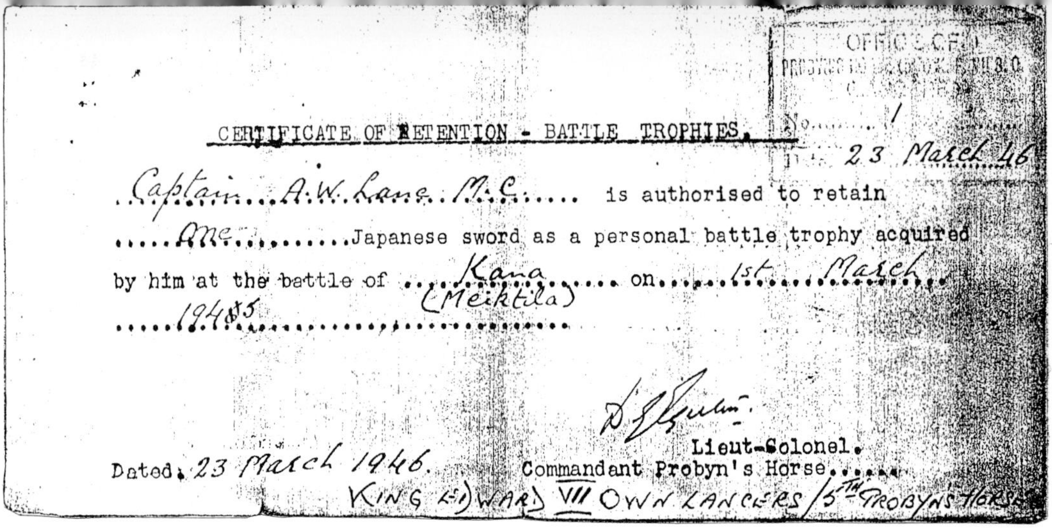
CERTIFICATE OF RETENTION - BATTLE TROPHIES.

No. 1

23 March 46

Captain A.W. Lane M.C. is authorised to retain One Japanese sword as a personal battle trophy acquired by him at the battle of Kana (Meiktila) on 1st March 1945

Dated 23 March 1946.

Lieut-Colonel.
Commandant Probyn's Horse.
KING EDWARD VII OWN LANCERS / 5TH PROBYNS HORSE

**Plate 307** *British authorisation certificate to retain a sword captured or surrendered. This example is for Captain A. W. Lane MC to retain a sword captured at the battle of Kana (Meiktila) on 1 March 1945, but it was not signed until he wanted to return home on 23 March 1946.*

Which is the better of the two classes mentioned? It is not easily decided, because each has its own special feature, after all the answer is depend upon the liking and taste of everyone.

The main part of the so-called old age was the warlike or wargoing age, so in this term swords were absolutely needed and should take practical effects, therefore many famous sword-makers appeared and endeavoured themselves to let their works fit for the purpose mentioned above, thus the works are generally so hard and so sharp that they have a touch of weirdness. On the contrary in the new age peace had gradually returned and last the feudalism was perfected and the knighthood (chivalry) – so-called Bushido – was raised more and more, thus swords were of course esteemed no less than in the wargoing age untill it was said 'a sword is the spirit of a samurai (knight)'. In this way during the term also many famous sword-maker appeared and made their efforts to get great fame, and their works were artificated as well as practically effective, and thus they generally have a touch of nobility rather than weirdness.

On reflection 'Hizen no Tada-yoshi' – it is the name of the sword as well as the name of the maker, because Japanese swords are used to be called with the name of its own maker is usually enlifted into 'the new ones', but it rather stands on the middle of two ages, new and old. I we enlist it into the class of the new ones, it is the oldest and the first class of all new ones.

It was already authenticated by the most famous judge named Hon. Ami (certified) that the sword being delivered to Sir was a quite genuine one of that kind, and we can see the name of its maker engraved on the hilt of the sword: 'Hizen no kuni Tadayoshi' if used Japanese letter . . . namely, five letters. Hereupon we must take a special notice, because in other hand we always see his works on which the name is engraved as follows 'Hizen Tadayoshi' – if used Japanese letter . . . – namely four letters. Thus we call the former 'Goji Tadayoshi'

**Plate 308** *Certificate dated 16 June 1946 which confirms ownership of a 'delapidated 1935 pattern Army NCOs shin-guntō' by Wing Commander W. E. Moss, RAF. Reference to the sword's condition is most unusual.*

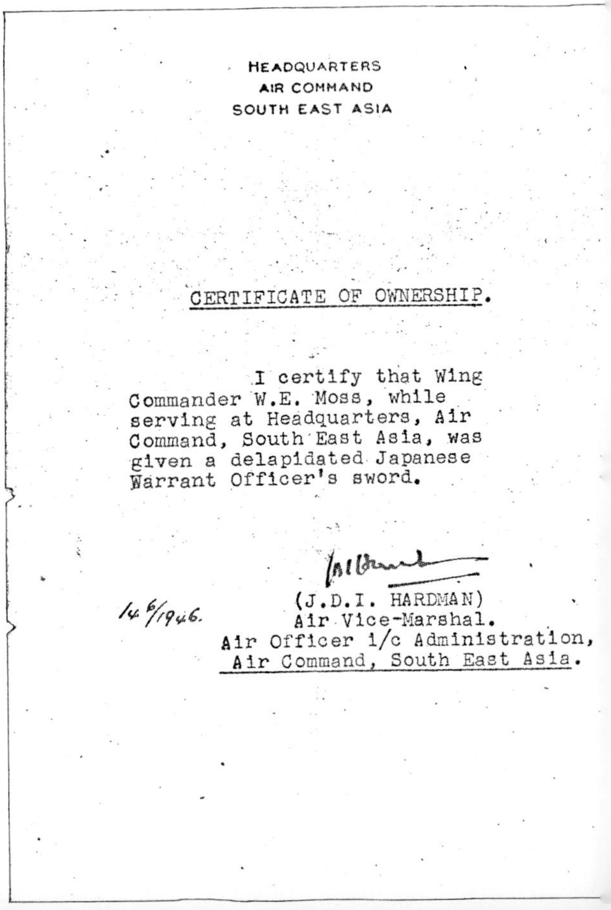
HEADQUARTERS
AIR COMMAND
SOUTH EAST ASIA

CERTIFICATE OF OWNERSHIP.

I certify that Wing Commander W.E. Moss, while serving at Headquarters, Air Command, South East Asia, was given a delapidated Japanese Warrant Officer's sword.

14/6/1946.

(J.D.I. HARDMAN)
Air Vice-Marshal.
Air Officer i/c Administration,
Air Command, South East Asia.

```
                                                    Serial No. 43

              WAR TROPHY CERTIFICATE
                      23 INDIAN DIVISION
                            SEAC.


      This is to certify that

      No. ......782...... Rank ...Colonel......... Name ...T.H.W. HIGHT...............

      Unit .......I.E.M.E. CENTRE............................

      a member of 23 Indian Division has been issued with the u/m Personal War Trophies vide ALFSEA Signal

      No. 2134/504 dated 21 November '46.


                          One Japanese Officer's Sword



      UNIT OFFICE
        STAMP

      Date: 23 Jul 1946                    Signature: ..................... Lt-Col.,
                                                C.I.E.M.E., 23rd Indian Division

      (N.B. This certificate is only valid if signed by an Officer of Field Rank).
```

**Plate 309** *Printed certificate issued by the 23rd Indian Division, South-East Asia Command, authorising a Colonel T. H. W. Hight to retain a captured or surrendered sword. The division was in Java at this time. (Ron Gregory).*

---

(Tadayoshi five letters) and the latter 'Yoji Tadayoshi (Tadayoshi four letters), and Tadayoshi the maker, seldom engraved five letters; namely only when we conceived his new work was a quite congenial one. Thereupon we can see that of all his works one which has five letters engraved is the best one and that the sword delivered to Sir is one of so-called Tadayoshi five letters. Tadayoshi means the individual name of this maker and so Hizen no kuni Tadayoshi or Hizen Tadayoshi means 'Tadayoshi being a native of the feudal district reigned over by feudal lord Nabeshima' and my old family also belonged to that feudal lord.

Excuse me if I have mistaken whatever or something which is difficult to understand is found.

This sword, a shin-guntō, has a red/black leather suspension strap (used by Field and General Officers) and a General Officers sword knot. A separate contemporary note confirms that the 'sword sash' (presumably the knot) was 'obtained from Major-General Saito, Japanese Commander on Bangka Island, at Pradjoe, 26 Feb 45'.[2]

The following fascinating extract is from a letter to the Australian 2nd Corps Chief of Staff, Brigadier Garrett, from the Japanese 17th Army Chief of Staff, Major-General Makata (Magata) Isaochi at the time of the surrender in New Guinea. It is dated 16 September 1945. Not only does it demonstrate the reverence in which swords were held but clearly confirms that some Japanese officers owned more than one sword. The broken English translation and certain Japanese words used in the text are retained. They are 'seito' (sword used with service dress), 'fukuto' (sword used when in dress uniform) and 'nipponto' (swords with hand-forged blades made in the traditional manner which naturally includes 'ancestral' blades).

'As you may already understand, nipponto are cherished by our officers as the swords of the "samurai", and the Japanese swords are to protect the right and we do not expect that they will be used as murderous weapons on behalf of injustice. There are two kinds of swords: one kind is made in a weapons factory and is given to NCOs and other ranks as Government issue regulation swords, and the other kind is the real nipponto, hand-made from ancient times, and most owned by officers are of this kind. These nipponto, forged by special process and are masterpieces of the swordsmiths paintaking craft will be finest with which no other sword in the world can compare. Our ancient "samurai" and present generation of officers would not grudge great sums of money to get such fine swords, and there are many which have been handed down from olden times, from ancestors as treasured swords of families. Jap officers loving care and respect for nipponto is very great. Therefore I would like to inform you on behalf of all Japanese officers that it is unbearable for them to part with such swords to anyone else.

At this time an Imperial prescript however has been published, in which we are bidden to surrender to you. We beg to inform you of our hopes and loving care regarding our swords especially these nipponto. Your Government regarding military swords as weapons, does not acknowledge the wearing of swords as dress, and we have been ordered to surrender all kinds of swords. Japanese officers are extremely dejected and troubled. But, since they knew that at present to obey your orders faithfully is the only [way] to show their loyalty to the Emperor, they willingly handed over their swords, renouncing absolutely their loving care for nipponto . . .

The nipponto handed over under such mental stress as described above we would like to request you to keep with great care as the symbol of the relation of friendship that accompanies same. For this reason our senior officers request that you will appoint personal custodians or receivers, as they hope, for the nipponto which it was desired would

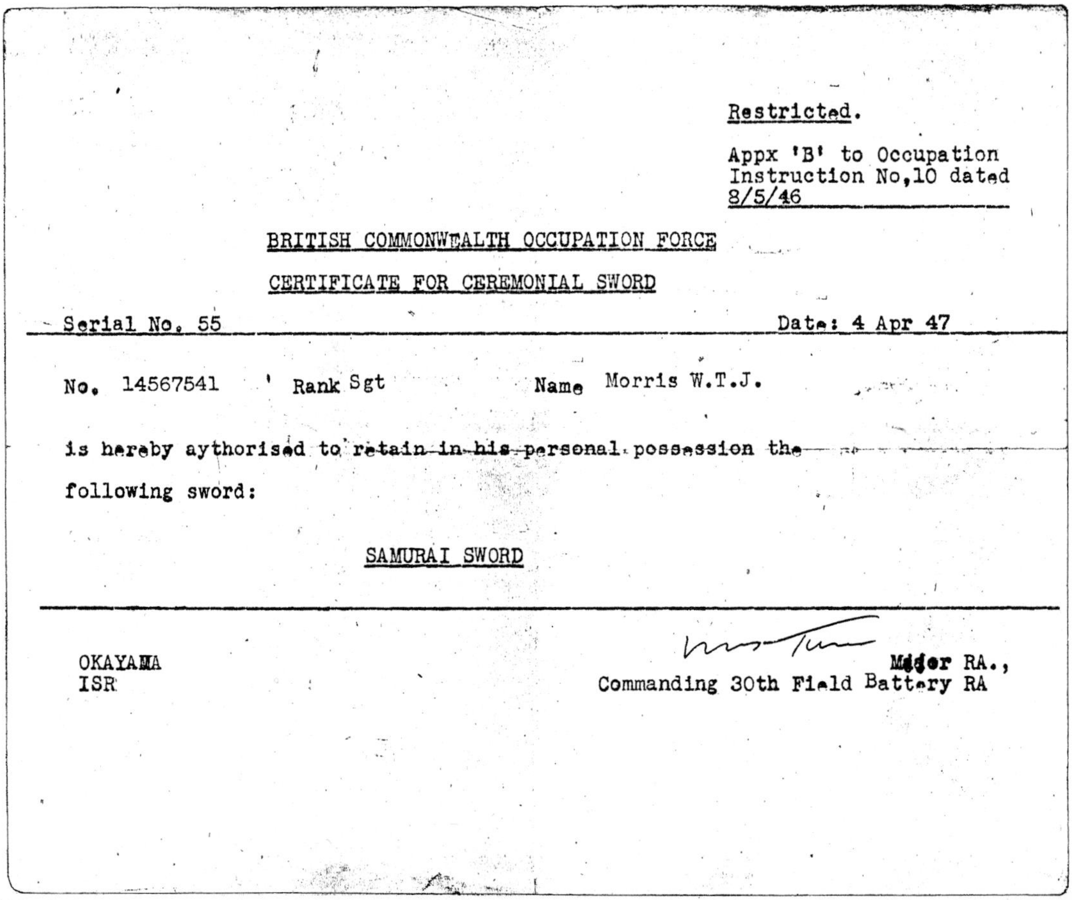

**Plate 310** *Certificate authorising a Sergeant Morris (probably Royal Artillery) to retain a sword obtained in Japan during the Allied occupation. (Ron Gregory).*

```
                                              Restricted.
                                              Appx 'B' to Occupation
                                              Instruction No. 10 dated
                                              8/5/46

         BRITISH COMMONWEALTH OCCUPATION FORCE
         CERTIFICATE FOR CEREMONIAL SWORD

   Serial No. 55                               Date: 4 Apr 47

   No. 14567541    Rank Sgt       Name Morris W.T.J.

   is hereby aythorised to retain in his personal possession the
   following sword:

                        SAMURAI SWORD


   OKAYAMA                                     Major RA.,
   ISR                       Commanding 30th Field Battery RA
```

be held by your receivers and custodians as individuals. Again, since a special mark has been set upon these historical nipponto and famous blades, it is requested for your special consideration that they may be entrusted to an authorised museum or to suitable battle-tried military men, so that they may be preserved from damage due to negligence or careless handling. The former possessors of the swords and blades above mentioned will feel greatly relieved of anxiety if your receivers and custodians would inform them of their ranks, names, units and addresses. And we should be very glad if this will lead to the exchange of letters of friendship in the future after peace.

Although we think you may already know, among our senior commanders are some who have one seito and fukuto. Apart from personal use, these fukuto are to be given to subordinates when they distinguish themselves in action.[3] The ones which Lt-General Kanda and myself carry at the time of the surrender signing ceremony the other day are actually our seito.[4] The above nipponto were made by the leading swordsmith of modern times at the request of the Yasukuni Shrine, which is the only shrine of the Japanese military man. Although they are of recent origin, we believe that they are sufficiently worthy to be held by your Corps Commander and yourself. Among these handed over today there is the fukuto of Commanding General Kanda. The said fukuto, an object of great craftmanship made by a famous swordsmith living near Kyoto about 600 years ago, with its dignity of practical worth, General was in the habit of wearing daily at his side. We understand that the order to hand over nipponto was issued by the supreme commander of the Australian forces. Therefore I request you to present it to C-in C General Blamey. I request that you give this matter careful consideration in accordance with the sincere hope of General Kanda.'

---

1 Other examples, not reproduced here, were published in *Military Swords of Japan 1868–1945* by the authors (see Bibliography).
2 Maj-Gen Saito appears to be the military commander of Bangka Island off south-east Sumatra. Pradjoe is believed to be the post-war Japanese assembly area near Palembang, Sumatra. This sword is now in the Clive Sinclair collection, England. The use of '. . .' in the text means the Japanese kanji (characters) have been omitted.
3 The awarding of one's dress, and presumably best, sword to a deserving subordinate has not been noted elsewhere.
4 Lt-Gen Kanda Masatane's seito has a Shōwa period blade by Emura (chief warden and swordsmith of Okayama prison). It is now in the Australian War Memorial Museum (cat. no. AWM 20314). The whereabouts of his fukuto is unknown to the authors.

*Plate 311* Document in Japanese and English giving details of blade manufacturer, owner and history. It was surrendered by Army Captain H.Takemura at Phnom Penh, French Indo-China on 23 January 1946. See page 252 for details. (Bruce Skelly).

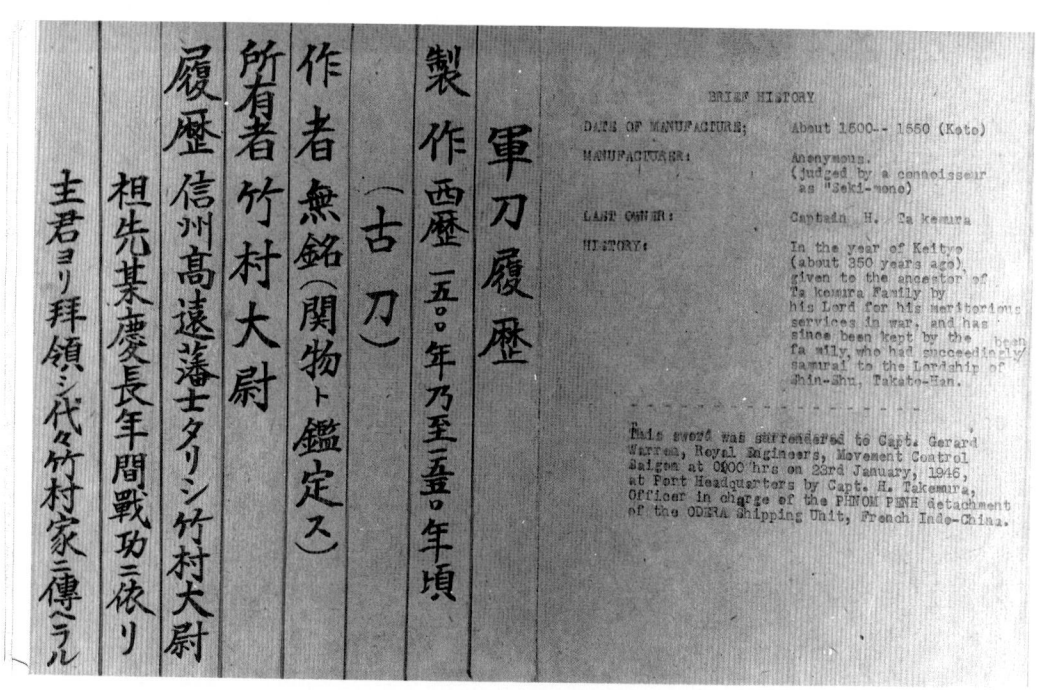

# Surrender/Transportation Labels

Labels of linen and sometimes silk, card or even wood can be found tied to the hilt or hanging ring of a sword surrendered or confiscated at the end of World War Two. Occasionally a piece of inscribed linen may actually be sewn around the hilt being non-removable unless deliberately cut off. These are 'surrender' or 'transportation' labels (or tags) tied on by the former Japanese owner either when the sword was shipped with his baggage or possibly upon his surrender, perhaps while under the impression that it would eventually be returned. However, none of the linen types has been seen in surrender ceremony photographs.

They are of great interest since they may reveal the owner's name, rank, unit and possibly location written in ink in his own handwriting. Condition varies from good and legible to smudged, torn and even incomplete. Information is variable ranging from just a surname to even details of the swordsmith, but the latter is rare.

Translating is often very difficult because of the handwriting style used, smudged characters or the use of a divisional or regimental codename or number. Without a list of the latter, the unit and last location (i.e. probable place of surrender) cannot be identified.[1] Even when fully translated it is often difficult for a non-Japanese speaker to make sense of the intended meaning. Nevertheless they are historically interesting and should be retained with the swords on which they came.

The majority, where a rank is given, belonged to Captains, Lieutenants, Warrant Officers and sometimes Sergeant-Majors. Ranks of Major and above appear to be scarce. Nearly all are found on Army swords but occasionally they may be found with naval kai-guntō. In rare cases these labels may confirm ownership either in conjunction with surrender documentation or information engraved on the blade tang. One such example with a signed blade tang dated August 1938 also included the name of the person for whom it was made – Kamiya Sadanori. A linen label attached translates as 'Kamiya Sadanori [of the] Defence Force'. Naturally confirmation on both blade and label is extremely rare.

It is not unknown for a paper label, with the normal ink inscriptions, to be stuck to a leather scabbard cover. However, it is easily torn or scratched and is often illegible or only partially readable.

Tie on labels can easily be moved from sword to sword, or used to increase monetary value, so the collector should accept their presence with caution. Some examples are shown in Plates 312 to 318.

---

1 The authors would much appreciate a copy of any unit code listing which also gives the equivalent Japanese kanji (characters) for the 1945 period, should any reader have access to such a thing.

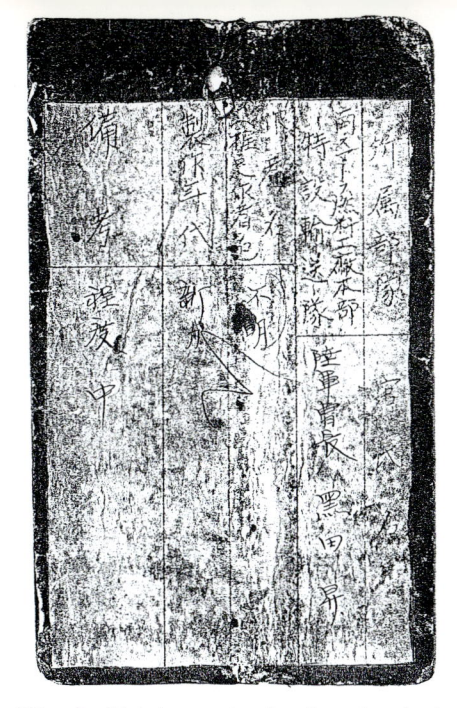

**Plate 312** Card label part printed and part handwritten in ink bearing the name Army Sergeant-Major Kuroda Nobori and stating that the swordsmith is unknown since unsigned. The reverse is divided into panels with English headings but generally unreadable except for Unit – Specialist Transportation Corps at SSOD. This may have been written by a Japanese sword appraiser (Kantaisha) for the surrender. (Richard Fuller).

**Plate 313** RIKUGUN (Army), GUNI (Medical Officer), TAI-I (Captain), NAKASHIMA, HIROYUKI, i.e. Army Medical Officer Captain Nakashima Hiroyuki. (He was a reserve officer and may, originally, have been a civilian doctor.) DAI (number), SHI (4), JU (10), NI (2), HEITAN (supply train or line of communications), CHIKU (area, sector, district), TAI (troop), HOMBU (headquarters), i.e. Troop Headquarters of No. 42 Supply (or Logistics) District. (By 1945 this unit was in Burma supplying the notorious Burma–Siam Railway). (Richard Fuller).

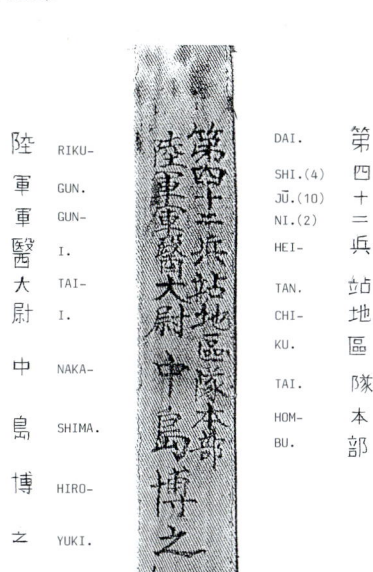

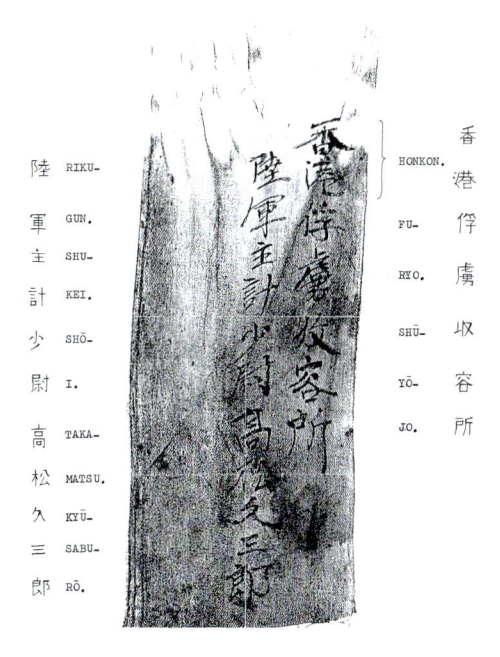

**Plate 314** RIKUGUN (Army), SHUKEI (Paymaster), SHŌI (2nd Lieutenant), TAKAMATSU (surname), KYUSABURŌ (male name), i.e. Army Paymaster 2nd Lieutenant Takamatsu Kyusaburō. HONKON (Hong Kong), FURYO (prisoner of war), SHUYOJŌ (internment camp), i.e. Hong Kong prisoner of war internment camp. (This would be the location of his post and not a reference to where he was interned after the cessation of hostilities.). (Mike Clark)

**Plate 315**
1. MATSUZAKI (surname), CHUI (1st Lieutenant).
   1st Lieutenant Matsuzaki.
2. KEIRI-BU Intendance Dept. (of Division HQ).
3. NITE (at), TODOKE (a report, notification), ZUMI (finished).
   Meaning uncertain.
4. BANBON (a place name), YASEN SŌKO (field depot or storehouse).
   Banbon field storehouse or depot.
5. HACHI (8), GATSU (month), NI (2), JU (10), HACHI (8), NICHI (day).
   8th month, 28th day i.e. 28 August. (Ron Gregory).

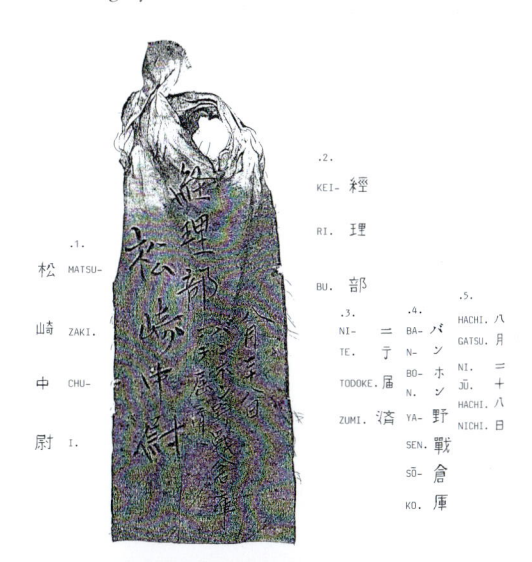

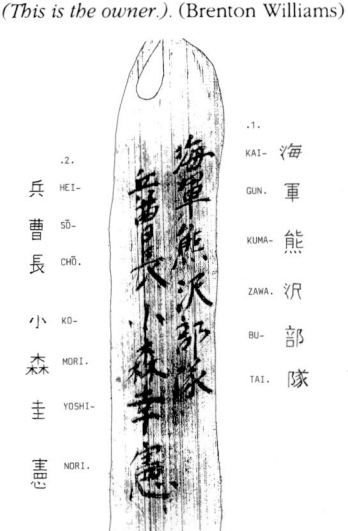

**Plate 318**  Silk surrender label.
1. TŌ MEI SEKI FUJIWARA YOSHINAO SAKU:
   TŌ (sword), MEI (inscription, signature), SEKI, FUJIWARA (family or clan name), YOSHINAO (male name), SAKU (made), i.e. the signature on the sword is 'made by Fujiwara Yoshinao of Seki'.
2. KAHŌ ŌITA-KEN USA-GUN HIURA-MACHI ŌAZA-KŌ SHU GA:
   KAHŌ (heirloom, family treasure), ŌITA, KEN (prefecture), USA, GUN (district, county), HIURA, MACHI (town), ŌAZA, KŌ (bay), SHU (necessarily, by all means), GA (congratulations, celebrate), i.e. family treasure. Oaza bay at Hiura town in the Usa district of Oita prefecture (which is the owner's address). The meaning of 'shu ga' is uncertain since it does not seem to be relevant. Perhaps it refers to the address as a street or block name?
3. KUBO (surname), YUSAKU (male name), i.e. Kubo Yasuku (which is the name of the owner).

It seems odd to refer to this sword as a 'family treasure' since the swordsmith, Fujiwara Yoshinao, was a Shōwa period smith who worked under the Army Blade Department at Seki. However, the blade is in old civilian katana mounts utilising old fuchi, kashira and seppa. It is probable that the owner was forced to hand over this sword in Japan by order of the American occupation forces. The reference to 'family treasure' was perhaps included to ensure that it was eventually returned since it was not a military mounted weapon. The tang is indeed signed SEKI FUJIWARA YOSHINAO SAKU i.e. made by Fujiwara Yoshinao of Seki. (Richard Fuller and Leo Monson Jr collection).

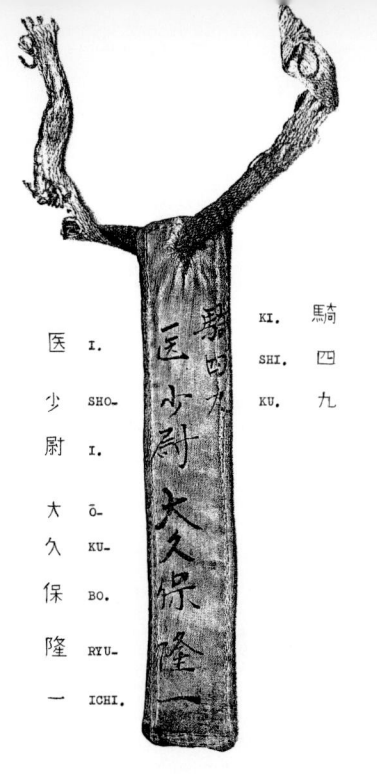

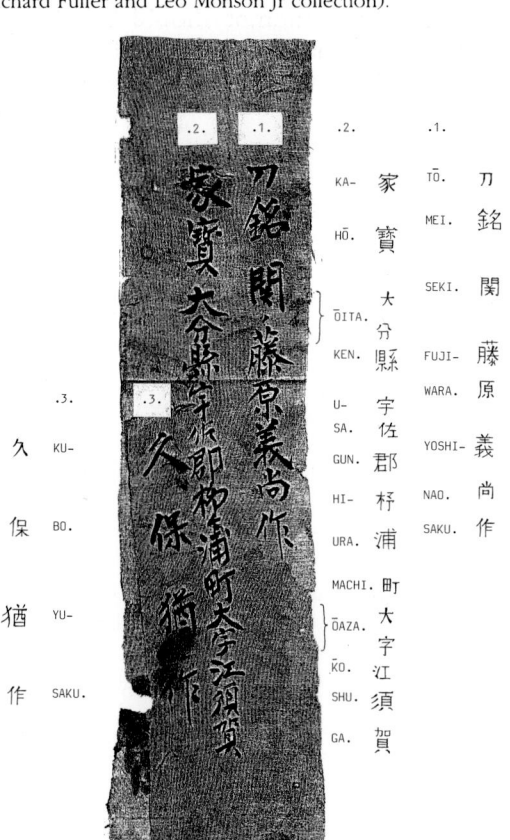

**Plate 316**  Good quality sword transportation tag of white linen with a red silk backing.
I (Doctor), SHOI (2nd Lieutenant), ŌKUBO (surname), RYUICHI (male name), i.e. 2nd Lieutenant Doctor Ōkubo Ryuichi.
KI (riding on a horse – probably an abbreviation of KIHEI i.e. cavalry), SHI (4), KU (9), i.e. 49th Cavalry? (Possibly the 49th Cavalry Regiment which was part of the 49th Division which surrendered in Burma at the cessation of hostilities in 1945). (I. Phillips)

**Plate 317**  Scarce naval transportation or surrender tag.
1. KAIGUN (navy), KUMAZAWA (surname), BUTAI (unit).
   The Kumazawa naval unit.
   ('Kumazawa' is the name of the Commanding Officer).
2. HEISŌCHŌ (Chief Petty Officer) KOMORI (surname), YOSHINORI (male name).
   Chief Petty Officer Komori Yoshinori.
   (This is the owner.). (Brenton Williams)

# Commemorative Plaques

A silver or brass plaque screwed, soldered or secured by bands to a scabbard, could be added after surrender either by the new Allied owner or before presentation to a third party. It may record the name, rank and unit of the recipient together with the location and date of the surrender, and sometimes include similar details of the original owner. Unfortunately it is easy for a modern dealer to add such items with spurious inscriptions to increase the sale value. Therefore every attempt should be made to validate the contents if it is judged to have affected the value. Typical genuine examples are as follows:

Presented to Lt.-Colonel Joubert
by H.Q.B.M.A. Malaya 1945
*(This stands for Headquarters British Military Administration.)*

Presented to
129th (Lowland) Field Regiment Royal Artillery (Lieut.-Colonel C.F. Younger R.A.)
by
The 7/10th Baluc. Hill 6052 Chin Hills Burma 28/29 January 1944
'F' Troop 493rd Fd. Bty., Bty. Commander Maj. P.M. Brown, R.A.
'F' Troop Commander Capt. D.W.B. Gordon, R.A.
F.O.O. Lt. M.I. Roy, R.A.
*(The 7/10 Baluchi Regiment was an Indian force which was a divisional reconnaissance battalion attached to the 17th Indian Light Division under Major-General D.T. Cowan in 1944.)*

Presented to 2nd Goorkhas on the disbandment of 3/2nd Goorkhas.
This Japanese sword was forged in about AD 1500[1]
*(This occurred in 1947 when the 3rd Battalion, which had fought through Burma, was disbanded. The sword is believed to have been surrendered in Malaya, 1945).*

Surrendered to Lt.-Col. R.C.W. Thomas in French Indo-China
24 Dec. 1945 by Lt.-Col. Miyahara H.Q. Japanese Army.
*(Lt-Col Miyahara Toshio also supplied a personal history with this sword. In 1945 he was Chief Staff Officer to HQ Traffic Facilities, Southern Army, Saigon. The signed blade is dated 1396.)*

Sword presented to Brigadier M.S.K. Maunsell D.S.O. O.B.E., Commander British Inter-Service Mission French Indo-China by Lieut. General Takazo Numata, Chief of Staff Japanese Forces Southern Regions. 8 June 1946.

---

[1] This undated blade is signed by Fujiwara Kanesaki of Inshū province. There were several smiths who used this signature content from the sixteenth to the late seventeenth century, but this is possibly fourth-generation and late seventeenth century. It was often the case that a Japanese officer, upon surrendering his sword, would say that it had been in his family for 'generations', which probably explains the dating given. Thus dating on plaques and surrender information must always be checked.

JAPANESE MILITARY AND CIVIL SWORDS AND DIRKS

*(This sword, accompanied by a letter, came through military channels from Numata after working with Maunsell who was Chief of Staff to the French Indo-China Control Commission. One of his jobs was to monitor the Japanese HQ so he worked with Numata on an almost daily basis until repatriation.)*

**Plate 319** *Lt-Gen George E. Stratemeyer USAAF (left), Air Commander of Eastern Air Command, with an Army Officers shin-guntō. There are three silver plaques secured by bands which are engraved with details of the presentation. The scabbard band (shibabiki) has been replaced the wrong way round. The number of bands is most unusual but research has failed to learn what they say or the current whereabouts of this sword.* Imperial War Museum.

# Collaboration, Emergency Issue, Reproduction and Fake Military Swords

There is great difficulty in establishing whether many swords, seemingly from World War Two, are (a) genuine, (b) wartime field-made replacements, (c) 'collaboration' swords, or (d) made as souvenirs after the cessation of hostilities. This is an area full of pitfalls for the military sword collector which, unfortunately, cannot be negotiated with any certainty.

## Collaborating Forces

Usually forgotten are the numerous collaborating forces which either fought with, or were maintained by, the Japanese Army. They could be equipped with Japanese weapons and may have worn Japanese-style uniforms. It is therefore to be expected that many of their officers and NCOs could, and did, carry some form of sword either traditional or based on the Japanese military pattern. Little attention has been paid to most of the various armed organisations so it is worth outlining them by country in alphabetical order:[1]

### Burma

A nationalist force known as the Burma Independence Army was formed in February 1940 but was disbanded by the Japanese because of dissension in their ranks caused by broken Japanese promises. Reformed as the Burma Defence Army with 55,000 men by April 1943. Renamed Burma National Army in September 1943 but was used for garrison duties. It changed sides and fought for the British from March 1945 becoming the Patriotic Burmese Forces. Clothing varied from native dress, British battledress and Japanese uniforms.

### China

By 1939 it was reported that 100,000 armed Chinese had defected to the Japanese. In March 1940 the Japanese established the 'Reformed National Government of the Republic of China' under Premier Wang Chin-wei at Nanking.[2] Nationalist Chinese and Japanese style uniforms appear to have been worn. Provisional and Reformed Government Chinese Officers have been photographed with Japanese shin-guntō.

### India

The Indian National Army or 'Azad Hind Fauj' was formed in January 1942 from 20,000 Indian prisoners of war, mostly held in Malaya. It increased to 40,000 by the summer of 1942 but was reduced by eighty per cent in late 1942. Peak operational membership was only one division (approx. 7,000) which fought in Burma in 1944. They wore either Indian khaki or Japanese uniform and are believed to have had their own insignia. It has not been established if officers carried swords, although it is known that their leader, Subhas Chandra Bose, was presented with a sword by members of the Malayan Indian community on 24 October 1943. Unfortunately the type is not known.

### Java

A large force called the Java Defence Army[3] (or Volunteer Army for the Defence of the Homeland) was formed which, by November 1944, consisted of about 33,000 men (sixty-six battalions) on Java and 1,500 men (three battalions) on Bali. They are believed to have had their own insignia and uniforms based on that of the Japanese Army. Officers also carried swords (see later in this chapter). A further recruitment of 25,000 in Java and 2,500 in Bali became Military Auxiliaries (Hei-ho) which were basically labour auxiliaries to the Japanese. The Japanese allowed such large numbers to bear arms because their own garrison forces were small and promises of independence, plus a hatred of the Dutch colonials, made the Javanese compliant and sympathetic.

### Korea

Korea was annexed by Japan in 1910. Its people could enlist but were mainly used as labourers and guards. Their officers seem to be mainly Japanese. They wore Japanese uniforms (see also 'Korean Swords and Dirks').

### Malaya

A Volunteer Corps (the Malay Volunteer Army) of 2,000 men was raised in early 1944 and increased to 5,000 by March 1944. It was used for policing and coastal defence. They appear to have mostly worn British uniform.

### Manchuria

After its occupation by the Japanese in 1932 they raised a Manchurian Army which had about 75,000 men in infantry and cavalry units (see also 'Swords and Dirks of Manchukuo (Manchuria)').

### Mongolia

Cavalry units were formed from recruits in May 1939 under Japanese officers. They fought alongside Japanese cavalry and presumably wore the same uniforms.

### North Borneo

An Indo-Chinese force of about 3,000 men was formed in March 1944. It is assumed they wore Japanese uniforms.

### Philippines

The Patriotic League of Filipinos was formed in December 1943 for construction and guard duties. Maximum membership was about 4,000.

## Collaboration swords

A steel works at Semerang in Java made sword blades for use by collaborating Indonesian officers of the Java Defence Army, although the actual pattern, or patterns, (if any were prescribed) has not been established.[4] Further, it has also been ascertained that such officers were allowed to carry swords provided the blade and mountings were Indonesian-made, although they could be based on Japanese designs. However, Japanese-made blades were not allowed.[5]

Quality must have varied but the blades are said to be heavy and often crude with a rounded back edge, rounded tang end, no file marks, a long 'kissaki' (point) and a rough habaki (mostly lacking the small flattened inner section against the cutting edge). Apparently many officers broke off the points of their blades between two stones rather than suffer the shame of surrendering them whole. Consequently many wakizashi have been found in post-war Indonesia with newly filed points, no 'yokote' and an unbalanced feel.

Yukio Yamaguchi, who has lived in Java, was told the Indonesians continued to make Japanese-style swords in the western city of Bandung after the Japanese surrender because of a scarcity of weapons.

It is thought that the sword in Plate 320 is almost certainly a Java Defence Army Officers pattern. The origin of the shin-guntō in Plates 320 to 324 is open to question.

A sword taken reputedly from a dead Korean officer in the Korean war of 1950–3 has been examined. It is a copy of a shin-guntō in a leather field scabbard with an external brass band suspension mount. The hilt is bound in Japanese fashion with lacquered leather, instead of braid, but has no menuki (hilt ornaments). The tsuba and kabuto-gane (pommel) are very poor quality cast brass copies of those used on a shin-guntō. Copper wire sarute (knot loop). Pressed brass fuchi (hilt collar) having a raised leaf motif on both sides. One-piece steel blade, sharpened by file, with four unidentified characters (Korean?) stamped on one side near a thin brass habaki. A similar wakizashi version has also been seen.

The condition and overall wear is certainly commensurate with use in the Korean war and, indeed, could possibly be of World War Two vintage. Swords apparently resembling this style have been reported in China. Whether locally made for Koreans serving under the Japanese in World War Two or used by Koreans (and Chinese) in the Korean war is a matter for speculation. There is also a possibility that they are no more than reproductions.

There are problems in distinguishing between 'collaboration', 'emergency issue' and 'fake' swords. Alas, there are no firm guidelines since many 'collaboration' swords do not seem to follow a set pattern, being locally made and based on the shin-guntō. Fittings may be fairly crude castings finished by hand but should be of acceptable quality if they were to be used on a sword intended for official use. Blades are locally hammered out or machine-made in shinogi-zukuri form and have no tempered edge (yakiba). The hilt binding is often missing so it is not possible to generalise on material, binding skill or even if menuki (hilt ornaments) were present. However the hilt binding on one example is typically Japanese with shin-guntō menuki. A brown leather field scabbard, often light tan coloured, is usual since easy to make.

Possibly the only criteria which can be used to assess such swords are age and quality. Does such an item look fifty years old and are the quality of fittings too bad, or even too good, for use? It is unfortunately a matter for personal judgement.

A number of different coloured shin-guntō pattern sword knots have been encountered, some attached to normal Japanese-made shin-guntō (but they could have been added post-war). They are fairly scarce and appear to be of wartime manufacture. The straps are wider than normal at 12.5mm (½"), being made from a braid or silk mixture, but in a different weave from their normal Japanese counterparts. Colours noted are: Maroon and blue straps, maroon and blue tassels; maroon and red straps, maroon and red tassels; green and blue straps, green and blue tassels; green and yellow straps, green and yellow tassels. Possibly there are other colours as well. They would seem to represent some form of ranking system, but in what order is unknown. Even the country of origin has not been established, but Indonesia, and in particular Java, is likely. It is thought they are genuine, and the sword pattern shown in Plate 320 is a likely candidate for use.

There is one unidentified shin-guntō style knot which closely resembles the Japanese weave pattern but is slightly coarser. The straps are reddish-brown externally and white internally where there are (deliberate?) reddish-brown edge stripes. The tassels seem to be predominately reddish-brown as is the slide which also has white diagonal threads. Strap width 10mm (3/16"). It was obtained separately, although reputably taken off a shin-guntō by the vendor.

JAPANESE MILITARY AND CIVIL SWORDS AND DIRKS

## A probable 'collaboration' sword

This unusual sword variation appears to be a 'pattern' rather than a 'one off' since several have been seen. Plain blackened steel hilt mounts including an ovoid tsuba (guard) which has an indistinct circular stamp.[6] Two aluminium seppa (washers). The hilt is bound with a narrow, tightly bound, red tape exposing a simulated samé of a white embossed canvas material. It is secured to the tang by two widely spaced wooden pegs. The menuki (hilt ornaments) are brass in the form of an unidentified stylised flower. Triangular steel sarute (knot loop). Retention is by means of leather loop and strap which passes through a hole in the tsuba to engage with a press stud on the scabbard cover.

Heavy machine-made blade of shinogi-zukuri form with light file marks on the tang and two widely spaced peg holes. Copper habaki (blade collar). Light tan leather-covered field scabbard with a steel throat and a single suspension mount having a large steel hanging ring.

Overall length of sword and scabbard 995mm (39 3/16"). Hilt length 264mm (10 3/8"). Blade length 678mm (26 11/16"). Scabbard length 745mm (29 3/16"). Weight of sword and scabbard 56 ounces.

There seems no doubt that this is a genuine wartime sword pattern, but probably not for Japanese use. It is likely to have been carried by an officer of a national unit which supported the Japanese. The favourite in this category is the Java Defence Army whose men could carry swords, but not those with Japanese-made blades. The steel works at Semerang in central Java certainly made blades since some have been seen bearing the inscription SHIYAWA-TŌ SUMARAN, i.e. sword (made at) Semerang on the island of Java. Unfortunately the mounting details of most of these items were not reported to the authors, but at least one fits the general description.

No example with a bona fide sword knot has been reported, but one of the shin-guntō knot variants of non-standard colours referred to earlier in this section is likely. Not a highly collectable

**Plate 320** *World War Two period sword probably made for use by one of the national forces which collaborated with the Japanese.* (Richard Fuller).

item it is, nevertheless, an interesting military sword pattern and seems to be fairly scarce.

The scabbard of this example has 1422706 CLARK written in faded ink while the leather fuchi cover has CLARK 706. Apparently this number was not allocated to a British serviceman of this name so the soldier's personal history has not been established to confirm whether or not it was brought from Java as a souvenir after his service.

## An enigmatic shin-guntō

This is an enigmatic and difficult sword type to appraise when compared to normal shin-guntō because of differences, some subtle, which lead one to 'feel' it is not Japanese. However, the consensus of opinion among those who have examined the known examples is that they are from the wartime period.

Only two examples of this sword are known, being those in Plates 321–324 and another one in poorer condition in the author's collection. There are only minor differences between them. Basically a standard shin-guntō with a plated

***Plate 321*** *An enigmatic shin-guntō with a dark green painted metal scabbard and sharply curved machine-made plated blade. Possibly made for, and used by, a collaborating foreign officer (see text and Plates 322–4). (Dr Terry Ingold).*

blade having a pronounced curve and dark green painted metal scabbard. The author's scabbard has been repainted black some time in the past and has wear to the base of the ishizuke (chap) which indicates use. The notable points are:

(i) Some fittings are longer than the norm: kabuto-gane (pommel) 47mm (norm 45mm); ishizuke (chape) 46mm (norm 41mm); fuchi (hilt collar) 18mm (norm 11–12mm).
(ii) Decoration of the fittings has more of a sculptured appearance than normal shin-guntō. The gap between sakura (cherry blossom) petals is also wider than normal giving a slightly distorted appearance. The overall effect leads one to conclude that it is not manufactured in Japan.
(iii) The author's example only has one menuki (hilt ornament) since that on the reverse was never fitted. The standard tape binding has sweat marks and is most definitely of wartime origin. The illustrated example has two menuki and a waxed tape binding.
(iv) An 'aoi'-shaped tsuba is used but is more rounded than usual and has four circular holes through it. The external rim and four sakura have been broken off the author's example to give a solid tsuba which matches the shape of the dai-seppa. It could be made in two separate sections, the outer being sweated or soldered to the inner at the four sakura, but this is uncertain.
(v) The brass dai-seppa (large washers) on each side of the tsuba are totally different in design from the normal shin-guntō equivalent shown in Plate 75. They also feature four heart-shaped (boar's eye) holes. Plate 323. Those on the author's sword show the remains of green paint similar to the scabbard, while those on the illustrated example are black.
(vi) The ashi (suspension mount) is a demountable hinged type (Fig. 11 (ii)) which has never been found singly before. The sakura at the top of the bands is wider and a slightly different appearance from the normal shin-guntō ashi. No reproduction of this mount has been reported and it would be expensive and pointless to reproduce when it would not (until 1986) be recognised as a scarce fitting.[7]
(vii) The blade is plated with a fake acid-etched yakiba (tempered edge) but is sharp and of substantial construction. Such blades have not been reported with normal shin-guntō before. The etching is different from that on parade sabres since the dividing line is extremely well-defined and can be felt in places with a fingernail.
(viii) There are two sets of machi (tang notches), the space between them being covered by the habaki (see Plate 324). This is normally a sign of a shortened blade, but there seems no reason for this when the blade is seemingly contemporary with the scabbard.
(ix) Tang rusting is light but is in keeping with a wartime dating.
(x) All seppa, dai-seppa, tsuba, habaki and blade tang are stamped with matching Western assembly numbers. That illustrated is '43' while the author's is '7'.

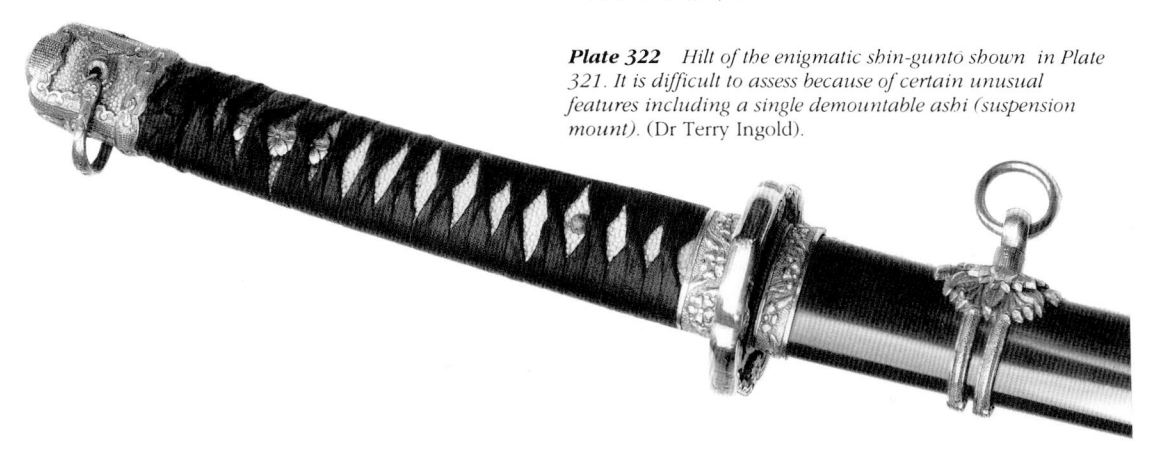

***Plate 322*** *Hilt of the enigmatic shin-guntō shown in Plate 321. It is difficult to assess because of certain unusual features including a single demountable ashi (suspension mount). (Dr Terry Ingold).*

# JAPANESE MILITARY AND CIVIL SWORDS AND DIRKS

To summarise, the demountable ashi appears to be a copy while the poorly formed sakura do not seem Japanese. The use of a plated blade could indicate post-war manufacture. It could also be argued that the number 7 example is earlier and uses an original grip, while that numbered 43 is post-war. However, the most likely explanation, given that they generally appear to be wartime, is that they were manufactured in an occupied country for an officer of a collaborating national force. Java is perhaps favourite since it had the largest standing force of this type under Japanese control.

**Plate 323** *Unusual dai-seppa and tsuba of the sword in Plates 321, 322. The tsuba (guard) is more rounded than that of a normal shin-guntō and has four circular holes. Strangely it appears to have been made of two separate sections. The dai-seppa (large washers) are of a most unusual shape and feature four heart-shaped (boar's eye) holes. Normal brass seppa (washers). All are stamped with matching assembly numbers, which in this case is '43'. (Dr Terry Ingold).*

**Plate 324** *Tang of the enigmatic shin-guntō shown in Plates 321 to 323. It has two peg holes although only secured by one. That in the author's collection only has one hole but is otherwise identical (except for the file nicks and numbering). (Dr Terry Ingold).*

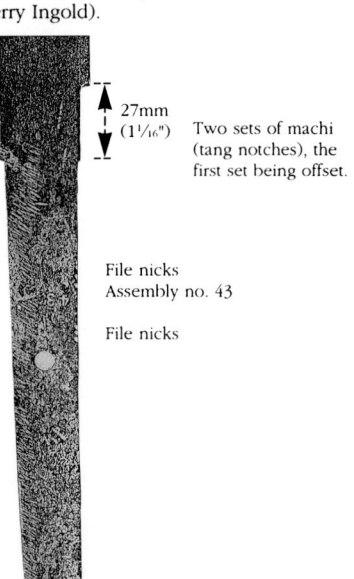

27mm (1¹/₁₆″) Two sets of machi (tang notches), the first set being offset.

File nicks
Assembly no. 43
File nicks

## Emergency issue swords

An 'emergency issue' sword is one that has been made in an occupied area for use by Japanese troops for promotion purposes or to replace lost, or damaged, swords when supplies from the homeland were no longer possible.

A field-made version of the 1935 pattern NCOs aluminium-hilted shin-guntō is known which has a crudely cast aluminium hilt and an officers-style field scabbard with a brown leather covering.[8] The one-piece steel blade of traditional shinogi-zukuri form appears to be locally made. The likelihood is that it is an 'emergency' item for a soldier promoted to NCO grade.

An example of a shin-guntō with locally made tsuba (guard) and reasonable quality hilt fittings of almost standard form has been found having a crudely scratched Japanese tang inscription which reads YAMAMURA TARŌ (the smith's or owner's name) and DAI NIHON GUNTŌ (great Japan Army sword).[9] Reference to Japan is only normally made on blades made outside of that country or for export. The last certainly does not apply. Unfortunately the hilt binding and scabbard are missing. In this instance the sword was obtained in Indonesia in the nineteen-eighties. Whether it was made by a bored Japanese soldier for his own pleasure (as is known to have happened) is unknown but the shin-guntō fittings and their quality seem to indicate 'emergency issue' for use by the Japanese.

Those with crude wooden, and rattan-bound, hilts and scabbards are probably native- or Australian troop-made souvenirs for sale to the unwary and unknowledgeable (see under 'Fakes'). Unfortunately there is no easy way to distinguish 'emergency' issue swords from those in other categories covered in this chapter.

## Reproduction military swords

It is a sad fact that reproduction military swords are now appearing in ever-increasing numbers. They range in quality from those with a very poor attention to detail with plain one-piece steel blades to those of good quality with plated blades. Some can be recognised by incorrect detailing, lacquered fittings, simulated samé, poor quality hilt binding, lack of wear and an apparent 'newness'. More experienced collectors may experience an 'incorrect feel' about the whole item.

Wear is a factor which must be considered, especially relating to hand sweat marks, rubbing on the base of the ishizuke (chape) where dragged on the ground and wear to the ashi (suspension mount) from swinging by the hanging ring. Check also for verdigris, wood shrinkage and tang rusting commensurate with a minimum age of fifty years, if genuine. A good Spanish-made replica shin-guntō was seen at an arms fair fitted with an original Company Officers sword knot to fool the collector. There are now reproduction brown leather Army sword belts and suspension straps available from Japan. Plaited and plain straps have been seen (Plate 300) but they usually lack a regain hook and are less substantial than originals. The collector is recommended to make up his own mind about the various factors to be considered, and not to buy if in doubt.

The following reproductions have been seen, either at arms fairs or in catalogues. They appear to originate, in the main, from Pakistan, India, Spain, Japan and Britain.

(i) Army Field Officers grade kyu-guntō. Correct design of fittings but the brass hilt has a 'lacquered' effect and the backstrap decoration is not so well defined as on originals. Smooth simulated samé grip of white, black or light orange colour. Machine-made grooved blade, similar to the NCOs shin-guntō without a yakiba and often heavily greased to deter close examination. Brass peg or screw securing the hilt to the tang.

(ii) Army Officers shin-guntō. Several types from poor to very good quality. Detailing of fittings varies as does the method and type of hilt binding. Shinogi-zukuri form blades often chromium-plated with an acid-etched yakiba. Tang markings, if any, are unknown. Condition is often mint with heavily gilded fittings. One type has a silvered scabbard with an end cap instead of a proper shin-guntō ishizuke (chape).

(iii) Army NCOs aluminium-hilted shin-guntō. Some are poorly detailed while others are excellent being almost indistinguishable from genuine examples. They even have arsenal stamps, although often not quite as clear as on originals. Those with Nagoya stamped blades have been found to have the numbering the wrong way up, i.e. reading parallel with the blade groove. Other identifying features are mint paintwork (sometimes deliberately chipped), unsharpened blades (sometimes sharpened with a file), no wear to the scabbard drag (shoe) paintwork and widely spaced blade numbering.

(iv) Poor quality Spanish-made replicas of various patterns are often seen in Spanish souvenir shops but are of a quality which should fool nobody. They include naval dirks with rough black leather scabbards and silvered fittings.

A Japanese company in Tokyo advertises civilian and military swords but does not appear to state they are reproductions, which some obviously are. Their 1987 catalogue illustrated kai-guntō, shin-guntō, Army and naval parade sabres, naval dirks with either leather of shagreen scabbards and three sword belts (see Plate 325). All brass fittings are heavily gilded and very bright.

Also offered for sale by this company are new naval kyu-guntō pattern sword knots plus Army shin-guntō knots for both Company and Field grades. There is also a General Officers grade knot which, for some unknown reason, has lightish brown and yellow straps and tassels. This is a totally different colour scheme to the original shin-guntō version. These modern knots are of the

# JAPANESE MILITARY AND CIVIL SWORDS AND DIRKS

same material and weave as originals but the straps seem to be thicker with a 'padded' feel to them. The naval kyu-guntō knot barrel has a larger zigzag pattern than an original plus very stiff metallic cords. Even in 1987 the advertised prices for such reproductions were considerably more than genuine examples of such swords in Western countries.

See also 'Shin-guntō with naval characteristics' earlier in this book.

Kai-guntō with stainless steel blades and utilising some genuine surplus parts obtained from Japan have been reported. They may be artificially aged or distressed by deliberately 'smoking' the hilt, fraying the binding or marking the scabbard. Whether 'fake' or 'reproduction' depends upon the degree of original fittings used.

**Plate 325** *Reproduction military swords, belts and knots shown in a Japanese catalogue dated 1987. Item 823 is described as a General Officers knot but is not the same colouring as the World War Two type (see text for details). The belts from top to bottom are Defence Agency (for current use), World War Two, Naval, and Army Officers of Company grade.*

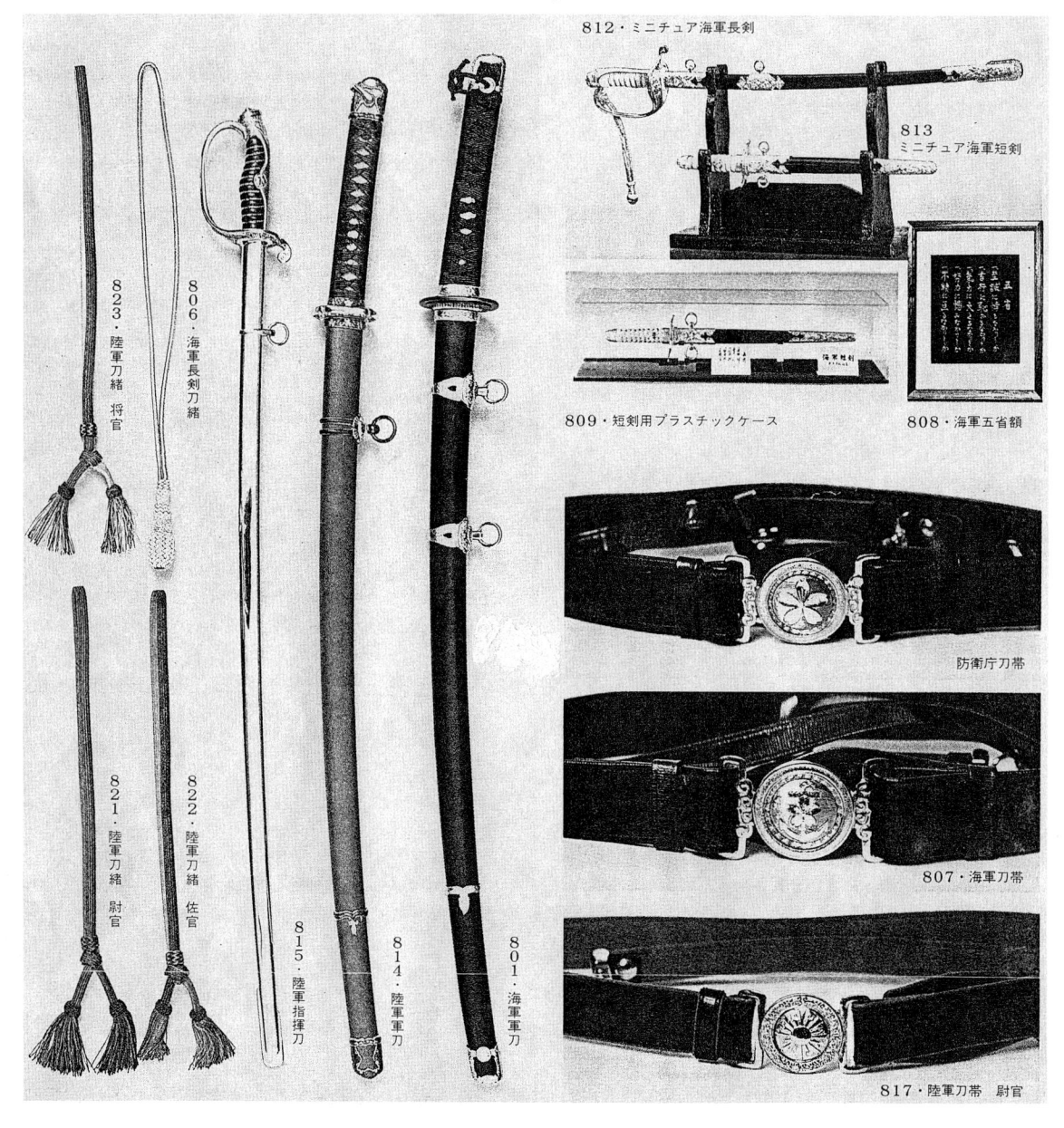

## Fake swords

A 'fake' is an item made to deceive, while a 'reproduction' is a copy but, unfortunately, many of the latter are sold as genuine, thus becoming fakes.

The so-called naval NCOs kai-guntō in Plate 326 is believed to be a fake since it is of a type which is not seen in wartime photographs or Japanese documentation either for their own or collaboration use. Another type is a military-style sword having mounts based on old tachi or katana but which are not of a quality or type which may be regarded as Japanese. Often they may be made of silver and of a quality too good for the remainder of the sword. Plate 327 shows just such an example.

It is known that enterprising Australian troops made fake 'samurai swords' for sale to souvenir-hungry GIs, but they would not be recognisable as pure shin- or kai-guntō. Apparently the tangs could have spurious Japanese characters engraved on them. Presumably the fittings were crude but they could be mistaken for 'emergency' or 'collaboration' swords (although there was then no distinction between the two). Possibly those with crude wooden rattan-bound hilts and/or scabbards could come from this source if they were not native-made. Certainly by 1946 Indian blacksmiths were making Japanese swords out of old car springs and selling them to Allied military personnel who would pay high prices for such 'souvenirs'.[9] Spanish souvenir shops are currently selling a range of poor quality military swords with silvered fittings which include patterns which never existed such as a naval kyu-guntō decorated in the manner of an Army Field Officers kyu-guntō.

Counterfeit signature gendaitō, especially those with signatures of Yasukuni Shrine smiths, have been reported in America. They are evidently produced surreptitiously in Japan and exported abroad where they are sold in full polish mounted in shira-saya. No doubt some will become available in original shin-guntō mounts to complete the deception. The buyers of such items, which can fetch high prices, are advised to seek a second opinion before purchase.

Spurious signatures were added to genuine unsigned Shōwa period blades obtained from China.

There can be no definite guidelines to identify reproduction or fake swords other than a regard for age, indications of 'non-Japanese manufacture' and an intuitive 'feel' that something is wrong.

**Plate 326** *A kai-guntō type often erroneously described as a late naval NCOs sword. Plain brass hilt and scabbard mounts pinned in position. Golden brown cotton tape hilt binding over narrow pieces of white samé. Thin blue-black leather scabbard covering. Crude tsuba (guard) and dai-seppa (large washer) cast integrally. Poor quality one-piece blade with a rounded back edge. An inferior, poorly made item. Probably an Indian or Far Eastern attempt at a naval kai-guntō. They are fairly common and seem to be immediately post-war period, probably sold to returning servicemen as the genuine article.* (Richard Fuller).

**Plate 327** *An example of a 'fake' Japanese sword made to imitate a traditional katana which has been mounted for military use. Engraved solid silver mounts and a blackened steel tsuba with poor quality engraving of sakura and leaves. The blade is made from a single piece of steel and the black lacquered wooden scabbard is of inferior quality. Note also the incorrect proportions of the hilt. Probably made in India, or the Far East, not long after the war ended.* (Brenton Williams).

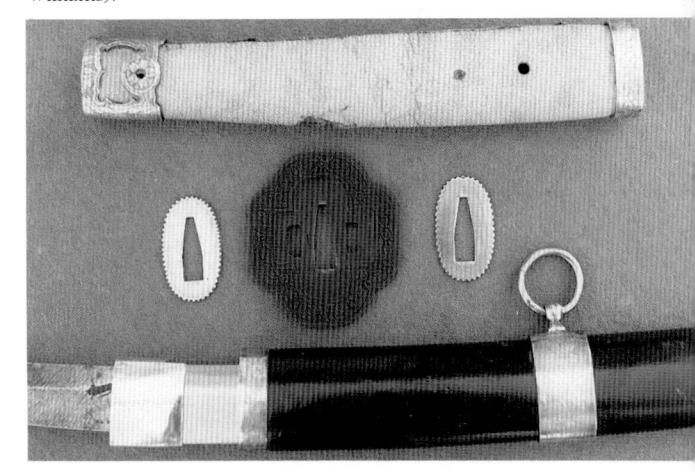

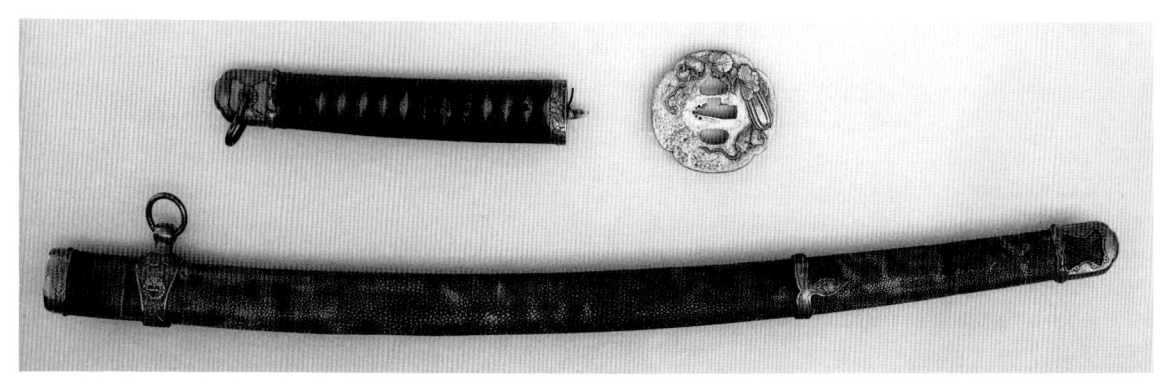

JAPANESE MILITARY AND CIVIL SWORDS AND DIRKS

*Plate 328  Shin-guntō with silvered military and civilian mounts. (Richard Fuller).*

## Shin-guntō with silvered mounts

A shin-guntō with a mixture of military and civilian fittings is shown in Plates 328, 329. The original regulation pattern shin-guntō hilt has silvered brass fittings. A large, heavy, silvered, cast brass tsuba is decorated with a melon and leaves in relief on one side and two leaves and tendrils on the other. There are faint Japanese characters near the tang hole. Blackened samé scabbard of poor quality utilising an original silvered brass ishizuke (chape). All other fittings are specially made of silvered metal. The kuchi-gane (throat) is decorated with raised chrysanthemum blooms but the mouth, which was separate, is missing. A single ashi (suspension mount) is similarly decorated but has the raised mon (family badge) of the Shibata family on both sides. Both are well detailed. The (shibabiki strengthening band) is in the form of a leaf. Both the ashi and shibabiki are a loose fit. These mounts were obtained without a blade. It is uncertain if this is a post-war scabbard made to be of a higher quality than normal or was actually made to the special order of a wealthy officer, although the former is suspected. Perhaps 'silvered' military fittings should be viewed with suspicion.

1 This section has, in general, been summarised from *The Armed Forces of WWII* by Andrew Mollow (see Bibliography).
2 There is no published information on Chinese Imperial, Republican and Nationalist military swords and dirks although some can be confused with Japanese weapons and were actually made in Japan. Research is ongoing into the preparation of a book tentatively called *Chinese Military Swords and Dirks (of the twentieth century)* which will, hopefully, show some such items. The author, Richard Fuller, would welcome any information and photographs for possible inclusion.
3 Known as 'Giyugun' (Volunteer Force) by the Japanese.
4 This has been confirmed by one-piece blades bearing the tang inscription SUMARAN (Semarang) and SHIYAWA-TŌ (Java sword). It is always written in 'katakana' script which is a Japanese syllabary used to write foreign words and is quite different from the normal Japanese kanji. A shin-guntō with such a blade and green metal scabbard is known. The standard mounts are of average quality but not Japanese-made. The kabuto-gane (pommel) is rather large. Nickel-plated habaki (blade collar) and seppa (hilt washers). Yellowish-white leather hilt covering under a normal tape binding. Maroon and blue tassels (Donald Barnes collection).
5 The authors are indebted to Jaap Platenga who supplied this information after interviewing a former Colonel of the Java Defence Army. Unfortunately the Colonel distrusted Europeans and was loath to provide further details.
6 The stamp appears to be a stylised version of 造 set in a circle, but this is not certain. This reads TSUKURU, meaning 'made' or 'construction', and is probably an inspection stamp.
7 The variations and scarcity of this mount were generally unrecorded and unknown until the publication of *Military Swords of Japan 1868–1945* by the authors in 1986.
8 Illustrated in Plate 51 (right) of *Military Swords of Japan 1868–1945* (see Bibliography).
9 Jaap Platenga collection.
9 *Monsoon Victory* by G. Hanley, 1946, also says Indian tradesmen could not resist the chance of money-making from a willing (if duped) market.

*Plate 329  The silvered metal kuchi-gane (throat) and ashi (suspension mount) of the shin-guntō in Plate 328. The raised 'wisteria and ichi' mon of the Shibata family is evident on the ashi band. The boss and sakura are standard shin-guntō*

# Miscellaneous Edged Weapons

During the preparation of this book certain unusual weapons have been located which do not fit into the various sections used, although they are associated. They have, therefore, been included in this chapter.

## Combination sword and pistol

A rare 'combination' weapon of a Nambu pistol (dated to September 1944) and a 610mm (24") sword blade of shinogi-zukuri form is known in America. The blade (signed Kanehisa and said to be c.1368) has a normal brass habaki, but the tang has been fixed to a Nambu pistol on the right side between the wooden grip and magazine housing so that the barrel is at forty-five degrees to the blade. The tang signature cannot be seen without removing the pistol grip so a copper plate bearing a copy of the characters has been mounted on the lower right grip. A normal shin-guntō metal scabbard is utilised. The balance of the sword, although lacking the normal hilt, is said to be good. Both the sword and the pistol can therefore be used by the same hand.

This appears to be a genuine wartime item made to the special order of an officer who obviously was a fighting man. Another such item is reported to be in the Military Weapons Museum in Aberdeen, Maryland, America. Obviously this was not a common practice.

## Unidentified dirk

This dirk is shown in Plates 330–333. The brass-mounted white samé-covered hilt is fitted with a kashira (pommel) and fuchi (hilt collar) decorated ensuite with open chrysanthemum blossoms and leaves. There is a small brass tsuba (guard). The gold mekugi (hilt ornaments) consist of a curled dragon on the obverse and a plain disc on the reverse. They surmount male and female screws which pass through the blade tang. Silvered metal scabbard engraved on both sides with a dragon. Brass locket and chape engraved ensuite with the hilt fittings. Opposing brass hanging rings.

Straight, lozenge section blade engraved on both sides with bonji (religious symbols). It may, in fact, be the tip of a 'yari' (pole arm) blade. The wooden scabbard liner has apparently been cut to receive a grooved blade, so the one fitted could be a replacement. Double copper habaki (blade collar). This item appears to be nineteenth century but the blade seems to be older.

Forestry Officials dirks are the only known patterns to have plain raised suspension bands together with 'boar's eye' (heart-shaped) scabbard mount recesses. However, all known variants have hilt backstraps. A tsuba is unknown on any form of naval or governmental dirk.

The dirk as a whole suggests that it was made for presentation purposes, but use at court by a member of the Imperial Household cannot be ruled out.

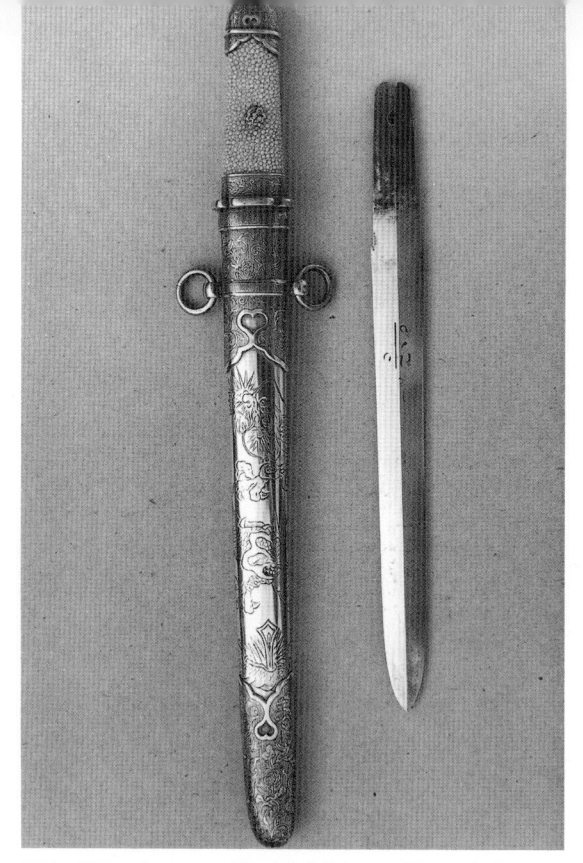

**Plate 330**  Ornate unidentified dirk, possibly made for presentation purposes. (Brenton Williams).

**Plate 331**  Obverse of the ornate dirk in Plate 330 showing the assembled blade with the double copper habaki (blade collar) (Brenton Williams).

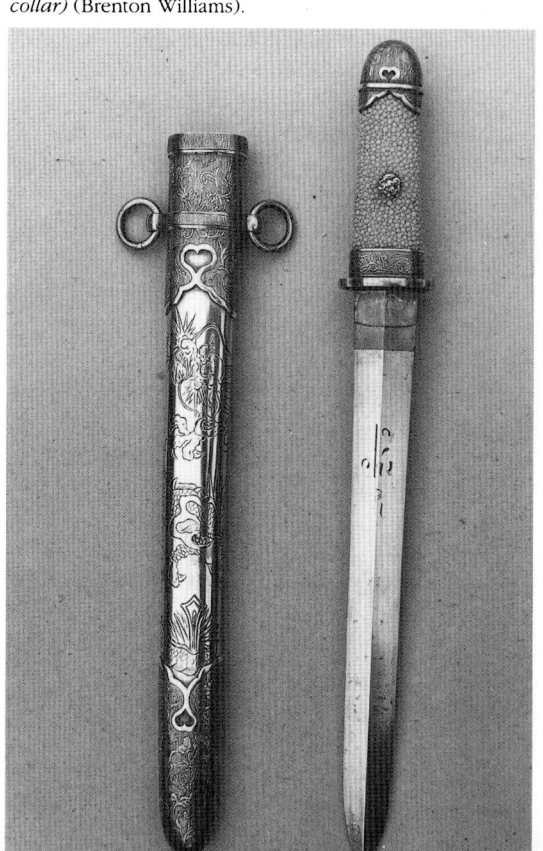

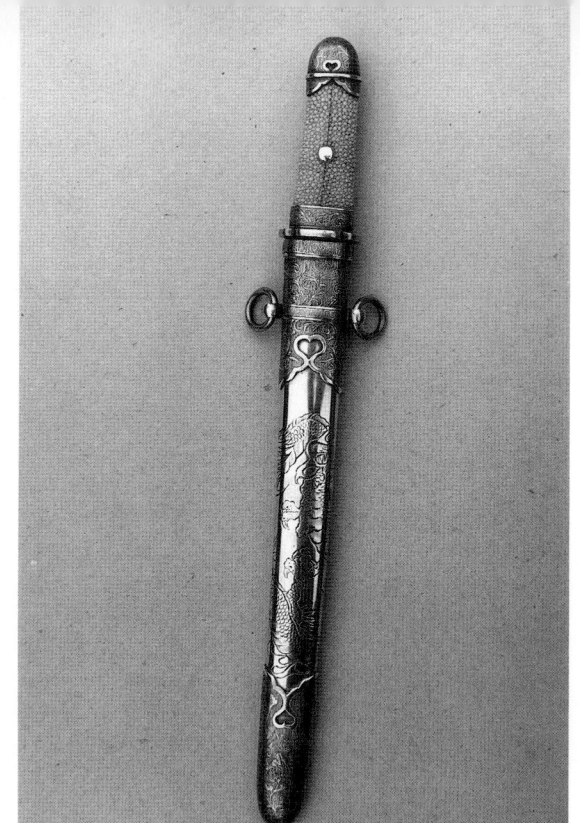

**Plate 332**  Reverse of the ornate dirk in Plate 330. (Brenton Williams).

**Plate 333**  Close-up of the hilt and top scabbard locket of the ornate dirk in Plate 330. The brass fittings appear to be hand-engraved. The gold curled dragon menuki is in the centre of the grip. (Brenton Williams).

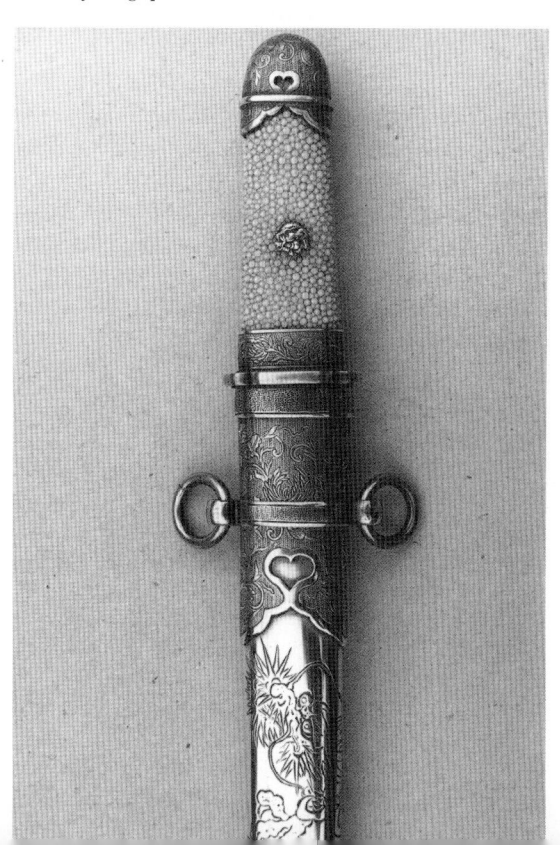

## Shōwa period boys' dirk

A military-style dirk[1] thought to have been carried by a child is shown in Plates 334, 335. Use was probably restricted to pageants or festivals when boys were dressed in replica military uniforms. Photographs of children with edged weapons are usually indistinct, thus preventing proper identification.

The quality of manufacture is inferior to those used by the military and civil organisations. Indeed it could be taken for Chinese except for the hilt sakura (cherry blossom) which indicates Japanese usage. Hilt and scabbard fittings are thin pressed brass profusely decorated with flowers and leaves. The wide black plastic grip has a brass wire binding and a sakura menuki (hilt ornament). Black lacquered scabbard decorated ensuite with the hilt fittings. Narrow straight blade of poor quality.

Overall length of dirk and scabbard 387mm (15¼"). Hilt length 89mm (3½"). Blade length 210mm (8¼"). Weight three ounces.

The lack of hanging rings indicates it was either carried in a frog or thrust through a belt.

1 The authors wish to thank Martin Hirons for bringing this item to their attention.

**Plate 334**  *Dirk thought to have been carried by a boy when dressed in military-style uniform during pageants in the nineteen-forties.* (Martin Hirons).

**Plate 335**  *Hilt and top scabbard mount of a boys' dirk.* (Martin Hirons).

## Miniature shin-guntō

An unusual miniature sword, shown in Plates 336, 337, which appears to be a two-hanger shin-guntō. The menuki (hilt ornaments), tsuba shape and two ashi (suspension mounts) emulate the shin-guntō while the kabutogane (pommel) is more like that of a kai-guntō. The shibabiki (strengthening band) is reminiscent of a shin-guntō but the ishizuke (chape) is non-military. The scabbard is black Bakelite, as are the habaki (blade collar) and hilt which are moulded as one item. Letter-opener quality steel blade.

Overall length of hilt and scabbard 161mm (6⁵⁄₁₆"). Hilt length 49mm (1¹⁵⁄₁₆"). Blade length (to habaki) 80mm (3⅛").

Dating is believed to be World War Two or before. Since the detailing of components is somewhat mixed, it appears to be just a letter opener and not a manufacturer's sample. Miniature Japanese swords in the style of katana or tachi are relatively common, but those representing military swords appear to be very rare.

# JAPANESE MILITARY AND CIVIL SWORDS AND DIRKS

**Plates 336, 337**  *Miniature shin-guntō-style sword.* (Richard Fuller)

## Japanese-made sword for Australian military use

Plates 338–340 show a typical British-style export cavalry sword for mounted and dress use. Steel mounts, black shagreen grip and brown leather service knot. The steel scabbard has an upper suspension band fitted with two opposing hanging rings and a lower band with a single hanging ring. The inside of the guard is stamped D ↑ D indicating issue by the Australian Defence Department.

The feature which makes this sword most unusual is a Japanese inscription stamped on the outside of the guard under the quillion. It reads DAI NIHON SEI, i.e. manufactured in Great Japan. Larry Johnson, in his book *Japanese Bayonets* (see Bibliography), says the Japanese began to manufacture arms for export 'in 1892 when the Tokyo Arsenal made 1,000 small arms and 100 sabres for the Military Department of the City of Melbourne, Australia.' Possibly this weapon is from that batch

**Plate 338**  *Steel hilt of a British-style cavalry sword manufactured in Japan for Australian use.* (Donald Barnes).

MISCELLANEOUS EDGED WEAPONS

since no report of repeat orders has been seen by the authors.

Overall length of sword and scabbard 1,000mm (39 3/8"). Hilt length 141mm (5 9/16"). Blade length 825mm (32½"). Scabbard length 859mm (33 7/16").

Another such sword is known (see Fig. 75) but it has a chromium-plated blade and hilt. A brown leather field scabbard is used, but unlike British swords, has two thickened sections near the base. The presence of the D↑D stamp was not reported. It seems likely this is the Officers version. (Fig. 75.).

**Plate 339** *Japanese inscription meaning 'manufactured in Great Japan' on a British-style Cavalry sword used by the Australian Army.* (Donald Barnes).

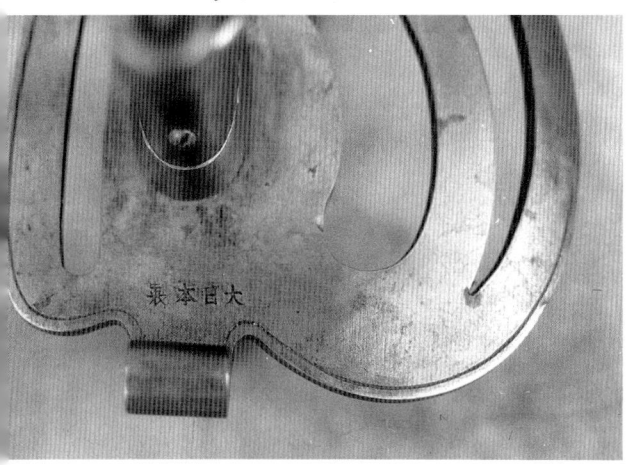

**Plate 340** *Australian Defence Department markings on a Japanese-made British-style Cavalry sword.* (Donald Barnes).

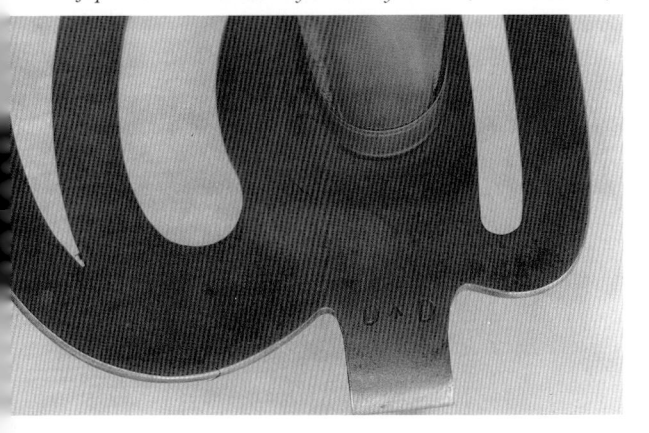

**Fig. 75** *Japanese-made Cavalry sword for Australian use, c.1892. This is believed to be the Officers version.*

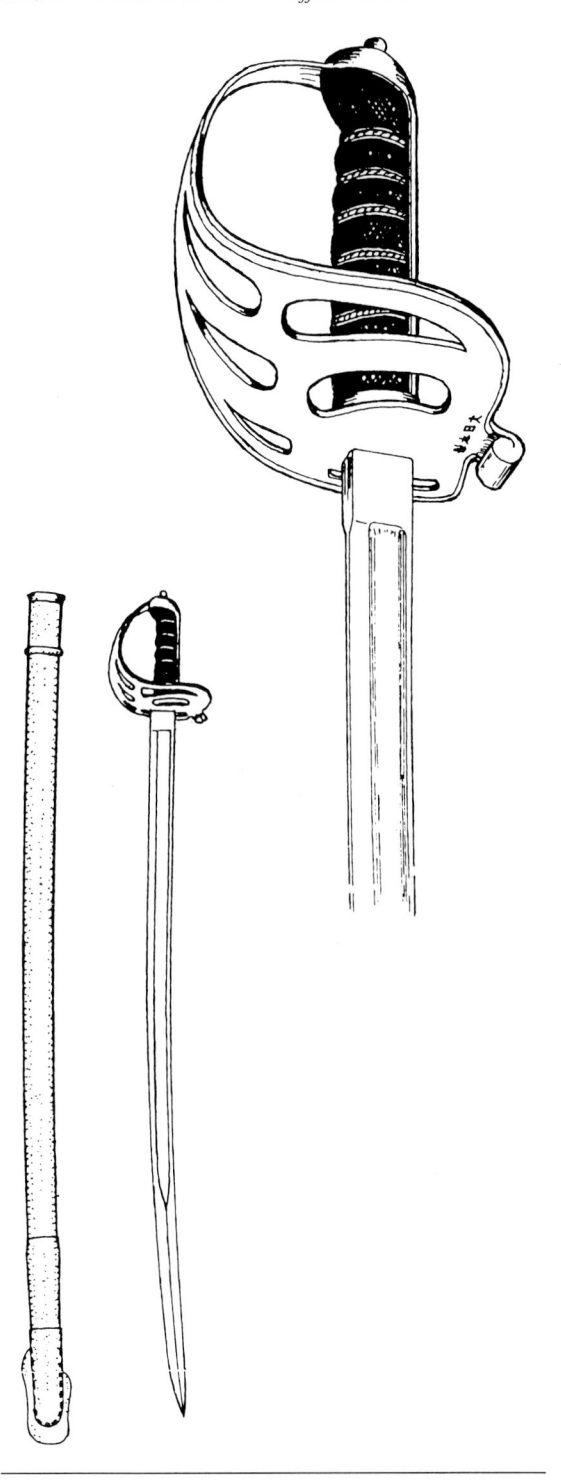

# Hints for Collectors

The collector is advised to consider the following general advice before buying a Japanese military sword.

(1) Ascertain the sword pattern is as advertised. Auction houses often briefly describe, or fail to properly identify, the model or pattern.

(2) Hilt fittings should be fairly tight, though the wood base does shrink over the years and allows some movement. An old tsuba may have been removed and replaced by a military example, so check for wear marks, verdigris, correct grading of seppa and matching assembly numbers.

(3) Check that the hilt-securing hole matches that on the tang if the peg is missing, by using a matchstick or holding the sword up to the light if necessary. If the holes do not match, the blade has been switched. An enlarged hilt peg hole may also indicate that this has occurred.

(4) Check the fittings. Tsuba should be correct for method of retaining the sword in the scabbard, e.g. a push-fit type does not normally have a slot for spring clip retention, although there are genuine exceptions. Similarly, a push-button spring clip is not found with a field scabbard unless a metal throat is provided with a slot.

(5) Check for Shōwa period blades by looking for the blunted cutting edge adjacent to the habaki.

(6) Compare the blade length against the scabbard. An old wakizashi blade (i.e. short) may be found in a much longer scabbard. Shōwa period blades should match to within 100–125mm (4"–5"). Blades should not rattle but should fit fairly tightly in the scabbard, although wood shrinkage and wear occurs.

(7) Count the number of peg holes on a tang if it is a Shōwa period blade. More than one could indicate that it has been switched. A new hole drilled to line up with that in the hilt may be artificially aged.

(8) Check a tang signature before buying if possible. The claim that 'it is a signed blade' is no guarantee of quality, age or even a genuine inscription.

(9) Check all blade tangs for abnormal file marks above a signature, indicating the removal of a military inspection/arsenal stamp.

(10) Acceptance of blade quality is a matter for the individual. Red stains are rust, not blood, as is sometimes claimed. Even the smallest fault or stress mark can devalue a good blade. Remember that military officers were not as condescending as modern experts and often took older blades, which had faults, to war.

(11) Check a shin-guntō grooved blade for signs of file marks near the habaki which indicates

that the numbers of a NCOs sword have been removed, thus confirming a switched blade.

(12) Ensure the blade and scabbard numbers match on Army NCOs and Cavalry Troopers swords.

(13) Beware undocumented claims that, for example, a sword comes from the Imperial Guard. Military swords have no divisional or regimental markings.

(14) Surrender/transportation tags with Japanese calligraphy often contain the owner's name, rank and unit. As they can easily be exchanged, it is a buyer's risk when accepting any claim about origin.

(15) Check that the overall condition is commensurate for age and military service. Look for wear to the scabbard drag, worn scabbard paintwork from hand sweat, worn suspension mount boss from continuous swinging when carried, dirty or greasy hilt binding and verdigris on fittings.

(16) Carefully check a 'mint' sword or fittings since it could be a 'whole' or 'parts' reproduction.

(17) Do not touch a naked blade with the fingers since even small sweat marks cause rusting.

(18) Do not grease blades. Scabbard debris adheres to the surface and may cause rusting.

(19) Never clean a blade with an abrasive material or wadding which can cause scratching to the mirror-like polish. Always use an approved blade-cleaning kit containing 'uchiko' powder.

(20) Japanese workmanship and attention to detail, even on issue swords, is good. Check for visible file marks on fittings, poorly defined decorative detailing or a sloppy fit which might indicate non-Japanese manufacture.

(21) Consider your own intuitive feelings. If in doubt, exercise extreme caution or don't buy!

(22) A blade tang is meant to be rusted and it acts as an indication of age. Do not clean off, or polish up, since this will devalue a blade even if the signature remains. As a general guide: uniformly black = Kōtō period; uniformly dark brown = Shintō period; light brown (perhaps with unrusted areas) = Meiji-Shōwa periods.

(23) If you wish to get a blade repolished go to a competent skilled person who has been recommended by other collectors for whom he has done work. Always ascertain the price first. It may be uneconomic to have a Shōwa period military blade repolished when compared to the current valuation of the whole sword.

# Bibliography

*A Photographic Record of the Russo–Japanese War* (P. F. Collier & Son, New York, 1905).

Bergamini, David, *Japan's Imperial Conspiracy* (Heinemann, London, 1971).

Bird, Craig A., 'The State of the Art. Contemporary Japanese Swordsmiths', Japanese Sword Society of the United States Newsletter, vol. 18 no. 4, 1986.

Cox, Malcolm E., 'Further explanation of Gendaitō/Showatō', To-ken Society of Great Britain Programme 156, 1992.

Creswell, Lt-Col H. T.; Hiraoka, Major J.; Namba, Major R., *A Dictionary of Military Terms* (The University of Chicago Press, 1942).

Dawson, Jim, *Swords of Imperial Japan 1868–1945* (Stenger-Scott Publishing Company, Georgia, U.S.A. 1996)

Decker, *Return of the Black Ships* (Vantage, 1978).

Derby, Harry L., *Hand Cannons of Japan* (Derby Publishing Co., USA, 1981).

*Die Japanische Armee in Iher Gengenwatigen Uniformierung* (published by Moritz Ruhl, Leipzig, Germany, 1910). German text.

Doron, Frank, *The Sino–Japanese War* (Macmillan Publishing, 1974).

Etsuko Yagyu, *The Changes of the Landing Forces Uniforms*. Japanese text.

Frenzel, Arnold, 'Gendaitō', Japanese Sword Society of the United States Newsletter, vol. 20 nos. 4, 6.

Fujishiro Okisato (translated by Leon Kapp), 'Yasukuni Shrine and the Tanren-kai', To-ken Society of Great Britain Programme 134, 1987.

Fuller, Richard, *A Dictionary of Japanese Sword Terms*, To-ken Society of Great Britain.

Fuller, Richard, *Shōkan: Hirohito's Samurai, Leaders of the Japanese Armed Forces* (Arms & Armour Press, London, 1992).

Fuller, Richard; Gregory, Ron, *The Oshigata Book* (Limited edition, privately printed, England, 1985).

Fuller, Richard; Gregory, Ron, *Military Swords of Japan 1868–1945* (Arms & Armour Press, England, 1986).

Fuller, Richard; Gregory, Ron, *Swordsmiths of Japan 1926–1945* (privately printed, limited edition, England, 1983).

Gregory, Ron, *Japanese Military Swords* (limited edition, privately printed, England, 1971).

Han Bing Siong, 'Japanese Zwaarden in

Nederlands Bezit', Nederlandse Tō-ken Vereniging. Dutch text.

Han Bing Siong, 'The enigma of stamps on contemporary Japanese swords (revisiting the premises necessary)', To-ken Society of Great Britain Programme 157, 1992.

Han Bing Siong, 'The Japanese and their swords', To-ken society of Great Britain Programme 101, 1978.

Han Bing Siong, 'The significance of the Yasukuni Shrine for the contemporary sword history', Parts I–IV, To-ken Society of Great Britain Programmes 141–145, 1989–90.

Han Bing Siong, 'Yasunori', To-ken Society of Great Britain Programme 91, 1976.

Han Bing Siong, A future (untitled) article on the origin of the shin-guntō.

Harries, Meirion and Susie, *Soldiers of the Sun. The Rise and Fall of the Imperial Japanese Army 1868–1945* (Heinemann, London, 1991).

Hawley, W. M., *Japanese Swordsmiths Revised* (privately published, California, 1981).

Hawley, W. M.; Kei Kaneda Chappelar, *Mon (The Japanese Family Crest)* (privately published, America).

Honeycutt, Jr, Fred L., editor and publisher of the reprint of *Taihei Kumiai – Catalog A, Rifles, Machine Guns & Others* (originally published in Tokyo, c.1935).

Honeycutt Jr, Fred L.; Anthony, F., *Military Rifles of Japan* (Julin Books, America, 1977 & 1983).

Hsu Long-hsuen; Chang Ming-kai, *History of the Sino–Japanese War 1937–1945* (Taiwan, 1971).

*Imperial Japanese Daggers 1883–1945*. Compiler unknown. America.

Johnson, Larry, *The Japanese Bayonet* (Cedar Ridge Press, Broken Arrow, Oklahoma, 1988).

Kanzan Satō, *The Japanese Sword* (Kodansha International Ltd, and Shibuno, New York, 1983).

Kapp. Leon and Hiroko; Yoshindo Yoshihara, *The Craft of the Japanese Sword* (Kodansha International, Tokyo and New York, 1987).

MacCarthy, Aidan, *A Doctor's War* (Robson Books, 1979).

May, Commander W. E.; Annis, P. G. W., *Swords for Sea Service,* two volumes (HMSO London, 1970).

Mollo, Andrew, *The Armed Forces of WWII* (Orbis Publishing Ltd, London, 1981).

Nagatsuka, R., *I was a Kamikaze* (New English Library, London, 1974).

Okochi, Tsunehira, *Teikoku Rikukaigun Guntō Monotagatari*. Japanese text.

Ono, Tadashi, *Gendai Tōkō Meikan*. Japanese text.

Ōta Rinichirō, *Nippon no Gunpuku (Japanese Military Uniforms – from Bakumatsu until today)* (National Literature Publication Society, Japan). Japanese text.

Peterson, James W., *Orders & Medals of Japan and Associated States* (The Orders and Medals Society of America, 1967).

Ritta Nakanishi, *Japanese Military Uniforms 1930–1945* (Dai Nihon Kaiga Co. Ltd, Tokyo, 1991). Japanese text with English captions.

Sasama (Yoshihiko), Yuzankaku, *Nippon no Gunso (Japanese Military Uniforms and War Attires throughout the centuries)*, vol. 2 (Tokyo, 1970). Japanese text.

Self, James; Nobuko Hirose, *Japanese Art Signatures* (Bamboo Publishing Ltd, London, 1987).

# JAPANESE MILITARY AND CIVIL SWORDS AND DIRKS

Tadao Nakata, *Imperial Japanese Army and Navy Uniforms & Equipments* (Arms & Armour Press, London, 1975). Japanese text with English supplement.

Terraine, John, *The Life and Times of Lord Mountbatten* (London, 1968).

*The Russo–Japanese War Fully Illustrated*, vol. 1, April 1904; vol. 2 June 1904 (Kinkodo Publishing Co., Tokyo, 1904).

Trotter, George, *Japanese Swords and Fittings in the Western Australia Museum* (Western Australia Museum, Perth, 1988).

Wilkinson-Latham, Robert, *Swords in Colour, including other Edged Weapons* (Blandford Press, Dorset, England, 1977).

Wilkinson-Latham, R.J., *Pictorial History of Swords and Bayonets* (Ian Allan Ltd, England, 1973).

Wilson, H. W., *Japan's Fight for Freedom (the Russo–Japanese War)* three volumes (London, 1904–5).

Woodward, David, *Armies of the World 1854–1914* (Sidgwick & Jackson, London, 1978).

Yumoto, John, *The Samurai Sword* (Tuttle, America, 1958).

# Japanese Sword Societies

(Some produce a monthly or bi-monthly newsletter for members)

Banzai
(The bulletin for the collector of Japanese militaria),
4001 Windemere Drive,
Tuscaloosa,
Alabama,
35405
USA

De Nedelandse Token Vereniging
(The Netherlands Token Society),
Ocarinalaan 556,
2287 Sj Rijswijk,
Netherlands

Florida Token Kai
17120 Gulf Boulevard,
N. Redington Beach,
Florida,
33708
USA

The Northern California Japanese Sword Club,
PO Box 1397,
Lafayette,
California,
94549
USA

The Southern California Japanese Sword Society,
1039 Katella,
Laguna Beach,
California,
92651
USA

The Japanese Sword Society of Canada,
RR#1
Mindemoya,
Ontario,
POP ISO
Canada

The Japanese Sword Society of Australia,
Box 2108
North Parramatta,
New South Wales,
2151
Australia

The Japanese Sword Society of the United States,
PO Box 712,
Breckenridge,
Texas,
76424
USA

To-ken Society of Great Britain,
340 Hurst Road,
Bexley,
Kent,
DA5 3LA
England

Northern To-ken Society (UK),
The Manse,
Trelogan,
Near Holywell,
Clwyd,
CH8 9BY
Wales

Sacramento Japanese Sword Club,
7680 Howerton Drive
Sacramento,
California,
95831–4105
USA

Metropolitan New York Japanese Sword Club,
Box 1119,
Rockefeller Center Station,
New York,
NY 10185
USA

# Index

Admirals (Flag Officers): Akinaga 130, Hasegawa 116, 117, Kamada 117, Kamimura 114, Koizumi 126, Kusaka 212, Miwa 107, Toyada 107, Ugaki 211, 212, Yamada 117, Yamamoto 210, 211, 249
  See Fleet Admirals
Admiral's dirk: 182
Admiral's swords: 114, 121, 122
anchors: 111, 123, 124, 125, 132, 133, 134
Army airborne, airforce:
  dirks 101
  insignia 103
  swords 103–106
Army, contemporary photographs:
  groups, 20, 23, 26, 33, 41, 56, 57, 91, 73, 81, 89, 96, 98, 107, 116, 117, 237, 251
  single, 2, 3, 28, 33, 34, 43, 48, 55, 64, 72, 73, 74, 76, 91, 96, 116, 157, 159, 237, 250
Army dirks: 101, 102
Army swords: (see Artillery, Cavalry, Kyu-guntō, shin-guntō)
  enlisted, NCOs 27, 78, 90, 91
  officers 19, 21–23, 78, 81, 82
arsenals: 26, 37, 61, 84, 85, 86, 90, 91, 119, 128, 130, 138, 147, 213, 219, 220, 225, 226, 227, 228, 231
Artillery swords: 19, 20, 24–26
Australian sword: 276, 277

badges, civil and colonial: 165, 170, 172, 175, 176, 177, 182, 186, 187, 194, 198, 199, 206
bamboo flower: 198, 199
blade refurbishment units: 221

blades:
  type and shapes: 31, 36, 49, 62, 79, 82, 86, 90, 109, 111, 114, 117, 119, 128, 132, 133, 154, 158, 160, 163, 170, 171, 188, 190, 192, 202, 203, 204, 214, 221, 265
  manufacture: 213–232
  prison: 221
boar's eye scabbard recesses: 120, 139, 140, 173, 178, 180, 195, 273
Borneo: 50
Boxer Rebellion: 18
Brauchitsch, Feldmarschall: 210
British Royal Navy: 110, 117
Burma: 12, 210, 253, 259, 260, 261, 263

Cavalry swords:
  NCOs, Troopers, 19, 20, 45, 46–48, 231
  Officers, 45, 49–53, 54, 58
Central China Railway: 92
cherry blossoms: see kadosakura, sakura
China: 11, 92, 93, 126, 168, 221, 225, 246, 248, 263
Chinese military swords: 49, 77, 89, 169, 185, 200, 201
chrysanthemum: see kiku
collaborating forces: 263–266
collaboration swords: 264–266
collecting: 278, 279
combat covers: 31, 48, 56, 57, 63, 64, 67, 68, 107, 128
contemporary photographs (see army, naval, surrender), civil: 93, 163, 171, 201, 223

court swords:
　civil 205, 206, 207
　military 21
cutlass, naval: 109, 110, 131

dates:
　nengo (reign eras) 16
　type 46, 47, 53, 54, 91
diplomatic corps swords: 161–163
dirks (see presentation, tanto)
　army: 101, 102
　boys: 275
　civil: 150, 158, 164–166, 168–170, 174–176, 178–180, 182, 183, 187, 189, 191, 192, 194–197, 198, 199, 208
　kaiten: 107
　kamikaze: 102, 104, 106–108
　naval candidates: 149–152
　naval midshipman: 144, 146
　naval officers: 144–152, 211
　naval petty officers: 144, 145
　naval prison governors: 140
　unidentified: 150, 208, 273, 274

Echizen shop: 164, 167, 231
edged weapons, miscellaneous: 273–277
emergency issue swords: 268
engineers swords: 20, 25
Etajima: 149, 152

fake swords: 271
Field Marshals: Hafa 153, Oyama 155, Terauchi 154
Field Marshal's swords (gensui-tō), 41, 153–155
Fire Bureau badges: 186
Fire Bureau dirks: 191, 194–197
flag officers: see admirals
Fleet Admirals: Togo 154, Yamamoto 155
Forestry officials dirks: 178–180
Formosa dirks: 164–166
　swords: 166, 167
foul weather hilt covers: leather 31, 56, 57, 67, 70, 72, 73
　linen bandage 31, 56, 70, 89
France: 45

gendaitō: 62, 216, 217, 220, 222, 223, 231, 232

Generals, Army: Akita 248, Araki 64, Ayabe 251, Baba 50, Itagaki 251, Kando 257, Kodama 43, Matsudo 116, Matsui 116, 117, Makata (Magata) 255, Nishi 33, Numata 261, Okasaki 96, Saito 257, Takehara 250, Testima 33, Yamashita 210, Yashida 101
General's swords: 21, 22, 30, 35, 37, 45
gensui-tō: (see Field Marshal's swords)
Göring, Reichsmarschall Hermann: 210, 212
Government-Generals Departments: see Formosa, Korea, Kwantung Leased Territories, Mandated Territories (South Sea Islands)
gunzoku: 71–74, 77

Hakkou: 17, 42, 191, 193
Hanabusa, Baron: 199
Hisashi: 17, 31, 40, 42, 44, 195
Hirohito, Emperor: 11, 43

Iida (scabbard seal), 69, 71
Imperial Guards: 88, 156, 159
Imperial Household: 156
Imperial Household:
　dirks 157, 158, 183
　swords 158, 159, 160
Imperial insignia: 17
India: 264
Indo-China: 240
Indonesia: 248

Japanese Self Defence Force (JSDF): 143
Japanese Sword Societies: 280, 281
Java Defence Force: 264, 265, 266

Kadosakura: 17, 18, 19, 29, 30, 32, 35, 38, 50, 52, 55, 60, 79, 172, 173, 202
Kai-guntō: 107, 119, 126, 130, 136, 137, 138
Kaikosha: 75, 97
Kaiten: (see dirks)
Kakihan: 229
Kamikaze: 106–108 (see dirks)
Kanezane, Asano: 99, 213, 232
Kang-te, Emperor: 174
Katana: 56, 68, 69, 89, 94–98, 221
Kempeitai: (see Police, Military)

Kiku (chrysanthemum): 17, 153, 156, 157, 158, 159, 160, 161, 207
Kiri: 17, 121, 122, 153, 157, 161, 162, 163, 170, 171, 182, 206, 207, 210
Korea: 168, 171, 264, 265
Korean:
   dirks 168–170
   swords 170, 171
Kwantung Leased Territories: 173, 186
Kyu-guntō:
   Army NCOs 29
   Army officers 29–34, 35, 49, 50, 54, 111, 231
   Army pattern for naval use 124, 125
   naval flag officers 114, 115
   naval NCOs 114, 115, 119
   naval officers 65, 113–118, 119, 135
   Police 29, 31, 192

labels:
   paper 97, 226, 227
   surrender, transportation 252–259
leather-covered swords: 54, 100, 105

MacArthur, General: 216, 248
Malaya: 32, 63, 264
Mandated Territories (South Sea Islands): 172, 186
   dirks 172, 173
   swords 173
Manchukuo (Manchuria): 141, 174, 186, 211, 217, 219, 221, 264
   dirks 174–176
   swords 174, 176
Mankefsu: 82, 99, 209, 217, 218, 219, 220, 221
Marine Artillery: 135
Marines (see Naval Landing Forces)
Medical Corps swords: 21–23
Meiji, Emperor: 16, 43, 157
Meiji period: 16, 131
Military Police (see police)
military ranks: 74, 117
Mikasa: 211, 221
Minatogawa Shrine: 128, 223
Min-Yun-Huan, Prince: 171
mon: 17, 31, 37, 52, 70
Mountbatten, Lord: 154, 155, 246, 250

namban tetsu: 217
naval airforce: 105
naval bandsmen dirk: 141, 142
naval contemporary photographs:
   groups 65, 120, 137, 141, 149, 155
   single 154, 241
Naval Landing Forces: 65, 68, 77, 81, 96, 128, 135–137, 138
naval dirks: 144–152, 211, 212
naval swords:
   Officers (see kai-guntō, kyu-guntō, parade sabres) 105, 111, 112, 135
   Petty Officers, (see kai-guntō, kyu-guntō, parade sabres) 105, 111, 135
   unidentified 131, 132
   prison 133, 134, 139, 140
   Warrant Officers 105
Netherlands Colonial sword: 110
North China Joint Stock Transportation Company: 92, 93

parade sabres:
   Army 3, 35–44, 52, 53, 170
   boys 44
   Imperial Household 160
   naval 119–122, 123
   Police 37, 42
photographs, contemporary (see Army, Civil, naval)
plaques: 261, 262
plum blossom: 17, 174, 177
Police badges: 17, 186
   dirks 31, 37, 39, 42, 46, 52, 187, 188, 189, 190, 191, 192, 193
   history 185, 186
   military (kempeitai) 46, 48, 88, 186, 187
   mounted 51, 186, 188, 189, 190
   ranks 192
   swords 31, 37, 39, 42, 52, 187, 188, 189, 190, 191, 192, 193
polishing, blades, 222, 223
presentation:
   dirks 147, 210, 211
   swords 39, 40, 209, 210, 211, 212
Pu-yi (see Kang-te)
prison labour figures: 226

prison swordsmiths: 224, 257

Railways Board, National:
   dirks 168, 182, 183
   swords 183
Red Cross Society: 198
   dirks 198, 199
   swords 199
reproduction swords: 269, 270
Rogge, Berhard: 210
Rommel, General-Feldmarschall Erwin: 210, 212
Russia (USSR): 248
Russo–Japanese war: 18, 23, 26, 28, 33, 94, 114, 149, 199

Siam (Thailand): 248
Sakura: 17, 18, 35, 40, 50, 80, 95, 111, 116, 124, 126, 128, 131, 135, 140, 146, 147, 148, 164, 167, 178, 195, 196, 202, 203, 208
samurai swords: 11, 94, 97, 256
Satsuma Rebellion: 185, 187, 188
seals: 230
Seki: 213, 215, 216, 229
Seki stamp: 213, 225, 226, 227, 228, 232
shin-guntō:
   officers 44, 54–77, 99, 104, 105, 107, 136, 137, 209, 210, 216, 250, 251, 255, 266, 267, 272
   naval characteristics 138
   NCOs (copper hilt) 83–87, 90
   NCOs (aluminium hilt) 54, 77, 83–90, 251
shira-saya: 67, 94, 100, 101, 210, 212
sho-stamp: 93, 97, 225
Shore Patrol swords, navy: 133, 134
shōwa period: 11
sidearms: 24–26
Sino–Japanese war: 18, 20
Soekarno, Achmed: 210
South Manchurian Railway Company: 92, 93, 218, 226, 227, 228
South Sea Islands (see Mandated Territories)
stamps (acceptance, arsenal, inspection): 12, 29, 37, 41, 46, 47, 48, 61, 66, 79, 84, 87, 88, 90, 91, 93, 119, 128, 138, 147, 180, 195, 217, 218, 219, 221, 224–229, 266
star stamps: 79, 217, 221, 226, 227, 228
suikosha: 228

surrender documentation: 252–360
surrender photographs: 81, 137, 247, 248, 250, 251, 262
surrender of swords: 34, 50, 81, 86, 101, 246–262
suspension methods: 44, 47, 58, 243–245
Suya Company: 12, 37, 41, 83, 87, 119, 226, 227
sword belts: 58, 136, 149, 233–245
sword knots and tassels:
   army 17, 31, 32, 36, 37, 42, 46, 48, 50, 57, 65, 74, 77, 80, 85, 87, 95, 105, 104, 108, 116, 133, 139, 140, 161, 177, 190, 201
   civil 206, 207
   naval 115, 116, 117, 119, 128, 136
   on unidentified swords 202, 205, 265
swords, civil: 105, 200–207
swordsmiths: 112, 155, 163, 210, 211, 213, 221, 222–225, 254, 255, 259, 261
sword terminology: 13–15

tachi: 54, 99, 126, 153, 174, 210, 250
Taishō period: 16
Taiwan (see Formosa)
tameshigiri: 11
tantō: 95, 101, 147
Tatsumi, Colonel Namio: 78
Tokyo Police Force: 185
transport swords: 19, 20
Tsingtao: 173
turtle-shell, 21, 30, 35, 37, 160, 199, 207

ubu-ha: 231
unidentified:
   dirks 150, 208
   swords civil 200–207
   swords military 131, 132

Wakizashi: 56, 62, 94–97, 105, 107, 112, 203, 221
war artist drawings: 20, 110, 149
Warrant Officers:
   Army 29, 35, 37, 54, 105
   Navy 105, 126
Wilkinson Sword Company Ltd: 110, 112, 144
Woodville, Richard Caton: 109, 112

Yasukuni Shrine: 75, 154, 222, 223, 232, 257
Yasuhuni Shrine smiths: 154, 222, 223